Maid-Sama!

Volumes 1-2

CONTENTS

Chapter 1 005

Chapter 2 037

Chapter 3 079

Chapter 4 111

Bonus Story: A Transparent World 143

Chapter 5 195

Chapter 6 237

Chapter 7 269

Chapter 8 299

Chapter 9 334

Shojo Beat

Maid-sama!

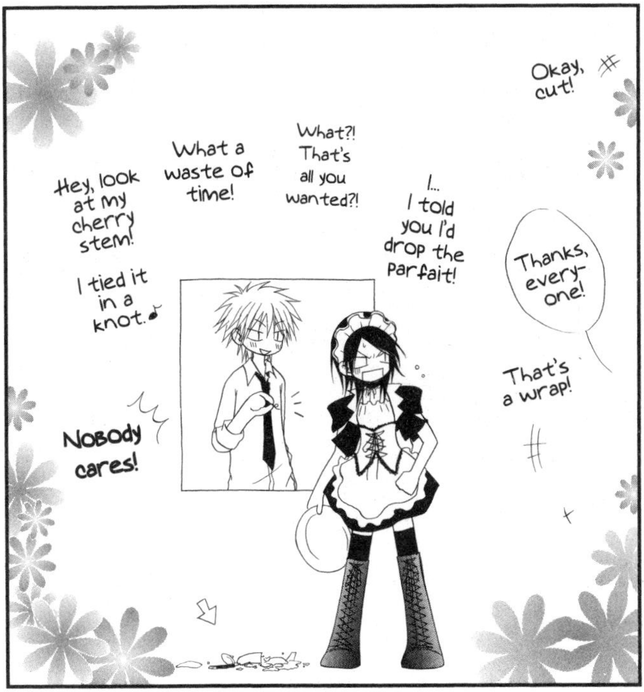
Okay, cut!
What?! That's all you wanted?!
What a waste of time!
Thanks, every-one!
I... I told you I'd drop the parfait!
Hey, look at my cherry stem!
I tied it in a knot.
That's a wrap!
Nobody cares!

Vol. 1

Story & Art by

Hiro Fujiwara

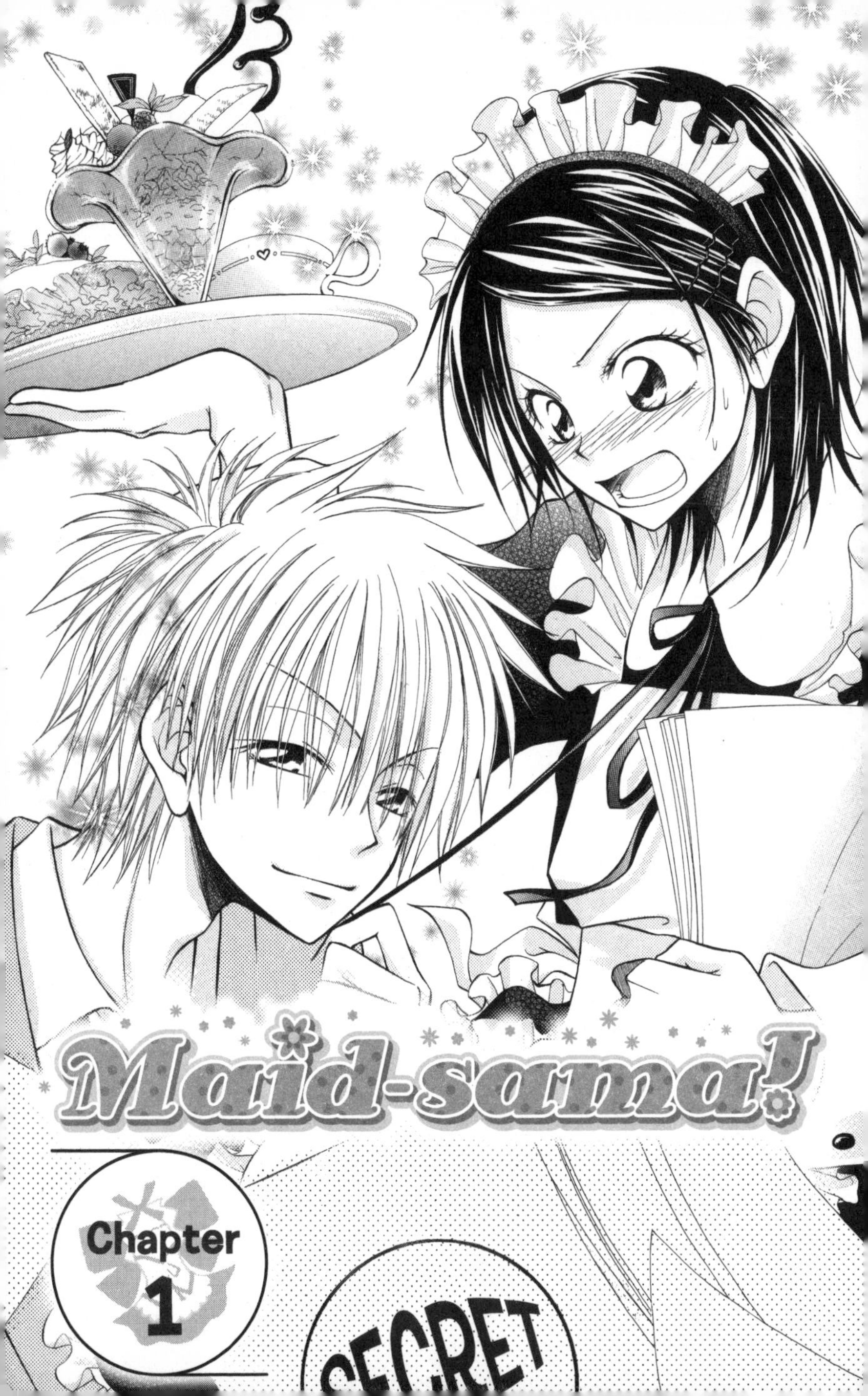
Maid-sama!
Chapter 1
SECRET

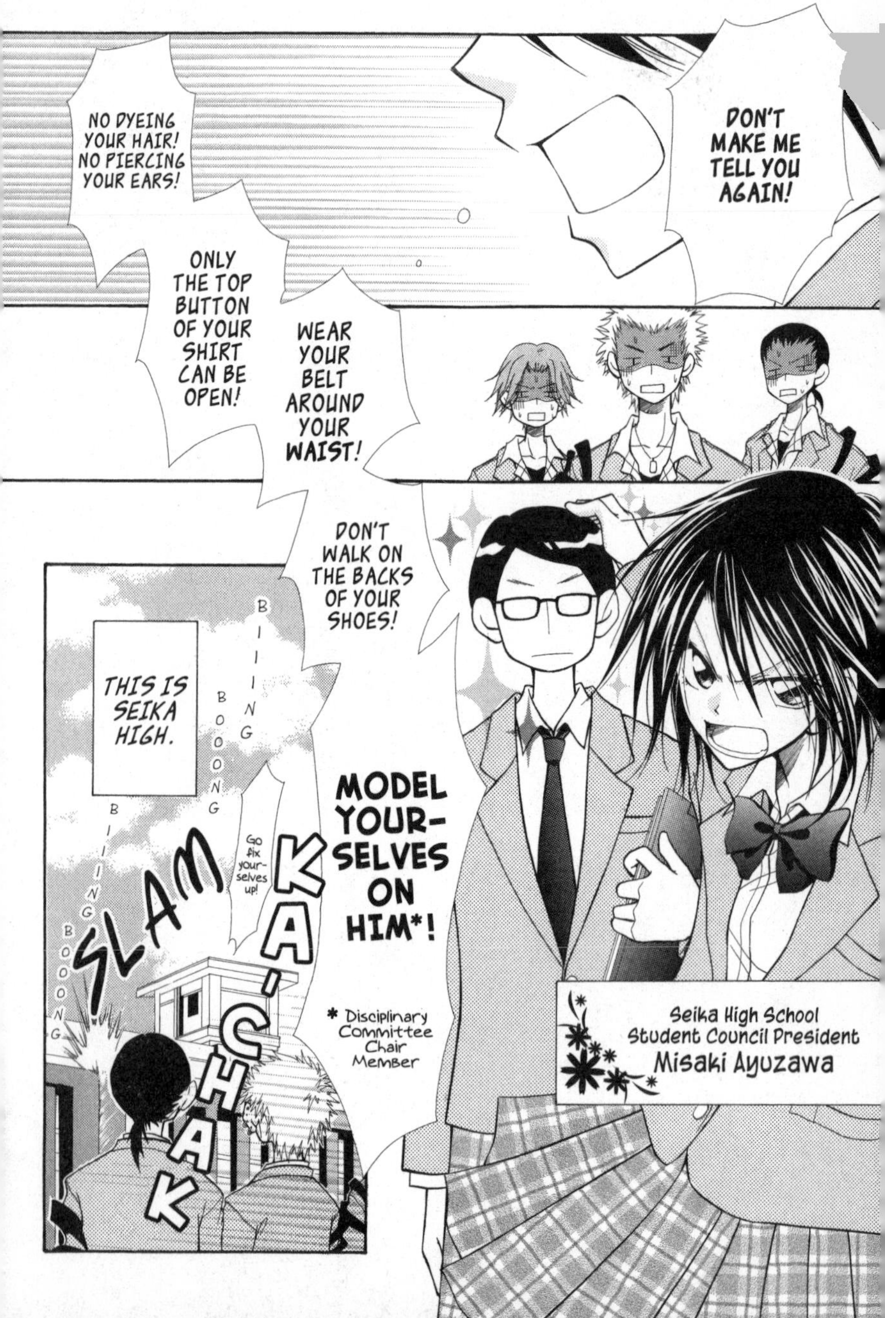
DON'T MAKE ME TELL YOU AGAIN!
NO DYEING YOUR HAIR! NO PIERCING YOUR EARS!
WEAR YOUR BELT AROUND YOUR WAIST!
ONLY THE TOP BUTTON OF YOUR SHIRT CAN BE OPEN!
DON'T WALK ON THE BACKS OF YOUR SHOES!
MODEL YOUR-SELVES ON HIM*!
Seika High School Student Council President Misaki Ayuzawa
* Disciplinary Committee Chair Member
THIS IS SEIKA HIGH.
BIIING
BOOOONG
Go fix your-selves up!
KA-CHAK
SLAM
BIIING
BOOOONG

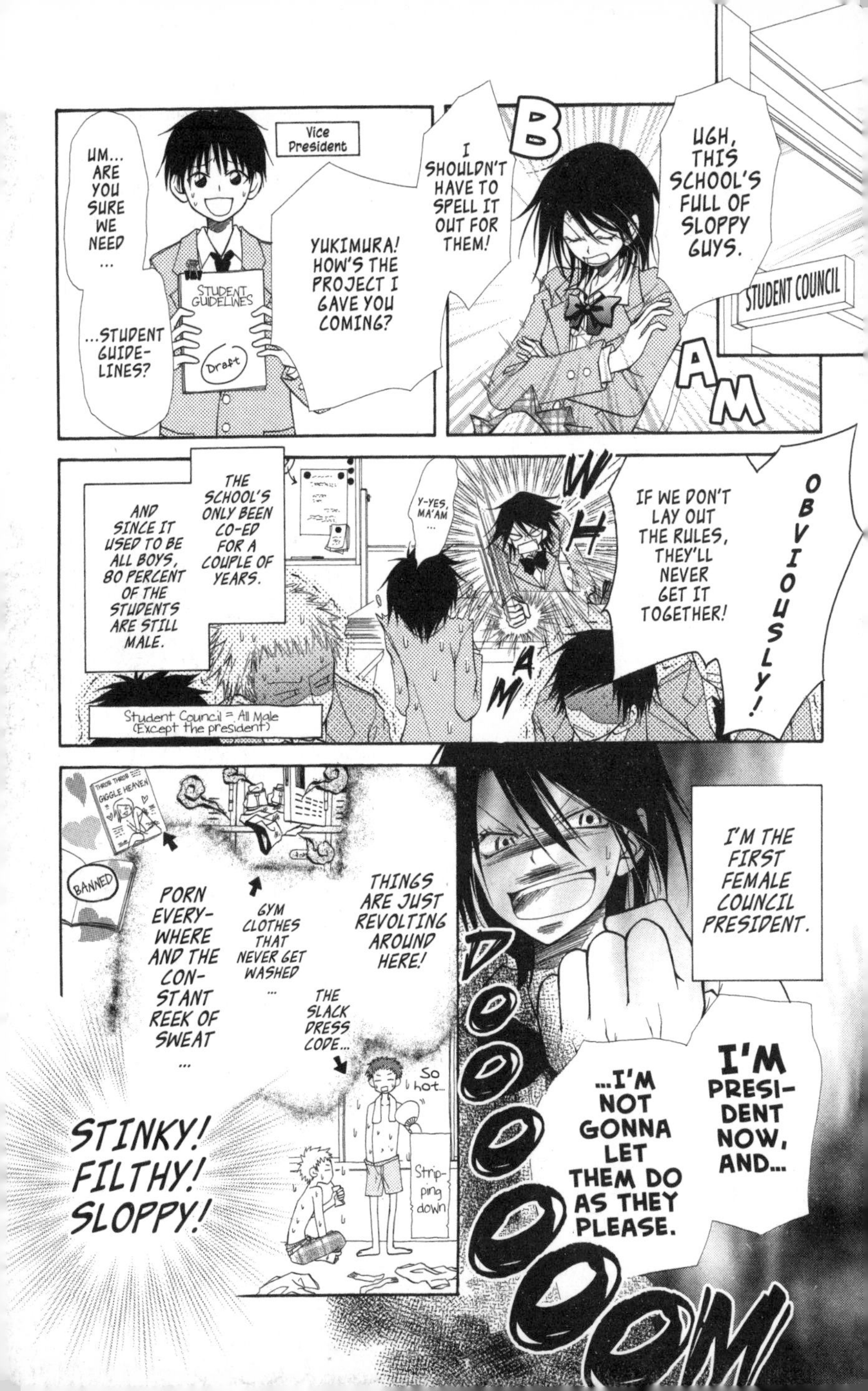
UGH, THIS SCHOOL'S FULL OF SLOPPY GUYS.
STUDENT COUNCIL
BAM
I SHOULDN'T HAVE TO SPELL IT OUT FOR THEM!
YUKIMURA! HOW'S THE PROJECT I GAVE YOU COMING?
Vice President
UM... ARE YOU SURE WE NEED ...
...STUDENT GUIDE-LINES?
STUDENT GUIDELINES
Draft
OBVIOUSLY!
IF WE DON'T LAY OUT THE RULES, THEY'LL NEVER GET IT TOGETHER!
WHAM
Y-YES, MA'AM ...
THE SCHOOL'S ONLY BEEN CO-ED FOR A COUPLE OF YEARS.
AND SINCE IT USED TO BE ALL BOYS, 80 PERCENT OF THE STUDENTS ARE STILL MALE.
Student Council = All Male (Except the president)
I'M THE FIRST FEMALE COUNCIL PRESIDENT.
I'M PRESI-DENT NOW, AND...
...I'M NOT GONNA LET THEM DO AS THEY PLEASE.
DOOOOOOOM
THINGS ARE JUST REVOLTING AROUND HERE!
THROB THROB GIGGLE HEAVEN
BANNED
PORN EVERY-WHERE AND THE CON-STANT REEK OF SWEAT ...
GYM CLOTHES THAT NEVER GET WASHED ...
THE SLACK DRESS CODE...
So hot...
Strip-ping down
STINKY! FILTHY! SLOPPY!

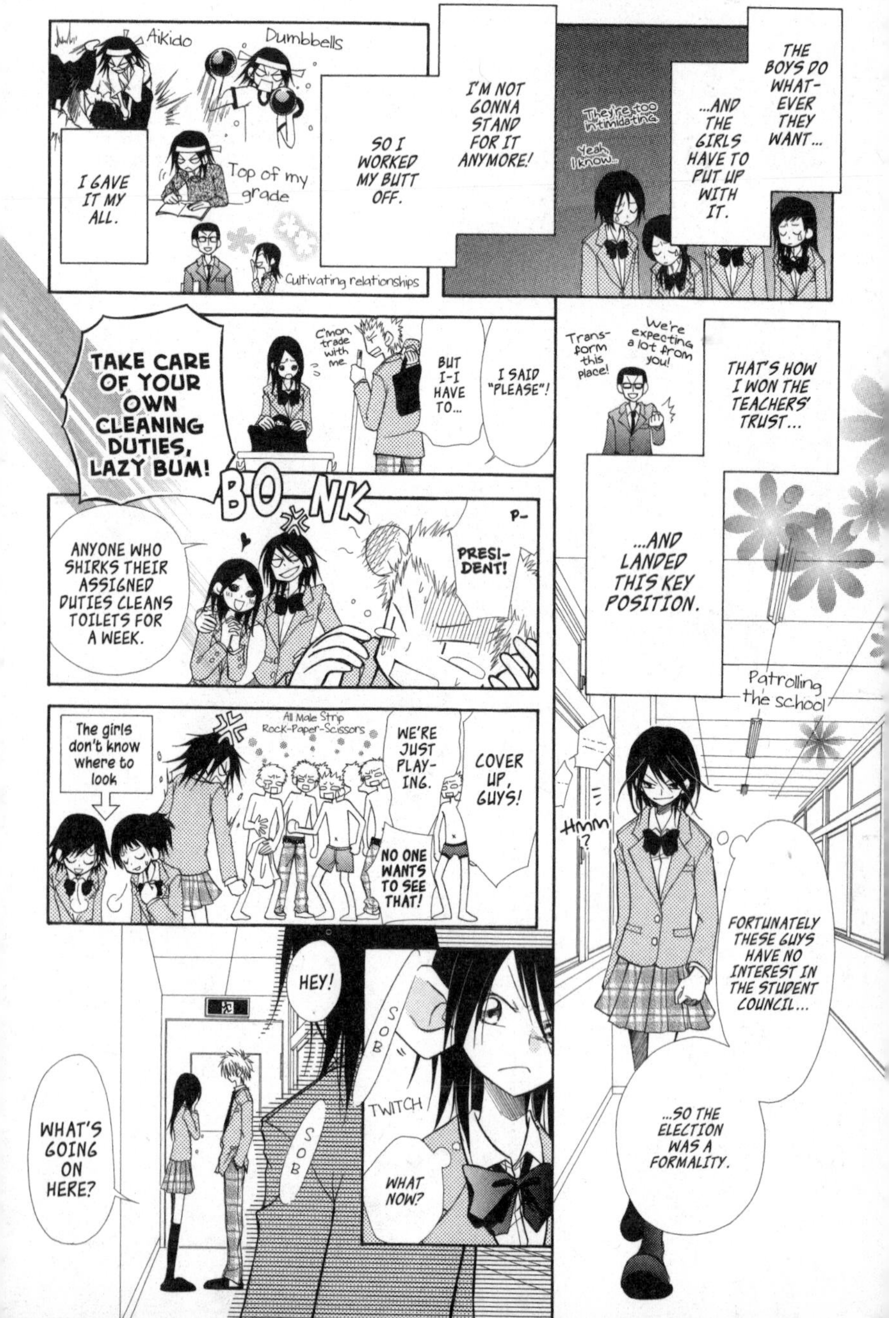
THE BOYS DO WHAT-EVER THEY WANT...
...AND THE GIRLS HAVE TO PUT UP WITH IT.
They're too intimidating.
Yeah, I know...
I'M NOT GONNA STAND FOR IT ANYMORE!
SO I WORKED MY BUTT OFF.
Dumbbells
Aikido
I GAVE IT MY ALL.
Top of my grade
Cultivating relationships
THAT'S HOW I WON THE TEACHERS' TRUST...
We're expecting a lot from you!
Trans-form this place!
...AND LANDED THIS KEY POSITION.
Patrolling the school
Hmm?
FORTUNATELY THESE GUYS HAVE NO INTEREST IN THE STUDENT COUNCIL...
...SO THE ELECTION WAS A FORMALITY.
I SAID "PLEASE"!
BUT I-I HAVE TO...
C'mon, trade with me.
TAKE CARE OF YOUR OWN CLEANING DUTIES, LAZY BUM!
BONK
P-
PRESI-DENT!
ANYONE WHO SHIRKS THEIR ASSIGNED DUTIES CLEANS TOILETS FOR A WEEK.
COVER UP, GUYS!
WE'RE JUST PLAY-ING.
All Male Strip Rock-Paper-Scissors
NO ONE WANTS TO SEE THAT!
The girls don't know where to look
HEY!
SOB
SOB
TWITCH
WHAT NOW?
WHAT'S GOING ON HERE?

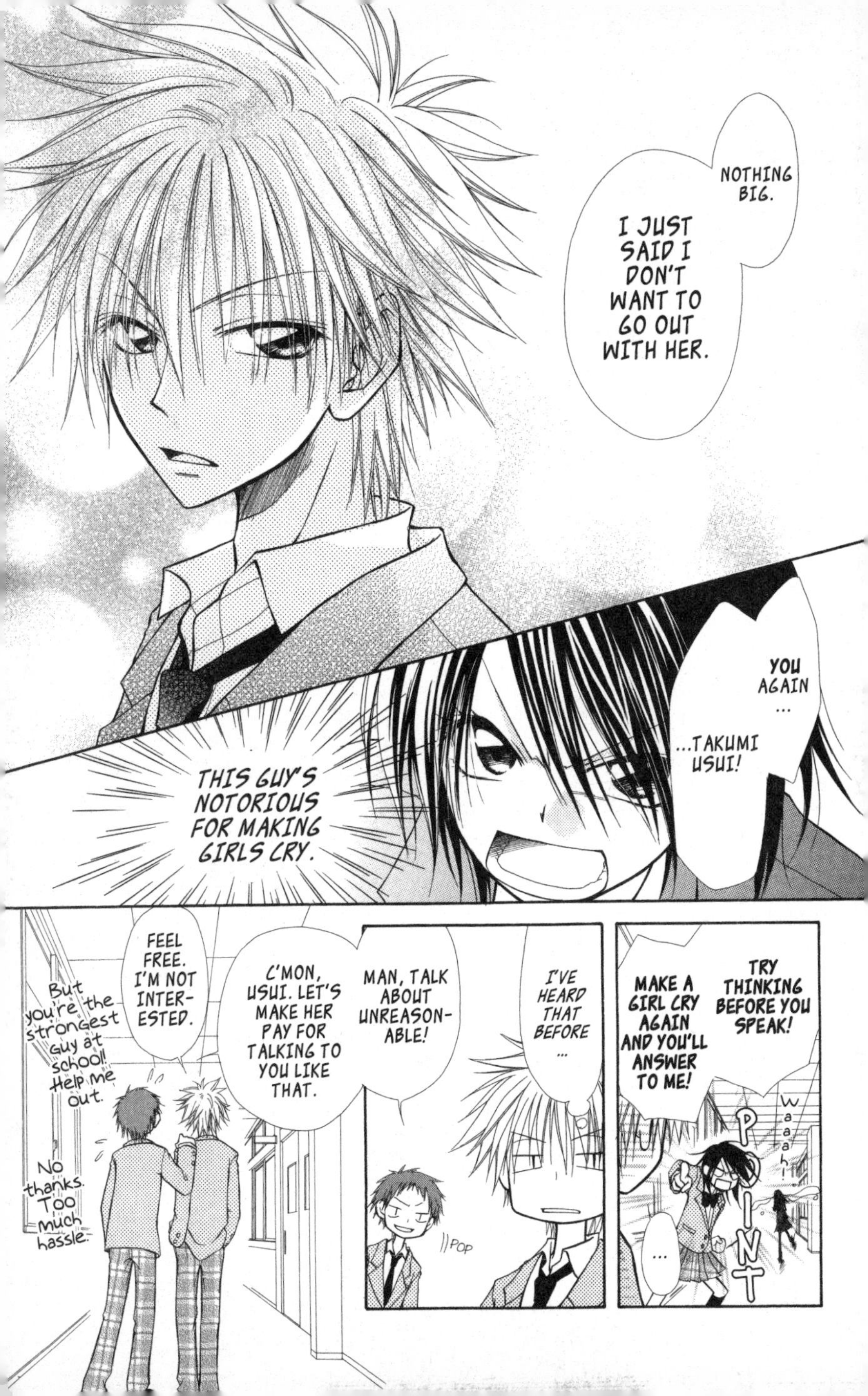
NOTHING BIG.
I JUST SAID I DON'T WANT TO GO OUT WITH HER.
YOU AGAIN...
...TAKUMI USUI!
THIS GUY'S NOTORIOUS FOR MAKING GIRLS CRY.
TRY THINKING BEFORE YOU SPEAK!
MAKE A GIRL CRY AGAIN AND YOU'LL ANSWER TO ME!
PINT
Waaah!
...
I'VE HEARD THAT BEFORE...
MAN, TALK ABOUT UNREASON-ABLE!
POP
C'MON, USUI. LET'S MAKE HER PAY FOR TALKING TO YOU LIKE THAT.
FEEL FREE. I'M NOT INTER-ESTED.
But you're the strongest guy at school! Help me out.
No thanks. Too much hassle.

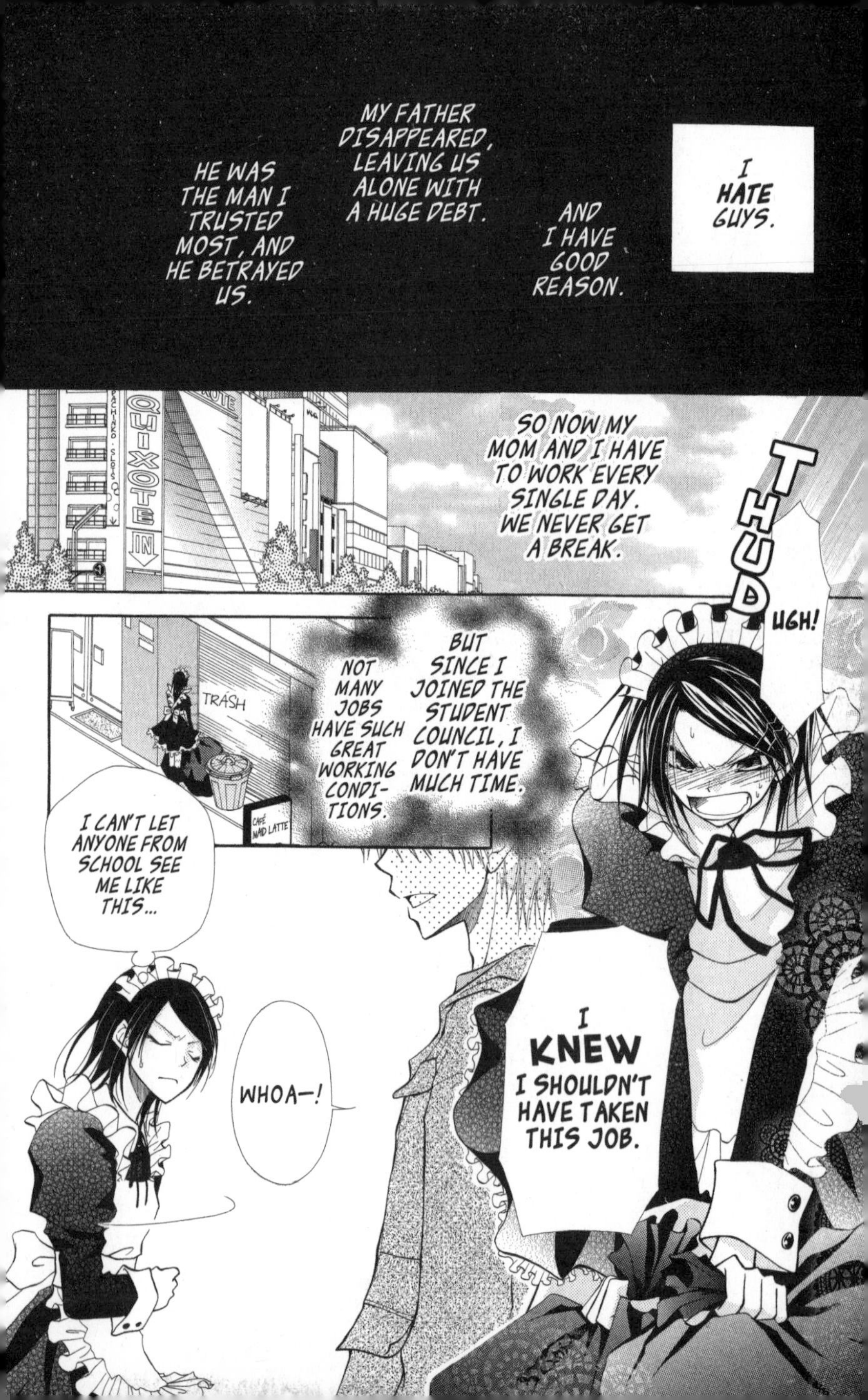
I HATE GUYS.
AND I HAVE GOOD REASON.
MY FATHER DISAPPEARED, LEAVING US ALONE WITH A HUGE DEBT.
HE WAS THE MAN I TRUSTED MOST, AND HE BETRAYED US.
SO NOW MY MOM AND I HAVE TO WORK EVERY SINGLE DAY. WE NEVER GET A BREAK.
QUIXOTE
PACHINKO · SLOTS
IN
THUD
UGH!
I KNEW I SHOULDN'T HAVE TAKEN THIS JOB.
BUT SINCE I JOINED THE STUDENT COUNCIL, I DON'T HAVE MUCH TIME.
NOT MANY JOBS HAVE SUCH GREAT WORKING CONDI-TIONS.
TRASH
CAFÉ MAID LATTE
I CAN'T LET ANYONE FROM SCHOOL SEE ME LIKE THIS...
WHOA—!

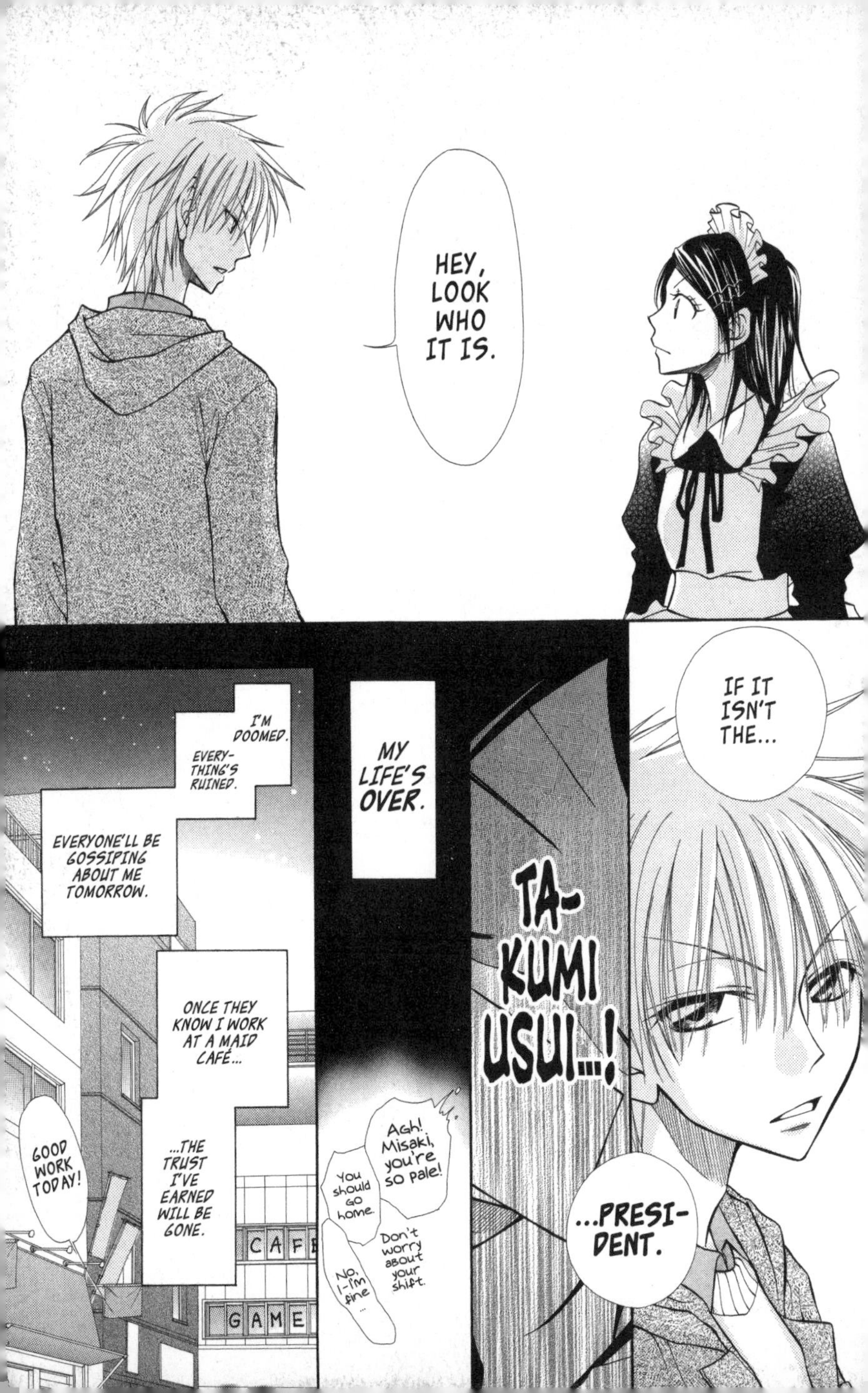
HEY, LOOK WHO IT IS.
IF IT ISN'T THE...
TA-KUMI USUI...!
...PRESIDENT.
MY LIFE'S OVER.
Agh! Misaki, you're so pale!
You should go home.
Don't worry about your shift.
No, I-I'm fine...
I'M DOOMED.
EVERY-THING'S RUINED.
EVERYONE'LL BE GOSSIPING ABOUT ME TOMORROW.
ONCE THEY KNOW I WORK AT A MAID CAFÉ...
...THE TRUST I'VE EARNED WILL BE GONE.
GOOD WORK TODAY!
CAFE
GAME

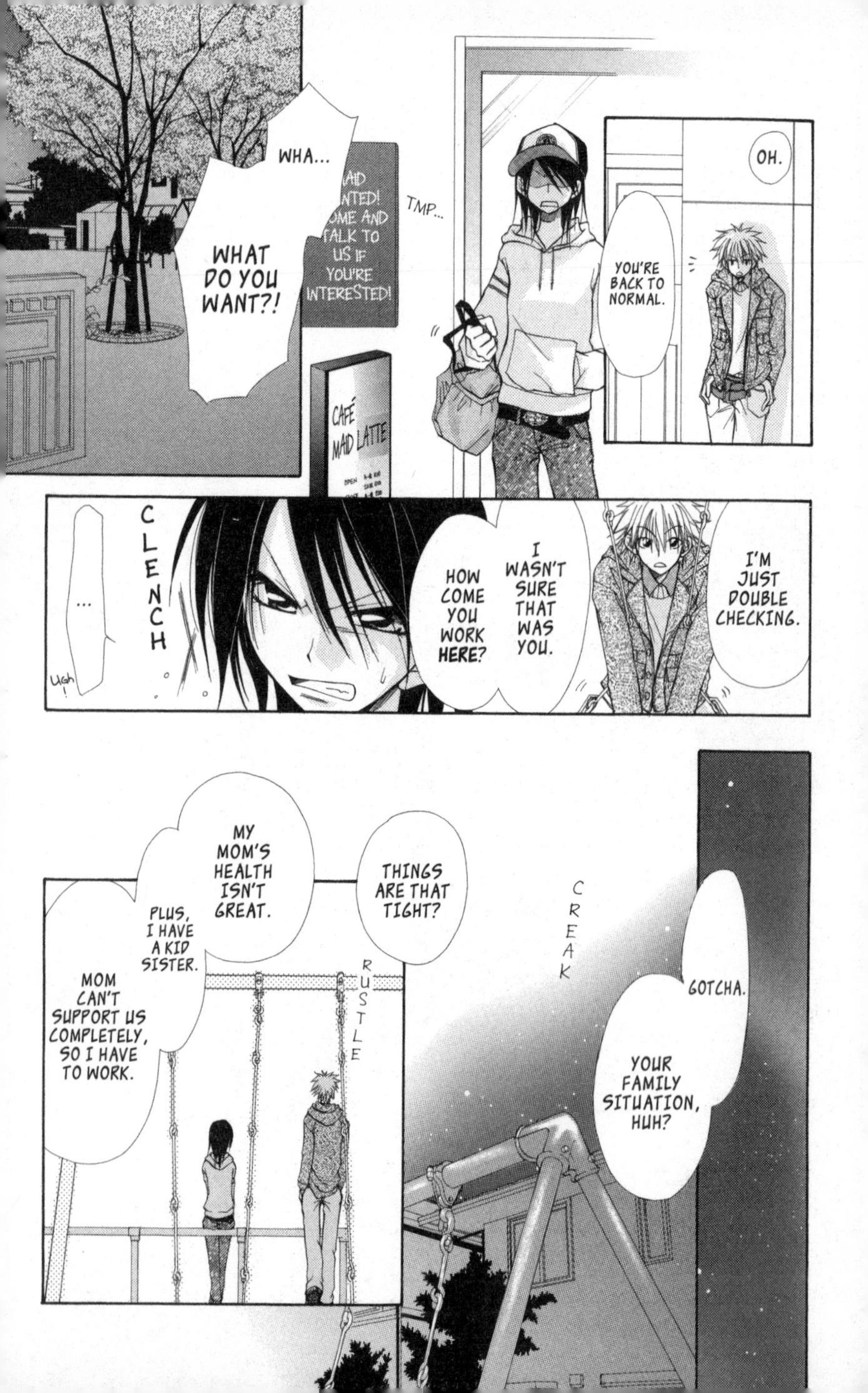
OH.
YOU'RE BACK TO NORMAL.
TMP...
AID NTED! OME AND TALK TO US IF YOU'RE INTERESTED!
CAFÉ MAID LATTE
WHA...
WHAT DO YOU WANT?!
I'M JUST DOUBLE CHECKING.
I WASN'T SURE THAT WAS YOU.
HOW COME YOU WORK HERE?
CLENCH
...
Ugh!
GOTCHA.
YOUR FAMILY SITUATION, HUH?
CREAK
THINGS ARE THAT TIGHT?
MY MOM'S HEALTH ISN'T GREAT.
PLUS, I HAVE A KID SISTER.
MOM CAN'T SUPPORT US COMPLETELY, SO I HAVE TO WORK.
RUSTLE

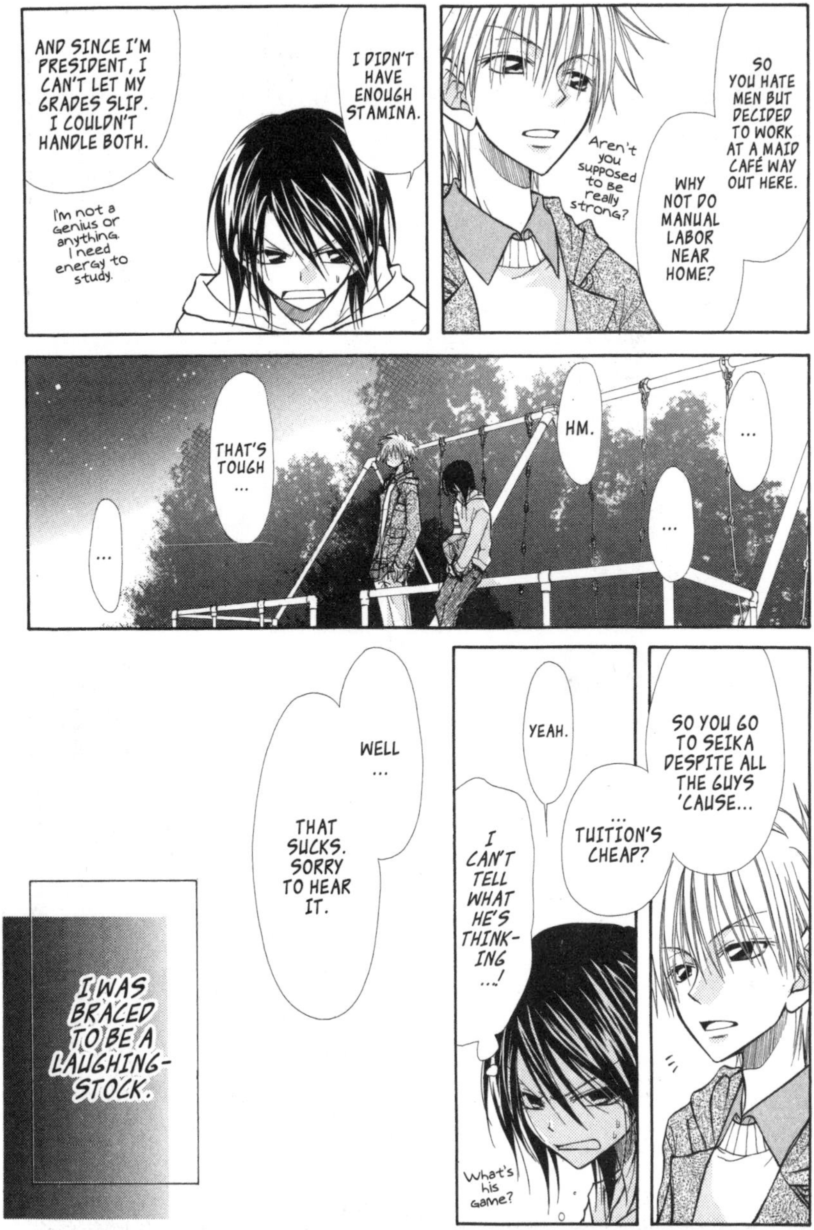
SO YOU HATE MEN BUT DECIDED TO WORK AT A MAID CAFÉ WAY OUT HERE.
WHY NOT DO MANUAL LABOR NEAR HOME?
Aren't you supposed to be really strong?
I DIDN'T HAVE ENOUGH STAMINA.
AND SINCE I'M PRESIDENT, I CAN'T LET MY GRADES SLIP. I COULDN'T HANDLE BOTH.
I'm not a genius or anything. I need energy to study.
...
HM.
...
THAT'S TOUGH ...
...
SO YOU GO TO SEIKA DESPITE ALL THE GUYS 'CAUSE...
... TUITION'S CHEAP?
YEAH.
I CAN'T TELL WHAT HE'S THINKING ...!
What's his game?
WELL ...
THAT SUCKS. SORRY TO HEAR IT.
I WAS BRACED TO BE A LAUGHING-STOCK.

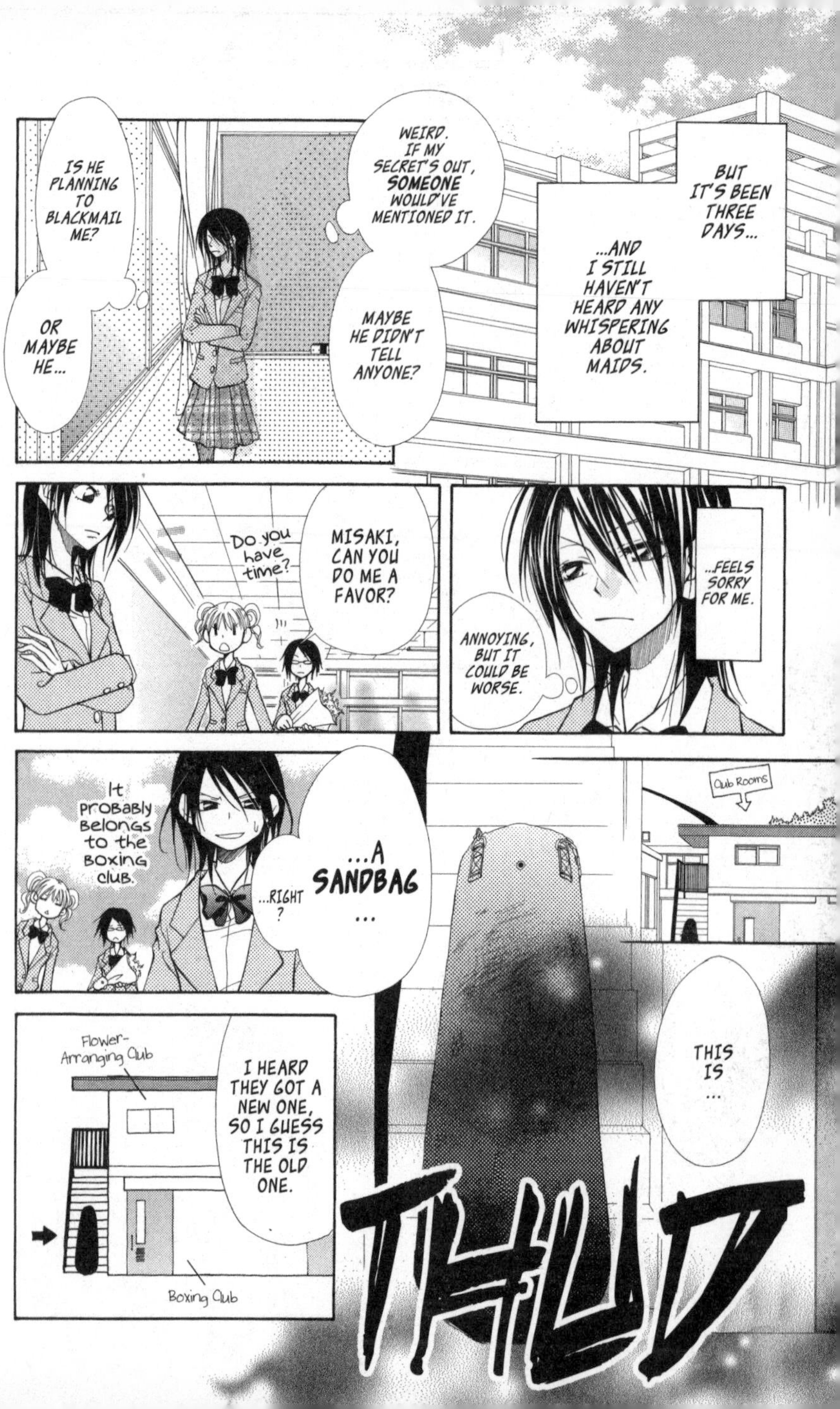
BUT IT'S BEEN THREE DAYS...
...AND I STILL HAVEN'T HEARD ANY WHISPERING ABOUT MAIDS.
WEIRD. IF MY SECRET'S OUT, SOMEONE WOULD'VE MENTIONED IT.
MAYBE HE DIDN'T TELL ANYONE?
IS HE PLANNING TO BLACKMAIL ME?
OR MAYBE HE...
...FEELS SORRY FOR ME.
ANNOYING, BUT IT COULD BE WORSE.
MISAKI, CAN YOU DO ME A FAVOR?
Do you have time?
Club Rooms
THIS IS...
THUD
...A SANDBAG...
...RIGHT?
It probably belongs to the boxing club.
I HEARD THEY GOT A NEW ONE, SO I GUESS THIS IS THE OLD ONE.
Flower-Arranging Club
Boxing Club

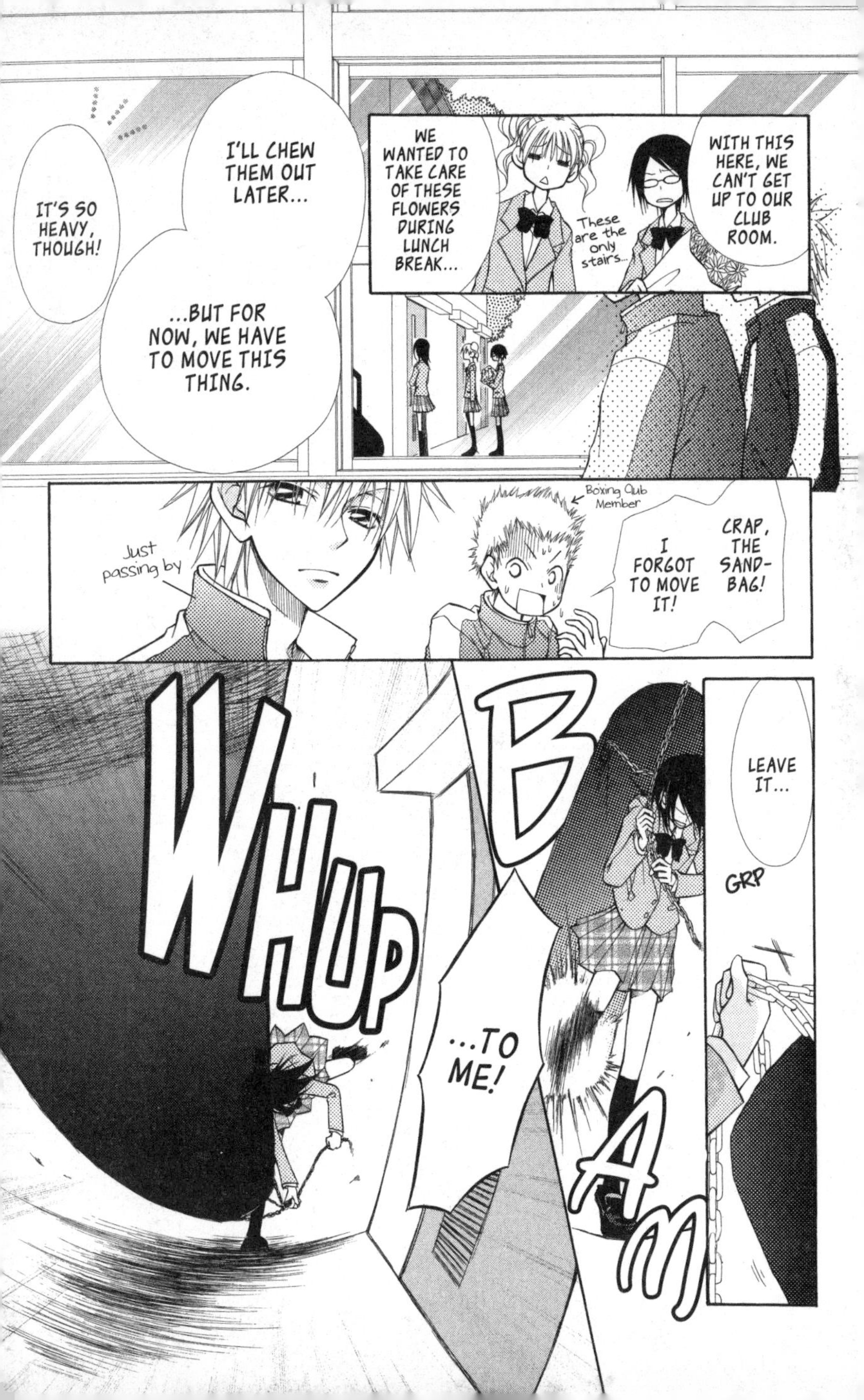
WITH THIS HERE, WE CAN'T GET UP TO OUR CLUB ROOM.
These are the only stairs...
WE WANTED TO TAKE CARE OF THESE FLOWERS DURING LUNCH BREAK...
I'LL CHEW THEM OUT LATER...
...BUT FOR NOW, WE HAVE TO MOVE THIS THING.
IT'S SO HEAVY, THOUGH!
CRAP, THE SAND-BAG!
I FORGOT TO MOVE IT!
Boxing Club Member
Just passing by
LEAVE IT...
GRP
...TO ME!
BAM
WHUP

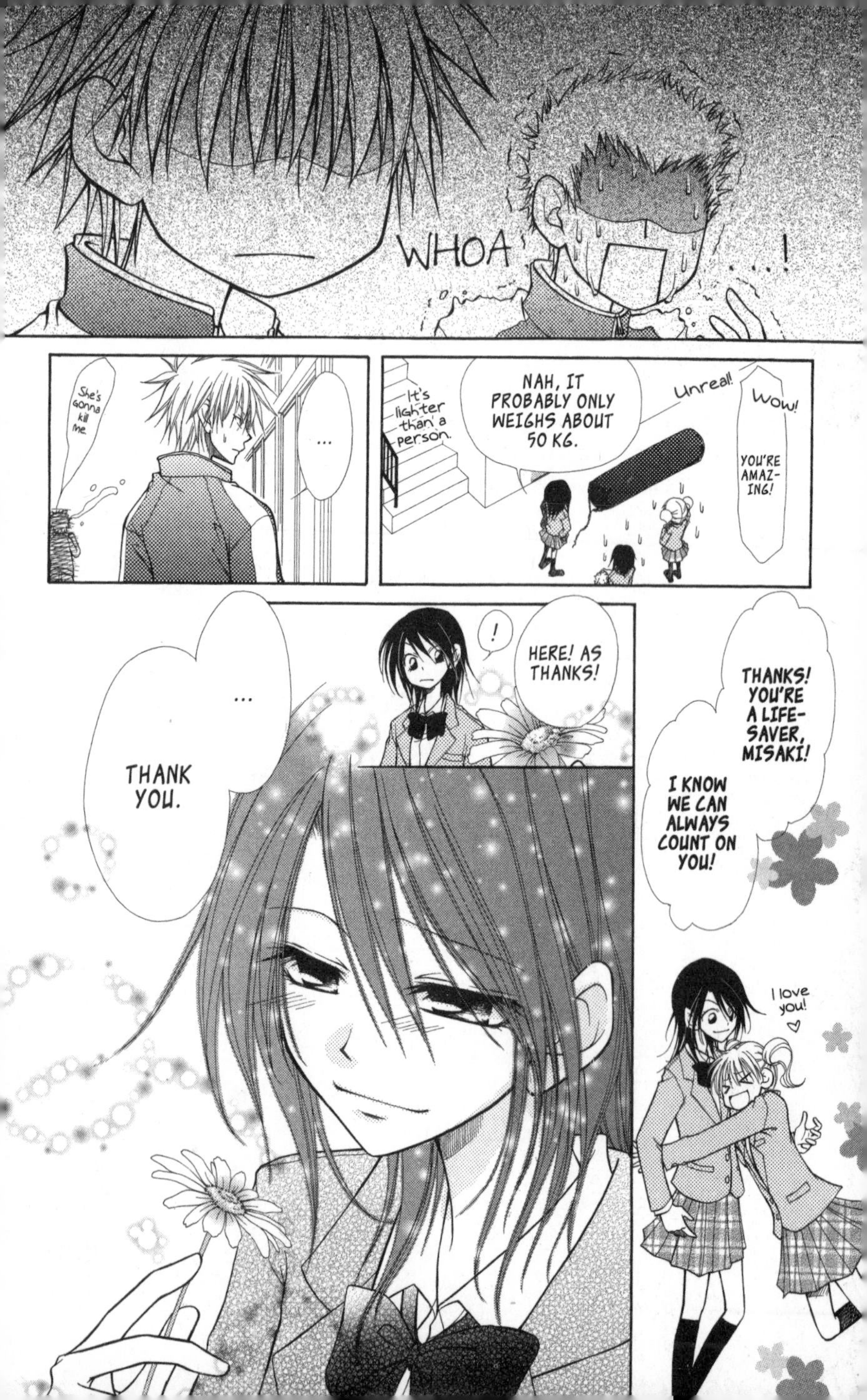
WHOA ...!
Wow!
YOU'RE AMAZ-ING!
Unreal!
NAH, IT PROBABLY ONLY WEIGHS ABOUT 50 KG.
It's lighter than a person.
...
She's gonna kill me.
THANKS! YOU'RE A LIFE-SAVER, MISAKI!
I KNOW WE CAN ALWAYS COUNT ON YOU!
I love you!
HERE! AS THANKS!
!
...
THANK YOU.

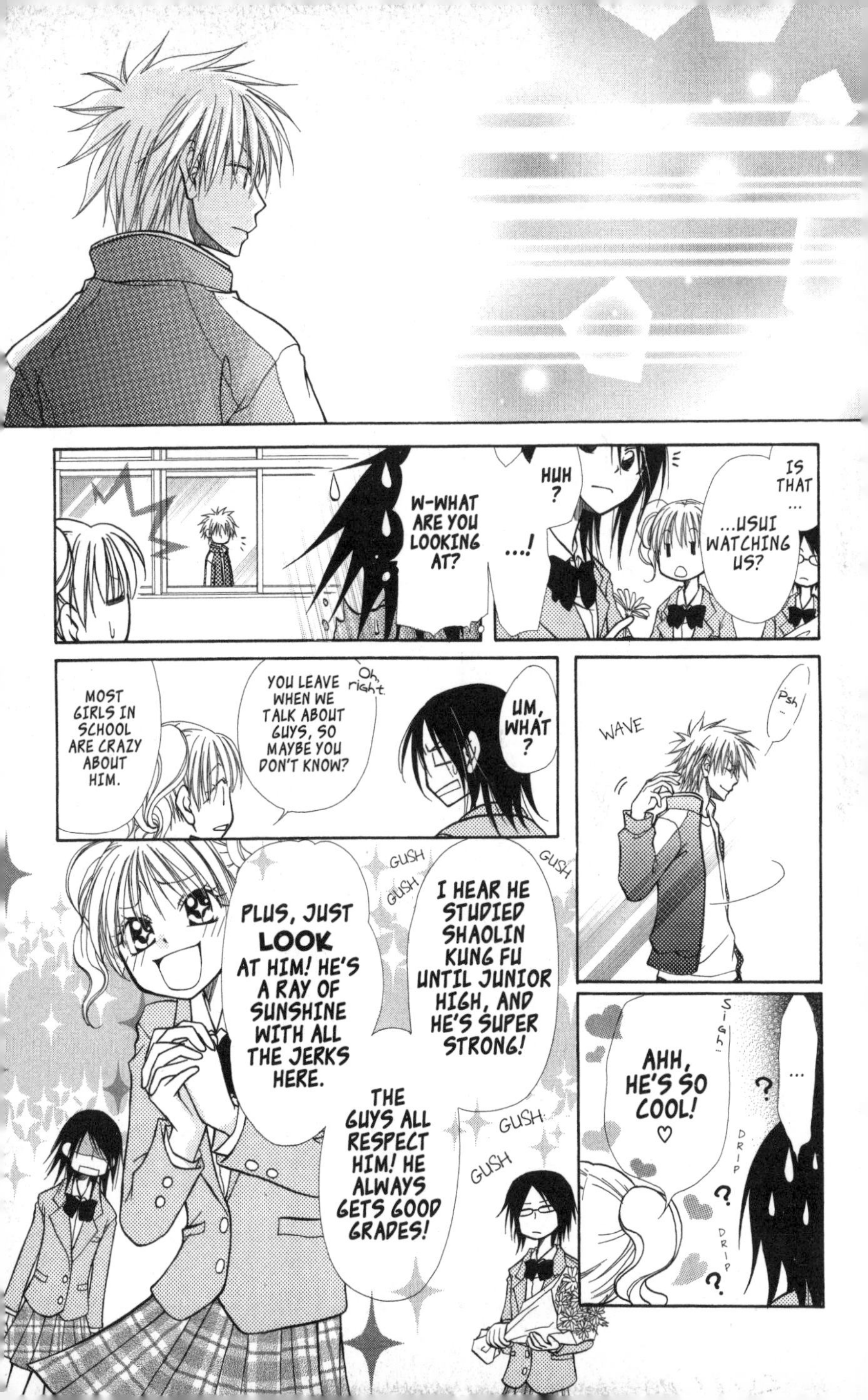
IS THAT... ...USUI WATCHING US?
HUH?
...!
W-WHAT ARE YOU LOOKING AT?
WAVE
Psh...
UM, WHAT?
Oh, right.
YOU LEAVE WHEN WE TALK ABOUT GUYS, SO MAYBE YOU DON'T KNOW?
MOST GIRLS IN SCHOOL ARE CRAZY ABOUT HIM.
GUSH
GUSH
GUSH
I HEAR HE STUDIED SHAOLIN KUNG FU UNTIL JUNIOR HIGH, AND HE'S SUPER STRONG!
PLUS, JUST LOOK AT HIM! HE'S A RAY OF SUNSHINE WITH ALL THE JERKS HERE.
GUSH
GUSH
THE GUYS ALL RESPECT HIM! HE ALWAYS GETS GOOD GRADES!
Sigh...
AHH, HE'S SO COOL! ♡
...
?
DRIP
?
DRIP
?

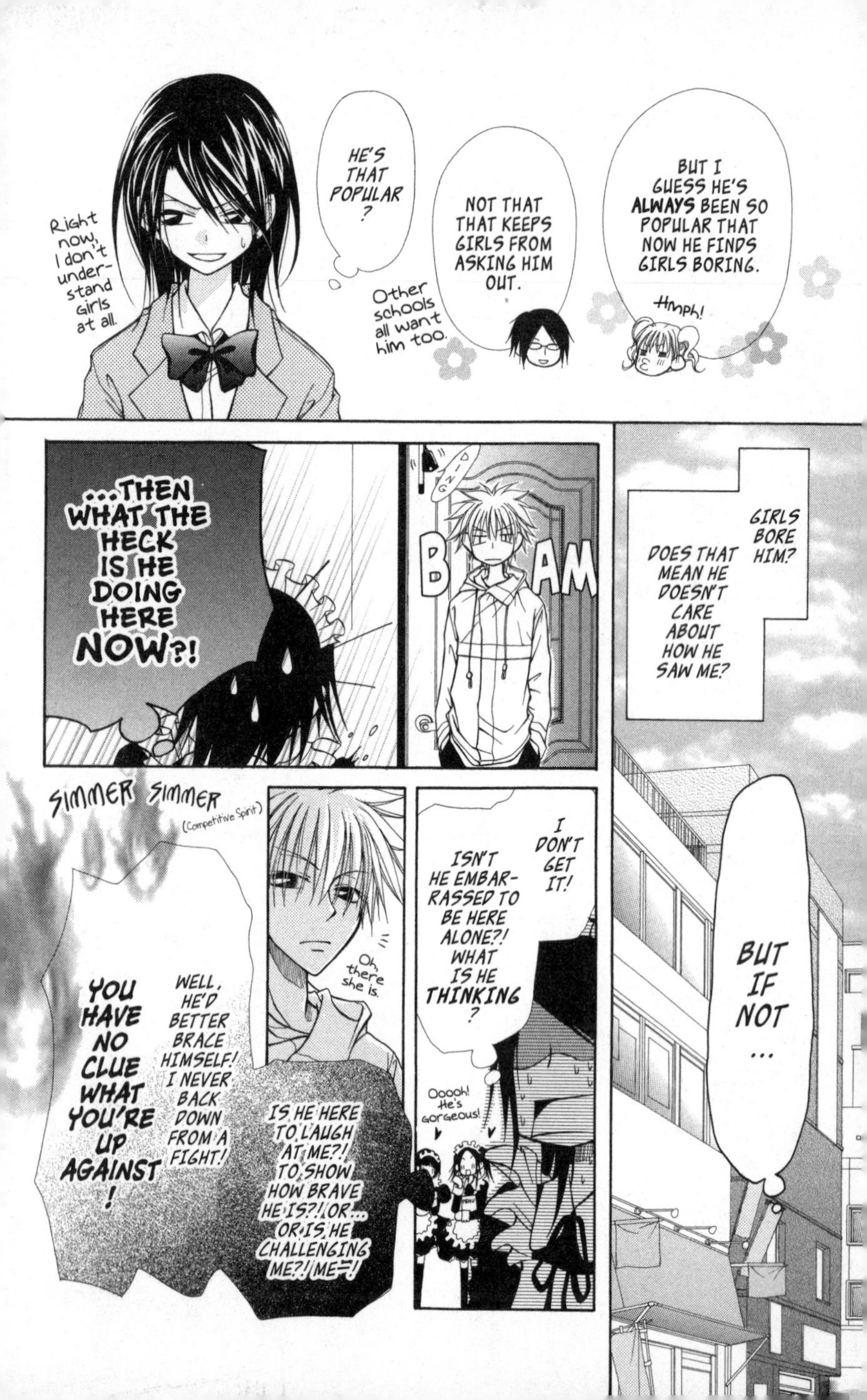
BUT I GUESS HE'S ALWAYS BEEN SO POPULAR THAT NOW HE FINDS GIRLS BORING.
Hmph!
NOT THAT THAT KEEPS GIRLS FROM ASKING HIM OUT.
Other schools all want him too.
HE'S THAT POPULAR?
Right now, I don't understand girls at all.
GIRLS BORE HIM?
DOES THAT MEAN HE DOESN'T CARE ABOUT HOW HE SAW ME?
BUT IF NOT...
DING
BAM
...THEN WHAT THE HECK IS HE DOING HERE NOW?!
I DON'T GET IT!
ISN'T HE EMBARRASSED TO BE HERE ALONE?! WHAT IS HE THINKING?
Ooooh! He's gorgeous!
Oh, there she is.
IS HE HERE TO LAUGH AT ME?! TO SHOW HOW BRAVE HE IS?! OR... OR IS HE CHALLENGING ME?! ME—!
SIMMER SIMMER
(Competitive Spirit)
WELL, HE'D BETTER BRACE HIMSELF! I NEVER BACK DOWN FROM A FIGHT!
YOU HAVE NO CLUE WHAT YOU'RE UP AGAINST!

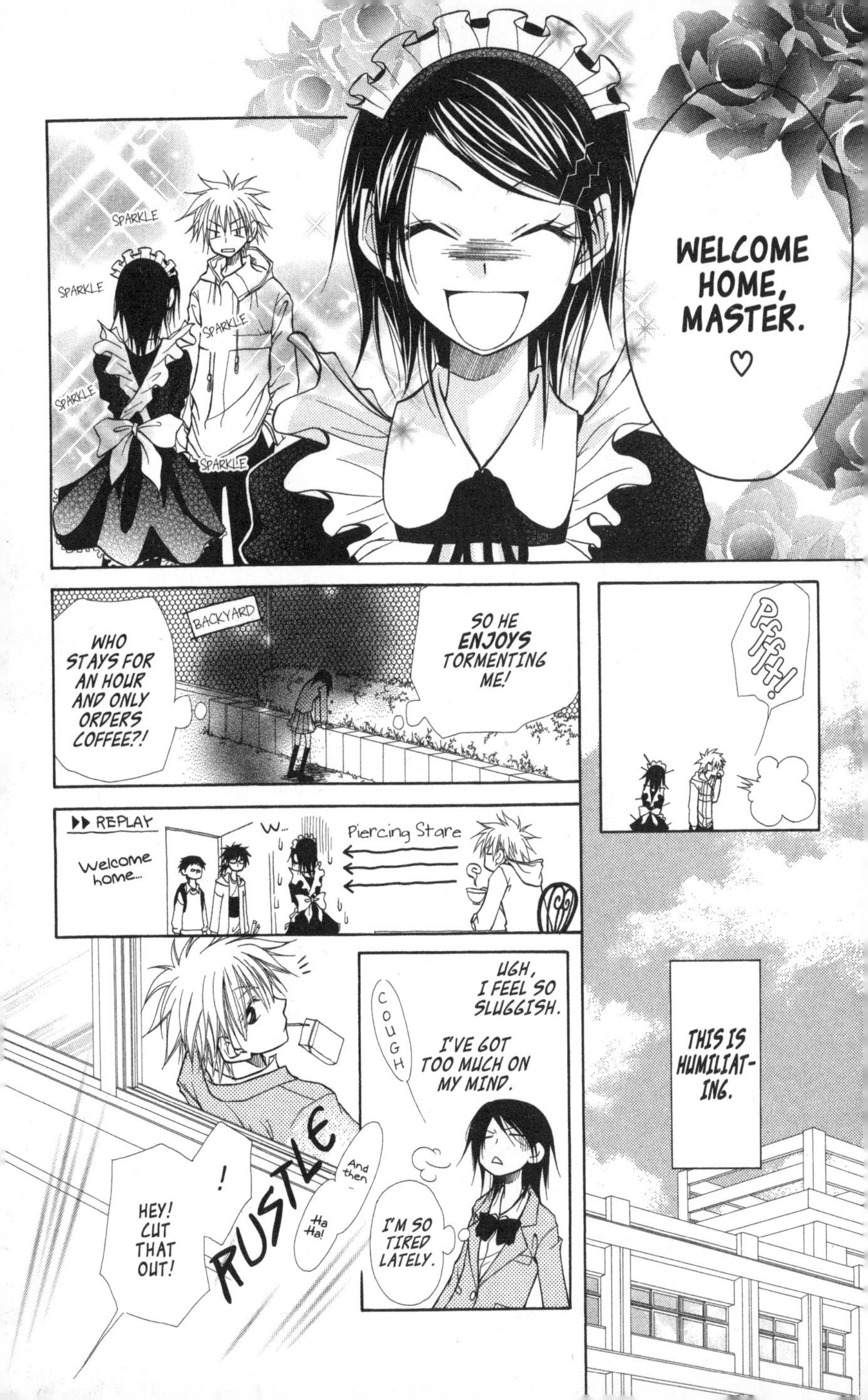
WELCOME HOME, MASTER. ♡
SPARKLE
SPARKLE
SPARKLE
SPARKLE
SPARKLE
Pffft!
SO HE ENJOYS TORMENTING ME!
BACKYARD
WHO STAYS FOR AN HOUR AND ONLY ORDERS COFFEE?!
▶▶ REPLAY
Piercing Stare
W...
Welcome home...
THIS IS HUMILIAT-ING.
UGH, I FEEL SO SLUGGISH.
COUGH
I'VE GOT TOO MUCH ON MY MIND.
I'M SO TIRED LATELY.
And then...
Ha Ha!
RUSTLE
!
HEY! CUT THAT OUT!

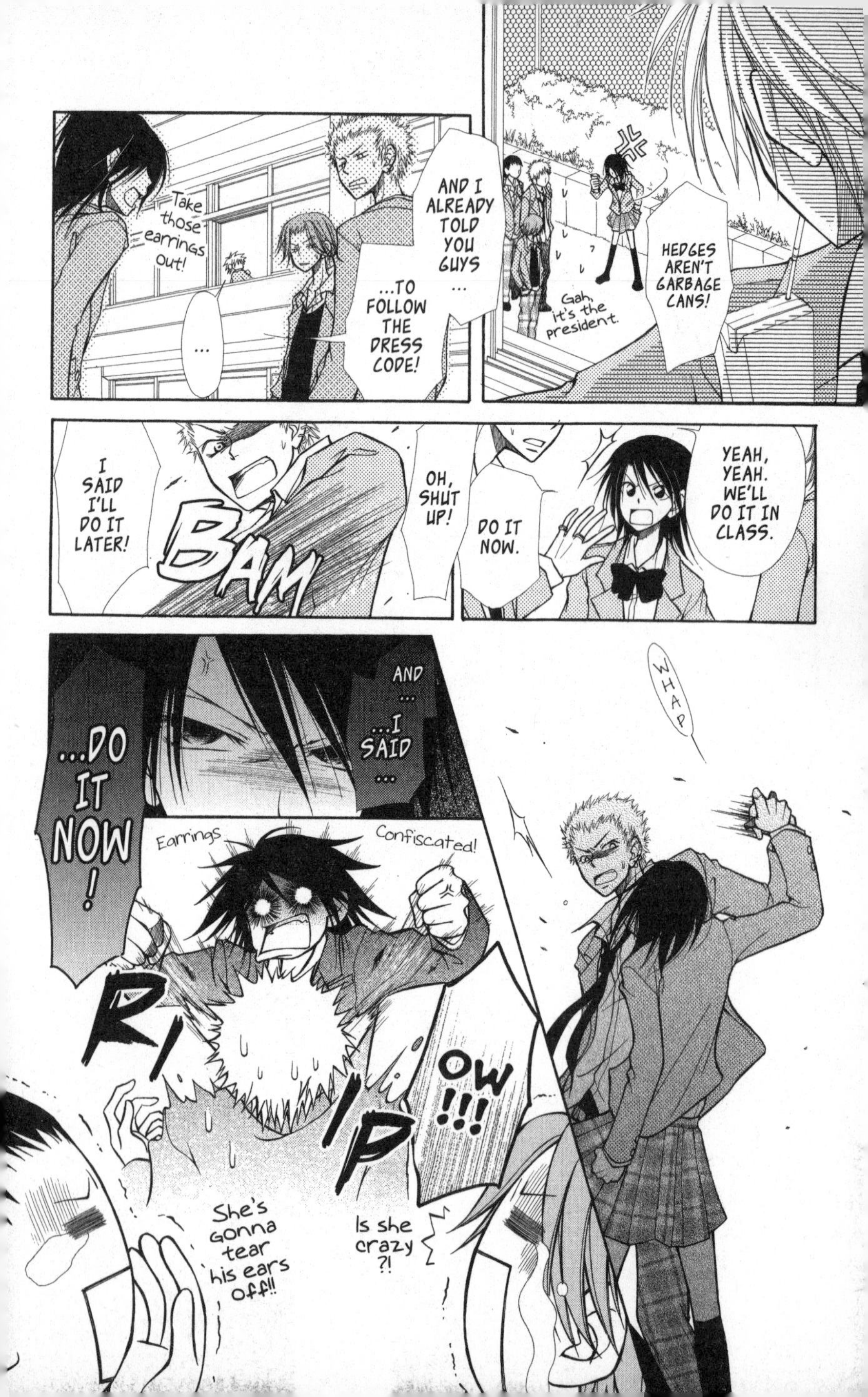
HEDGES AREN'T GARBAGE CANS!
Gah, it's the president.
AND I ALREADY TOLD YOU GUYS ...
...TO FOLLOW THE DRESS CODE!
Take those earrings out!
...
YEAH, YEAH. WE'LL DO IT IN CLASS.
DO IT NOW.
OH, SHUT UP!
I SAID I'LL DO IT LATER!
BAM
WHAP
AND ...
...I SAID ...
...DO IT NOW!
Earrings Confiscated!
RIP
OW!!!
Is she crazy?!
She's gonna tear his ears off!!

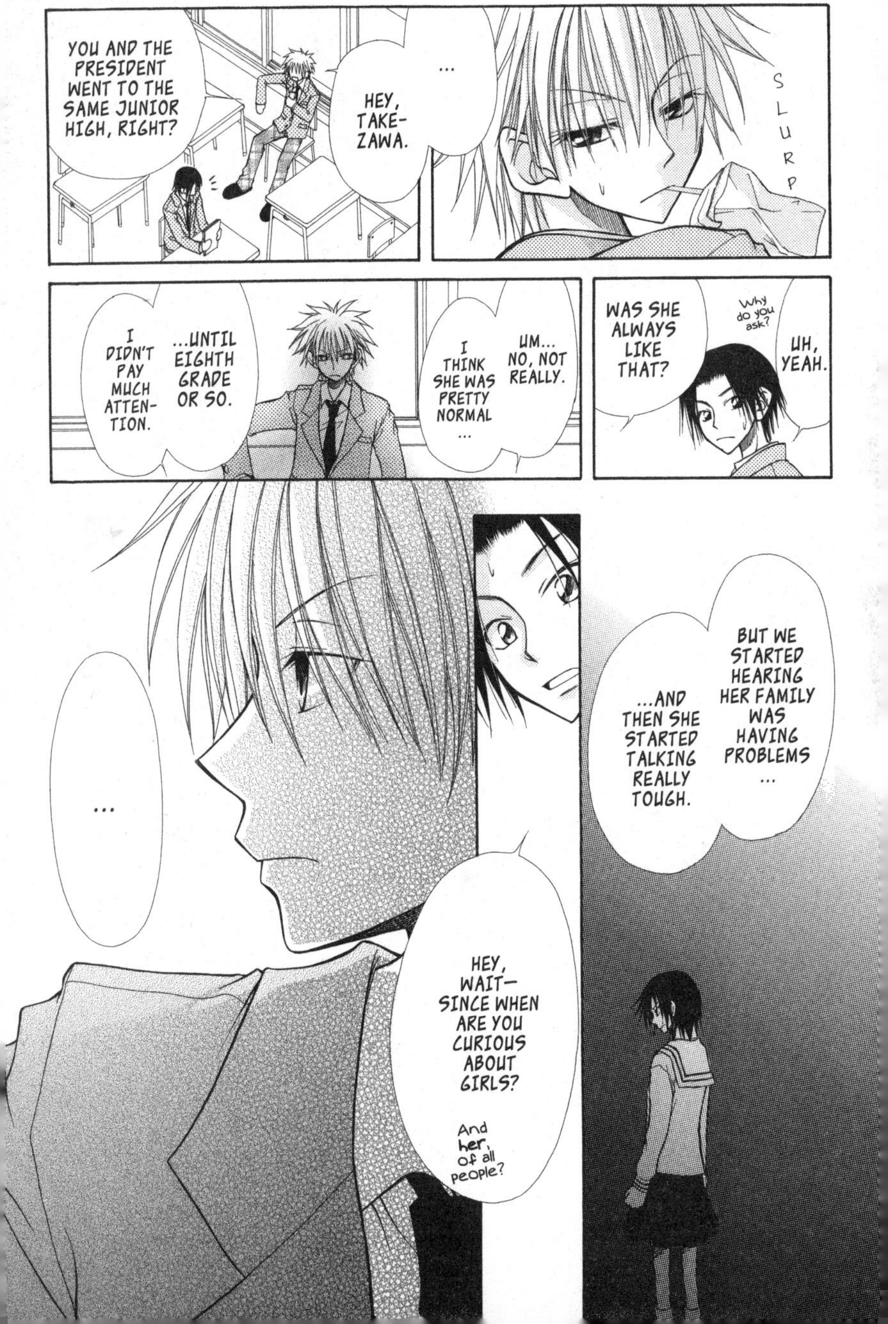
SLURP
... HEY, TAKE-ZAWA.
YOU AND THE PRESIDENT WENT TO THE SAME JUNIOR HIGH, RIGHT?
UH, YEAH.
Why do you ask?
WAS SHE ALWAYS LIKE THAT?
UM... NO, NOT REALLY.
I THINK SHE WAS PRETTY NORMAL...
...UNTIL EIGHTH GRADE OR SO.
I DIDN'T PAY MUCH ATTEN-TION.
BUT WE STARTED HEARING HER FAMILY WAS HAVING PROBLEMS...
...AND THEN SHE STARTED TALKING REALLY TOUGH.
...
HEY, WAIT— SINCE WHEN ARE YOU CURIOUS ABOUT GIRLS?
And her, of all people?

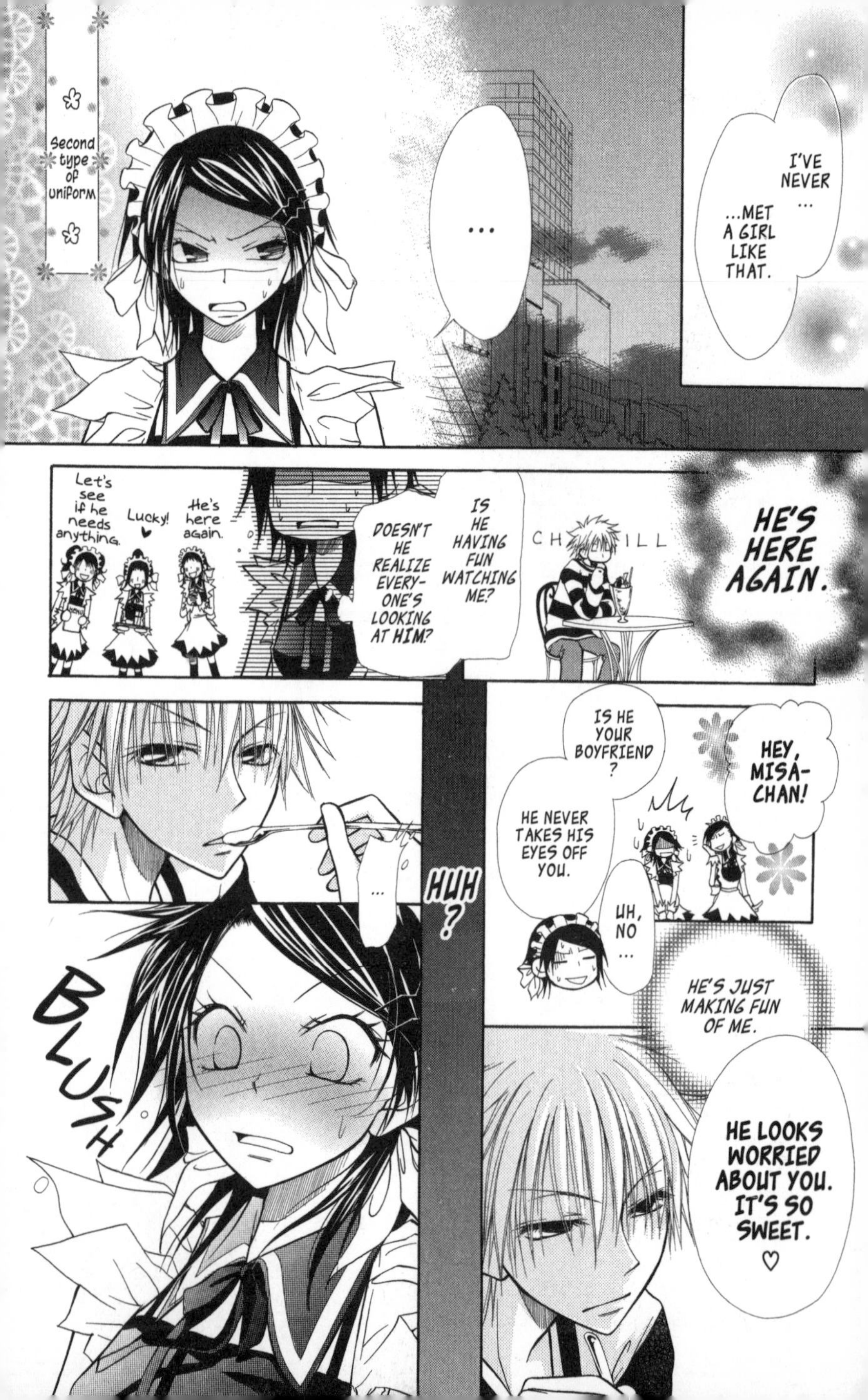
I'VE NEVER ...
...MET A GIRL LIKE THAT.
...
Second type of uniform
HE'S HERE AGAIN.
IS HE HAVING FUN WATCHING ME?
DOESN'T HE REALIZE EVERYONE'S LOOKING AT HIM?
He's here again.
Lucky! ♥
Let's see if he needs anything.
HEY, MISÁ-CHAN!
IS HE YOUR BOYFRIEND?
HE NEVER TAKES HIS EYES OFF YOU.
UH, NO ...
HUH?
...
HE'S JUST MAKING FUN OF ME.
HE LOOKS WORRIED ABOUT YOU. IT'S SO SWEET. ♡
BLUSH

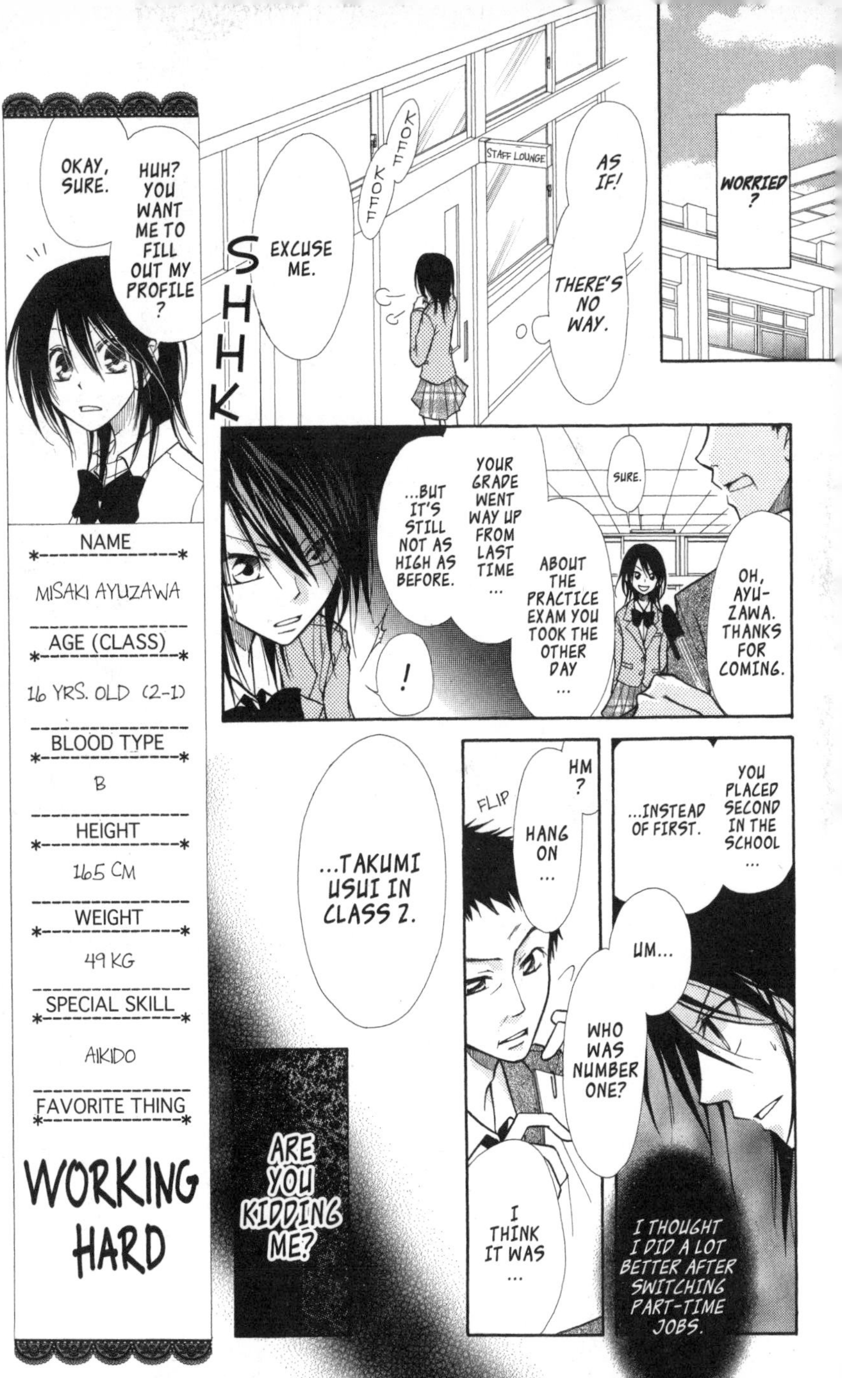
WORRIED?
AS IF!
THERE'S NO WAY.
STAFF LOUNGE
KOFF KOFF
EXCUSE ME.
SHHK
OH, AYUZAWA. THANKS FOR COMING.
SURE.
ABOUT THE PRACTICE EXAM YOU TOOK THE OTHER DAY...
YOUR GRADE WENT WAY UP FROM LAST TIME...
...BUT IT'S STILL NOT AS HIGH AS BEFORE.
!
YOU PLACED SECOND IN THE SCHOOL...
...INSTEAD OF FIRST.
HM?
FLIP
HANG ON...
UM...
WHO WAS NUMBER ONE?
I THINK IT WAS...
...TAKUMI USUI IN CLASS 2.
I THOUGHT I DID A LOT BETTER AFTER SWITCHING PART-TIME JOBS.
ARE YOU KIDDING ME?
HUH? YOU WANT ME TO FILL OUT MY PROFILE?
OKAY, SURE.
NAME
MISAKI AYUZAWA
AGE (CLASS)
16 YRS. OLD (2-1)
BLOOD TYPE
B
HEIGHT
165 CM
WEIGHT
49 KG
SPECIAL SKILL
AIKIDO
FAVORITE THING
WORKING HARD

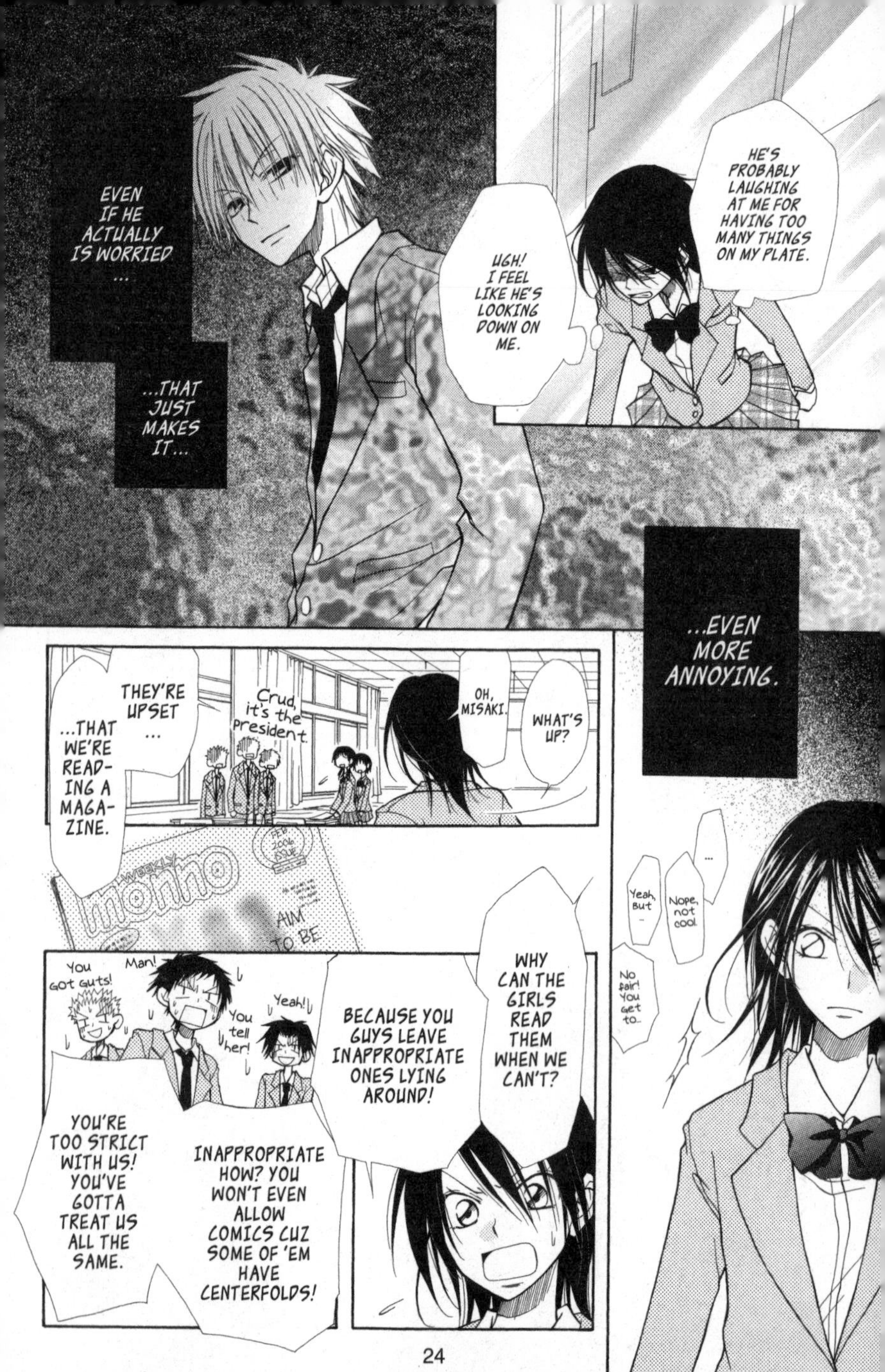
HE'S PROBABLY LAUGHING AT ME FOR HAVING TOO MANY THINGS ON MY PLATE.
UGH! I FEEL LIKE HE'S LOOKING DOWN ON ME.
EVEN IF HE ACTUALLY IS WORRIED ...
...THAT JUST MAKES IT...
...EVEN MORE ANNOYING.
...
Nope, not cool.
Yeah, but ...
No fair! You get to...
OH, MISAKI.
WHAT'S UP?
Crud, it's the President.
THEY'RE UPSET ...
...THAT WE'RE READING A MAGAZINE.
FEB 2006 ISSUE
WEEKLY monno
AIM TO BE
WHY CAN THE GIRLS READ THEM WHEN WE CAN'T?
BECAUSE YOU GUYS LEAVE INAPPROPRIATE ONES LYING AROUND!
Man!
You Got Guts!
Yeah!
You tell her!
YOU'RE TOO STRICT WITH US! YOU'VE GOTTA TREAT US ALL THE SAME.
INAPPROPRIATE HOW? YOU WON'T EVEN ALLOW COMICS CUZ SOME OF 'EM HAVE CENTERFOLDS!

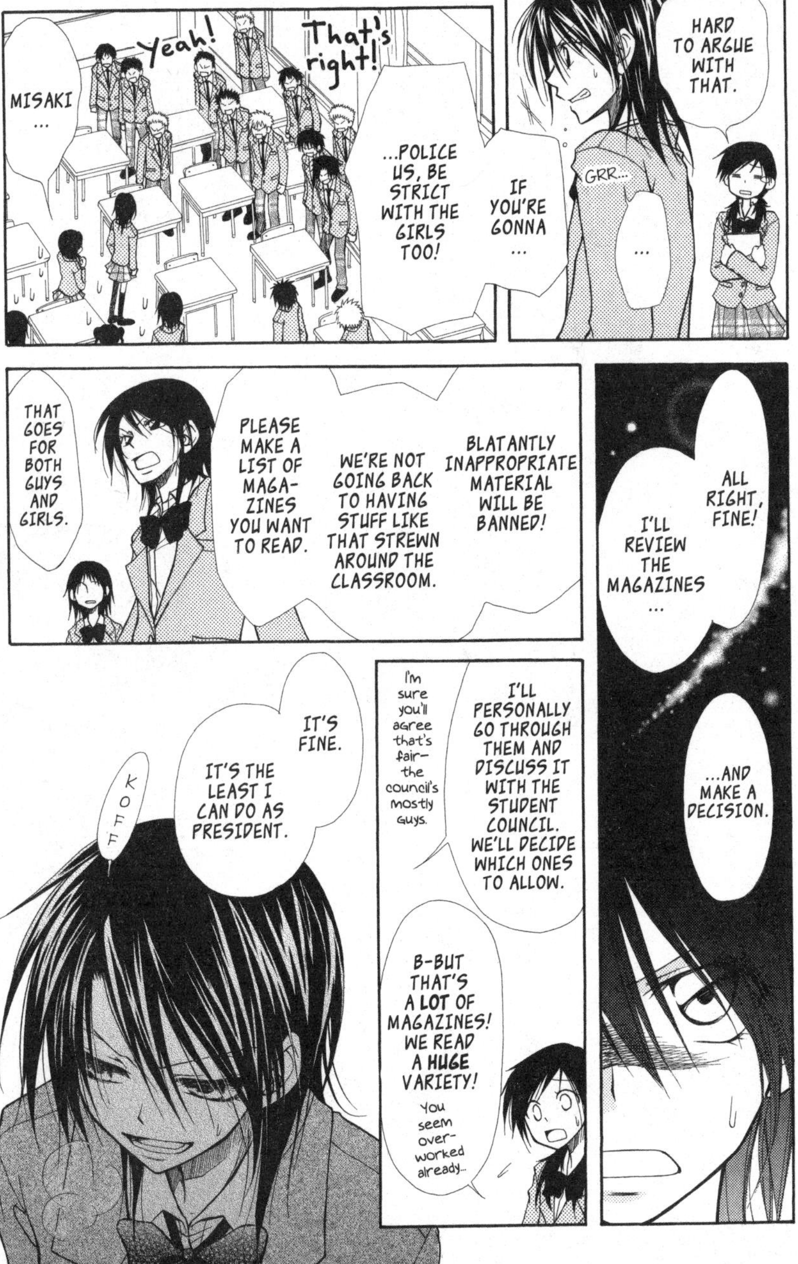
HARD TO ARGUE WITH THAT.
GRR...
...
IF YOU'RE GONNA ...
...POLICE US, BE STRICT WITH THE GIRLS TOO!
That's right!
Yeah!
MISAKI ...
ALL RIGHT, FINE!
I'LL REVIEW THE MAGAZINES ...
...AND MAKE A DECISION.
BLATANTLY INAPPROPRIATE MATERIAL WILL BE BANNED!
WE'RE NOT GOING BACK TO HAVING STUFF LIKE THAT STREWN AROUND THE CLASSROOM.
PLEASE MAKE A LIST OF MAGA-ZINES YOU WANT TO READ.
THAT GOES FOR BOTH GUYS AND GIRLS.
I'LL PERSONALLY GO THROUGH THEM AND DISCUSS IT WITH THE STUDENT COUNCIL. WE'LL DECIDE WHICH ONES TO ALLOW.
I'm sure you'll agree that's fair—the council's mostly guys.
B-BUT THAT'S A LOT OF MAGAZINES! WE READ A HUGE VARIETY!
You seem over-worked already...
IT'S FINE.
IT'S THE LEAST I CAN DO AS PRESIDENT.
KOFF

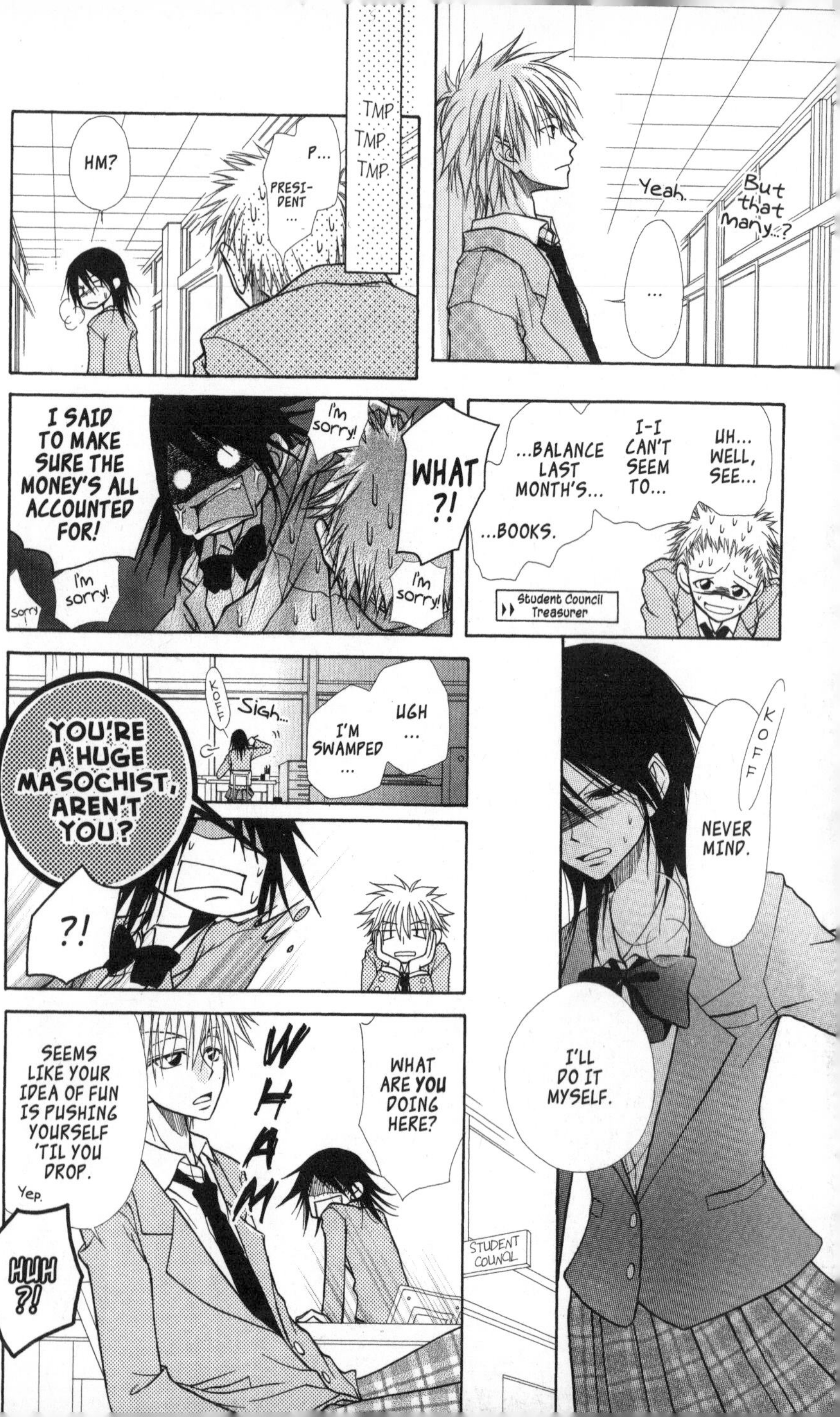
But that many...?
Yeah.
...
TMP
TMP
TMP
P...
PRESIDENT...
HM?
UH... WELL, SEE...
I-I CAN'T SEEM TO...
...BALANCE LAST MONTH'S...
...BOOKS.
Student Council Treasurer
WHAT?!
I'm sorry!
I SAID TO MAKE SURE THE MONEY'S ALL ACCOUNTED FOR!
I'm sorry!
I'm sorry!
sorry
KOFF
NEVER MIND.
I'LL DO IT MYSELF.
STUDENT COUNCIL
UGH...
I'M SWAMPED...
Sigh...
KOFF
YOU'RE A HUGE MASOCHIST, AREN'T YOU?
?!
WHAT ARE YOU DOING HERE?
WHAM
SEEMS LIKE YOUR IDEA OF FUN IS PUSHING YOURSELF 'TIL YOU DROP.
Yep.
HUH?!

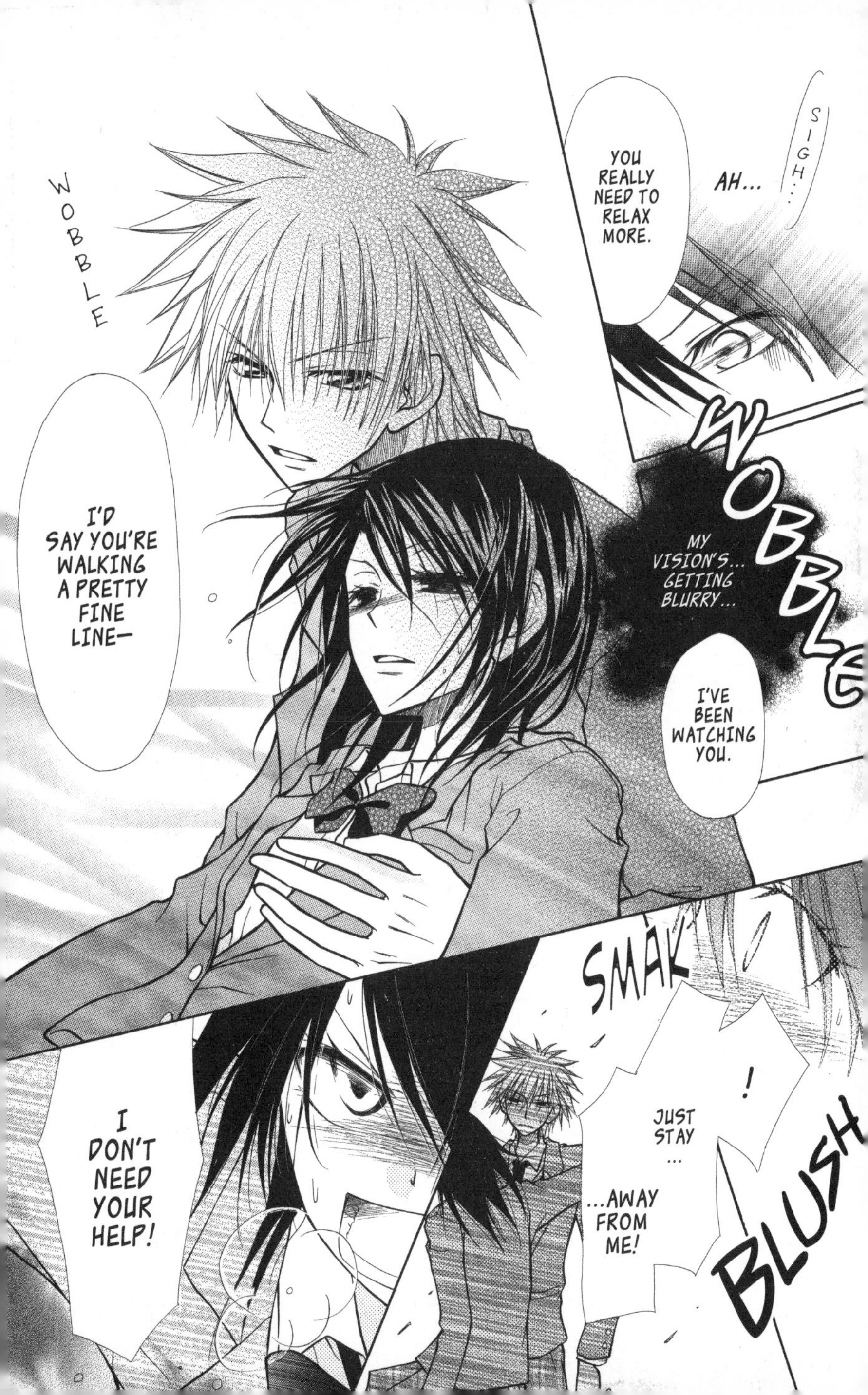
SIGH...
AH...
YOU REALLY NEED TO RELAX MORE.
WOBBLE
WOBBLE
MY VISION'S... GETTING BLURRY...
I'VE BEEN WATCHING YOU.
I'D SAY YOU'RE WALKING A PRETTY FINE LINE—
SMAK
!
BLUSH
JUST STAY ...
...AWAY FROM ME!
I DON'T NEED YOUR HELP!

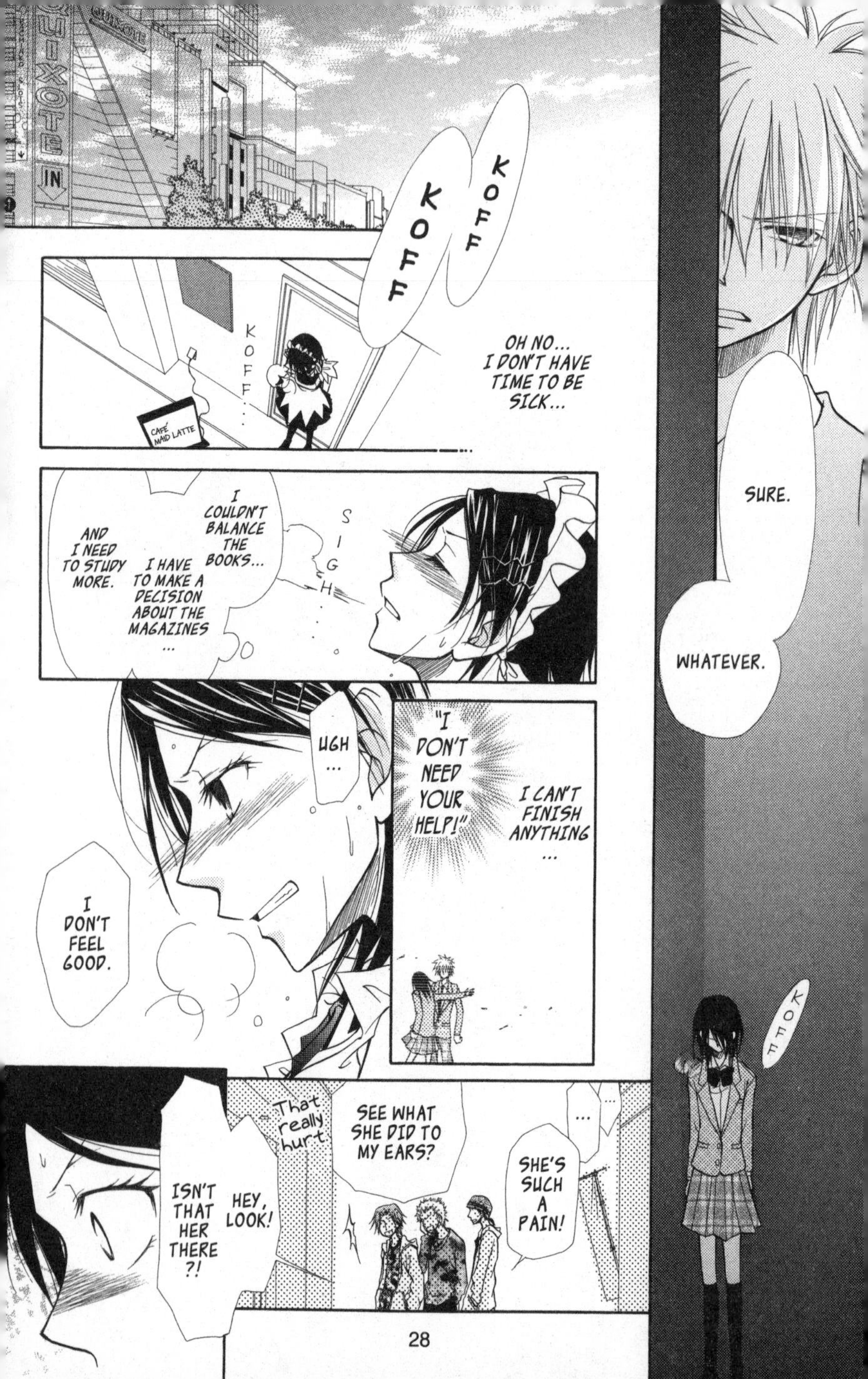
SURE.
WHATEVER.
KOFF
KOFF KOFF
KOFF...
OH NO... I DON'T HAVE TIME TO BE SICK...
SIGH...
I COULDN'T BALANCE THE BOOKS...
I HAVE TO MAKE A DECISION ABOUT THE MAGAZINES...
AND I NEED TO STUDY MORE.
"I DON'T NEED YOUR HELP!"
I CAN'T FINISH ANYTHING...
UGH...
I DON'T FEEL GOOD.
...
...
SHE'S SUCH A PAIN!
SEE WHAT SHE DID TO MY EARS?
That really hurt.
HEY, LOOK!
ISN'T THAT HER THERE?!

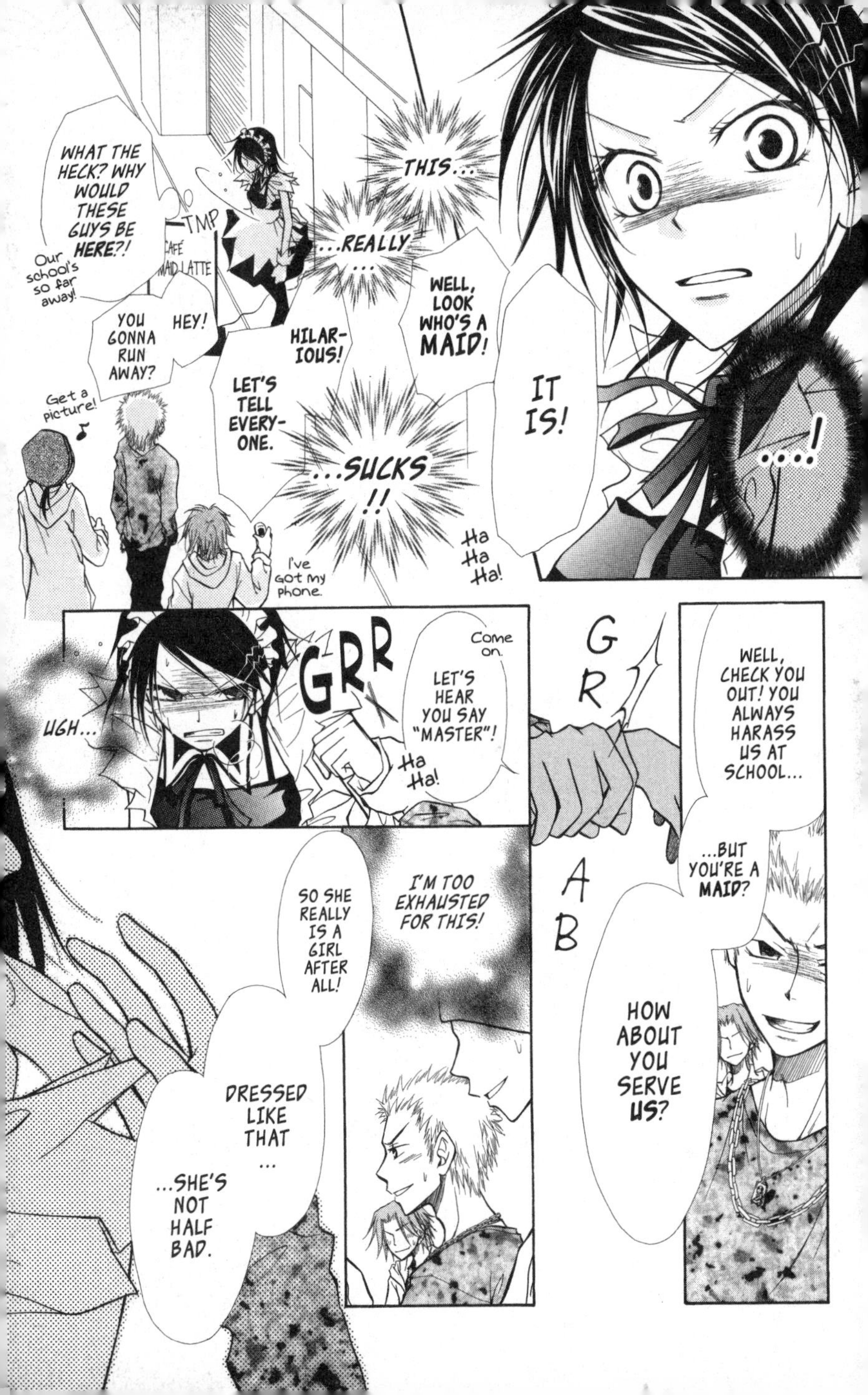
....!
IT IS!
WELL, LOOK WHO'S A MAID!
HILAR-IOUS!
THIS...
...REALLY...
...SUCKS!!
WHAT THE HECK? WHY WOULD THESE GUYS BE HERE?!
Our school's so far away!
TMP
CAFÉ MAID LATTE
HEY!
YOU GONNA RUN AWAY?
LET'S TELL EVERY-ONE.
Get a picture!
I've got my phone.
Ha Ha Ha!
GRAB
WELL, CHECK YOU OUT! YOU ALWAYS HARASS US AT SCHOOL...
...BUT YOU'RE A MAID?
HOW ABOUT YOU SERVE US?
Come on.
LET'S HEAR YOU SAY "MASTER"!
GRR
Ha Ha!
UGH...
I'M TOO EXHAUSTED FOR THIS!
SO SHE REALLY IS A GIRL AFTER ALL!
DRESSED LIKE THAT...
...SHE'S NOT HALF BAD.

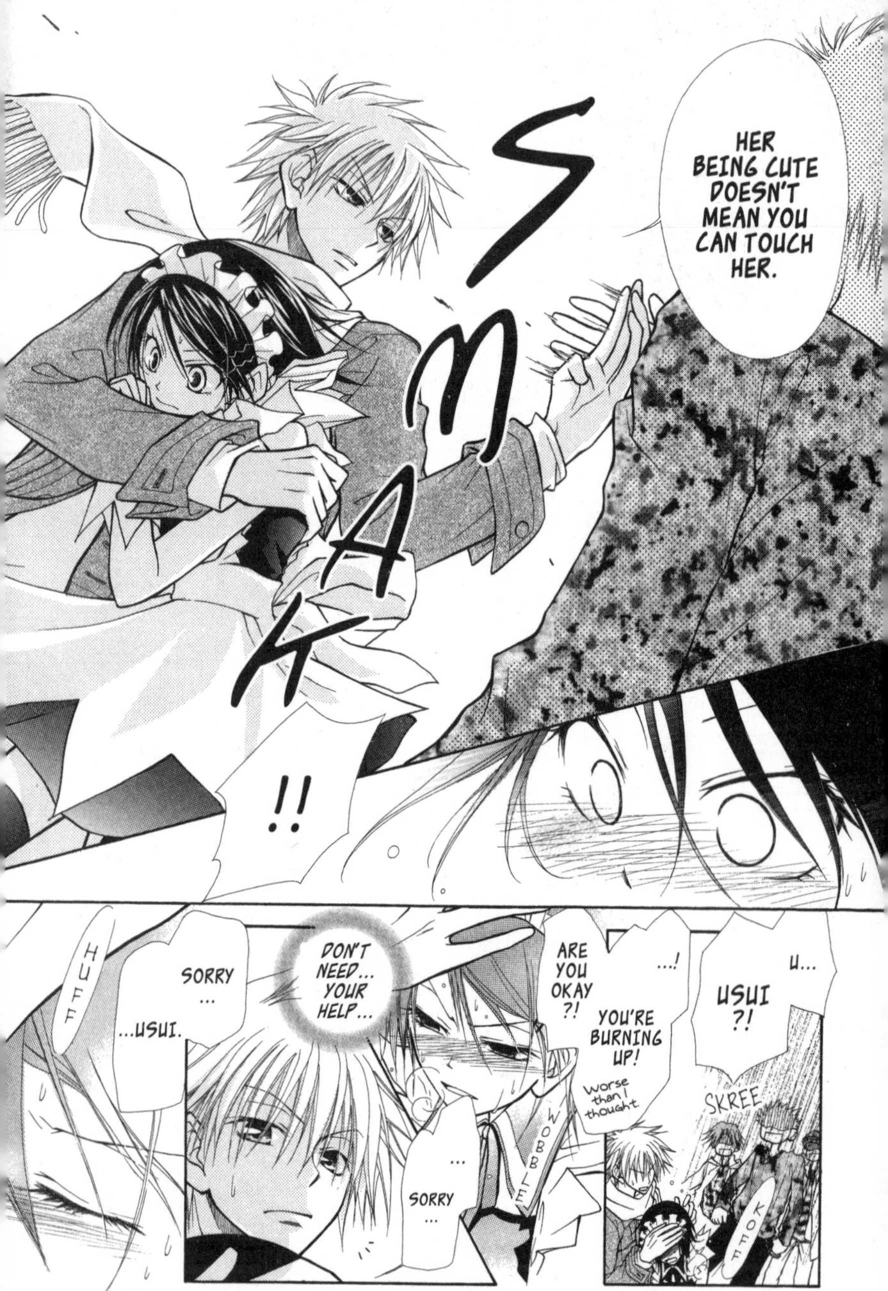
HER BEING CUTE DOESN'T MEAN YOU CAN TOUCH HER.
SMACK
!!
U... USUI ?!
SKREE
KOFF
...!
ARE YOU OKAY ?!
YOU'RE BURNING UP!
Worse than I thought.
WOBBLE
DON'T NEED... YOUR HELP...
... SORRY ...
HUFF
SORRY ...
...USUI.

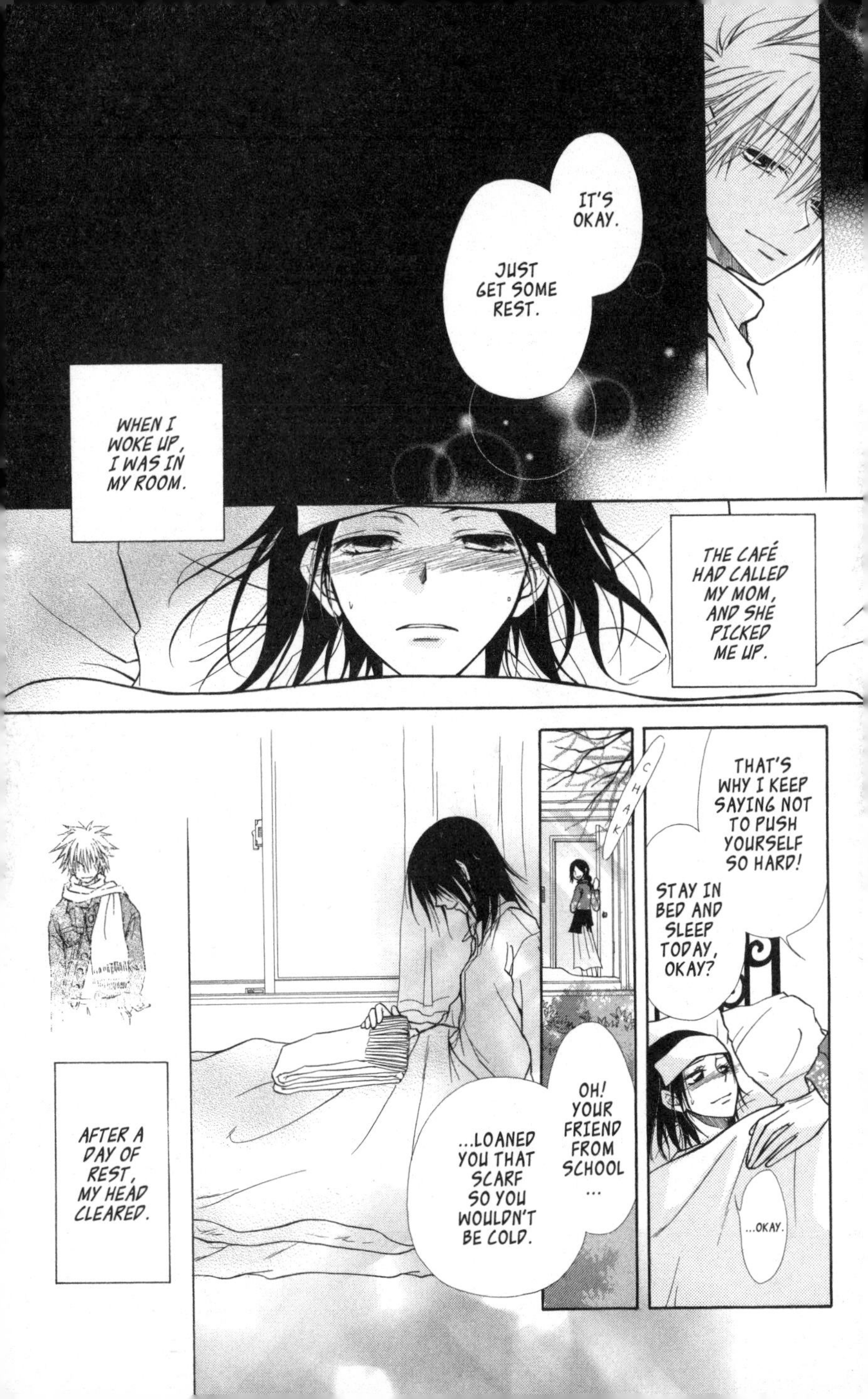
IT'S OKAY.
JUST GET SOME REST.
WHEN I WOKE UP, I WAS IN MY ROOM.
THE CAFÉ HAD CALLED MY MOM, AND SHE PICKED ME UP.
THAT'S WHY I KEEP SAYING NOT TO PUSH YOURSELF SO HARD!
STAY IN BED AND SLEEP TODAY, OKAY?
...OKAY.
CHAK
OH! YOUR FRIEND FROM SCHOOL...
...LOANED YOU THAT SCARF SO YOU WOULDN'T BE COLD.
AFTER A DAY OF REST, MY HEAD CLEARED.

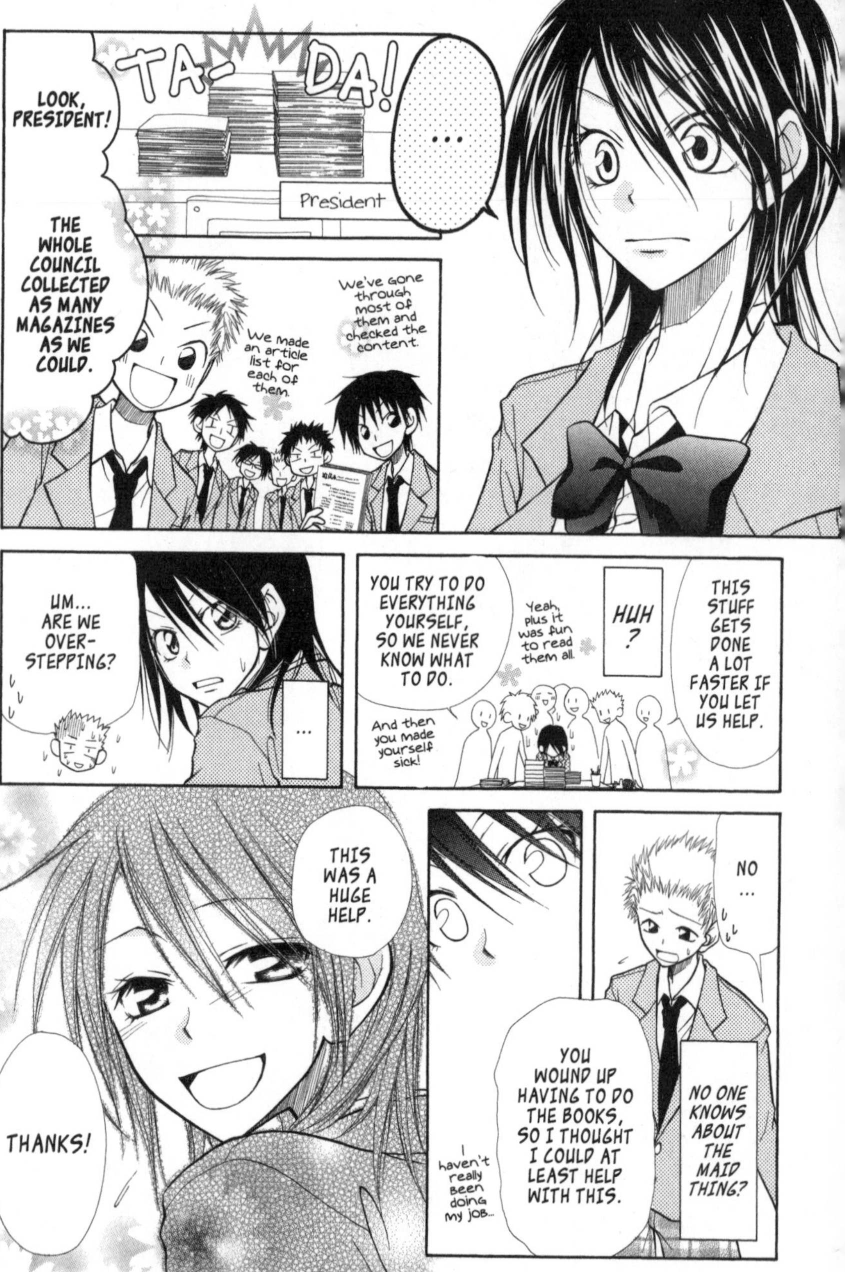
TA-DA!
LOOK, PRESIDENT!
President
...
THE WHOLE COUNCIL COLLECTED AS MANY MAGAZINES AS WE COULD.
We've gone through most of them and checked the content.
We made an article list for each of them.
THIS STUFF GETS DONE A LOT FASTER IF YOU LET US HELP.
HUH?
Yeah, plus it was fun to read them all.
YOU TRY TO DO EVERYTHING YOURSELF, SO WE NEVER KNOW WHAT TO DO.
And then you made yourself sick!
...
UM... ARE WE OVER-STEPPING?
NO...
NO ONE KNOWS ABOUT THE MAID THING?
YOU WOUND UP HAVING TO DO THE BOOKS, SO I THOUGHT I COULD AT LEAST HELP WITH THIS.
I haven't really been doing my job...
THIS WAS A HUGE HELP.
THANKS!

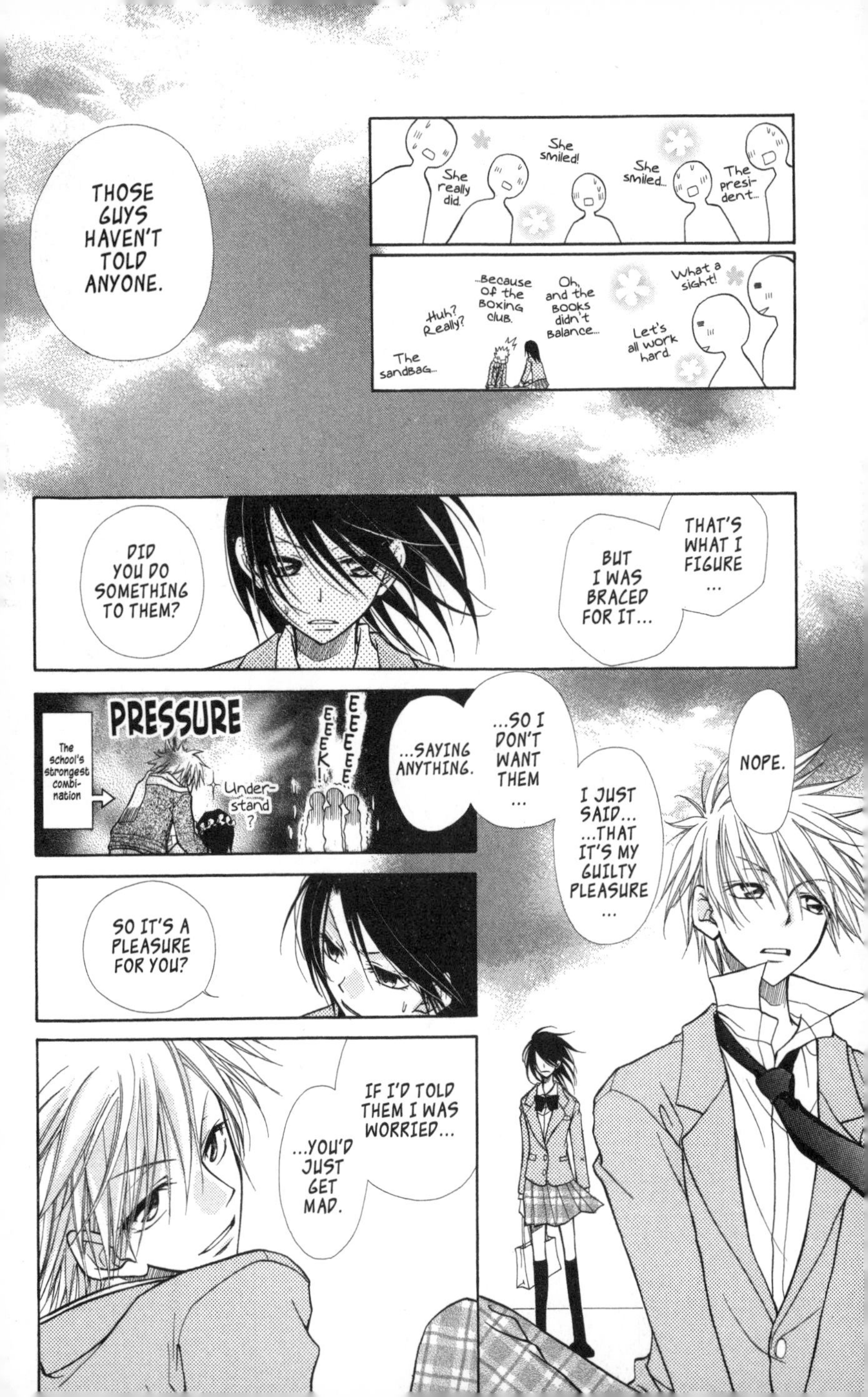
The president...
She smiled...
She smiled!
She really did.
What a sight!
Let's all work hard.
Oh, and the books didn't balance...
...Because of the boxing club.
Huh? Really?
The sandbag...
THOSE GUYS HAVEN'T TOLD ANYONE.
THAT'S WHAT I FIGURE ...
BUT I WAS BRACED FOR IT...
DID YOU DO SOMETHING TO THEM?
NOPE.
I JUST SAID... ...THAT IT'S MY GUILTY PLEASURE ...
...SO I DON'T WANT THEM ...
...SAYING ANYTHING.
EEEEEE
EEEK!
Understand?
PRESSURE
The school's strongest combination
SO IT'S A PLEASURE FOR YOU?
IF I'D TOLD THEM I WAS WORRIED...
...YOU'D JUST GET MAD.

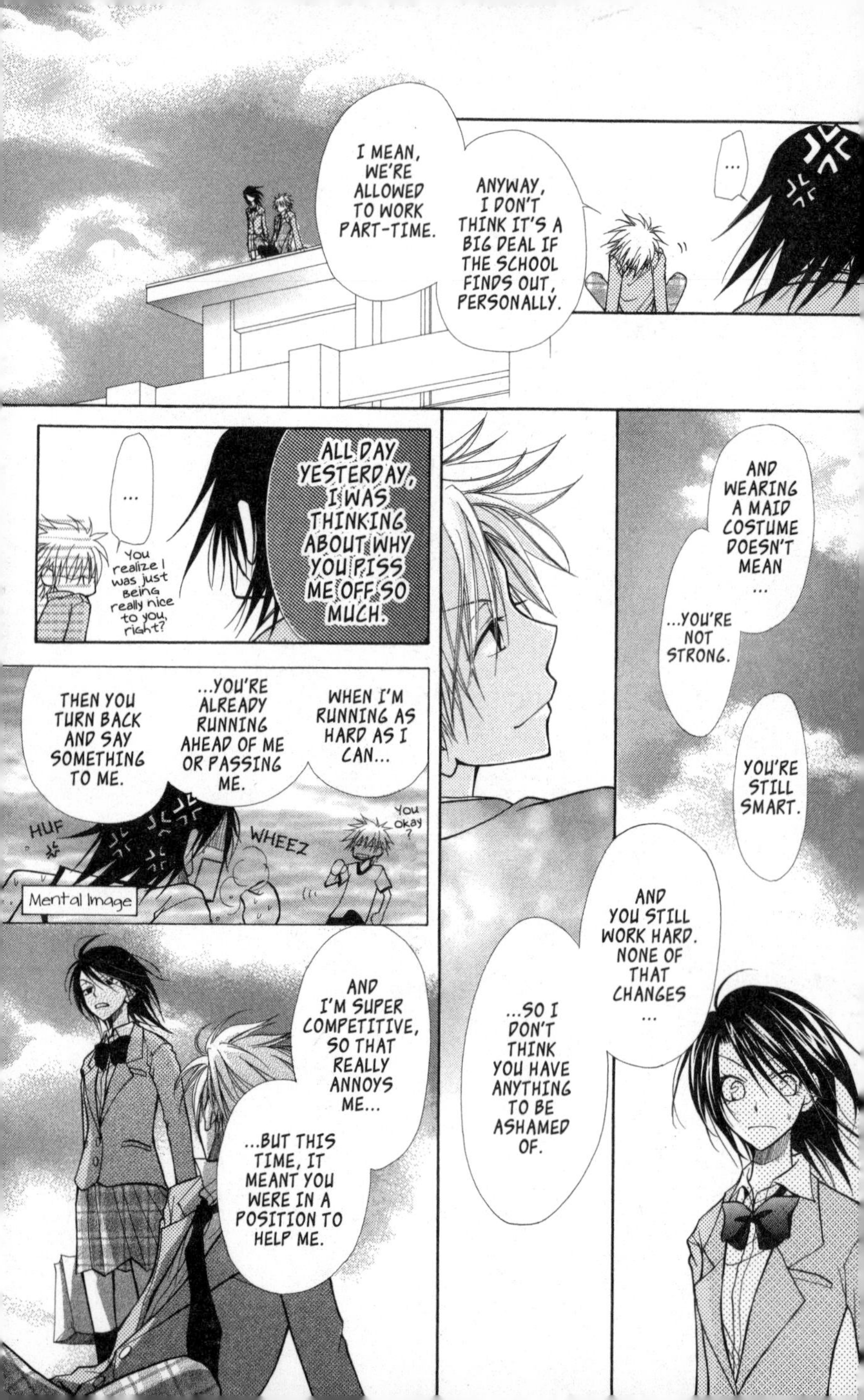
...
ANYWAY, I DON'T THINK IT'S A BIG DEAL IF THE SCHOOL FINDS OUT, PERSONALLY.
I MEAN, WE'RE ALLOWED TO WORK PART-TIME.
AND WEARING A MAID COSTUME DOESN'T MEAN ...
...YOU'RE NOT STRONG.
YOU'RE STILL SMART.
AND YOU STILL WORK HARD. NONE OF THAT CHANGES ...
...SO I DON'T THINK YOU HAVE ANYTHING TO BE ASHAMED OF.
ALL DAY YESTERDAY, I WAS THINKING ABOUT WHY YOU PISS ME OFF SO MUCH.
...
You realize I was just being really nice to you, right?
WHEN I'M RUNNING AS HARD AS I CAN...
...YOU'RE ALREADY RUNNING AHEAD OF ME OR PASSING ME.
THEN YOU TURN BACK AND SAY SOMETHING TO ME.
You okay?
WHEEZ
HUF
Mental Image
AND I'M SUPER COMPETITIVE, SO THAT REALLY ANNOYS ME...
...BUT THIS TIME, IT MEANT YOU WERE IN A POSITION TO HELP ME.

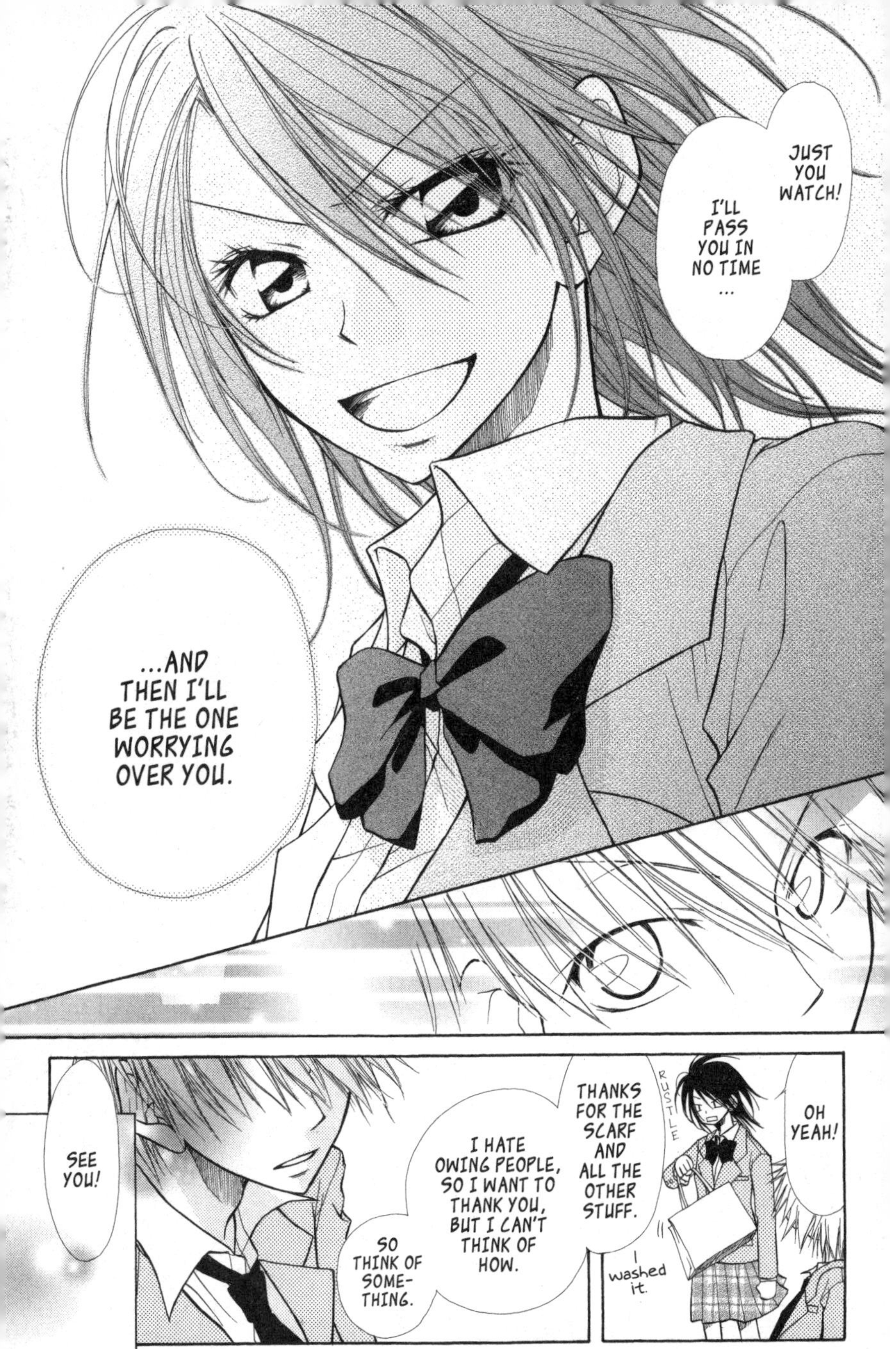
JUST YOU WATCH!
I'LL PASS YOU IN NO TIME ...
...AND THEN I'LL BE THE ONE WORRYING OVER YOU.
OH YEAH!
RUSTLE
THANKS FOR THE SCARF AND ALL THE OTHER STUFF.
I washed it.
I HATE OWING PEOPLE, SO I WANT TO THANK YOU, BUT I CAN'T THINK OF HOW.
SO THINK OF SOME-THING.
SEE YOU!

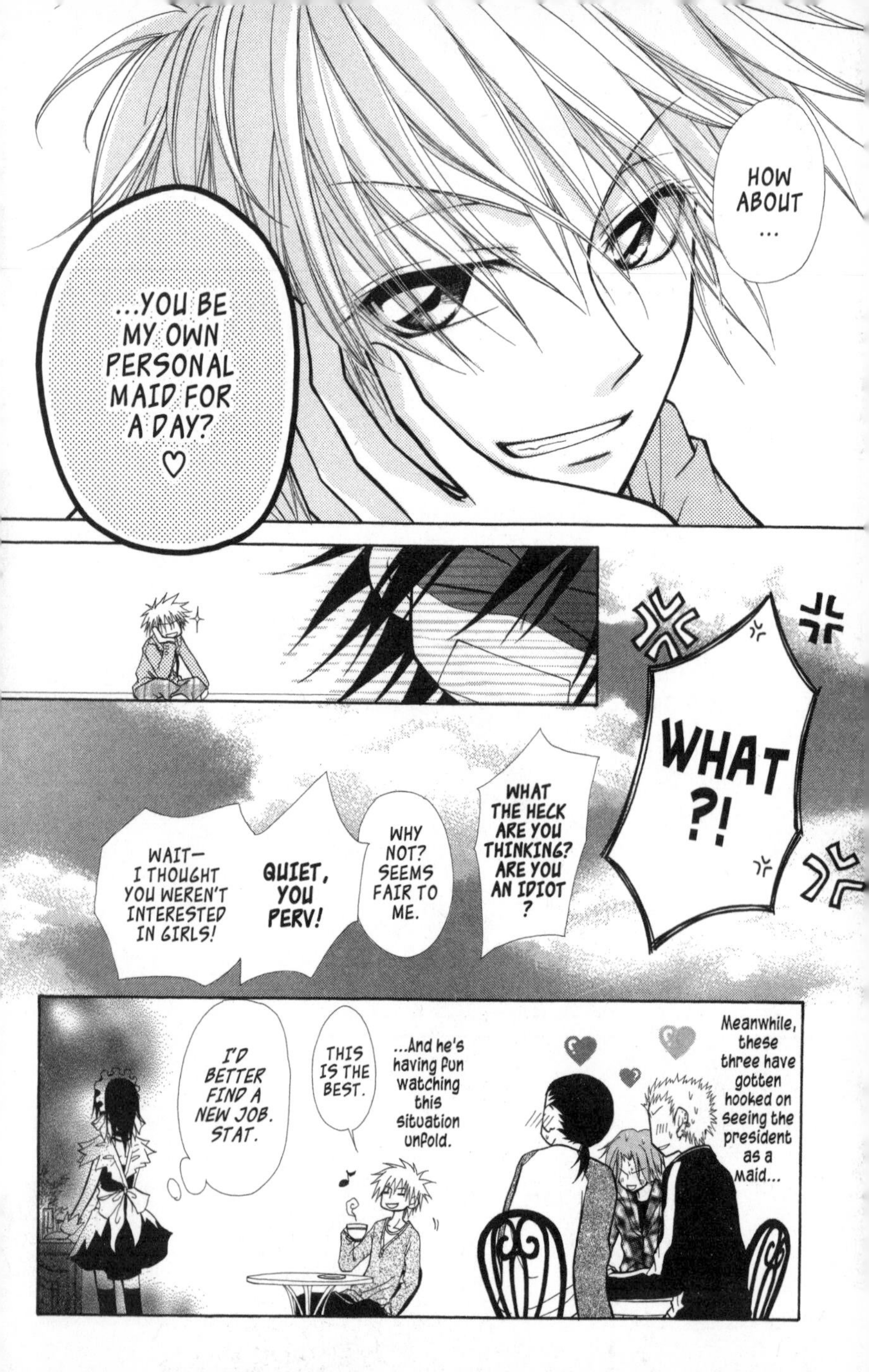
HOW ABOUT ...
...YOU BE MY OWN PERSONAL MAID FOR A DAY? ♡
WHAT ?!
WHAT THE HECK ARE YOU THINKING? ARE YOU AN IDIOT ?
WHY NOT? SEEMS FAIR TO ME.
QUIET, YOU PERV!
WAIT— I THOUGHT YOU WEREN'T INTERESTED IN GIRLS!
Meanwhile, these three have gotten hooked on seeing the president as a maid...
...And he's having fun watching this situation unfold.
THIS IS THE BEST.
I'D BETTER FIND A NEW JOB. STAT.

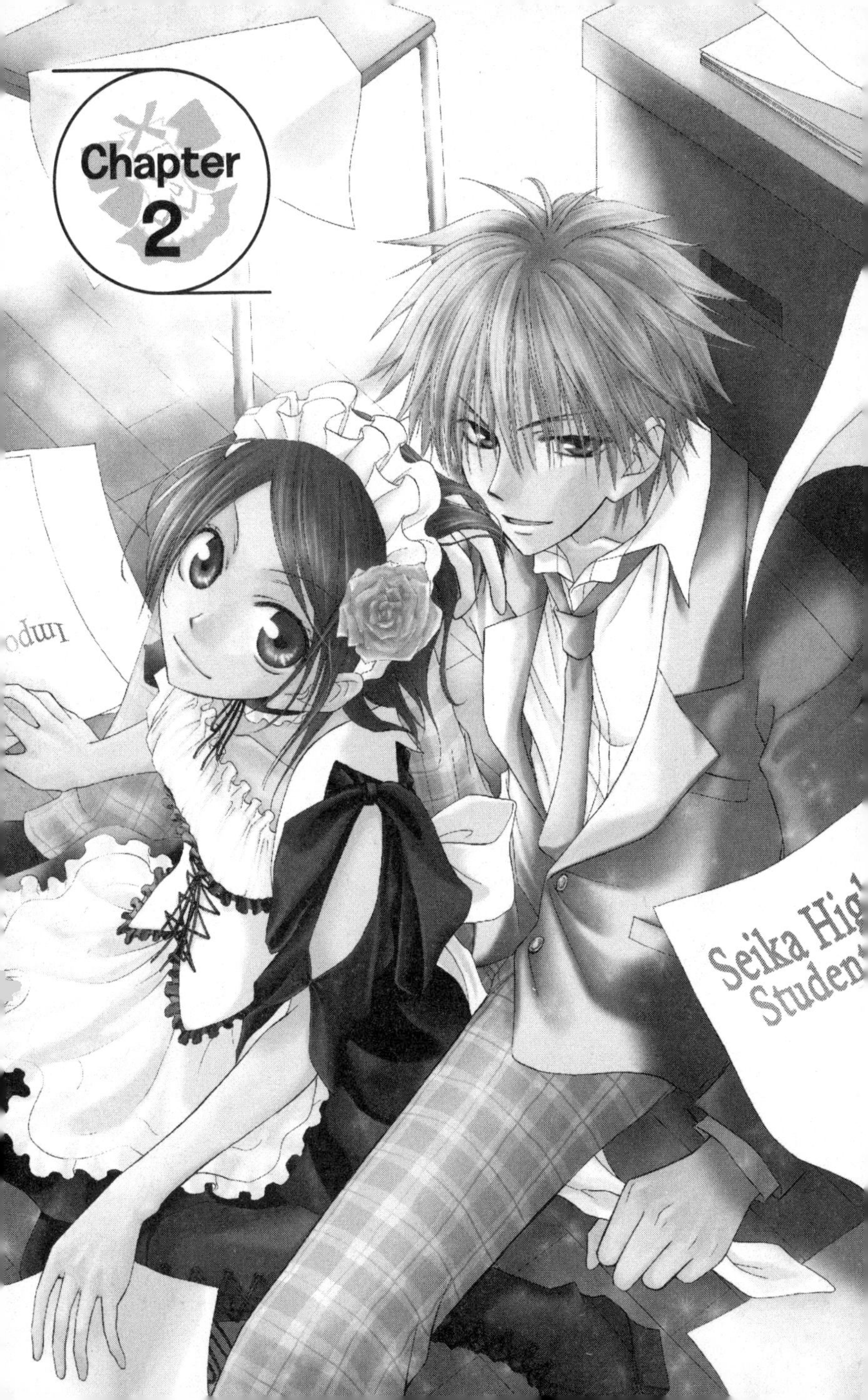
Chapter 2

café Maid Latte UNIFORM

All cutesy!

Would you like a rice omelet?

When the serialization of *Maid-sama* was announced, I decided I should come up with an original maid costume. After giving it a lot of thought, this is what I dreamed up. I wanted something totally unique, and after a lot of trial and error, this was my design. But frankly, even I'm not quite sure how it's all put together. (Seriously...!) I imagine the fabric for the shoulders is easy to wash.

It's secured here.

◆◆◆ Misaki's wearing boots...

◆ Honoka, who has a calming influence on the others, wears white knee socks with loafers. On the first day of work, the café manager offers her discriminating advice.

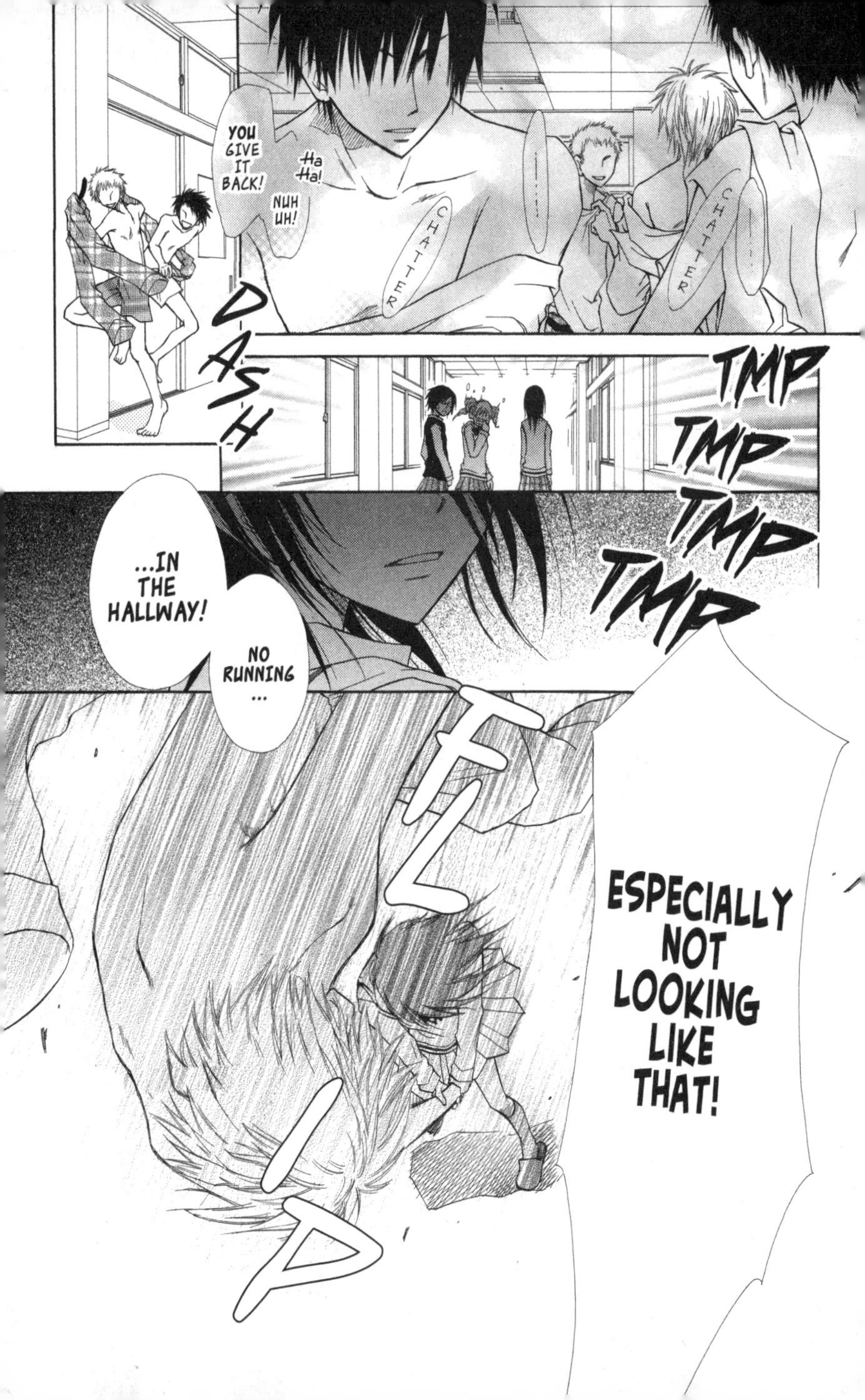

...!
CHATTER
...!
CHATTER
YOU GIVE IT BACK!
Ha Ha!
NUH UH!
DASH
TMP TMP TMP TMP
NO RUNNING...
...IN THE HALLWAY!
ESPECIALLY NOT LOOKING LIKE THAT!
FLIP

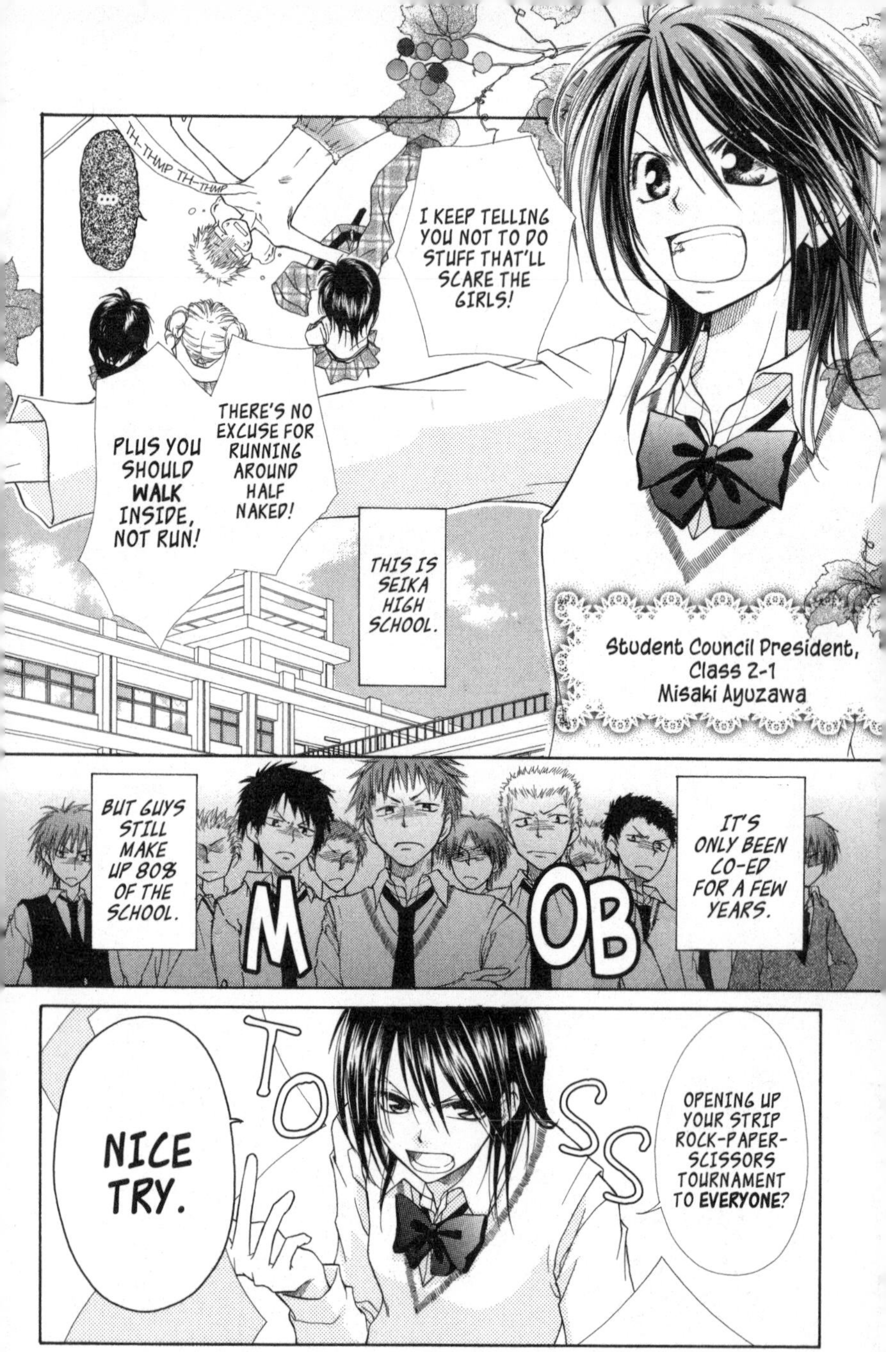
I KEEP TELLING YOU NOT TO DO STUFF THAT'LL SCARE THE GIRLS!
THERE'S NO EXCUSE FOR RUNNING AROUND HALF NAKED!
PLUS YOU SHOULD WALK INSIDE, NOT RUN!
TH-THMP TH-THMP
...
THIS IS SEIKA HIGH SCHOOL.
Student Council President, Class 2-1 Misaki Ayuzawa
IT'S ONLY BEEN CO-ED FOR A FEW YEARS.
BUT GUYS STILL MAKE UP 80% OF THE SCHOOL.
MOB
OPENING UP YOUR STRIP ROCK-PAPER-SCISSORS TOURNAMENT TO EVERYONE?
TOSS
NICE TRY.

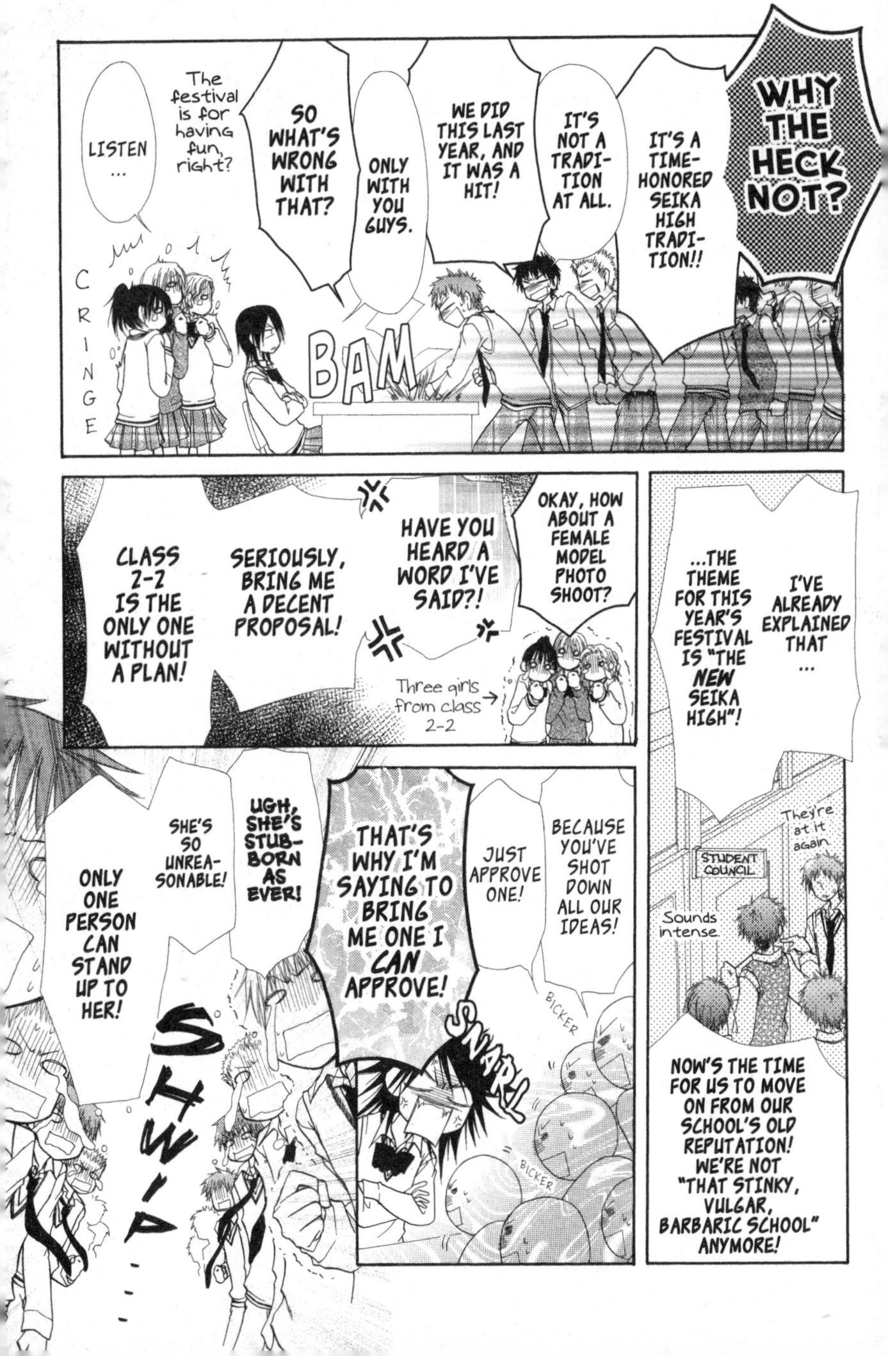
WHY THE HECK NOT?
IT'S A TIME-HONORED SEIKA HIGH TRADITION!!
IT'S NOT A TRADITION AT ALL.
WE DID THIS LAST YEAR, AND IT WAS A HIT!
ONLY WITH YOU GUYS.
SO WHAT'S WRONG WITH THAT?
The festival is for having fun, right?
LISTEN ...
BAM
CRINGE
I'VE ALREADY EXPLAINED THAT ...
...THE THEME FOR THIS YEAR'S FESTIVAL IS "THE NEW SEIKA HIGH"!
They're at it again
STUDENT COUNCIL
Sounds intense.
NOW'S THE TIME FOR US TO MOVE ON FROM OUR SCHOOL'S OLD REPUTATION! WE'RE NOT "THAT STINKY, VULGAR, BARBARIC SCHOOL" ANYMORE!
OKAY, HOW ABOUT A FEMALE MODEL PHOTO SHOOT?
HAVE YOU HEARD A WORD I'VE SAID?!
SERIOUSLY, BRING ME A DECENT PROPOSAL!
CLASS 2-2 IS THE ONLY ONE WITHOUT A PLAN!
Three girls from class 2-2
BECAUSE YOU'VE SHOT DOWN ALL OUR IDEAS!
JUST APPROVE ONE!
THAT'S WHY I'M SAYING TO BRING ME ONE I CAN APPROVE!
SNARL
BICKER
BICKER
UGH, SHE'S STUBBORN AS EVER!
SHE'S SO UNREASONABLE!
ONLY ONE PERSON CAN STAND UP TO HER!
SHWA...

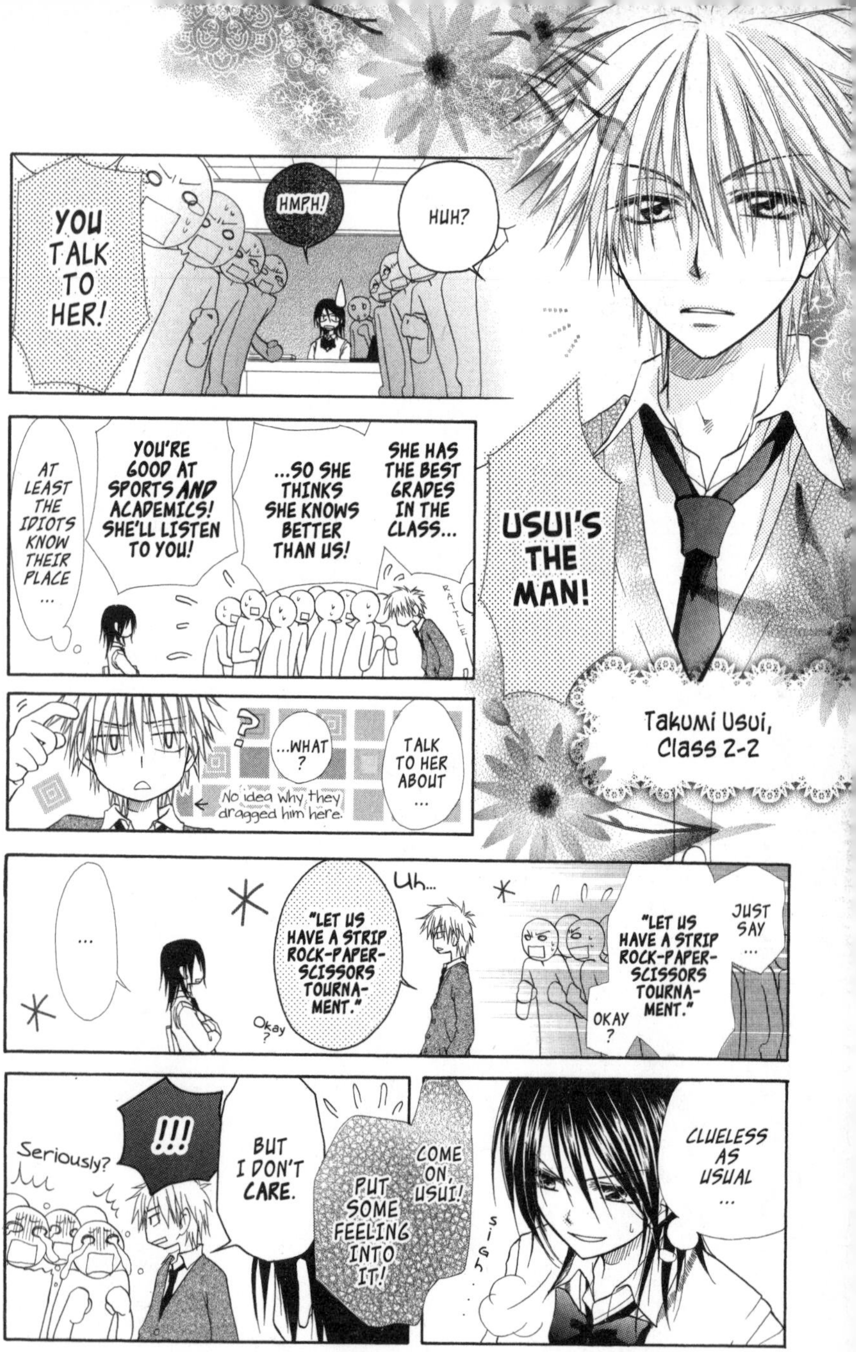
USUI'S THE MAN!
Takumi Usui, Class 2-2
HUH?
HMPH!
YOU TALK TO HER!
SHE HAS THE BEST GRADES IN THE CLASS...
...SO SHE THINKS SHE KNOWS BETTER THAN US!
YOU'RE GOOD AT SPORTS AND ACADEMICS! SHE'LL LISTEN TO YOU!
RATTLE
AT LEAST THE IDIOTS KNOW THEIR PLACE...
TALK TO HER ABOUT...
...WHAT?
No idea why they dragged him here.
JUST SAY...
"LET US HAVE A STRIP ROCK-PAPER-SCISSORS TOURNAMENT."
OKAY?
Uh...
"LET US HAVE A STRIP ROCK-PAPER-SCISSORS TOURNAMENT."
Okay?
...
CLUELESS AS USUAL...
SIGH
COME ON, USUI!
PUT SOME FEELING INTO IT!
BUT I DON'T CARE.
!!!
Seriously?

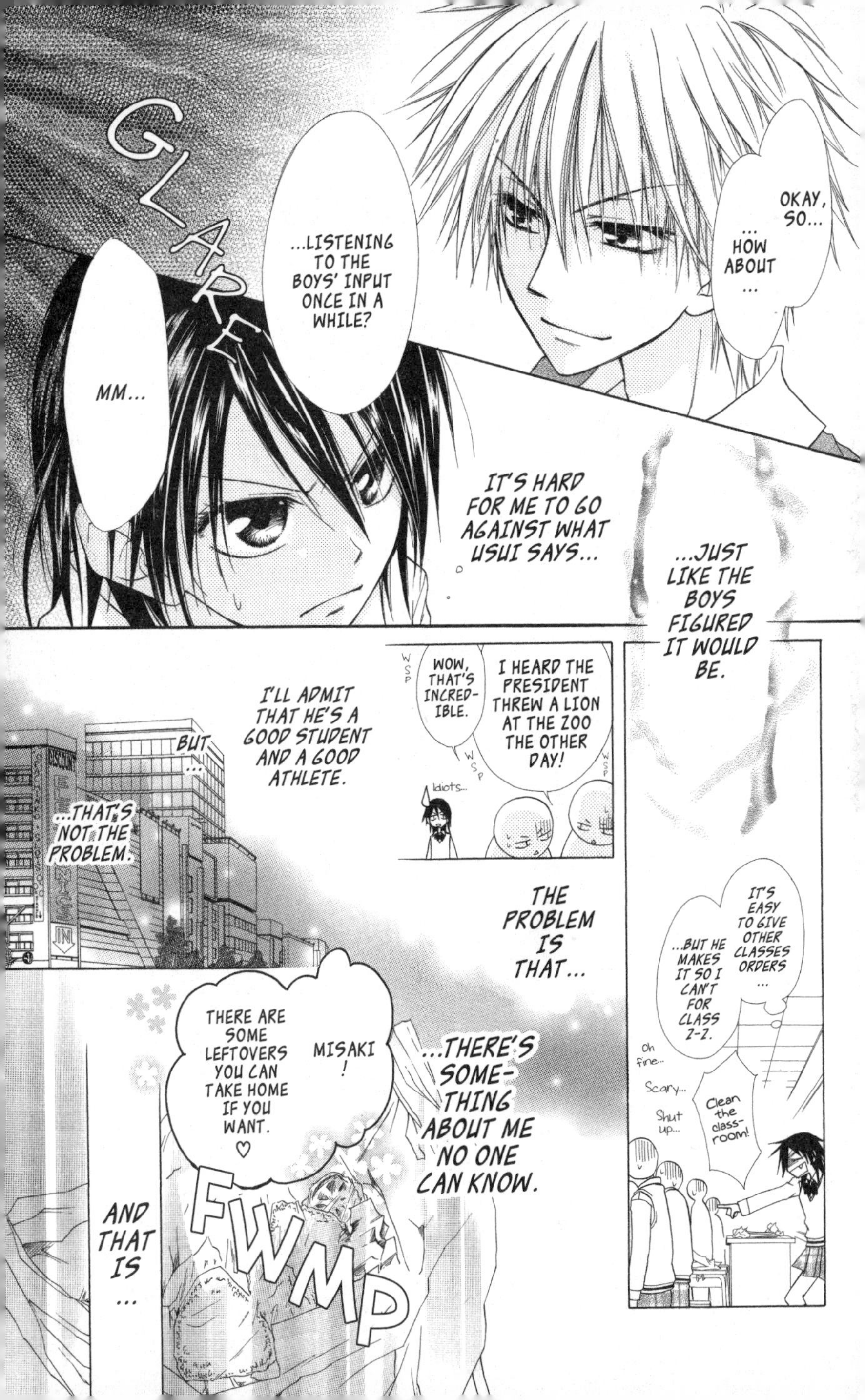
OKAY, SO... ...HOW ABOUT...
...LISTENING TO THE BOYS' INPUT ONCE IN A WHILE?
GLARE
MM...
IT'S HARD FOR ME TO GO AGAINST WHAT USUI SAYS...
...JUST LIKE THE BOYS FIGURED IT WOULD BE.
IT'S EASY TO GIVE OTHER CLASSES ORDERS...
...BUT HE MAKES IT SO I CAN'T FOR CLASS 2-2.
Clean the classroom!
Oh fine...
Scary...
Shut up...
WSP
I HEARD THE PRESIDENT THREW A LION AT THE ZOO THE OTHER DAY!
WSP
WOW, THAT'S INCREDIBLE.
WSP
Idiots...
I'LL ADMIT THAT HE'S A GOOD STUDENT AND A GOOD ATHLETE.
BUT...
...THAT'S NOT THE PROBLEM.
DISCOUNT
IN
THE PROBLEM IS THAT...
...THERE'S SOME-THING ABOUT ME NO ONE CAN KNOW.
MISAKI!
THERE ARE SOME LEFTOVERS YOU CAN TAKE HOME IF YOU WANT. ♡
FWMP
AND THAT IS...

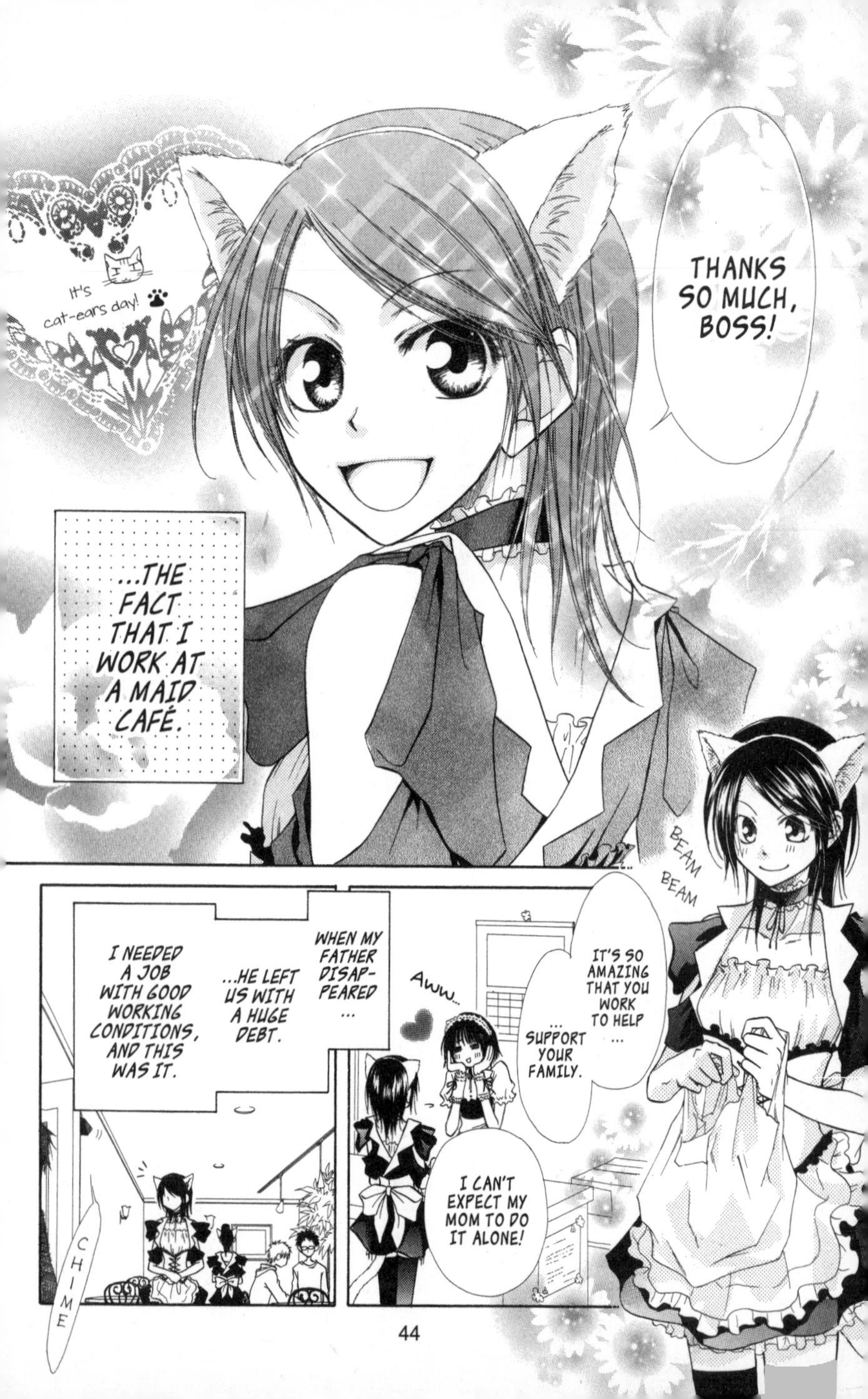
THANKS SO MUCH, BOSS!
It's cat-ears day!
...THE FACT THAT I WORK AT A MAID CAFÉ.
BEAM BEAM
IT'S SO AMAZING THAT YOU WORK TO HELP ...
... SUPPORT YOUR FAMILY.
AWW...
I CAN'T EXPECT MY MOM TO DO IT ALONE!
WHEN MY FATHER DISAPPEARED ...
...HE LEFT US WITH A HUGE DEBT.
I NEEDED A JOB WITH GOOD WORKING CONDITIONS, AND THIS WAS IT.
CHIME

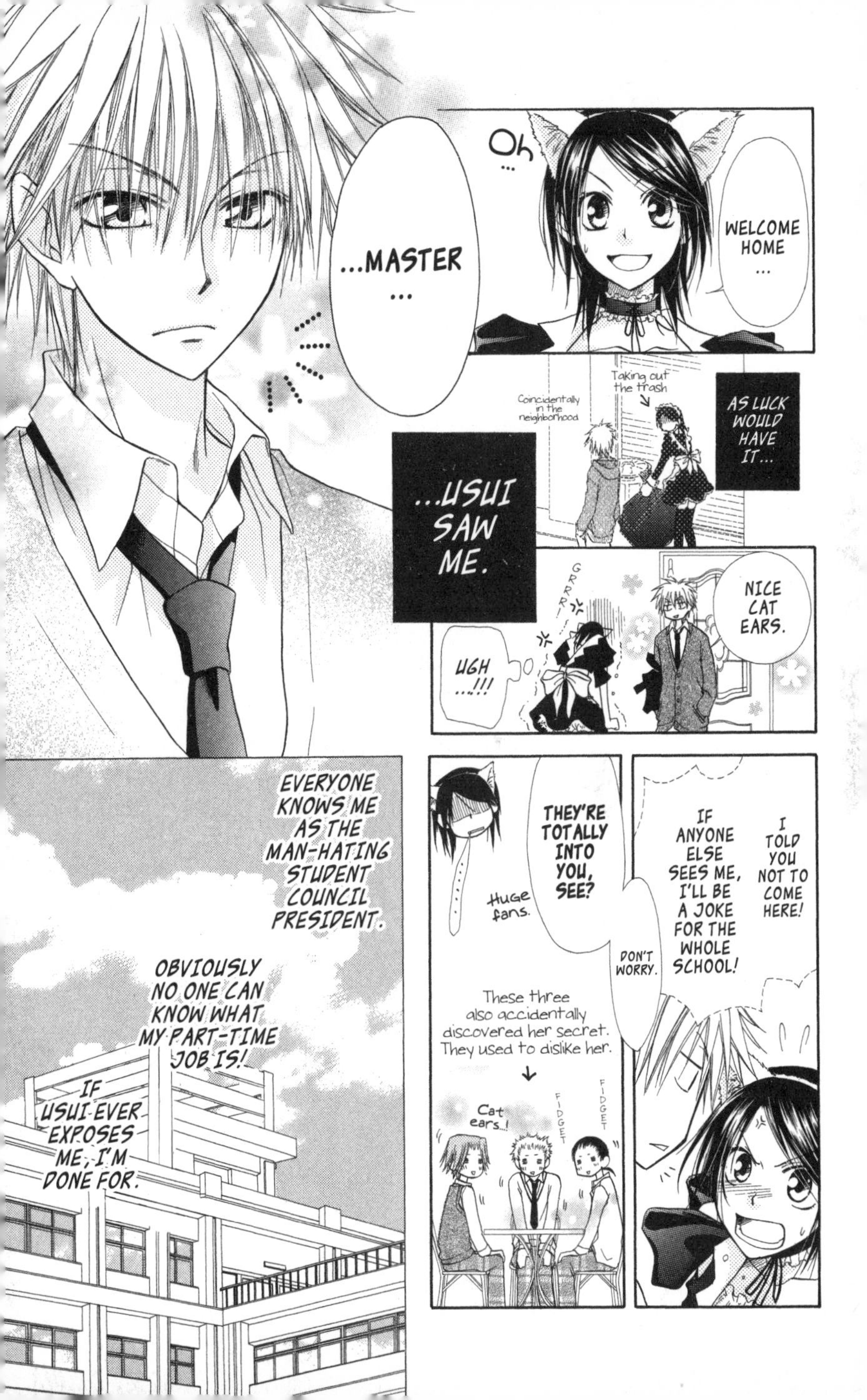
WELCOME HOME ...
Oh ...
AS LUCK WOULD HAVE IT...
Taking out the trash
Coincidentally in the neighborhood
...USUI SAW ME.
NICE CAT EARS.
GRRR!
UGH ...!!!
...MASTER ...
I TOLD YOU NOT TO COME HERE!
IF ANYONE ELSE SEES ME, I'LL BE A JOKE FOR THE WHOLE SCHOOL!
DON'T WORRY.
THEY'RE TOTALLY INTO YOU, SEE?
Huge fans.
These three also accidentally discovered her secret. They used to dislike her.
FIDGET
FIDGET
Cat ears..!
EVERYONE KNOWS ME AS THE MAN-HATING STUDENT COUNCIL PRESIDENT.
OBVIOUSLY NO ONE CAN KNOW WHAT MY PART-TIME JOB IS!
IF USUI EVER EXPOSES ME, I'M DONE FOR.

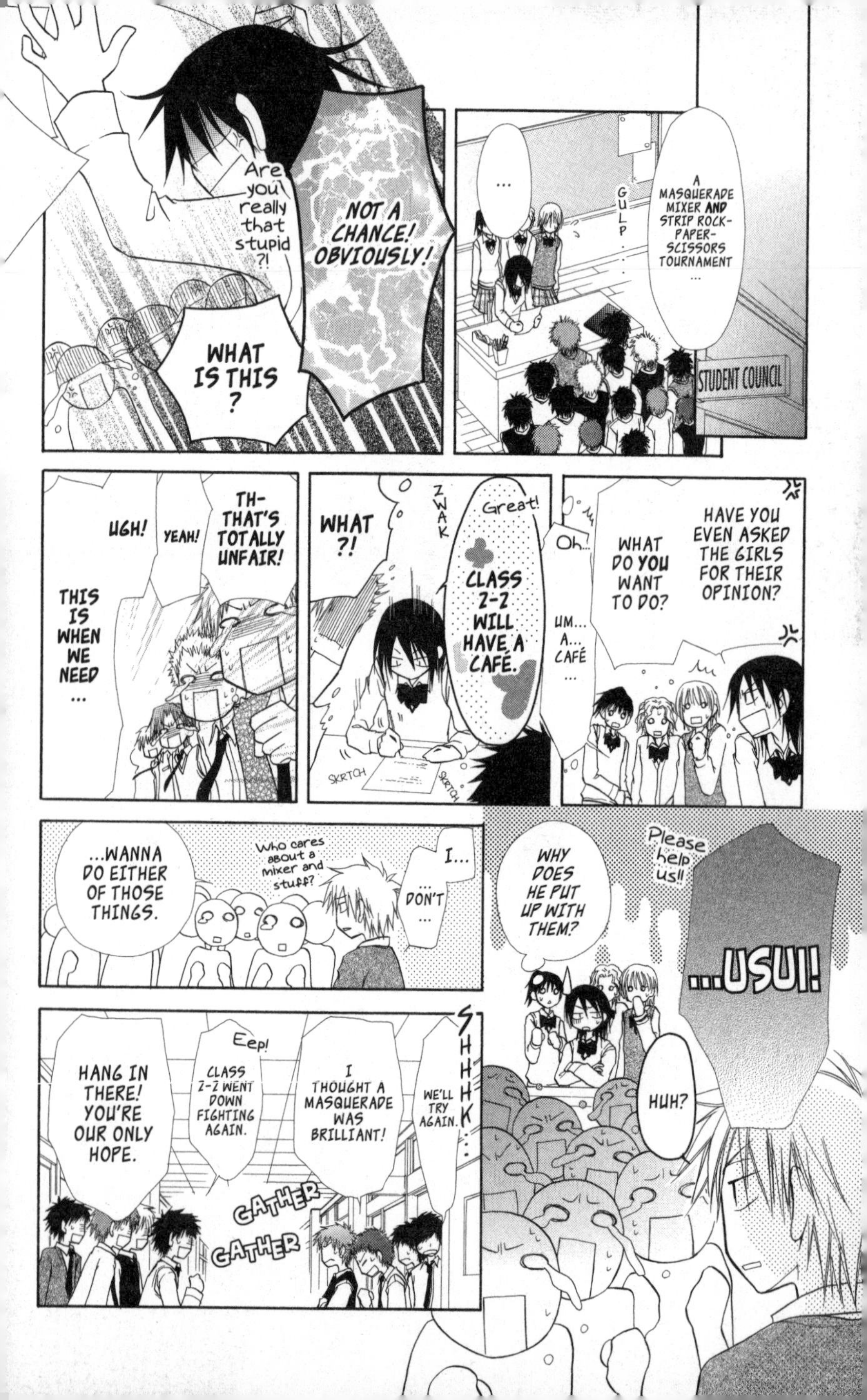
A MASQUERADE MIXER AND STRIP ROCK-PAPER-SCISSORS TOURNAMENT ...
GULP...
...
STUDENT COUNCIL
NOT A CHANCE! OBVIOUSLY!
Are you really that stupid?!
WHAT IS THIS?
HAVE YOU EVEN ASKED THE GIRLS FOR THEIR OPINION?
WHAT DO YOU WANT TO DO?
Oh...
UM... A... CAFÉ...
Great!
CLASS 2-2 WILL HAVE A CAFÉ.
ZWAK
WHAT?!
SKRTCH
SKRTCH
TH-THAT'S TOTALLY UNFAIR!
YEAH!
UGH!
THIS IS WHEN WE NEED...
...USUI!
Please help us!!
WHY DOES HE PUT UP WITH THEM?
HUH?
I...
...DON'T...
Who cares about a mixer and stuff?
...WANNA DO EITHER OF THOSE THINGS.
SHHHK...
WE'LL TRY AGAIN.
I THOUGHT A MASQUERADE WAS BRILLIANT!
Eep!
CLASS 2-2 WENT DOWN FIGHTING AGAIN.
HANG IN THERE! YOU'RE OUR ONLY HOPE.
GATHER
GATHER

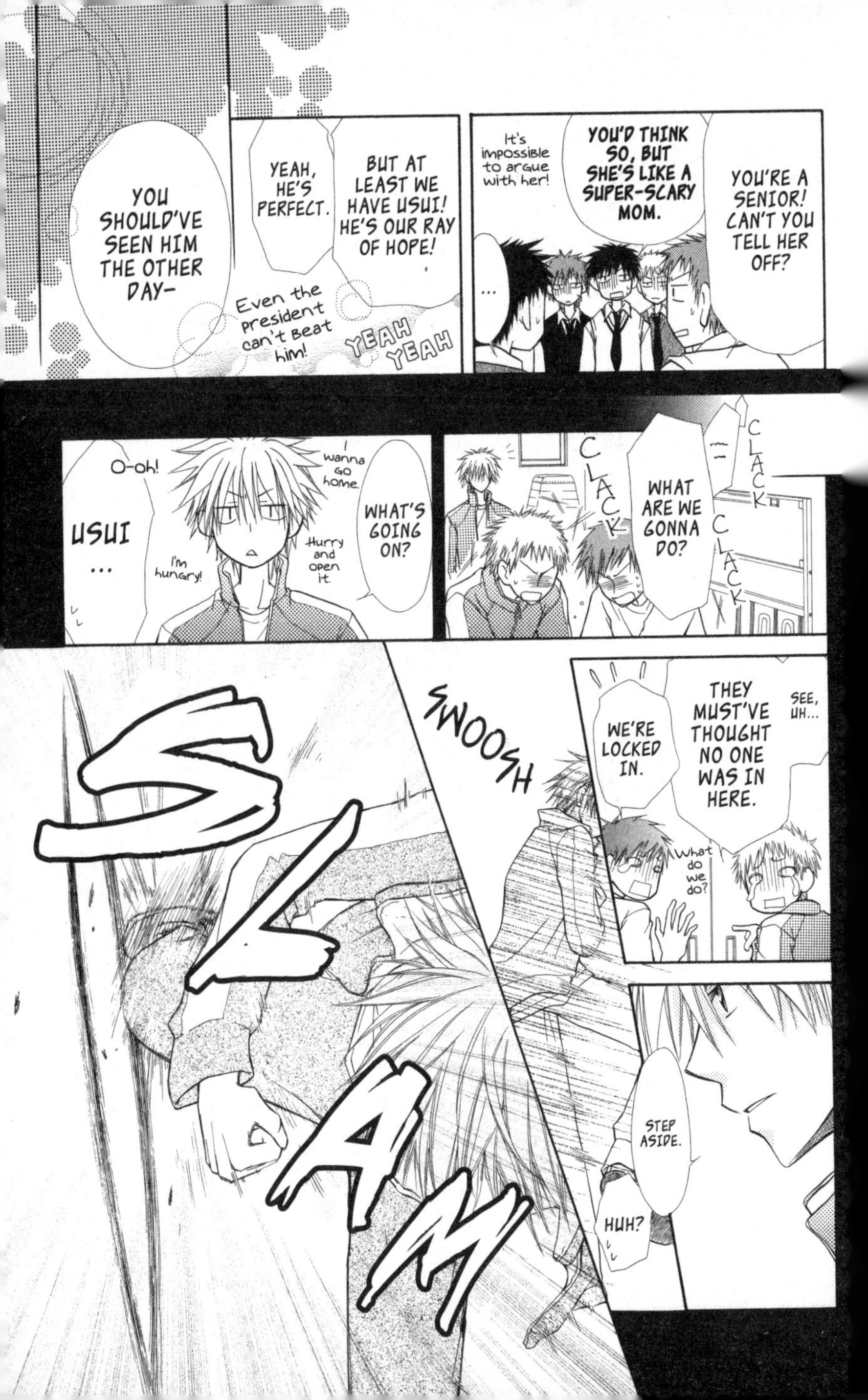
YOU'RE A SENIOR! CAN'T YOU TELL HER OFF?
YOU'D THINK SO, BUT SHE'S LIKE A SUPER-SCARY MOM.
It's impossible to argue with her!
...
BUT AT LEAST WE HAVE USUI! HE'S OUR RAY OF HOPE!
YEAH, HE'S PERFECT.
Even the president can't beat him!
YEAH YEAH
YOU SHOULD'VE SEEN HIM THE OTHER DAY–
CLACK CLACK
...
WHAT ARE WE GONNA DO?
CLACK CLACK
WHAT'S GOING ON?
I wanna go home.
Hurry and open it.
I'm hungry!
O-oh!
USUI...
SEE, UH...
THEY MUST'VE THOUGHT NO ONE WAS IN HERE.
WE'RE LOCKED IN.
What do we do?
STEP ASIDE.
HUH?
SWOOSH
SLAM

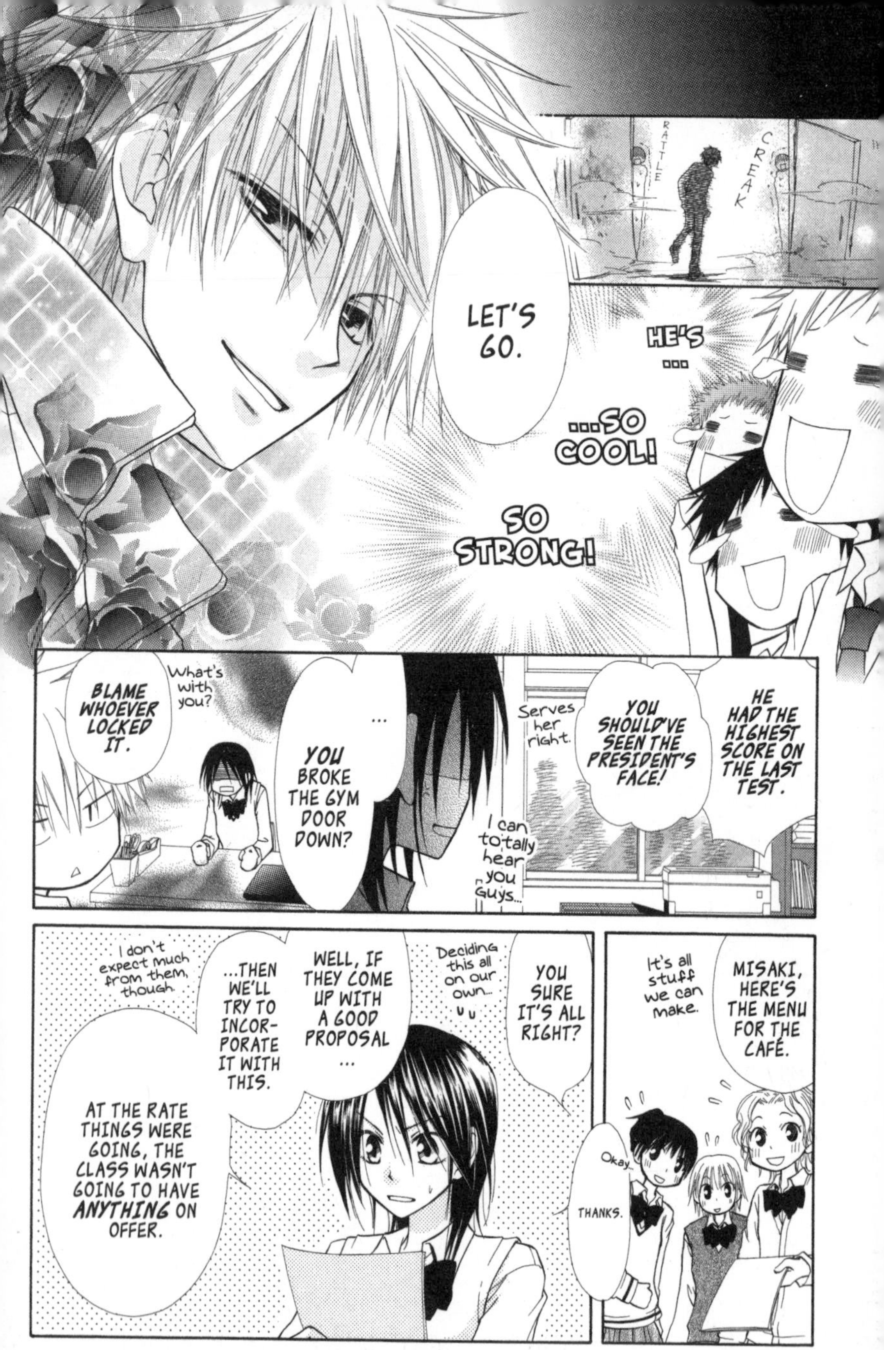
RATTLE
CREAK
LET'S GO.
HE'S...
...SO COOL!
SO STRONG!
HE HAD THE HIGHEST SCORE ON THE LAST TEST.
YOU SHOULD'VE SEEN THE PRESIDENT'S FACE!
Serves her right.
I can totally hear you guys...
...
YOU BROKE THE GYM DOOR DOWN?
What's with you?
BLAME WHOEVER LOCKED IT.
MISAKI, HERE'S THE MENU FOR THE CAFÉ.
It's all stuff we can make.
Okay...
THANKS.
YOU SURE IT'S ALL RIGHT?
Deciding this all on our own...
WELL, IF THEY COME UP WITH A GOOD PROPOSAL...
...THEN WE'LL TRY TO INCOR-PORATE IT WITH THIS.
I don't expect much from them, though.
AT THE RATE THINGS WERE GOING, THE CLASS WASN'T GOING TO HAVE ANYTHING ON OFFER.

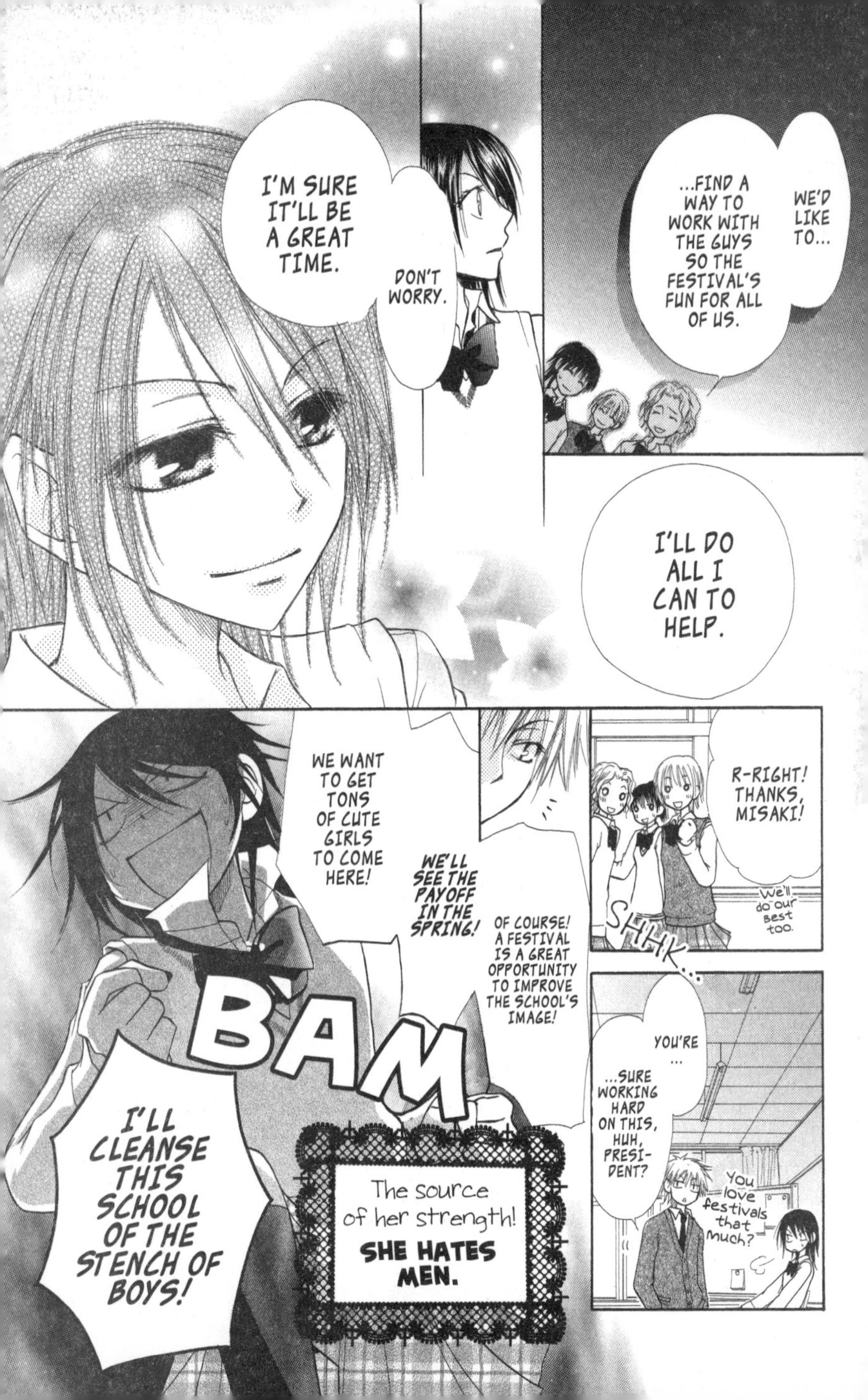
WE'D LIKE TO...
...FIND A WAY TO WORK WITH THE GUYS SO THE FESTIVAL'S FUN FOR ALL OF US.
DON'T WORRY.
I'M SURE IT'LL BE A GREAT TIME.
I'LL DO ALL I CAN TO HELP.
R-RIGHT! THANKS, MISAKI!
We'll do our best too.
SHHHK...
YOU'RE ...
...SURE WORKING HARD ON THIS, HUH, PRESIDENT?
You love festivals that much?
OF COURSE! A FESTIVAL IS A GREAT OPPORTUNITY TO IMPROVE THE SCHOOL'S IMAGE!
WE'LL SEE THE PAYOFF IN THE SPRING!
WE WANT TO GET TONS OF CUTE GIRLS TO COME HERE!
BAM
I'LL CLEANSE THIS SCHOOL OF THE STENCH OF BOYS!
The source of her strength!
SHE HATES MEN.

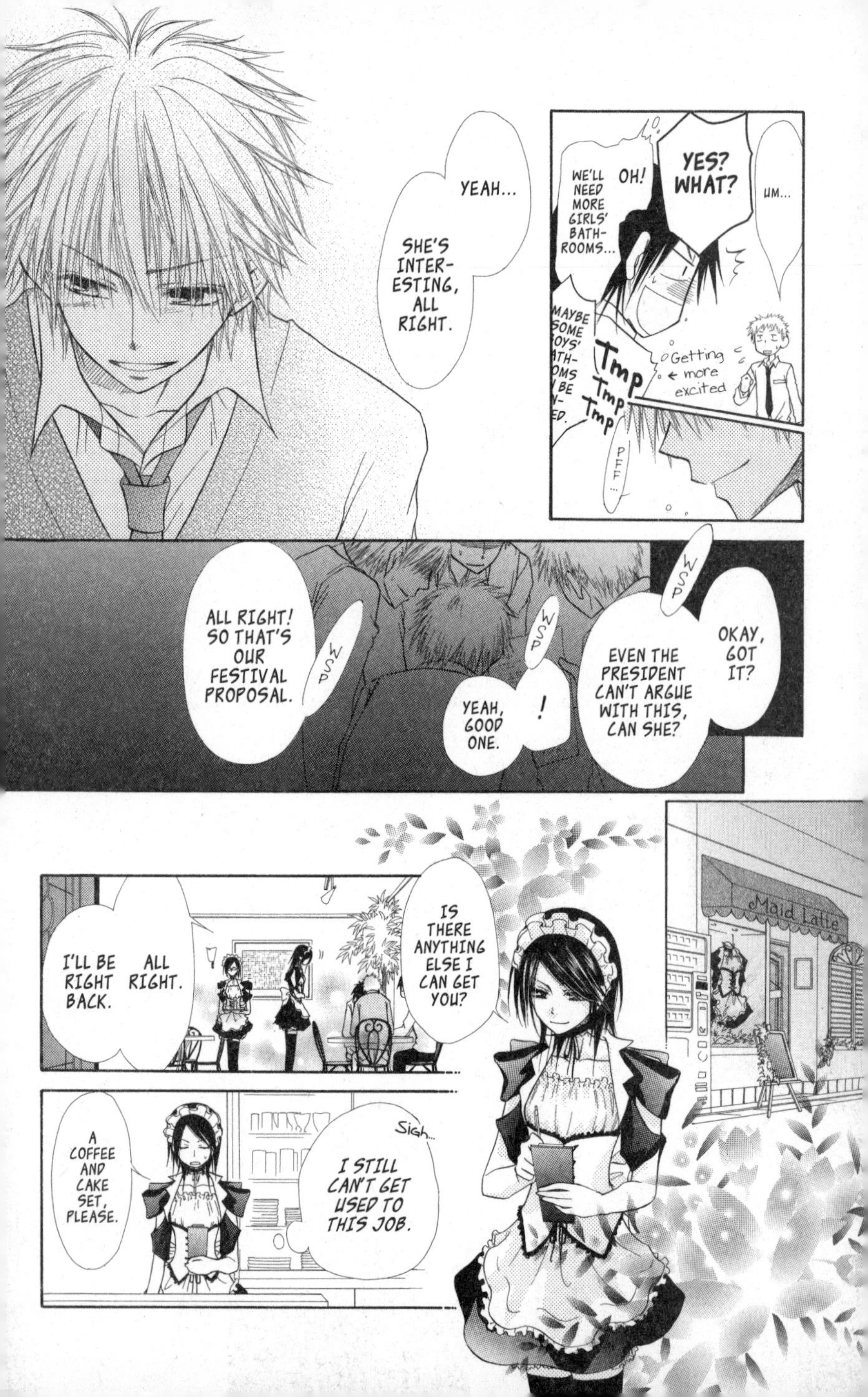
UM...
YES? WHAT?
OH!
WE'LL NEED MORE GIRLS' BATH-ROOMS...
Getting more excited
Tmp Tmp Tmp
MAYBE SOME
PFF...
YEAH...
SHE'S INTER-ESTING, ALL RIGHT.
WSP
OKAY, GOT IT?
EVEN THE PRESIDENT CAN'T ARGUE WITH THIS, CAN SHE?
WSP
!
YEAH, GOOD ONE.
WSP
ALL RIGHT! SO THAT'S OUR FESTIVAL PROPOSAL.
Maid Latte
IS THERE ANYTHING ELSE I CAN GET YOU?
ALL RIGHT.
I'LL BE RIGHT BACK.
Sigh...
I STILL CAN'T GET USED TO THIS JOB.
A COFFEE AND CAKE SET, PLEASE.

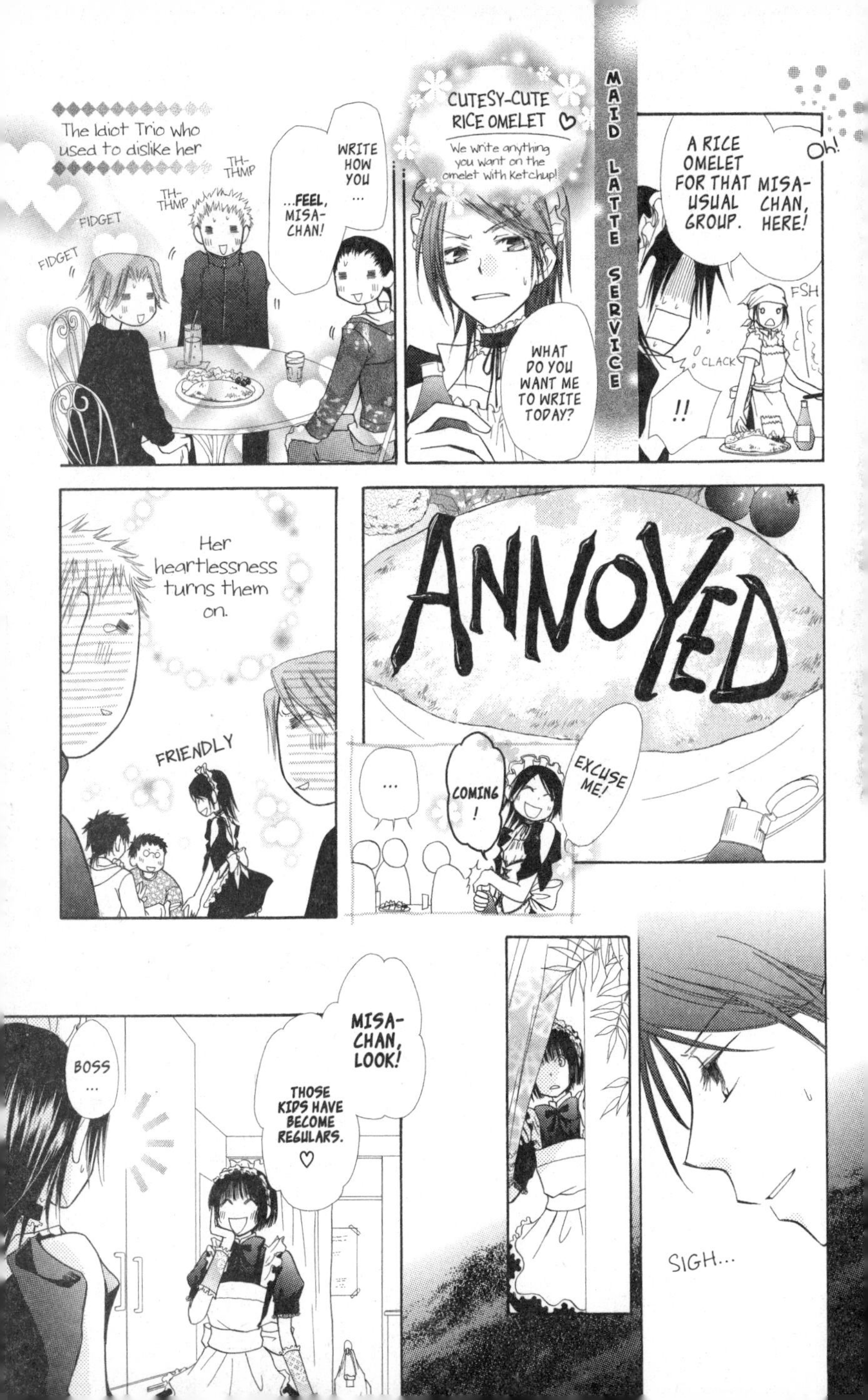
MAID LATTE SERVICE
Oh!
A RICE OMELET FOR THAT USUAL GROUP.
MISA-CHAN, HERE!
FSH
CLACK
!!
CUTESY-CUTE RICE OMELET ♡
We write anything you want on the omelet with Ketchup!
WHAT DO YOU WANT ME TO WRITE TODAY?
WRITE HOW YOU ...
...FEEL, MISA-CHAN!
TH-THMP
TH-THMP
FIDGET
FIDGET
The Idiot Trio Who used to dislike her
ANNOYED
EXCUSE ME!
COMING!
...
Her heartlessness turns them on.
FRIENDLY
SIGH...
MISA-CHAN, LOOK!
THOSE KIDS HAVE BECOME REGULARS. ♡
BOSS ...

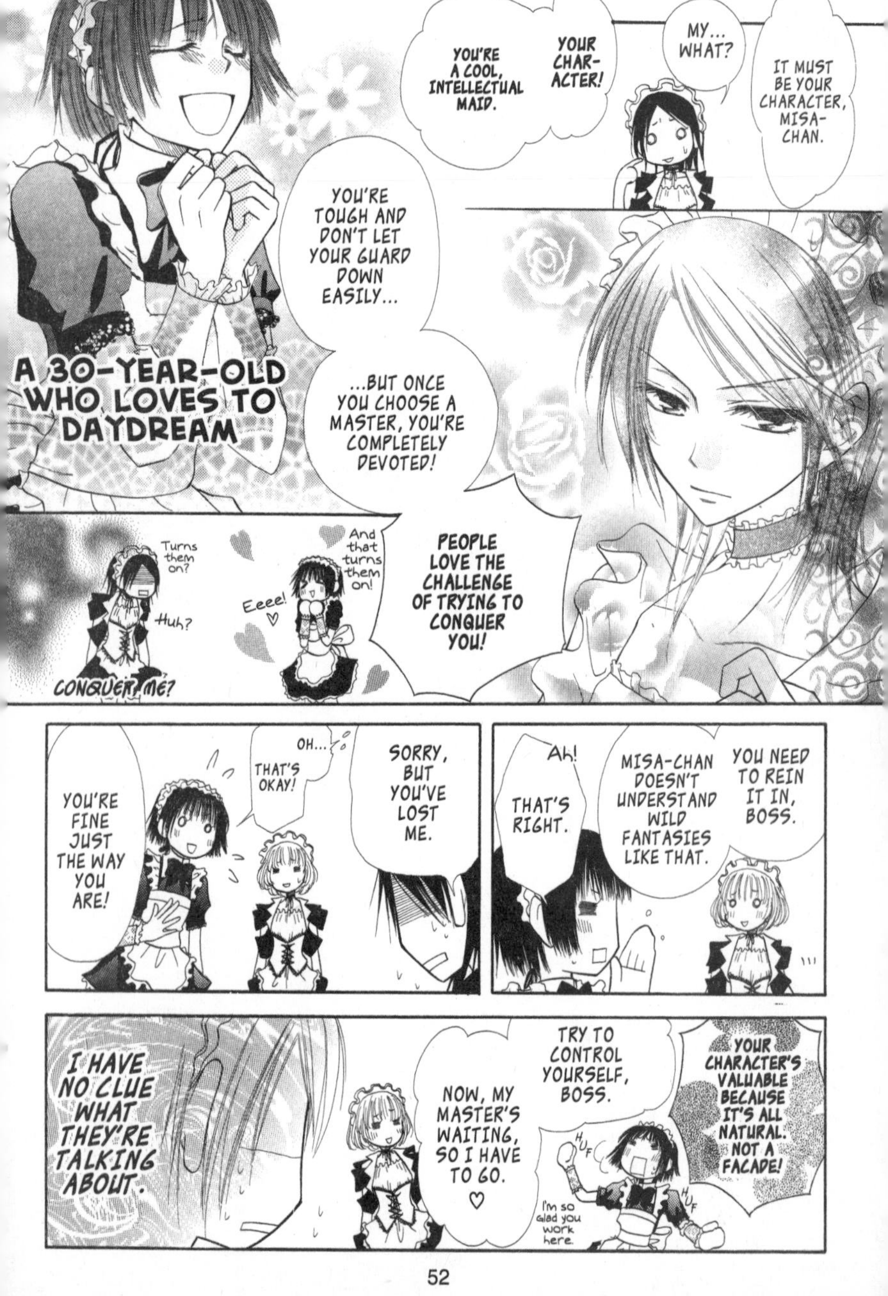
IT MUST BE YOUR CHARACTER, MISA-CHAN.
MY... WHAT?
YOUR CHARACTER!
YOU'RE A COOL, INTELLECTUAL MAID.
YOU'RE TOUGH AND DON'T LET YOUR GUARD DOWN EASILY...
...BUT ONCE YOU CHOOSE A MASTER, YOU'RE COMPLETELY DEVOTED!
PEOPLE LOVE THE CHALLENGE OF TRYING TO CONQUER YOU!
A 30-YEAR-OLD WHO LOVES TO DAYDREAM
And that turns them on!
Eeee! ♡
Turns them on?
Huh?
CONQUER ME?
YOU NEED TO REIN IT IN, BOSS.
MISA-CHAN DOESN'T UNDERSTAND WILD FANTASIES LIKE THAT.
Ah!
THAT'S RIGHT.
SORRY, BUT YOU'VE LOST ME.
OH...
THAT'S OKAY!
YOU'RE FINE JUST THE WAY YOU ARE!
YOUR CHARACTER'S VALUABLE BECAUSE IT'S ALL NATURAL. NOT A FACADE!
HUF
HUF
I'm so glad you work here.
TRY TO CONTROL YOURSELF, BOSS.
NOW, MY MASTER'S WAITING, SO I HAVE TO GO. ♡
I HAVE NO CLUE WHAT THEY'RE TALKING ABOUT.

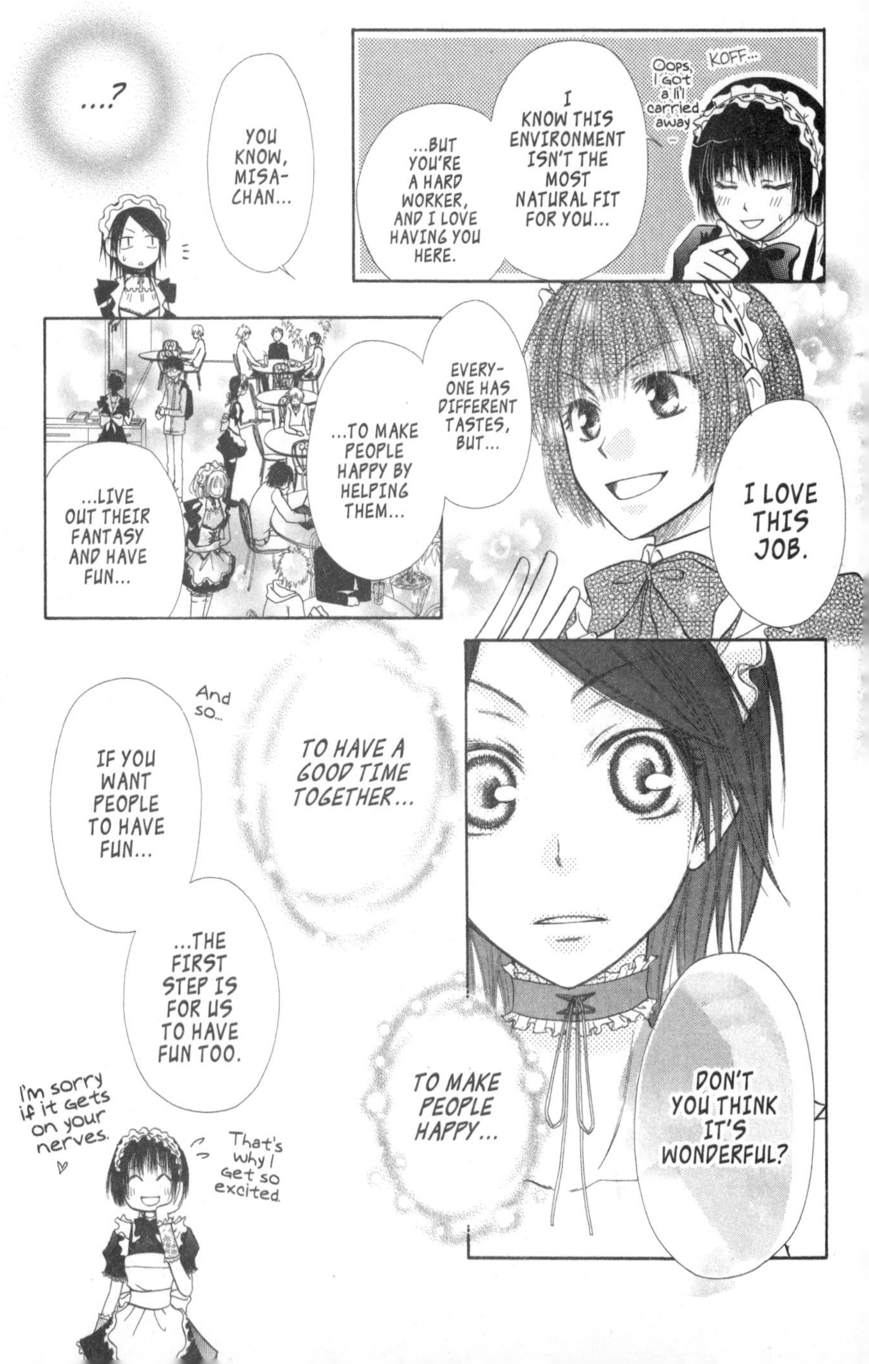
KOFF...
Oops, I got a li'l carried away...
I KNOW THIS ENVIRONMENT ISN'T THE MOST NATURAL FIT FOR YOU...
...BUT YOU'RE A HARD WORKER, AND I LOVE HAVING YOU HERE.
YOU KNOW, MISA-CHAN...
...?
I LOVE THIS JOB.
EVERYONE HAS DIFFERENT TASTES, BUT...
...TO MAKE PEOPLE HAPPY BY HELPING THEM...
...LIVE OUT THEIR FANTASY AND HAVE FUN...
DON'T YOU THINK IT'S WONDERFUL?
TO MAKE PEOPLE HAPPY...
TO HAVE A GOOD TIME TOGETHER...
And so...
IF YOU WANT PEOPLE TO HAVE FUN...
...THE FIRST STEP IS FOR US TO HAVE FUN TOO.
That's why I get so excited.
I'm sorry if it gets on your nerves.

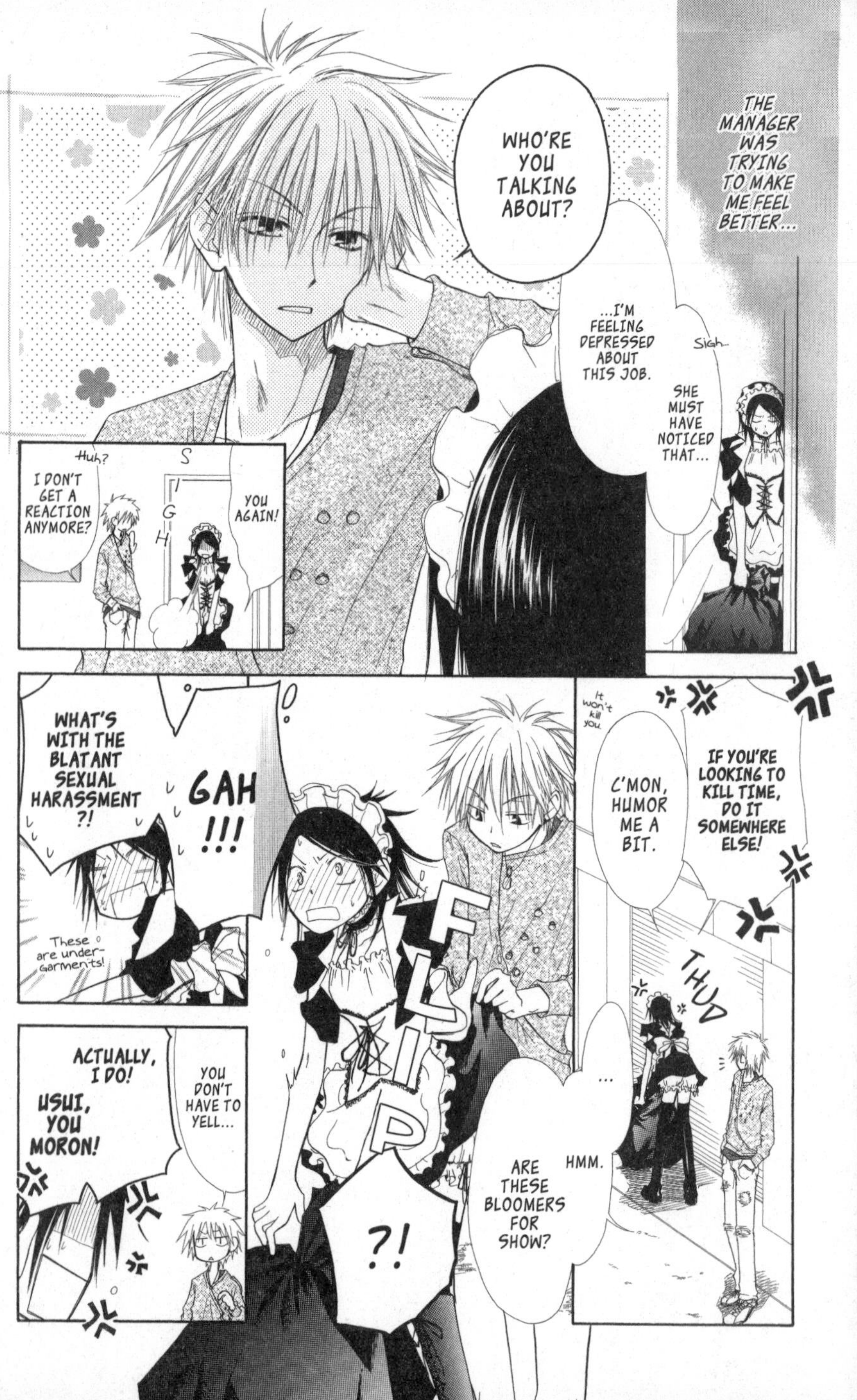
THE MANAGER WAS TRYING TO MAKE ME FEEL BETTER...
Sigh..
SHE MUST HAVE NOTICED THAT...
...I'M FEELING DEPRESSED ABOUT THIS JOB.
WHO'RE YOU TALKING ABOUT?
YOU AGAIN!
SIGH
Huh?
I DON'T GET A REACTION ANYMORE?
IF YOU'RE LOOKING TO KILL TIME, DO IT SOMEWHERE ELSE!
C'MON, HUMOR ME A BIT.
It won't kill you.
THUD
...
HMM.
ARE THESE BLOOMERS FOR SHOW?
FLIP
?!
GAH!!!
WHAT'S WITH THE BLATANT SEXUAL HARASSMENT?!
These are under-garments!
YOU DON'T HAVE TO YELL...
ACTUALLY, I DO!
USUI, YOU MORON!

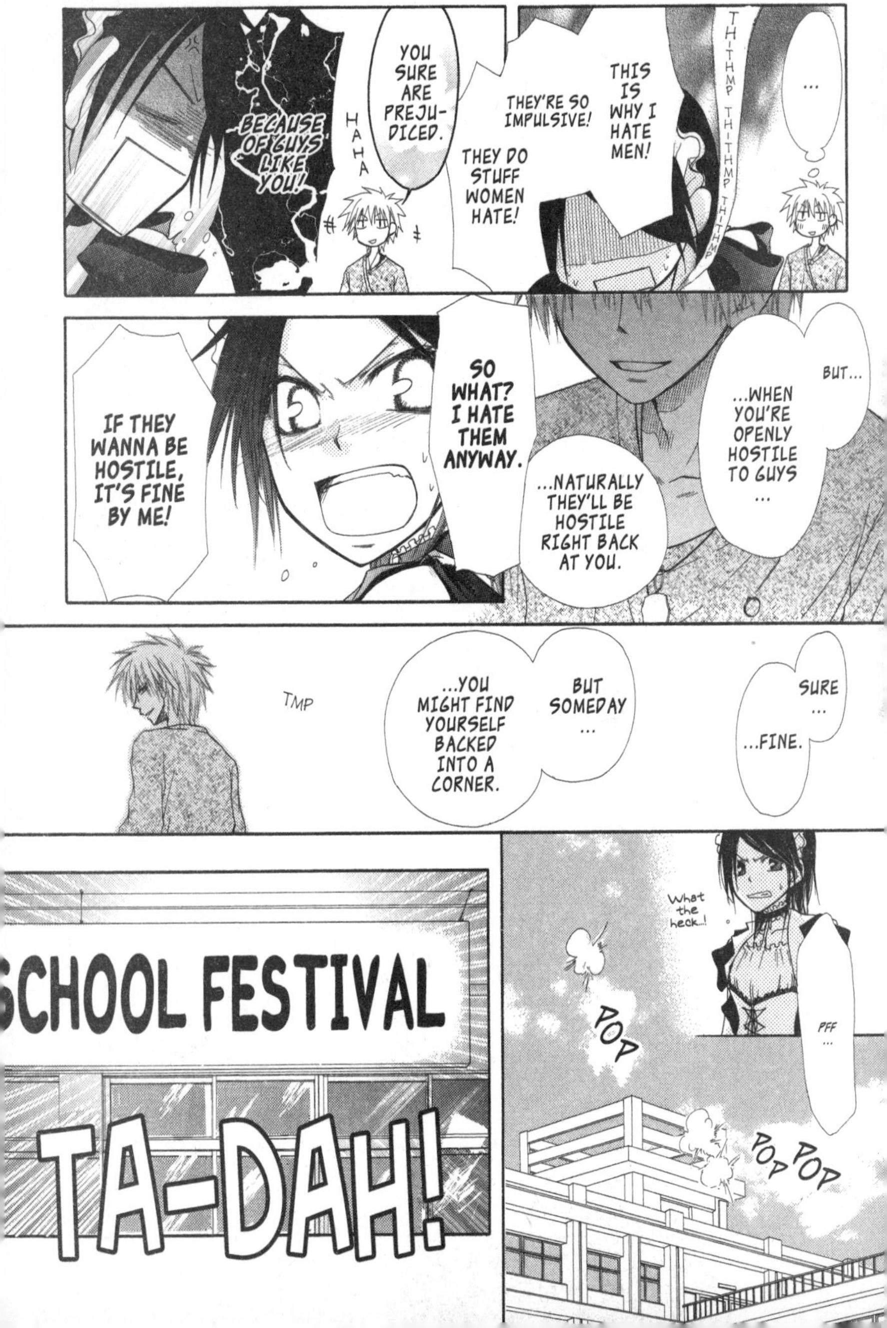
...
THITHMP THITHMP THITHMP
THIS IS WHY I HATE MEN!
THEY'RE SO IMPULSIVE!
THEY DO STUFF WOMEN HATE!
YOU SURE ARE PREJU-DICED.
HAHA
BECAUSE OF GUYS LIKE YOU!
BUT...
...WHEN YOU'RE OPENLY HOSTILE TO GUYS ...
...NATURALLY THEY'LL BE HOSTILE RIGHT BACK AT YOU.
SO WHAT? I HATE THEM ANYWAY.
IF THEY WANNA BE HOSTILE, IT'S FINE BY ME!
SURE ...
...FINE.
BUT SOMEDAY ...
...YOU MIGHT FIND YOURSELF BACKED INTO A CORNER.
TMP
What the heck...!
POP
PFF ...
POP POP POP
SCHOOL FESTIVAL
TA-DAH!

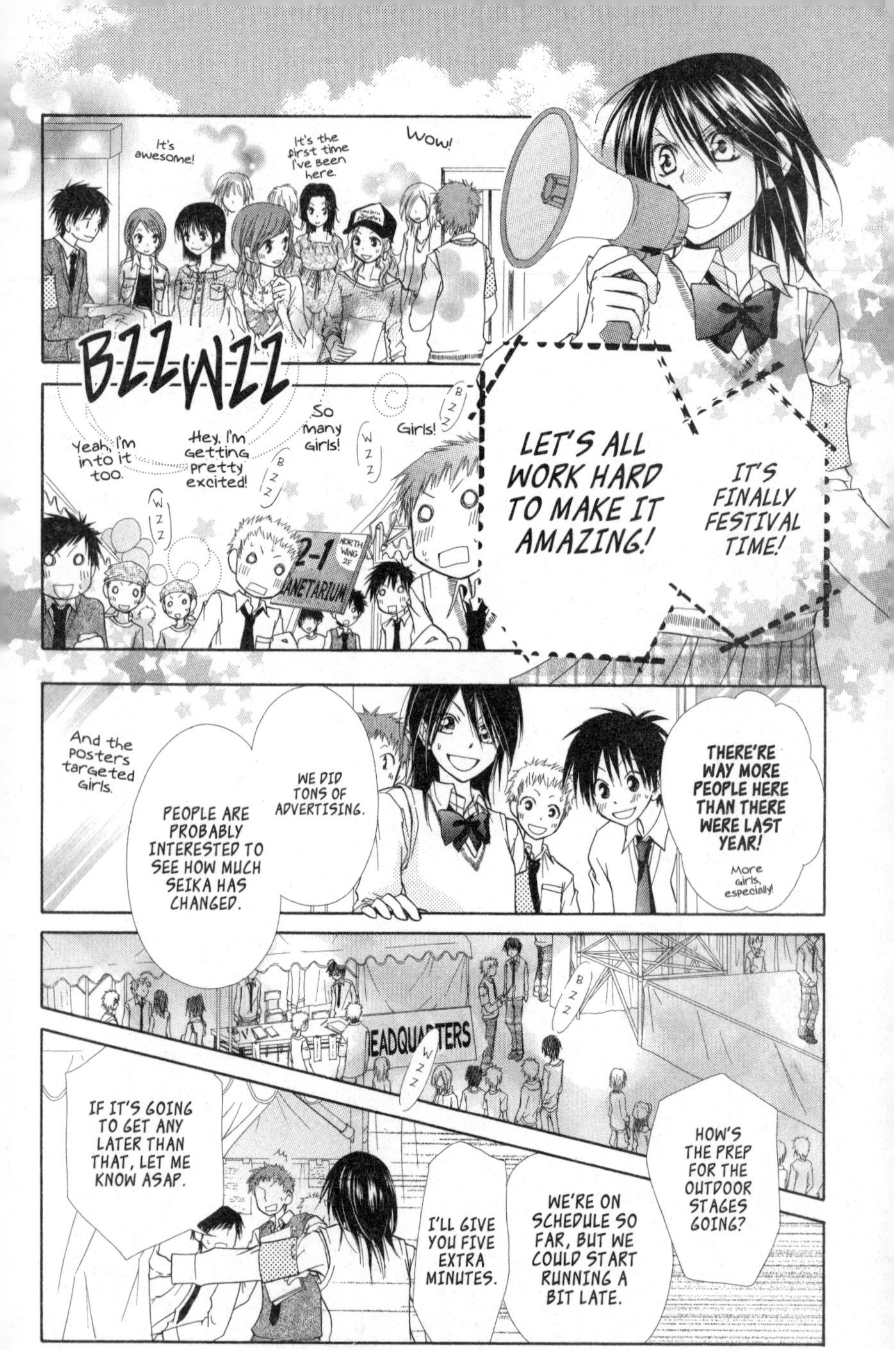

IT'S FINALLY FESTIVAL TIME!
LET'S ALL WORK HARD TO MAKE IT AMAZING!
Wow!
It's the first time I've been here.
It's awesome!
BZZWZZ
Girls!
BZZ
So many girls!
WZZ
BZZ
Hey, I'm getting pretty excited!
Yeah, I'm into it too.
WZZ
2-1
NORTH WING 2F
THERE'RE WAY MORE PEOPLE HERE THAN THERE WERE LAST YEAR!
More girls, especially!
WE DID TONS OF ADVERTISING.
PEOPLE ARE PROBABLY INTERESTED TO SEE HOW MUCH SEIKA HAS CHANGED.
And the posters targeted girls.
BZZ
WZZ
HOW'S THE PREP FOR THE OUTDOOR STAGES GOING?
WE'RE ON SCHEDULE SO FAR, BUT WE COULD START RUNNING A BIT LATE.
I'LL GIVE YOU FIVE EXTRA MINUTES.
IF IT'S GOING TO GET ANY LATER THAN THAT, LET ME KNOW ASAP.

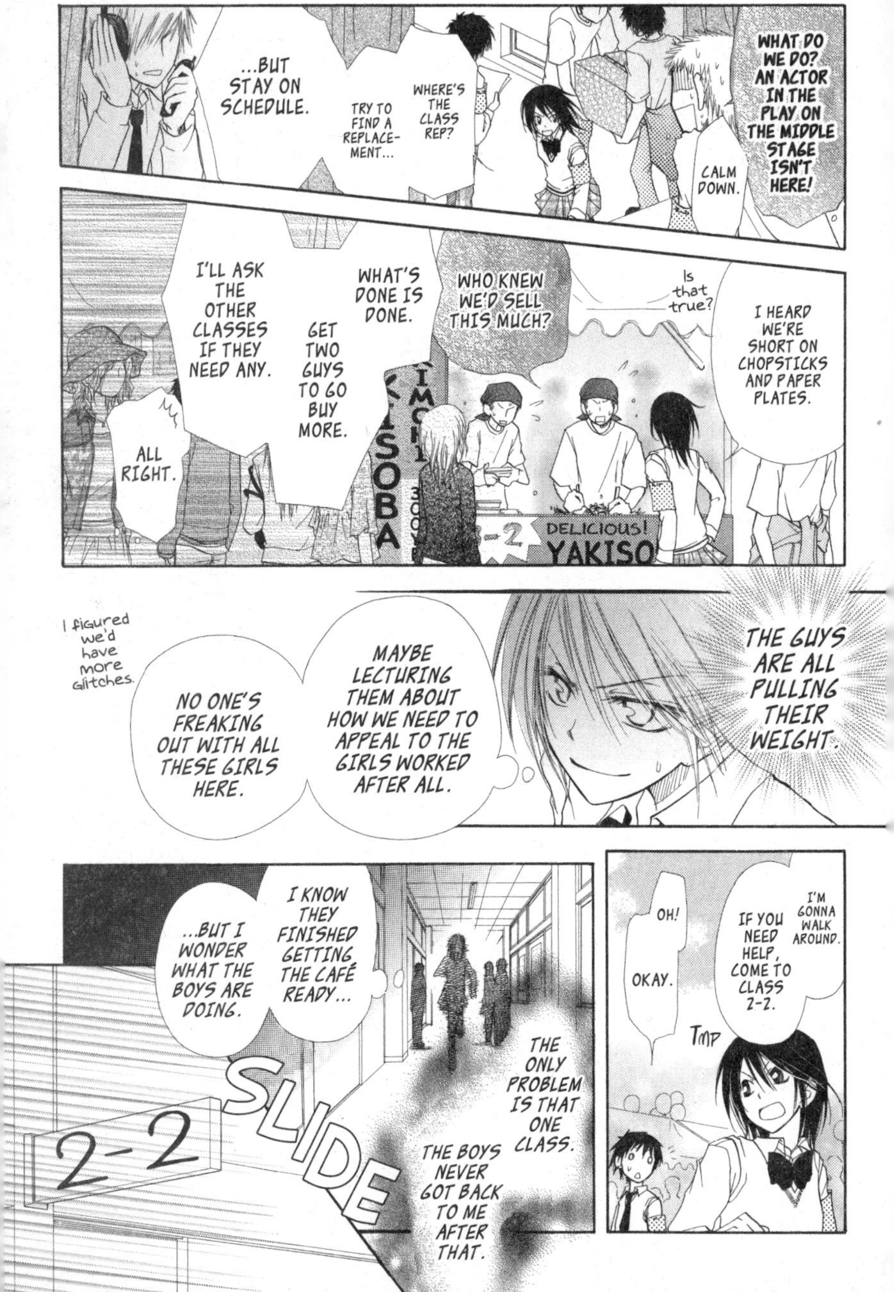
WHAT DO WE DO? AN ACTOR IN THE PLAY ON THE MIDDLE STAGE ISN'T HERE!
CALM DOWN.
WHERE'S THE CLASS REP?
TRY TO FIND A REPLACEMENT...
...BUT STAY ON SCHEDULE.
I HEARD WE'RE SHORT ON CHOPSTICKS AND PAPER PLATES.
Is that true?
WHO KNEW WE'D SELL THIS MUCH?
DELICIOUS! YAKISO
YAKISOBA
WHAT'S DONE IS DONE.
GET TWO GUYS TO GO BUY MORE.
I'LL ASK THE OTHER CLASSES IF THEY NEED ANY.
ALL RIGHT.
THE GUYS ARE ALL PULLING THEIR WEIGHT.
MAYBE LECTURING THEM ABOUT HOW WE NEED TO APPEAL TO THE GIRLS WORKED AFTER ALL.
NO ONE'S FREAKING OUT WITH ALL THESE GIRLS HERE.
I figured we'd have more glitches.
I'M GONNA WALK AROUND.
IF YOU NEED HELP, COME TO CLASS 2-2.
OH!
OKAY.
TMP
I KNOW THEY FINISHED GETTING THE CAFÉ READY...
...BUT I WONDER WHAT THE BOYS ARE DOING.
THE ONLY PROBLEM IS THAT ONE CLASS.
THE BOYS NEVER GOT BACK TO ME AFTER THAT.
SLIDE
2-2

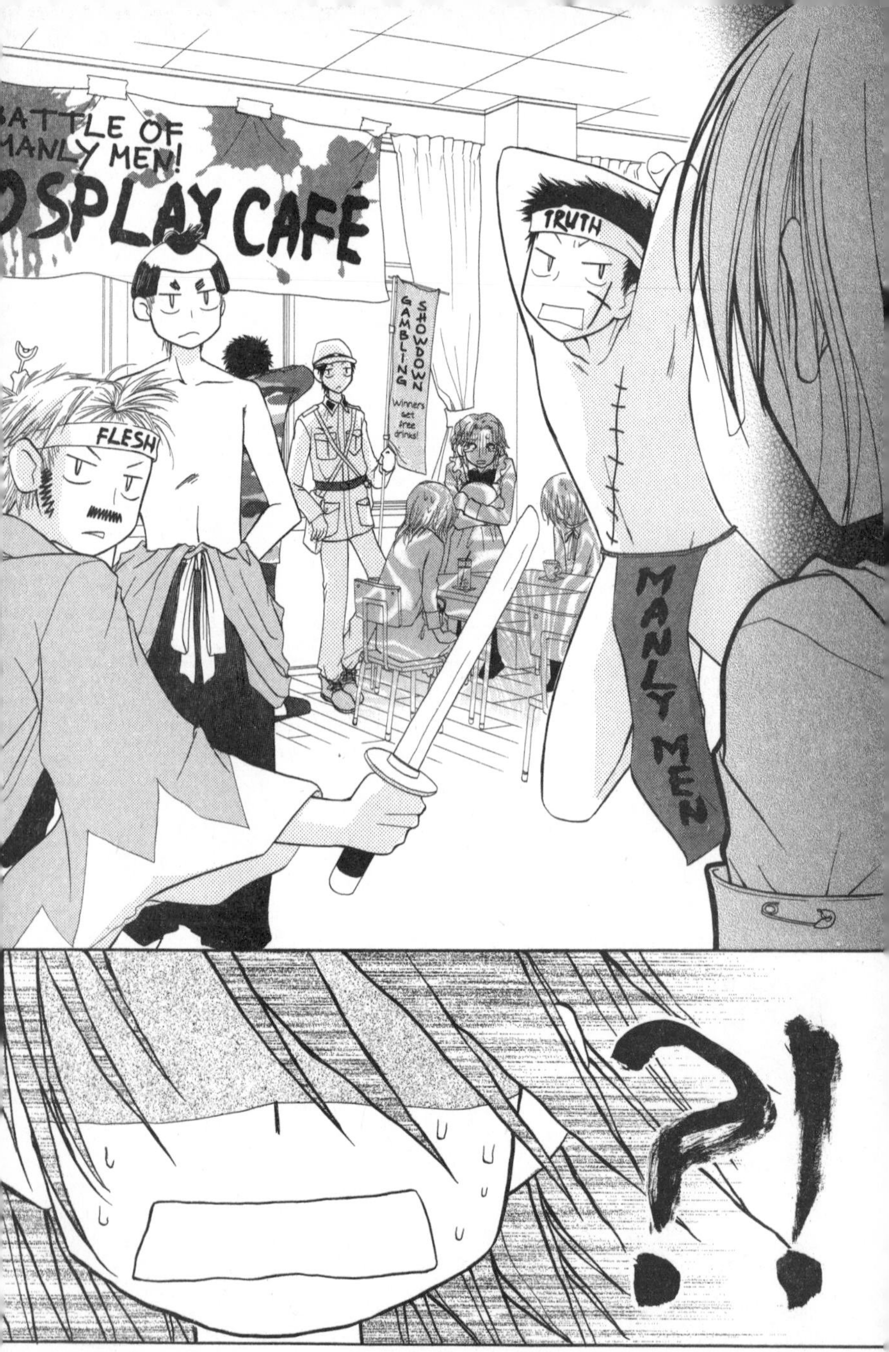
BATTLE OF MANLY MEN!
OSPLAY CAFÉ
TRUTH
GAMBLING SHOWDOWN
Winners get free drinks!
FLESH
MANLY MEN
?!

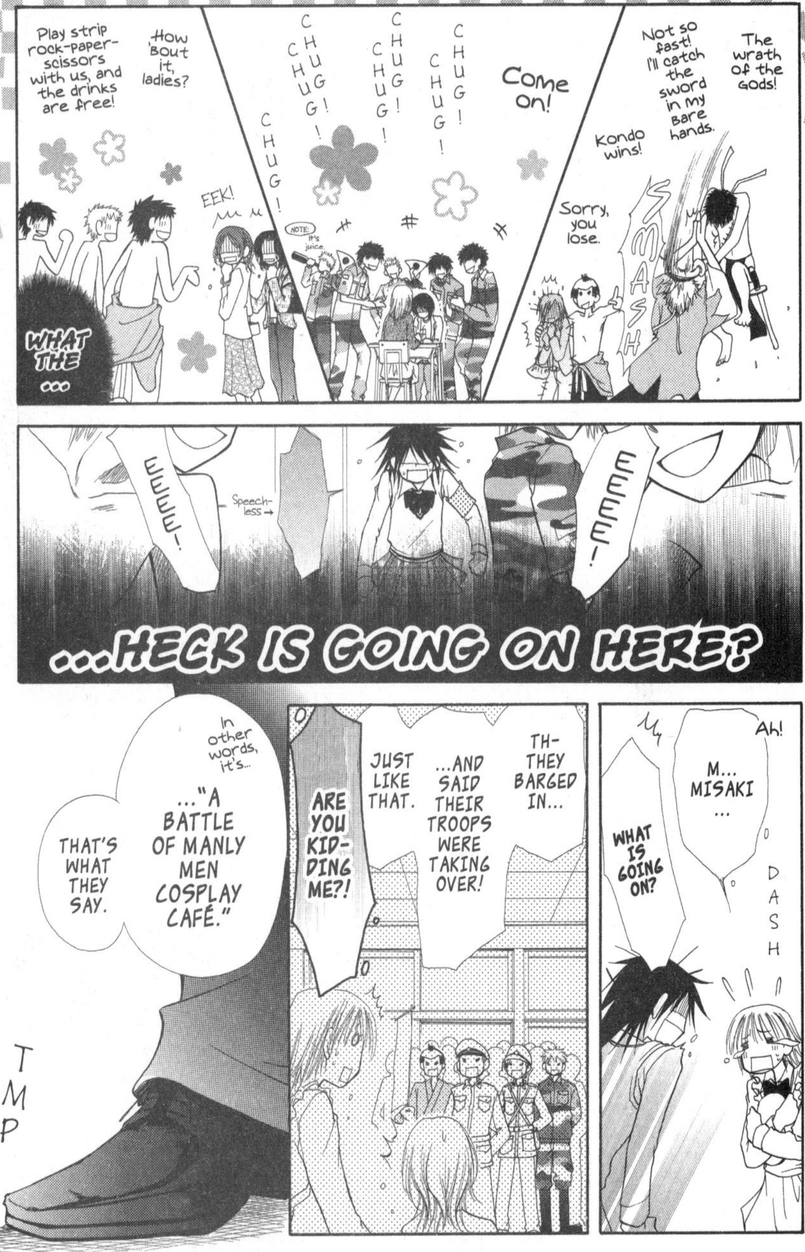
The wrath of the Gods!
Not so fast! I'll catch the sword in my bare hands.
Kondo wins!
Sorry, you lose.
SMASH
Come on!
CHUG! CHUG! CHUG! CHUG! CHUG! CHUG!
NOTE: It's juice.
How 'bout it, ladies?
Play strip rock-paper-scissors with us, and the drinks are free!
EEK!
WHAT THE...
EEEEE!
Speechless →
EEEEE!
...HECK IS GOING ON HERE?
Ah!
M... MISAKI...
WHAT IS GOING ON?
DASH
TH-THEY BARGED IN...
...AND SAID THEIR TROOPS WERE TAKING OVER!
JUST LIKE THAT.
ARE YOU KIDDING ME?!
In other words, it's...
..."A BATTLE OF MANLY MEN COSPLAY CAFÉ."
THAT'S WHAT THEY SAY.
TMP

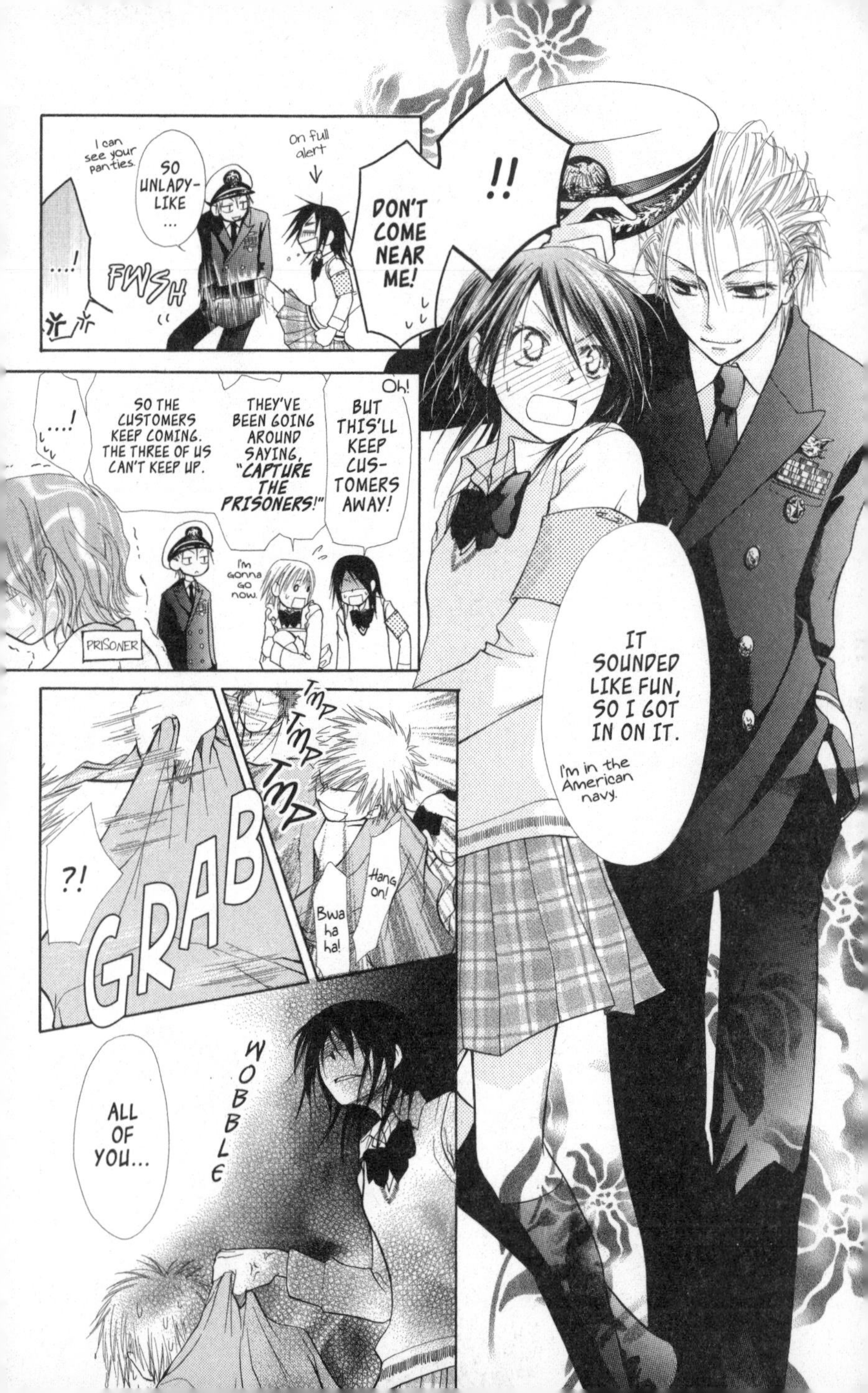
!!
DON'T COME NEAR ME!
IT SOUNDED LIKE FUN, SO I GOT IN ON IT.
I'm in the American navy.
On full alert
SO UNLADY-LIKE ...
I can see your panties.
FWSH
....!
Oh!
BUT THIS'LL KEEP CUS-TOMERS AWAY!
THEY'VE BEEN GOING AROUND SAYING, "CAPTURE THE PRISONERS!"
I'm gonna go now.
SO THE CUSTOMERS KEEP COMING. THE THREE OF US CAN'T KEEP UP.
....!
PRISONER
TMP TMP TMP TMP
Hang on!
Bwa ha ha!
GRAB
?!
WOBBLE
ALL OF YOU...

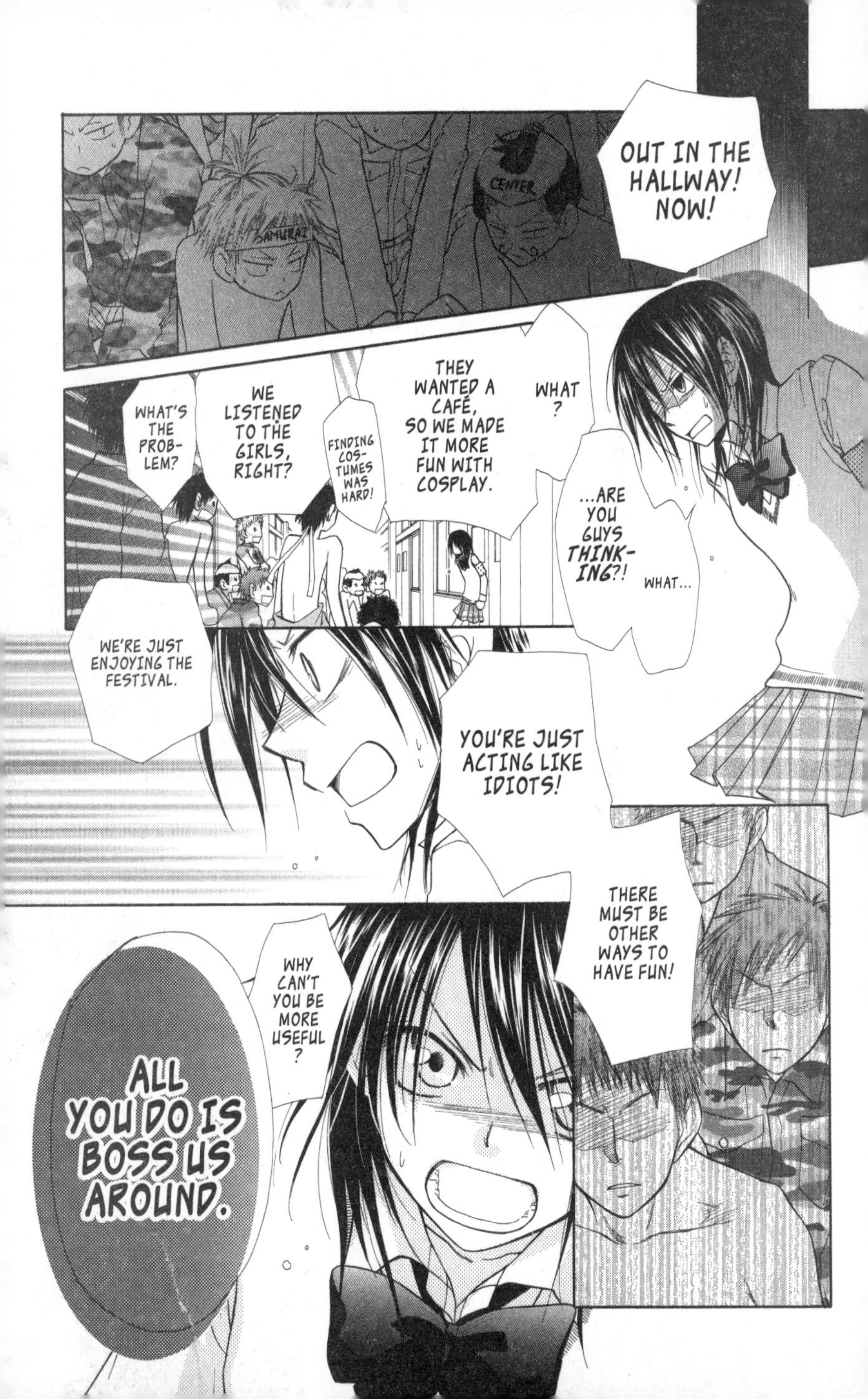
OUT IN THE HALLWAY! NOW!
WHAT...
...ARE YOU GUYS THINKING?!
WHAT?
THEY WANTED A CAFÉ, SO WE MADE IT MORE FUN WITH COSPLAY.
FINDING COS-TUMES WAS HARD!
WE LISTENED TO THE GIRLS, RIGHT?
WHAT'S THE PROB-LEM?
WE'RE JUST ENJOYING THE FESTIVAL.
YOU'RE JUST ACTING LIKE IDIOTS!
THERE MUST BE OTHER WAYS TO HAVE FUN!
WHY CAN'T YOU BE MORE USEFUL?
ALL YOU DO IS BOSS US AROUND.

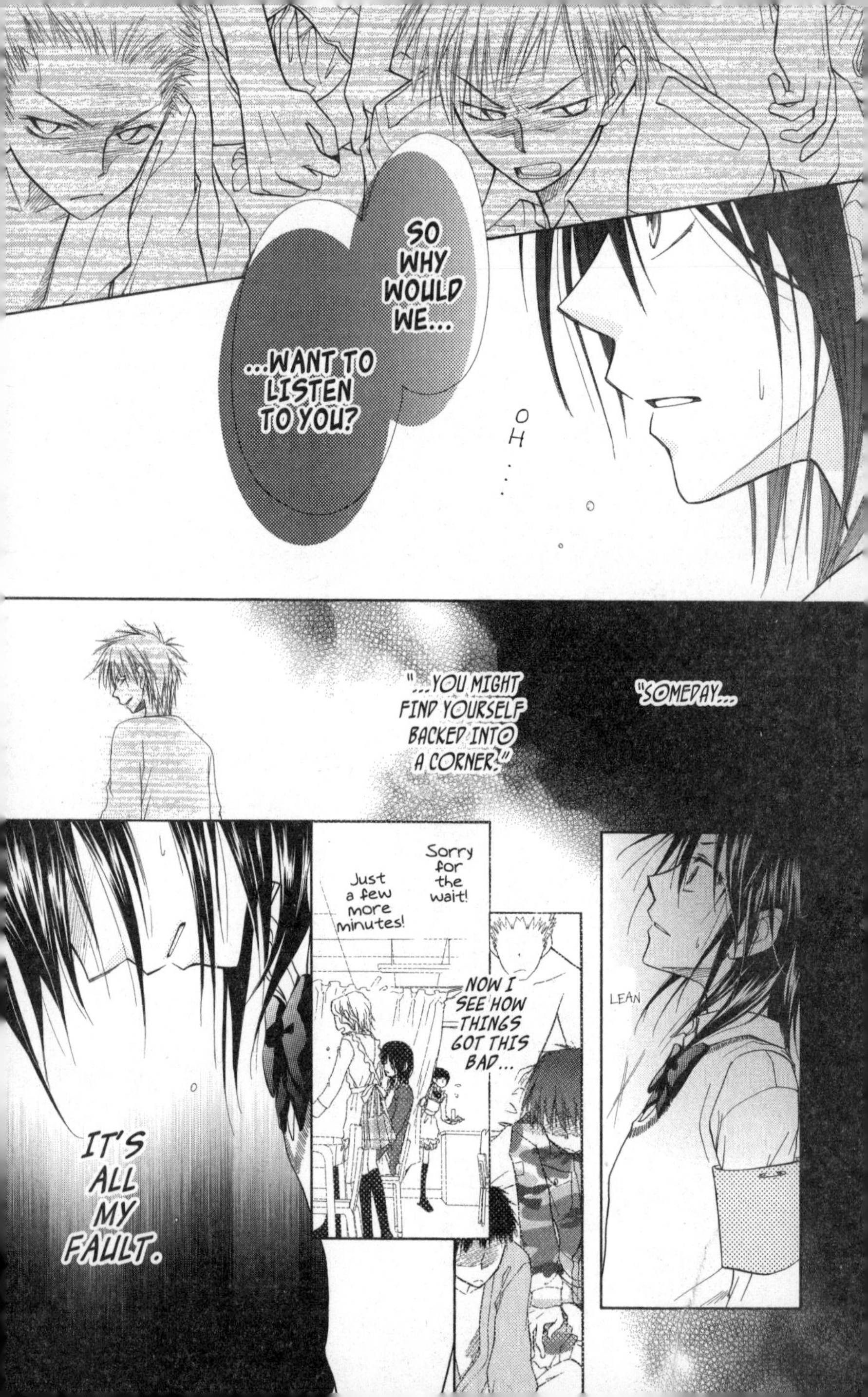
SO WHY WOULD WE...
...WANT TO LISTEN TO YOU?
OH...
"SOMEDAY...
"...YOU MIGHT FIND YOURSELF BACKED INTO A CORNER."
LEAN
Sorry for the wait!
Just a few more minutes!
NOW I SEE HOW THINGS GOT THIS BAD...
IT'S ALL MY FAULT.

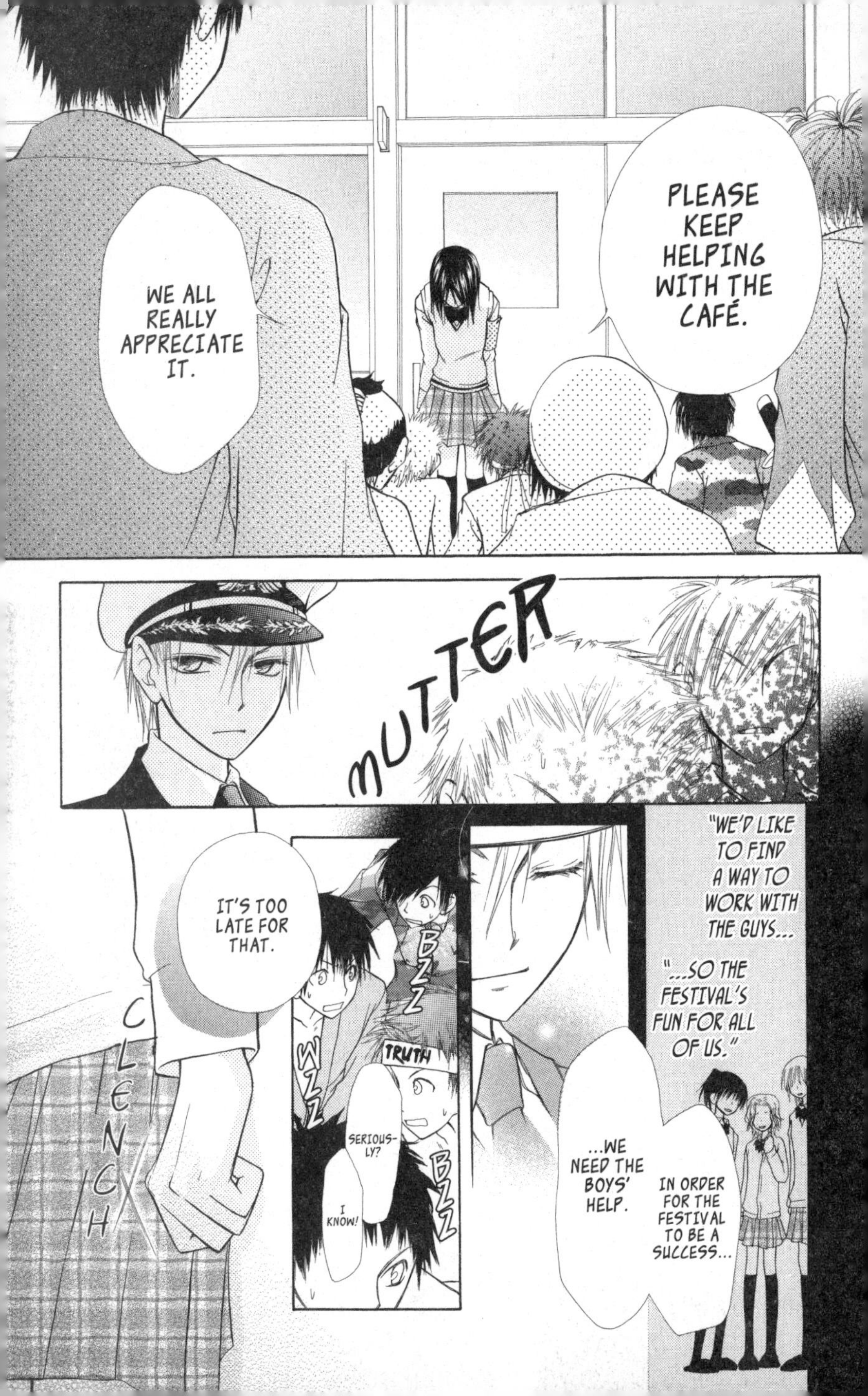
PLEASE KEEP HELPING WITH THE CAFÉ.
WE ALL REALLY APPRECIATE IT.
MUTTER
"WE'D LIKE TO FIND A WAY TO WORK WITH THE GUYS...
"...SO THE FESTIVAL'S FUN FOR ALL OF US."
IN ORDER FOR THE FESTIVAL TO BE A SUCCESS...
...WE NEED THE BOYS' HELP.
BZZ
TRUTH
SERIOUS-LY?
I KNOW!
WZZ
BZZ
IT'S TOO LATE FOR THAT.
CLENCH

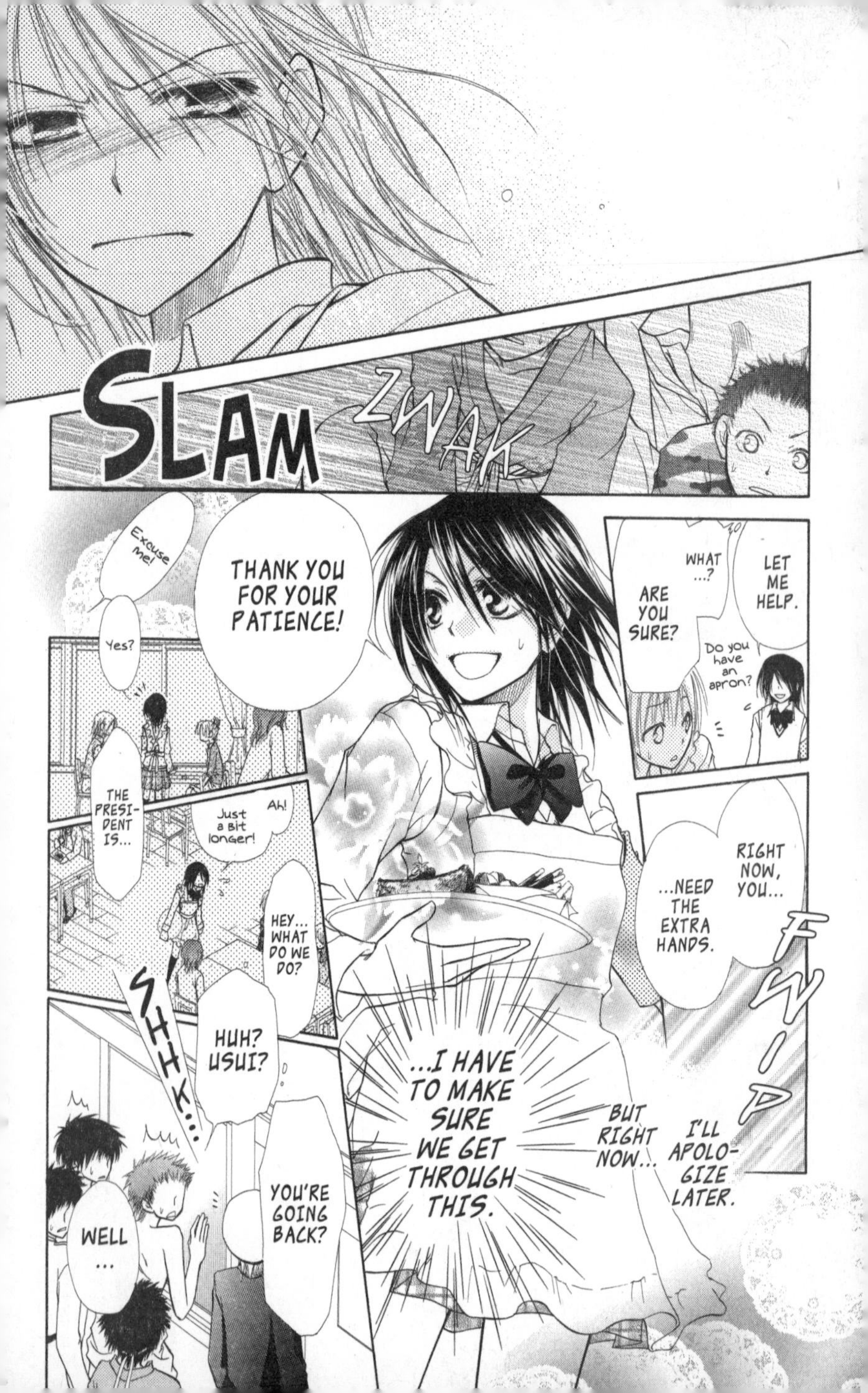
SLAM
ZWAK
LET ME HELP.
WHAT ...?
ARE YOU SURE?
Do you have an apron?
RIGHT NOW, YOU...
...NEED THE EXTRA HANDS.
FWIP
THANK YOU FOR YOUR PATIENCE!
Excuse me!
Yes?
THE PRESI-DENT IS...
Ah!
Just a bit longer!
HEY... WHAT DO WE DO?
I'LL APOLO-GIZE LATER.
BUT RIGHT NOW...
...I HAVE TO MAKE SURE WE GET THROUGH THIS.
HUH? USUI?
SHHK...
YOU'RE GOING BACK?
WELL ...

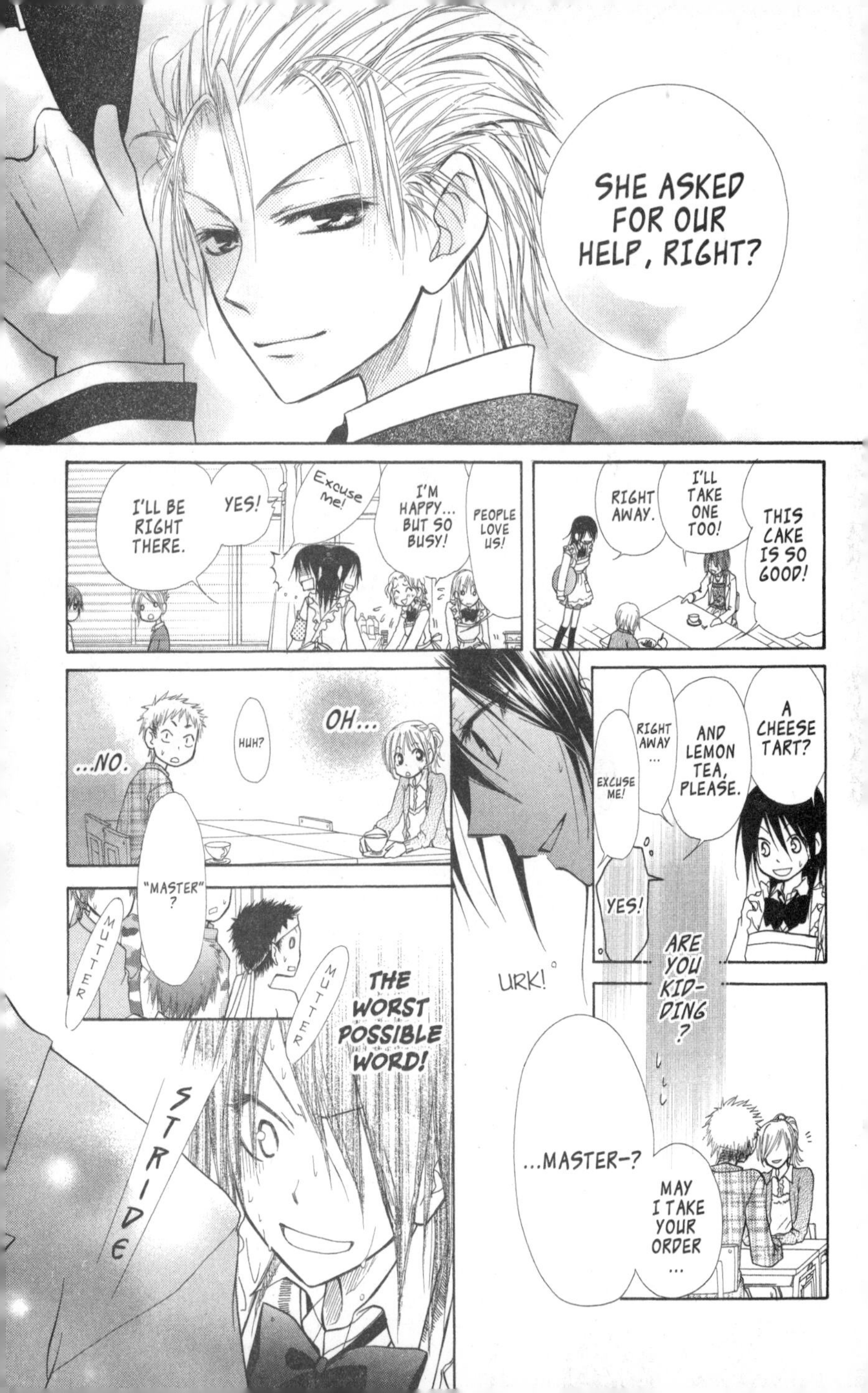

SHE ASKED FOR OUR HELP, RIGHT?
THIS CAKE IS SO GOOD!
I'LL TAKE ONE TOO!
RIGHT AWAY.
PEOPLE LOVE US!
I'M HAPPY... BUT SO BUSY!
Excuse me!
YES!
I'LL BE RIGHT THERE.
A CHEESE TART?
AND LEMON TEA, PLEASE.
RIGHT AWAY...
EXCUSE ME!
YES!
OH...
HUH?
...NO.
"MASTER"?
MUTTER
MUTTER
THE WORST POSSIBLE WORD!
ARE YOU KID-DING?
URK!
...MASTER-?
MAY I TAKE YOUR ORDER...
STRIDE

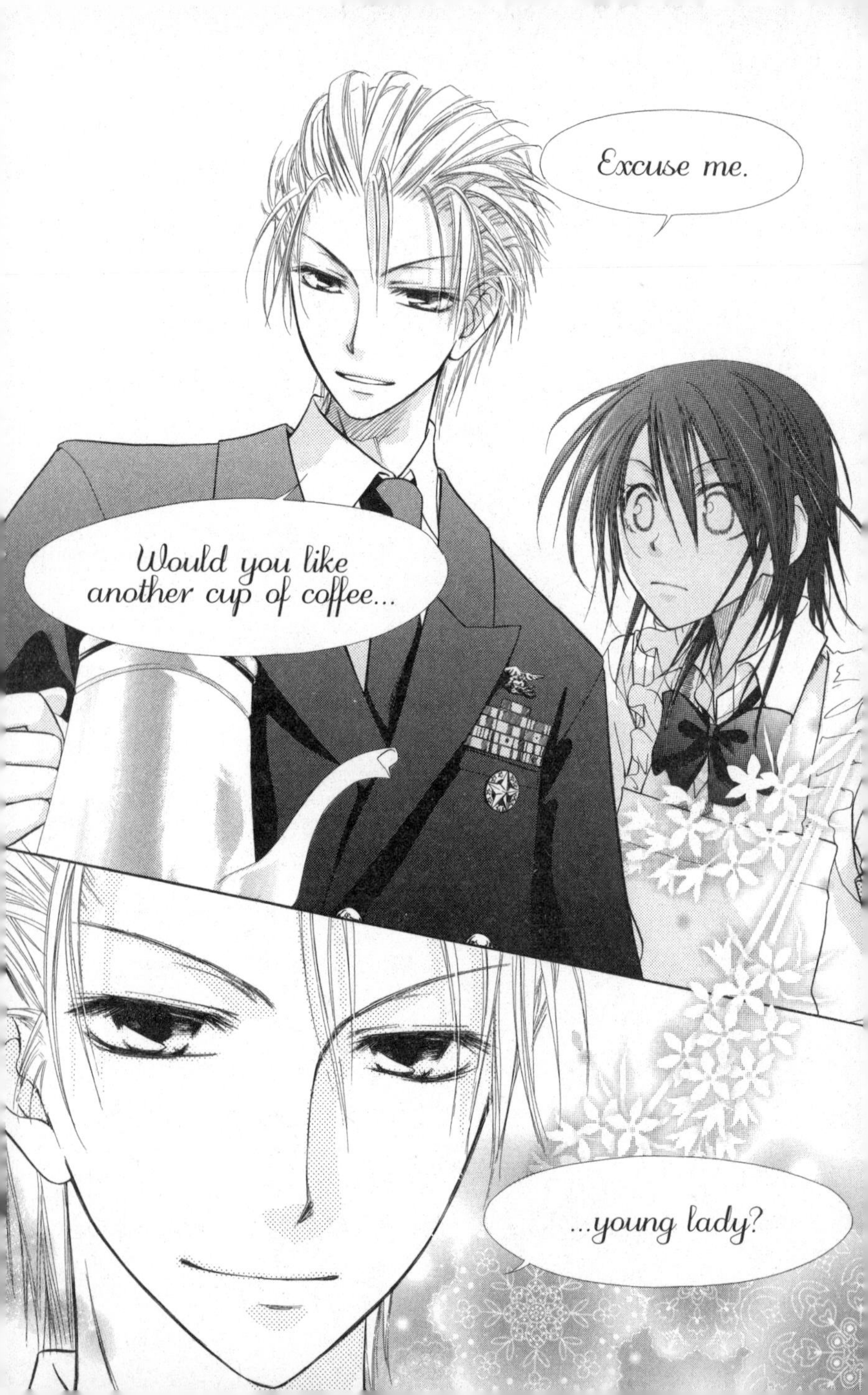
Excuse me.
Would you like another cup of coffee...
...young lady?

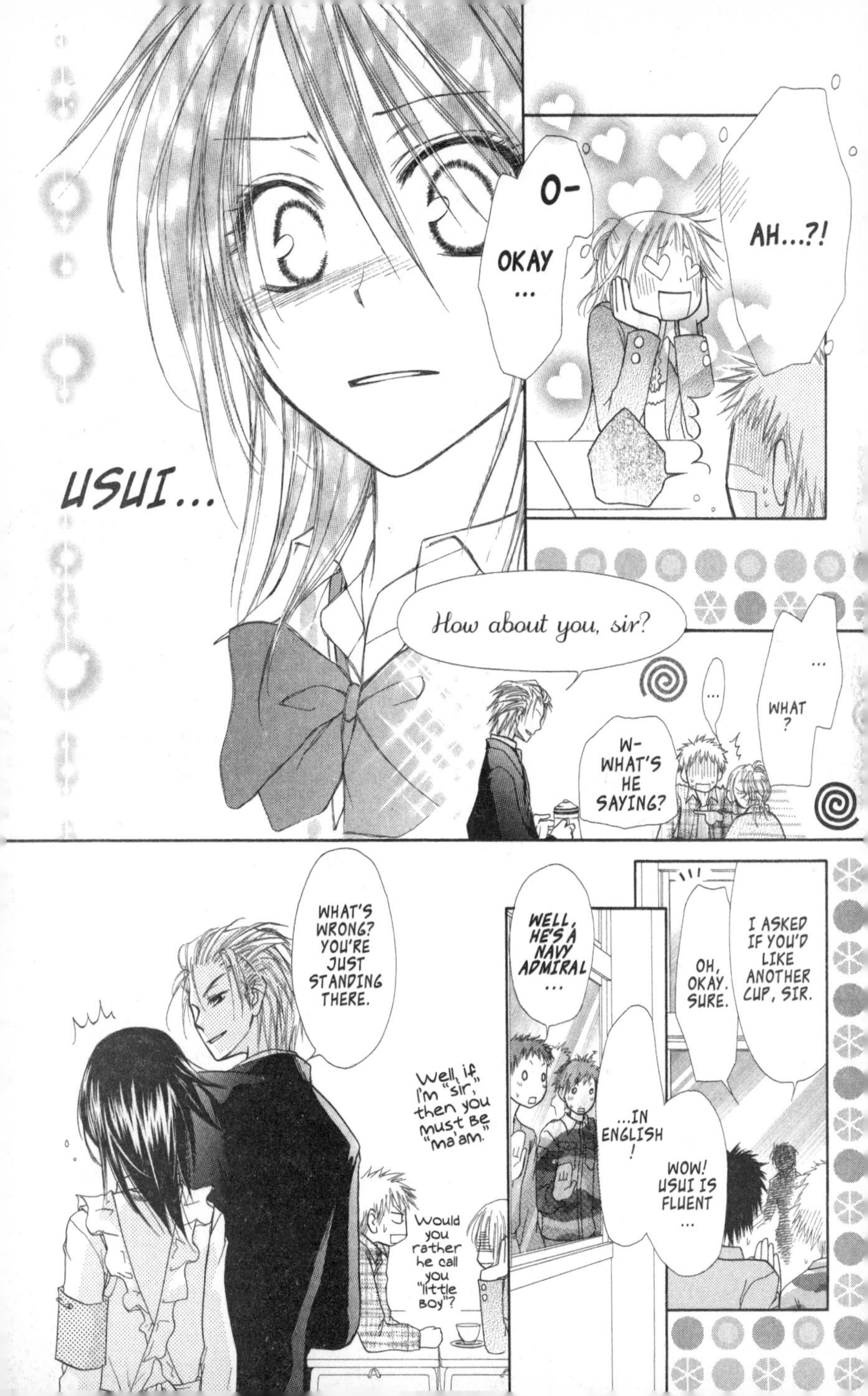
AH...?!
O-
OKAY
...
How about you, sir?
...
WHAT?
...
W-
WHAT'S
HE
SAYING?
USUI...
I ASKED
IF YOU'D
LIKE
ANOTHER
CUP, SIR.
OH,
OKAY.
SURE.
WELL,
HE'S A
NAVY
ADMIRAL
...
...IN
ENGLISH
!
WOW!
USUI IS
FLUENT
...
WHAT'S
WRONG?
YOU'RE
JUST
STANDING
THERE.
Well, if
I'm "sir,"
then you
must be
"ma'am."
Would
you
rather
he call
you
"little
boy"?

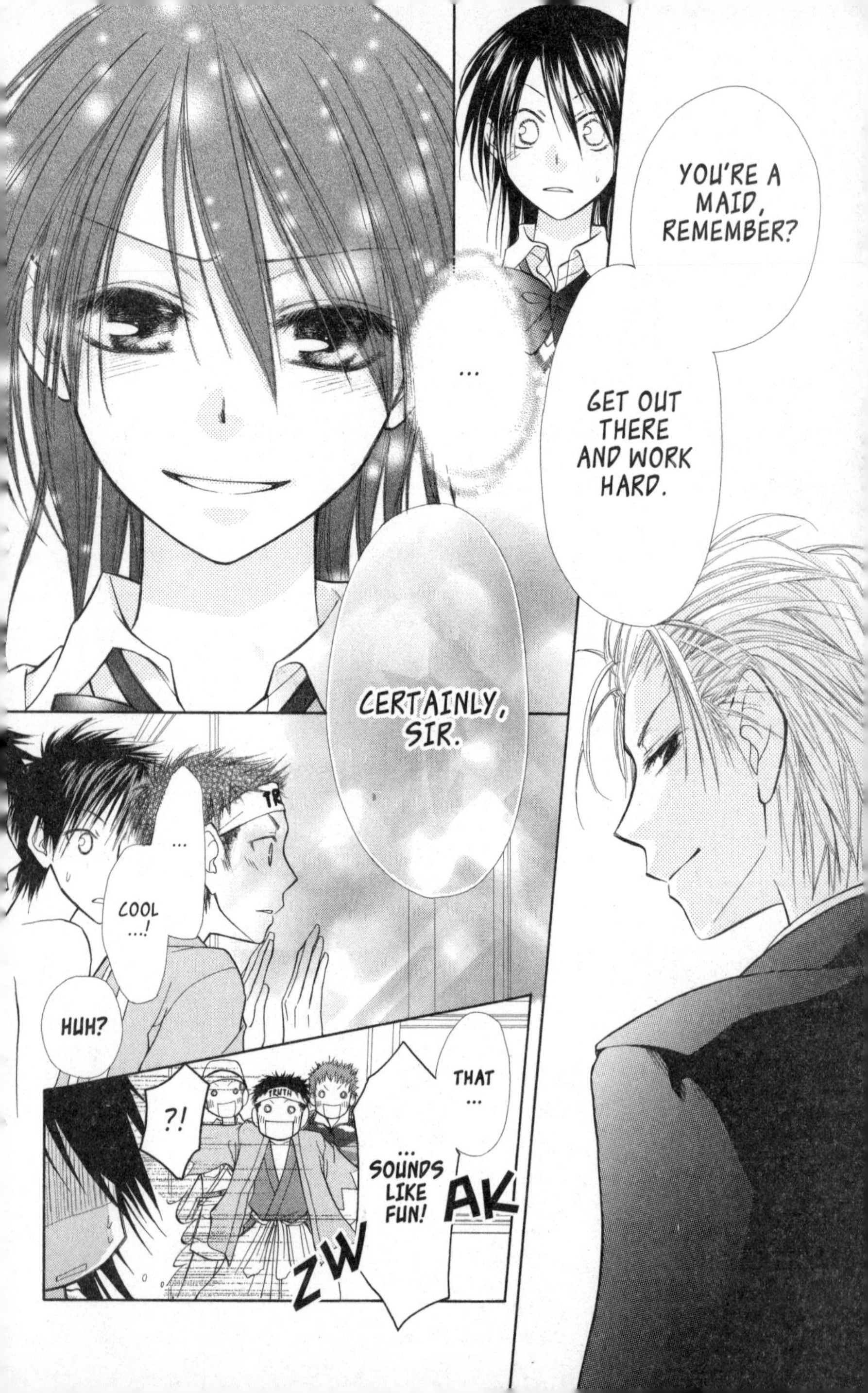
YOU'RE A MAID, REMEMBER?
GET OUT THERE AND WORK HARD.
...
CERTAINLY, SIR.
...
COOL ...!
HUH?
THAT ...
... SOUNDS LIKE FUN!
?!
ZWAK

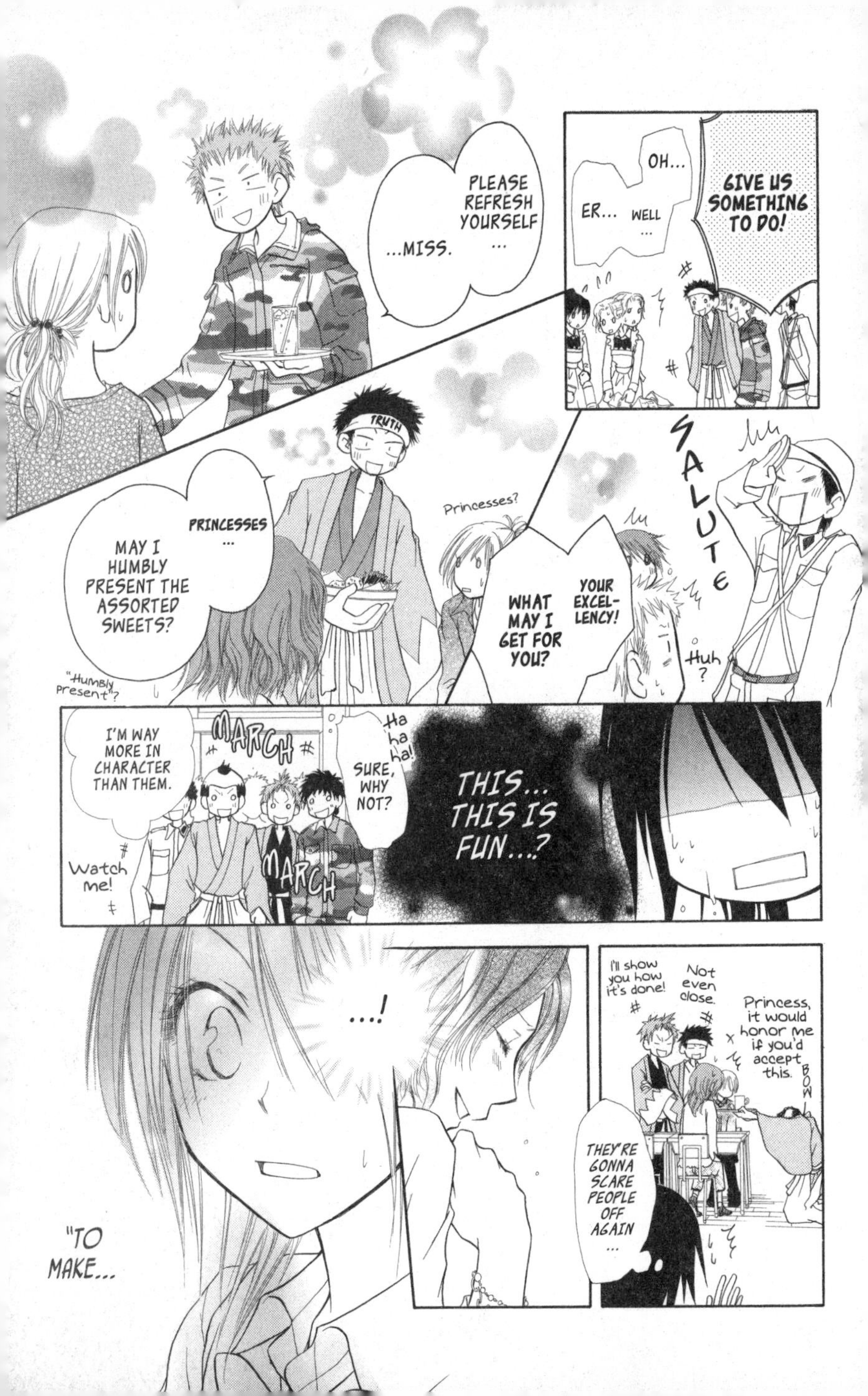
GIVE US SOMETHING TO DO!
OH...
ER... WELL...
PLEASE REFRESH YOURSELF...
...MISS.
SALUTE
YOUR EXCELLENCY!
WHAT MAY I GET FOR YOU?
Huh?
Princesses?
PRINCESSES...
MAY I HUMBLY PRESENT THE ASSORTED SWEETS?
"Humbly present"?
THIS... THIS IS FUN...?
Ha ha ha!
SURE, WHY NOT?
MARCH
MARCH
I'M WAY MORE IN CHARACTER THAN THEM.
Watch me!
Princess, it would honor me if you'd accept this.
BOW
Not even close.
I'll show you how it's done!
THEY'RE GONNA SCARE PEOPLE OFF AGAIN...
...!
"TO MAKE...

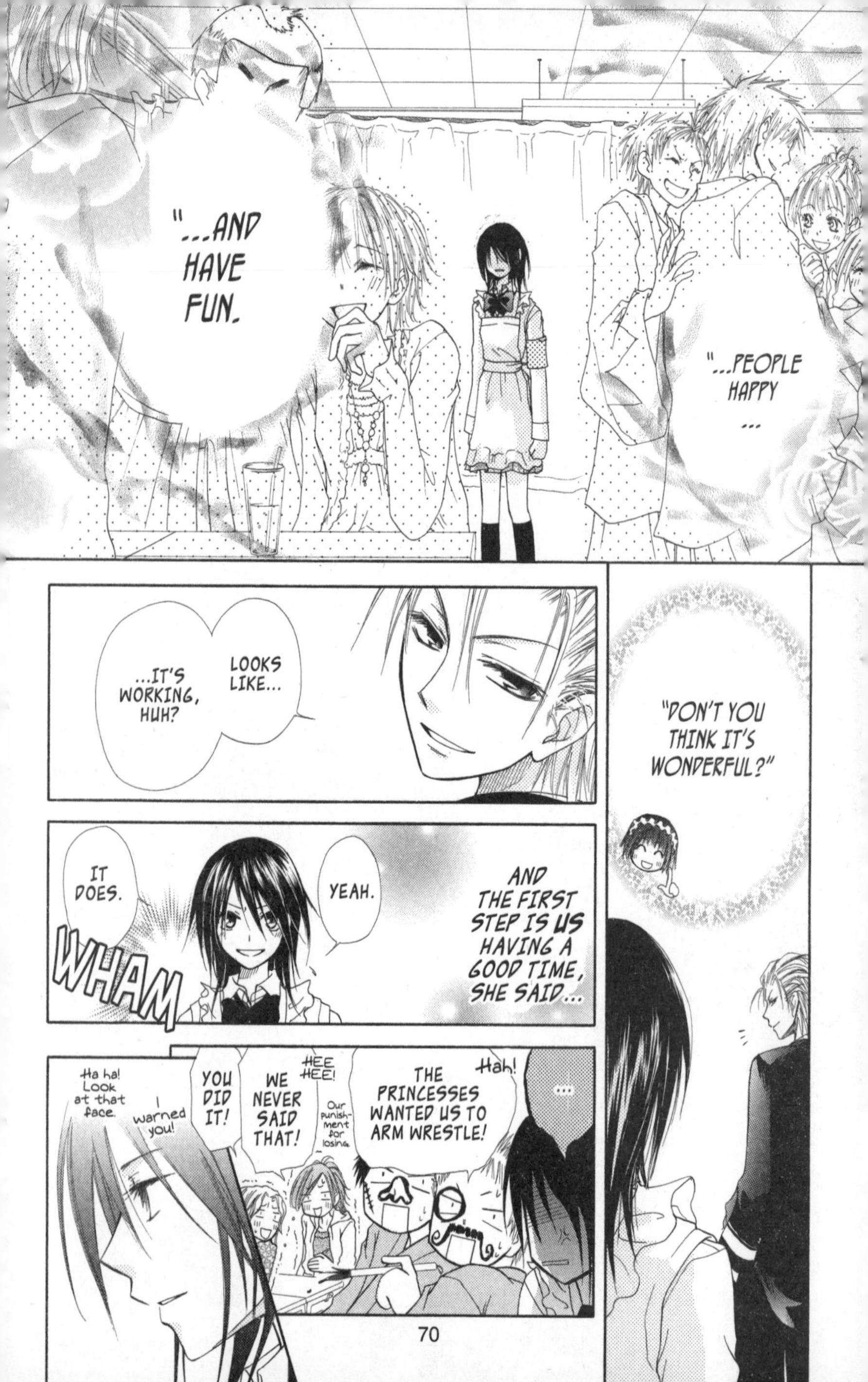
"...PEOPLE HAPPY ...
"...AND HAVE FUN.
"DON'T YOU THINK IT'S WONDERFUL?"
LOOKS LIKE...
...IT'S WORKING, HUH?
AND THE FIRST STEP IS US HAVING A GOOD TIME, SHE SAID...
YEAH.
IT DOES.
WHAM
...
Hah!
THE PRINCESSES WANTED US TO ARM WRESTLE!
Our punishment for losing.
HEE HEE!
WE NEVER SAID THAT!
YOU DID IT!
I warned you!
Ha ha! Look at that face.

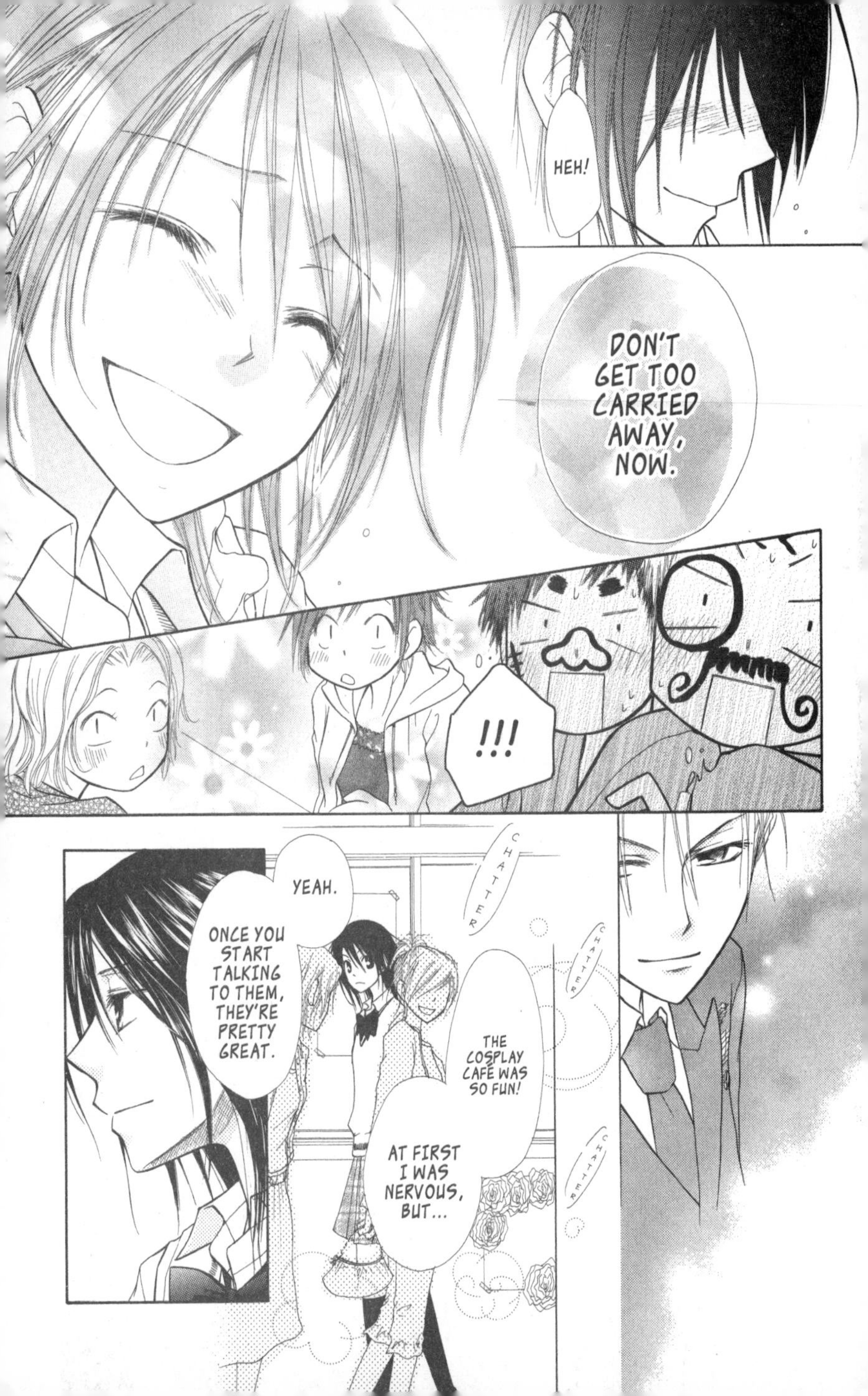
HEH!
DON'T GET TOO CARRIED AWAY, NOW.
!!!
CHATTER
CHATTER
CHATTER
THE COSPLAY CAFE WAS SO FUN!
AT FIRST I WAS NERVOUS, BUT...
YEAH.
ONCE YOU START TALKING TO THEM, THEY'RE PRETTY GREAT.

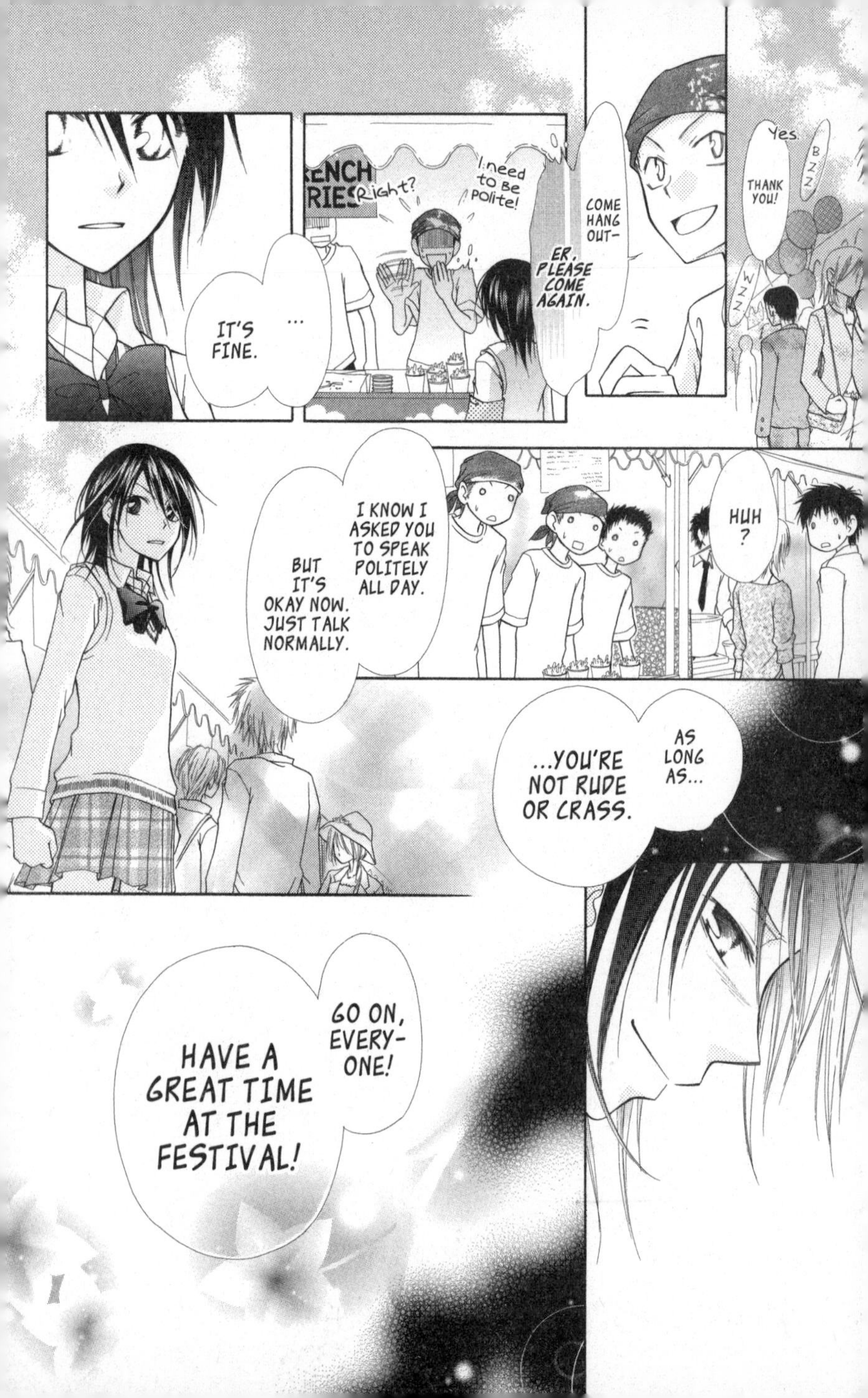

Yes.
BZZ
THANK YOU!
WZZ
COME HANG OUT-
ER, PLEASE COME AGAIN.
I need to be polite!
Right?
RENCH RIES
...
IT'S FINE.
HUH?
I KNOW I ASKED YOU TO SPEAK POLITELY ALL DAY.
BUT IT'S OKAY NOW. JUST TALK NORMALLY.
AS LONG AS...
...YOU'RE NOT RUDE OR CRASS.
GO ON, EVERYONE!
HAVE A GREAT TIME AT THE FESTIVAL!

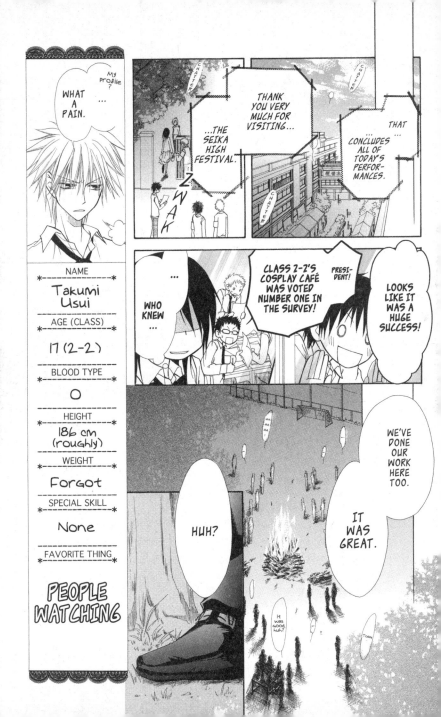

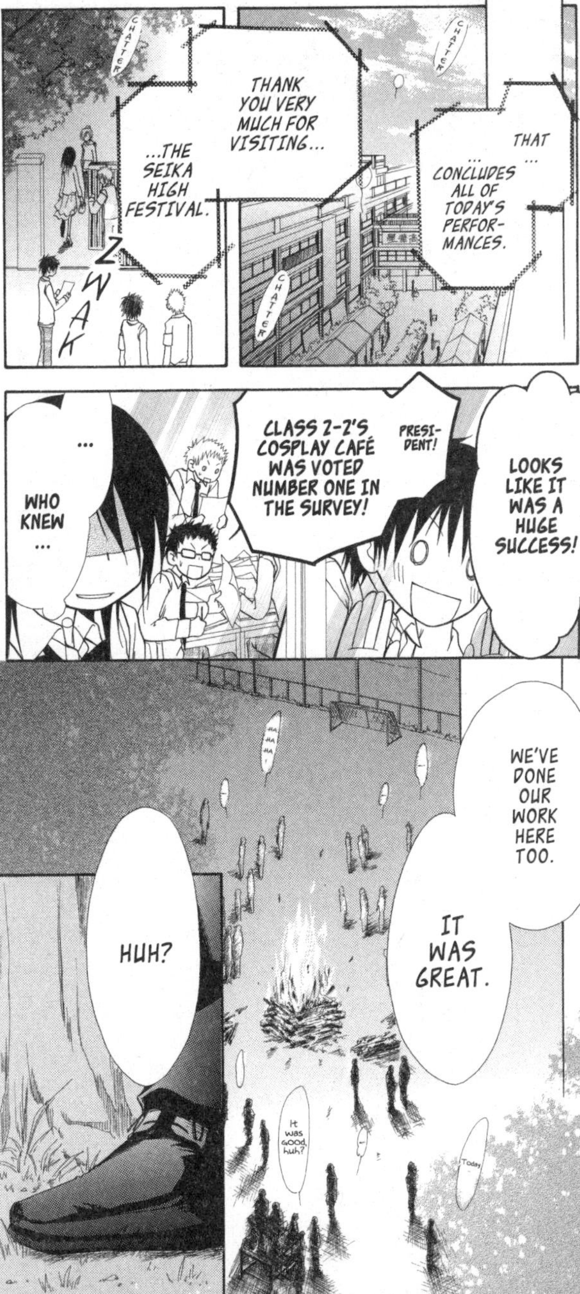
CHATTER
CHATTER
THAT... CONCLUDES ALL OF TODAY'S PERFORMANCES.
THANK YOU VERY MUCH FOR VISITING...
CHATTER
...THE SEIKA HIGH FESTIVAL.
ZWAK
LOOKS LIKE IT WAS A HUGE SUCCESS!
PRESI-DENT!
CLASS 2-2'S COSPLAY CAFÉ WAS VOTED NUMBER ONE IN THE SURVEY!
...
WHO KNEW...
WE'VE DONE OUR WORK HERE TOO.
IT WAS GREAT.
HA HA HA HA
Today...
It was good, huh?
HUH?

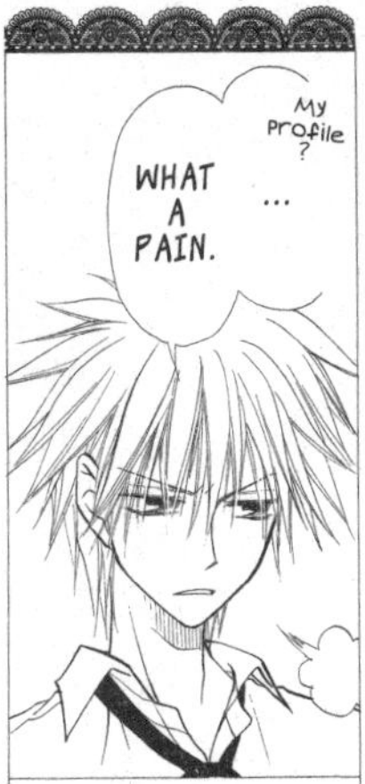
My profile?
...
WHAT A PAIN.

NAME

Takumi Usui

AGE (CLASS)

17 (2-2)

BLOOD TYPE

O

HEIGHT

186 cm (roughly)

WEIGHT

Forgot

SPECIAL SKILL

None

FAVORITE THING

PEOPLE WATCHING

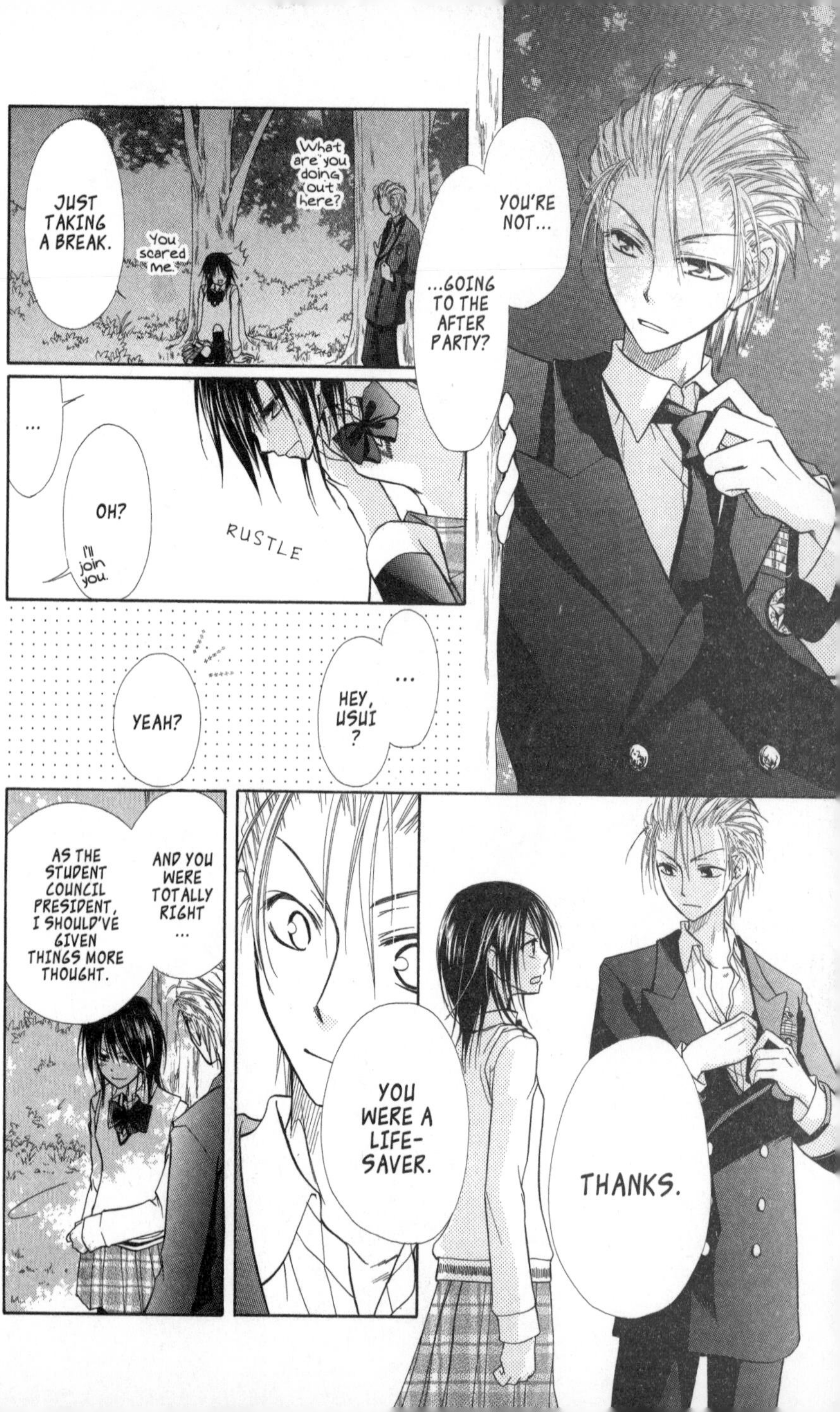
YOU'RE NOT...
...GOING TO THE AFTER PARTY?
What are you doing out here?
JUST TAKING A BREAK.
You scared me.
...
OH?
I'll join you.
RUSTLE
... HEY, USUI?
YEAH?
THANKS.
YOU WERE A LIFE-SAVER.
AND YOU WERE TOTALLY RIGHT...
AS THE STUDENT COUNCIL PRESIDENT, I SHOULD'VE GIVEN THINGS MORE THOUGHT.

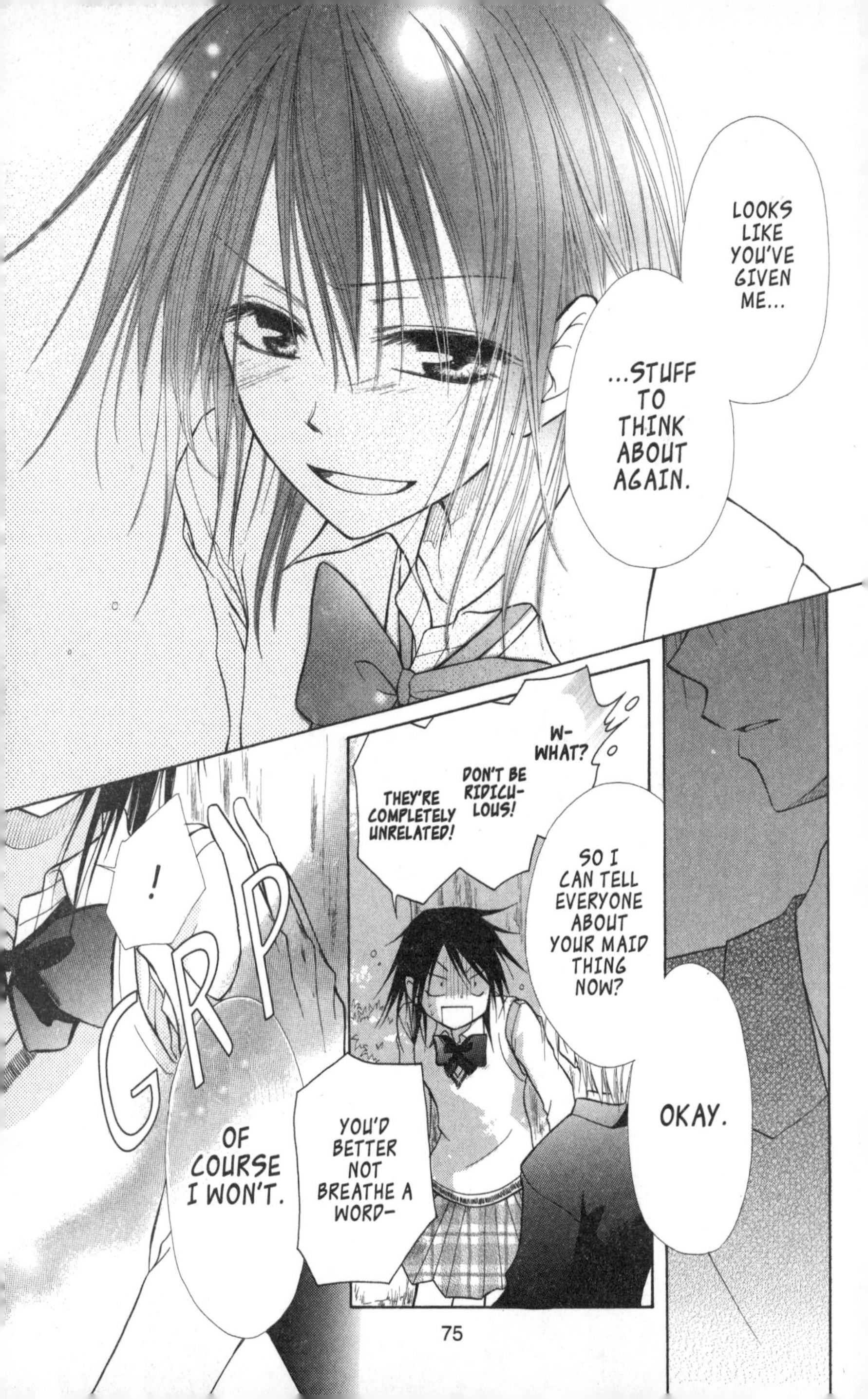
LOOKS LIKE YOU'VE GIVEN ME...
...STUFF TO THINK ABOUT AGAIN.
W-WHAT?
DON'T BE RIDICULOUS!
THEY'RE COMPLETELY UNRELATED!
SO I CAN TELL EVERYONE ABOUT YOUR MAID THING NOW?
OKAY.
YOU'D BETTER NOT BREATHE A WORD-
!
GRIP
OF COURSE I WON'T.

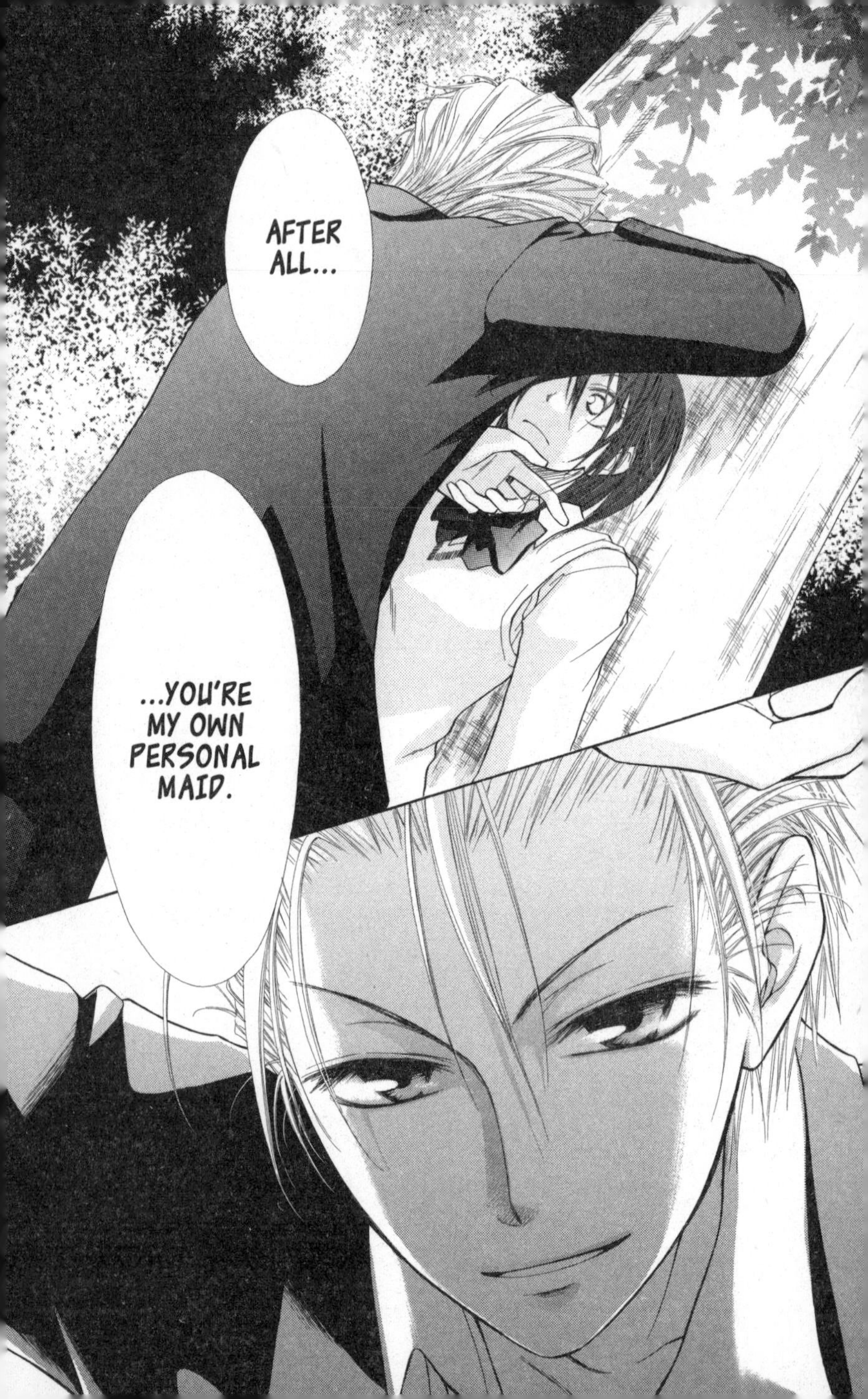
AFTER ALL...
...YOU'RE MY OWN PERSONAL MAID.

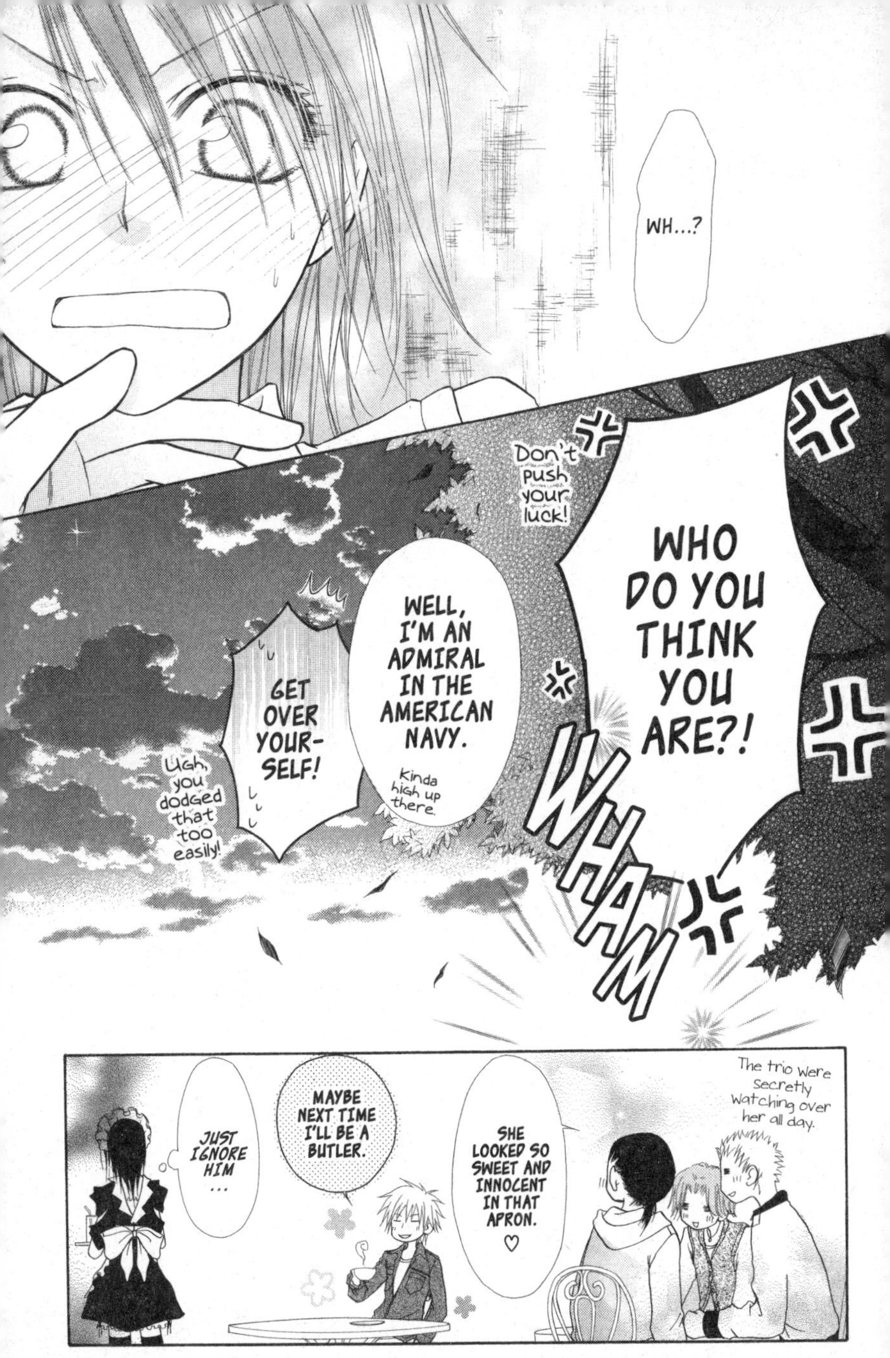
WH...?
WHO DO YOU THINK YOU ARE?!
Don't push your luck!
WHAM
WELL, I'M AN ADMIRAL IN THE AMERICAN NAVY.
Kinda high up there.
GET OVER YOUR-SELF!
Ugh, you dodged that too easily!
The trio were secretly watching over her all day.
SHE LOOKED SO SWEET AND INNOCENT IN THAT APRON. ♡
MAYBE NEXT TIME I'LL BE A BUTLER.
JUST IGNORE HIM ...

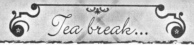

While Preparing for the School Festival

A Day in the Life of a Boy from Class 2-2!

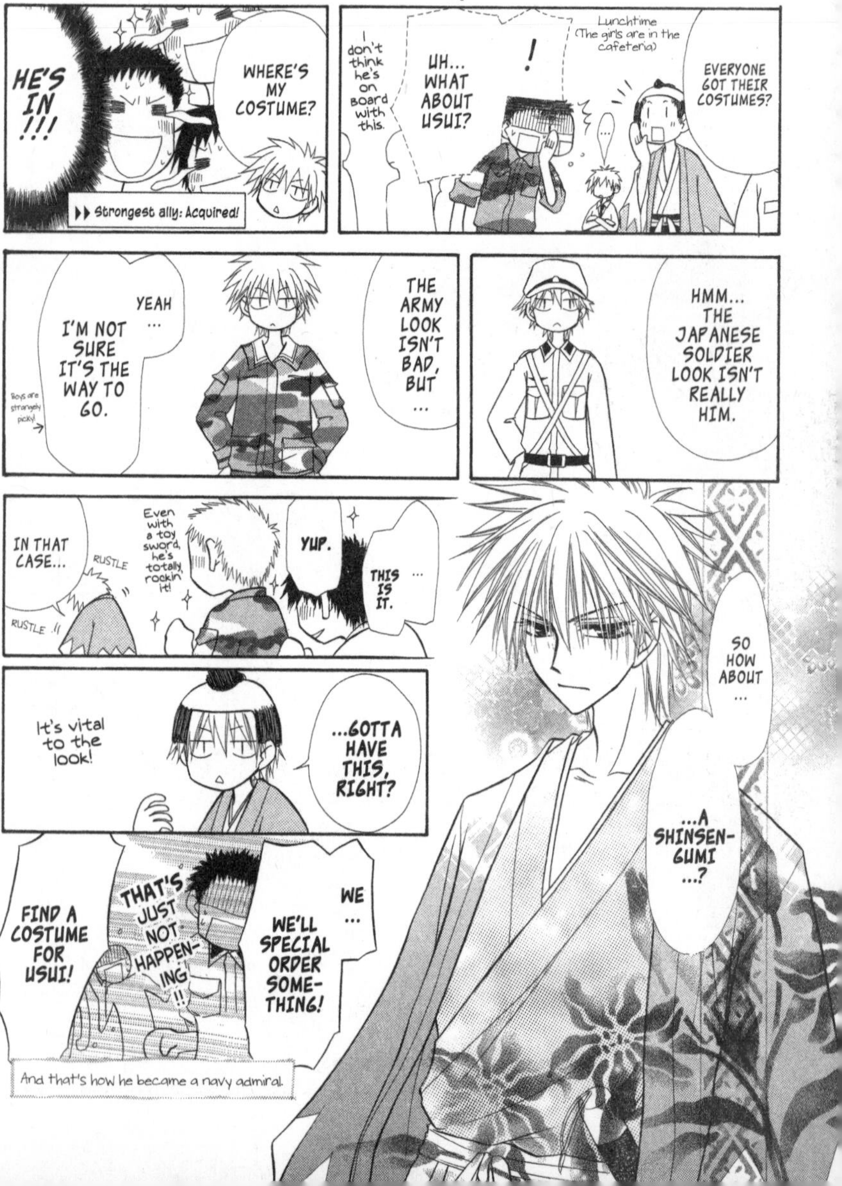
Lunchtime (The girls are in the cafeteria)
EVERYONE GOT THEIR COSTUMES?
...
!
UH... WHAT ABOUT USUI?
I don't think he's on board with this.
WHERE'S MY COSTUME?
HE'S IN!!!
Strongest ally: Acquired!
HMM... THE JAPANESE SOLDIER LOOK ISN'T REALLY HIM.
THE ARMY LOOK ISN'T BAD, BUT...
YEAH...
I'M NOT SURE IT'S THE WAY TO GO.
Boys are strangely picky!
SO HOW ABOUT...
...A SHINSEN-GUMI...?
THIS IS IT...
YUP.
Even with a toy sword, he's totally rockin' it!
IN THAT CASE...
RUSTLE
RUSTLE
...GOTTA HAVE THIS, RIGHT?
It's vital to the look!
WE...
WE'LL SPECIAL ORDER SOMETHING!
THAT'S JUST NOT HAPPENING!!
FIND A COSTUME FOR USUI!
And that's how he became a navy admiral.

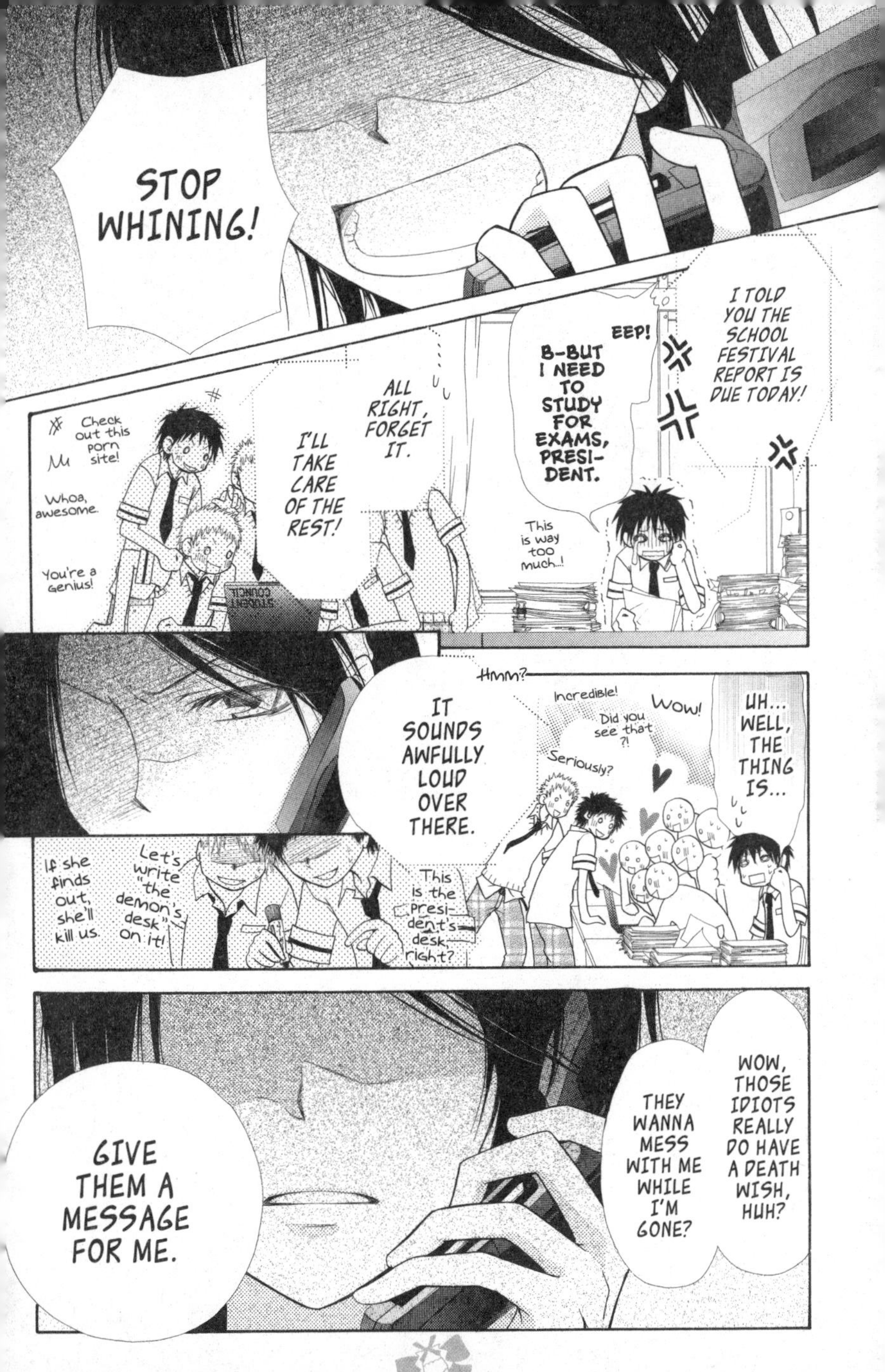
STOP WHINING!
I TOLD YOU THE SCHOOL FESTIVAL REPORT IS DUE TODAY!
EEP!
B-BUT I NEED TO STUDY FOR EXAMS, PRESIDENT.
This is way too much...!
ALL RIGHT, FORGET IT.
I'LL TAKE CARE OF THE REST!
Check out this porn site!
Whoa, awesome.
You're a genius!
UH... WELL, THE THING IS...
Wow!
Incredible!
Did you see that?!
Seriously?
Hmm?
IT SOUNDS AWFULLY LOUD OVER THERE.
This is the president's desk, right?
Let's write "the demon's desk" on it!
If she finds out, she'll kill us.
WOW, THOSE IDIOTS REALLY DO HAVE A DEATH WISH, HUH?
THEY WANNA MESS WITH ME WHILE I'M GONE?
GIVE THEM A MESSAGE FOR ME.

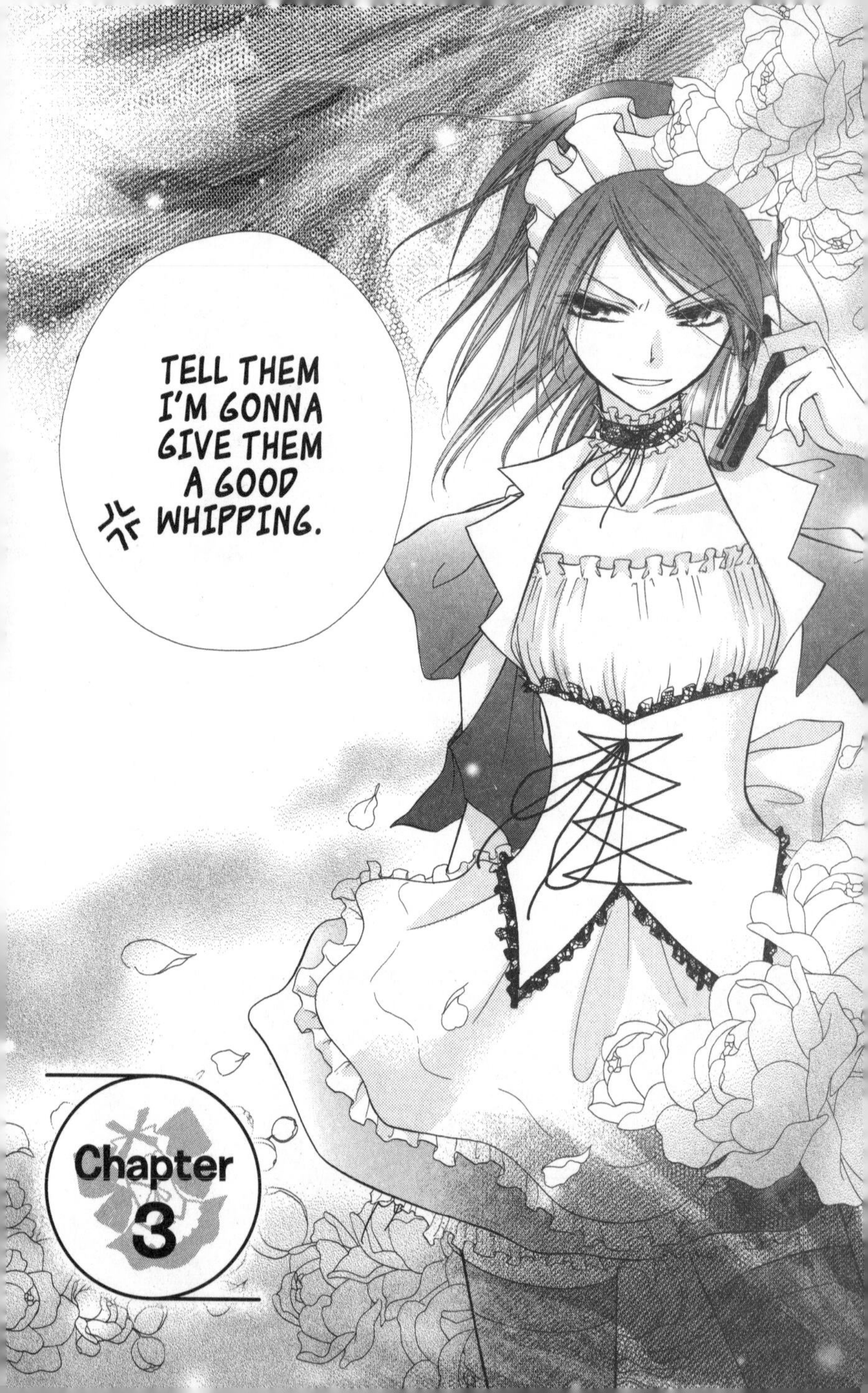
TELL THEM I'M GONNA GIVE THEM A GOOD WHIPPING.
Chapter 3

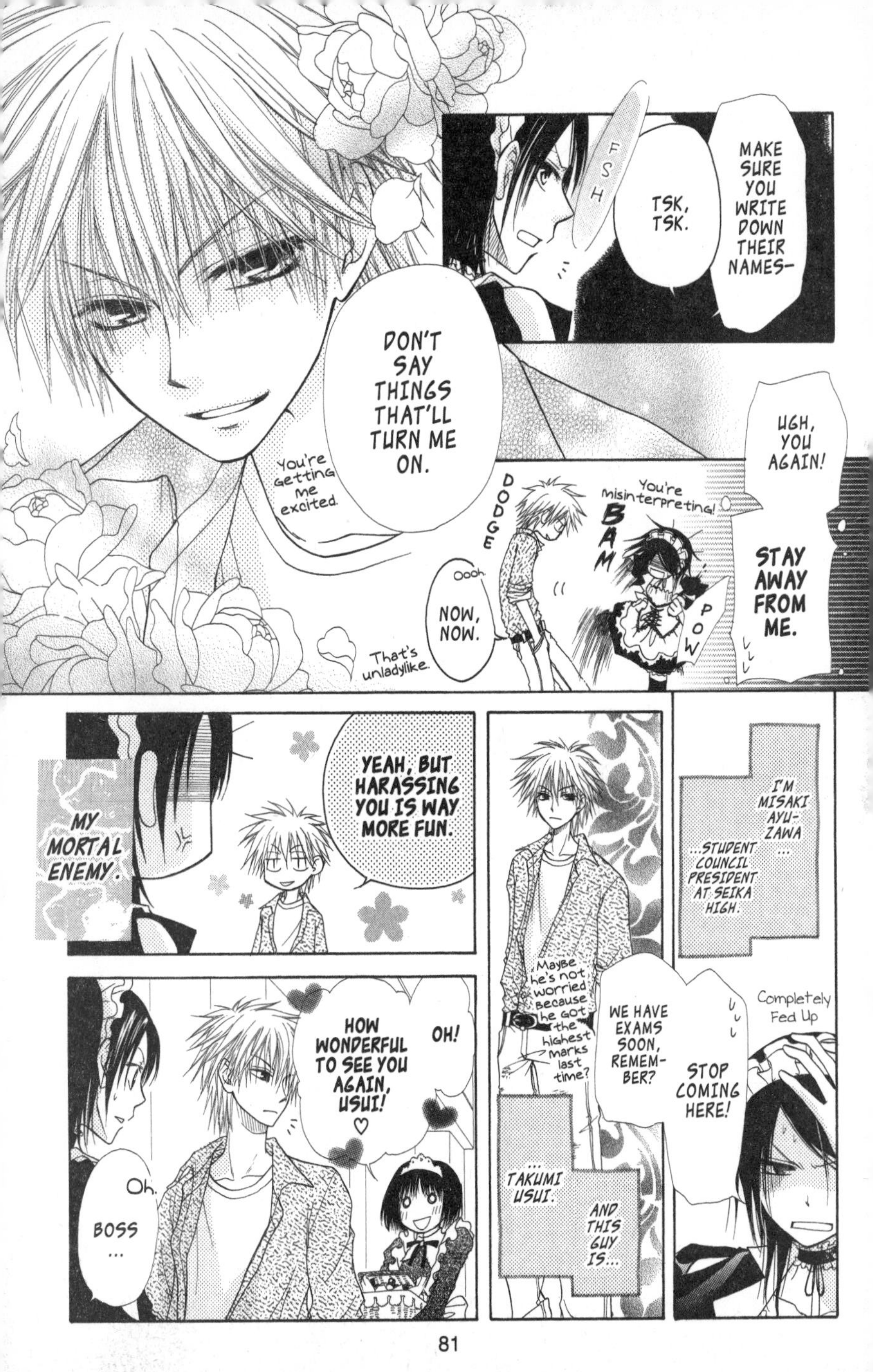
MAKE SURE YOU WRITE DOWN THEIR NAMES—
TSK, TSK.
FSH
DON'T SAY THINGS THAT'LL TURN ME ON.
You're getting me excited.
UGH, YOU AGAIN!
STAY AWAY FROM ME.
POW
You're misinterpreting!
BAM
DODGE
Oooh.
NOW, NOW.
That's unladylike.
I'M MISAKI AYUZAWA ...
...STUDENT COUNCIL PRESIDENT AT SEIKA HIGH.
Completely Fed Up
STOP COMING HERE!
WE HAVE EXAMS SOON, REMEMBER?
Maybe he's not worried because he got the highest marks last time?
AND THIS GUY IS...
...TAKUMI USUI.
YEAH, BUT HARASSING YOU IS WAY MORE FUN.
MY MORTAL ENEMY.
OH!
HOW WONDERFUL TO SEE YOU AGAIN, USUI! ♡
Oh.
BOSS ...

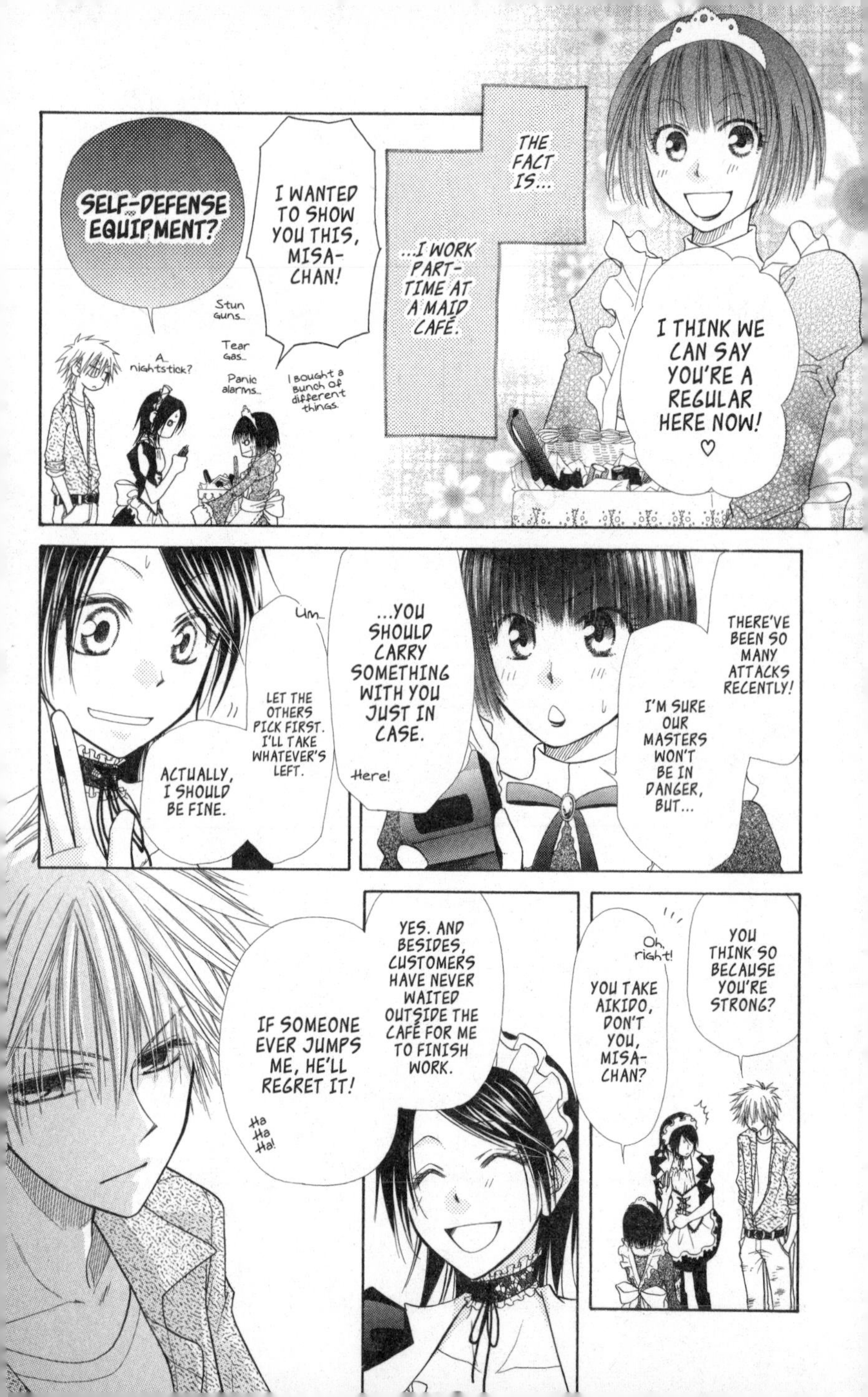
I THINK WE CAN SAY YOU'RE A REGULAR HERE NOW! ♡
THE FACT IS...
...I WORK PART-TIME AT A MAID CAFÉ.
I WANTED TO SHOW YOU THIS, MISA-CHAN!
I bought a bunch of different things.
Stun guns...
Tear gas...
Panic alarms...
A... nightstick?
SELF-DEFENSE EQUIPMENT?
THERE'VE BEEN SO MANY ATTACKS RECENTLY!
I'M SURE OUR MASTERS WON'T BE IN DANGER, BUT...
...YOU SHOULD CARRY SOMETHING WITH YOU JUST IN CASE.
Here!
Um...
LET THE OTHERS PICK FIRST. I'LL TAKE WHATEVER'S LEFT.
ACTUALLY, I SHOULD BE FINE.
YOU THINK SO BECAUSE YOU'RE STRONG?
Oh, right!
YOU TAKE AIKIDO, DON'T YOU, MISA-CHAN?
YES. AND BESIDES, CUSTOMERS HAVE NEVER WAITED OUTSIDE THE CAFÉ FOR ME TO FINISH WORK.
IF SOMEONE EVER JUMPS ME, HE'LL REGRET IT!
Ha Ha Ha!

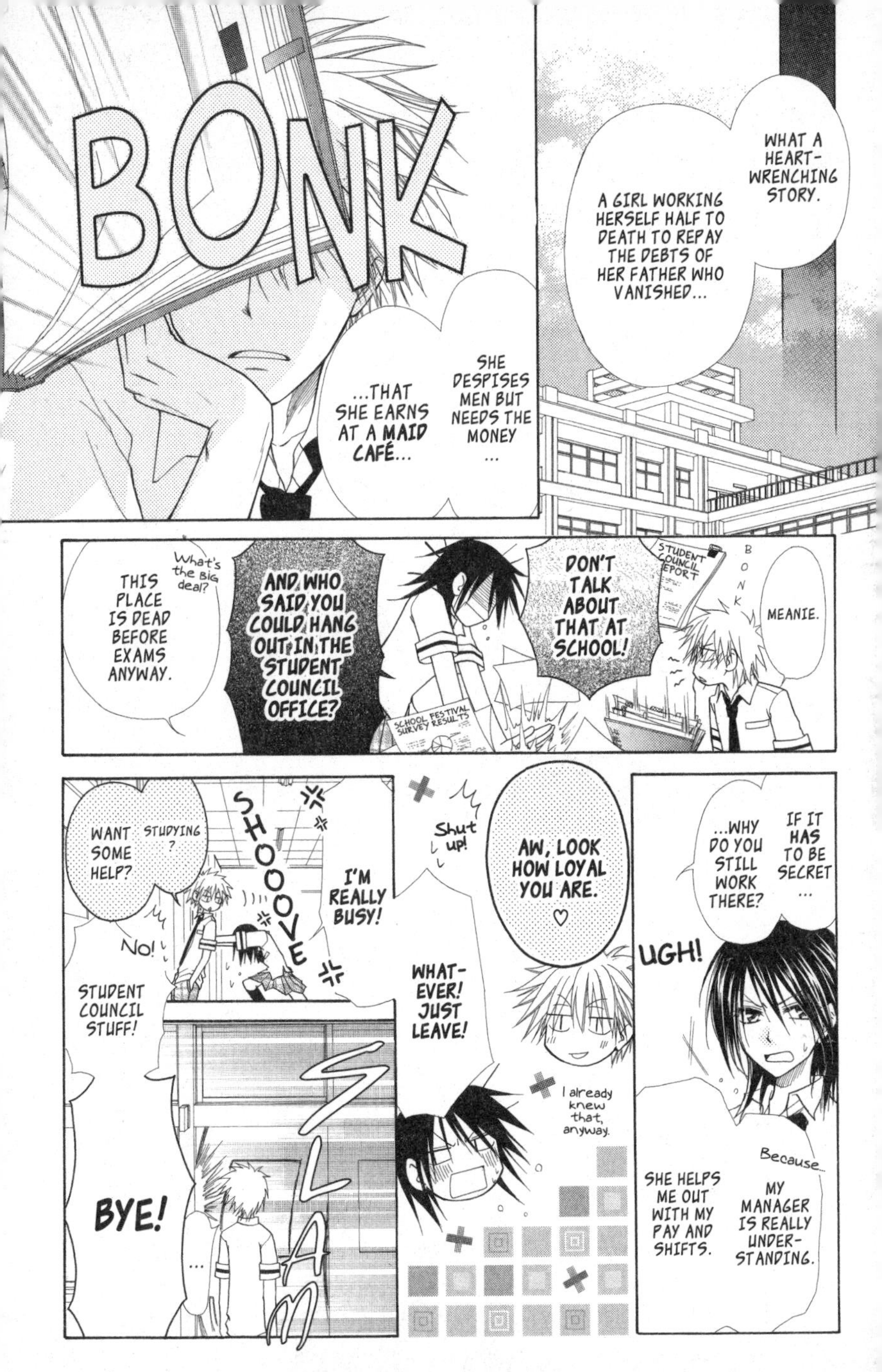
WHAT A HEART-WRENCHING STORY.
A GIRL WORKING HERSELF HALF TO DEATH TO REPAY THE DEBTS OF HER FATHER WHO VANISHED...
SHE DESPISES MEN BUT NEEDS THE MONEY ...
...THAT SHE EARNS AT A MAID CAFÉ...
BONK
MEANIE.
BONK
STUDENT COUNCIL REPORT
DON'T TALK ABOUT THAT AT SCHOOL!
SCHOOL FESTIVAL SURVEY RESULTS
AND WHO SAID YOU COULD HANG OUT IN THE STUDENT COUNCIL OFFICE?
What's the big deal?
THIS PLACE IS DEAD BEFORE EXAMS ANYWAY.
IF IT HAS TO BE SECRET ...
...WHY DO YOU STILL WORK THERE?
UGH!
Because...
MY MANAGER IS REALLY UNDER-STANDING.
SHE HELPS ME OUT WITH MY PAY AND SHIFTS.
AW, LOOK HOW LOYAL YOU ARE. ♡
Shut up!
I'M REALLY BUSY!
WHAT-EVER! JUST LEAVE!
I already knew that, anyway.
SHOOOVE
STUDYING?
WANT SOME HELP?
No!
STUDENT COUNCIL STUFF!
SLAM
BYE!
...

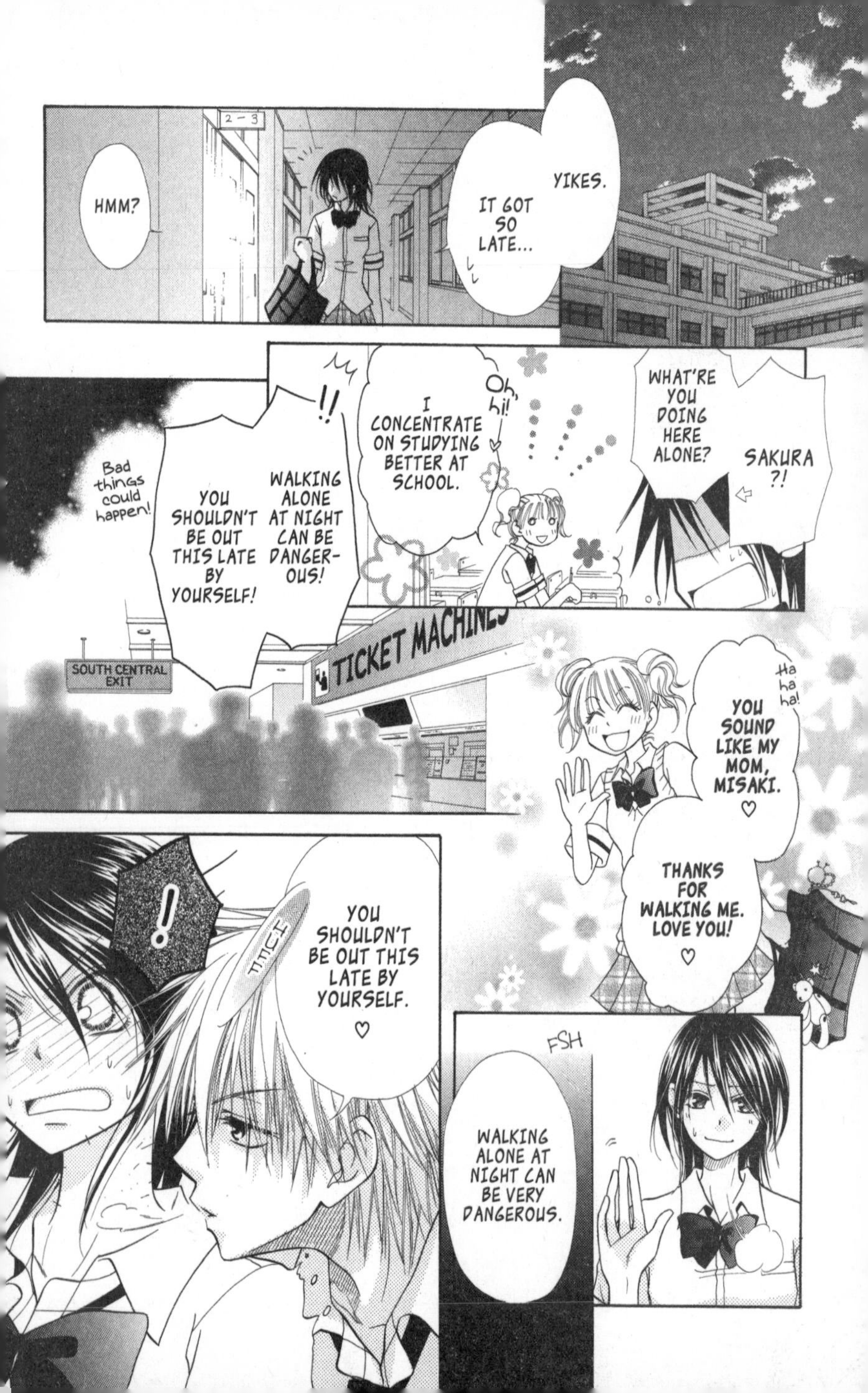
YIKES.
IT GOT SO LATE...
HMM?
SAKURA?!
WHAT'RE YOU DOING HERE ALONE?
Oh, hi!
I CONCENTRATE ON STUDYING BETTER AT SCHOOL.
!!
WALKING ALONE AT NIGHT CAN BE DANGER-OUS!
YOU SHOULDN'T BE OUT THIS LATE BY YOURSELF!
Bad things could happen!
Ha ha ha!
YOU SOUND LIKE MY MOM, MISAKI. ♡
THANKS FOR WALKING ME. LOVE YOU! ♡
TICKET MACHINES
SOUTH CENTRAL EXIT
FSH
WALKING ALONE AT NIGHT CAN BE VERY DANGEROUS.
YOU SHOULDN'T BE OUT THIS LATE BY YOURSELF. ♡

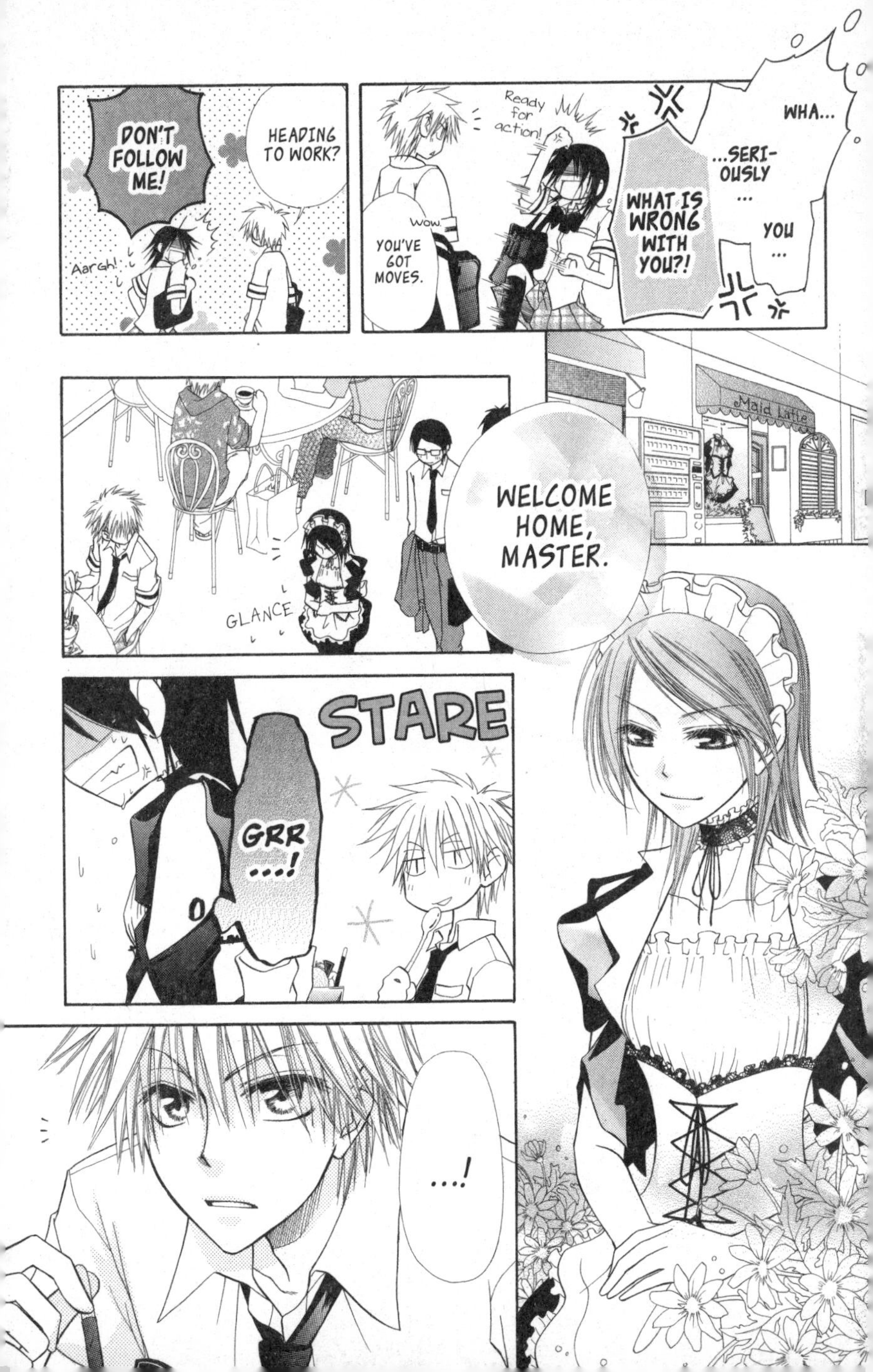
WHA...
...SERIOUSLY ... YOU ...
WHAT IS WRONG WITH YOU?!
Ready for action!
Wow.
YOU'VE GOT MOVES.
HEADING TO WORK?
DON'T FOLLOW ME!
Aargh!
Maid Latte
WELCOME HOME, MASTER.
GLANCE
STARE
GRR ...!
...!

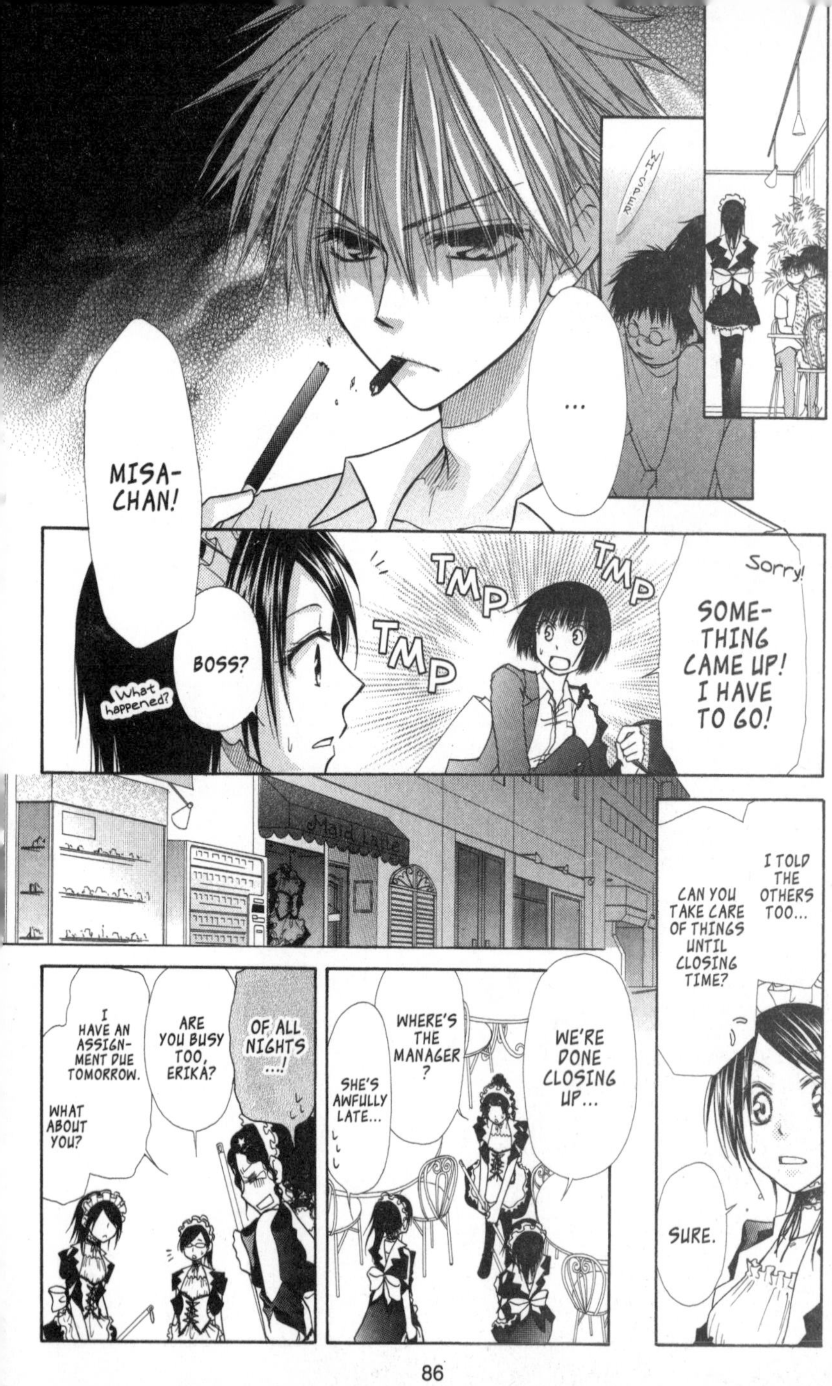
WHI-SPER
...
MISA-CHAN!
Sorry!
SOME-THING CAME UP! I HAVE TO GO!
TMP
TMP
TMP
BOSS?
What happened?
I TOLD THE OTHERS TOO...
CAN YOU TAKE CARE OF THINGS UNTIL CLOSING TIME?
SURE.
WE'RE DONE CLOSING UP...
WHERE'S THE MANAGER?
SHE'S AWFULLY LATE...
OF ALL NIGHTS...!
ARE YOU BUSY TOO, ERIKA?
I HAVE AN ASSIGN-MENT DUE TOMORROW.
WHAT ABOUT YOU?

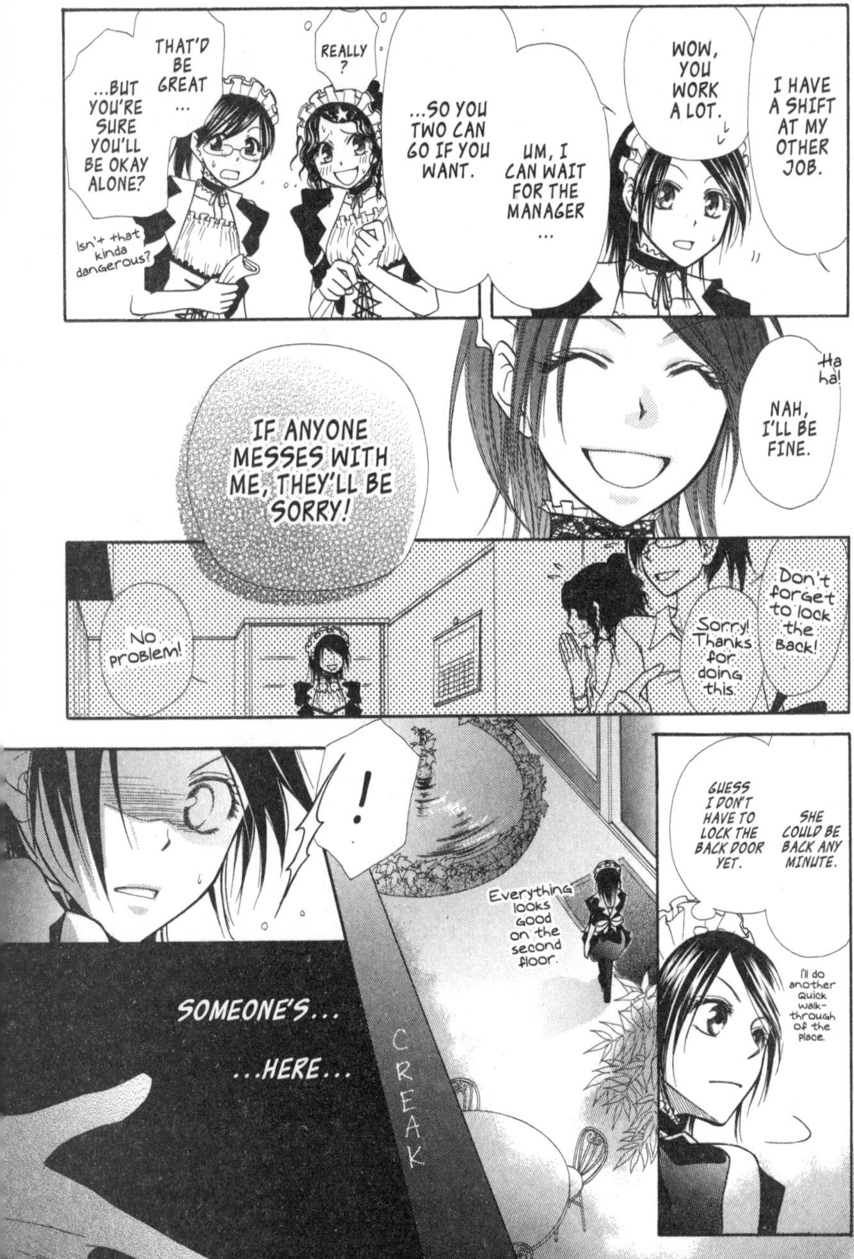
I HAVE A SHIFT AT MY OTHER JOB.
WOW, YOU WORK A LOT.
UM, I CAN WAIT FOR THE MANAGER...
...SO YOU TWO CAN GO IF YOU WANT.
REALLY?
THAT'D BE GREAT...
...BUT YOU'RE SURE YOU'LL BE OKAY ALONE?
Isn't that kinda dangerous?
Ha ha!
NAH, I'LL BE FINE.
IF ANYONE MESSES WITH ME, THEY'LL BE SORRY!
Don't forget to lock the back!
Sorry! Thanks for doing this.
No problem!
GUESS I DON'T HAVE TO LOCK THE BACK DOOR YET.
SHE COULD BE BACK ANY MINUTE.
I'll do another quick walk-through of the place.
Everything looks good on the second floor.
!
CREAK
SOMEONE'S...
...HERE...

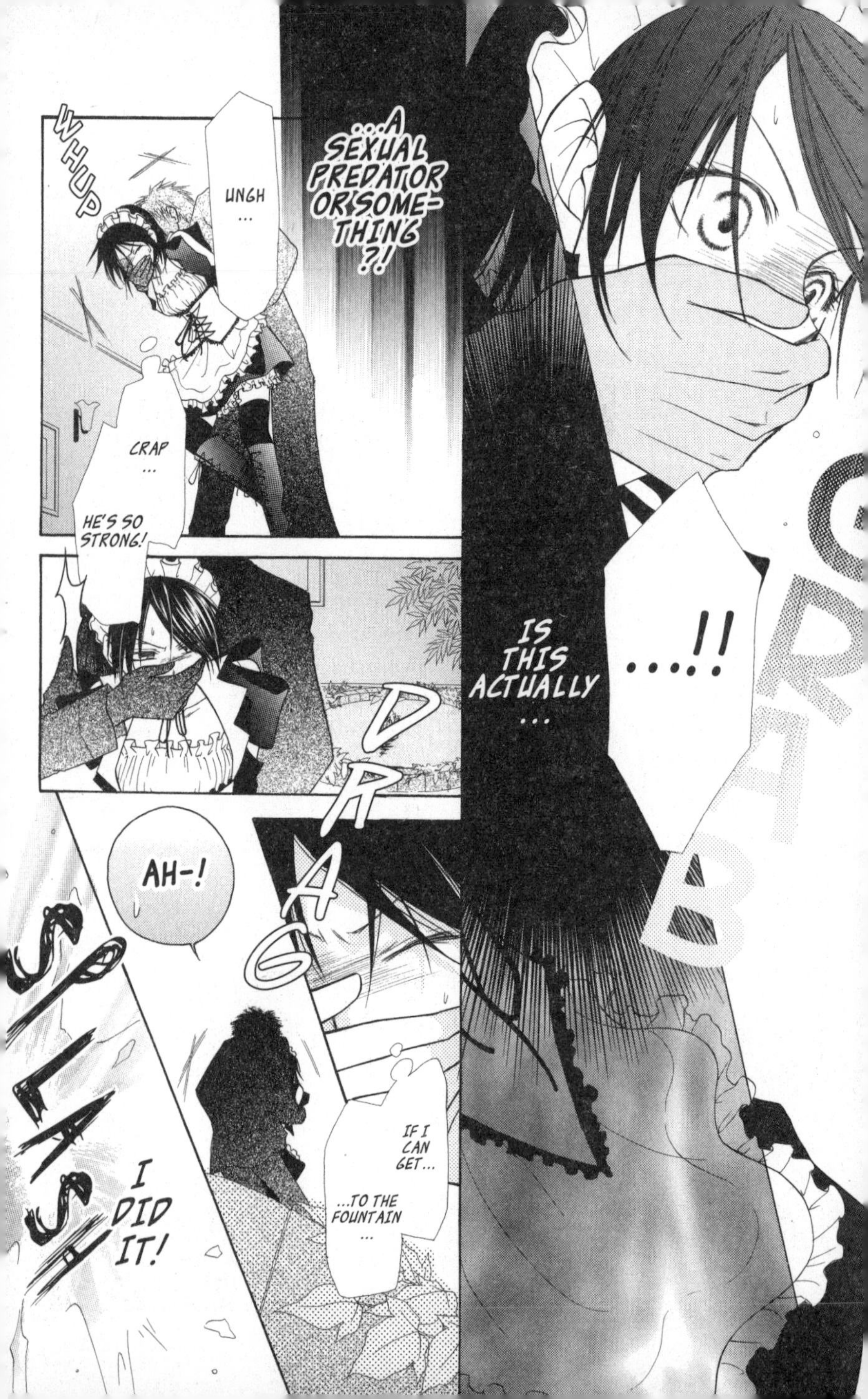
GRAB
...!!
IS THIS ACTUALLY...
...A SEXUAL PREDATOR OR SOME-THING?!
WHUP
UNGH...
CRAP...
HE'S SO STRONG!
DRAG
AH-!
IF I CAN GET...
...TO THE FOUNTAIN...
I DID IT!
SPLASH

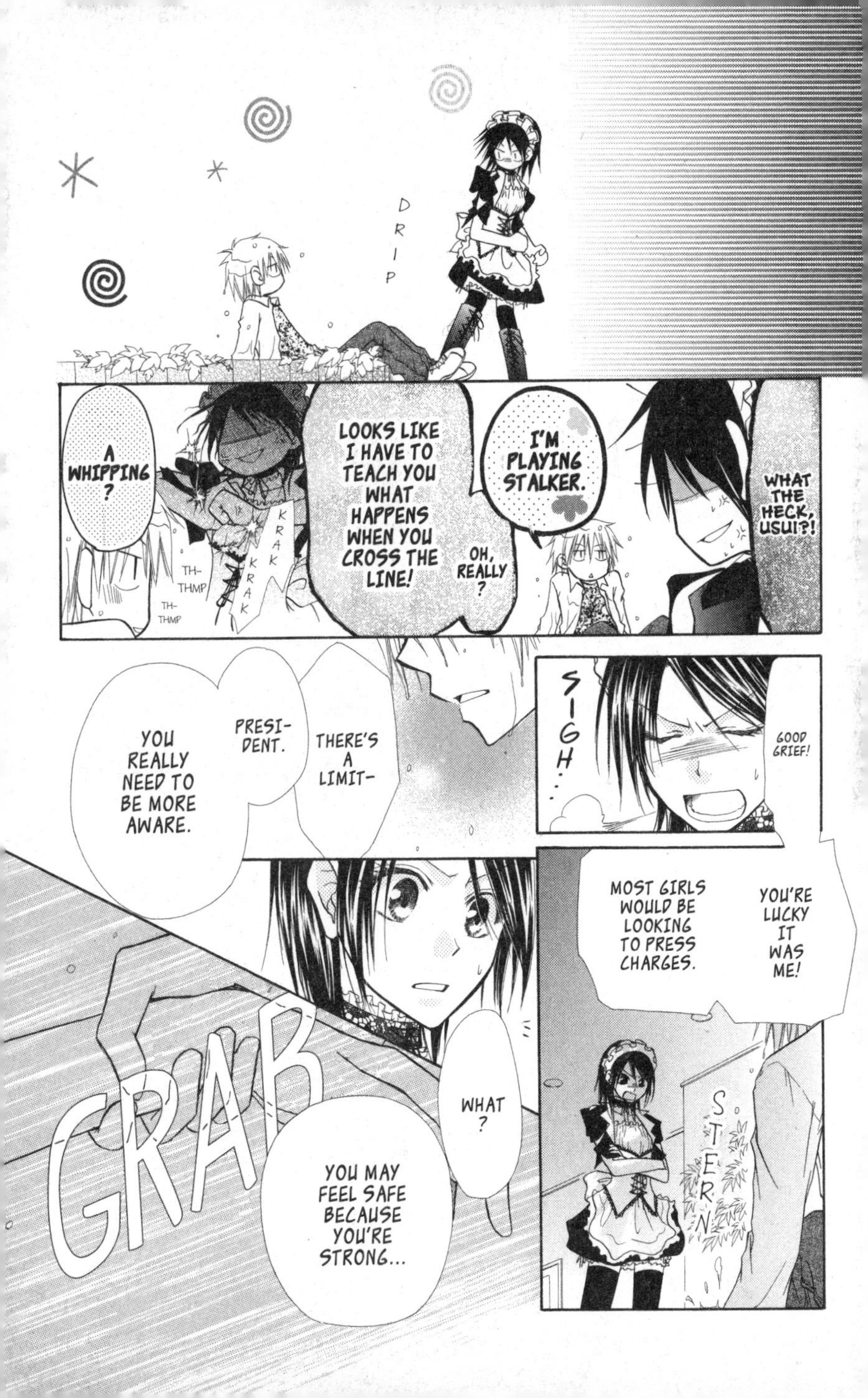
DRIP
WHAT THE HECK, USUI?!
I'M PLAYING STALKER.
OH, REALLY?
LOOKS LIKE I HAVE TO TEACH YOU WHAT HAPPENS WHEN YOU CROSS THE LINE!
A WHIPPING?
KRAK KRAK
KRAK
TH-THMP
TH-THMP
GOOD GRIEF!
SIGH...
THERE'S A LIMIT-
PRESIDENT.
YOU REALLY NEED TO BE MORE AWARE.
YOU'RE LUCKY IT WAS ME!
MOST GIRLS WOULD BE LOOKING TO PRESS CHARGES.
STERN
WHAT?
YOU MAY FEEL SAFE BECAUSE YOU'RE STRONG...
GRAB

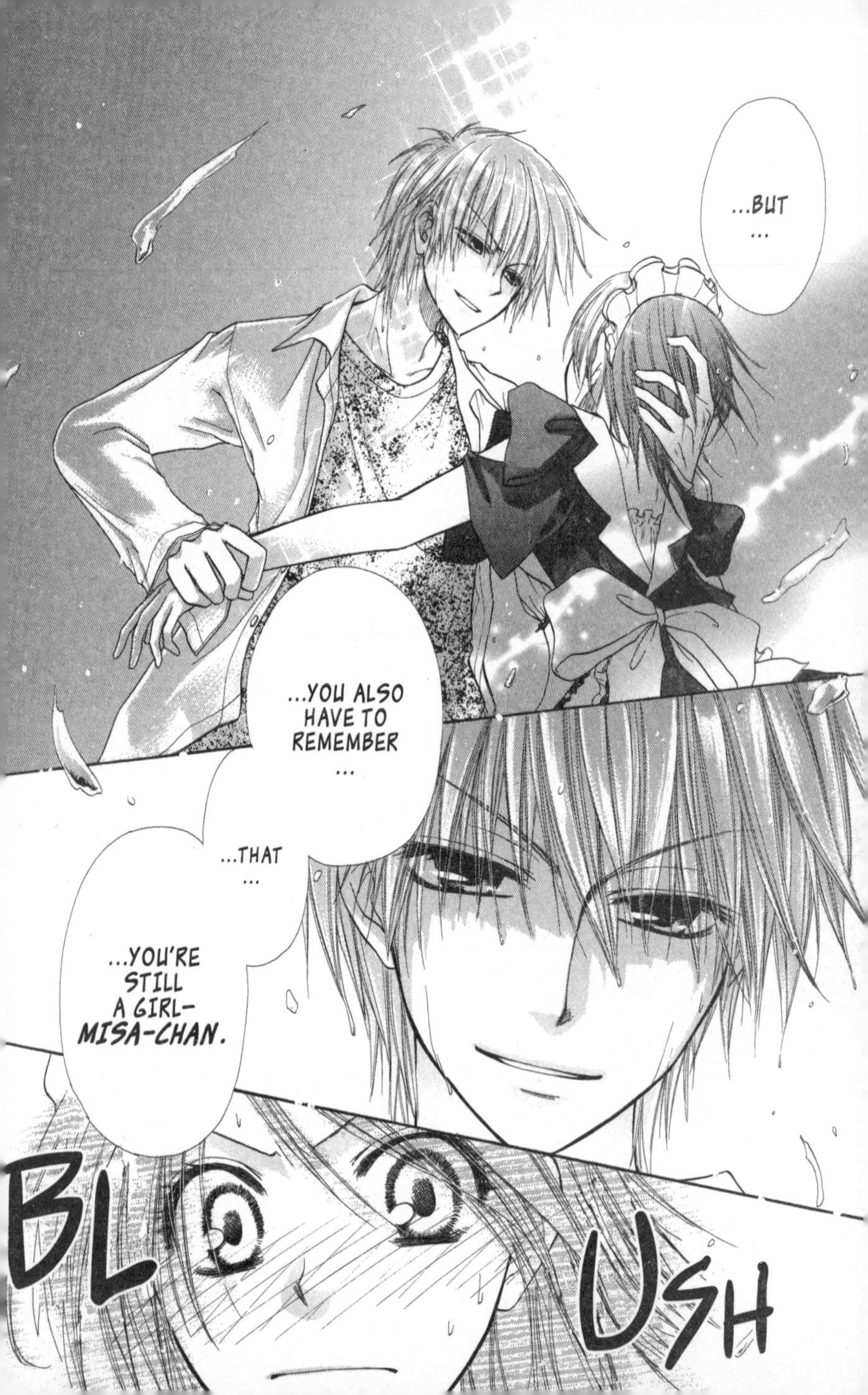
...BUT ...
...YOU ALSO HAVE TO REMEMBER ...
...THAT ...
...YOU'RE STILL A GIRL– MISA-CHAN.
BLUSH

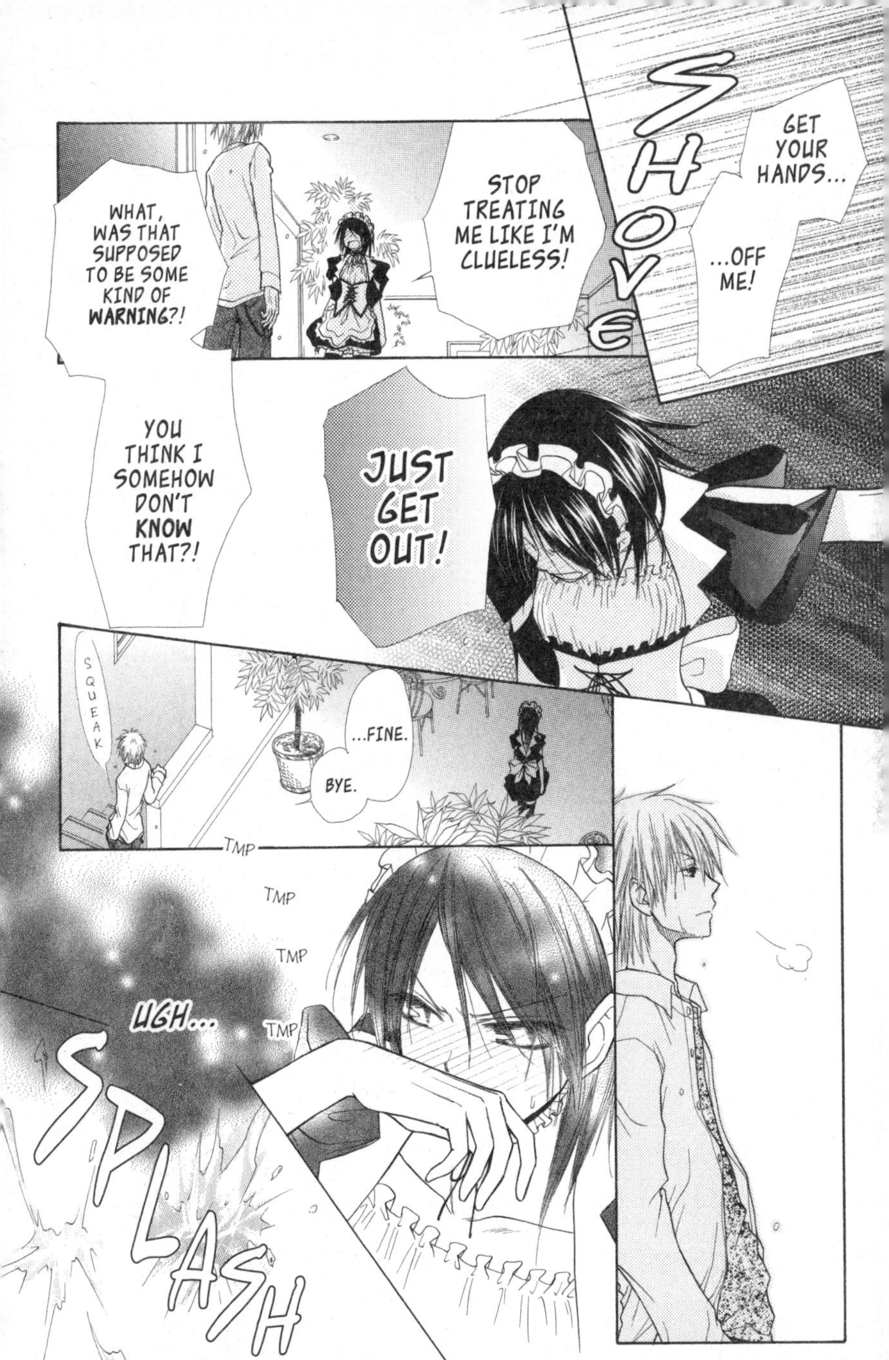
SHOVE
GET YOUR HANDS...
...OFF ME!
STOP TREATING ME LIKE I'M CLUELESS!
WHAT, WAS THAT SUPPOSED TO BE SOME KIND OF WARNING?!
JUST GET OUT!
YOU THINK I SOMEHOW DON'T KNOW THAT?!
...FINE.
BYE.
SQUEAK
TMP
TMP
TMP
TMP
UGH...
SPLASH

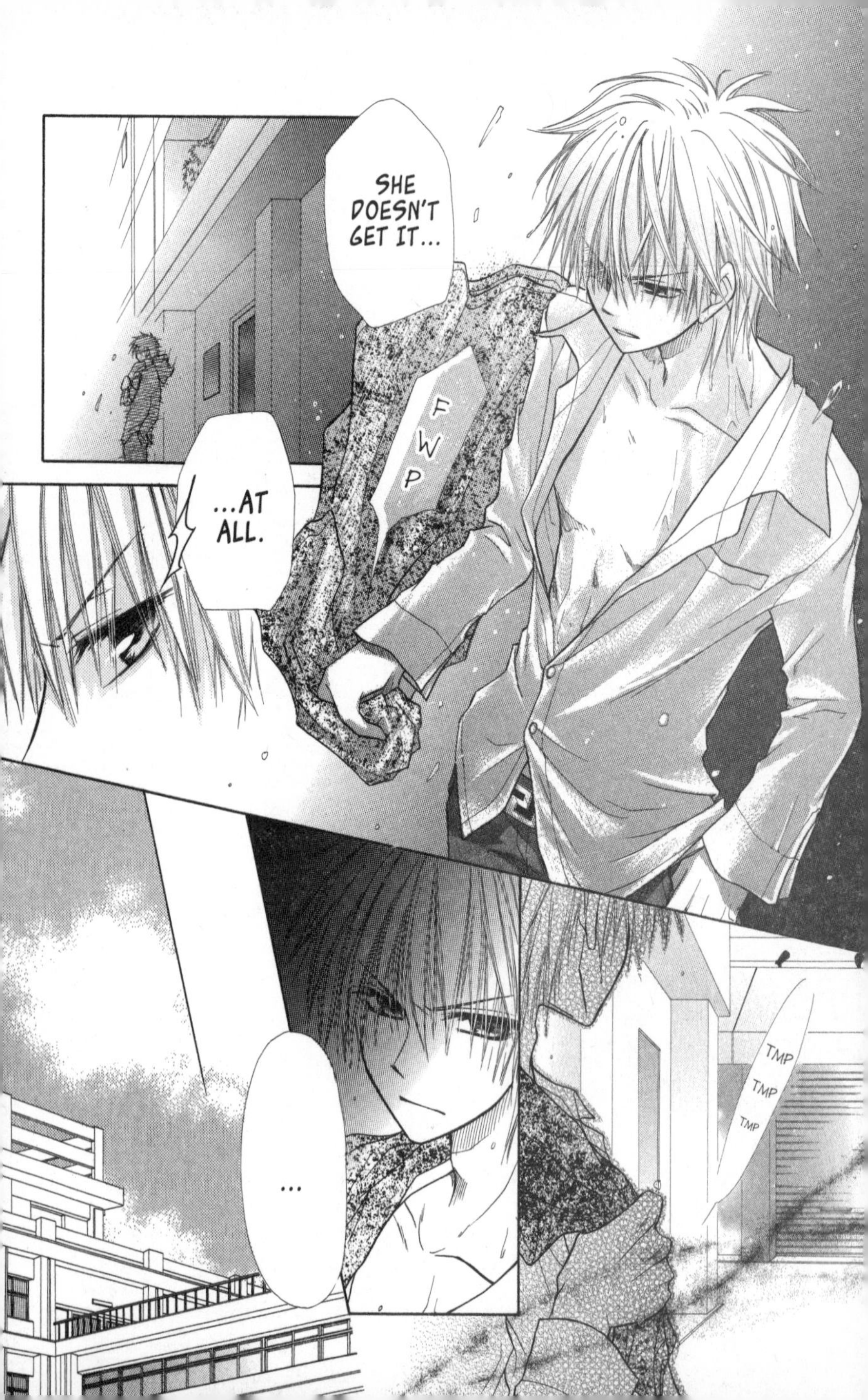
SHE DOESN'T GET IT...
FWP
...AT ALL.
TMP TMP TMP
...

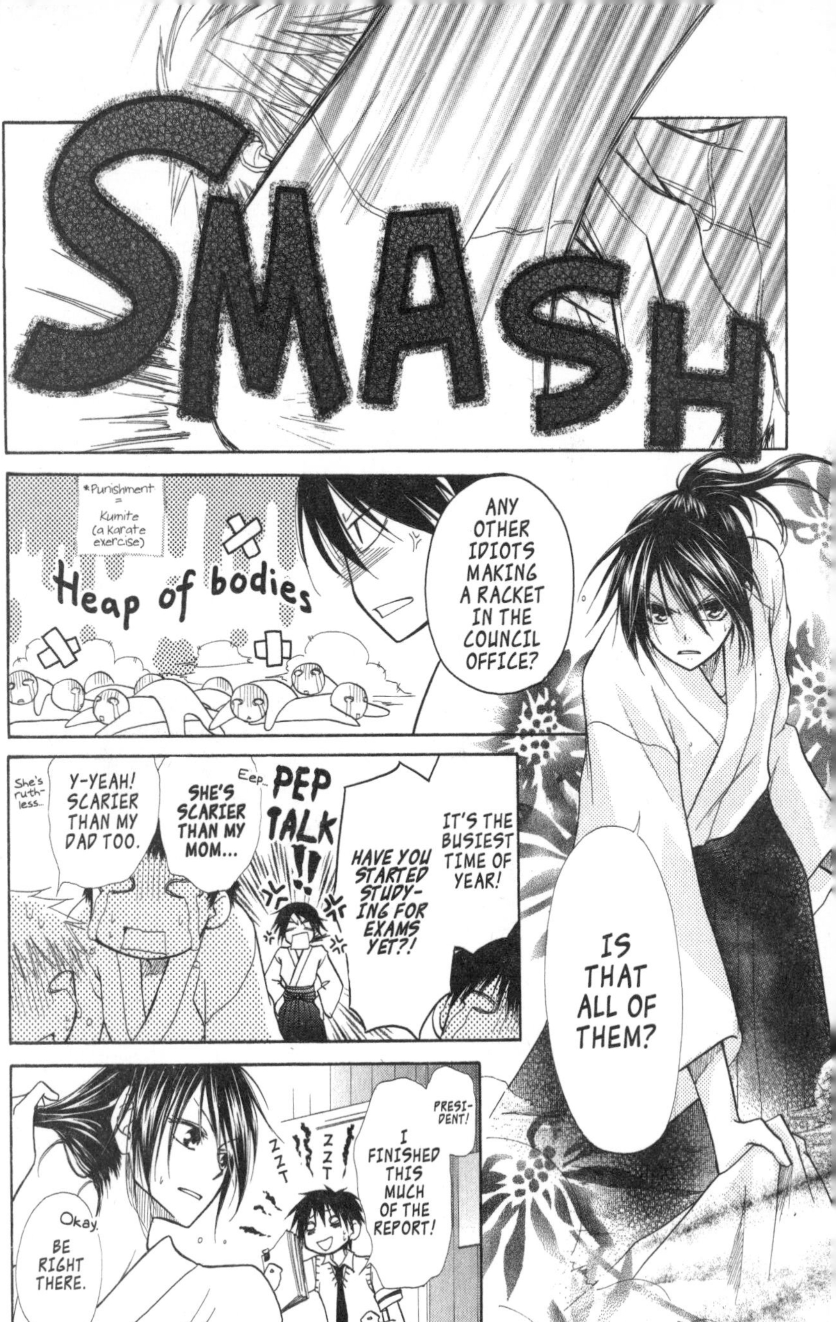
SMASH
IS THAT ALL OF THEM?
ANY OTHER IDIOTS MAKING A RACKET IN THE COUNCIL OFFICE?
Heap of bodies
*Punishment = Kumite (a karate exercise)
IT'S THE BUSIEST TIME OF YEAR!
HAVE YOU STARTED STUDYING FOR EXAMS YET?!
PEP TALK!!
Eep...
SHE'S SCARIER THAN MY MOM...
Y-YEAH! SCARIER THAN MY DAD TOO.
She's ruthless...
PRESIDENT!
I FINISHED THIS MUCH OF THE REPORT!
ZZT ZZT
Okay.
BE RIGHT THERE.

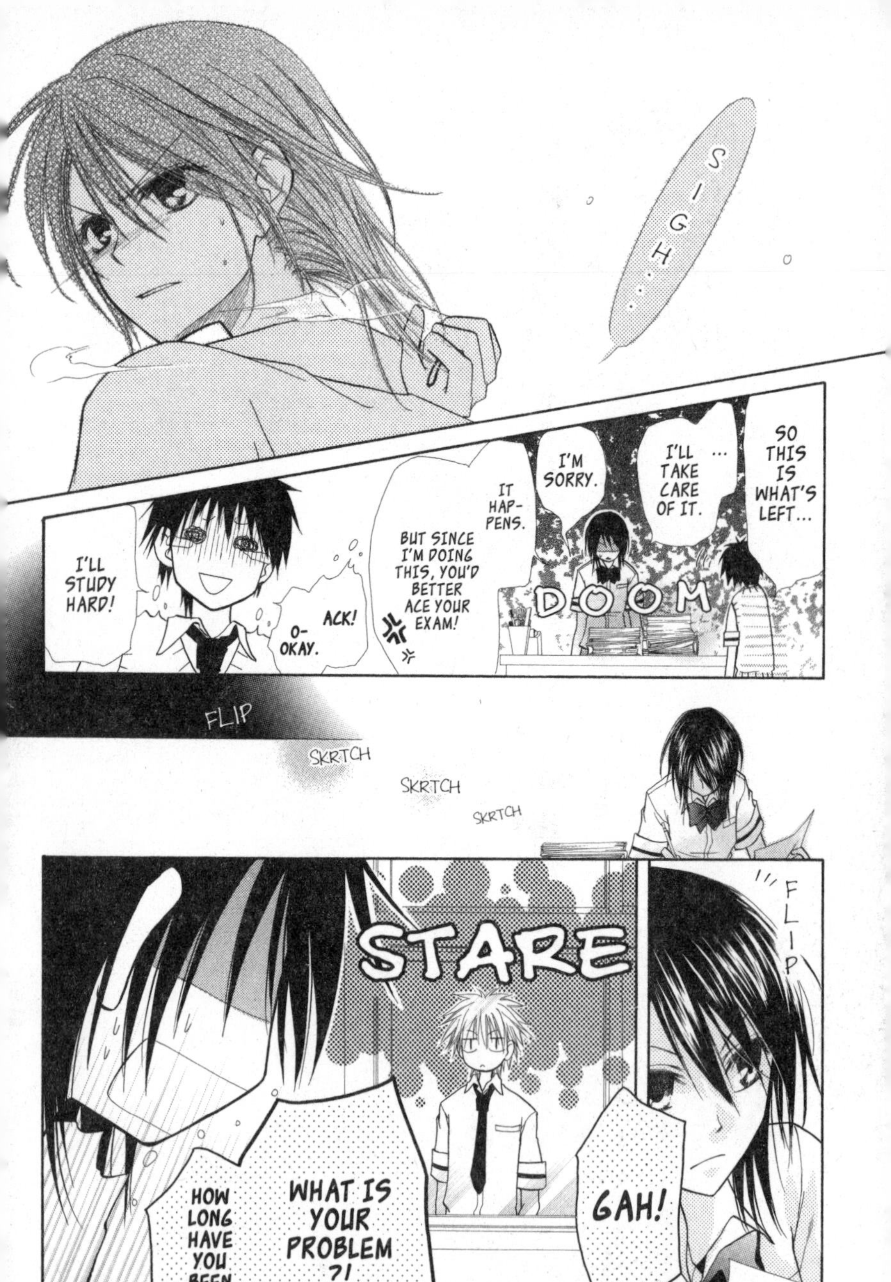
SIGH...
SO THIS IS WHAT'S LEFT...
...
I'LL TAKE CARE OF IT.
I'M SORRY.
IT HAP-PENS.
DOOM
BUT SINCE I'M DOING THIS, YOU'D BETTER ACE YOUR EXAM!
ACK!
O-OKAY.
I'LL STUDY HARD!
FLIP
SKRTCH
SKRTCH
SKRTCH
FLIP
GAH!
STARE
WHAT IS YOUR PROBLEM?!
HOW LONG HAVE YOU BEEN THERE?!

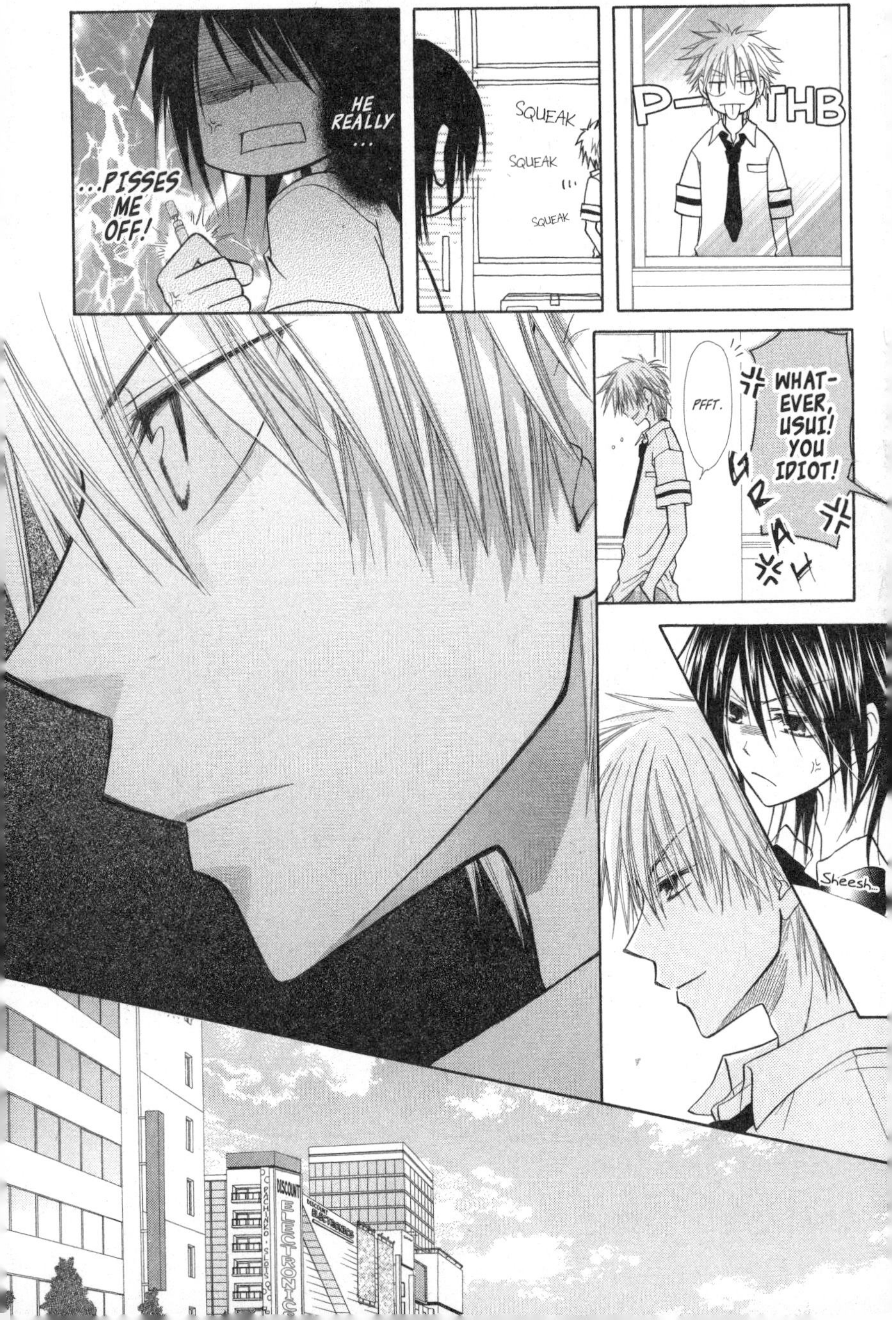
P-THB
SQUEAK
SQUEAK
SQUEAK
HE REALLY...
...PISSES ME OFF!
PFFT.
WHATEVER, USUI! YOU IDIOT!
GRAAH
Sheesh...

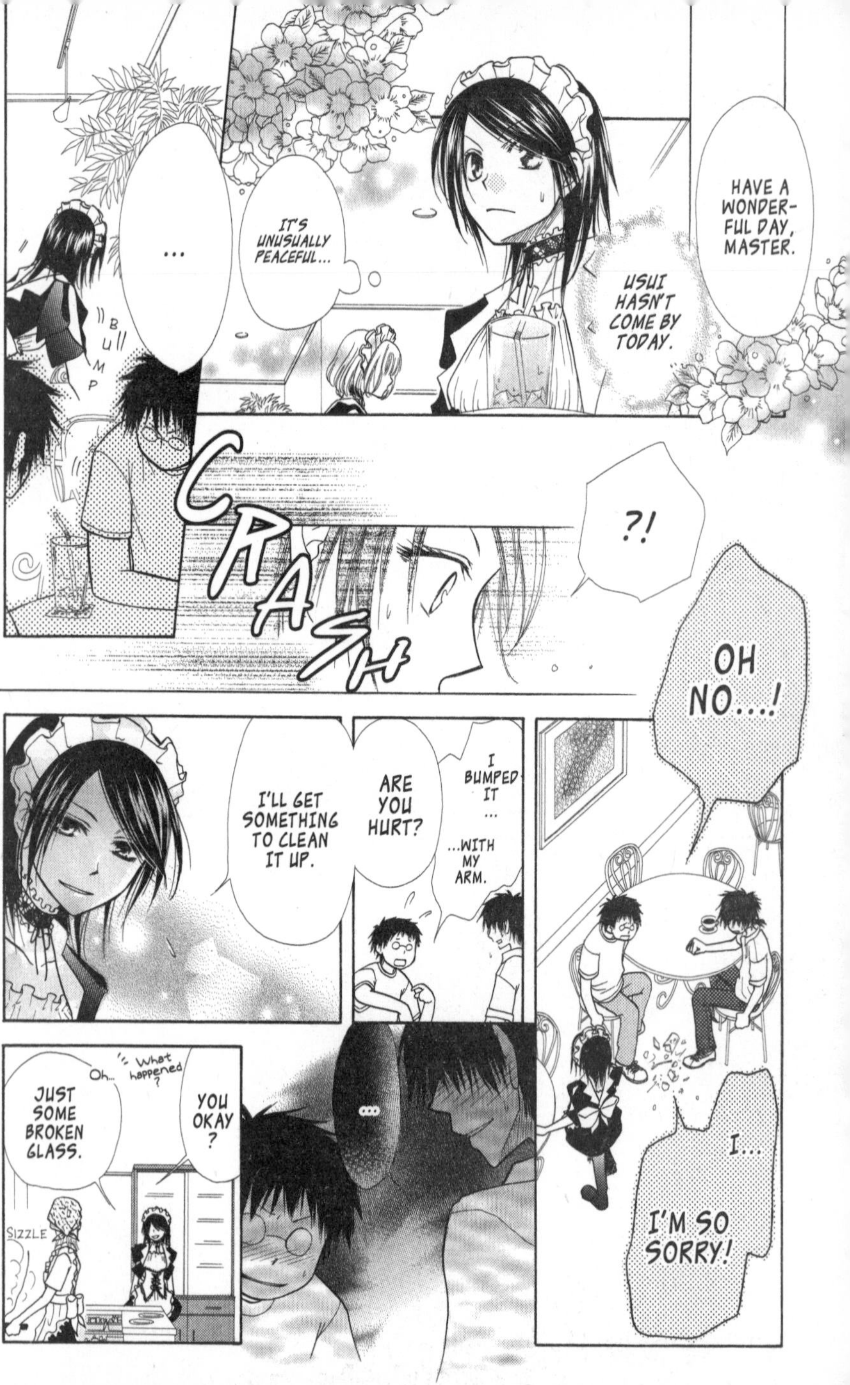
HAVE A WONDERFUL DAY, MASTER.
USUI HASN'T COME BY TODAY.
IT'S UNUSUALLY PEACEFUL...
...
BUMP
CRASH
?!
OH NO...!
I...
I'M SO SORRY!
I BUMPED IT ... ...WITH MY ARM.
ARE YOU HURT?
I'LL GET SOMETHING TO CLEAN IT UP.
...
YOU OKAY?
What happened?
Oh...
JUST SOME BROKEN GLASS.
SIZZLE

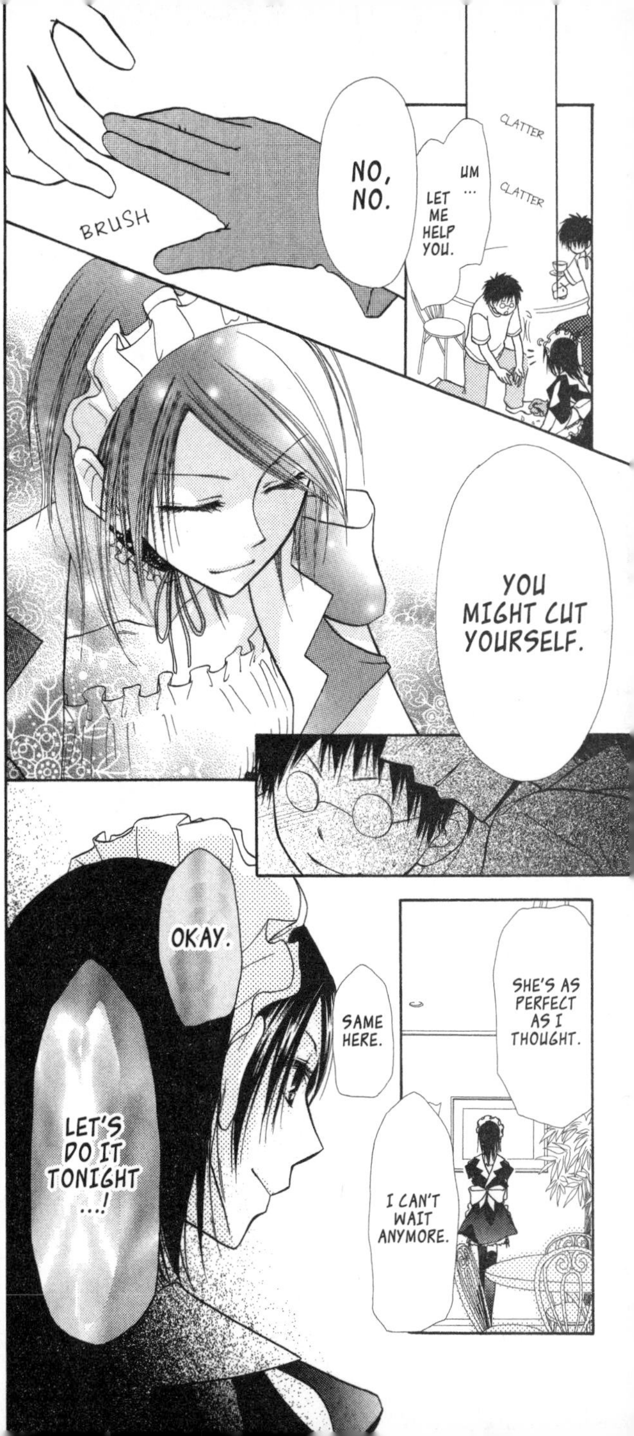
CLATTER
CLATTER
UM ...
LET ME HELP YOU.
NO, NO.
BRUSH
YOU MIGHT CUT YOURSELF.
SHE'S AS PERFECT AS I THOUGHT.
I CAN'T WAIT ANYMORE.
OKAY.
SAME HERE.
LET'S DO IT TONIGHT ...!

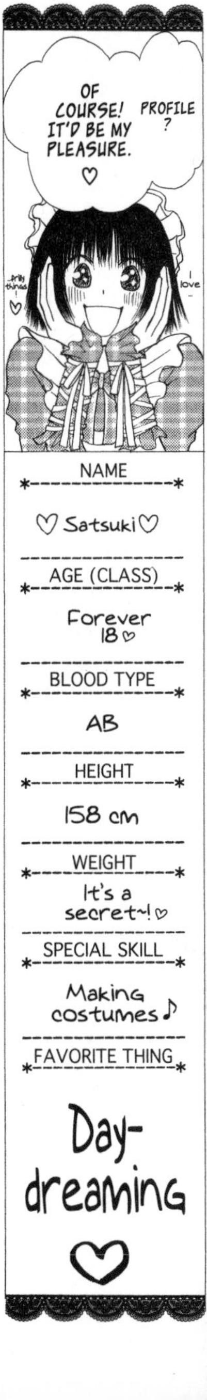
PROFILE ?
OF COURSE! IT'D BE MY PLEASURE. ♡
I love
frilly things! ♡

NAME

♡ Satsuki ♡

AGE (CLASS)

Forever 18 ♡

BLOOD TYPE

AB

HEIGHT

158 cm

WEIGHT

It's a secret~! ♡

SPECIAL SKILL

Making costumes ♪

FAVORITE THING

Day-dreaming ♡

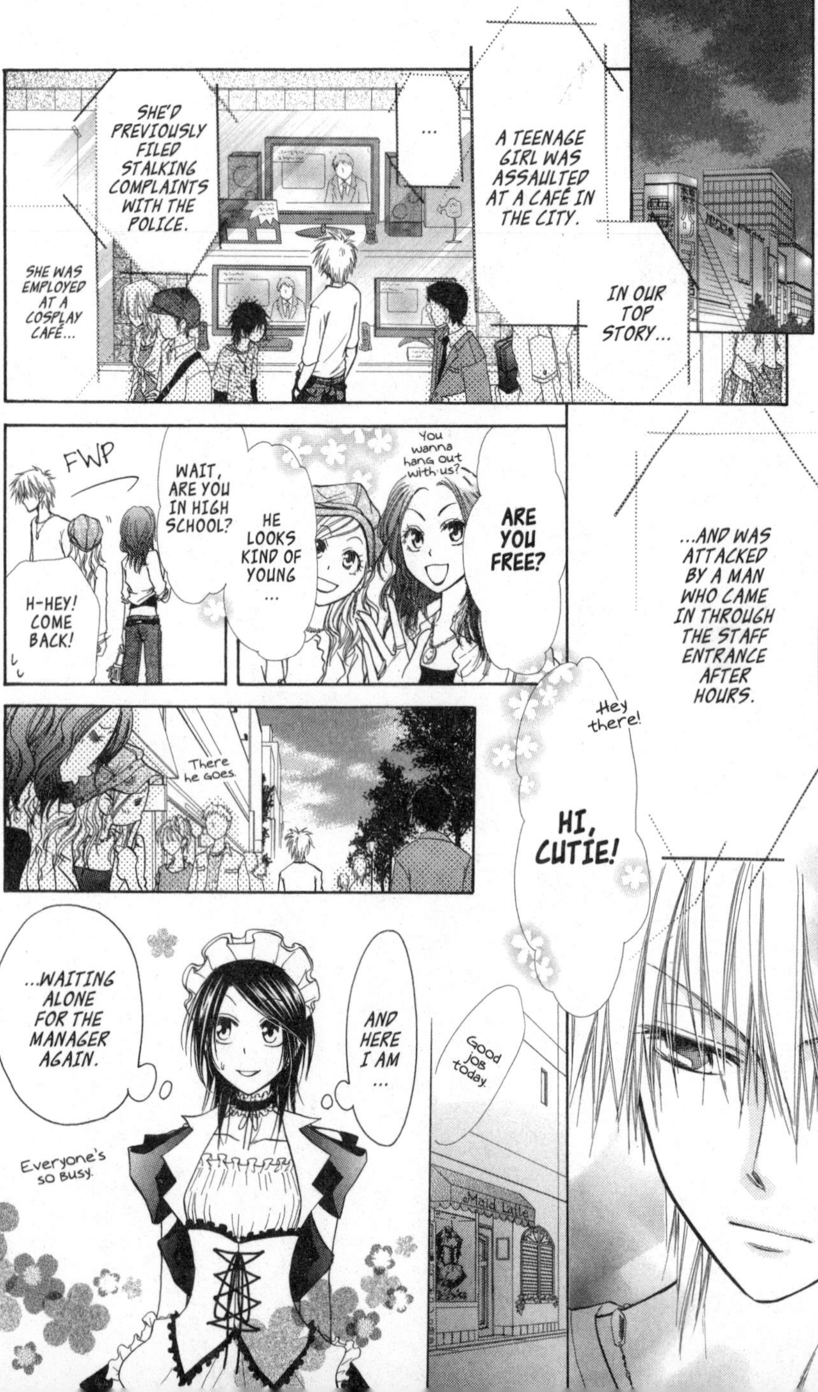
IN OUR TOP STORY...
A TEENAGE GIRL WAS ASSAULTED AT A CAFÉ IN THE CITY.
...
SHE'D PREVIOUSLY FILED STALKING COMPLAINTS WITH THE POLICE.
SHE WAS EMPLOYED AT A COSPLAY CAFÉ...
...AND WAS ATTACKED BY A MAN WHO CAME IN THROUGH THE STAFF ENTRANCE AFTER HOURS.
Hey there!
HI, CUTIE!
ARE YOU FREE?
You wanna hang out with us?
HE LOOKS KIND OF YOUNG...
WAIT, ARE YOU IN HIGH SCHOOL?
FWP
H-HEY! COME BACK!
There he goes.
Good job today.
AND HERE I AM...
...WAITING ALONE FOR THE MANAGER AGAIN.
Everyone's so busy.

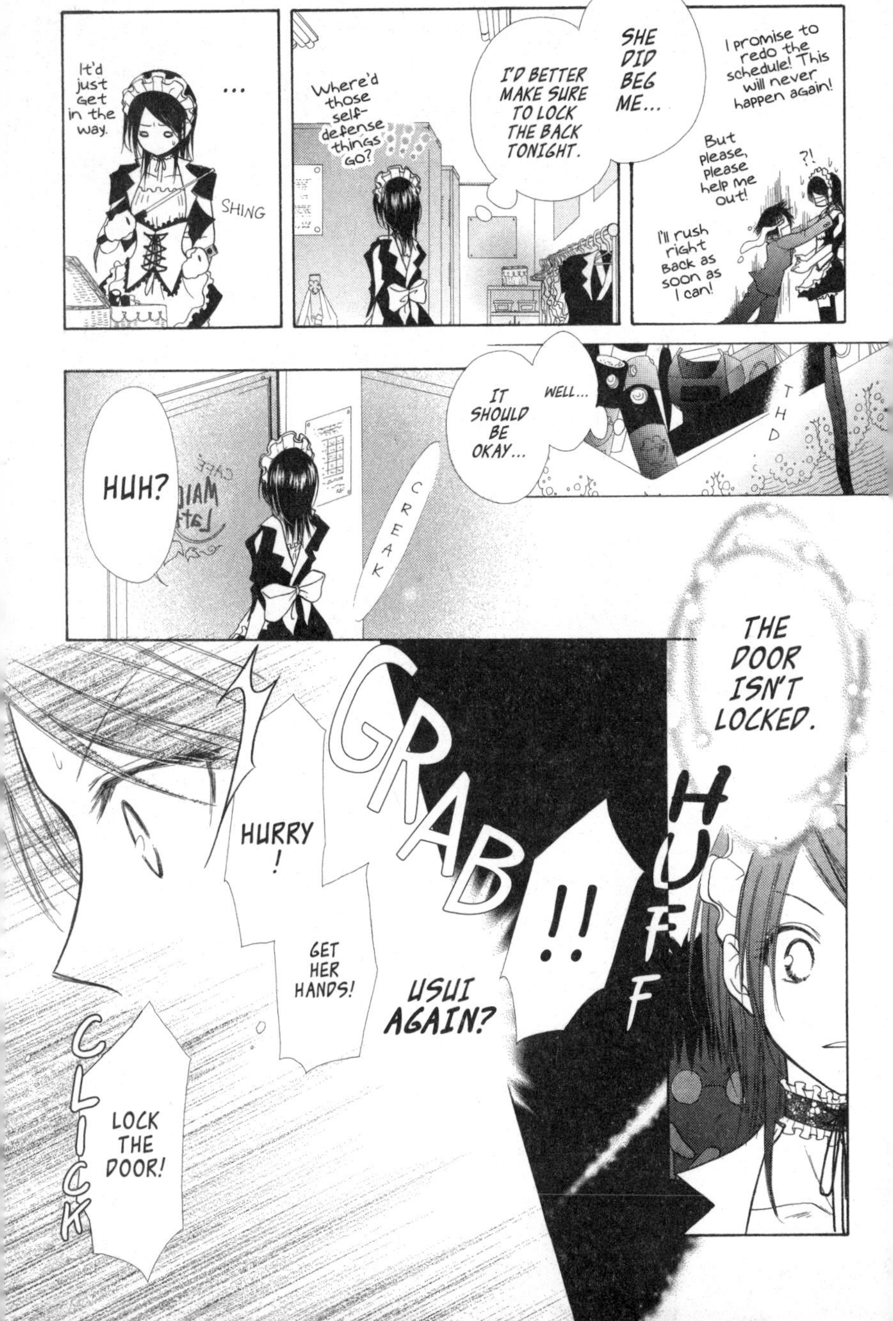
I promise to redo the schedule! This will never happen again!
?!
But please, please help me out!
I'll rush right back as soon as I can!
SHE DID BEG ME...
I'D BETTER MAKE SURE TO LOCK THE BACK TONIGHT.
Where'd those self-defense things go?
...
It'd just get in the way.
SHING
WELL...
IT SHOULD BE OKAY...
THD
CREAK
HUH?
THE DOOR ISN'T LOCKED.
HUFF
GRAB!!
USUI AGAIN?
HURRY!
GET HER HANDS!
LOCK THE DOOR!
CLICK

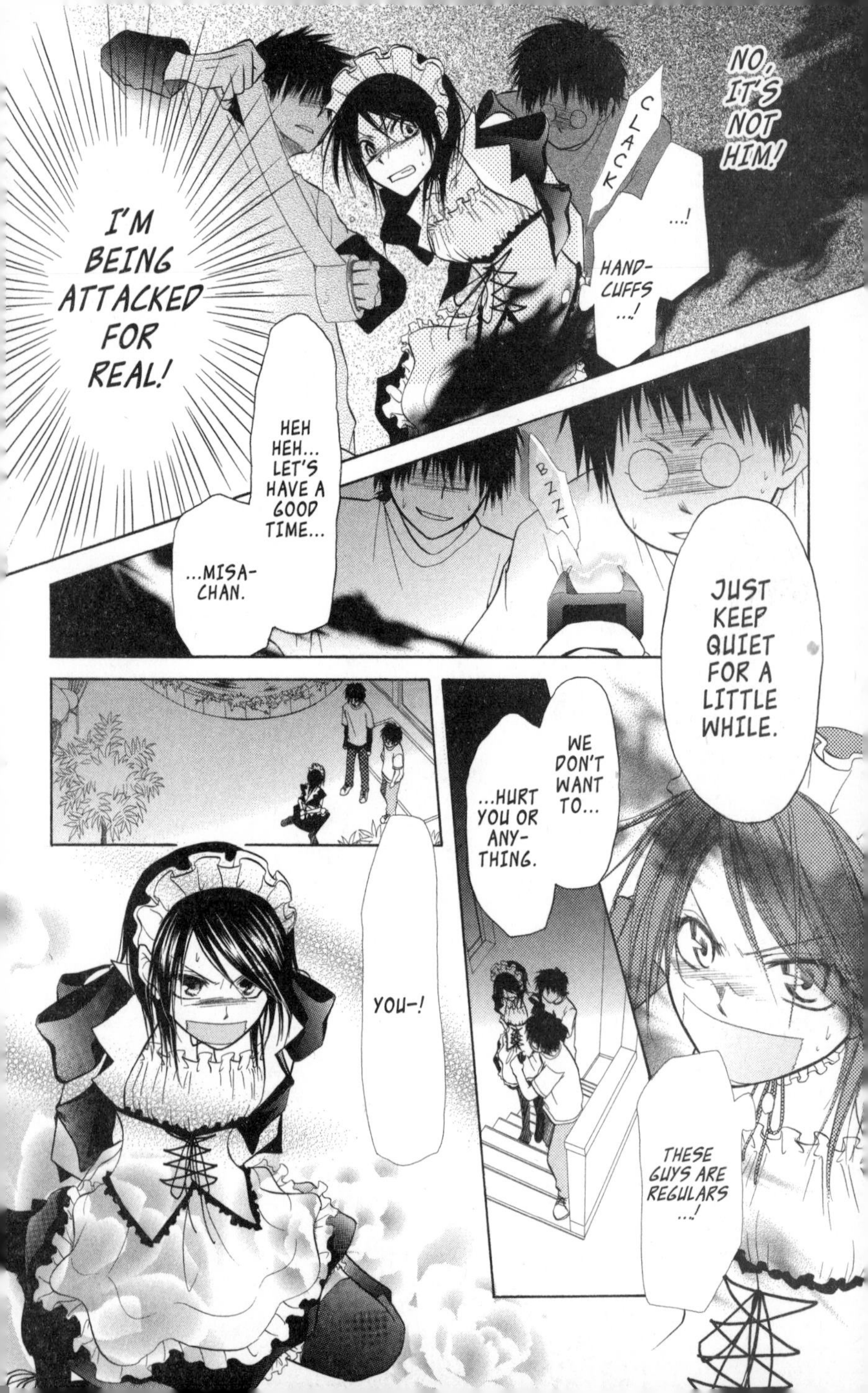
NO, IT'S NOT HIM!
CLACK
...!
HAND-CUFFS ...!
I'M BEING ATTACKED FOR REAL!
JUST KEEP QUIET FOR A LITTLE WHILE.
BZZT
HEH HEH... LET'S HAVE A GOOD TIME...
...MISA-CHAN.
WE DON'T WANT TO...
...HURT YOU OR ANY-THING.
THESE GUYS ARE REGULARS ...!
YOU-!

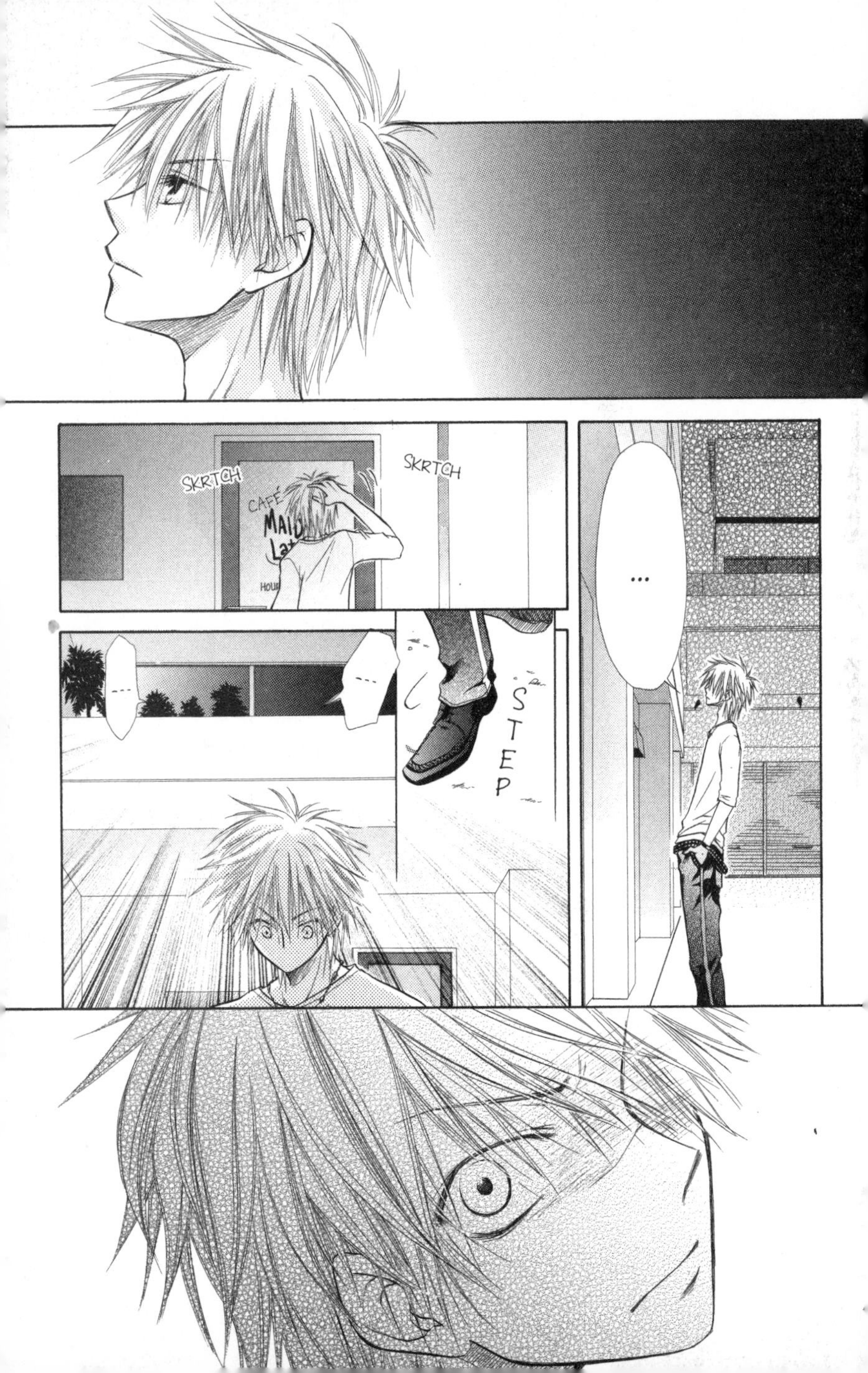
...
SKRTCH
SKRTCH
CAFÉ
MAID
STEP
...
...

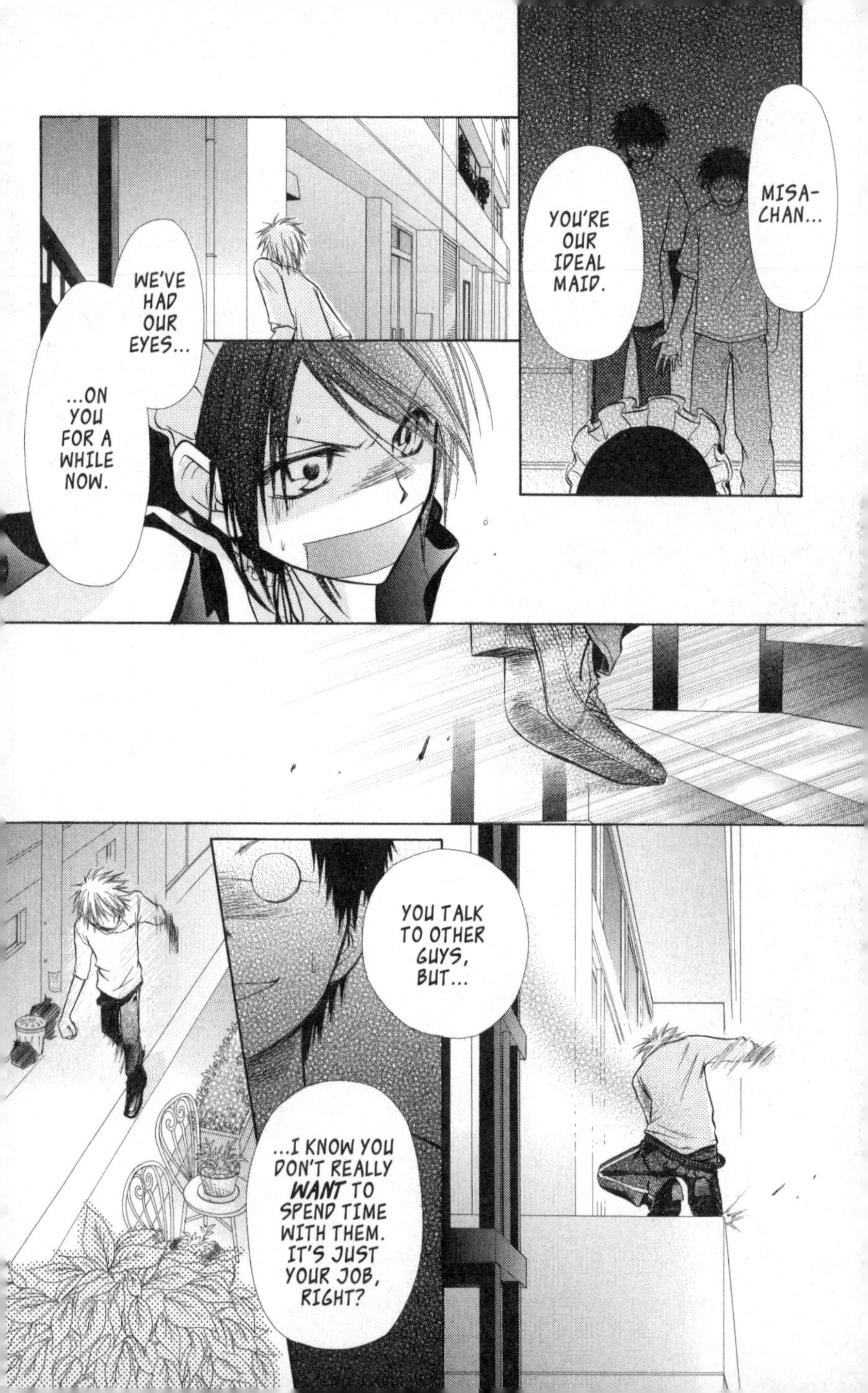
MISA-CHAN...
YOU'RE OUR IDEAL MAID.
WE'VE HAD OUR EYES...
...ON YOU FOR A WHILE NOW.
YOU TALK TO OTHER GUYS, BUT...
...I KNOW YOU DON'T REALLY **WANT** TO SPEND TIME WITH THEM. IT'S JUST YOUR JOB, RIGHT?

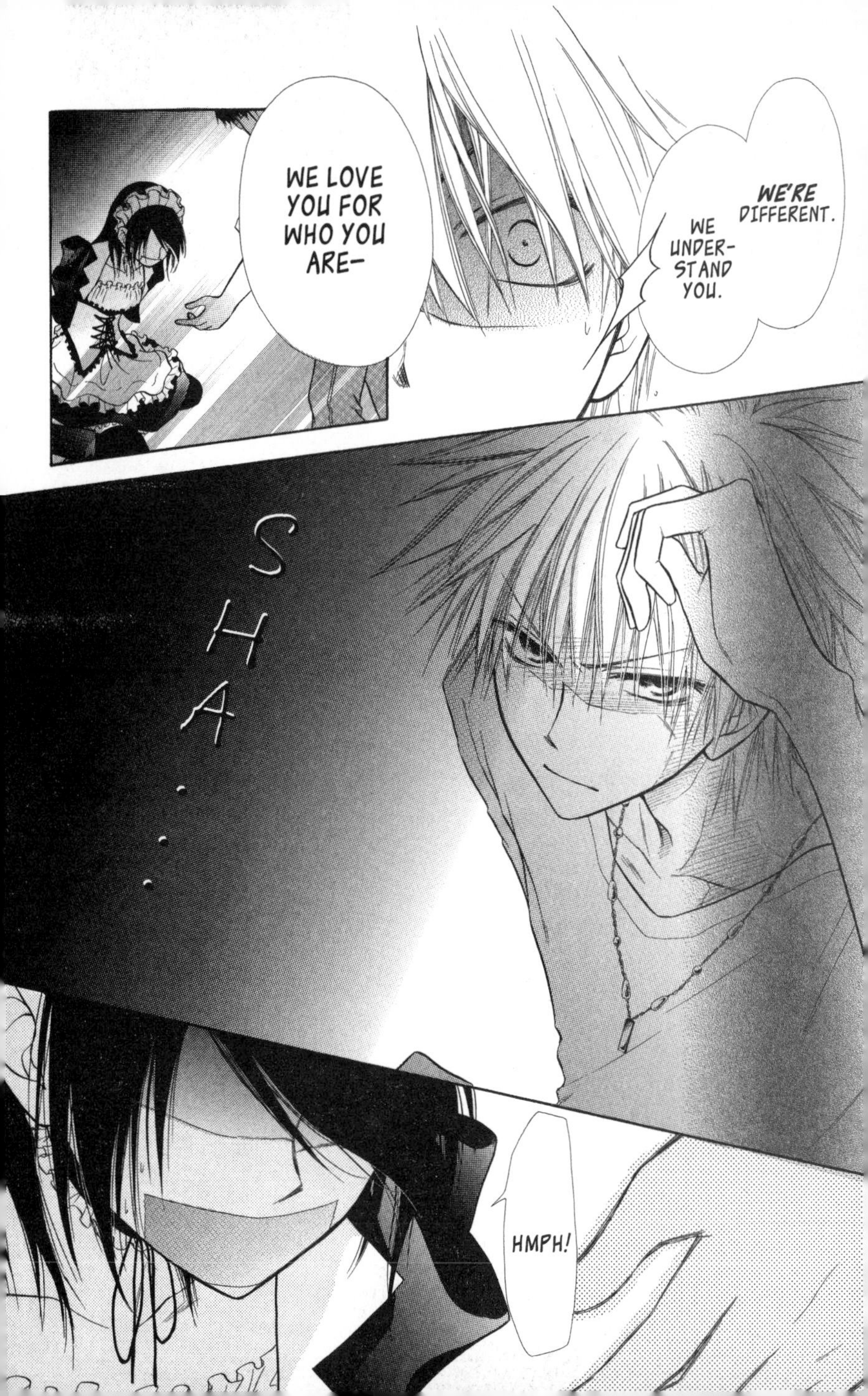
WE'RE DIFFERENT.
WE UNDER-STAND YOU.
WE LOVE YOU FOR WHO YOU ARE-
SHA...
HMPH!

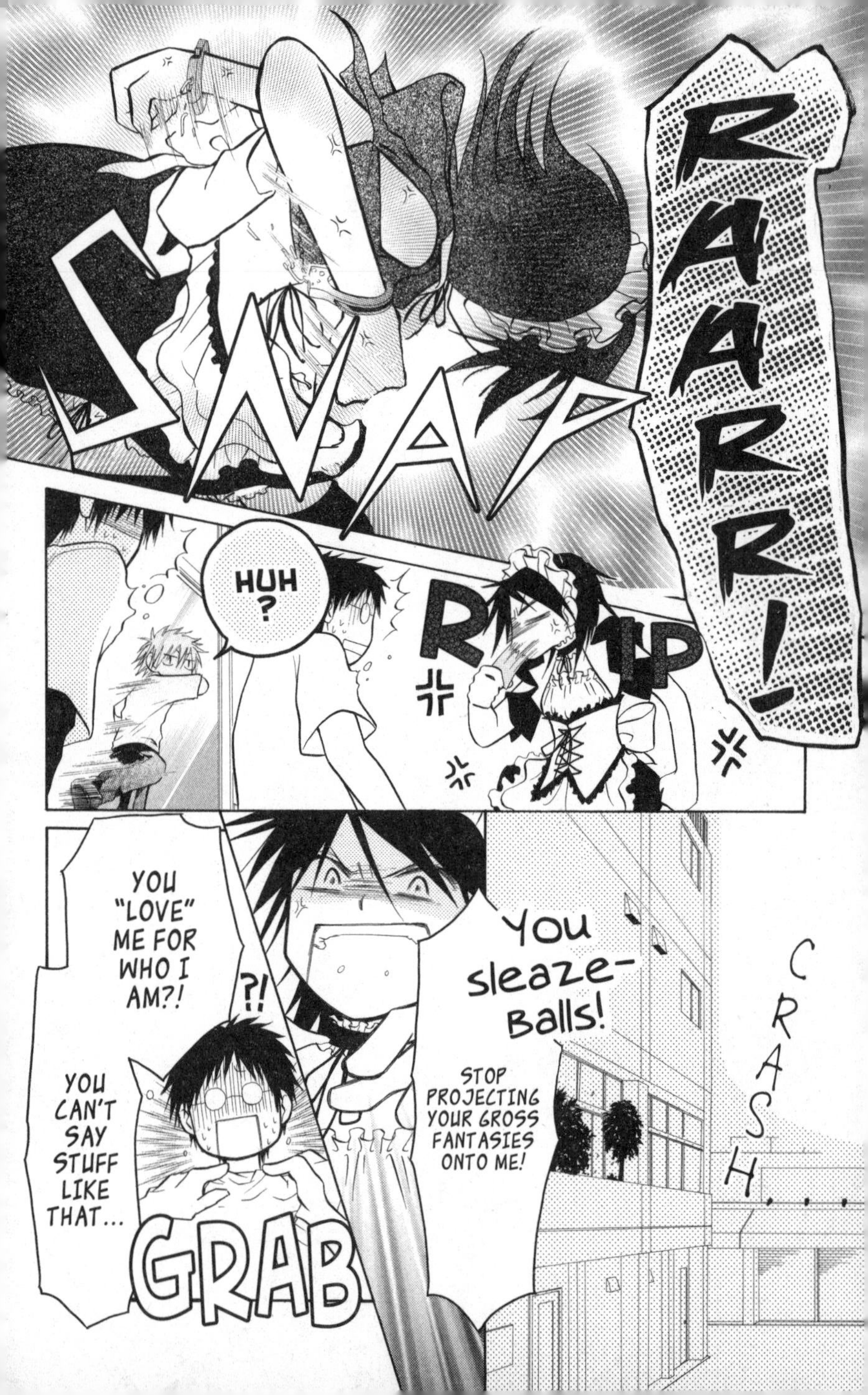
RAARR!
SNAP
RIP
HUH?
You sleaze-Balls!
STOP PROJECTING YOUR GROSS FANTASIES ONTO ME!
CRASH...
YOU "LOVE" ME FOR WHO I AM?!
?!
YOU CAN'T SAY STUFF LIKE THAT...
GRAB

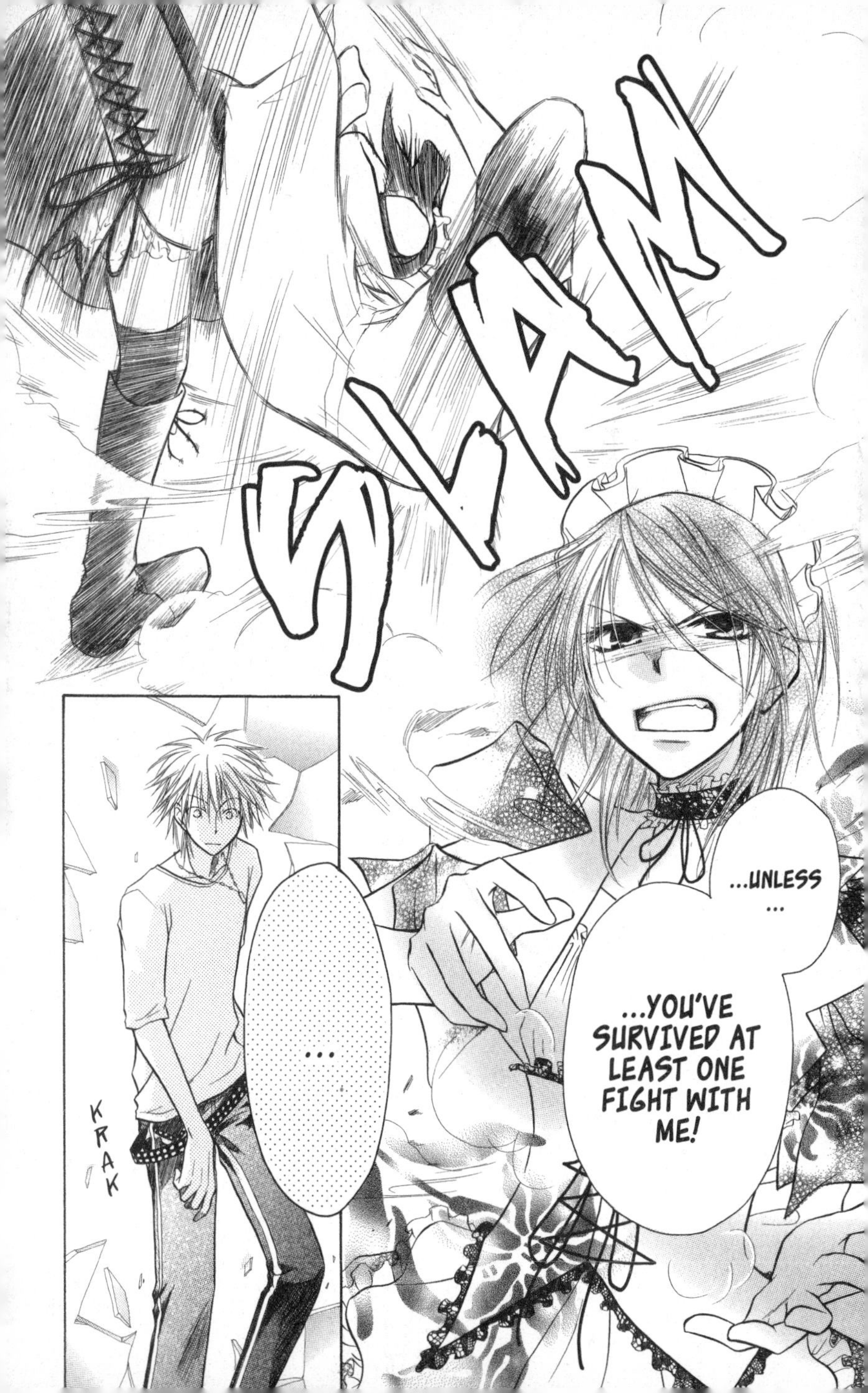
SLAM
...UNLESS ...
...YOU'VE SURVIVED AT LEAST ONE FIGHT WITH ME!
...
KRAK

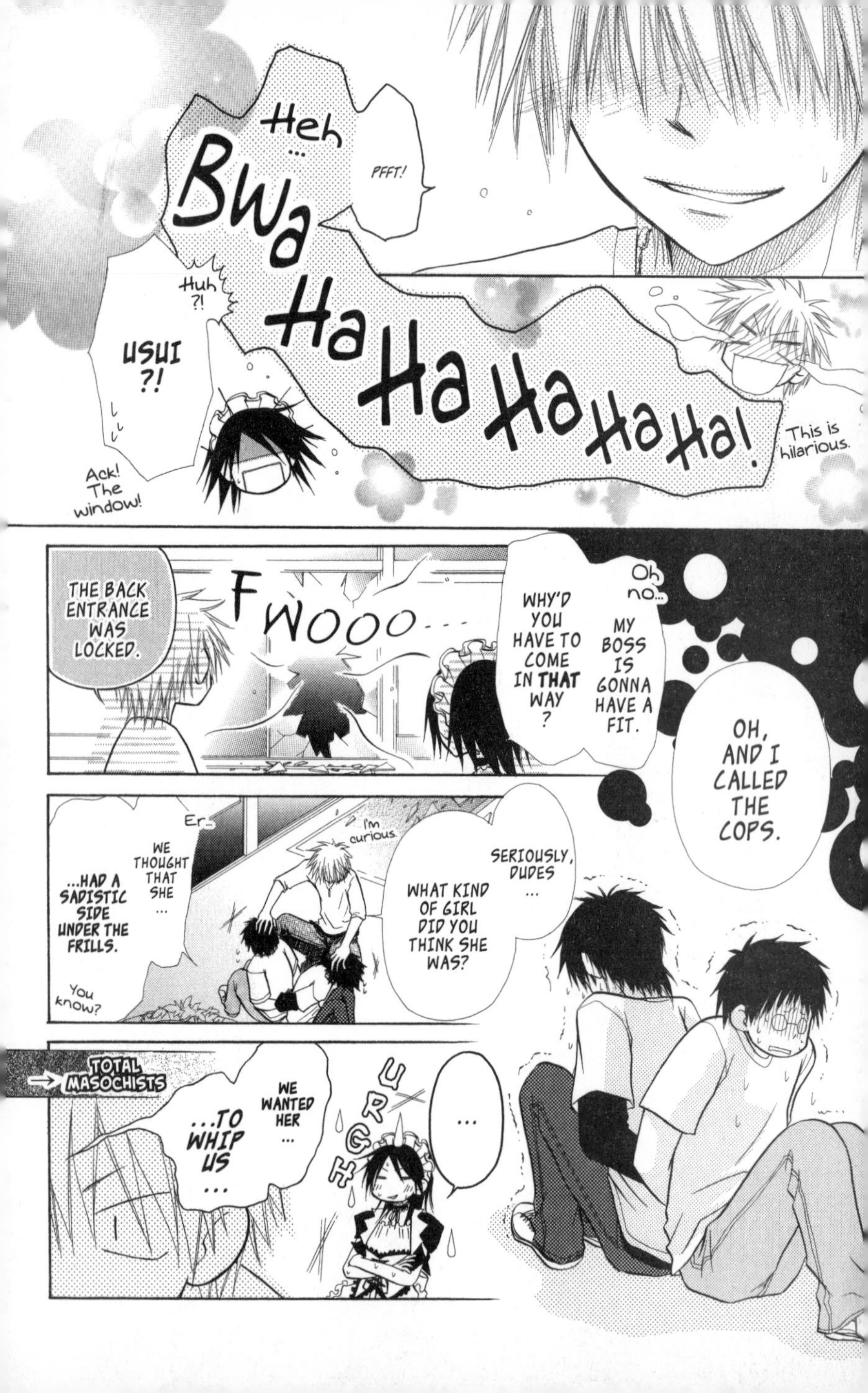
Heh...
PFFT!
BWA HA HA HA HA HA!
This is hilarious.
Huh?!
USUI?!
Ack! The window!
Oh no...
MY BOSS IS GONNA HAVE A FIT.
OH, AND I CALLED THE COPS.
WHY'D YOU HAVE TO COME IN THAT WAY?
FWOOO...
THE BACK ENTRANCE WAS LOCKED.
SERIOUSLY, DUDES...
WHAT KIND OF GIRL DID YOU THINK SHE WAS?
I'm curious.
Er...
WE THOUGHT THAT SHE...
...HAD A SADISTIC SIDE UNDER THE FRILLS.
You know?
...
HGRU
WE WANTED HER...
...TO WHIP US...
TOTAL MASOCHISTS

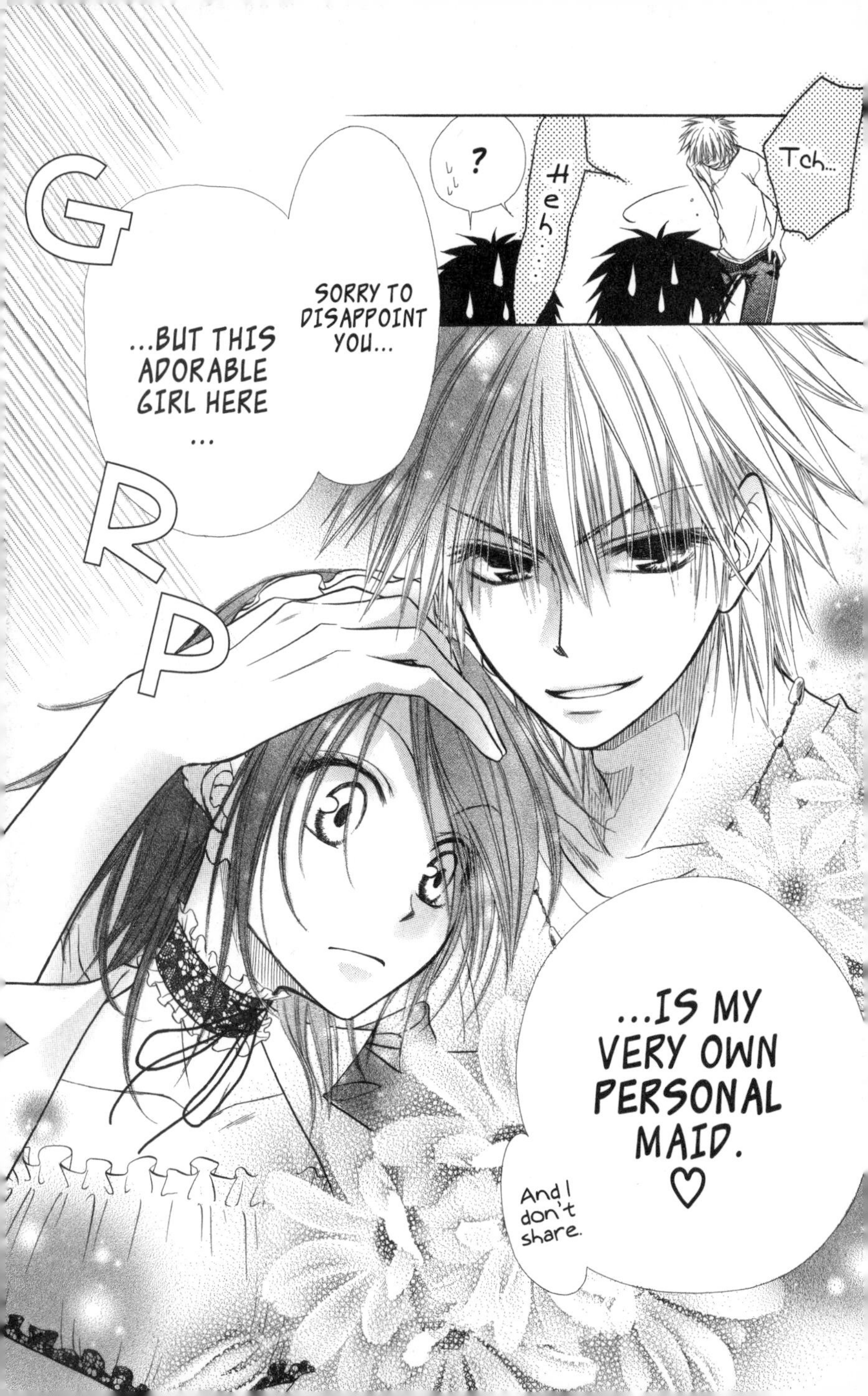
Tch...
Heh...
?
SORRY TO DISAPPOINT YOU...
...BUT THIS ADORABLE GIRL HERE ...
GRP
...IS MY VERY OWN PERSONAL MAID. ♡
And I don't share.

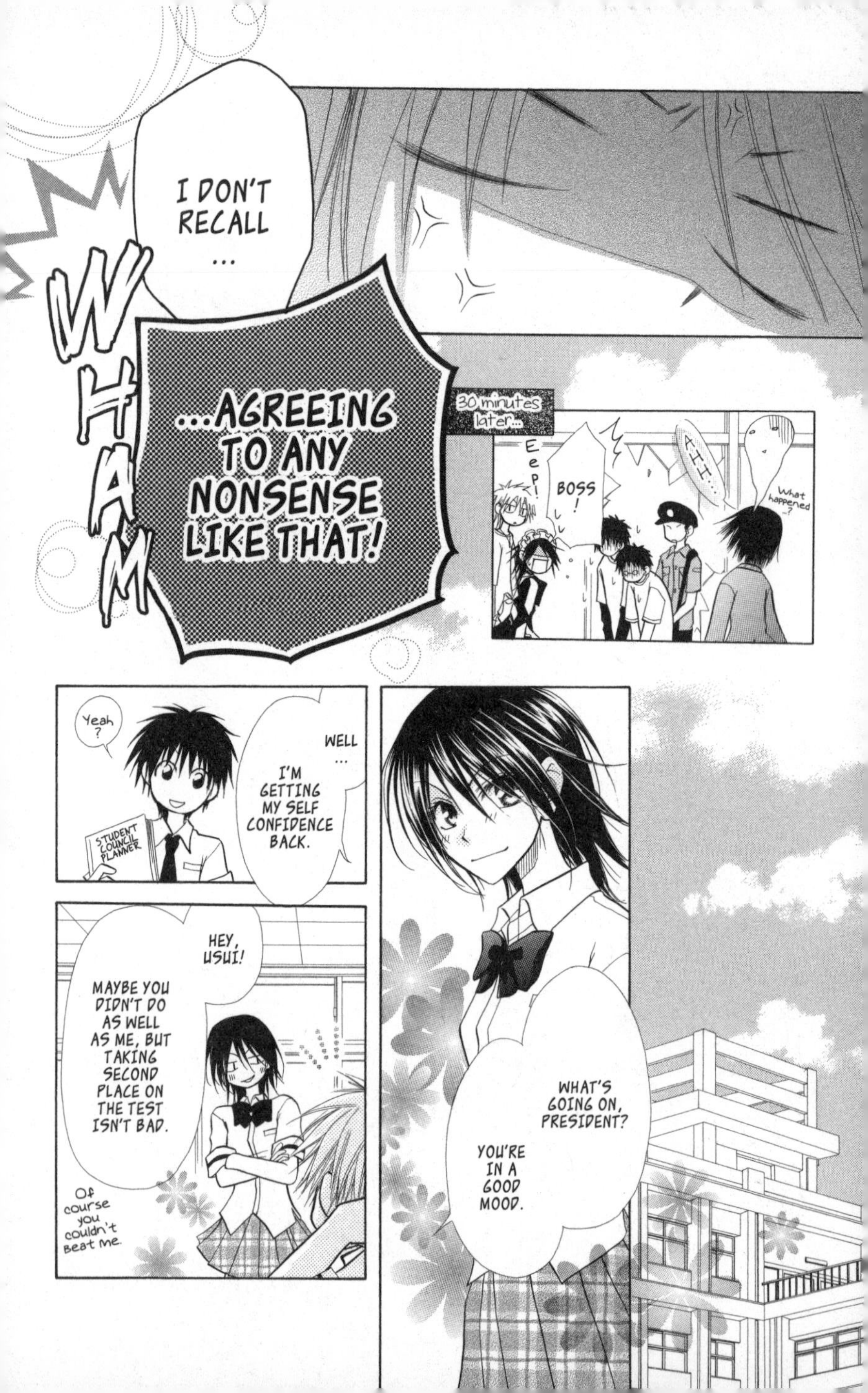
I DON'T RECALL ...
WHAM
...AGREEING TO ANY NONSENSE LIKE THAT!
30 minutes later...
What happened ...?
AHH...
BOSS!
Eep!
WHAT'S GOING ON, PRESIDENT?
YOU'RE IN A GOOD MOOD.
WELL ...
I'M GETTING MY SELF CONFIDENCE BACK.
Yeah?
STUDENT COUNCIL PLANNER
HEY, USUI!
MAYBE YOU DIDN'T DO AS WELL AS ME, BUT TAKING SECOND PLACE ON THE TEST ISN'T BAD.
Of course you couldn't beat me.

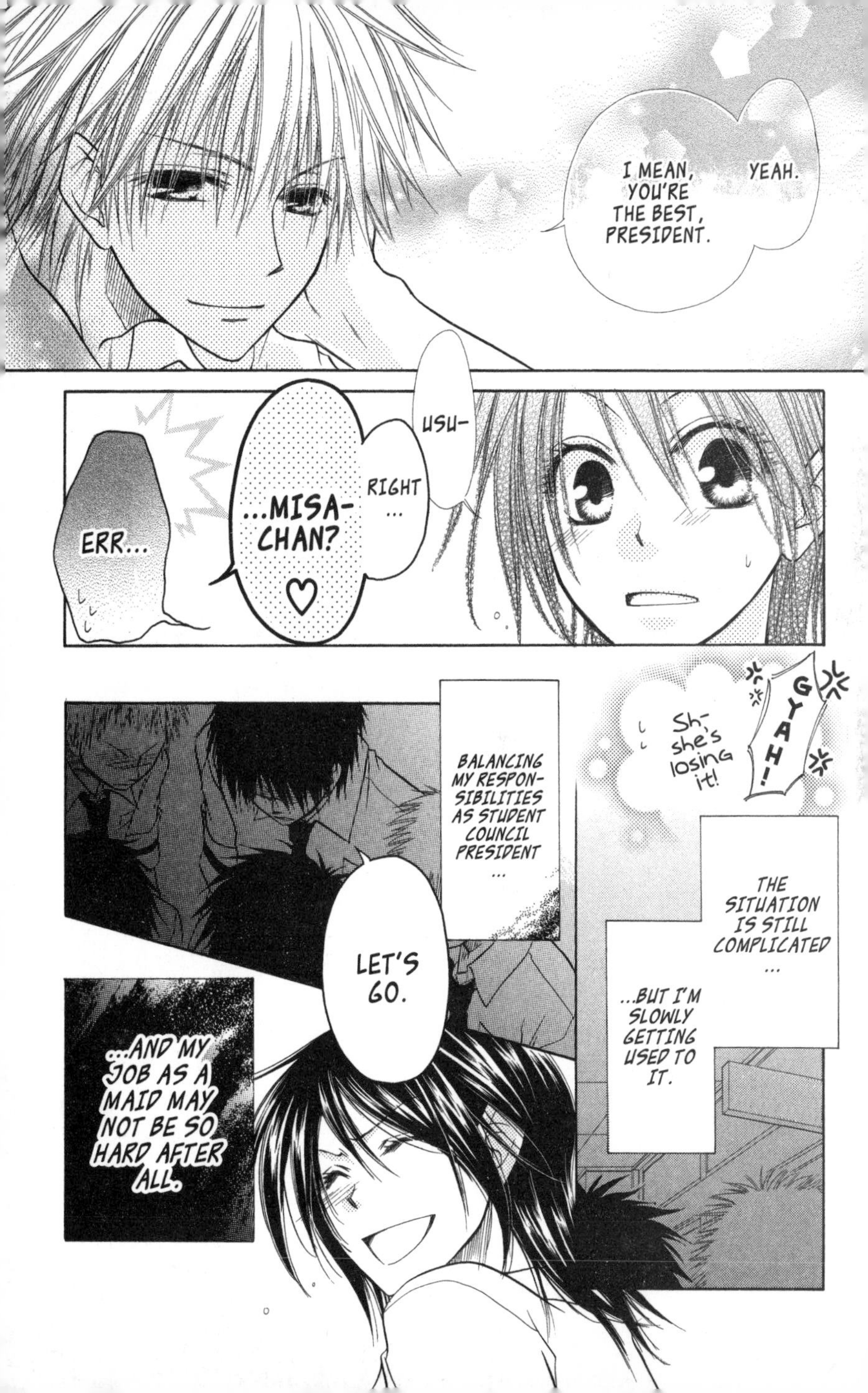
YEAH.
I MEAN, YOU'RE THE BEST, PRESIDENT.
USU-
RIGHT...
...MISA-CHAN? ♡
ERR...
GYAH!!
Sh-she's losing it!
THE SITUATION IS STILL COMPLICATED...
...BUT I'M SLOWLY GETTING USED TO IT.
BALANCING MY RESPONSIBILITIES AS STUDENT COUNCIL PRESIDENT...
LET'S GO.
...AND MY JOB AS A MAID MAY NOT BE SO HARD AFTER ALL.

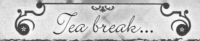

Maid Latte Lounge

-THE OTHER MAIDS TALK ABOUT MISAKI-

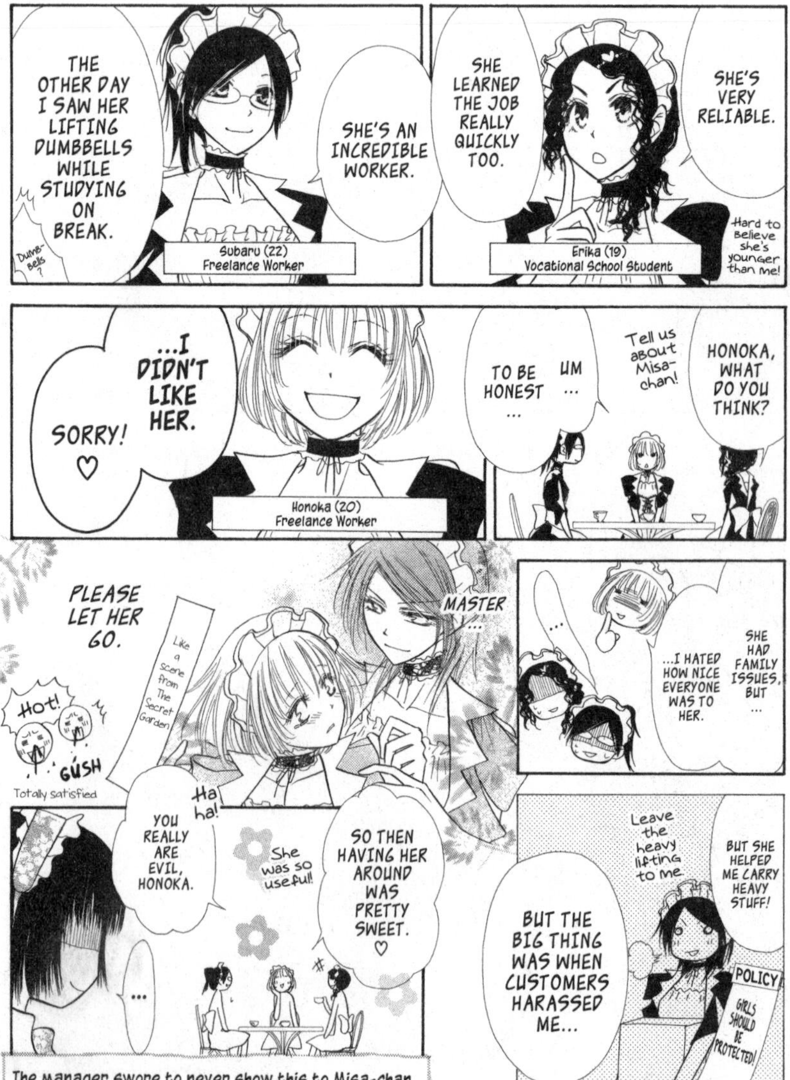
SHE'S VERY RELIABLE.
SHE LEARNED THE JOB REALLY QUICKLY TOO.
Hard to believe she's younger than me!
Erika (19) Vocational School Student
SHE'S AN INCREDIBLE WORKER.
THE OTHER DAY I SAW HER LIFTING DUMBBELLS WHILE STUDYING ON BREAK.
Dumb-bells?
Subaru (22) Freelance Worker
HONOKA, WHAT DO YOU THINK?
Tell us about Misa-chan!
UM ...
TO BE HONEST ...
...I DIDN'T LIKE HER.
SORRY! ♡
Honoka (20) Freelance Worker
SHE HAD FAMILY ISSUES, BUT ...
...I HATED HOW NICE EVERYONE WAS TO HER.
...
MASTER ...
PLEASE LET HER GO.
Like a scene from The Secret Garden
Hot!
GUSH
Totally satisfied
BUT SHE HELPED ME CARRY HEAVY STUFF!
Leave the heavy lifting to me.
BUT THE BIG THING WAS WHEN CUSTOMERS HARASSED ME...
POLICY
GIRLS SHOULD BE PROTECTED!
SO THEN HAVING HER AROUND WAS PRETTY SWEET. ♡
She was so useful!
Ha ha!
YOU REALLY ARE EVIL, HONOKA.
...
The manager swore to never show this to Misa-chan.

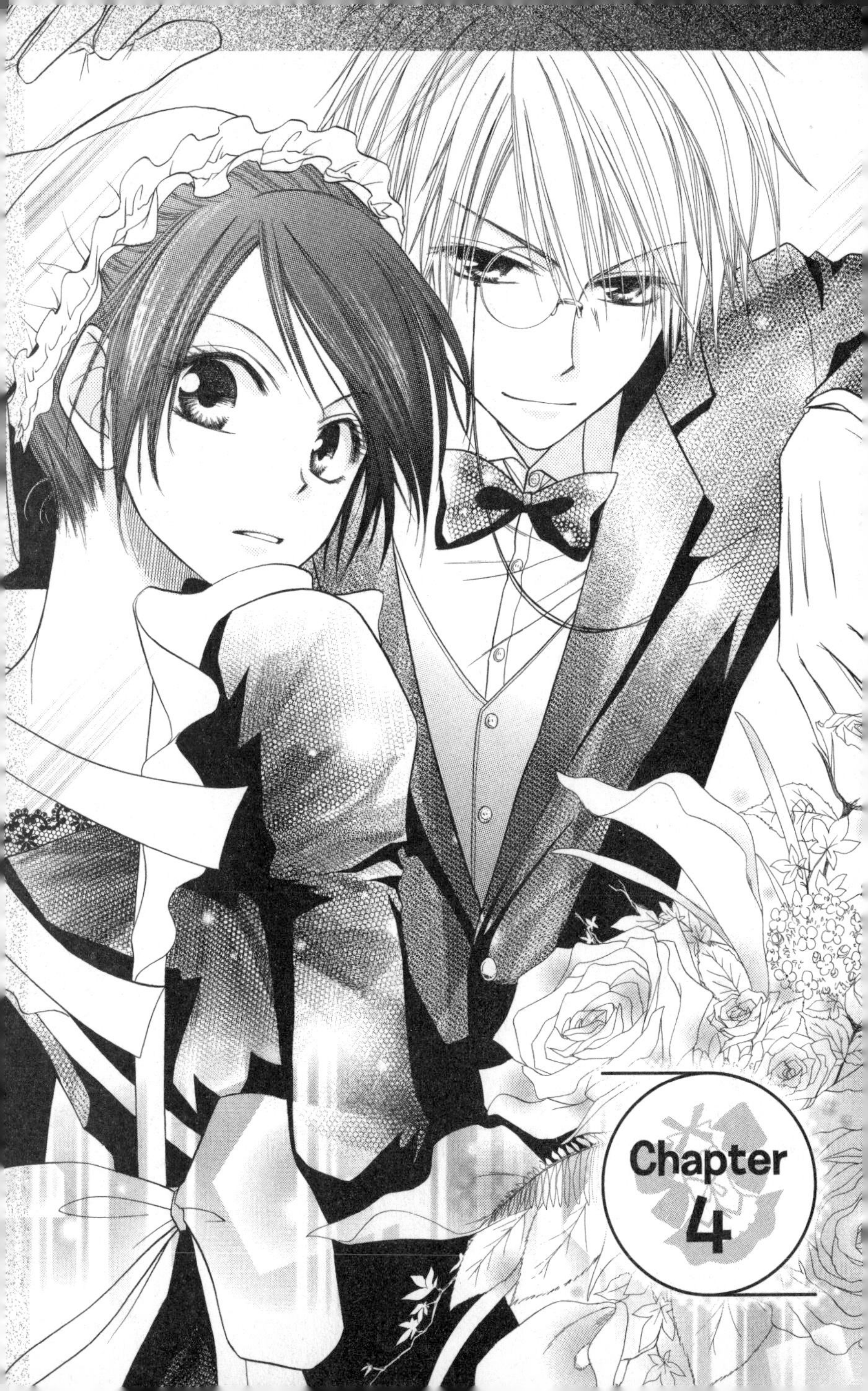
Chapter
4

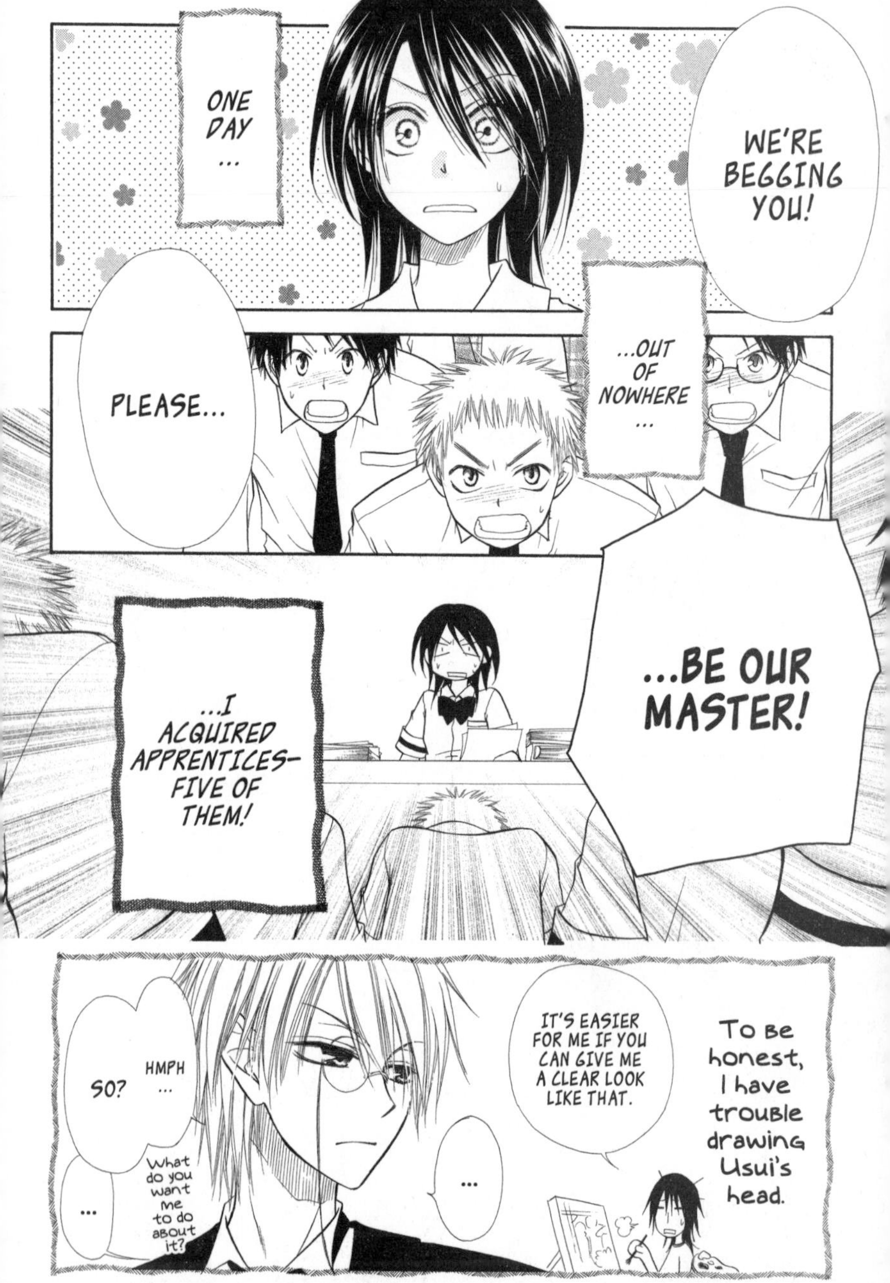
ONE DAY ...
WE'RE BEGGING YOU!
...OUT OF NOWHERE ...
PLEASE...
...BE OUR MASTER!
...I ACQUIRED APPRENTICES- FIVE OF THEM!
To be honest, I have trouble drawing Usui's head.
IT'S EASIER FOR ME IF YOU CAN GIVE ME A CLEAR LOOK LIKE THAT.
...
HMPH ...
SO?
What do you want me to do about it?
...

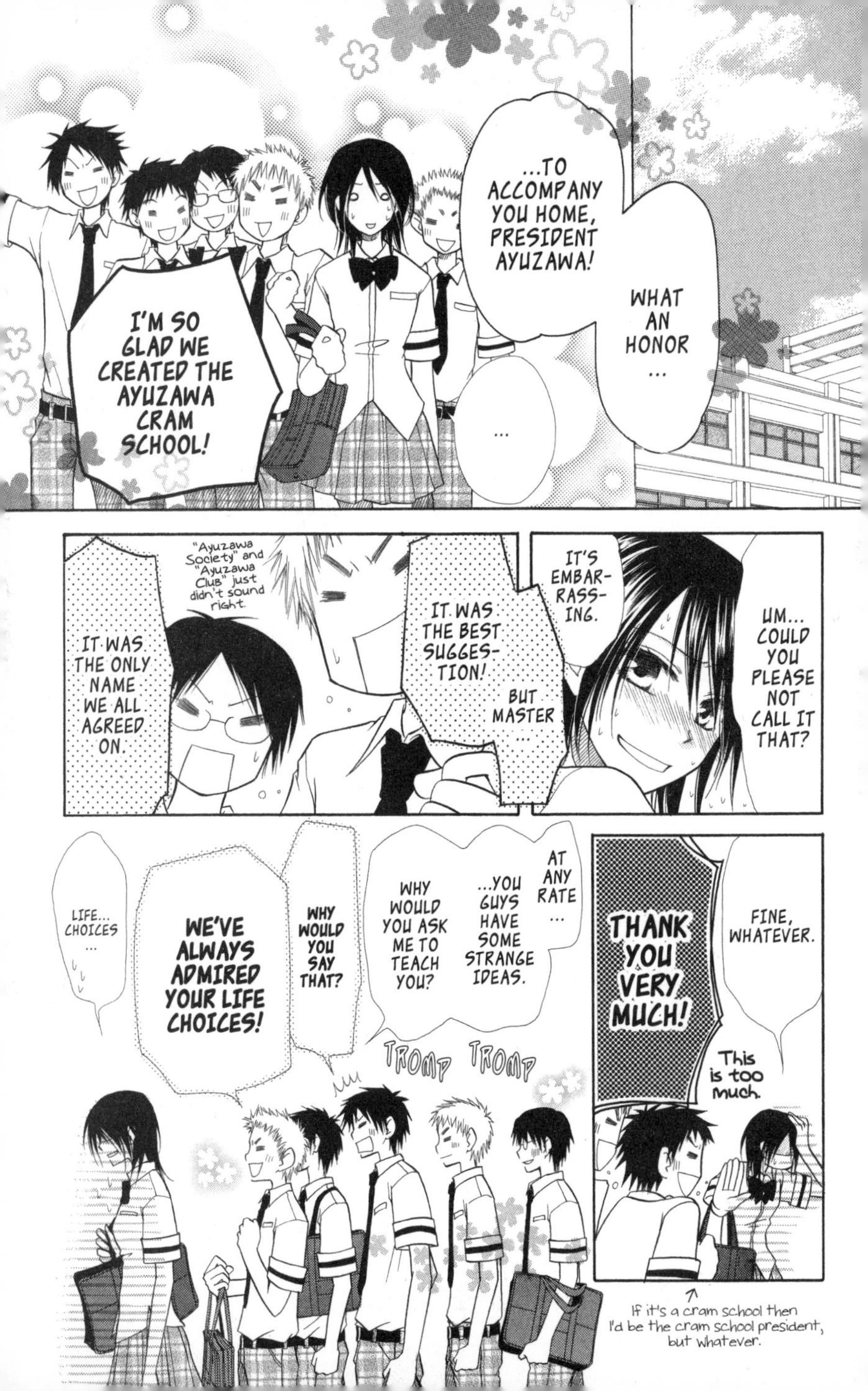
...TO ACCOMPANY YOU HOME, PRESIDENT AYUZAWA!
WHAT AN HONOR...
...
I'M SO GLAD WE CREATED THE AYUZAWA CRAM SCHOOL!
UM... COULD YOU PLEASE NOT CALL IT THAT?
IT'S EMBARRASSING.
IT WAS THE BEST SUGGESTION!
BUT MASTER...
"Ayuzawa Society" and "Ayuzawa Club" just didn't sound right.
IT WAS THE ONLY NAME WE ALL AGREED ON.
FINE, WHATEVER.
THANK YOU VERY MUCH!
This is too much.
If it's a cram school then I'd be the cram school president, but whatever.
AT ANY RATE...
...YOU GUYS HAVE SOME STRANGE IDEAS.
WHY WOULD YOU ASK ME TO TEACH YOU?
WHY WOULD YOU SAY THAT?
TROMP TROMP
WE'VE ALWAYS ADMIRED YOUR LIFE CHOICES!
LIFE... CHOICES...

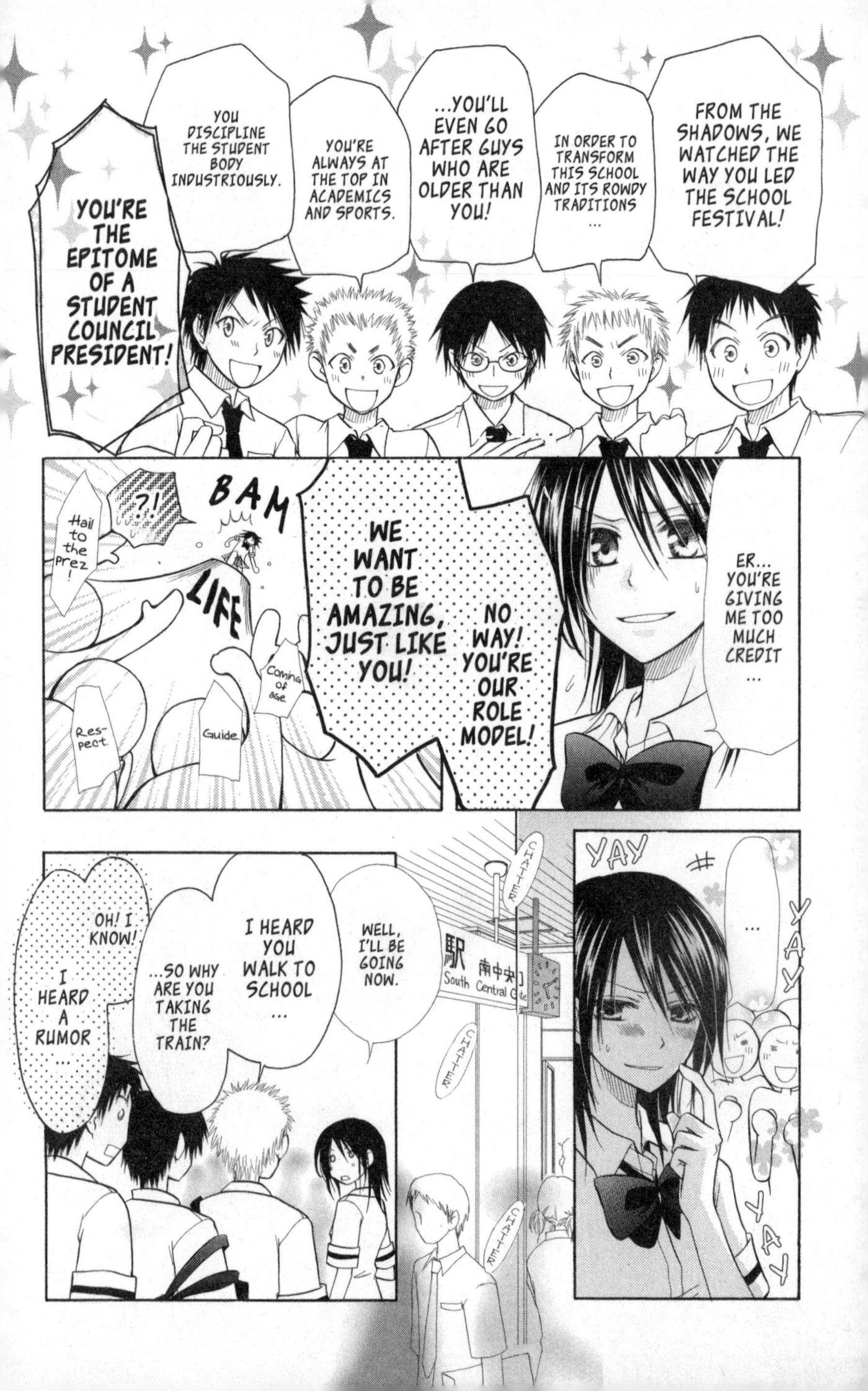
FROM THE SHADOWS, WE WATCHED THE WAY YOU LED THE SCHOOL FESTIVAL!
IN ORDER TO TRANSFORM THIS SCHOOL AND ITS ROWDY TRADITIONS ...
...YOU'LL EVEN GO AFTER GUYS WHO ARE OLDER THAN YOU!
YOU'RE ALWAYS AT THE TOP IN ACADEMICS AND SPORTS.
YOU DISCIPLINE THE STUDENT BODY INDUSTRIOUSLY.
YOU'RE THE EPITOME OF A STUDENT COUNCIL PRESIDENT!
ER... YOU'RE GIVING ME TOO MUCH CREDIT ...
NO WAY! YOU'RE OUR ROLE MODEL!
WE WANT TO BE AMAZING, JUST LIKE YOU!
BAM
?!
Hail to the Prez!
LIFE
Coming of age.
Guide.
Res-pect.
YAY
#
...
YAY
YAY
CHATTER
駅
南中央口
South Central G
CHATTER
CHATTER
WELL, I'LL BE GOING NOW.
I HEARD YOU WALK TO SCHOOL ...
...SO WHY ARE YOU TAKING THE TRAIN?
OH! I KNOW!
I HEARD A RUMOR ...

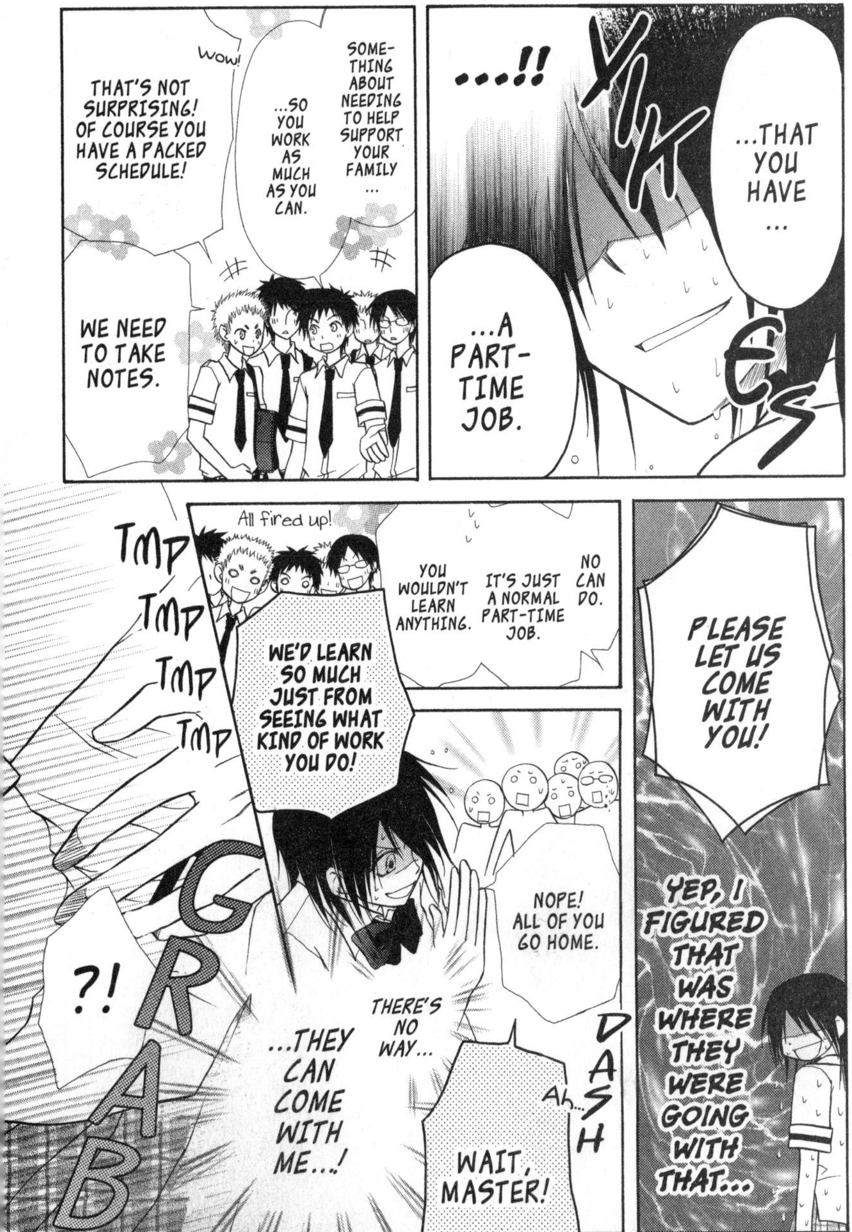

...THAT YOU HAVE ...
...A PART-TIME JOB.
YIKES
...!!
SOME-THING ABOUT NEEDING TO HELP SUPPORT YOUR FAMILY ...
...SO YOU WORK AS MUCH AS YOU CAN.
Wow!
THAT'S NOT SURPRISING! OF COURSE YOU HAVE A PACKED SCHEDULE!
WE NEED TO TAKE NOTES.
PLEASE LET US COME WITH YOU!
YEP, I FIGURED THAT WAS WHERE THEY WERE GOING WITH THAT...
NO CAN DO.
IT'S JUST A NORMAL PART-TIME JOB.
YOU WOULDN'T LEARN ANYTHING.
All fired up!
WE'D LEARN SO MUCH JUST FROM SEEING WHAT KIND OF WORK YOU DO!
NOPE! ALL OF YOU GO HOME.
DASH
Ah...
WAIT, MASTER!
THERE'S NO WAY...
...THEY CAN COME WITH ME...!
TMP
TMP
TMP
TMP
GRAB
?!

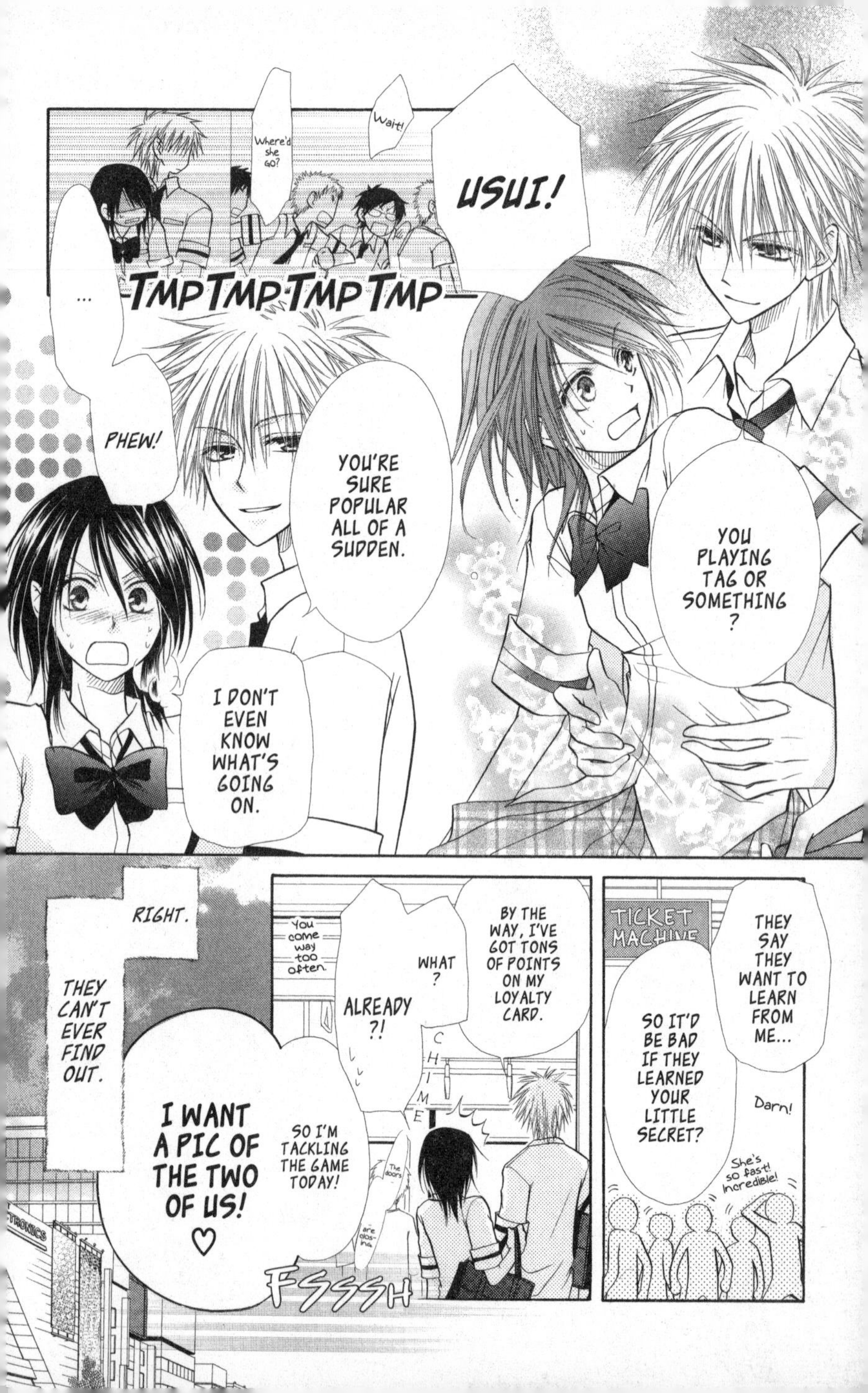
USUI!
Wait!
Where'd she go?
TMP TMP TMP TMP
...
YOU PLAYING TAG OR SOMETHING?
YOU'RE SURE POPULAR ALL OF A SUDDEN.
PHEW!
I DON'T EVEN KNOW WHAT'S GOING ON.
TICKET MACHINE
THEY SAY THEY WANT TO LEARN FROM ME...
SO IT'D BE BAD IF THEY LEARNED YOUR LITTLE SECRET?
Darn!
She's so fast! Incredible!
BY THE WAY, I'VE GOT TONS OF POINTS ON MY LOYALTY CARD.
WHAT?
ALREADY?!
You come way too often.
CHIME
SO I'M TACKLING THE GAME TODAY!
The doors are closing.
FSSSH
RIGHT.
THEY CAN'T EVER FIND OUT.
I WANT A PIC OF THE TWO OF US! ♡
-TRONICS

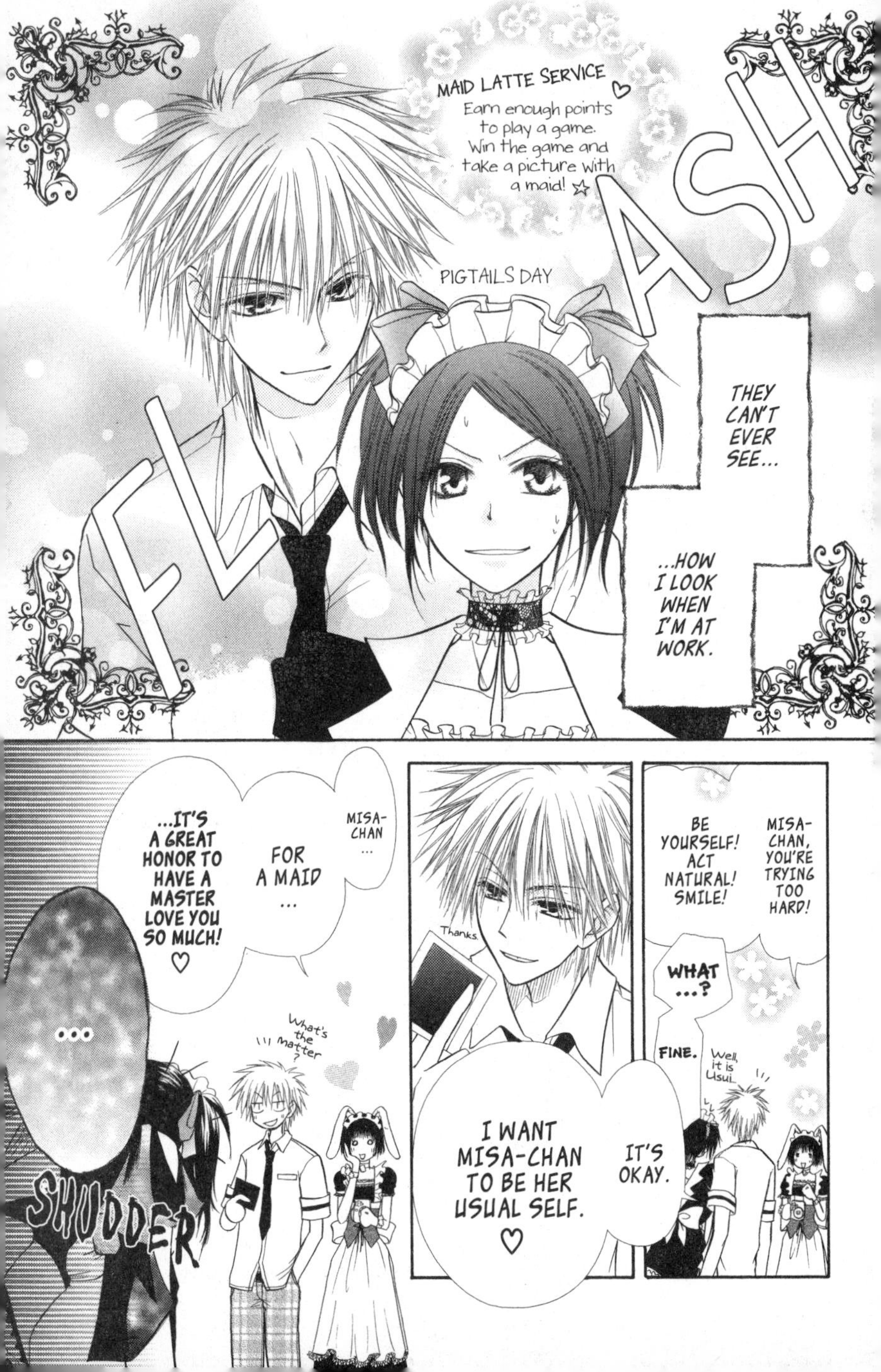
MAID LATTE SERVICE ♡
Earn enough points to play a game. Win the game and take a picture with a maid! ☆
FLASH
PIGTAILS DAY
THEY CAN'T EVER SEE...
...HOW I LOOK WHEN I'M AT WORK.
MISA-CHAN, YOU'RE TRYING TOO HARD!
BE YOURSELF! ACT NATURAL! SMILE!
WHAT...?
Well, it is Usui...
FINE.
Thanks.
IT'S OKAY.
I WANT MISA-CHAN TO BE HER USUAL SELF. ♡
MISA-CHAN...
FOR A MAID...
...IT'S A GREAT HONOR TO HAVE A MASTER LOVE YOU SO MUCH! ♡
What's the matter?
...
SHUDDER

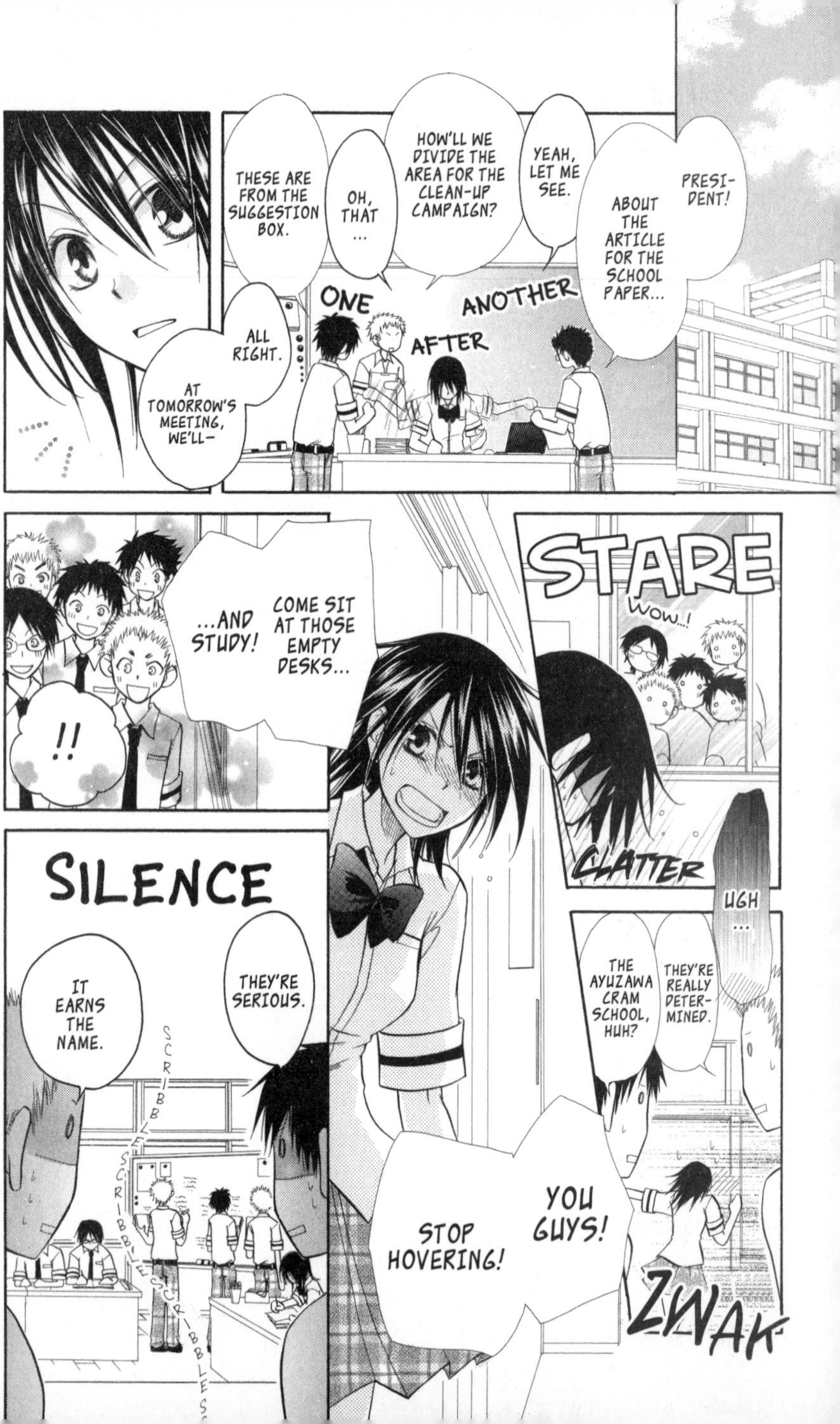
PRESI-DENT!
ABOUT THE ARTICLE FOR THE SCHOOL PAPER...
YEAH, LET ME SEE.
HOW'LL WE DIVIDE THE AREA FOR THE CLEAN-UP CAMPAIGN?
OH, THAT ...
THESE ARE FROM THE SUGGESTION BOX.
ONE AFTER ANOTHER
ALL RIGHT.
AT TOMORROW'S MEETING, WE'LL–
STARE
WOW...!
CLATTER
COME SIT AT THOSE EMPTY DESKS...
...AND STUDY!
!!
UGH ...
THEY'RE REALLY DETERM-MINED.
THE AYUZAWA CRAM SCHOOL, HUH?
YOU GUYS!
STOP HOVERING!
ZWAK
SILENCE
THEY'RE SERIOUS.
IT EARNS THE NAME.
SCRIBBLE
SCRIBBLE
SCRIBBLES

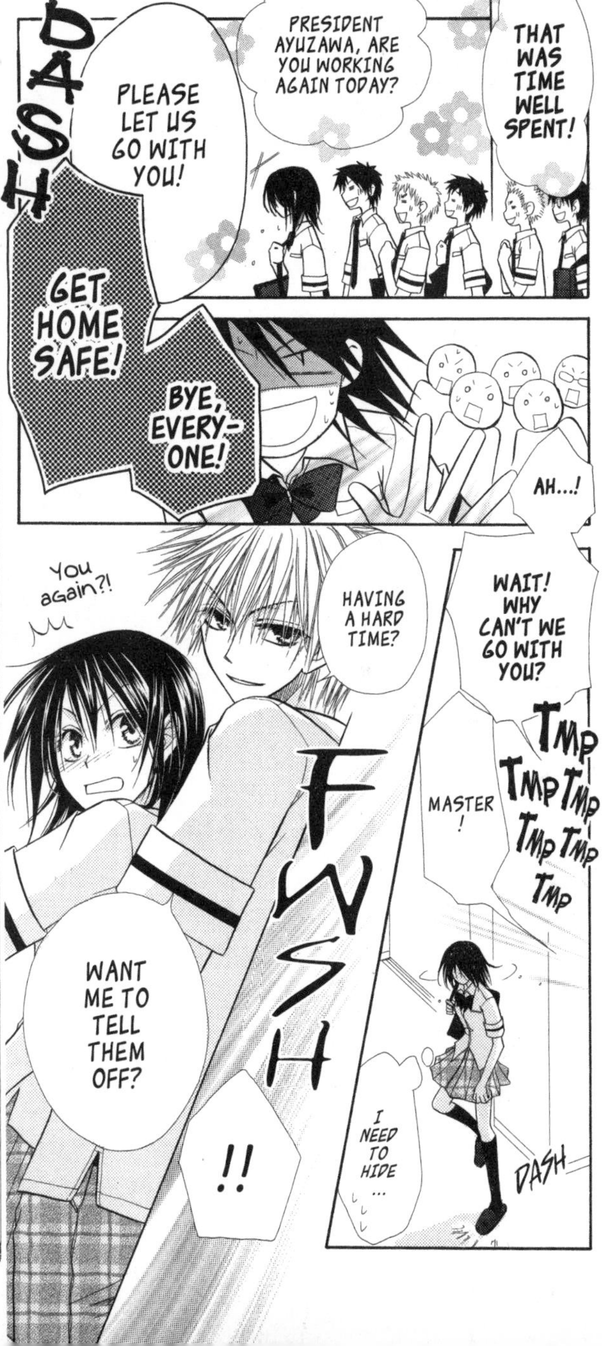
THAT WAS TIME WELL SPENT!
PRESIDENT AYUZAWA, ARE YOU WORKING AGAIN TODAY?
PLEASE LET US GO WITH YOU!
DASH
AH...!
BYE, EVERYONE!
GET HOME SAFE!
WAIT! WHY CAN'T WE GO WITH YOU?
MASTER!
TMP TMP TMP TMP TMP TMP TMP
I NEED TO HIDE...
DASH
HAVING A HARD TIME?
You again?!
FWSH
WANT ME TO TELL THEM OFF?
!!

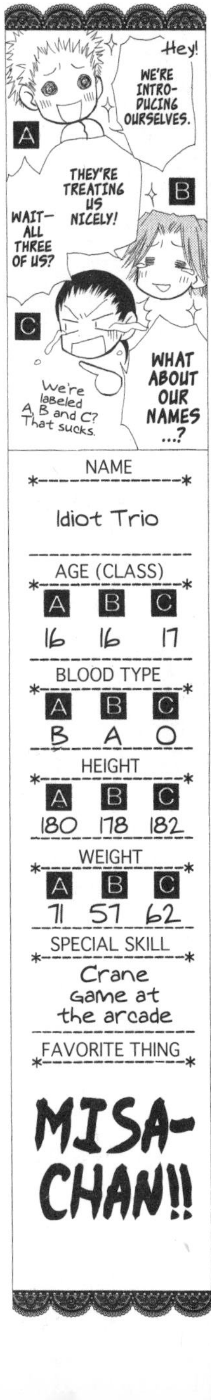
Hey!
WE'RE INTRODUCING OURSELVES.
A
THEY'RE TREATING US NICELY!
B
WAIT—ALL THREE OF US?
C
WHAT ABOUT OUR NAMES...?
We're labeled A, B and C? That sucks.

NAME

Idiot Trio

AGE (CLASS)

A	B	C
16	16	17

BLOOD TYPE

A	B	C
B	A	O

HEIGHT

A	B	C
180	178	182

WEIGHT

A	B	C
71	57	62

SPECIAL SKILL

Crane game at the arcade

FAVORITE THING

MISA-CHAN!!

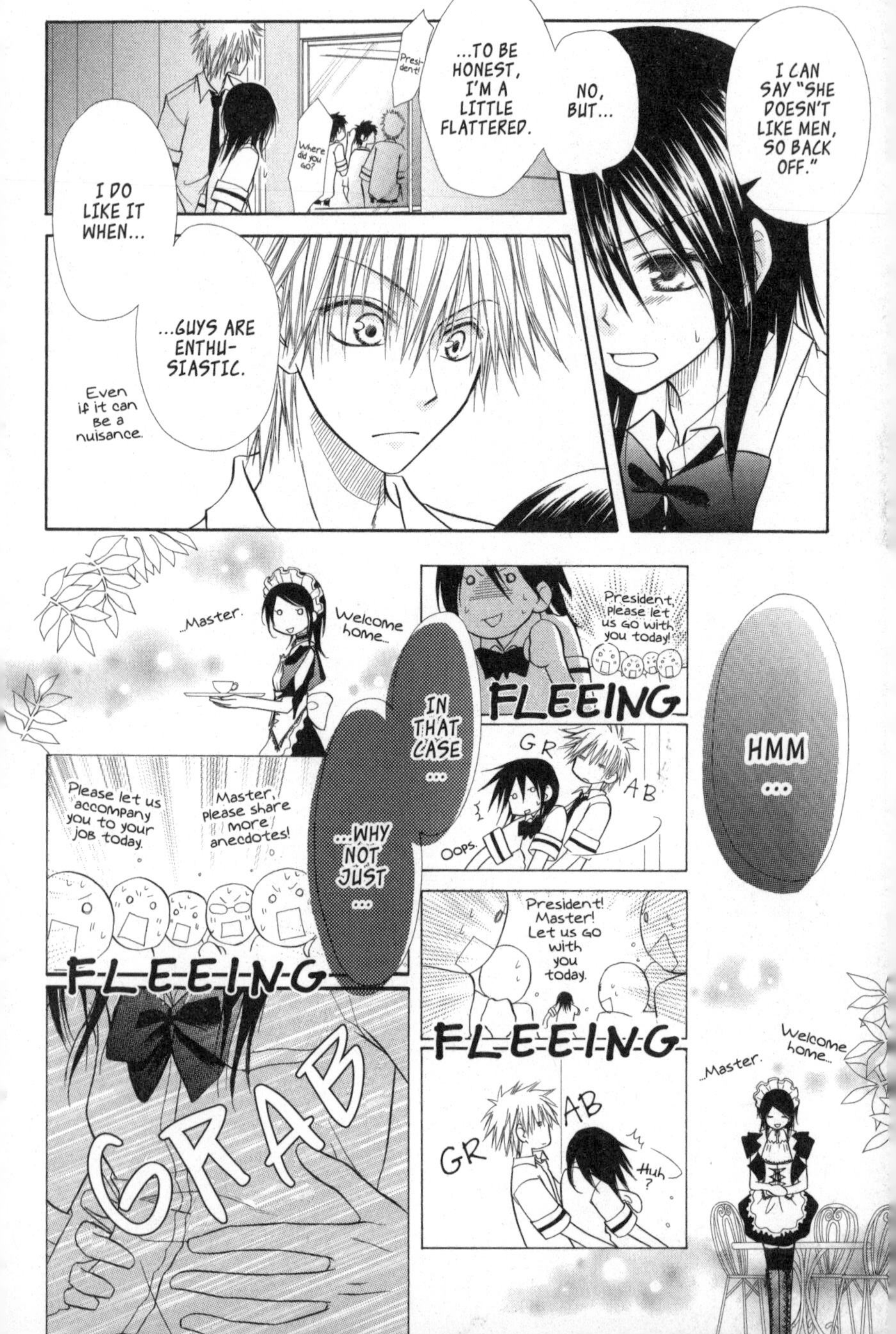
I CAN SAY "SHE DOESN'T LIKE MEN, SO BACK OFF."
NO, BUT...
...TO BE HONEST, I'M A LITTLE FLATTERED.
Presi-dent!
Where did you go?
I DO LIKE IT WHEN...
...GUYS ARE ENTHU-SIASTIC.
Even if it can be a nuisance.
HMM...
President, please let us go with you today!
FLEEING
GR
AB
Oops.
President! Master! Let us go with you today.
FLEEING
AB
GR
Huh?
Welcome home...
...Master.
Welcome home...
...Master.
IN THAT CASE...
...WHY NOT JUST...
Master, please share more anecdotes!
Please let us accompany you to your job today.
FLEEING
GRAB

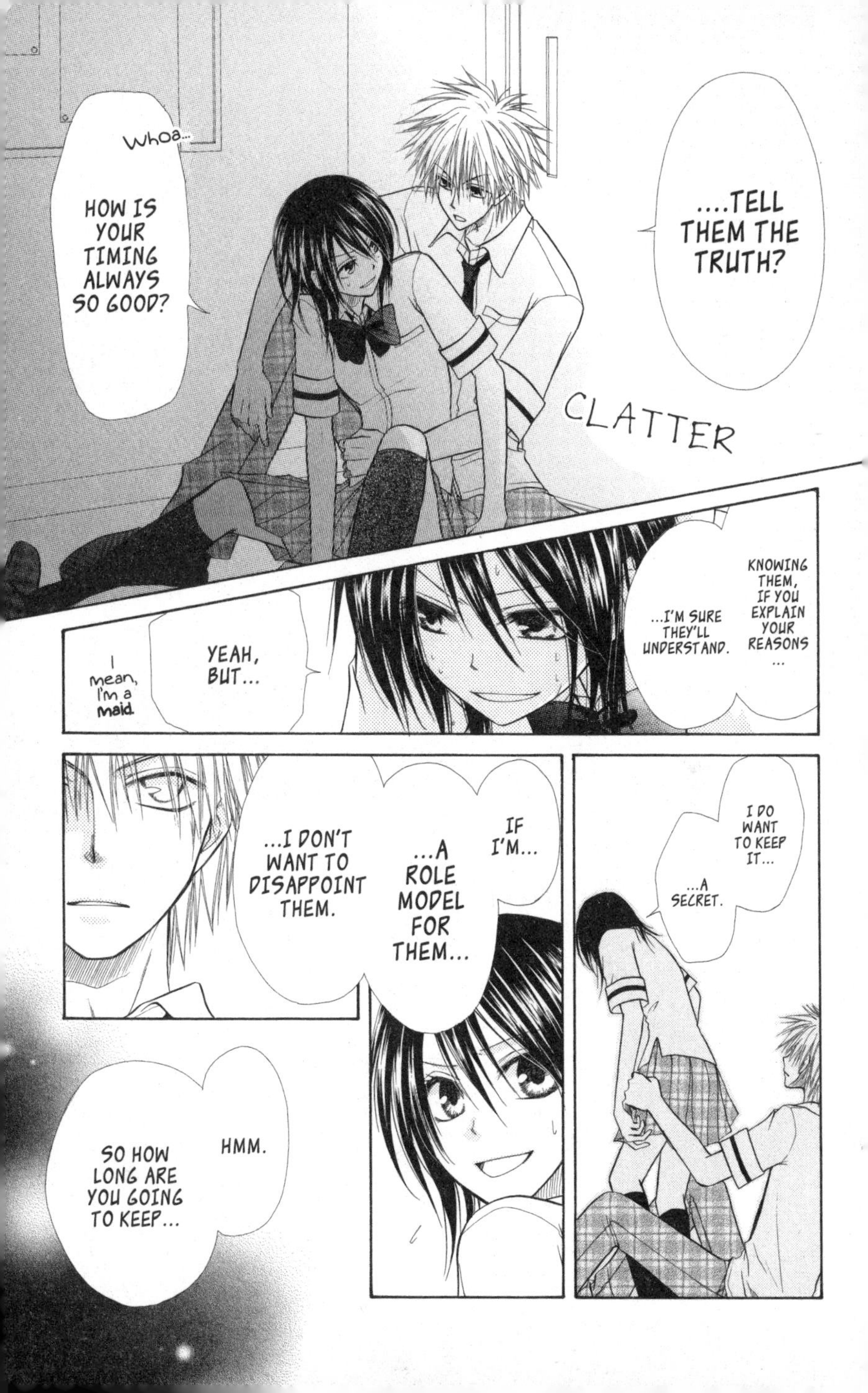
....TELL THEM THE TRUTH?
Whoa...
HOW IS YOUR TIMING ALWAYS SO GOOD?
CLATTER
KNOWING THEM, IF YOU EXPLAIN YOUR REASONS ...
...I'M SURE THEY'LL UNDERSTAND.
YEAH, BUT...
I mean, I'm a maid.
I DO WANT TO KEEP IT...
...A SECRET.
IF I'M...
...A ROLE MODEL FOR THEM...
...I DON'T WANT TO DISAPPOINT THEM.
HMM.
SO HOW LONG ARE YOU GOING TO KEEP...

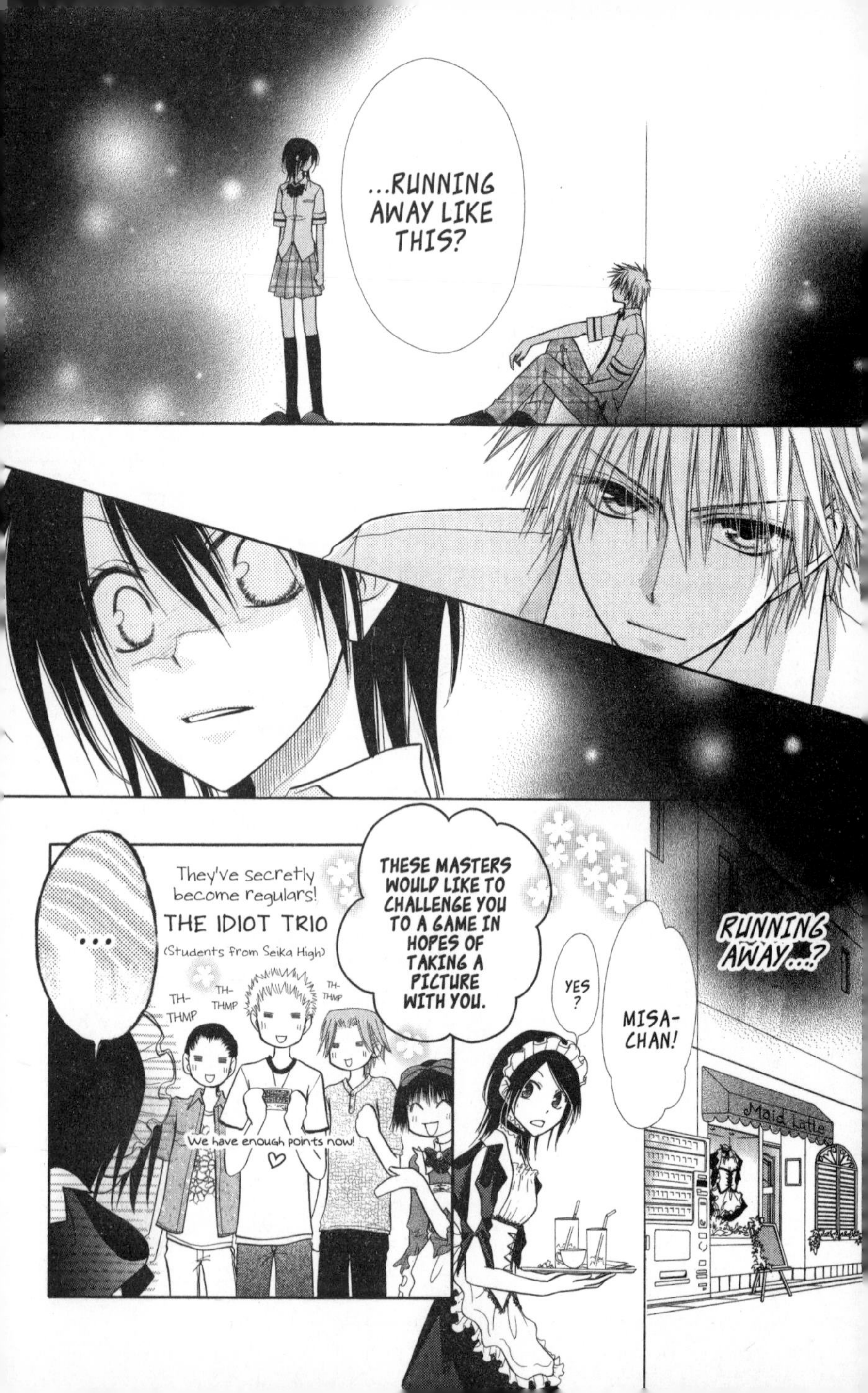
...RUNNING AWAY LIKE THIS?
RUNNING AWAY...?
MISA-CHAN!
YES?
THESE MASTERS WOULD LIKE TO CHALLENGE YOU TO A GAME IN HOPES OF TAKING A PICTURE WITH YOU.
They've secretly become regulars!
THE IDIOT TRIO
(Students from Seika High)
TH-THMP
TH-THMP
TH-THMP
...
We have enough points now!

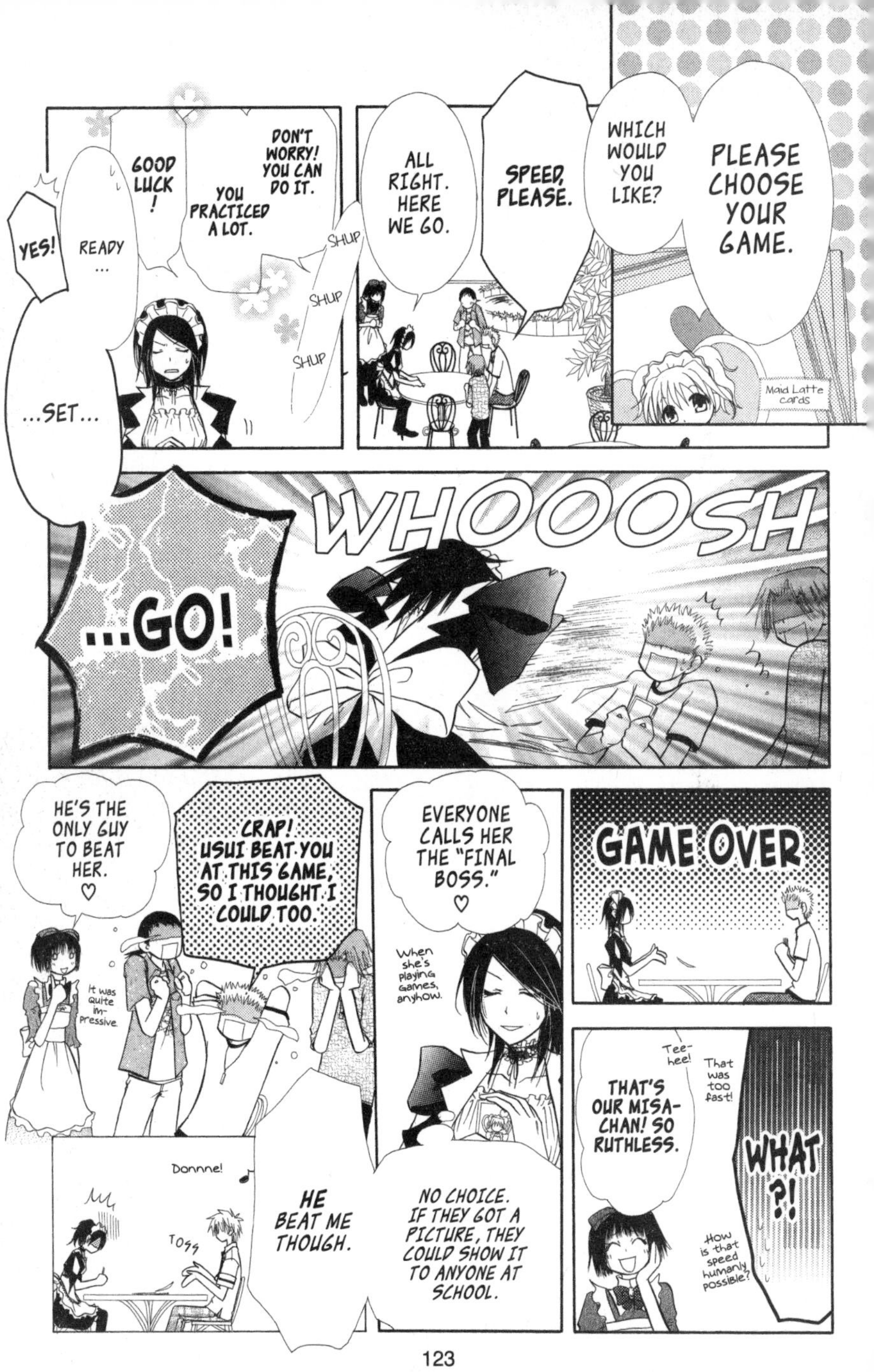
PLEASE CHOOSE YOUR GAME.
WHICH WOULD YOU LIKE?
Maid Latte cards
SPEED, PLEASE.
ALL RIGHT. HERE WE GO.
SHUP
SHUP
SHUP
DON'T WORRY! YOU CAN DO IT.
YOU PRACTICED A LOT.
GOOD LUCK!
READY...
YES!
...SET...
WHOOOSH
...GO!
GAME OVER
WHAT?!
That was too fast!
Tee-hee!
THAT'S OUR MISA-CHAN! SO RUTHLESS.
How is that speed humanly possible?
EVERYONE CALLS HER THE "FINAL BOSS." ♡
When she's playing games, anyhow.
CRAP! USUI BEAT YOU AT THIS GAME, SO I THOUGHT I COULD TOO.
HE'S THE ONLY GUY TO BEAT HER. ♡
It was quite impressive.
NO CHOICE. IF THEY GOT A PICTURE, THEY COULD SHOW IT TO ANYONE AT SCHOOL.
HE BEAT ME THOUGH.
Donnne!
TOSS

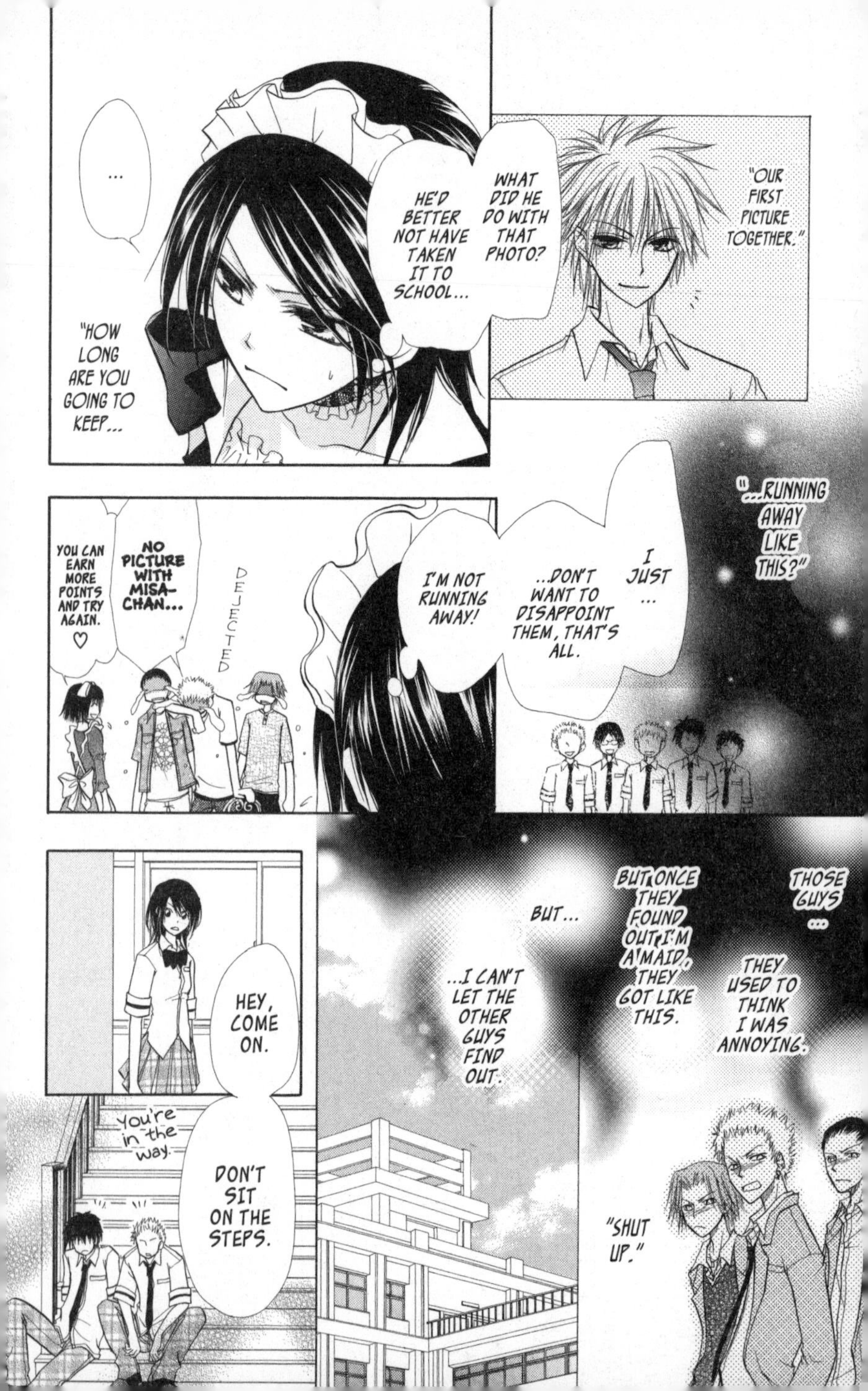
"OUR FIRST PICTURE TOGETHER."
WHAT DID HE DO WITH THAT PHOTO?
HE'D BETTER NOT HAVE TAKEN IT TO SCHOOL...
...
"HOW LONG ARE YOU GOING TO KEEP...
"...RUNNING AWAY LIKE THIS?"
I JUST ...
...DON'T WANT TO DISAPPOINT THEM, THAT'S ALL.
I'M NOT RUNNING AWAY!
NO PICTURE WITH MISA-CHAN...
DEJECTED
YOU CAN EARN MORE POINTS AND TRY AGAIN. ♡
THOSE GUYS...
THEY USED TO THINK I WAS ANNOYING.
BUT ONCE THEY FOUND OUT I'M A MAID, THEY GOT LIKE THIS.
BUT...
...I CAN'T LET THE OTHER GUYS FIND OUT.
"SHUT UP."
HEY, COME ON.
DON'T SIT ON THE STEPS.
You're in the way.

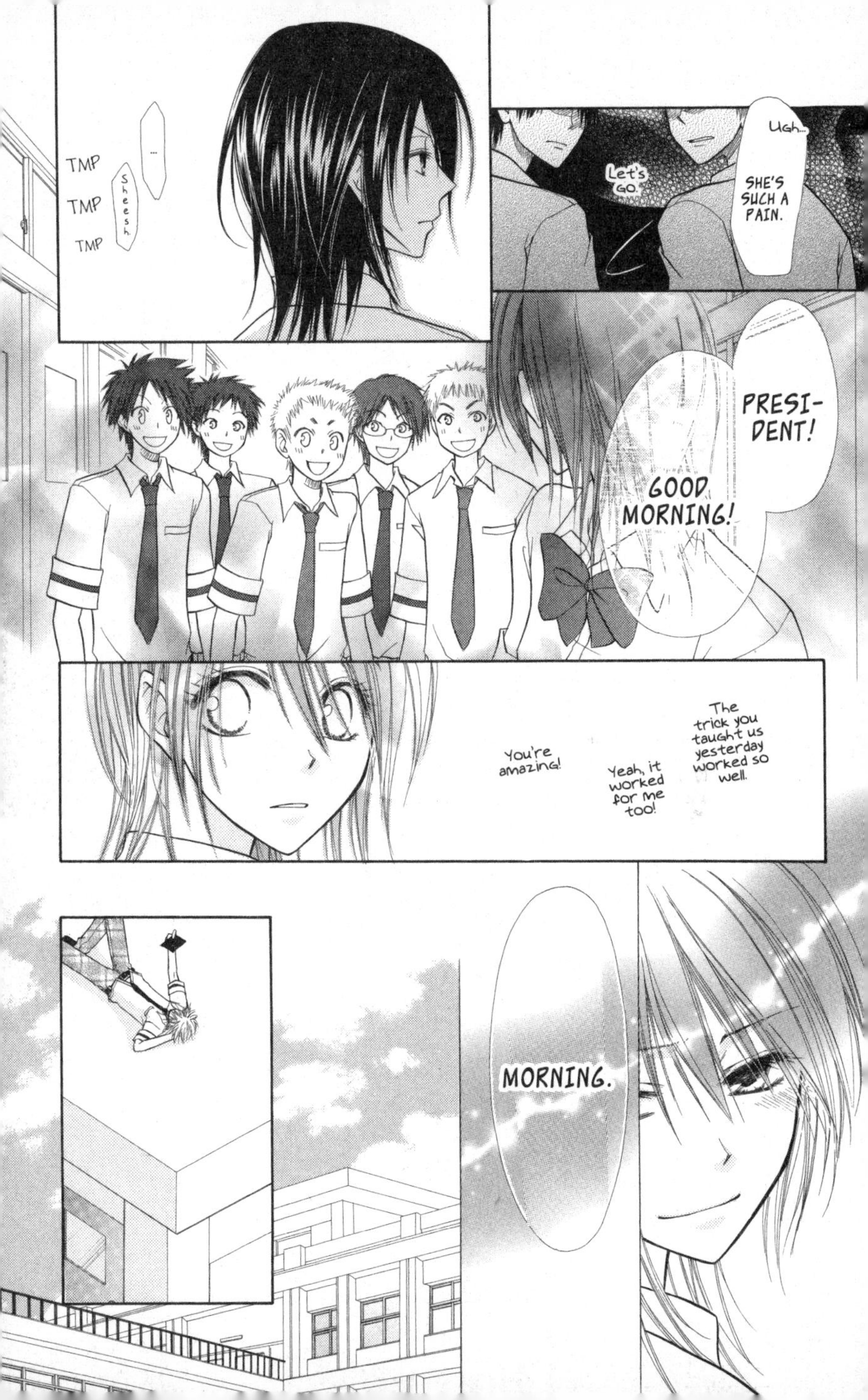
Ugh...
SHE'S SUCH A PAIN.
Let's go.
...
Sheesh.
TMP TMP TMP
PRESIDENT!
GOOD MORNING!
The trick you taught us yesterday worked so well.
Yeah, it worked for me too!
You're amazing!
MORNING.

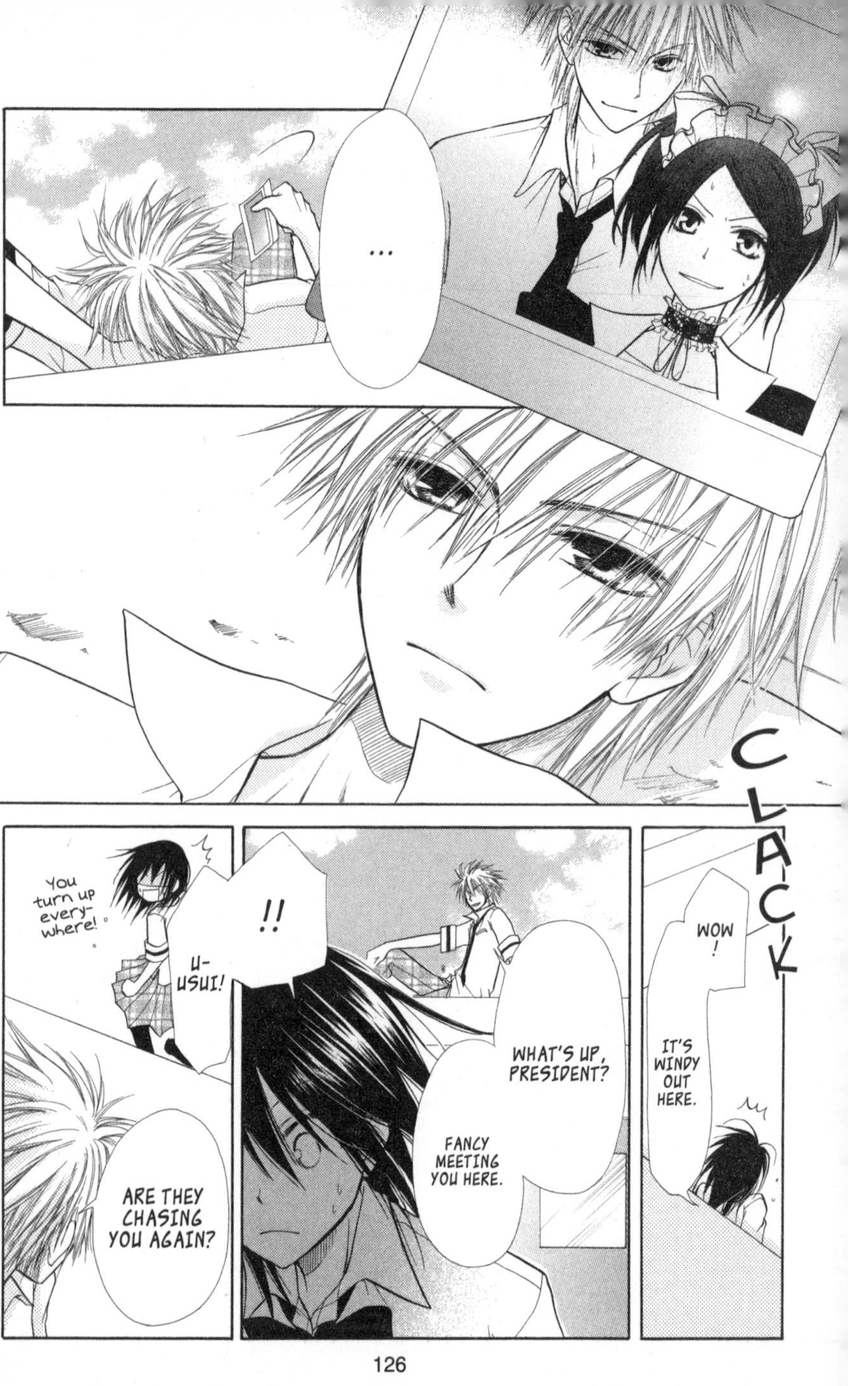
...
CLACK
WOW!
IT'S WINDY OUT HERE.
WHAT'S UP, PRESIDENT?
FANCY MEETING YOU HERE.
!!
U-USUI!
You turn up every-where!
ARE THEY CHASING YOU AGAIN?

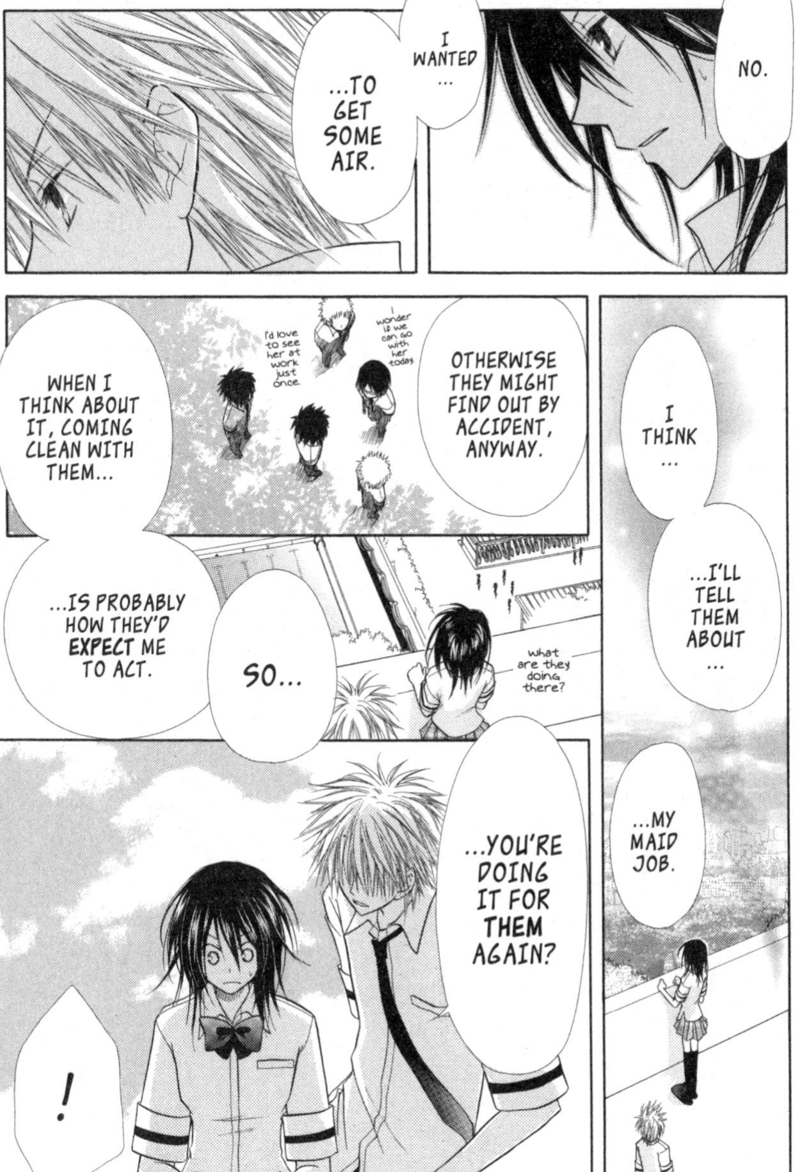
NO.
I WANTED ...
...TO GET SOME AIR.
I THINK ...
...I'LL TELL THEM ABOUT ...
...MY MAID JOB.
OTHERWISE THEY MIGHT FIND OUT BY ACCIDENT, ANYWAY.
I wonder if we can go with her today.
I'd love to see her at work just once.
WHEN I THINK ABOUT IT, COMING CLEAN WITH THEM...
what are they doing there?
...IS PROBABLY HOW THEY'D **EXPECT** ME TO ACT.
SO...
...YOU'RE DOING IT FOR **THEM** AGAIN?
!

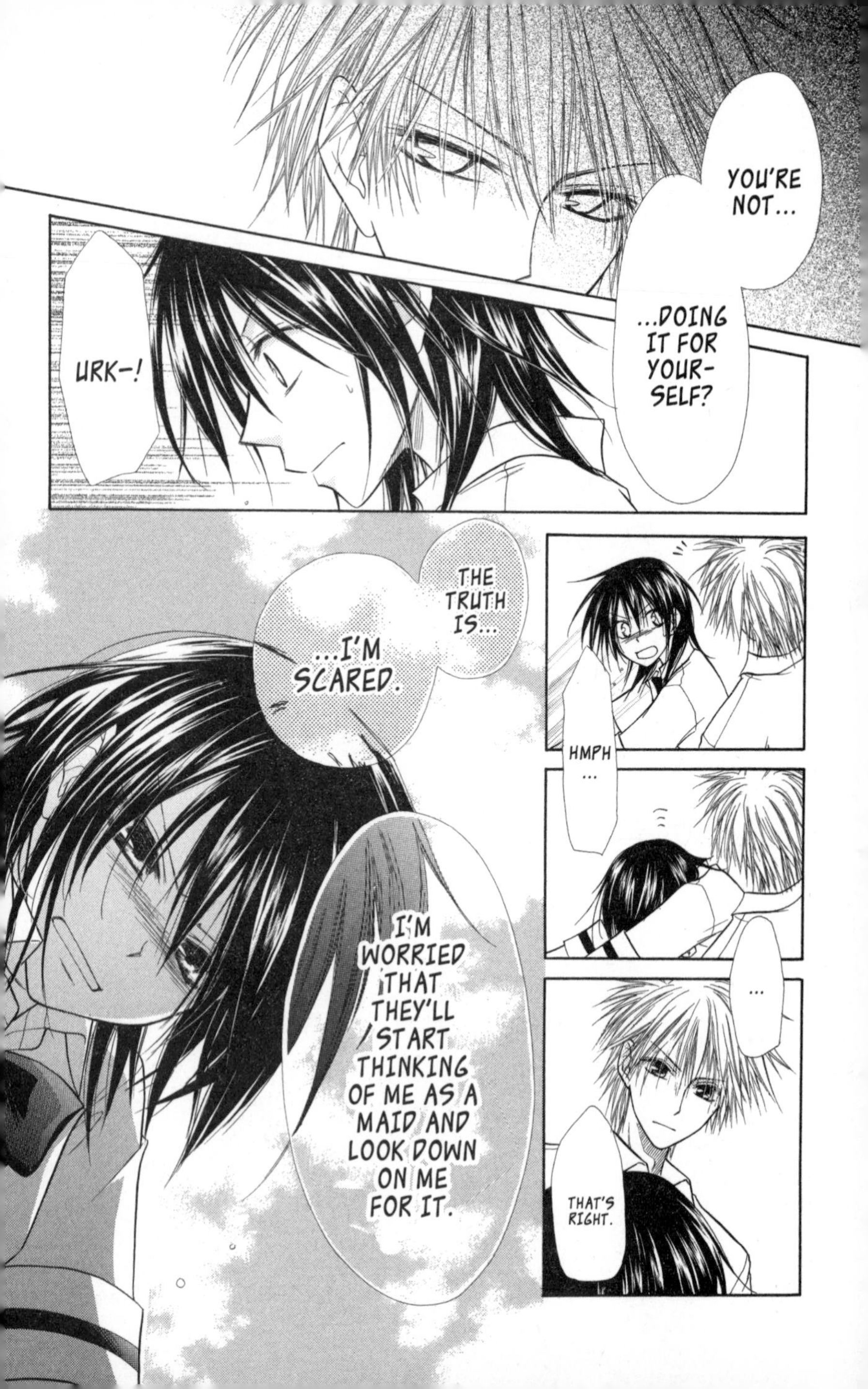
YOU'RE NOT...
...DOING IT FOR YOURSELF?
URK—!
HMPH...
...
THAT'S RIGHT.
THE TRUTH IS...
...I'M SCARED.
I'M WORRIED THAT THEY'LL START THINKING OF ME AS A MAID AND LOOK DOWN ON ME FOR IT.

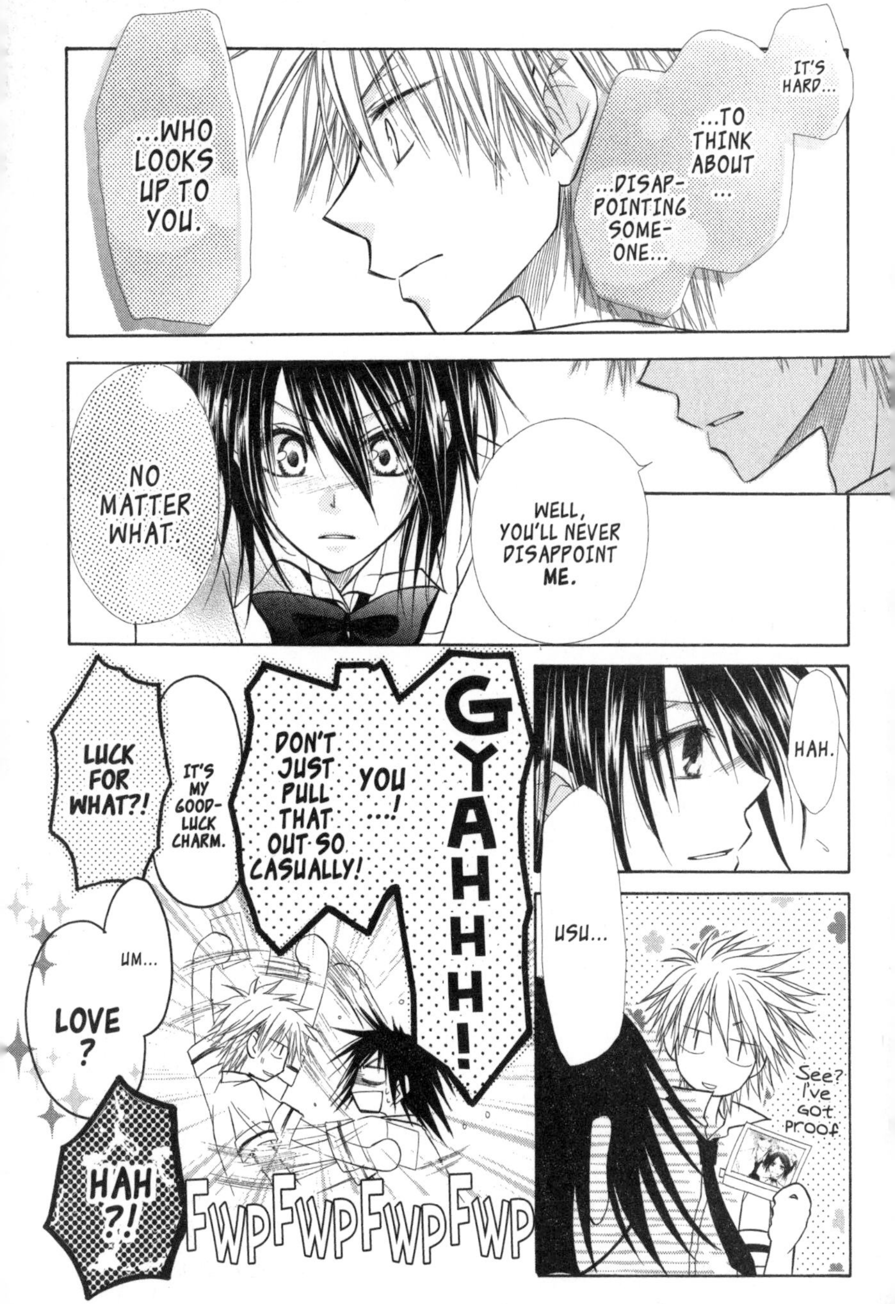
IT'S HARD...
...TO THINK ABOUT...
...DISAPPOINTING SOMEONE...
...WHO LOOKS UP TO YOU.
WELL, YOU'LL NEVER DISAPPOINT ME.
NO MATTER WHAT.
HAH.
USU...
See? I've got proof
GYAHHH!
YOU...!
DON'T JUST PULL THAT OUT SO CASUALLY!
IT'S MY GOOD-LUCK CHARM.
LUCK FOR WHAT?!
UM...
LOVE?
HAH?!
FWPFWPFWPFWP

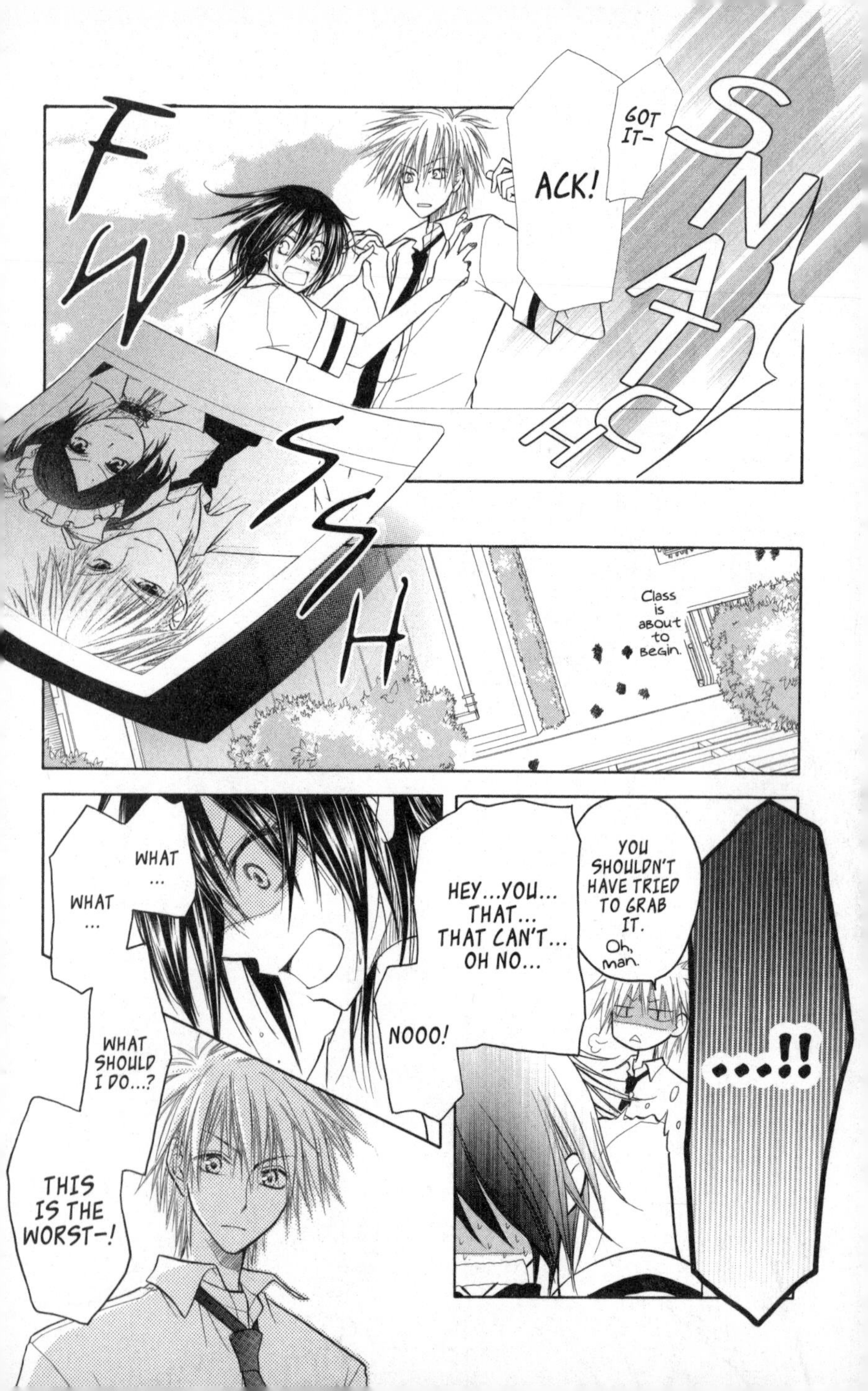
SNATCH
GOT IT–
ACK!
FWSSH
Class is about to begin.
...!!
YOU SHOULDN'T HAVE TRIED TO GRAB IT.
Oh, man.
HEY...YOU... THAT... THAT CAN'T... OH NO...
WHAT ...
WHAT ...
NOOO!
WHAT SHOULD I DO...?
THIS IS THE WORST–!

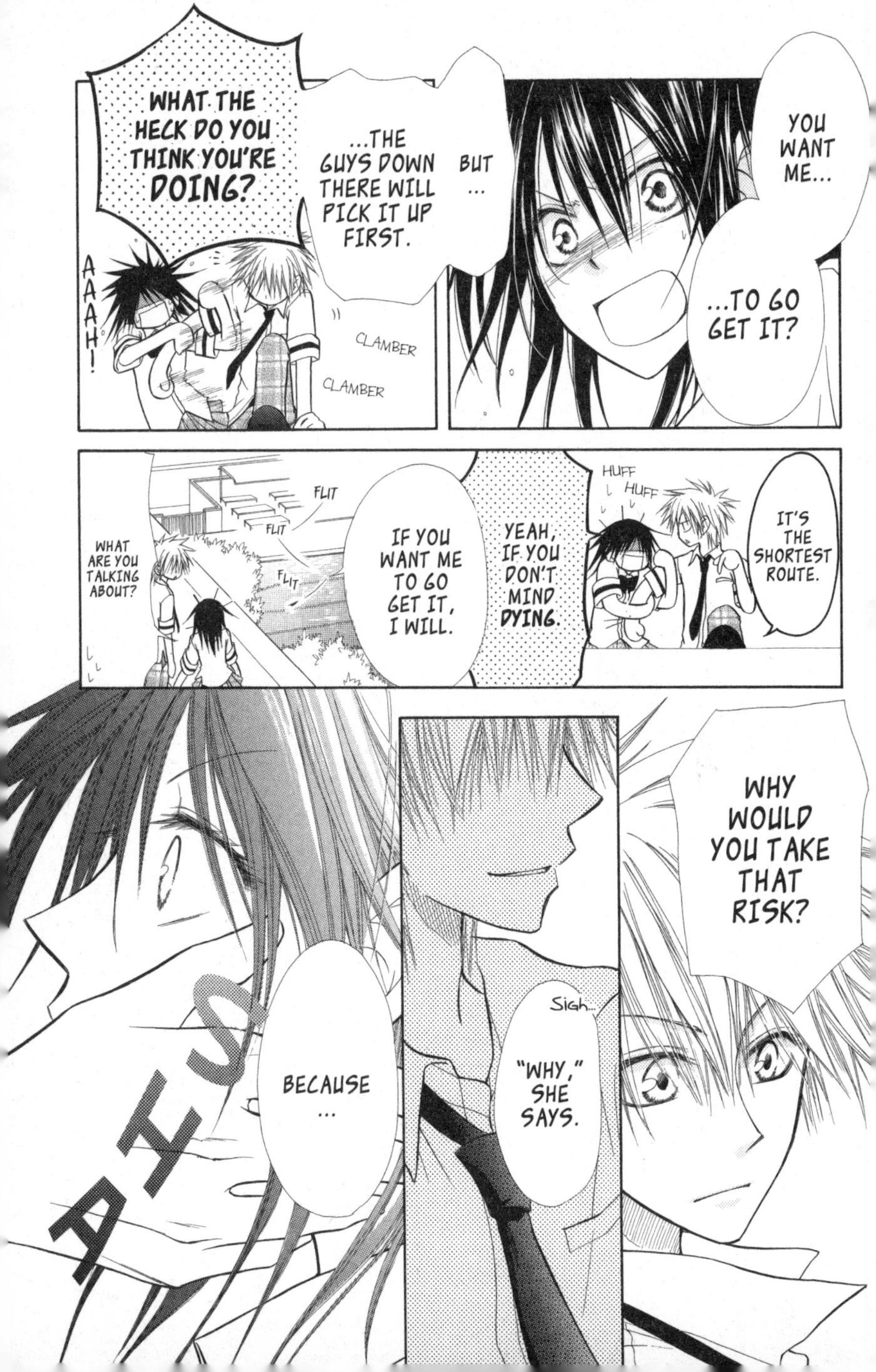
YOU WANT ME...
...TO GO GET IT?
BUT ...
...THE GUYS DOWN THERE WILL PICK IT UP FIRST.
WHAT THE HECK DO YOU THINK YOU'RE DOING?
AAAAH!
CLAMBER
CLAMBER
IT'S THE SHORTEST ROUTE.
HUFF
HUFF
YEAH, IF YOU DON'T MIND DYING.
IF YOU WANT ME TO GO GET IT, I WILL.
FLIT
FLIT
FLIT
WHAT ARE YOU TALKING ABOUT?
WHY WOULD YOU TAKE THAT RISK?
Sigh...
"WHY," SHE SAYS.
BECAUSE ...

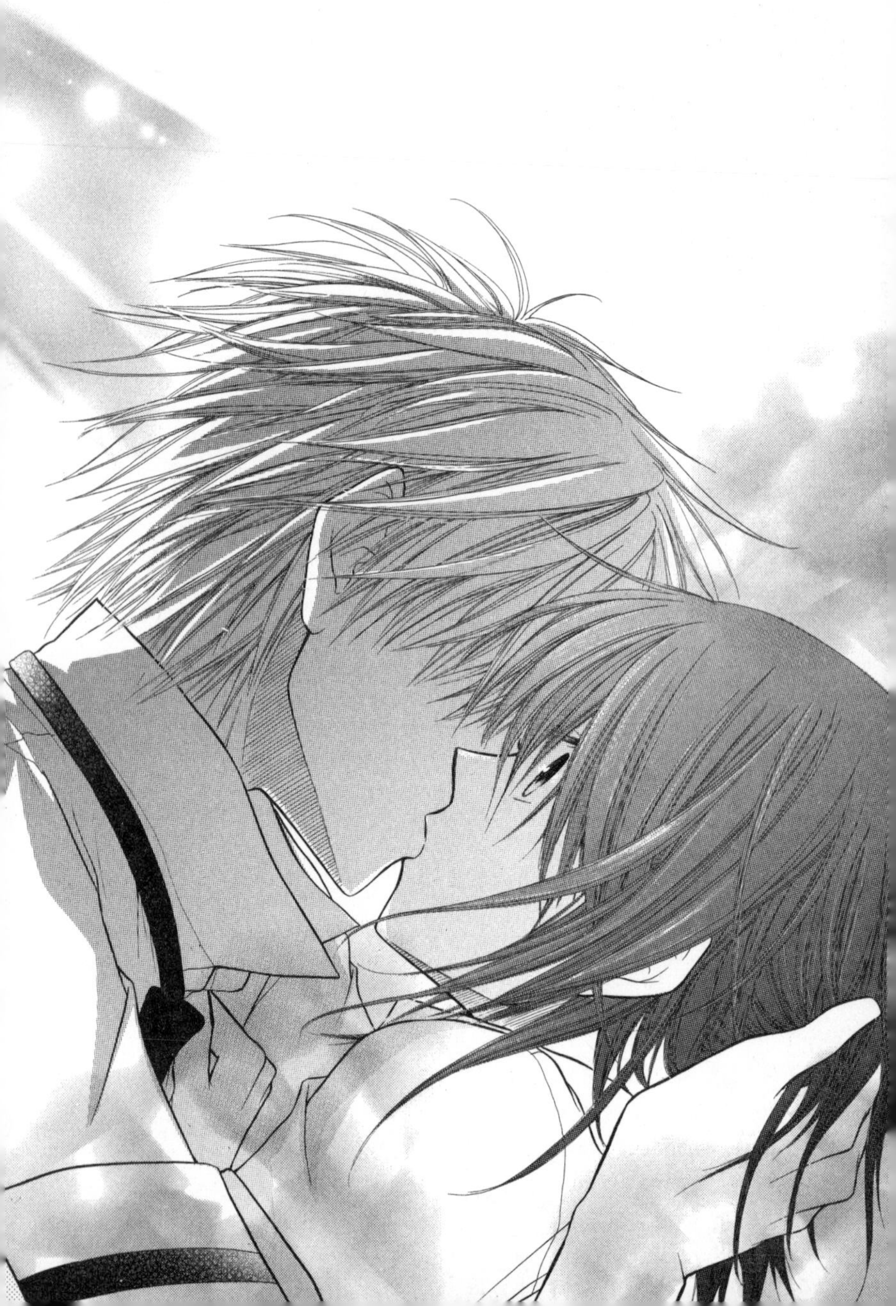

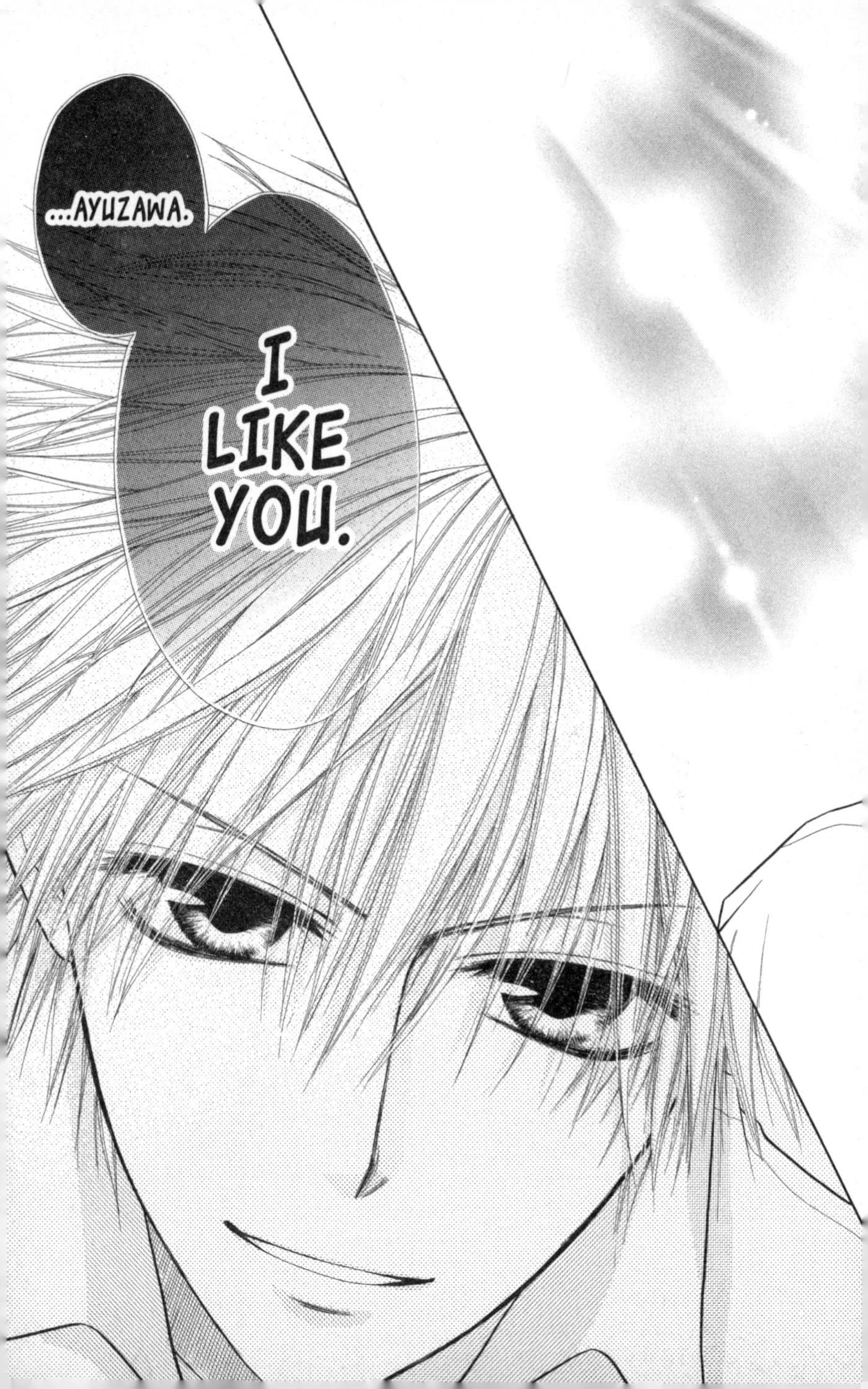
...AYUZAWA.
I LIKE YOU.

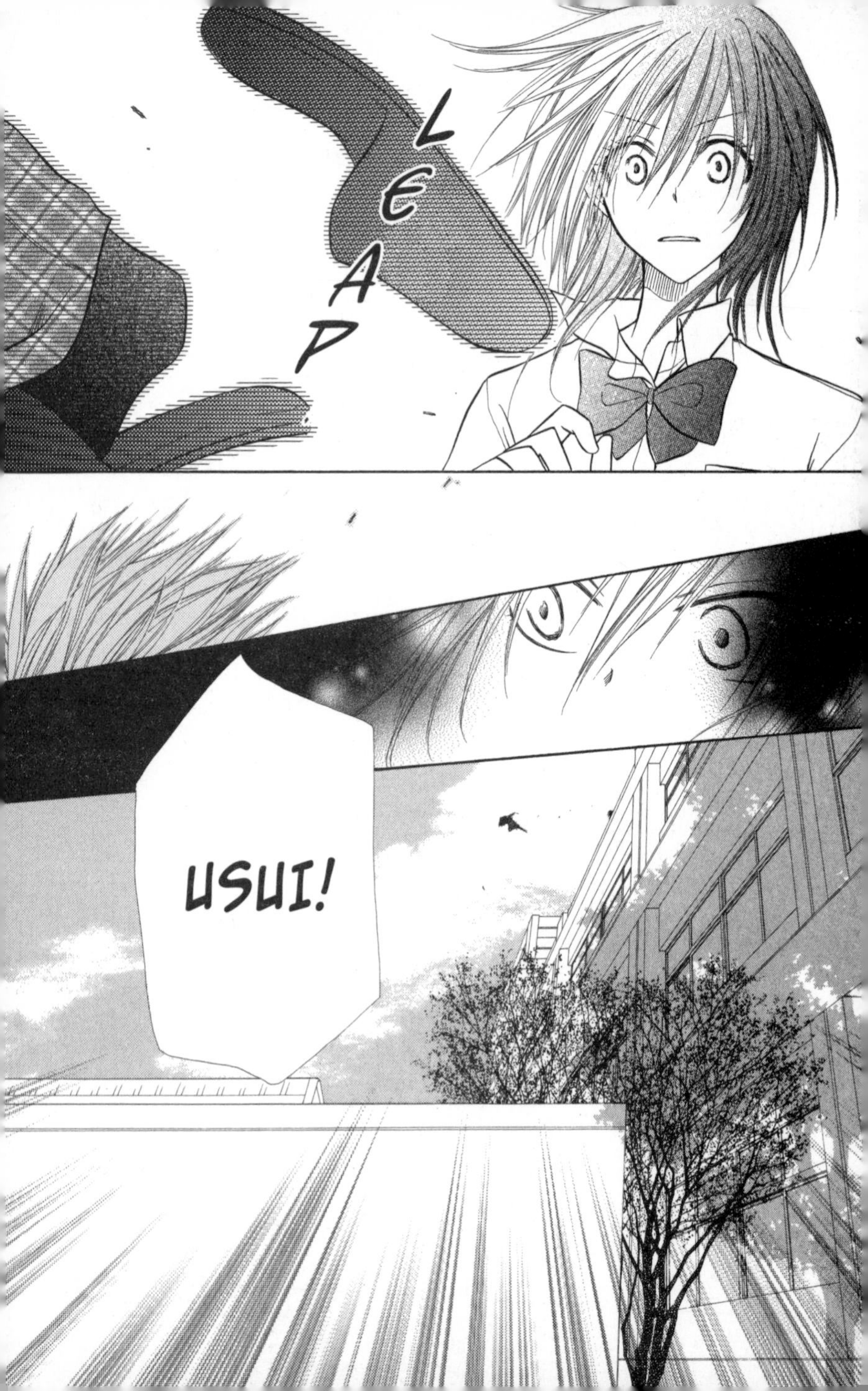
LEAP
USUI!

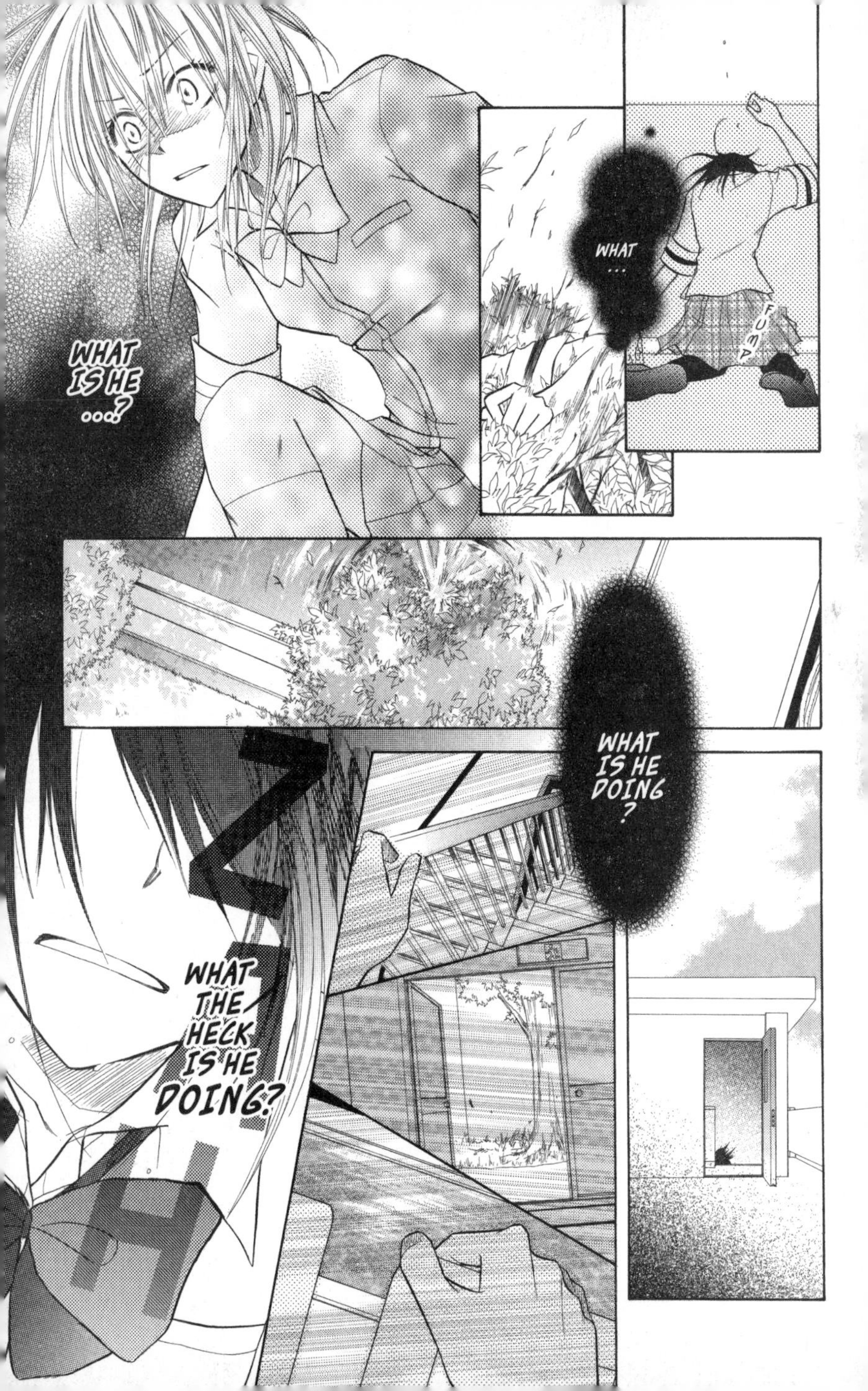
FUMP
WHAT...
WHAT IS HE...?
WHAT IS HE DOING?
WHAT THE HECK IS HE DOING?

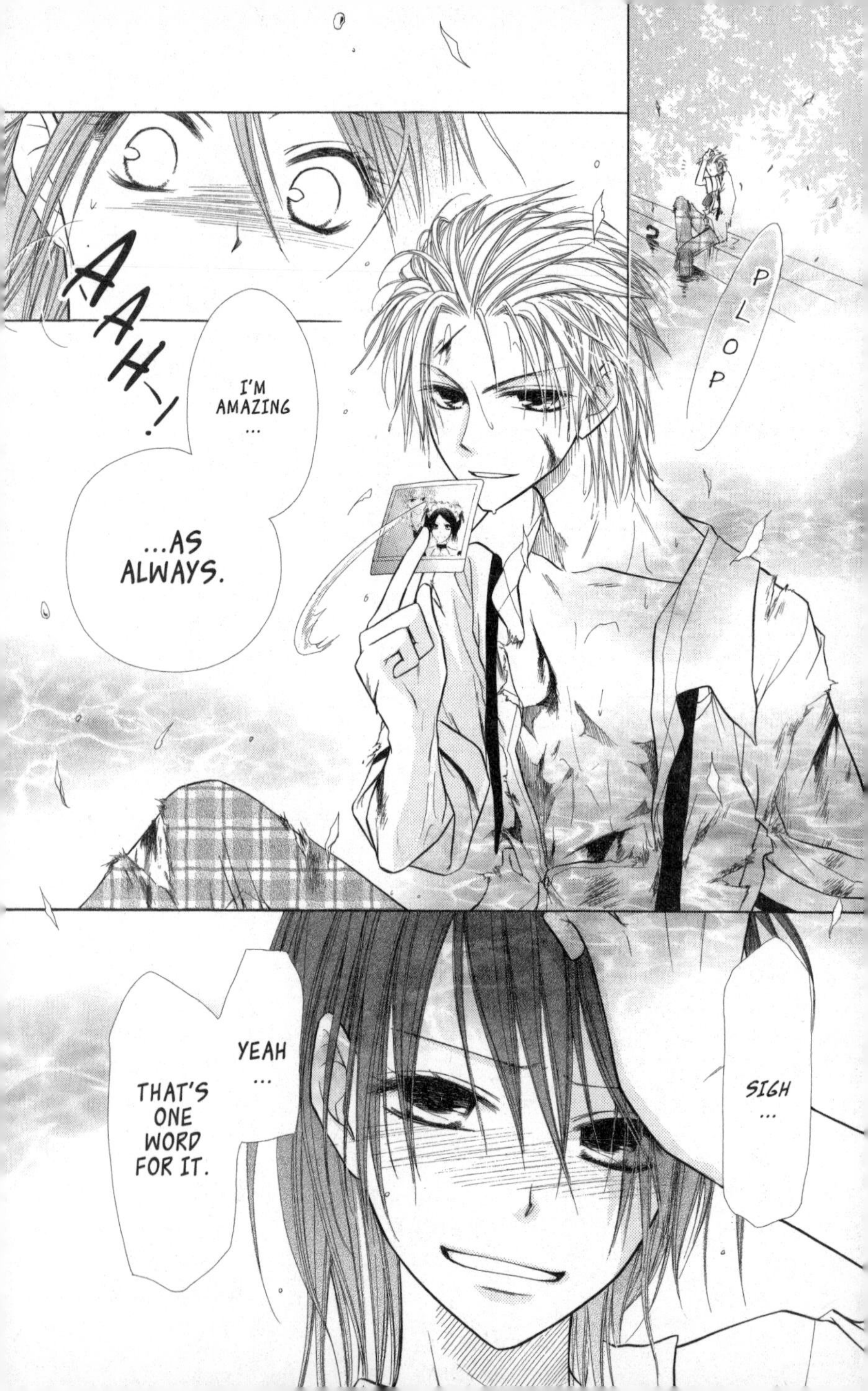
PLOP
AAAH-!
I'M AMAZING ...
...AS ALWAYS.
SIGH ...
YEAH ...
THAT'S ONE WORD FOR IT.

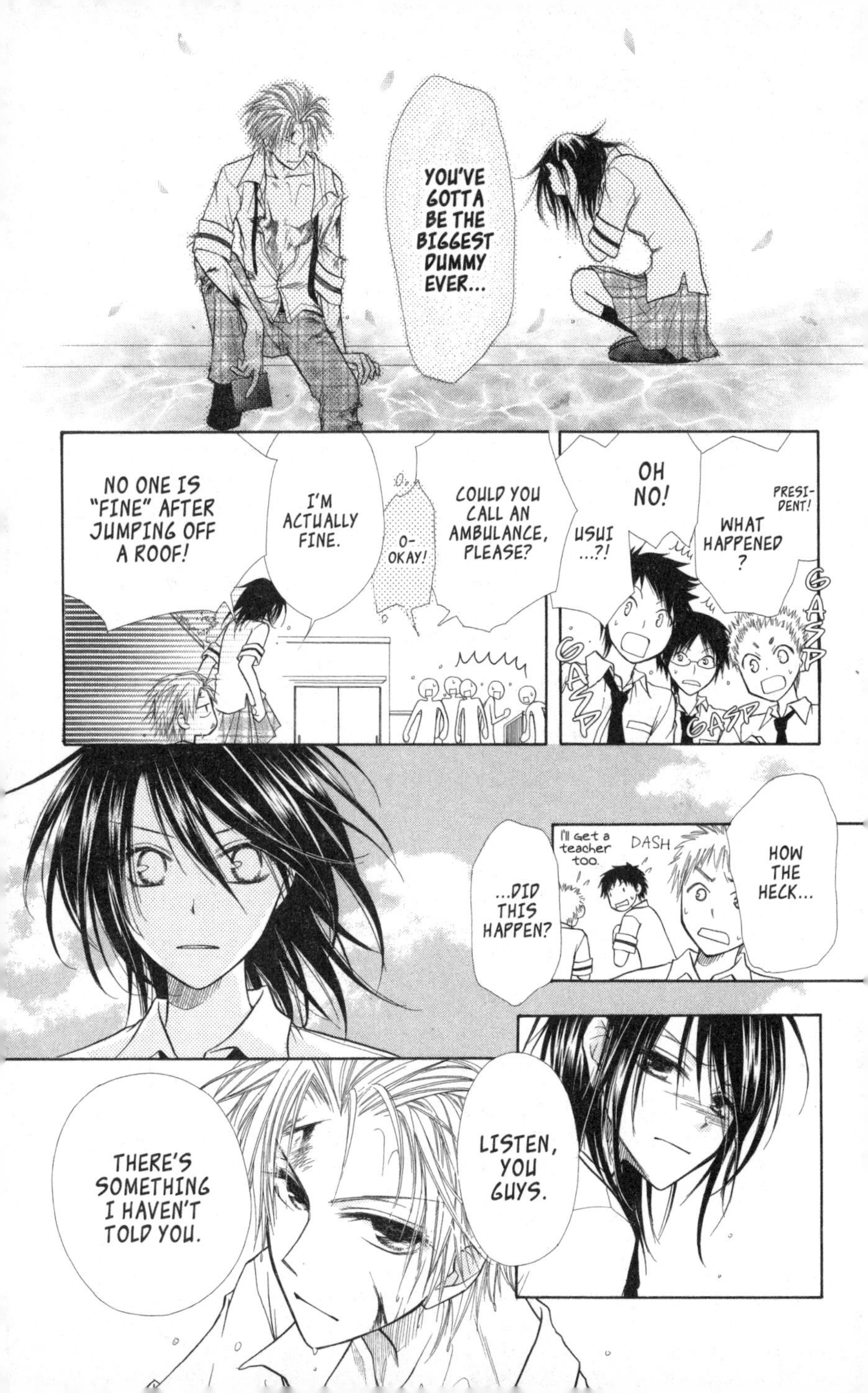
YOU'VE GOTTA BE THE BIGGEST DUMMY EVER...
PRESI-DENT!
OH NO!
WHAT HAPPENED?
USUI...?!
GASP
GASP
GASP
COULD YOU CALL AN AMBULANCE, PLEASE?
O-OKAY!
I'M ACTUALLY FINE.
NO ONE IS "FINE" AFTER JUMPING OFF A ROOF!
HOW THE HECK...
DASH
I'll get a teacher too.
...DID THIS HAPPEN?
LISTEN, YOU GUYS.
THERE'S SOMETHING I HAVEN'T TOLD YOU.

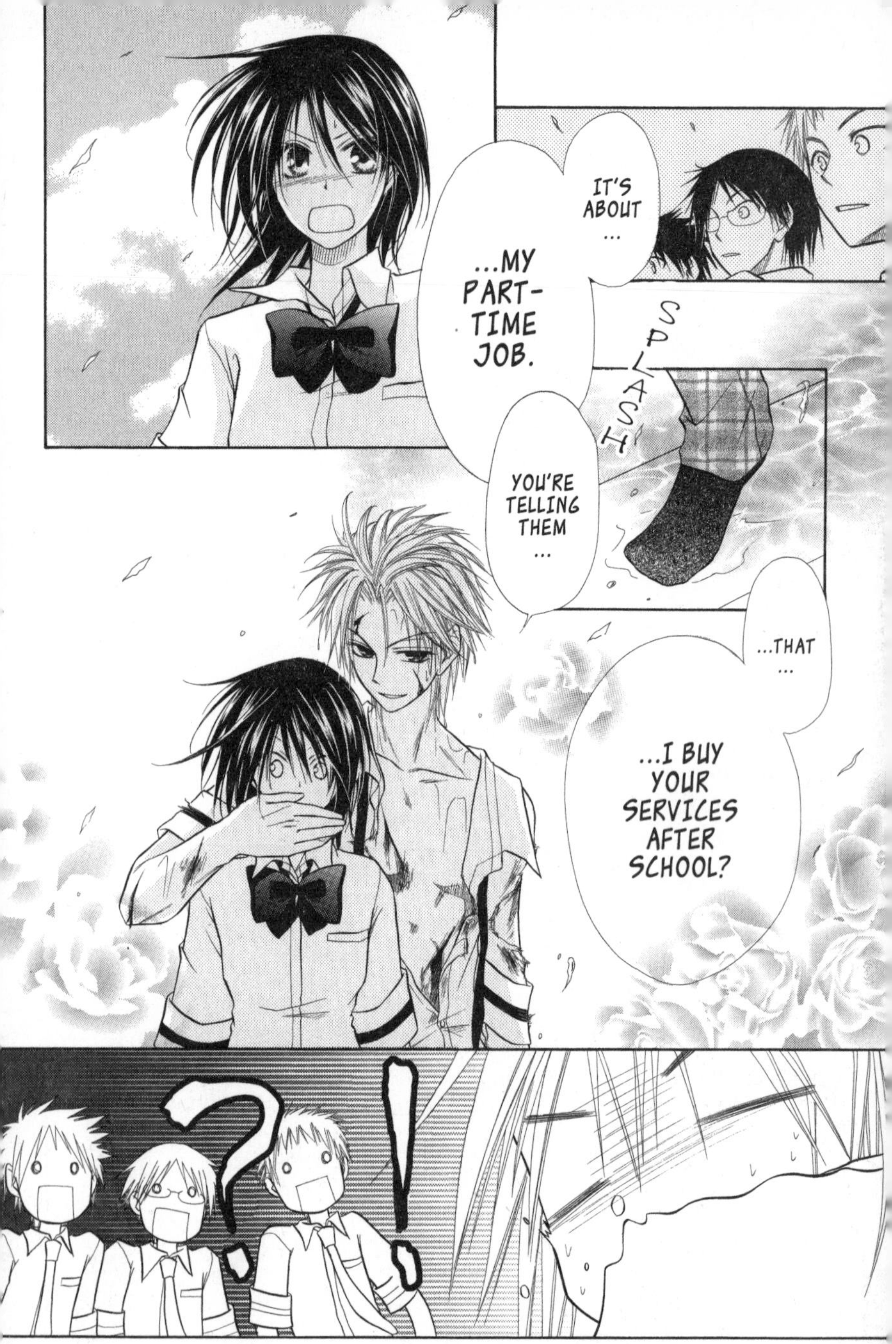
IT'S ABOUT ...
...MY PART-TIME JOB.
SPLASH
YOU'RE TELLING THEM ...
...THAT ...
...I BUY YOUR SERVICES AFTER SCHOOL?
?
!

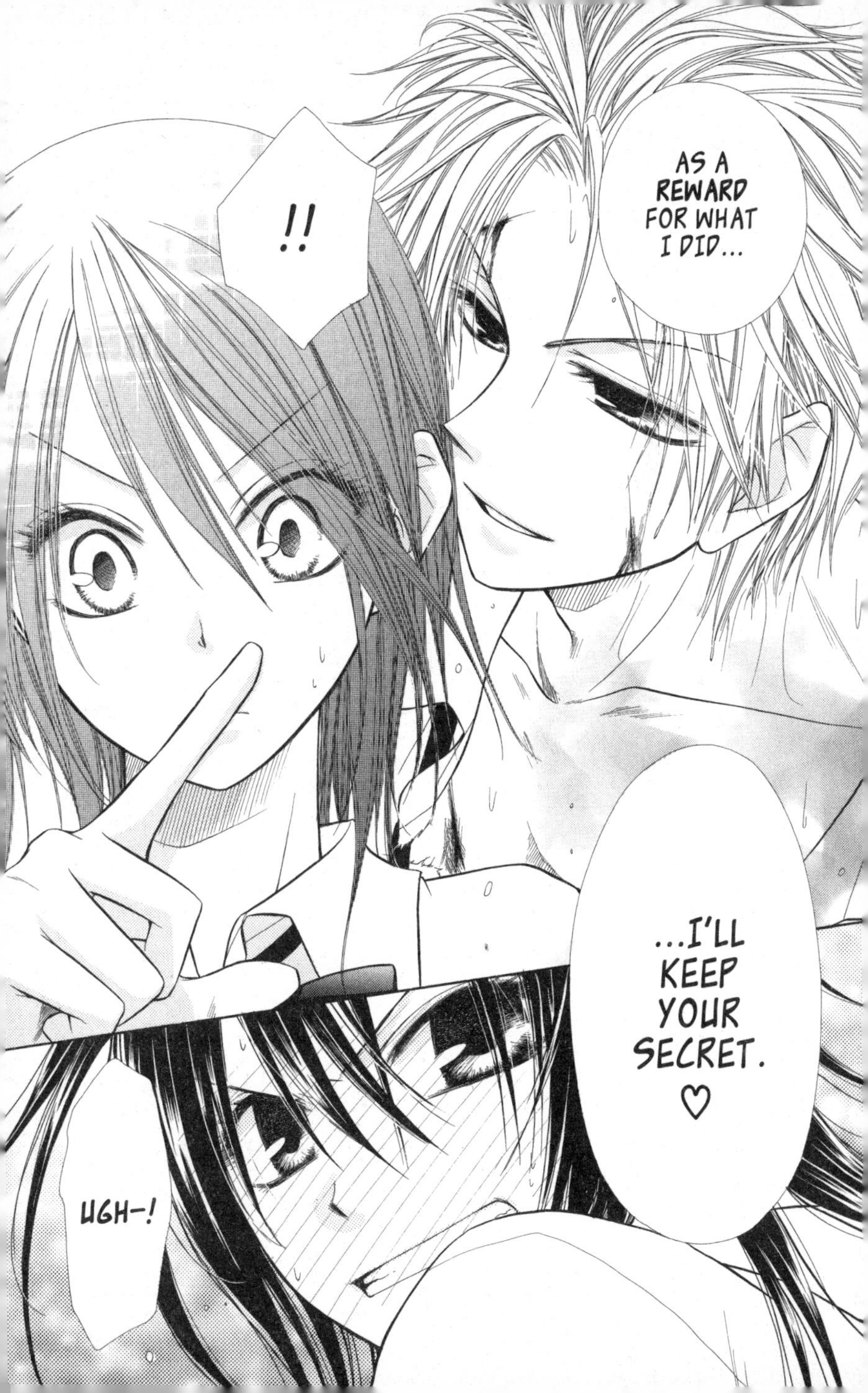
AS A REWARD FOR WHAT I DID...
!!
...I'LL KEEP YOUR SECRET. ♡
UGH-!

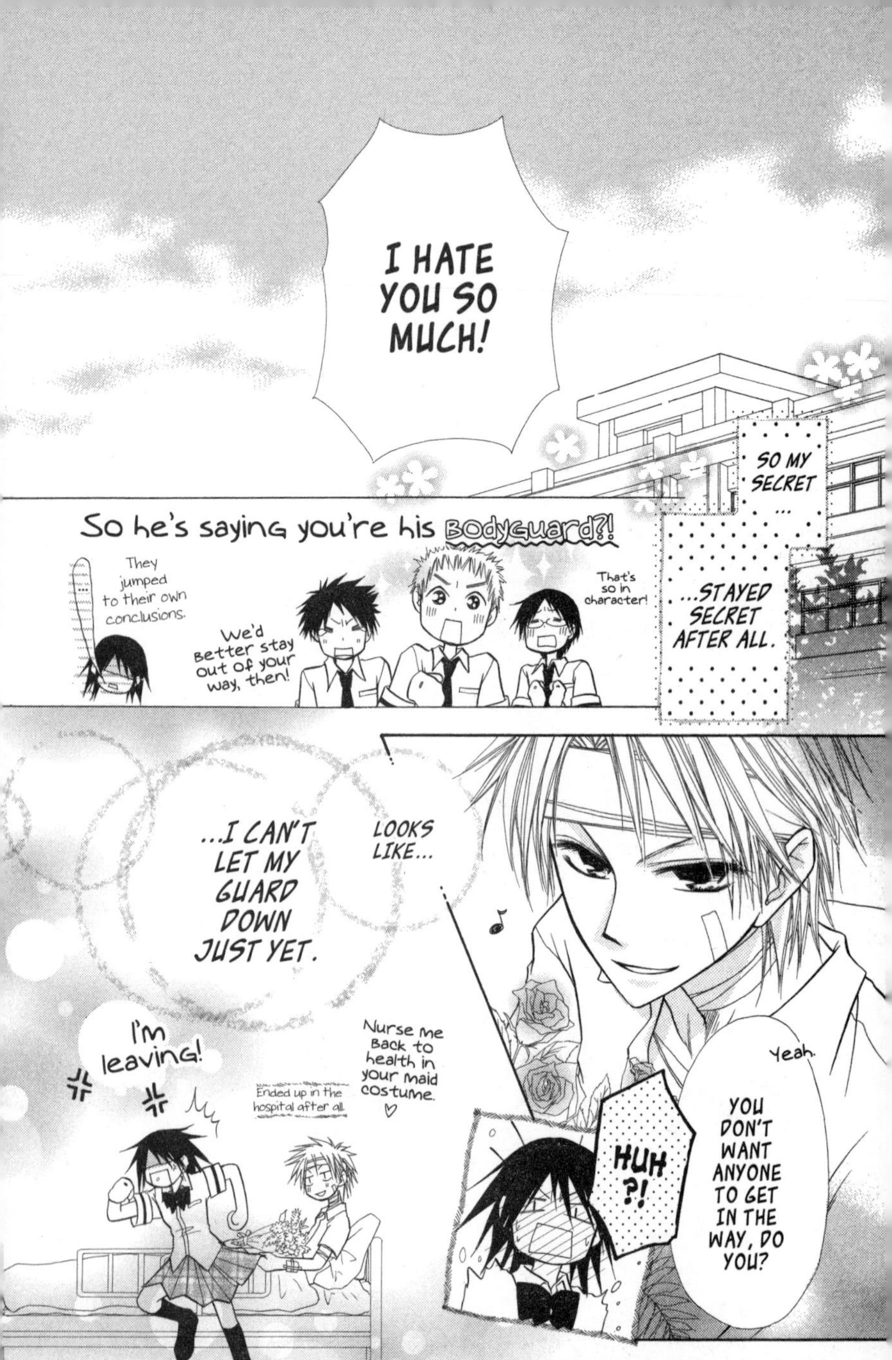

I HATE YOU SO MUCH!
SO MY SECRET ...
...STAYED SECRET AFTER ALL.
So he's saying you're his Bodyguard?!
That's so in character!
We'd better stay out of your way, then!
They jumped to their own conclusions.
LOOKS LIKE...
...I CAN'T LET MY GUARD DOWN JUST YET.
Yeah.
YOU DON'T WANT ANYONE TO GET IN THE WAY, DO YOU?
HUH?!
Nurse me back to health in your maid costume. ♡
Ended up in the hospital after all.
I'm leaving!

MAID-SAMA! ① / THE END

Tea break...

Their mental picture!

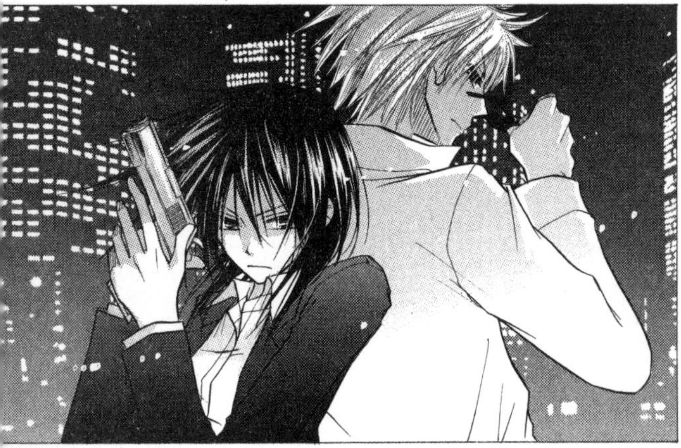

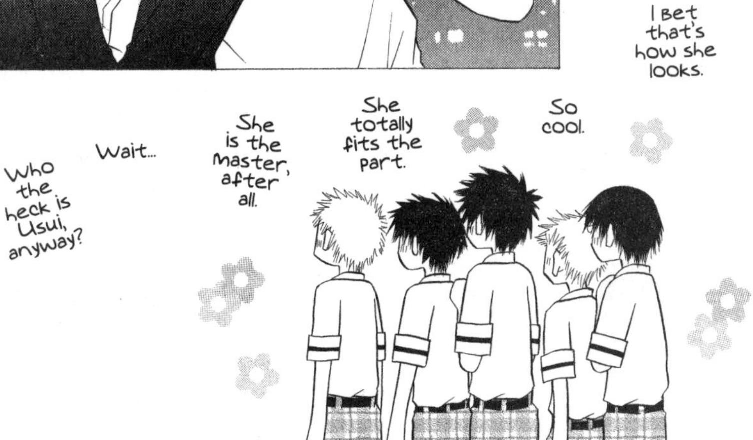
I bet that's how she looks.
So cool.
She totally fits the part.
She is the master, after all.
Wait...
Who the heck is Usui, anyway?

This next story is a one-shot manga story from before I wrote *Maid-sama*. With *Maid*, I kind of let loose and did whatever I wanted. So if you find the energy levels between the two stories quite different, well, there's your explanation!

But overall, this is a more subdued and gentle piece. I hope you can put yourself into that frame of mind and read it too.

Here's to subdued and gentle.

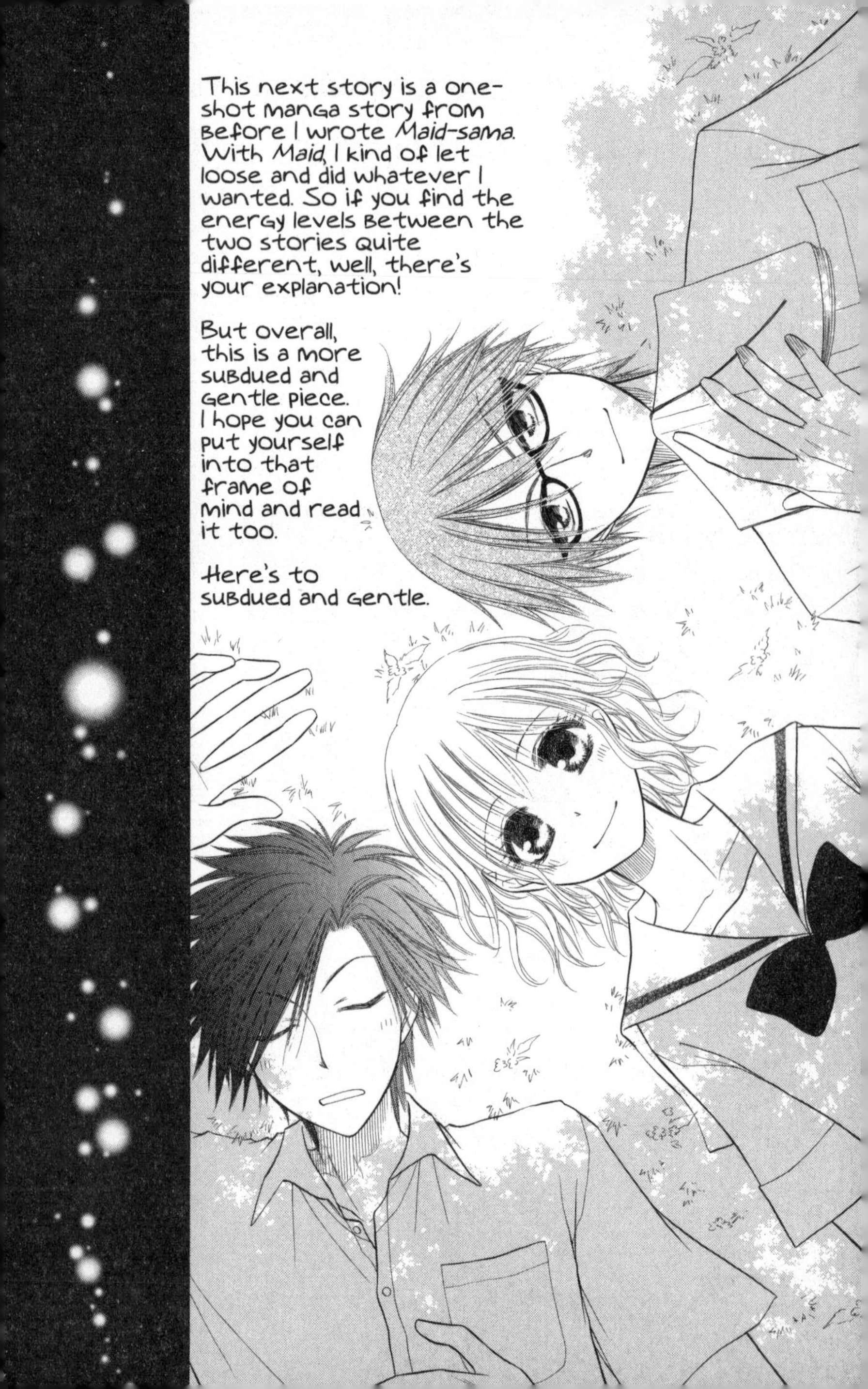

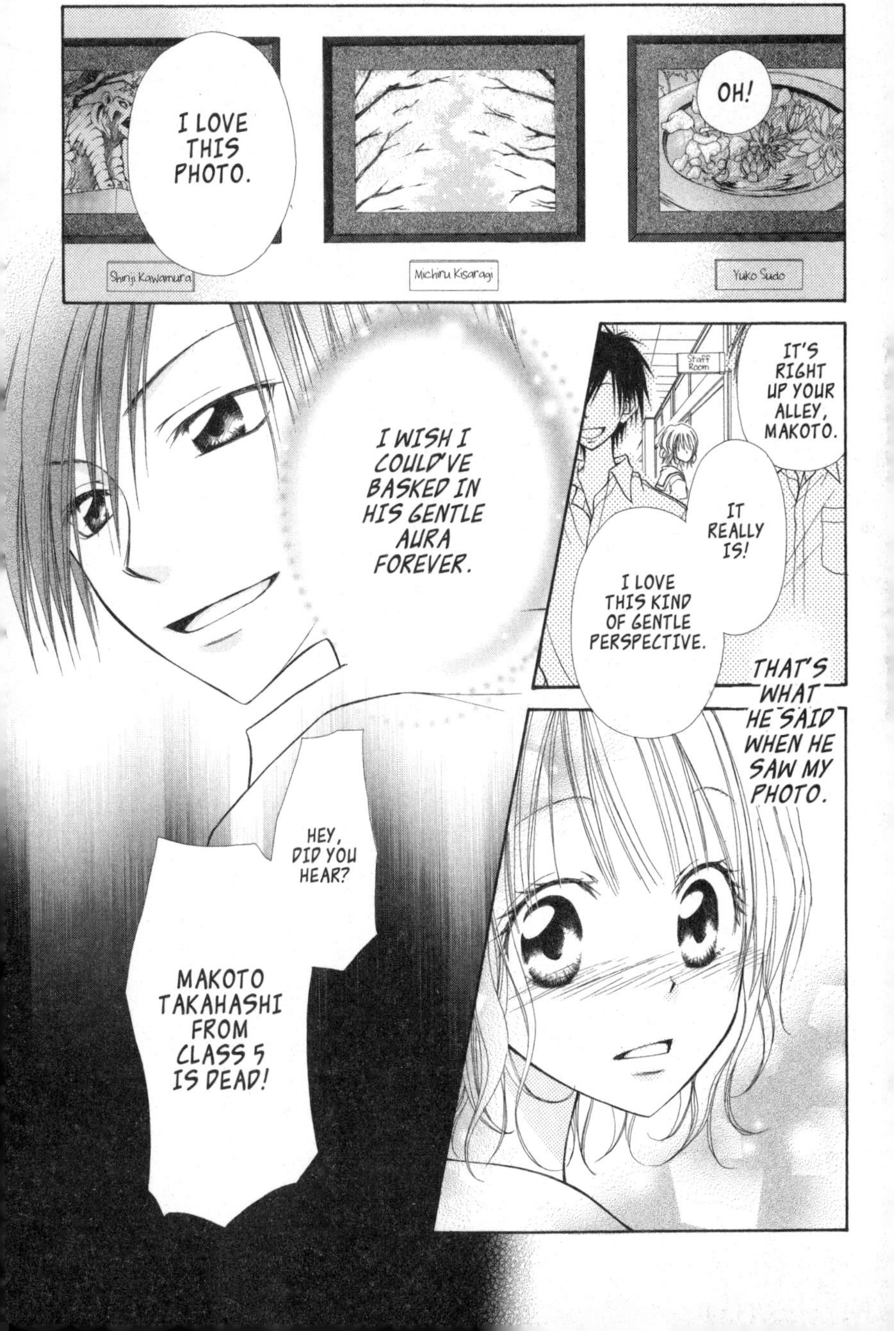
OH!
I LOVE THIS PHOTO.
Yuko Sudo
Michiru Kisaragi
Shinji Kawamura
IT'S RIGHT UP YOUR ALLEY, MAKOTO.
Staff Room
IT REALLY IS!
I LOVE THIS KIND OF GENTLE PERSPECTIVE.
THAT'S WHAT HE SAID WHEN HE SAW MY PHOTO.
I WISH I COULD'VE BASKED IN HIS GENTLE AURA FOREVER.
HEY, DID YOU HEAR?
MAKOTO TAKAHASHI FROM CLASS 5 IS DEAD!

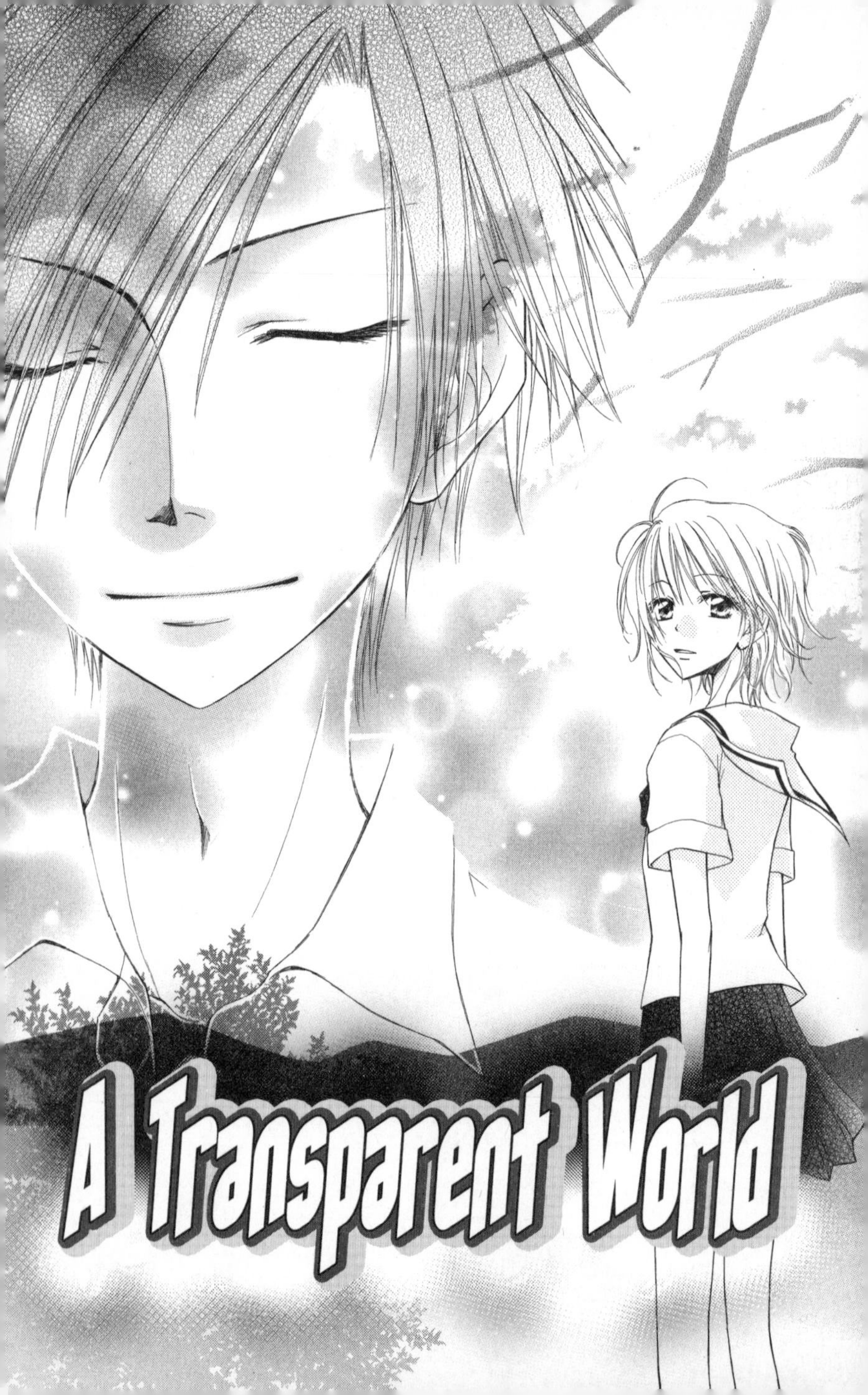
A Transparent World

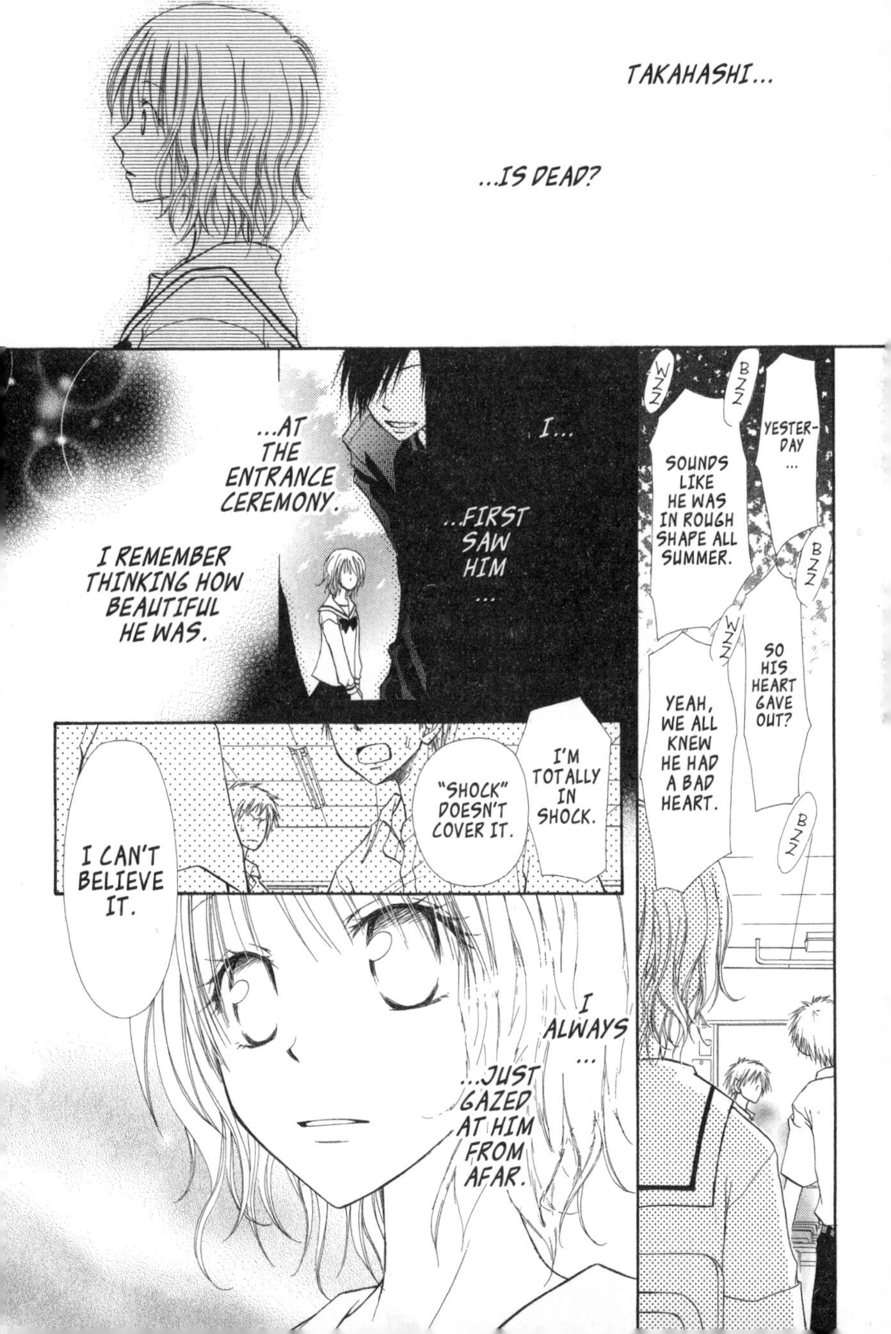
TAKAHASHI...
...IS DEAD?
BZZ
YESTER-DAY...
WZZ
SOUNDS LIKE HE WAS IN ROUGH SHAPE ALL SUMMER.
BZZ
SO HIS HEART GAVE OUT?
WZZ
YEAH, WE ALL KNEW HE HAD A BAD HEART.
BZZ
I...
...FIRST SAW HIM...
...AT THE ENTRANCE CEREMONY.
I REMEMBER THINKING HOW BEAUTIFUL HE WAS.
I'M TOTALLY IN SHOCK.
"SHOCK" DOESN'T COVER IT.
I CAN'T BELIEVE IT.
I ALWAYS...
...JUST GAZED AT HIM FROM AFAR.

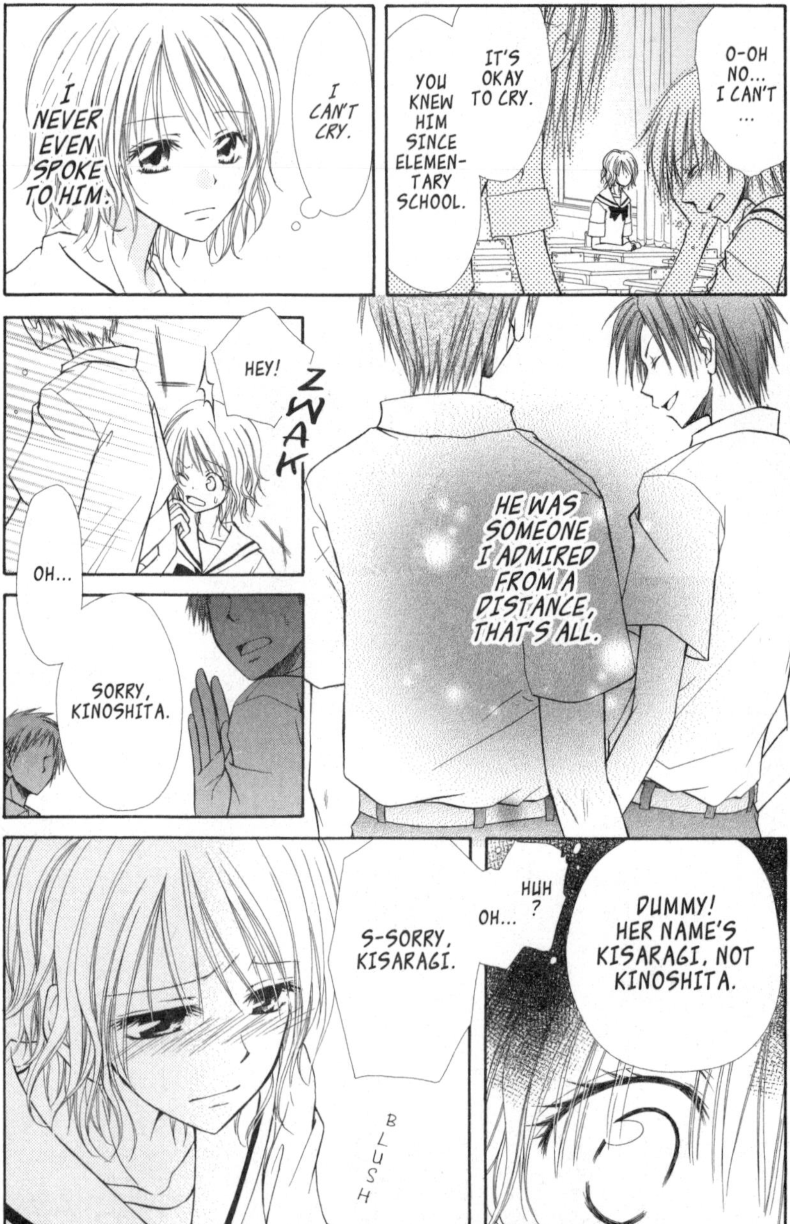
O-OH NO... I CAN'T...
IT'S OKAY TO CRY.
YOU KNEW HIM SINCE ELEMENTARY SCHOOL.
I CAN'T CRY.
I NEVER EVEN SPOKE TO HIM.
HE WAS SOMEONE I ADMIRED FROM A DISTANCE, THAT'S ALL.
HEY!
ZWAK
OH...
SORRY, KINOSHITA.
DUMMY! HER NAME'S KISARAGI, NOT KINOSHITA.
HUH?
OH...
S-SORRY, KISARAGI.
BLUSH

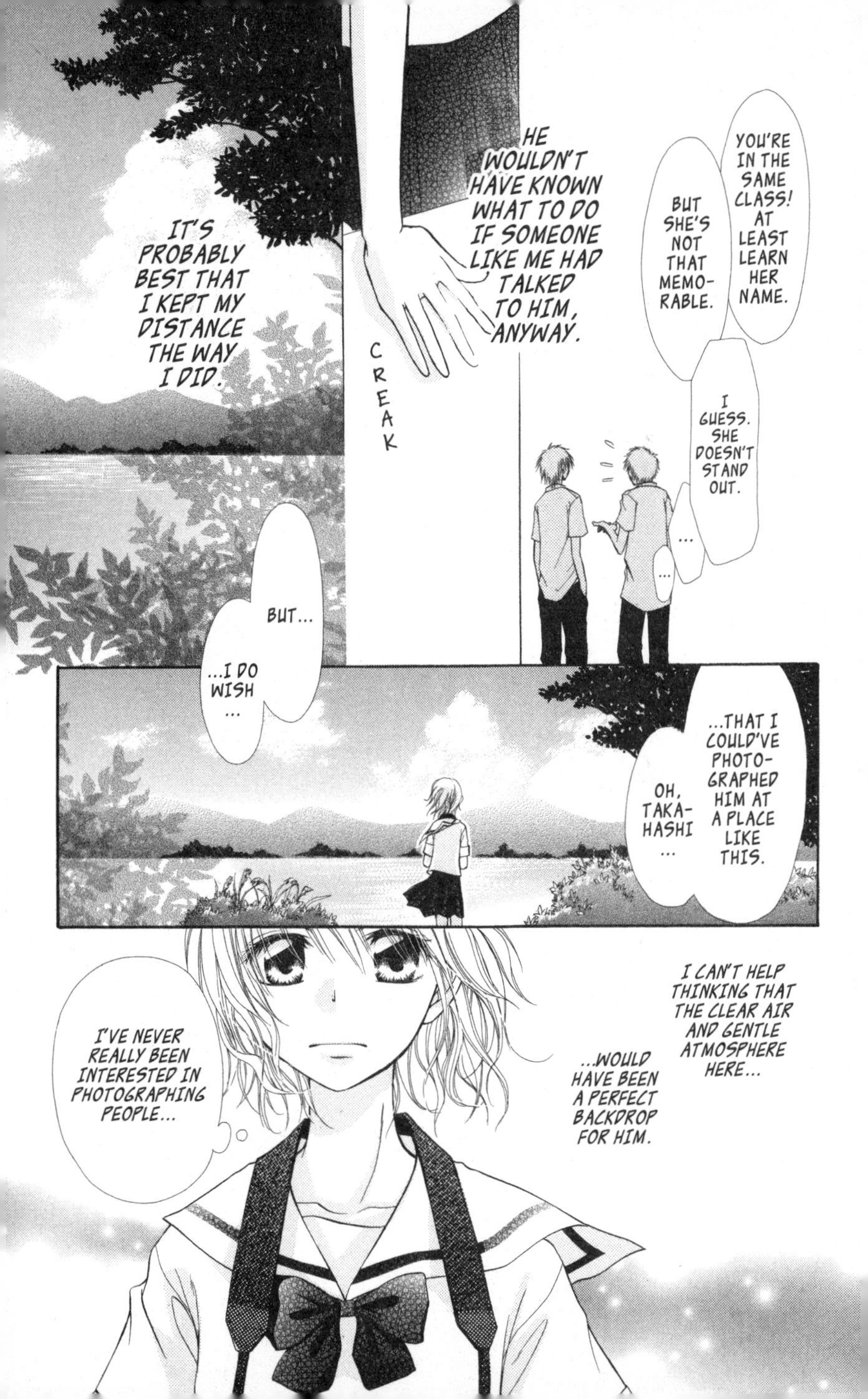
YOU'RE IN THE SAME CLASS! AT LEAST LEARN HER NAME.
BUT SHE'S NOT THAT MEMORABLE.
I GUESS. SHE DOESN'T STAND OUT.
...
...
HE WOULDN'T HAVE KNOWN WHAT TO DO IF SOMEONE LIKE ME HAD TALKED TO HIM, ANYWAY.
CREAK
IT'S PROBABLY BEST THAT I KEPT MY DISTANCE THE WAY I DID.
BUT...
...I DO WISH...
...THAT I COULD'VE PHOTOGRAPHED HIM AT A PLACE LIKE THIS.
OH, TAKAHASHI...
I CAN'T HELP THINKING THAT THE CLEAR AIR AND GENTLE ATMOSPHERE HERE...
...WOULD HAVE BEEN A PERFECT BACKDROP FOR HIM.
I'VE NEVER REALLY BEEN INTERESTED IN PHOTOGRAPHING PEOPLE...

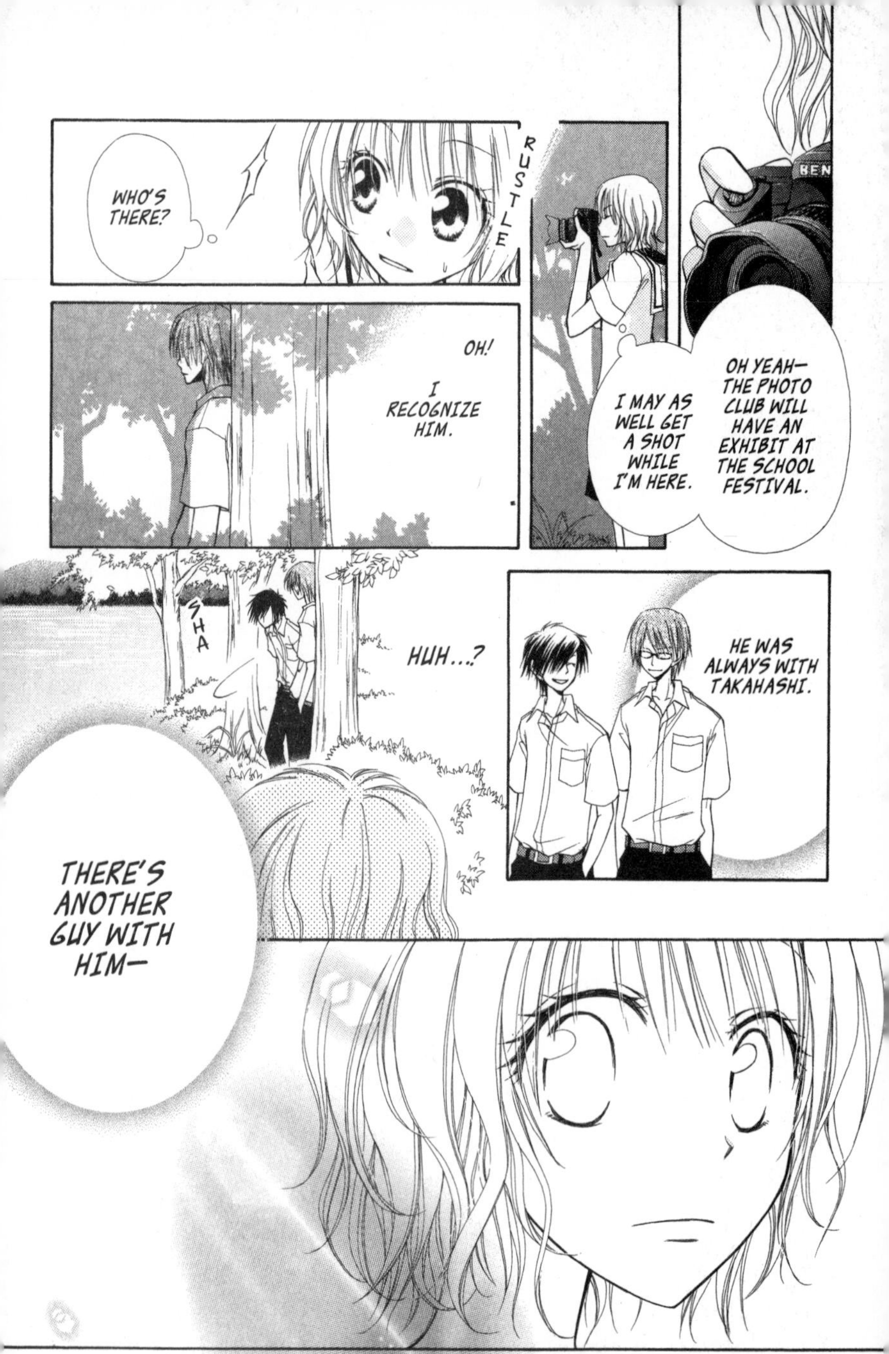
BEN
OH YEAH— THE PHOTO CLUB WILL HAVE AN EXHIBIT AT THE SCHOOL FESTIVAL.
I MAY AS WELL GET A SHOT WHILE I'M HERE.
RUSTLE
WHO'S THERE?
OH!
I RECOGNIZE HIM.
HE WAS ALWAYS WITH TAKAHASHI.
HUH...?
SHA
THERE'S ANOTHER GUY WITH HIM—

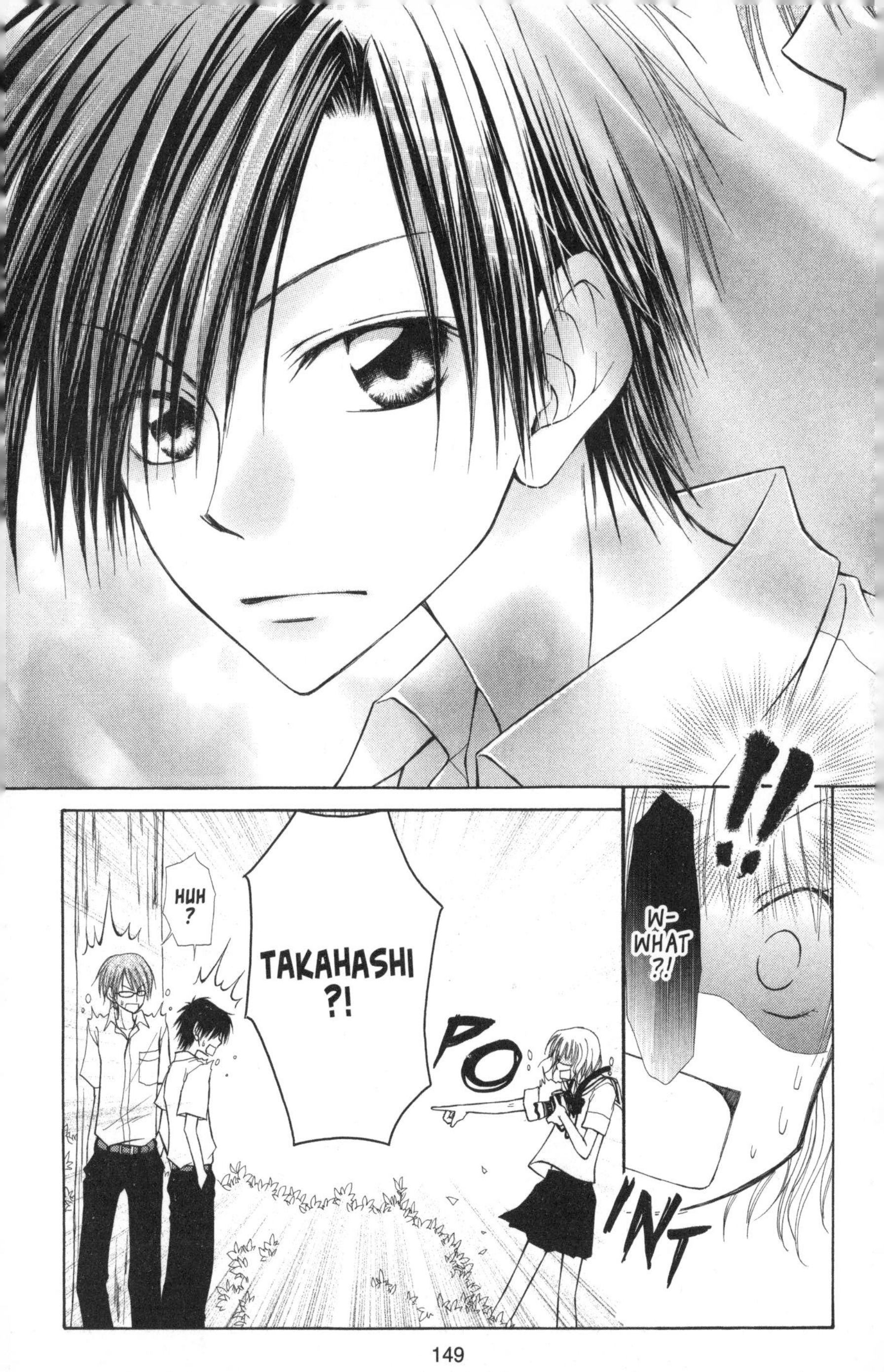
!!
W-WHAT?!
TAKAHASHI?!
HUH?
POINT

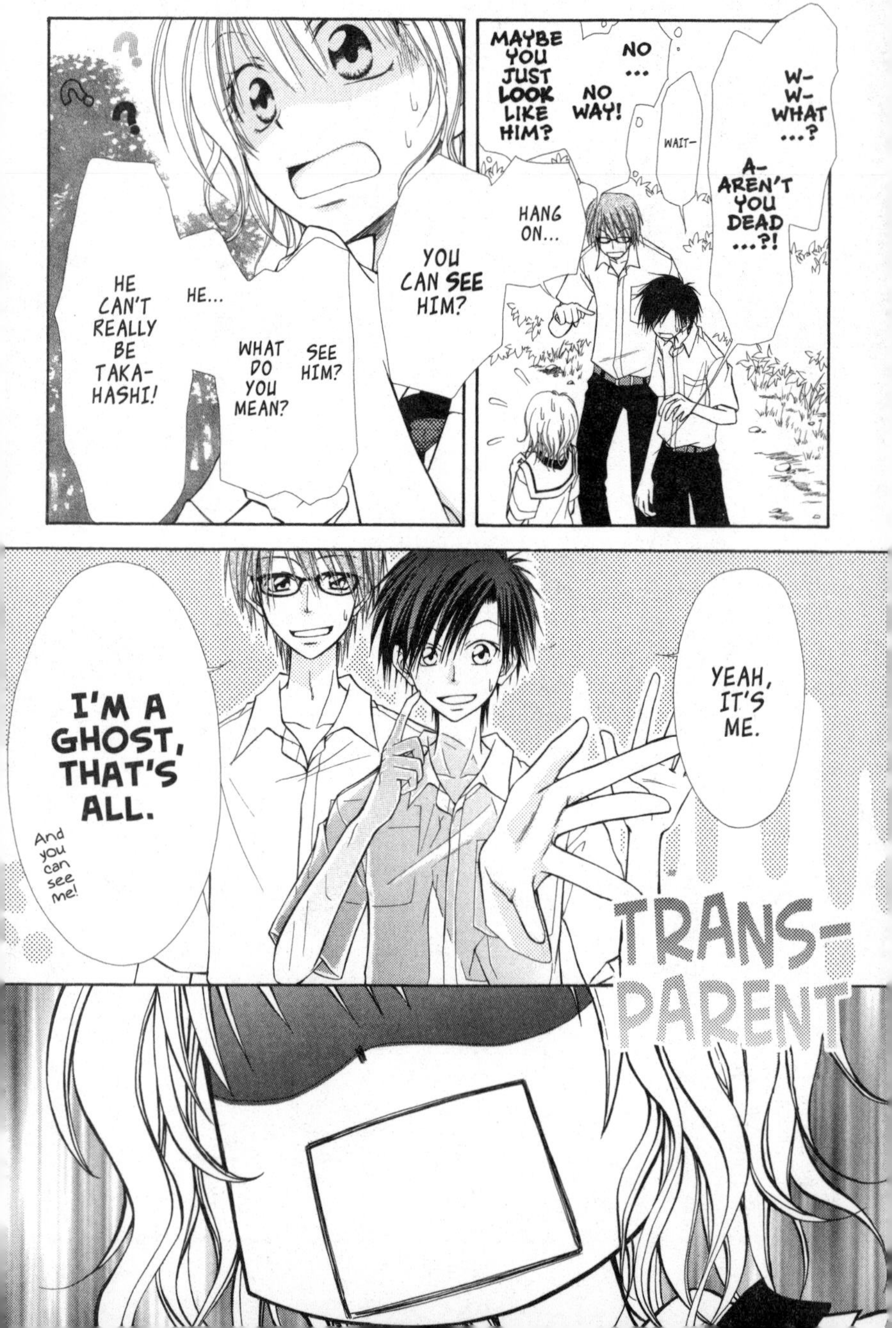
W-W-WHAT...?
A-AREN'T YOU DEAD...?!
WAIT—
NO...
NO WAY!
MAYBE YOU JUST LOOK LIKE HIM?
HANG ON...
YOU CAN SEE HIM?
SEE HIM?
WHAT DO YOU MEAN?
HE...
HE CAN'T REALLY BE TAKA-HASHI!
YEAH, IT'S ME.
I'M A GHOST, THAT'S ALL.
And you can see me!
TRANS-PARENT

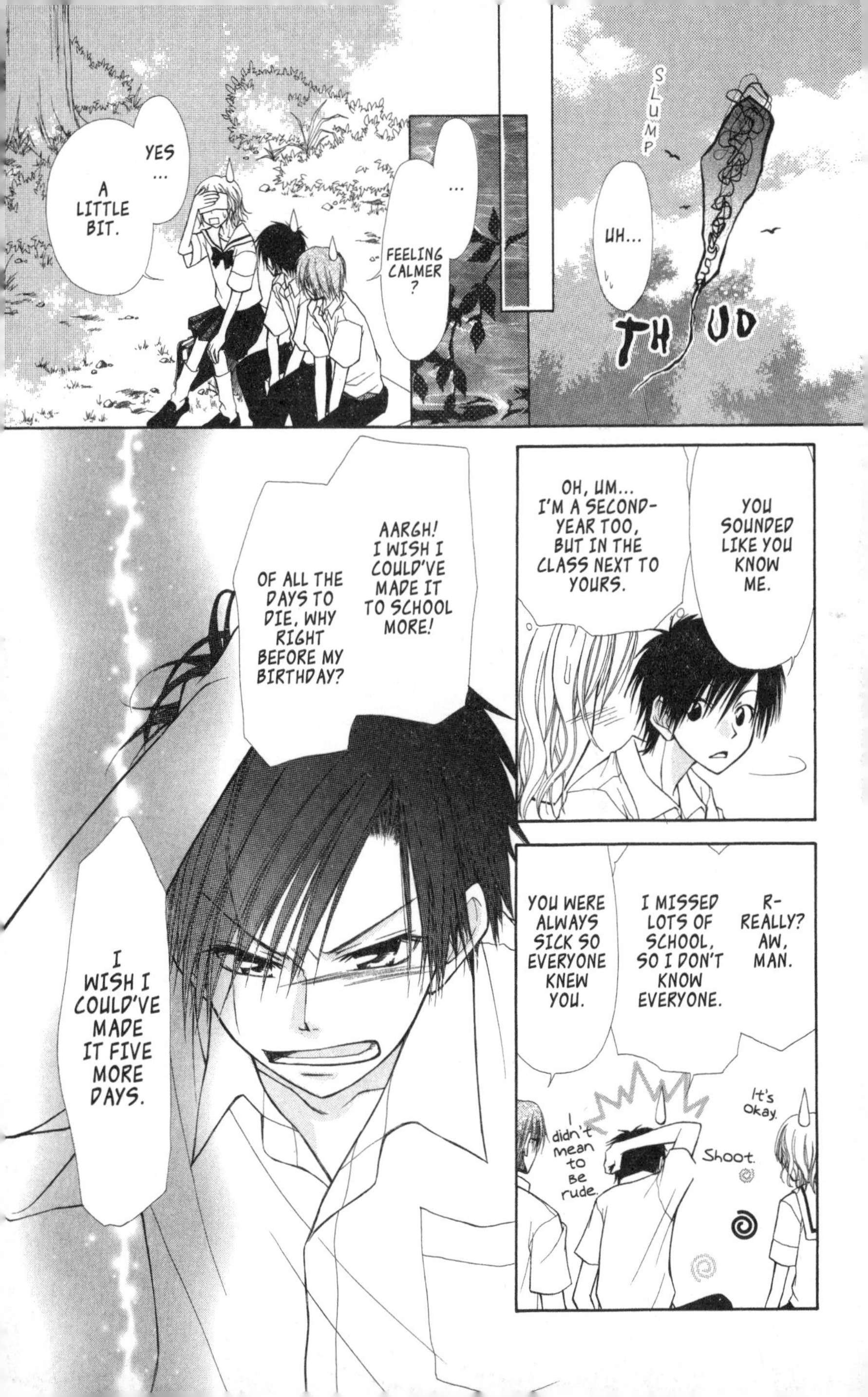
SLUMP
UH...
THUD
...
FEELING CALMER?
YES... A LITTLE BIT.
YOU SOUNDED LIKE YOU KNOW ME.
OH, UM... I'M A SECOND-YEAR TOO, BUT IN THE CLASS NEXT TO YOURS.
R-REALLY? AW, MAN.
I MISSED LOTS OF SCHOOL, SO I DON'T KNOW EVERYONE.
YOU WERE ALWAYS SICK SO EVERYONE KNEW YOU.
It's okay.
Shoot.
I didn't mean to be rude.
AARGH! I WISH I COULD'VE MADE IT TO SCHOOL MORE!
OF ALL THE DAYS TO DIE, WHY RIGHT BEFORE MY BIRTHDAY?
I WISH I COULD'VE MADE IT FIVE MORE DAYS.

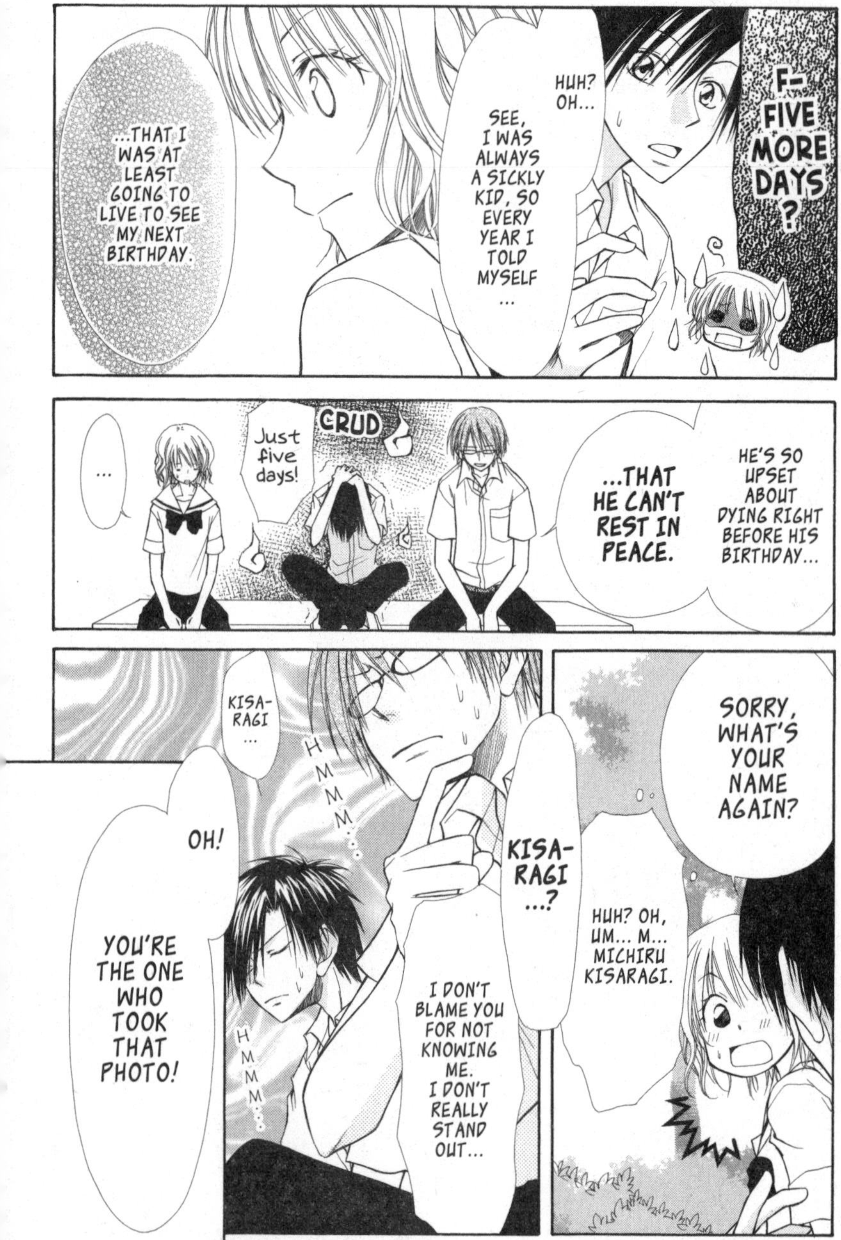
F- FIVE MORE DAYS?
HUH? OH...
SEE, I WAS ALWAYS A SICKLY KID, SO EVERY YEAR I TOLD MYSELF ...
...THAT I WAS AT LEAST GOING TO LIVE TO SEE MY NEXT BIRTHDAY.
HE'S SO UPSET ABOUT DYING RIGHT BEFORE HIS BIRTHDAY...
...THAT HE CAN'T REST IN PEACE.
CRUD
Just five days!
...
SORRY, WHAT'S YOUR NAME AGAIN?
HUH? OH, UM... M... MICHIRU KISARAGI.
KISARAGI ...
HMMM...
KISA-RAGI ...?
I DON'T BLAME YOU FOR NOT KNOWING ME. I DON'T REALLY STAND OUT...
HMMM...
OH!
YOU'RE THE ONE WHO TOOK THAT PHOTO!

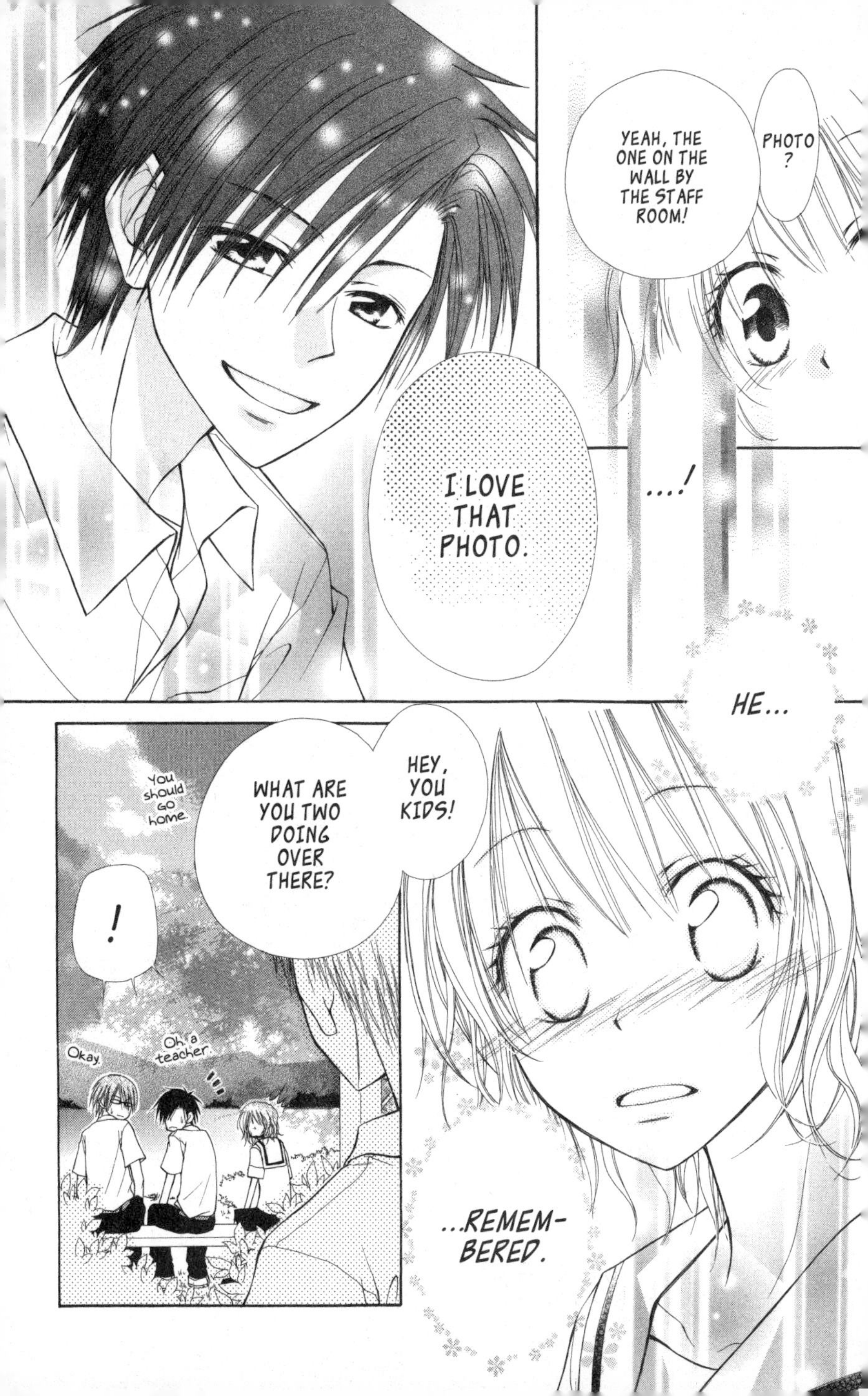
PHOTO?
YEAH, THE ONE ON THE WALL BY THE STAFF ROOM!
...!
I LOVE THAT PHOTO.
HE...
...REMEM-BERED.
HEY, YOU KIDS!
WHAT ARE YOU TWO DOING OVER THERE?
You should go home.
!
Oh a teacher.
Okay.

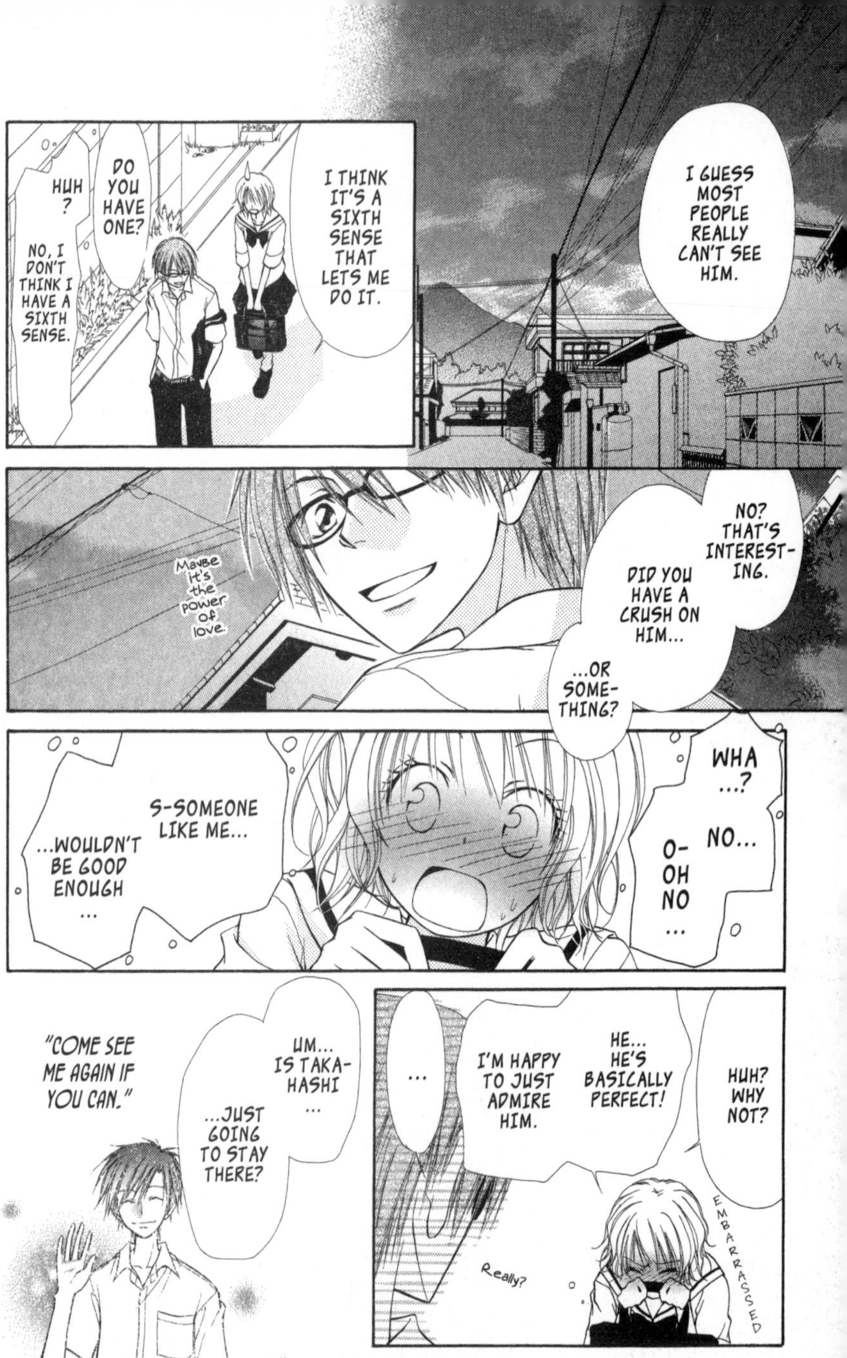
I GUESS MOST PEOPLE REALLY CAN'T SEE HIM.
I THINK IT'S A SIXTH SENSE THAT LETS ME DO IT.
DO YOU HAVE ONE?
HUH?
NO, I DON'T THINK I HAVE A SIXTH SENSE.
NO? THAT'S INTEREST-ING.
DID YOU HAVE A CRUSH ON HIM...
...OR SOME-THING?
Maybe it's the power of love.
WHA...?
NO...
O-OH NO...
S-SOMEONE LIKE ME...
...WOULDN'T BE GOOD ENOUGH...
HUH? WHY NOT?
HE... HE'S BASICALLY PERFECT!
I'M HAPPY TO JUST ADMIRE HIM.
...
EMBARRASSED
Really?
UM... IS TAKA-HASHI...
...JUST GOING TO STAY THERE?
"COME SEE ME AGAIN IF YOU CAN."

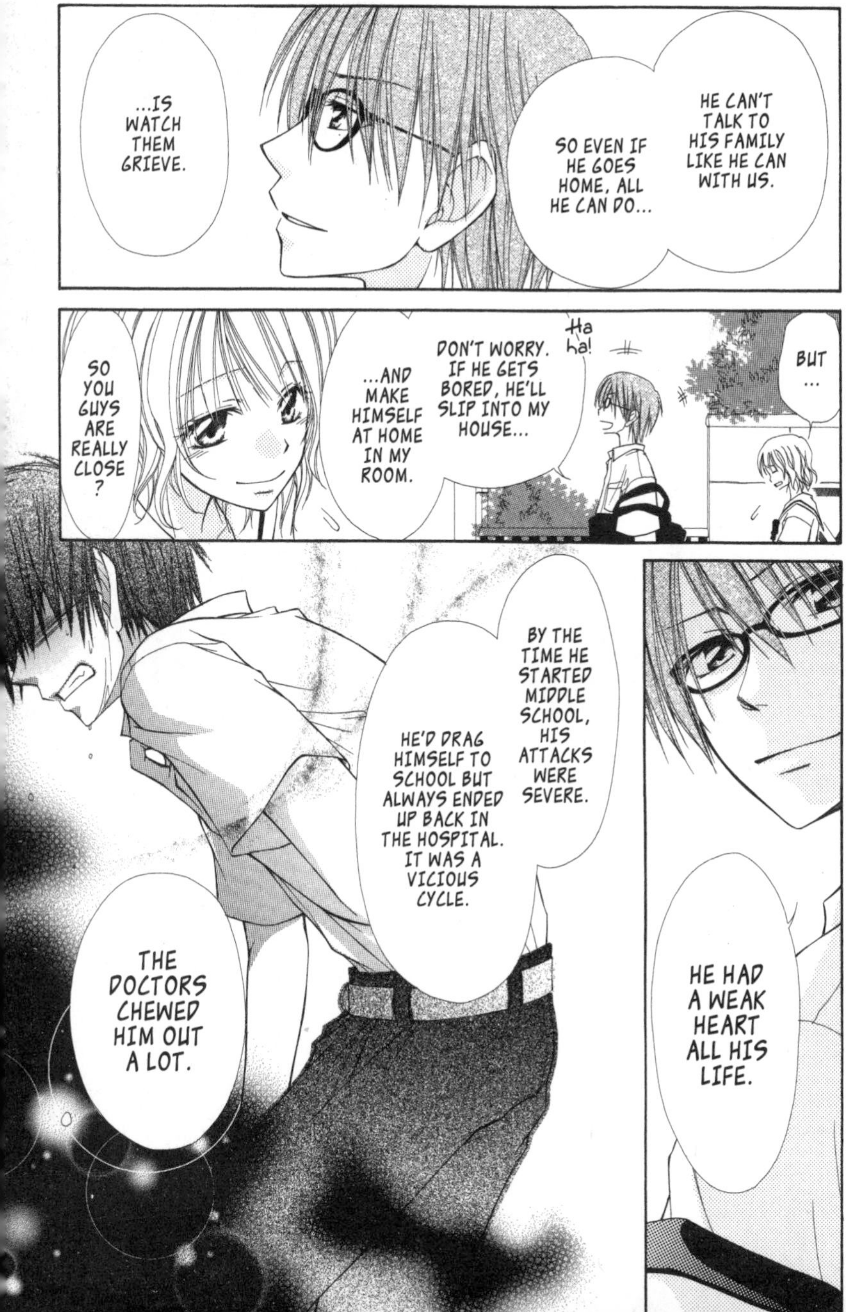
HE CAN'T TALK TO HIS FAMILY LIKE HE CAN WITH US.
SO EVEN IF HE GOES HOME, ALL HE CAN DO...
...IS WATCH THEM GRIEVE.
BUT ...
Ha ha!
DON'T WORRY. IF HE GETS BORED, HE'LL SLIP INTO MY HOUSE...
...AND MAKE HIMSELF AT HOME IN MY ROOM.
SO YOU GUYS ARE REALLY CLOSE?
HE HAD A WEAK HEART ALL HIS LIFE.
BY THE TIME HE STARTED MIDDLE SCHOOL, HIS ATTACKS WERE SEVERE.
HE'D DRAG HIMSELF TO SCHOOL BUT ALWAYS ENDED UP BACK IN THE HOSPITAL. IT WAS A VICIOUS CYCLE.
THE DOCTORS CHEWED HIM OUT A LOT.

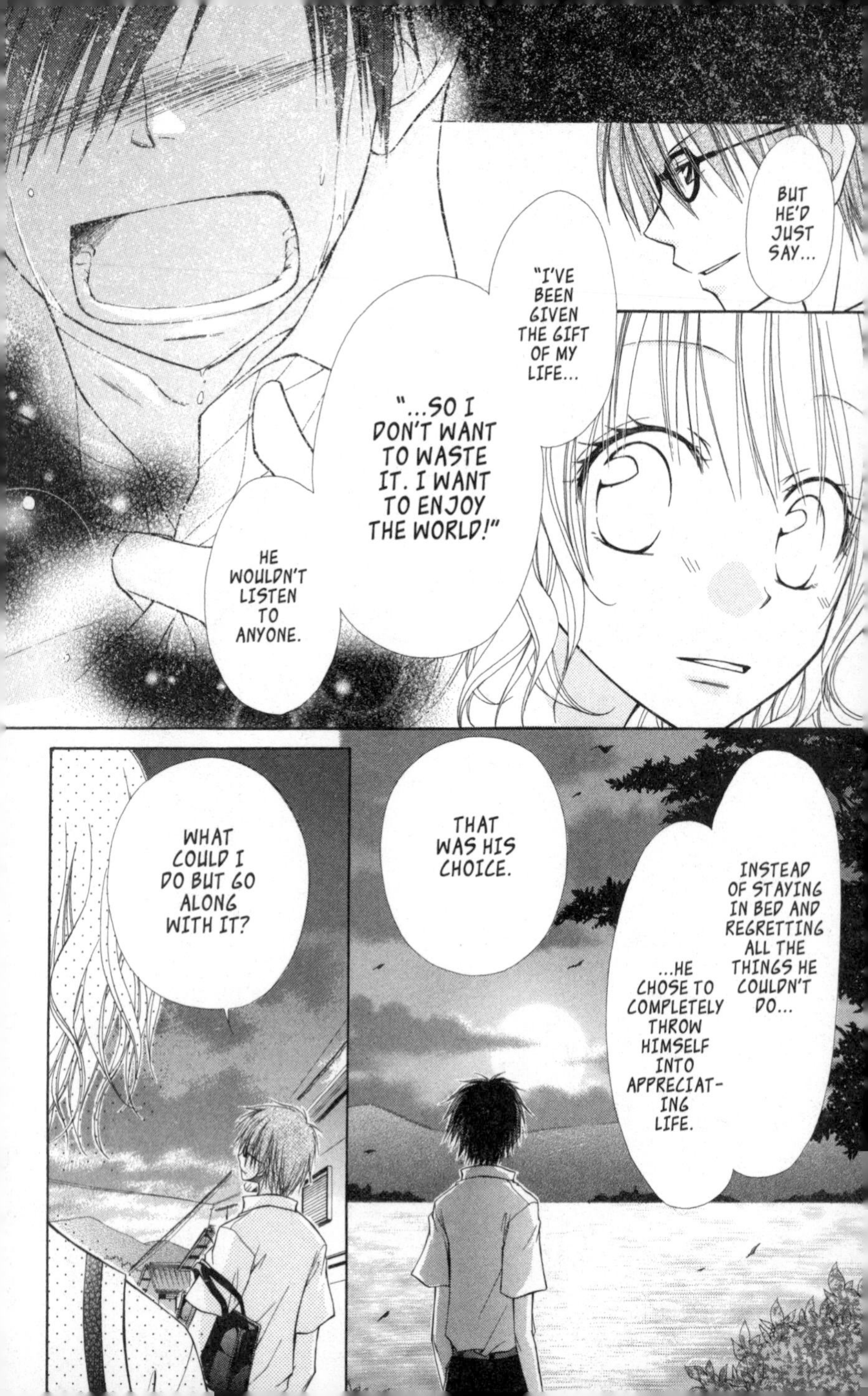
BUT HE'D JUST SAY...
"I'VE BEEN GIVEN THE GIFT OF MY LIFE...
"...SO I DON'T WANT TO WASTE IT. I WANT TO ENJOY THE WORLD!"
HE WOULDN'T LISTEN TO ANYONE.
INSTEAD OF STAYING IN BED AND REGRETTING ALL THE THINGS HE COULDN'T DO...
...HE CHOSE TO COMPLETELY THROW HIMSELF INTO APPRECIAT-ING LIFE.
THAT WAS HIS CHOICE.
WHAT COULD I DO BUT GO ALONG WITH IT?

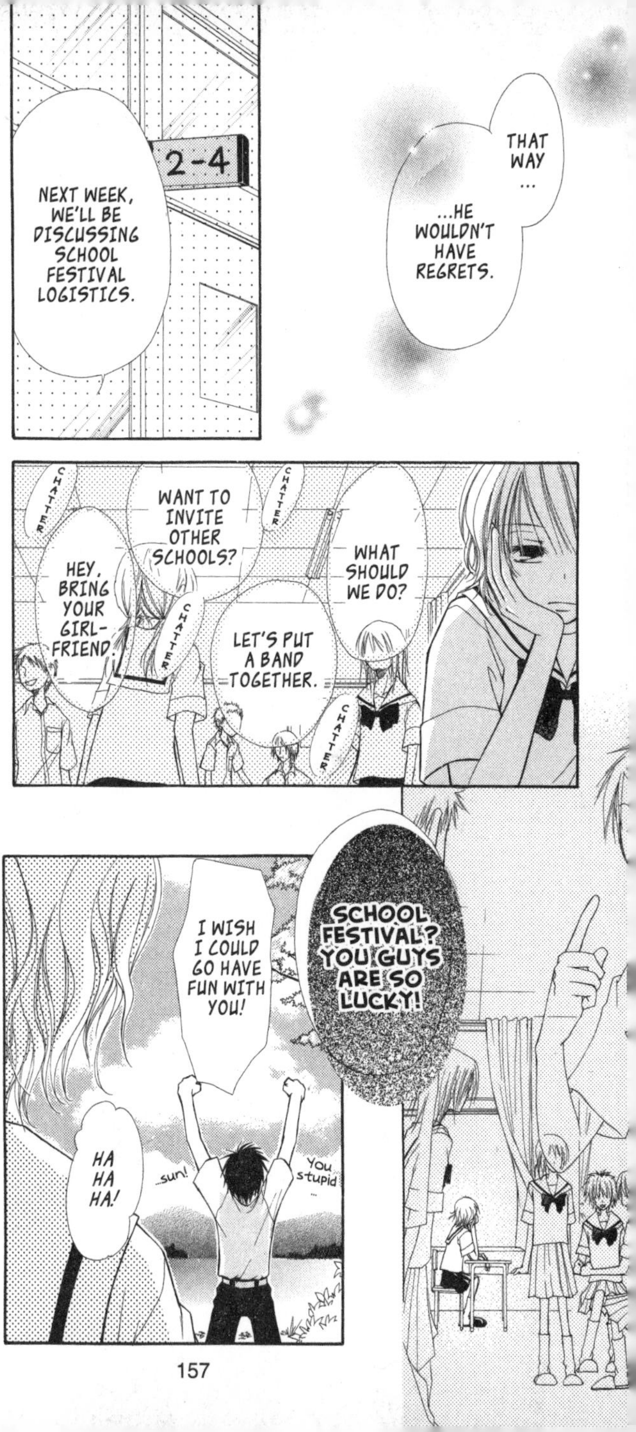
THAT WAY ...
...HE WOULDN'T HAVE REGRETS.
NEXT WEEK, WE'LL BE DISCUSSING SCHOOL FESTIVAL LOGISTICS.
2-4
CHATTER
WHAT SHOULD WE DO?
CHATTER
WANT TO INVITE OTHER SCHOOLS?
LET'S PUT A BAND TOGETHER.
CHATTER
CHATTER
HEY, BRING YOUR GIRL-FRIEND.
SCHOOL FESTIVAL? YOU GUYS ARE SO LUCKY!
I WISH I COULD GO HAVE FUN WITH YOU!
You stupid ...
...sun!
HA HA HA!

Finally, let's introduce the author!

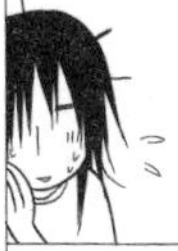

Hiro Fujiwara

Sex: Female

Blood type: B

Birthday: December 23

Birthplace: Hyogo Prefecture

• Most-asked question •

"What made you decide to be a manga artist?"

As long as I can remember, that was my dream. The first time I ever wrote a decent piece of manga was in 8th grade.

My love for drawing manga is the only reason I've made it this far.

———————

I'm so grateful for the support of the people around me. Without them, I'd never have made it to where I am today.

Thank you so much to everyone who encourages me, sends letters, helps me and pushes me to keep going.

With your encouragement, I'll keep working hard!

Yay!

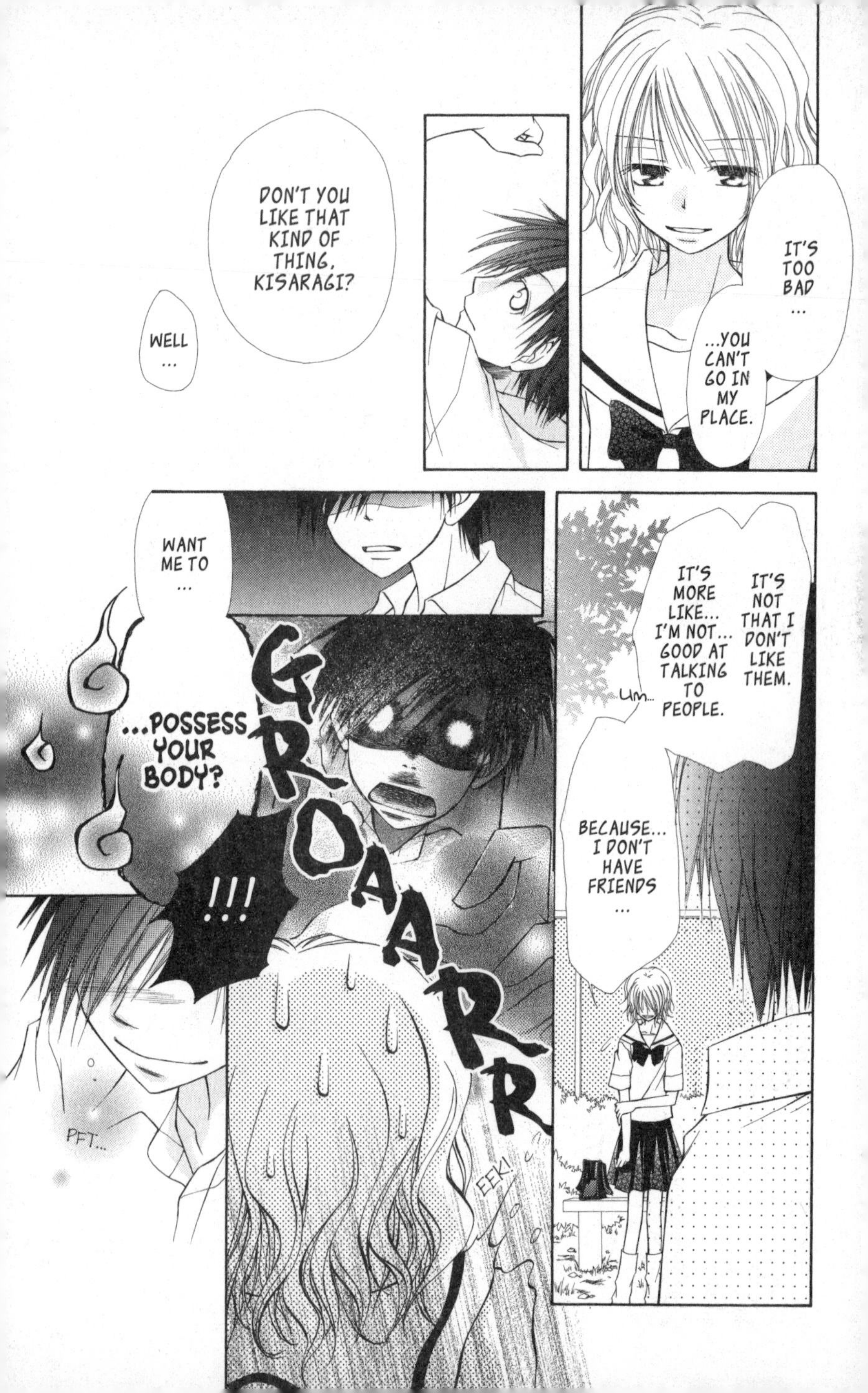
IT'S TOO BAD ...
...YOU CAN'T GO IN MY PLACE.
DON'T YOU LIKE THAT KIND OF THING, KISARAGI?
WELL ...
IT'S NOT THAT I DON'T LIKE THEM.
IT'S MORE LIKE... I'M NOT... GOOD AT TALKING TO PEOPLE.
Um...
BECAUSE... I DON'T HAVE FRIENDS ...
WANT ME TO ...
...POSSESS YOUR BODY?
GROAARR
!!!
EEK!
PFT...

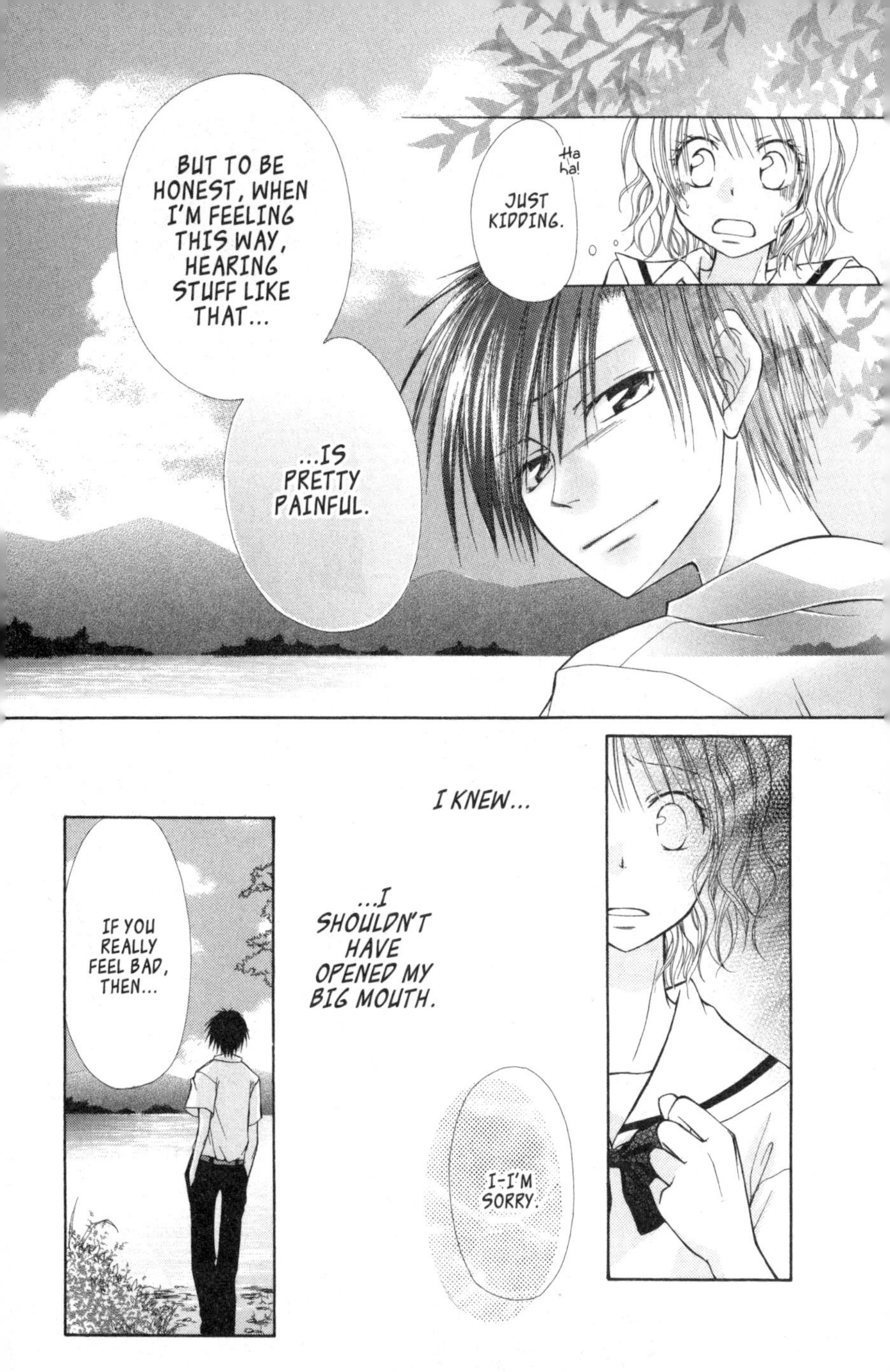
Ha ha!
JUST KIDDING.
BUT TO BE HONEST, WHEN I'M FEELING THIS WAY, HEARING STUFF LIKE THAT...
...IS PRETTY PAINFUL.
I KNEW...
...I SHOULDN'T HAVE OPENED MY BIG MOUTH.
I-I'M SORRY.
IF YOU REALLY FEEL BAD, THEN...

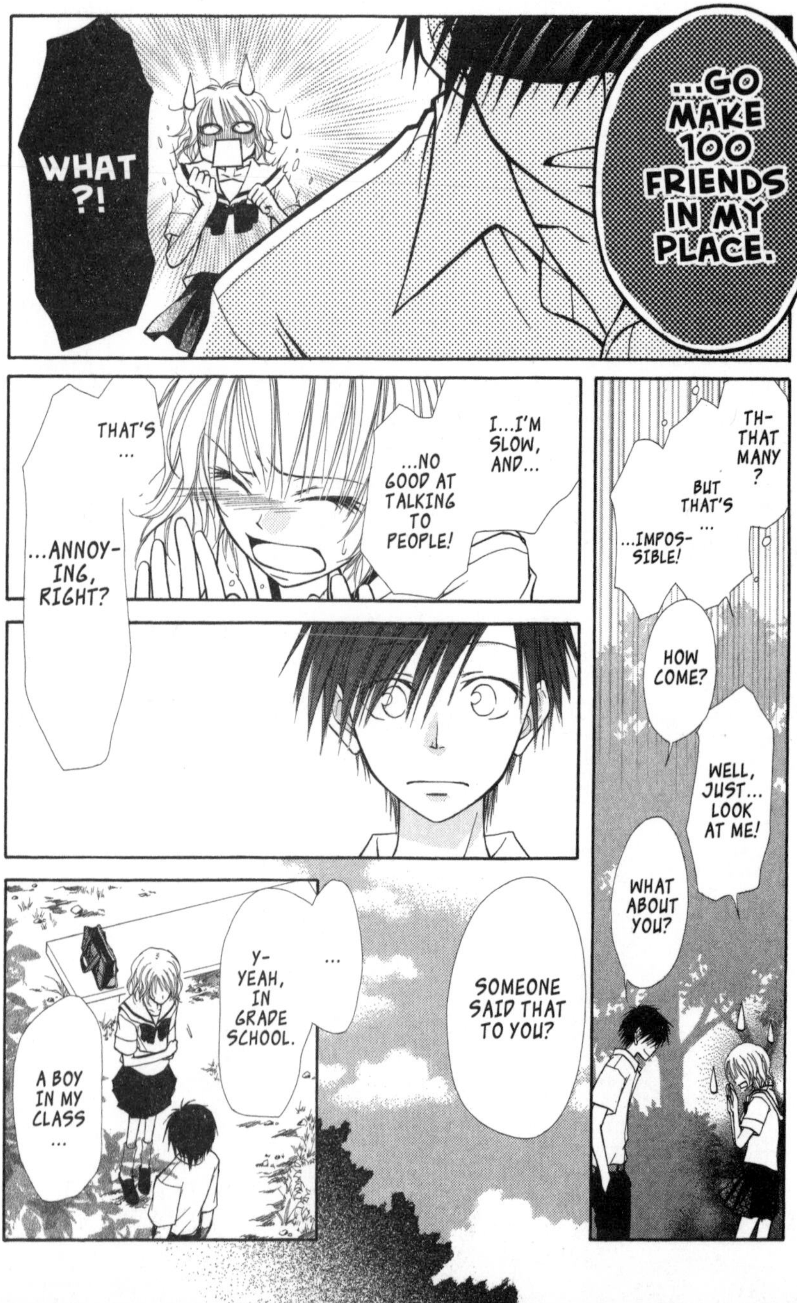
...GO MAKE 100 FRIENDS IN MY PLACE.
WHAT ?!
TH-THAT MANY?
BUT THAT'S ...
...IMPOSSIBLE!
HOW COME?
WELL, JUST... LOOK AT ME!
WHAT ABOUT YOU?
I...I'M SLOW, AND...
...NO GOOD AT TALKING TO PEOPLE!
THAT'S ...
...ANNOYING, RIGHT?
SOMEONE SAID THAT TO YOU?
...
Y-YEAH, IN GRADE SCHOOL.
A BOY IN MY CLASS ...

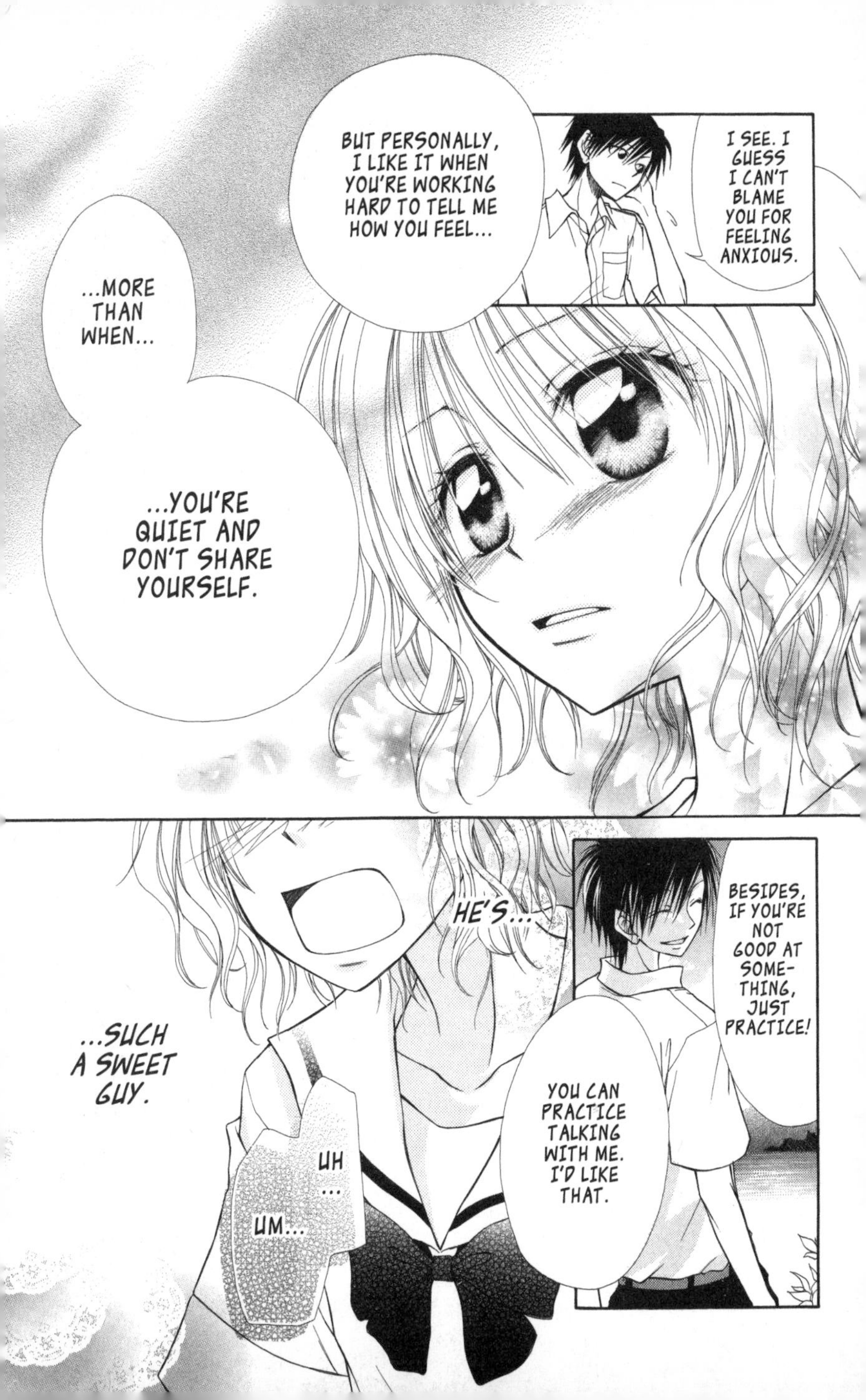
I SEE. I GUESS I CAN'T BLAME YOU FOR FEELING ANXIOUS.
BUT PERSONALLY, I LIKE IT WHEN YOU'RE WORKING HARD TO TELL ME HOW YOU FEEL...
...MORE THAN WHEN...
...YOU'RE QUIET AND DON'T SHARE YOURSELF.
BESIDES, IF YOU'RE NOT GOOD AT SOME-THING, JUST PRACTICE!
YOU CAN PRACTICE TALKING WITH ME. I'D LIKE THAT.
HE'S...
UH...
UM...
...SUCH A SWEET GUY.

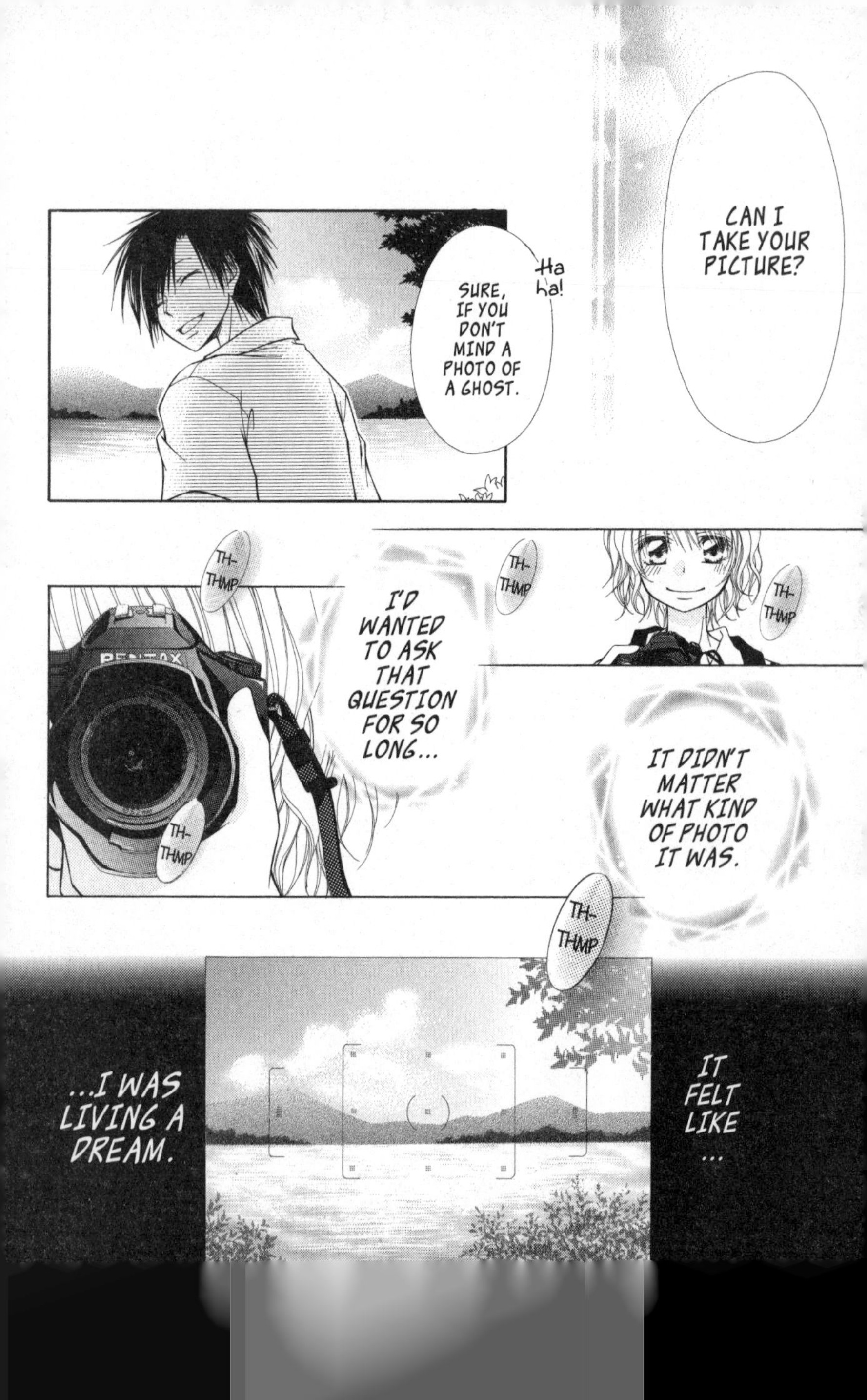
CAN I TAKE YOUR PICTURE?
Ha ha!
SURE, IF YOU DON'T MIND A PHOTO OF A GHOST.
TH-THMP
TH-THMP
TH-THMP
I'D WANTED TO ASK THAT QUESTION FOR SO LONG...
TH-THMP
IT DIDN'T MATTER WHAT KIND OF PHOTO IT WAS.
TH-THMP
IT FELT LIKE ...
...I WAS LIVING A DREAM.

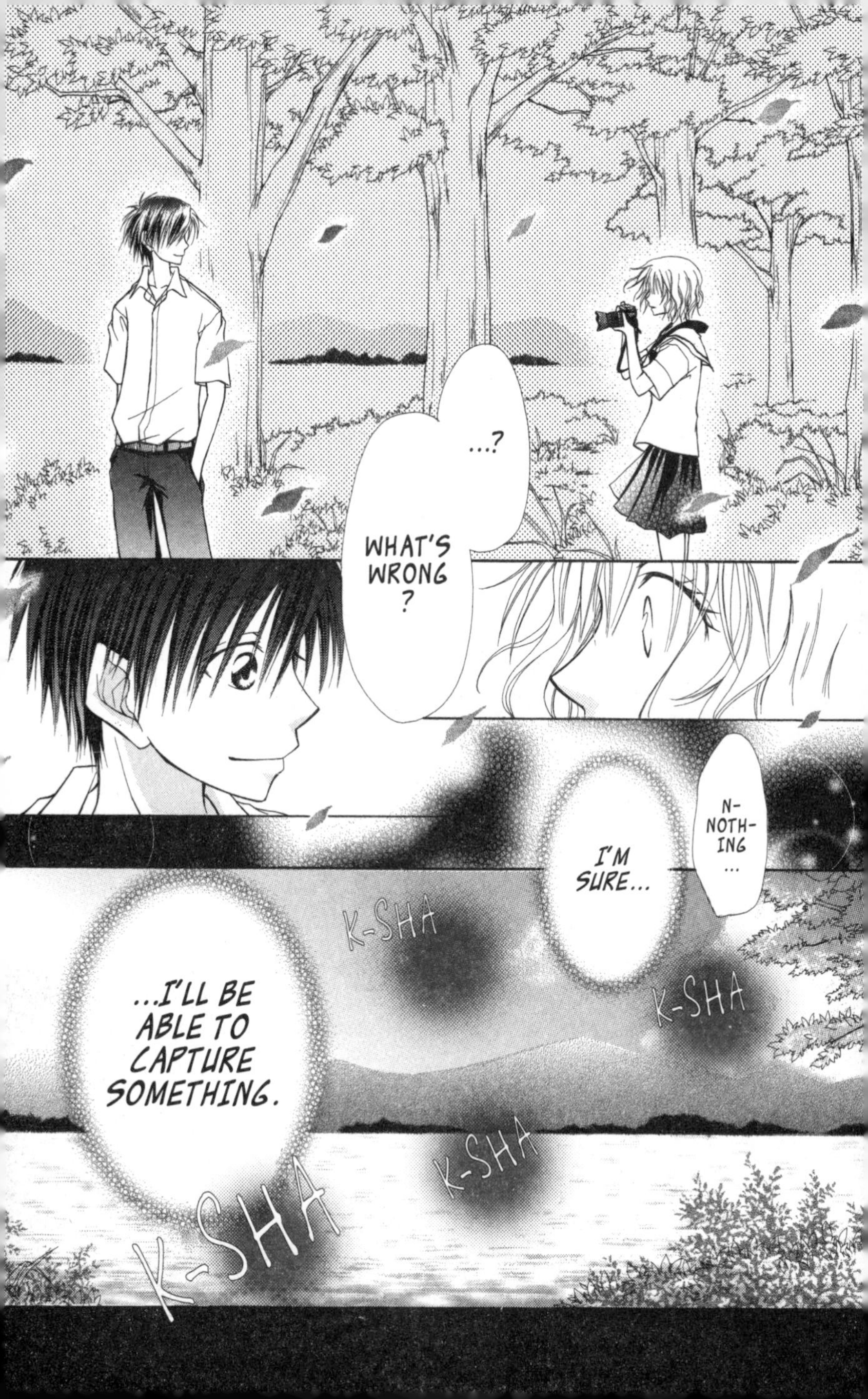
...? WHAT'S WRONG?
N-NOTHING...
I'M SURE...
K-SHA
K-SHA
...I'LL BE ABLE TO CAPTURE SOMETHING.
K-SHA
K-SHA

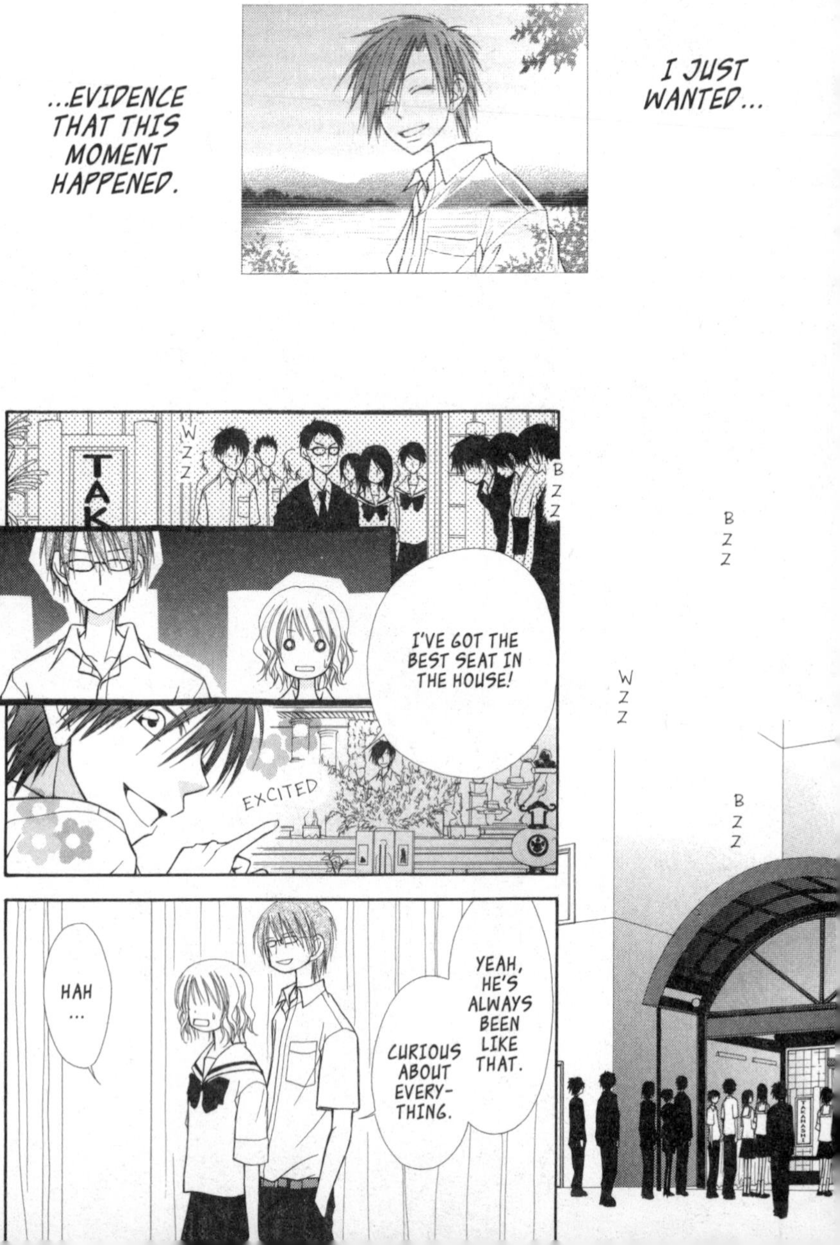
I JUST WANTED...
...EVIDENCE THAT THIS MOMENT HAPPENED.
BZZ
WZZ
BZZ
WZZ
BZZ
I'VE GOT THE BEST SEAT IN THE HOUSE!
EXCITED
YEAH, HE'S ALWAYS BEEN LIKE THAT.
CURIOUS ABOUT EVERY-THING.
HAH...

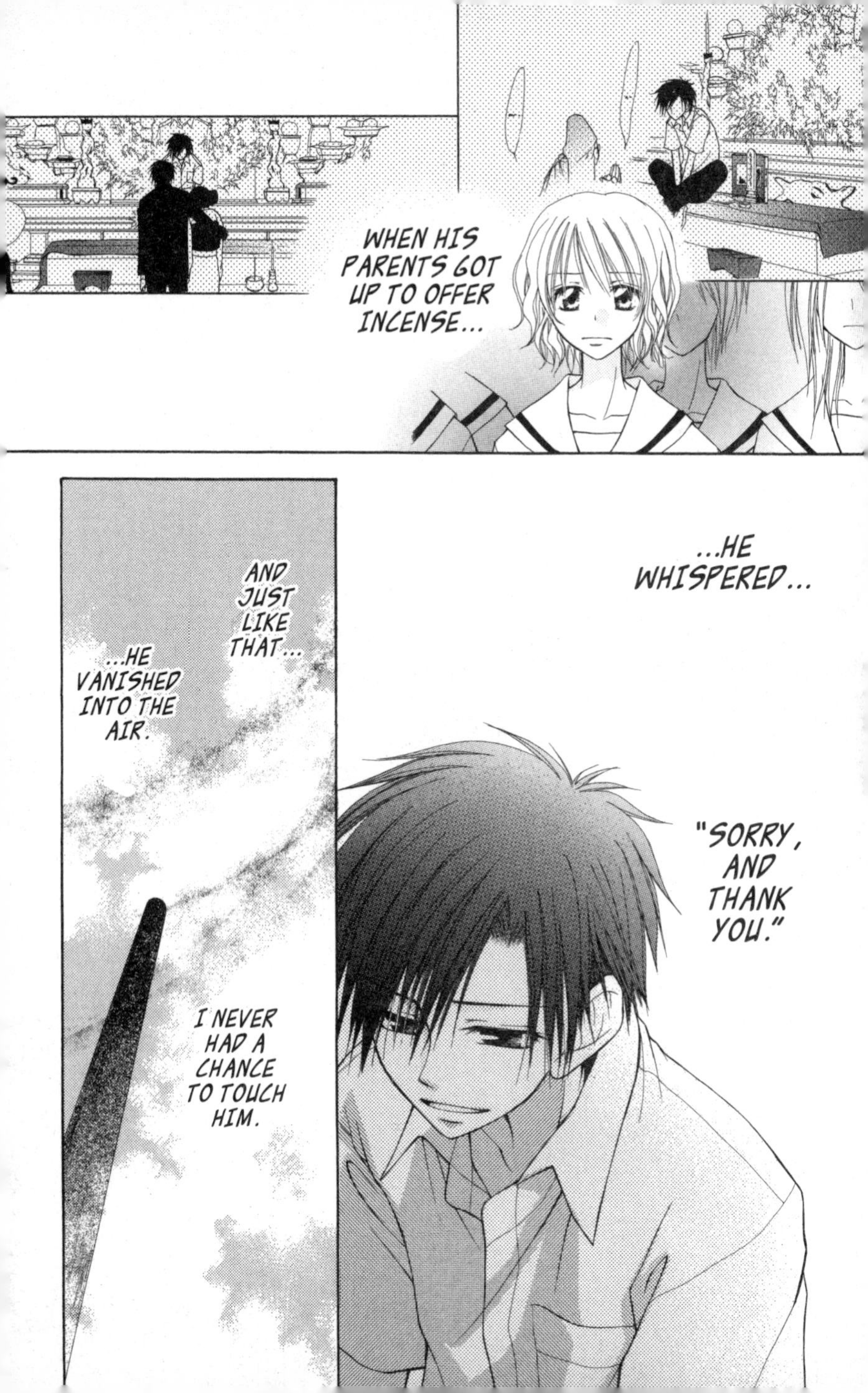
WHEN HIS PARENTS GOT UP TO OFFER INCENSE...
...HE WHISPERED...
"SORRY, AND THANK YOU."
AND JUST LIKE THAT...
...HE VANISHED INTO THE AIR.
I NEVER HAD A CHANCE TO TOUCH HIM.

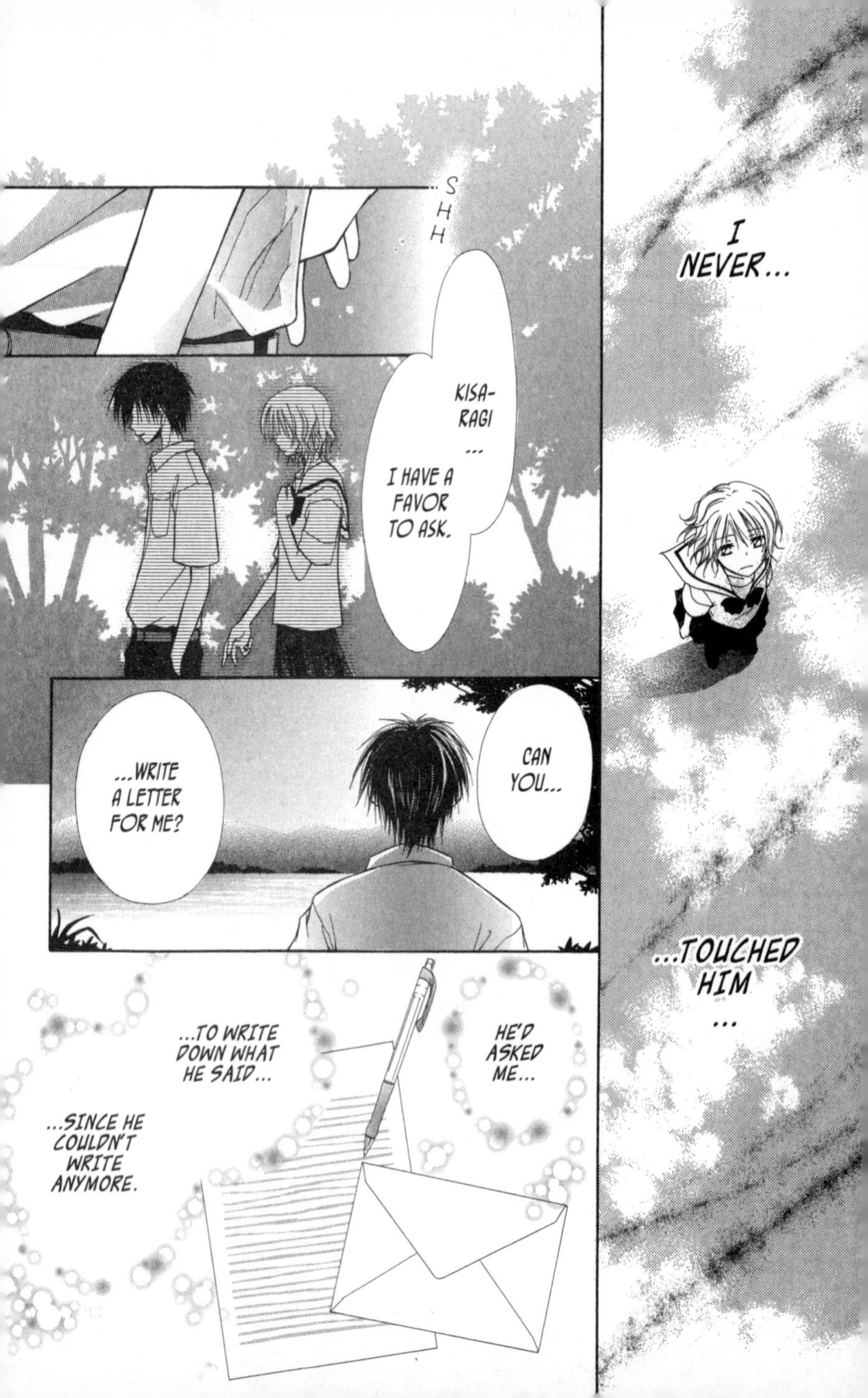
I NEVER...
...TOUCHED HIM...
SHHH
KISA-RAGI...
I HAVE A FAVOR TO ASK.
CAN YOU...
...WRITE A LETTER FOR ME?
HE'D ASKED ME...
...TO WRITE DOWN WHAT HE SAID...
...SINCE HE COULDN'T WRITE ANYMORE.

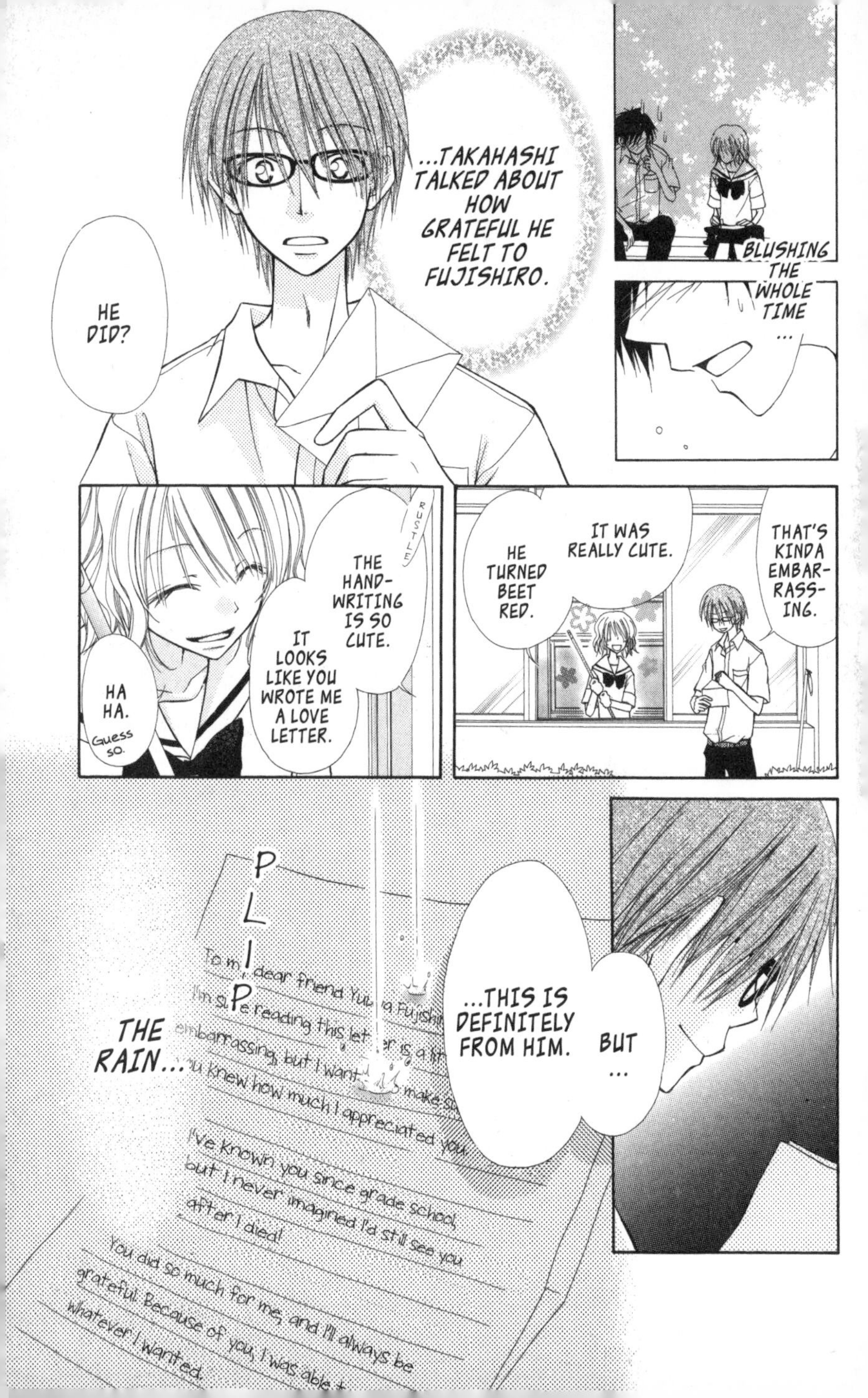
BLUSHING THE WHOLE TIME...
...TAKAHASHI TALKED ABOUT HOW GRATEFUL HE FELT TO FUJISHIRO.
HE DID?
THAT'S KINDA EMBARRASSING.
IT WAS REALLY CUTE.
HE TURNED BEET RED.
RUSTLE
THE HAND-WRITING IS SO CUTE.
IT LOOKS LIKE YOU WROTE ME A LOVE LETTER.
HA HA.
Guess so.
BUT...
...THIS IS DEFINITELY FROM HIM.
PLIP
THE RAIN...
I've known you since grade school, but I never imagined I'd still see you after I died!
You did so much for me, and I'll always be grateful. Because of you, I was able to whatever I wanted.

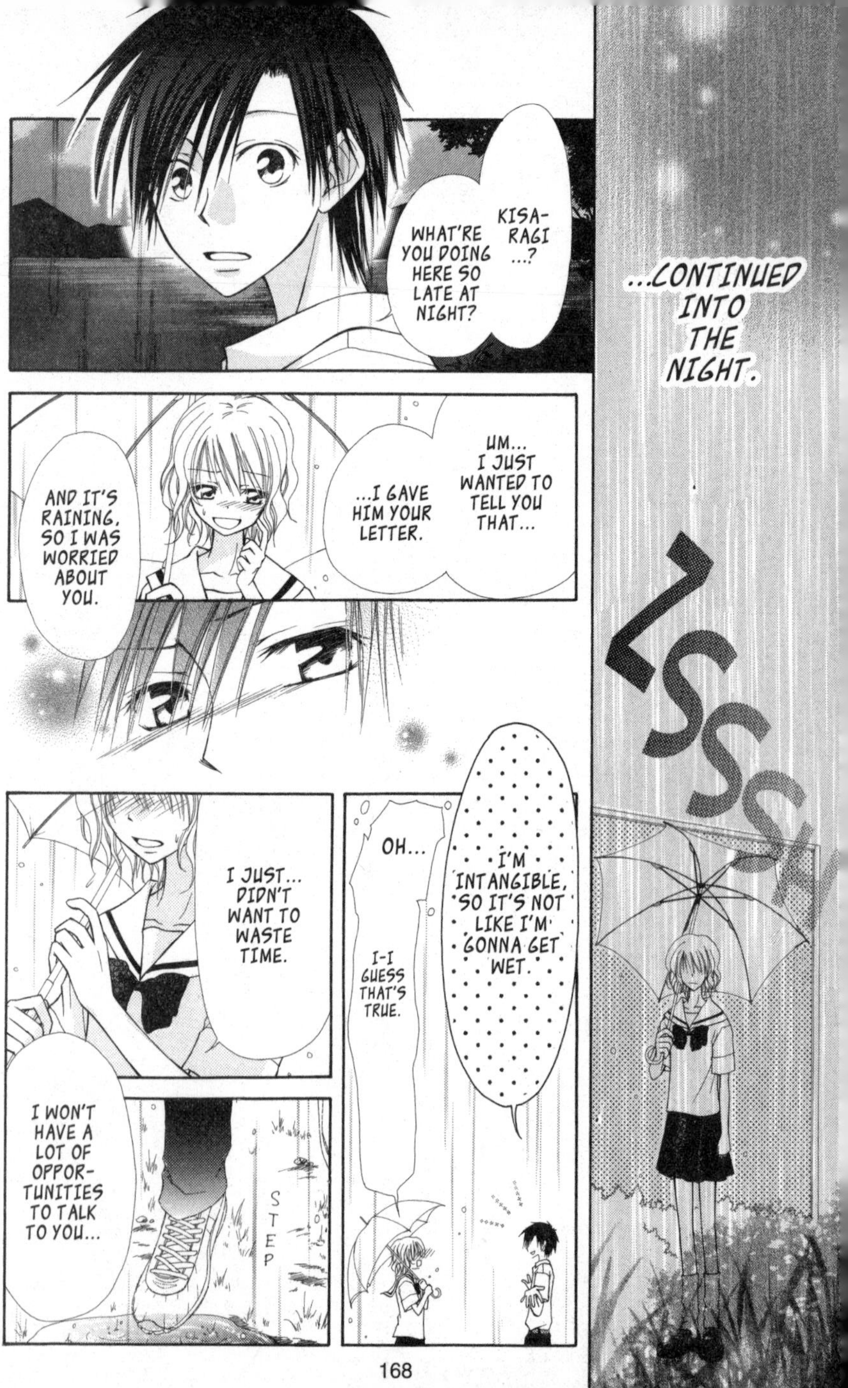
...CONTINUED INTO THE NIGHT.
ZSSSH
KISA-RAGI ...?
WHAT'RE YOU DOING HERE SO LATE AT NIGHT?
UM... I JUST WANTED TO TELL YOU THAT...
...I GAVE HIM YOUR LETTER.
AND IT'S RAINING, SO I WAS WORRIED ABOUT YOU.
I'M INTANGIBLE, SO IT'S NOT LIKE I'M GONNA GET WET.
OH...
I-I GUESS THAT'S TRUE.
I JUST... DIDN'T WANT TO WASTE TIME.
I WON'T HAVE A LOT OF OPPOR-TUNITIES TO TALK TO YOU...
STEP

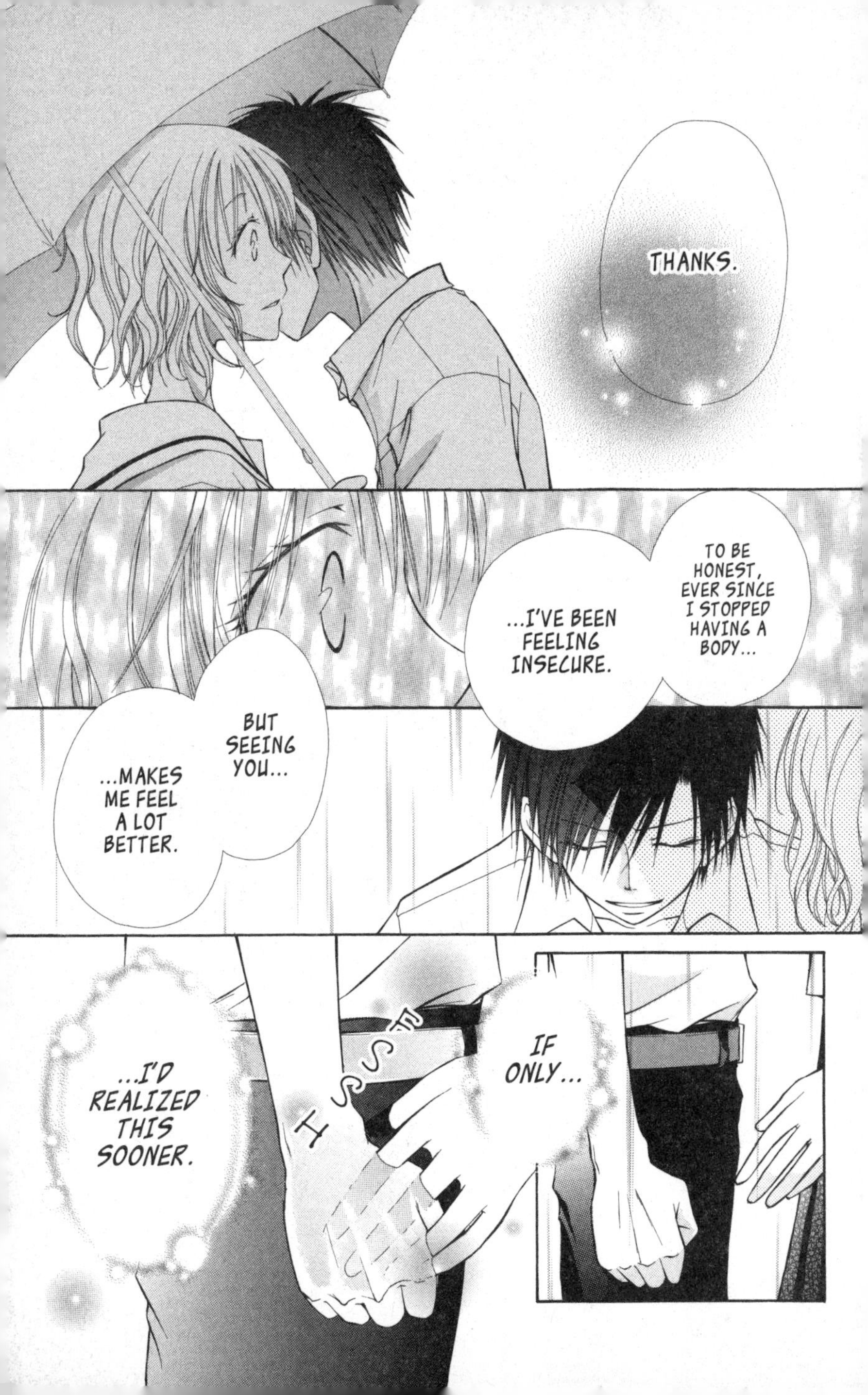
THANKS.
TO BE HONEST, EVER SINCE I STOPPED HAVING A BODY...
...I'VE BEEN FEELING INSECURE.
BUT SEEING YOU...
...MAKES ME FEEL A LOT BETTER.
IF ONLY...
...I'D REALIZED THIS SOONER.

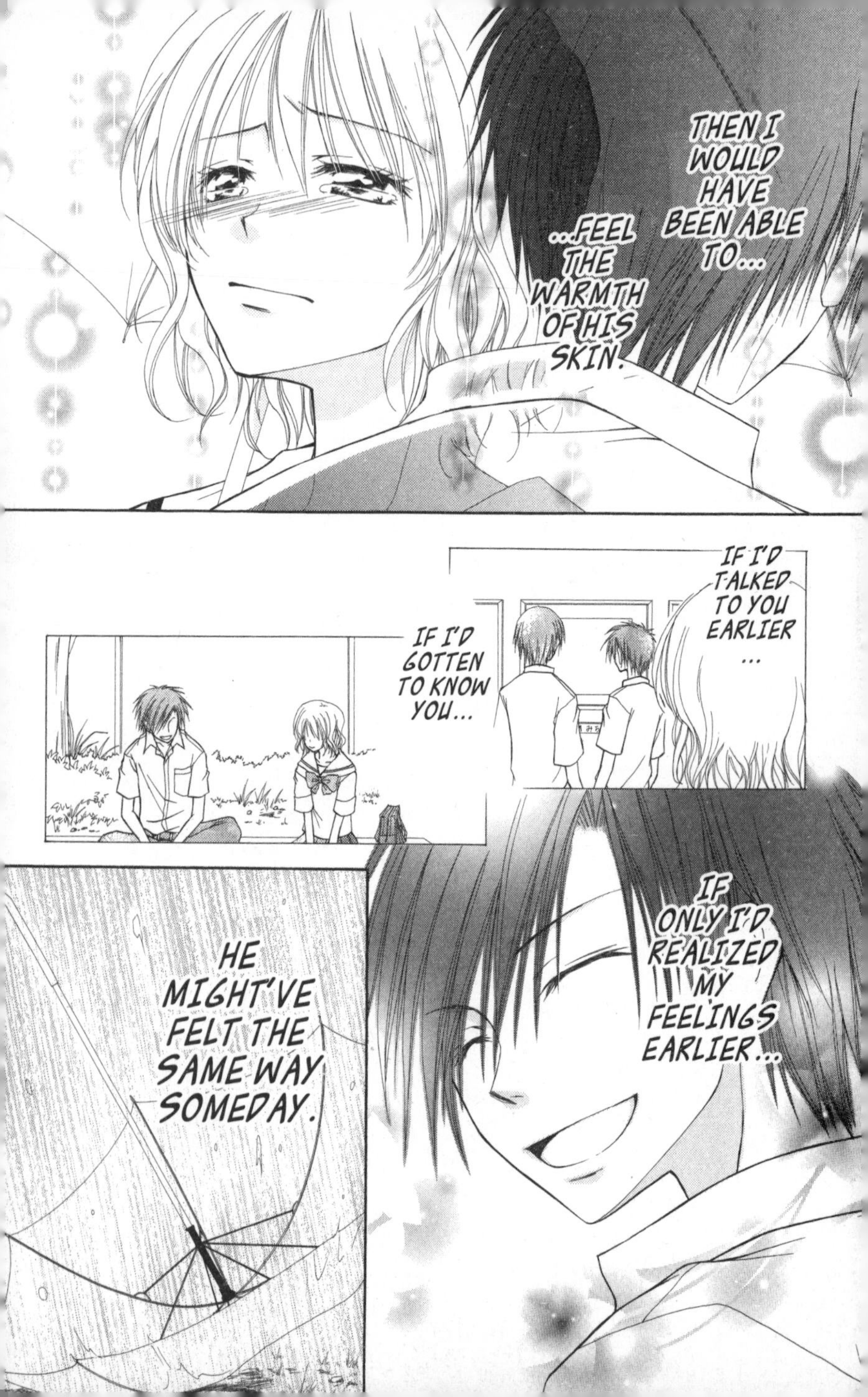
THEN I WOULD HAVE BEEN ABLE TO...
...FEEL THE WARMTH OF HIS SKIN.
IF I'D TALKED TO YOU EARLIER...
IF I'D GOTTEN TO KNOW YOU...
IF ONLY I'D REALIZED MY FEELINGS EARLIER...
HE MIGHT'VE FELT THE SAME WAY SOMEDAY.

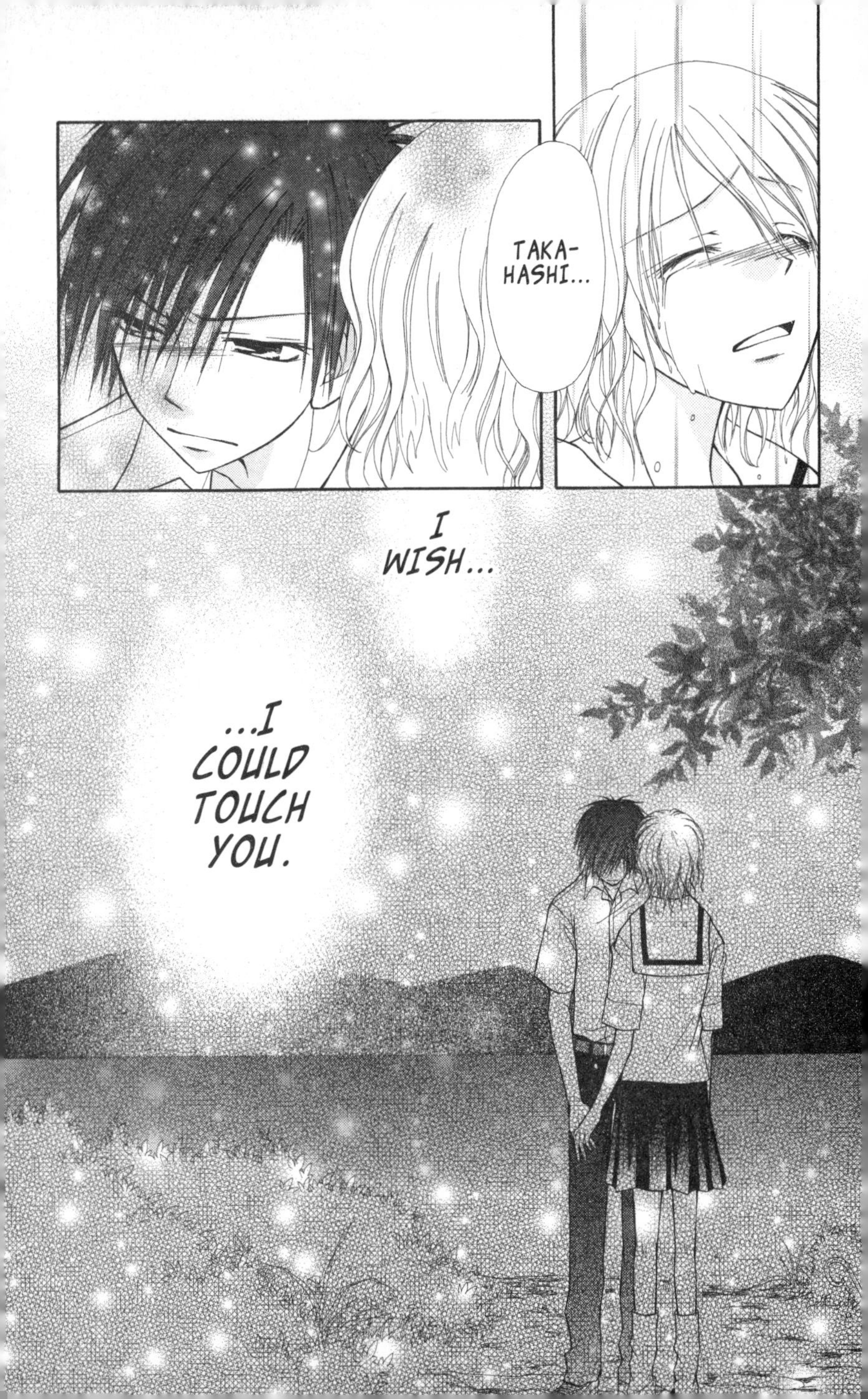
TAKA-HASHI...
I WISH...
...I COULD TOUCH YOU.

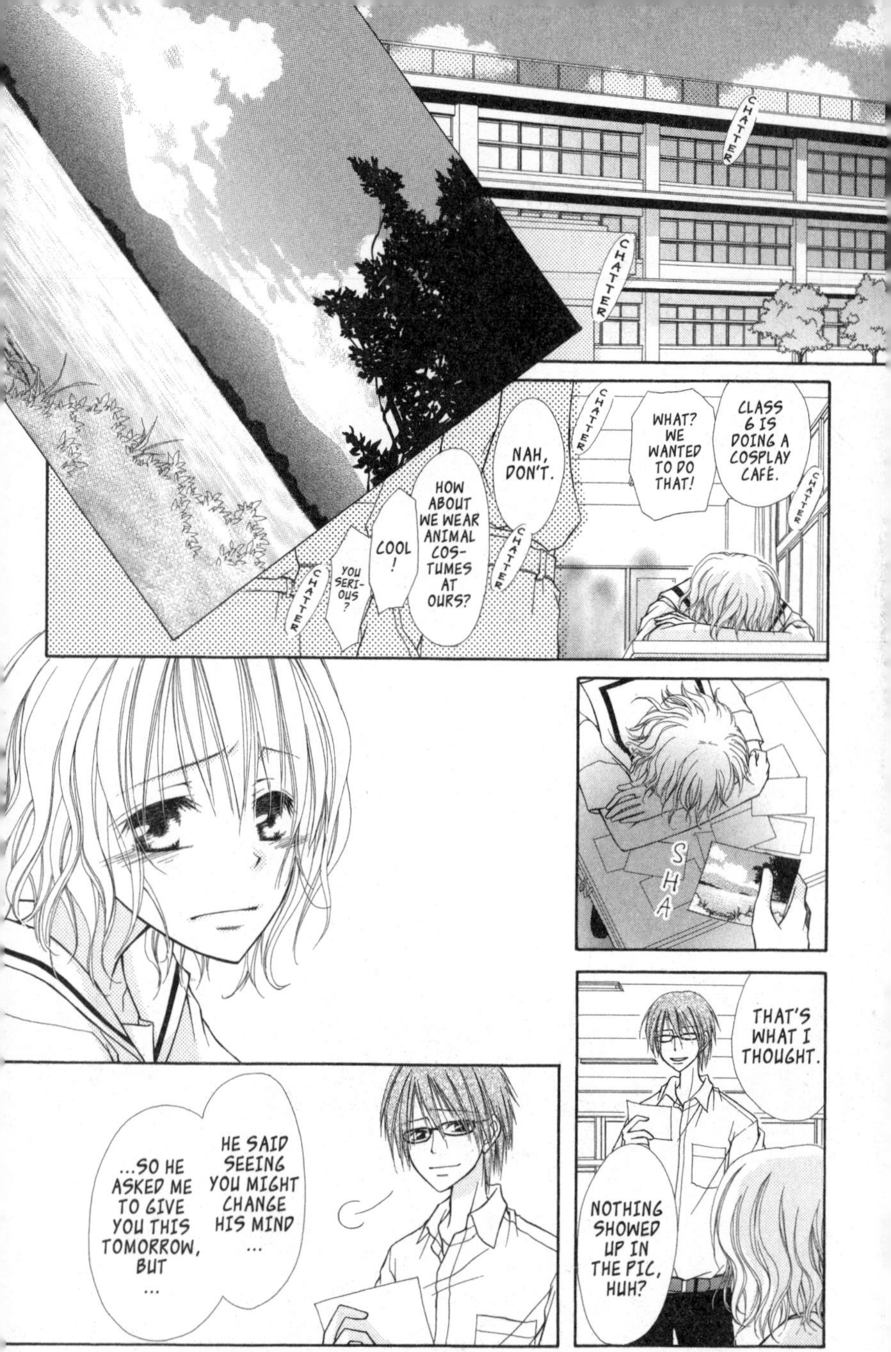
CHATTER
CHATTER
CLASS 6 IS DOING A COSPLAY CAFÉ.
CHATTER
WHAT? WE WANTED TO DO THAT!
CHATTER
NAH, DON'T.
CHATTER
HOW ABOUT WE WEAR ANIMAL COS-TUMES AT OURS?
COOL!
YOU SERI-OUS?
CHATTER
SHA
THAT'S WHAT I THOUGHT.
NOTHING SHOWED UP IN THE PIC, HUH?
HE SAID SEEING YOU MIGHT CHANGE HIS MIND...
...SO HE ASKED ME TO GIVE YOU THIS TOMORROW, BUT...

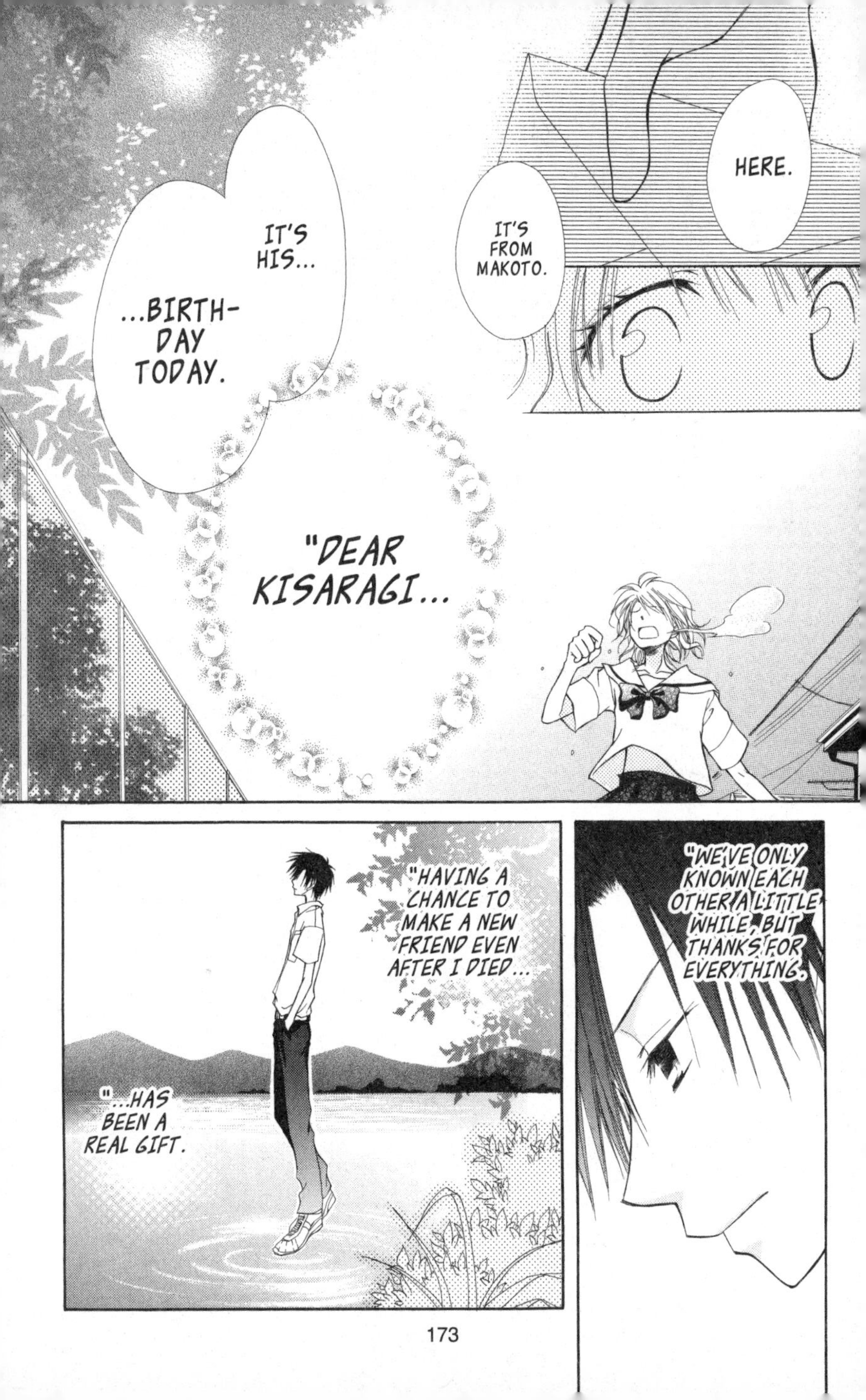
HERE.
IT'S FROM MAKOTO.
IT'S HIS...
...BIRTH-DAY TODAY.
"DEAR KISARAGI...
"WE'VE ONLY KNOWN EACH OTHER A LITTLE WHILE, BUT THANKS FOR EVERYTHING.
"HAVING A CHANCE TO MAKE A NEW FRIEND EVEN AFTER I DIED...
"...HAS BEEN A REAL GIFT.

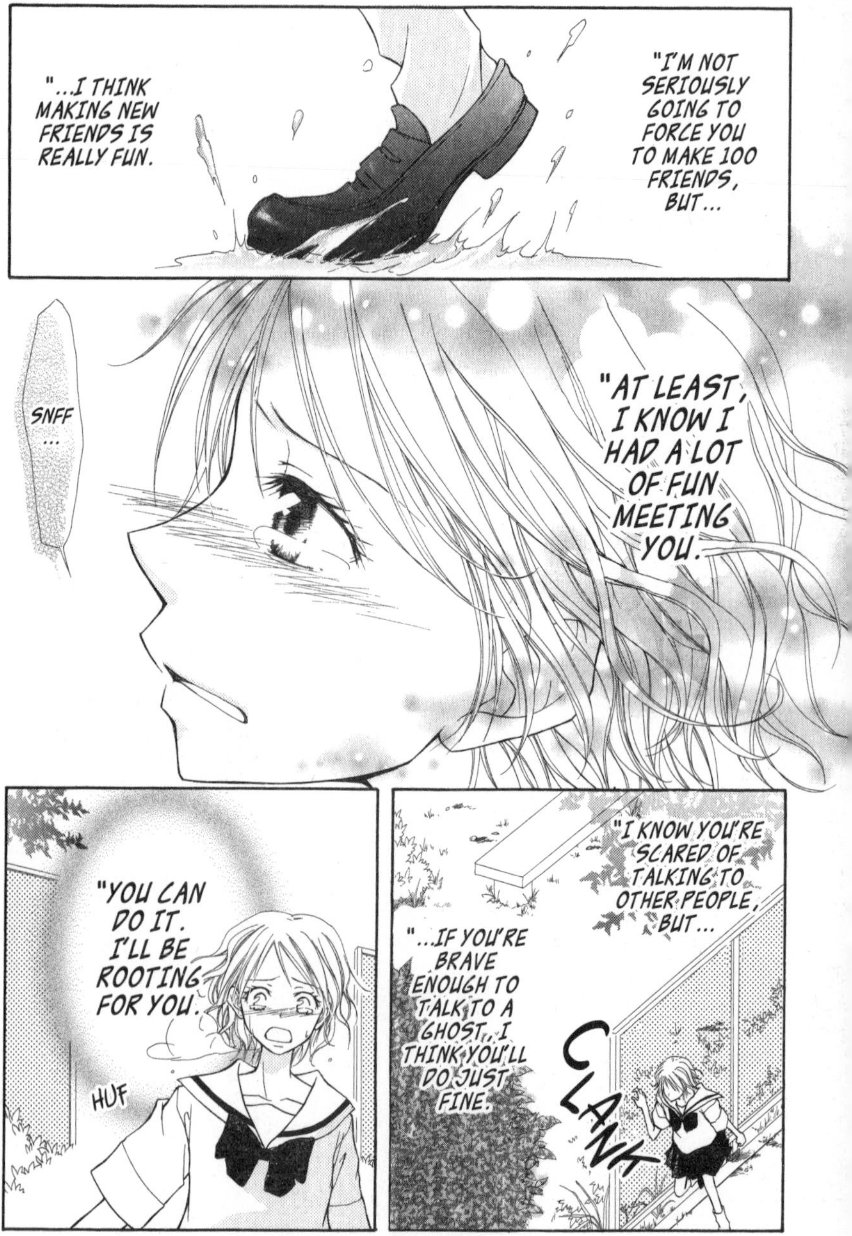
"I'M NOT SERIOUSLY GOING TO FORCE YOU TO MAKE 100 FRIENDS, BUT...
"...I THINK MAKING NEW FRIENDS IS REALLY FUN.
"AT LEAST, I KNOW I HAD A LOT OF FUN MEETING YOU.
SNFF ...
"I KNOW YOU'RE SCARED OF TALKING TO OTHER PEOPLE, BUT...
"...IF YOU'RE BRAVE ENOUGH TO TALK TO A GHOST, I THINK YOU'LL DO JUST FINE.
CLANK
"YOU CAN DO IT. I'LL BE ROOTING FOR YOU.
HUF

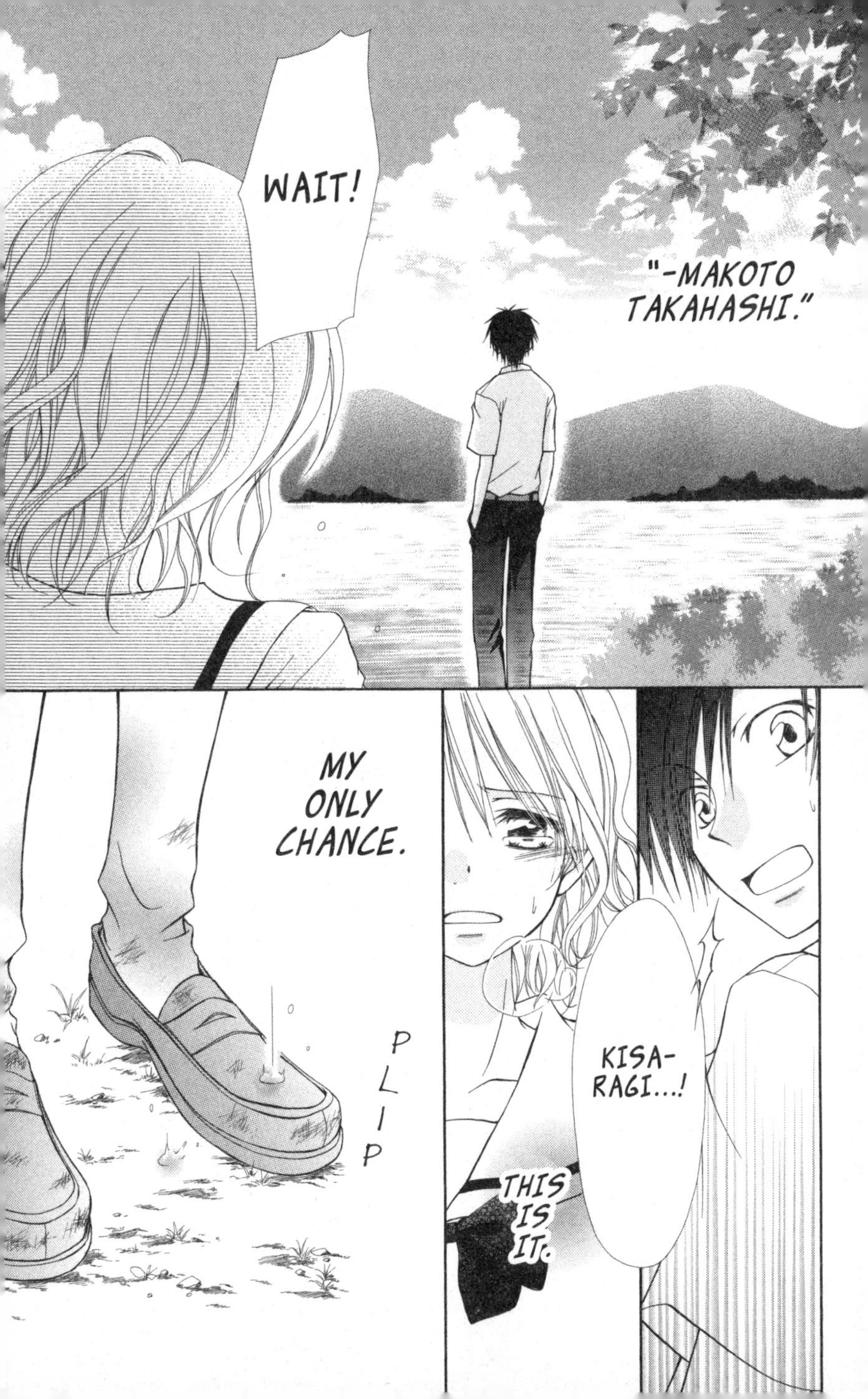
"-MAKOTO TAKAHASHI."
WAIT!
KISA-RAGI...!
THIS IS IT.
MY ONLY CHANCE.
PLIP

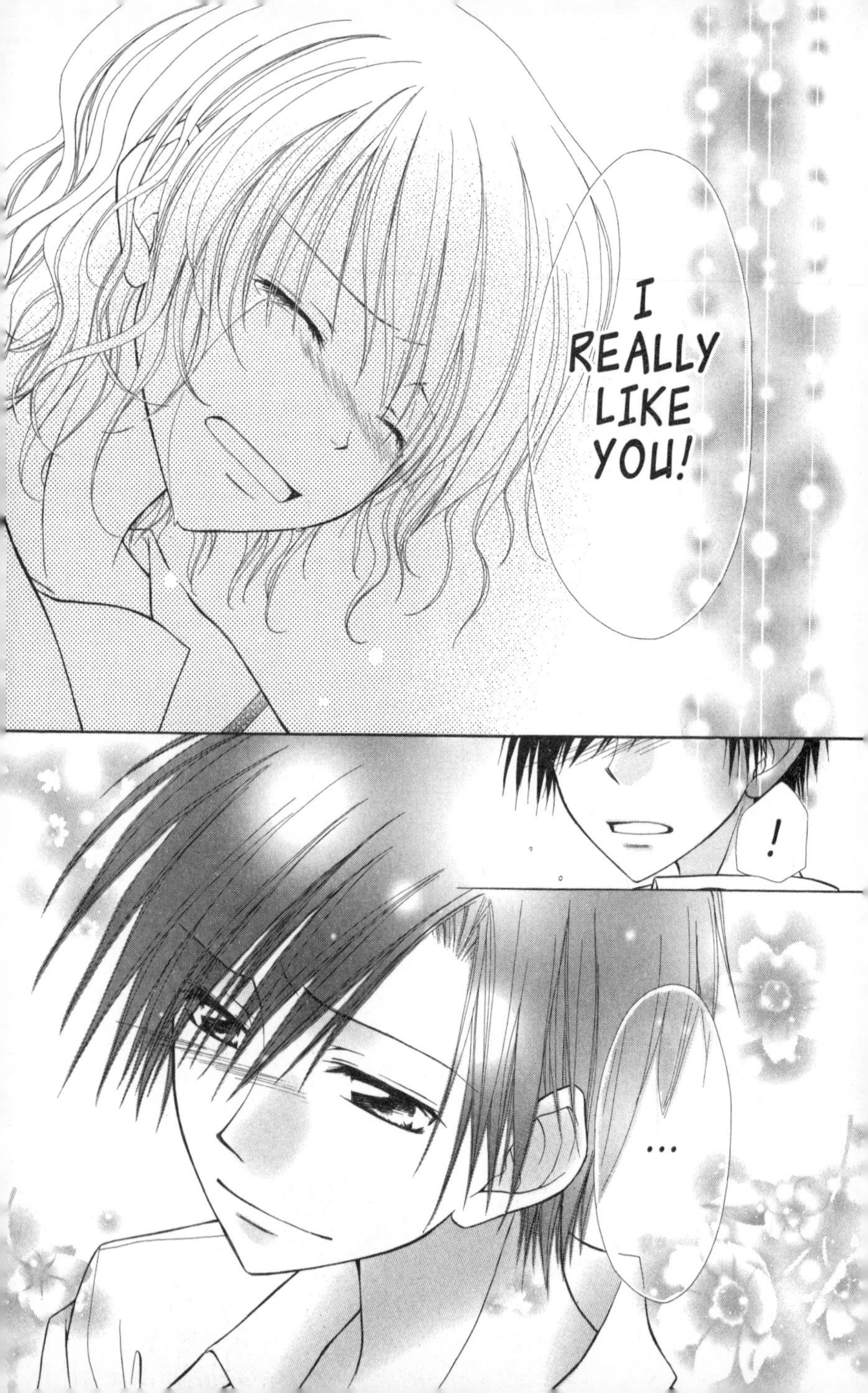
I REALLY LIKE YOU!
!
...

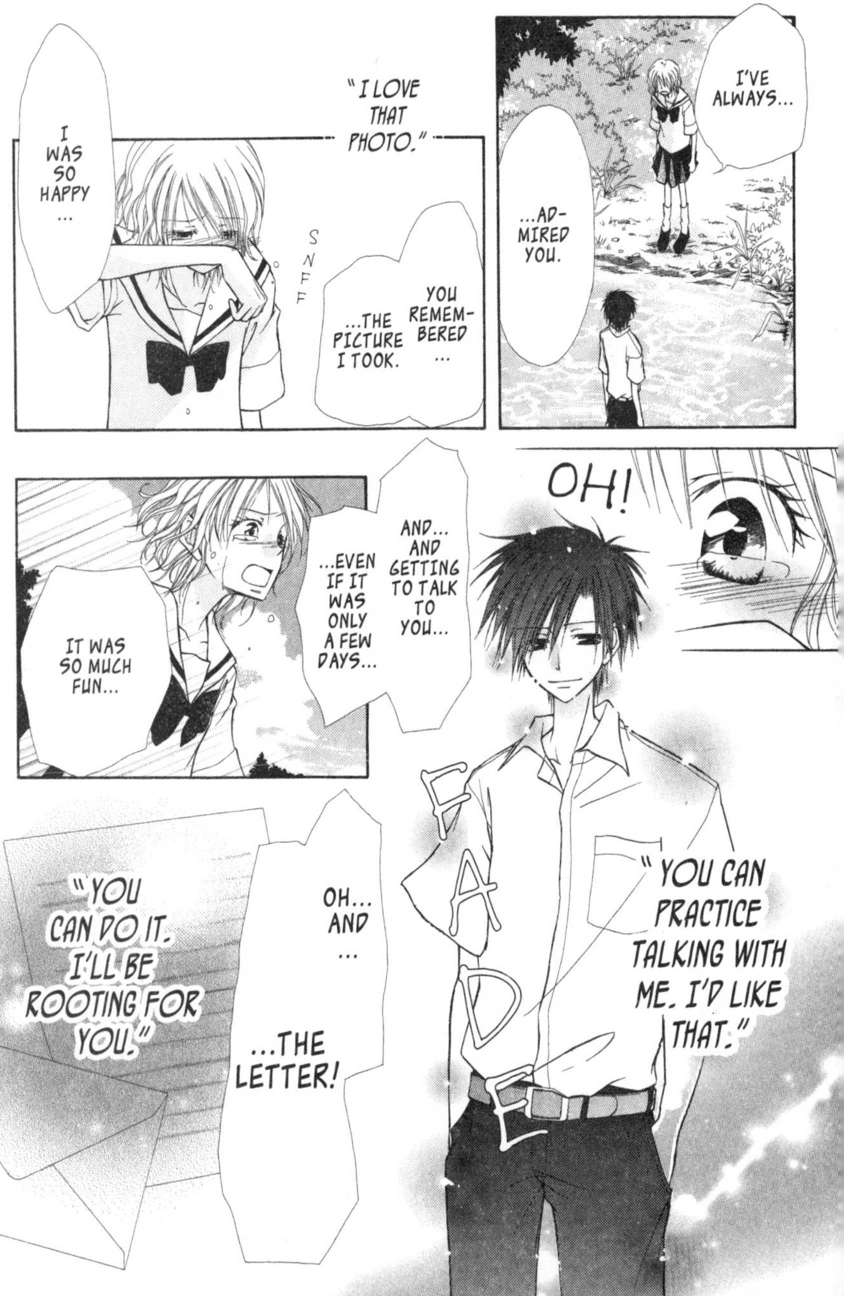
I'VE ALWAYS...
...ADMIRED YOU.
"I LOVE THAT PHOTO."
YOU REMEMBERED...
...THE PICTURE I TOOK.
SNFF
I WAS SO HAPPY...
OH!
AND... AND GETTING TO TALK TO YOU...
...EVEN IF IT WAS ONLY A FEW DAYS...
IT WAS SO MUCH FUN...
"YOU CAN PRACTICE TALKING WITH ME. I'D LIKE THAT."
FADE
OH... AND...
...THE LETTER!
"YOU CAN DO IT. I'LL BE ROOTING FOR YOU."

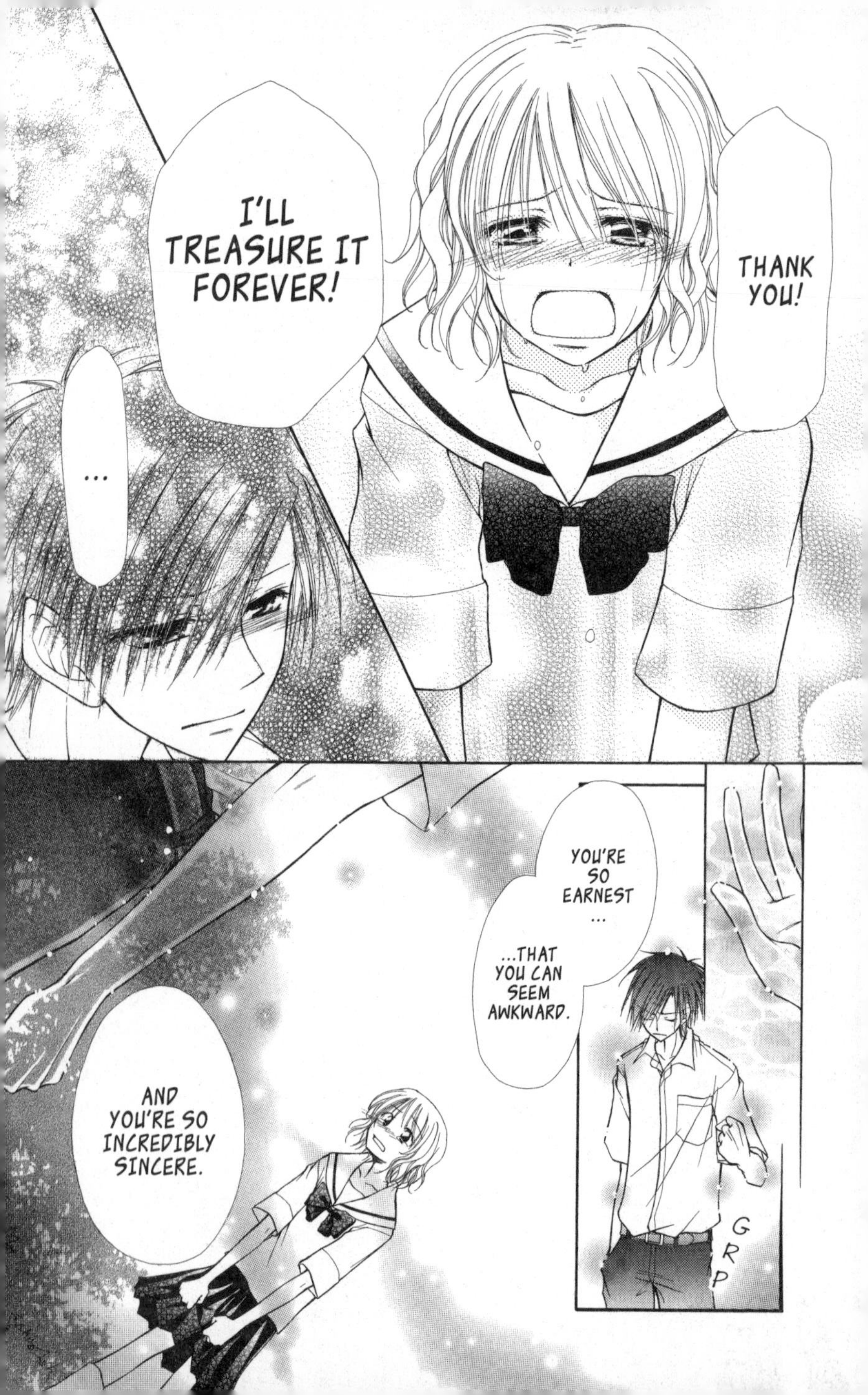
THANK YOU!
I'LL TREASURE IT FOREVER!
...
YOU'RE SO EARNEST ...
...THAT YOU CAN SEEM AWKWARD.
GRP
AND YOU'RE SO INCREDIBLY SINCERE.

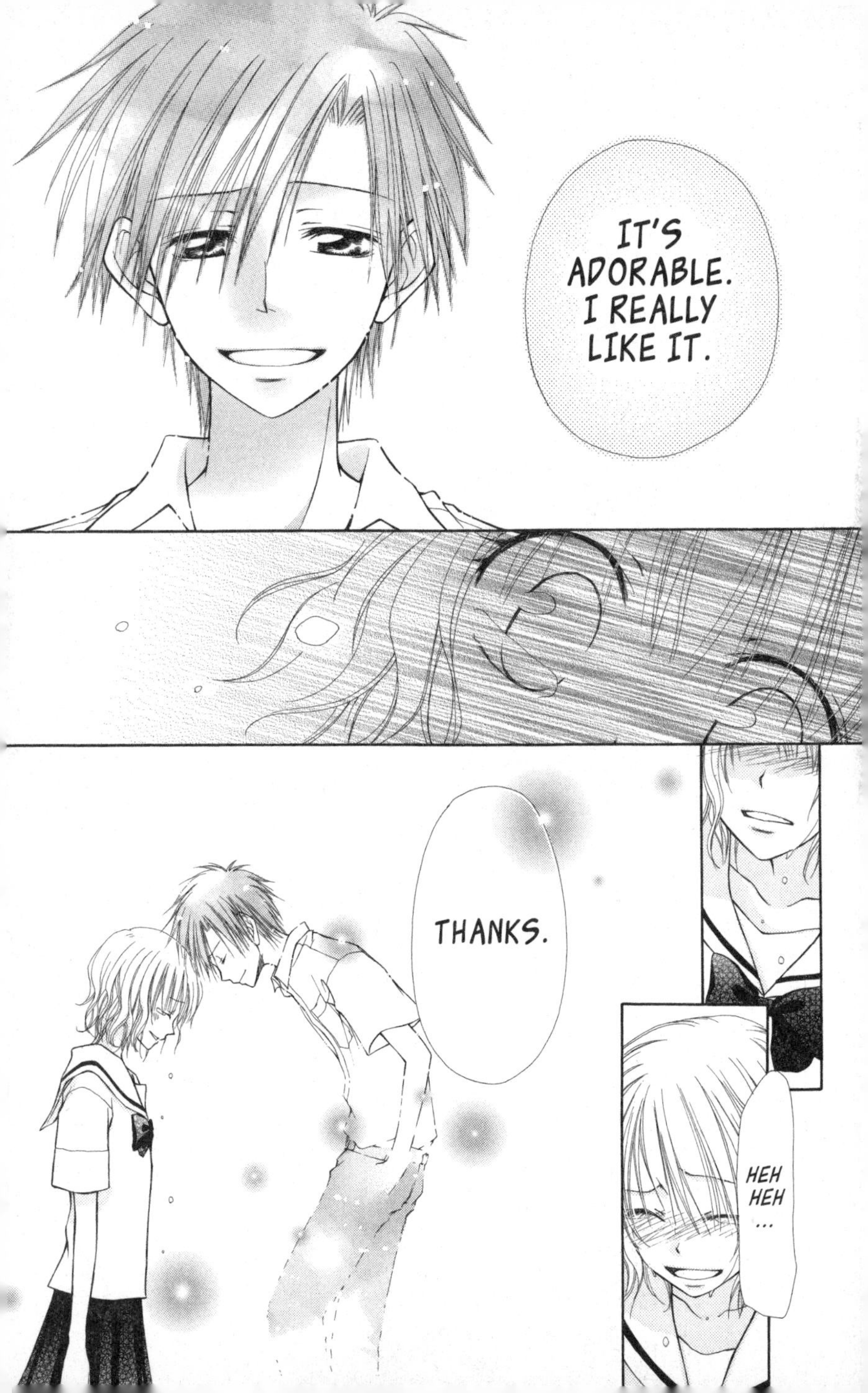
IT'S ADORABLE. I REALLY LIKE IT.
THANKS.
HEH HEH ...

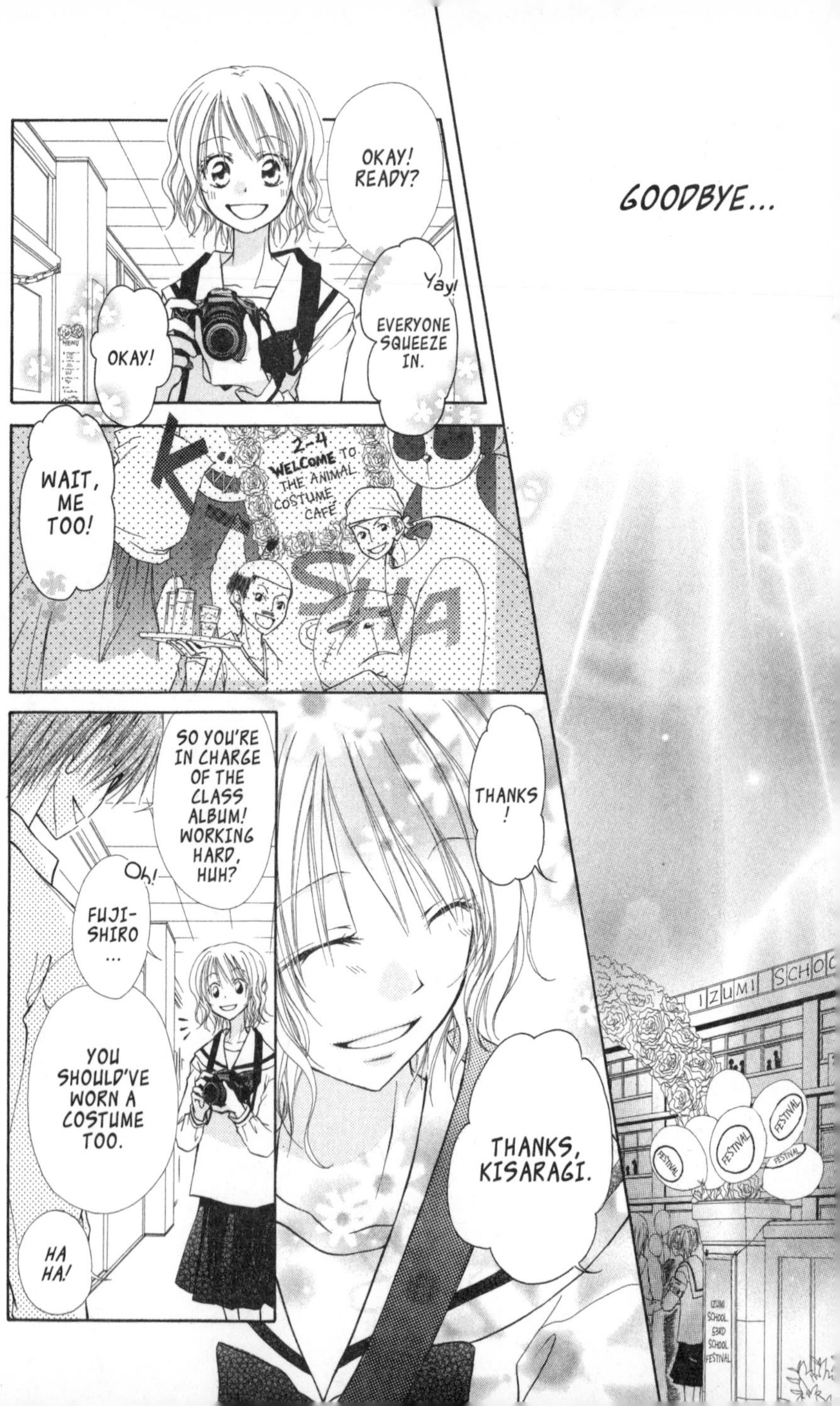
GOODBYE...
IZUMI SCHOO
FESTIVAL
FESTIVAL
FESTIVAL
FESTIVAL
IZUMI SCHOOL 53RD SCHOOL FESTIVAL
OKAY! READY?
Yay!
EVERYONE SQUEEZE IN.
OKAY!
2-4 WELCOME TO THE ANIMAL COSTUME CAFE
WAIT, ME TOO!
THANKS, KISARAGI.
THANKS!
SO YOU'RE IN CHARGE OF THE CLASS ALBUM! WORKING HARD, HUH?
Oh!
FUJI-SHIRO...
YOU SHOULD'VE WORN A COSTUME TOO.
HA HA!

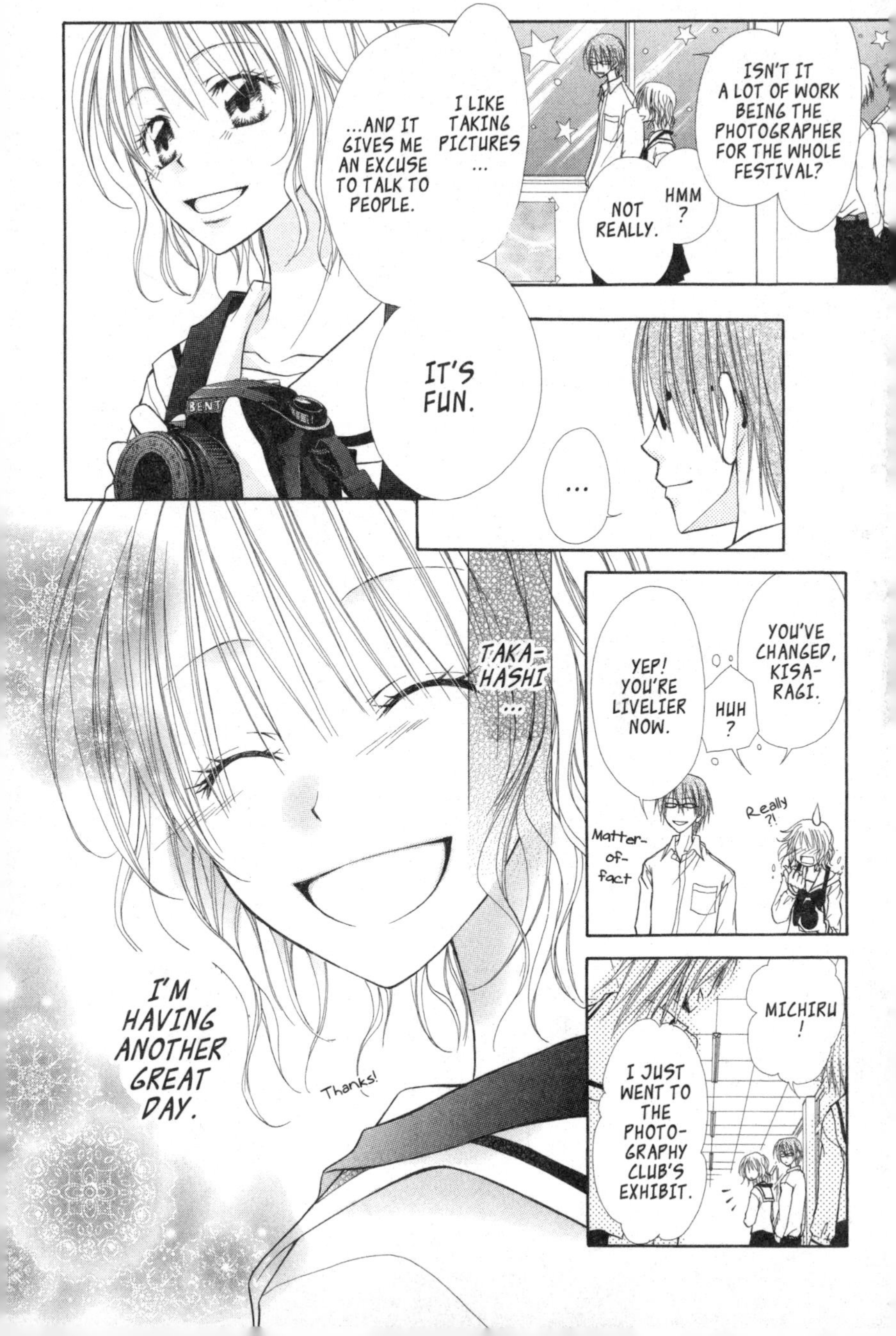
ISN'T IT A LOT OF WORK BEING THE PHOTOGRAPHER FOR THE WHOLE FESTIVAL?
HMM?
NOT REALLY.
I LIKE TAKING PICTURES...
...AND IT GIVES ME AN EXCUSE TO TALK TO PEOPLE.
IT'S FUN.
...
YOU'VE CHANGED, KISARAGI.
HUH?
YEP! YOU'RE LIVELIER NOW.
Matter-of-fact
Really?!
MICHIRU!
I JUST WENT TO THE PHOTOGRAPHY CLUB'S EXHIBIT.
TAKAHASHI...
I'M HAVING ANOTHER GREAT DAY.
Thanks!

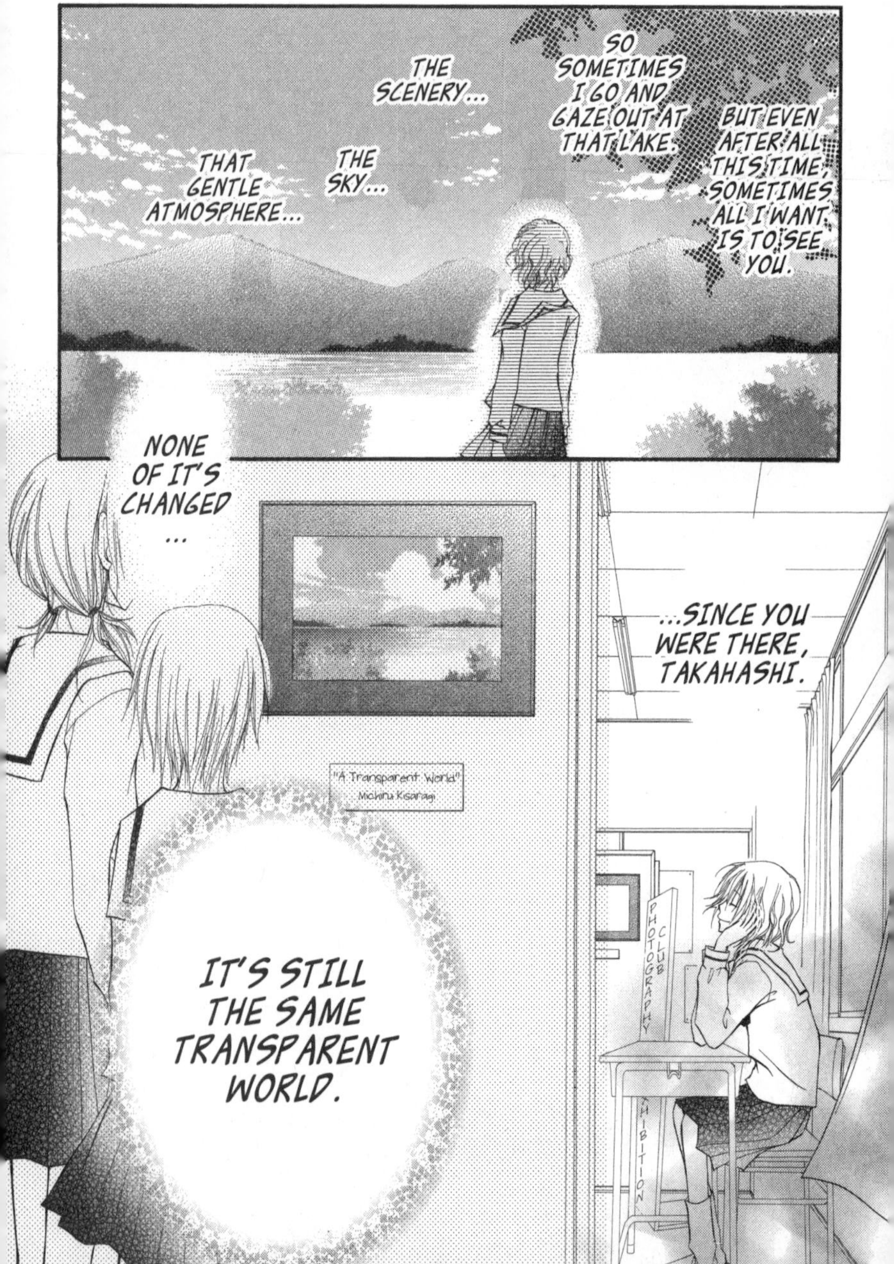
BUT EVEN AFTER ALL THIS TIME, SOMETIMES ALL I WANT IS TO SEE YOU.
SO SOMETIMES I GO AND GAZE OUT AT THAT LAKE.
THE SCENERY...
THE SKY...
THAT GENTLE ATMOSPHERE...
NONE OF IT'S CHANGED ...
"A Transparent World" Michiru Kisaragi
...SINCE YOU WERE THERE, TAKAHASHI.
PHOTOGRAPHY CLUB
HIBITION
IT'S STILL THE SAME TRANSPARENT WORLD.

A TRANSPARENT WORLD / THE END

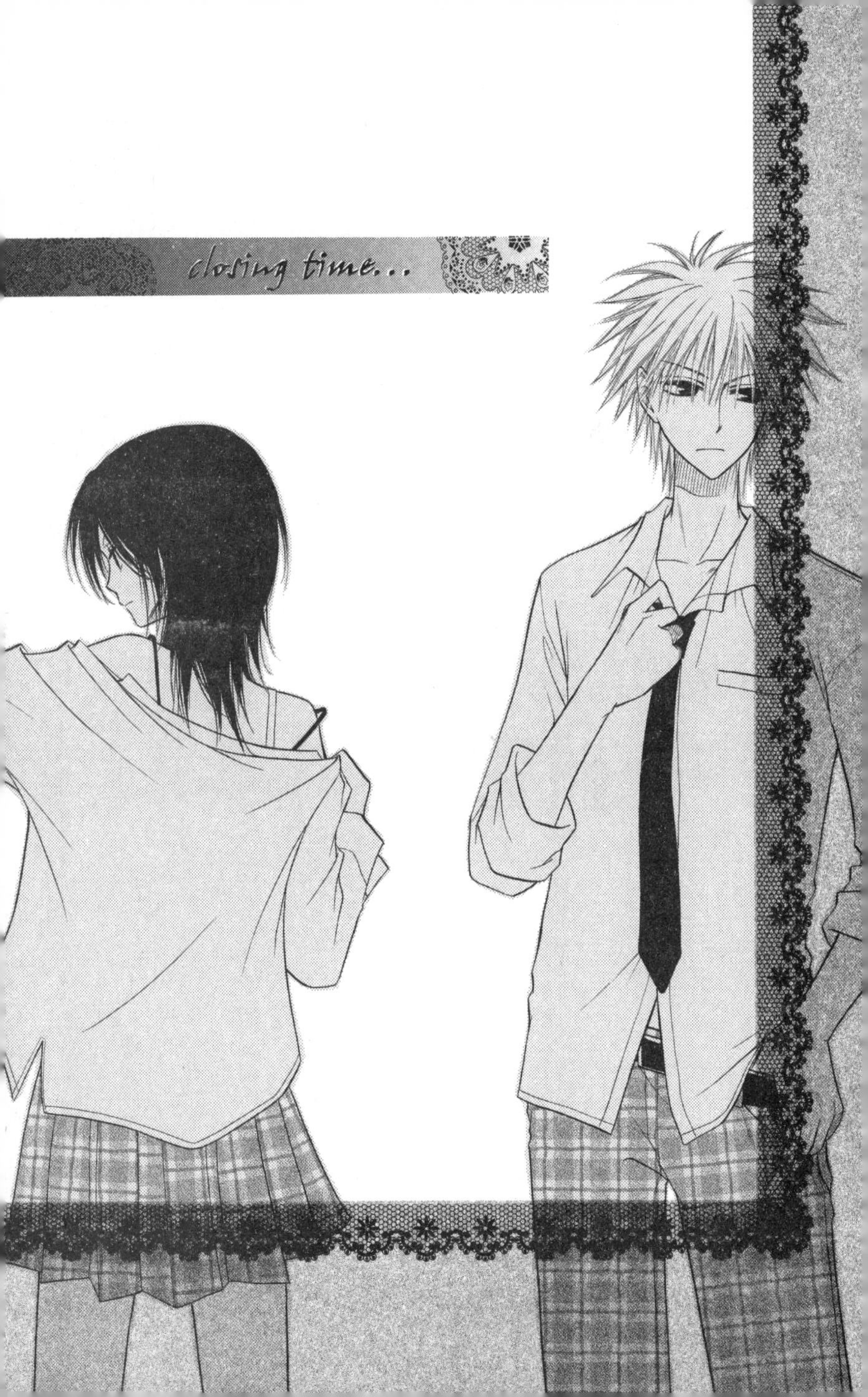
closing time...

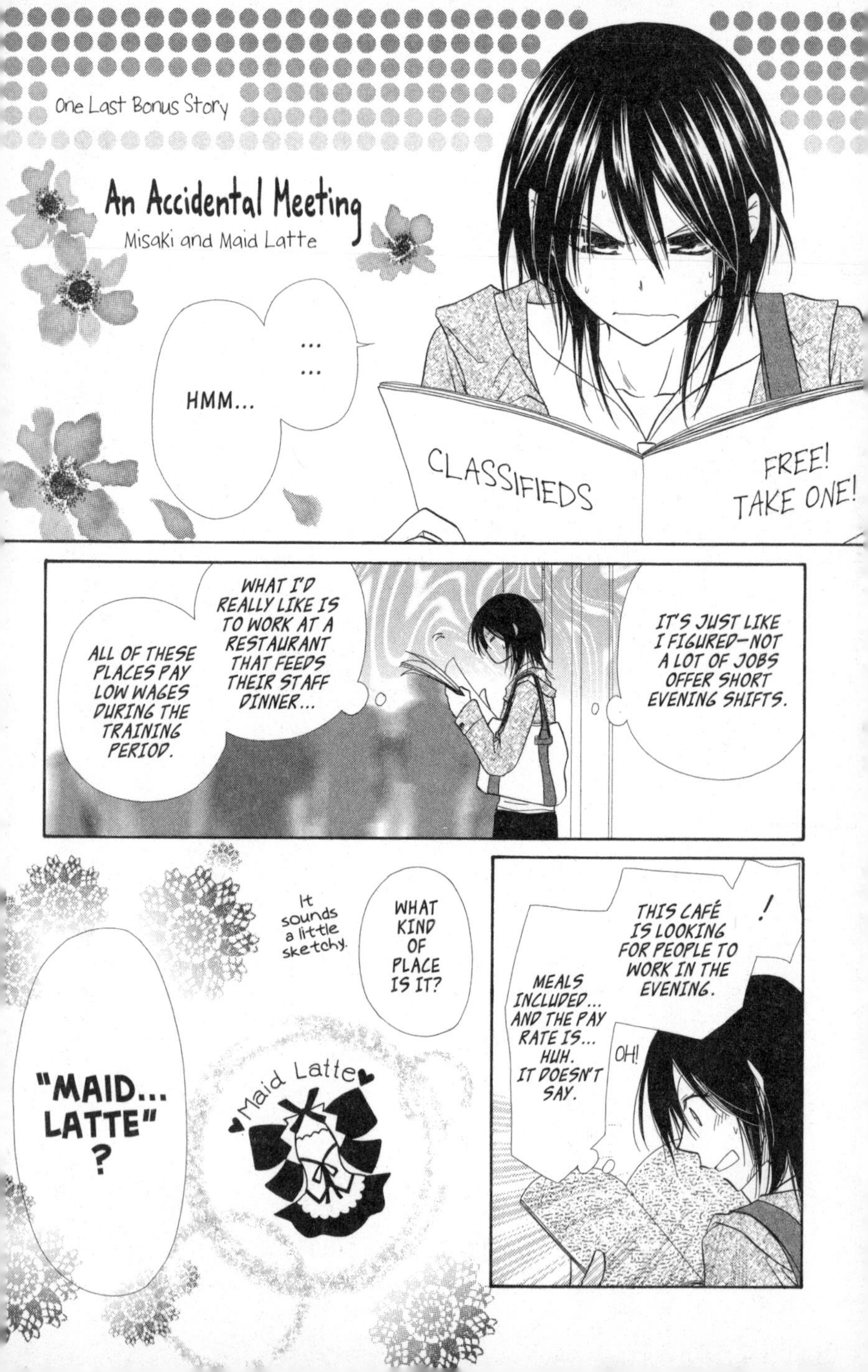
One Last Bonus Story
An Accidental Meeting
Misaki and Maid Latte
... ...
HMM...
CLASSIFIEDS
FREE! TAKE ONE!
IT'S JUST LIKE I FIGURED—NOT A LOT OF JOBS OFFER SHORT EVENING SHIFTS.
WHAT I'D REALLY LIKE IS TO WORK AT A RESTAURANT THAT FEEDS THEIR STAFF DINNER...
ALL OF THESE PLACES PAY LOW WAGES DURING THE TRAINING PERIOD.
!
THIS CAFÉ IS LOOKING FOR PEOPLE TO WORK IN THE EVENING.
MEALS INCLUDED... AND THE PAY RATE IS... HUH. IT DOESN'T SAY.
OH!
WHAT KIND OF PLACE IS IT?
It sounds a little sketchy.
Maid Latte
"MAID... LATTE"?

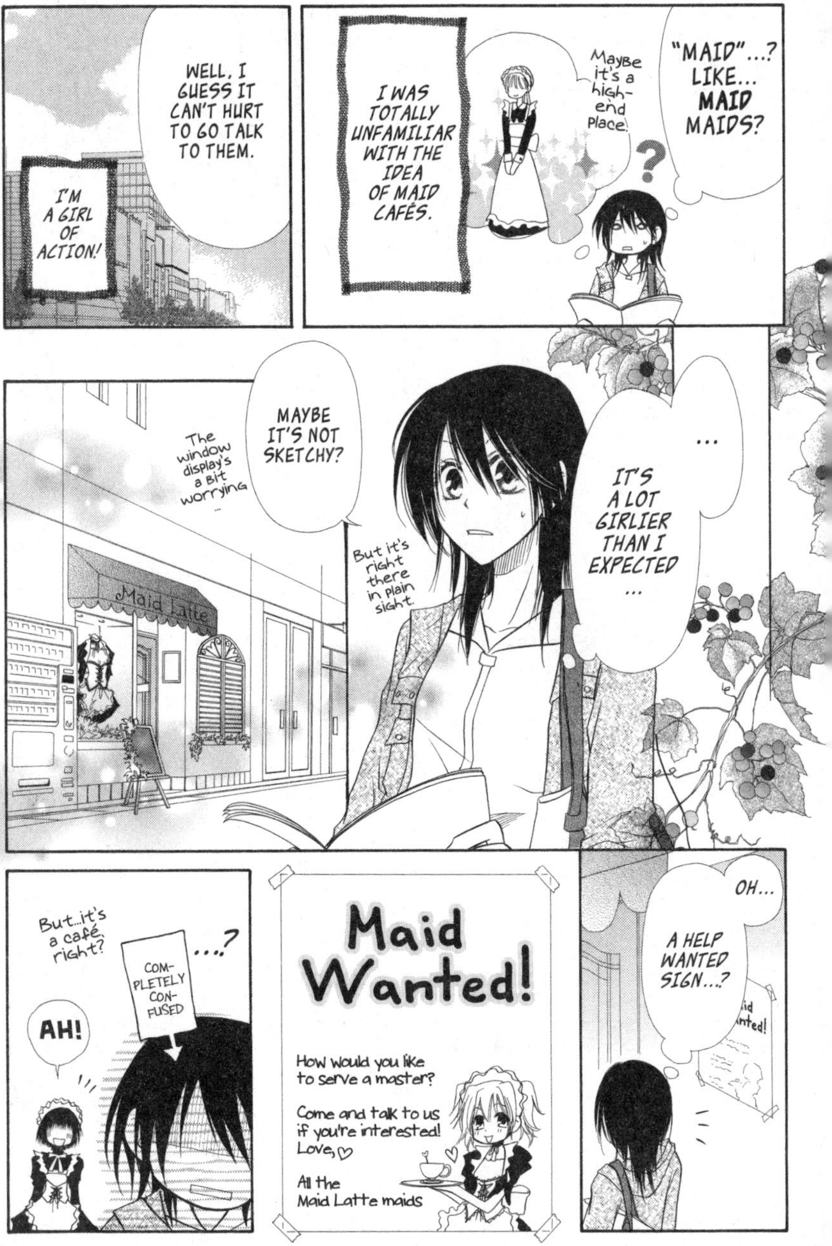
"MAID"...? LIKE... MAID MAIDS?
Maybe it's a high-end place.
I WAS TOTALLY UNFAMILIAR WITH THE IDEA OF MAID CAFÉS.
WELL, I GUESS IT CAN'T HURT TO GO TALK TO THEM.
I'M A GIRL OF ACTION!
...
IT'S A LOT GIRLIER THAN I EXPECTED...
But it's right there in plain sight.
MAYBE IT'S NOT SKETCHY?
The window display's a bit worrying...
Maid Latte
OH...
A HELP WANTED SIGN...?
Maid Wanted!
How would you like to serve a master?
Come and talk to us if you're interested! Love, ♡
All the Maid Latte maids
...?
COMPLETELY CONFUSED
But...it's a café, right?
AH!

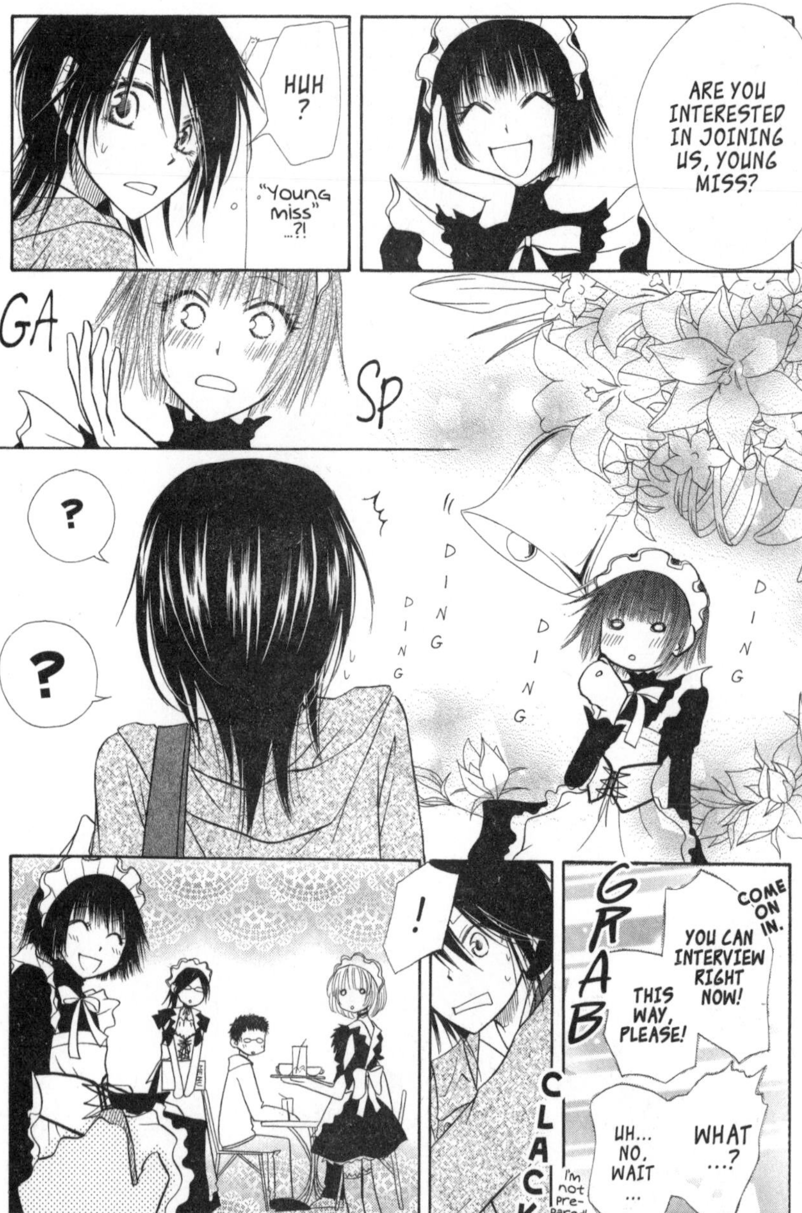
ARE YOU INTERESTED IN JOINING US, YOUNG MISS?
HUH?
"Young miss" ...?!
GA
SP
DING DING
DING DING
?
?
COME ON IN.
YOU CAN INTERVIEW RIGHT NOW!
THIS WAY, PLEASE!
GRAB
WHAT ...?
UH... NO. WAIT ...
CLACK
I'm not pre-pared!
!

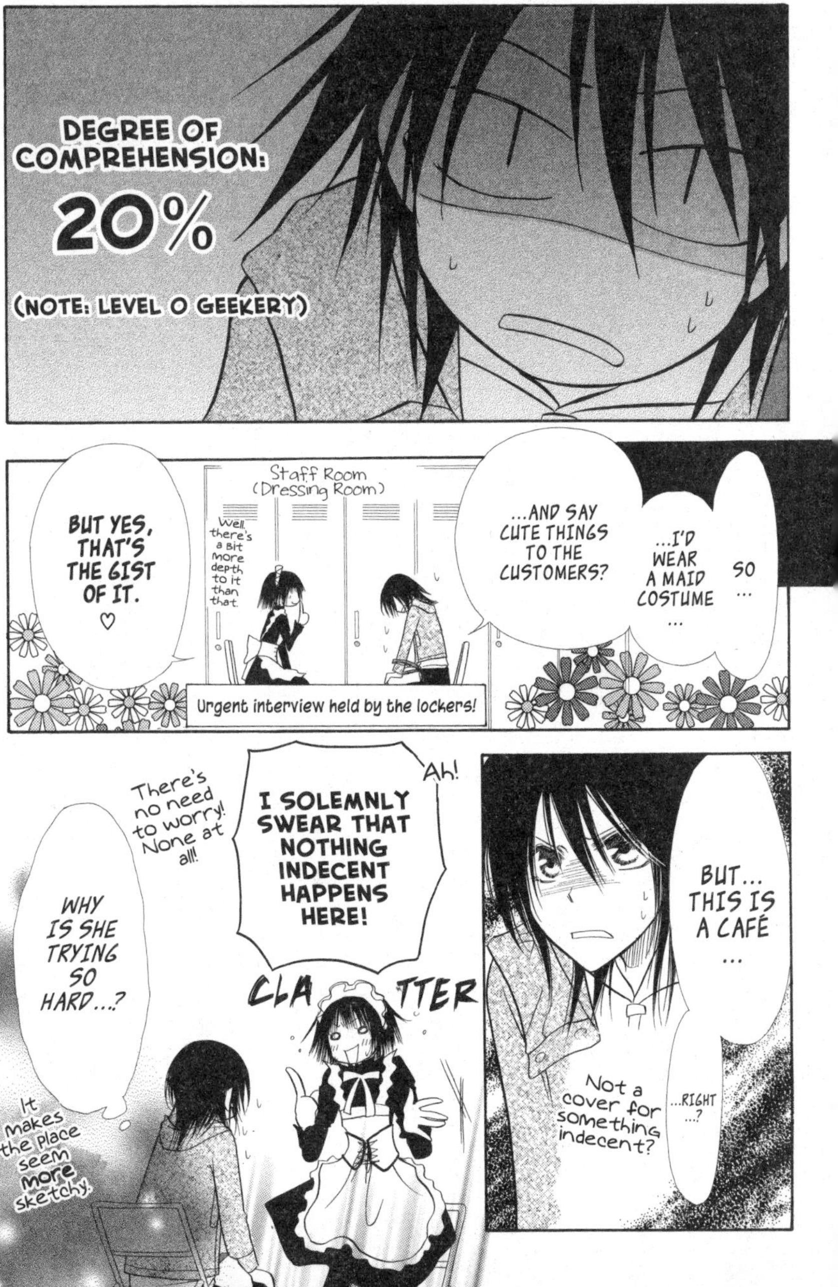
DEGREE OF COMPREHENSION:
20%
(NOTE: LEVEL 0 GEEKERY)
SO ...
...I'D WEAR A MAID COSTUME ...
...AND SAY CUTE THINGS TO THE CUSTOMERS?
Staff Room (Dressing Room)
Well, there's a bit more depth to it than that.
BUT YES, THAT'S THE GIST OF IT. ♡
Urgent interview held by the lockers!
BUT... THIS IS A CAFÉ ...
...RIGHT ...?
Not a cover for something indecent?
Ah!
I SOLEMNLY SWEAR THAT NOTHING INDECENT HAPPENS HERE!
There's no need to worry! None at all!
CLATTER
WHY IS SHE TRYING SO HARD...?
It makes the place seem more sketchy.

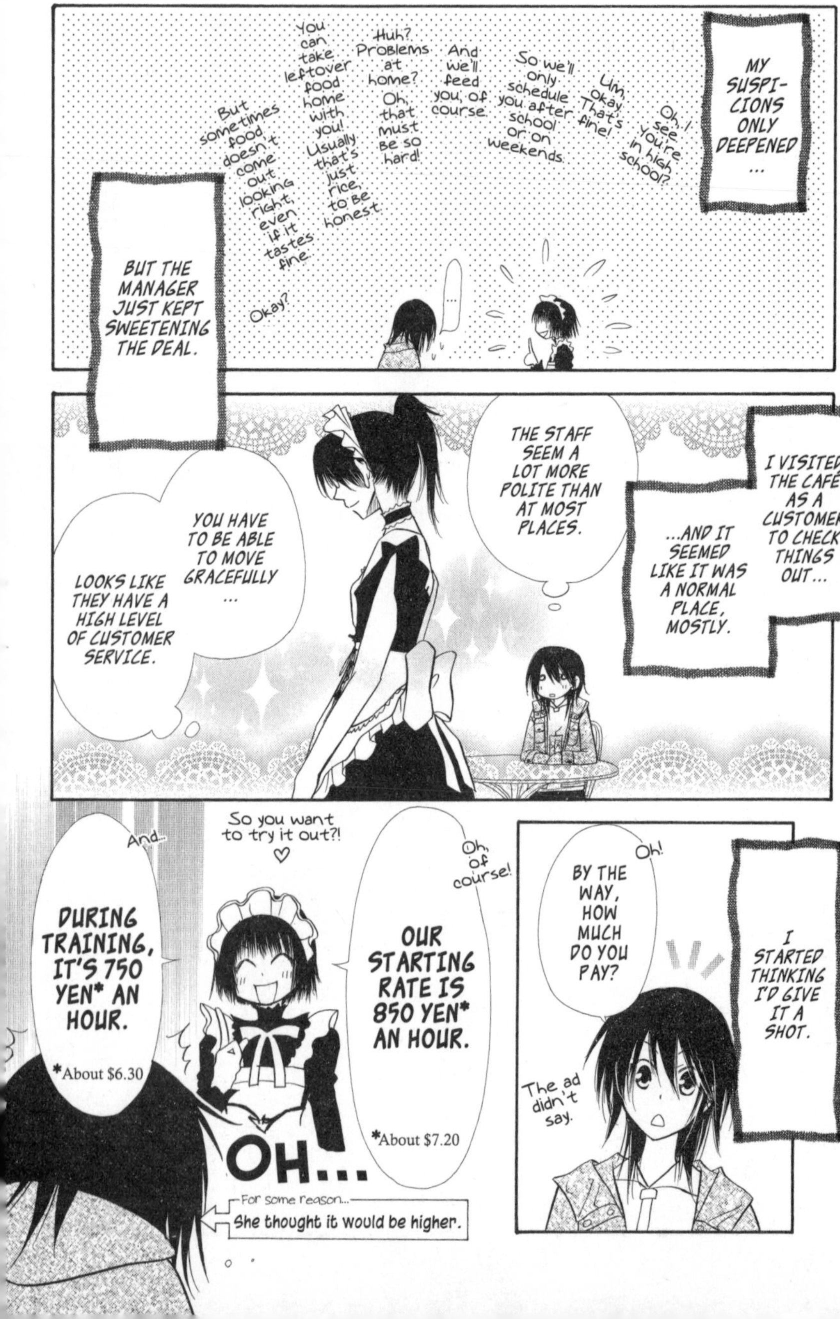
MY SUSPICIONS ONLY DEEPENED...
Oh... I see. You're in high school?
Um, okay. That's fine!
So we'll only schedule you after school or on weekends.
And we'll feed you, of course.
Huh? Problems at home?
Oh, that must be so hard!
You can take leftover food home with you! Usually that's just rice, to be honest.
But sometimes food doesn't come out looking right, even if it tastes fine.
Okay?
...
BUT THE MANAGER JUST KEPT SWEETENING THE DEAL.
I VISITED THE CAFÉ AS A CUSTOMER TO CHECK THINGS OUT...
...AND IT SEEMED LIKE IT WAS A NORMAL PLACE, MOSTLY.
THE STAFF SEEM A LOT MORE POLITE THAN AT MOST PLACES.
YOU HAVE TO BE ABLE TO MOVE GRACEFULLY...
LOOKS LIKE THEY HAVE A HIGH LEVEL OF CUSTOMER SERVICE.
I STARTED THINKING I'D GIVE IT A SHOT.
Oh!
BY THE WAY, HOW MUCH DO YOU PAY?
The ad didn't say.
So you want to try it out?! ♡
Oh, of course!
OUR STARTING RATE IS 850 YEN* AN HOUR.
*About $7.20
And...
DURING TRAINING, IT'S 750 YEN* AN HOUR.
*About $6.30
OH...
For some reason...
She thought it would be higher.

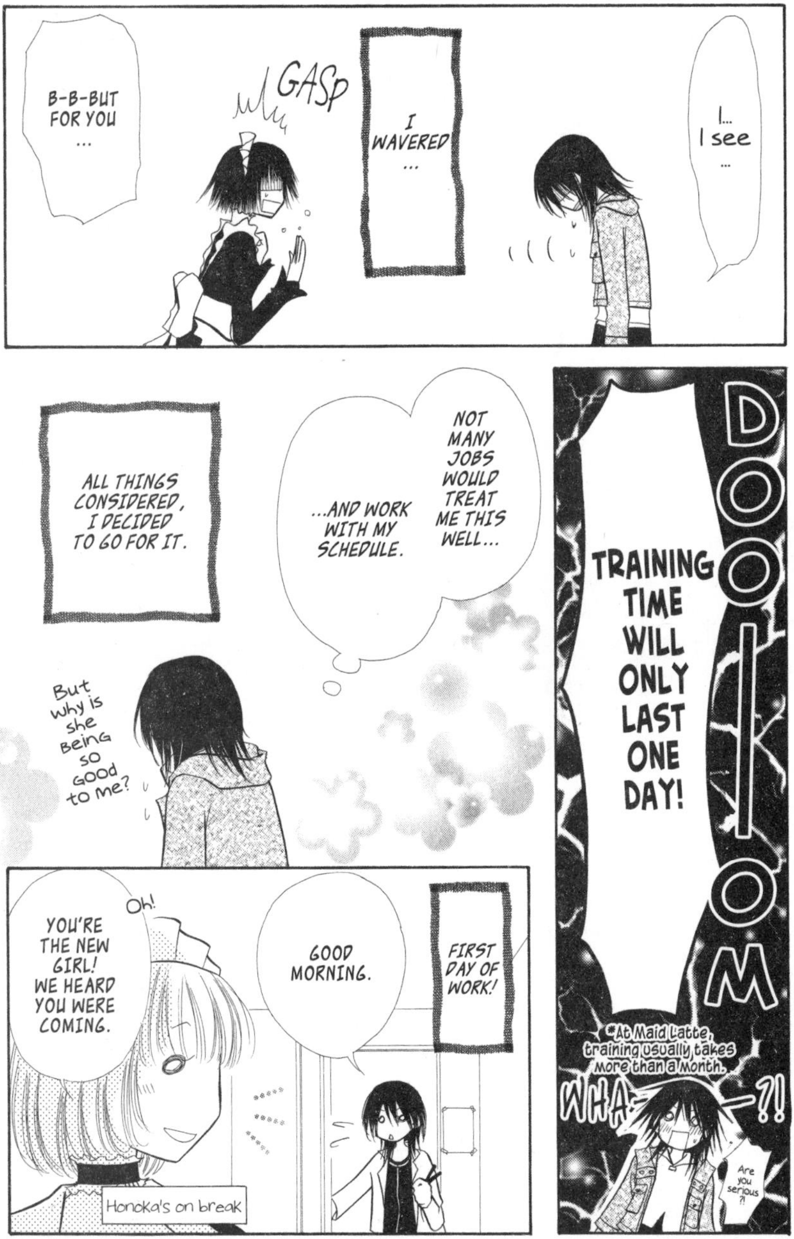
I... I see ...
I WAVERED ...
GASP
B-B-BUT FOR YOU ...
DOO—OOM
TRAINING TIME WILL ONLY LAST ONE DAY!
*At Maid Latte, training usually takes more than a month.
WHA—?!
Are you serious?!
NOT MANY JOBS WOULD TREAT ME THIS WELL...
...AND WORK WITH MY SCHEDULE.
ALL THINGS CONSIDERED, I DECIDED TO GO FOR IT.
But why is she being so good to me?
FIRST DAY OF WORK!
GOOD MORNING.
Oh!
YOU'RE THE NEW GIRL! WE HEARD YOU WERE COMING.
Honoka's on break

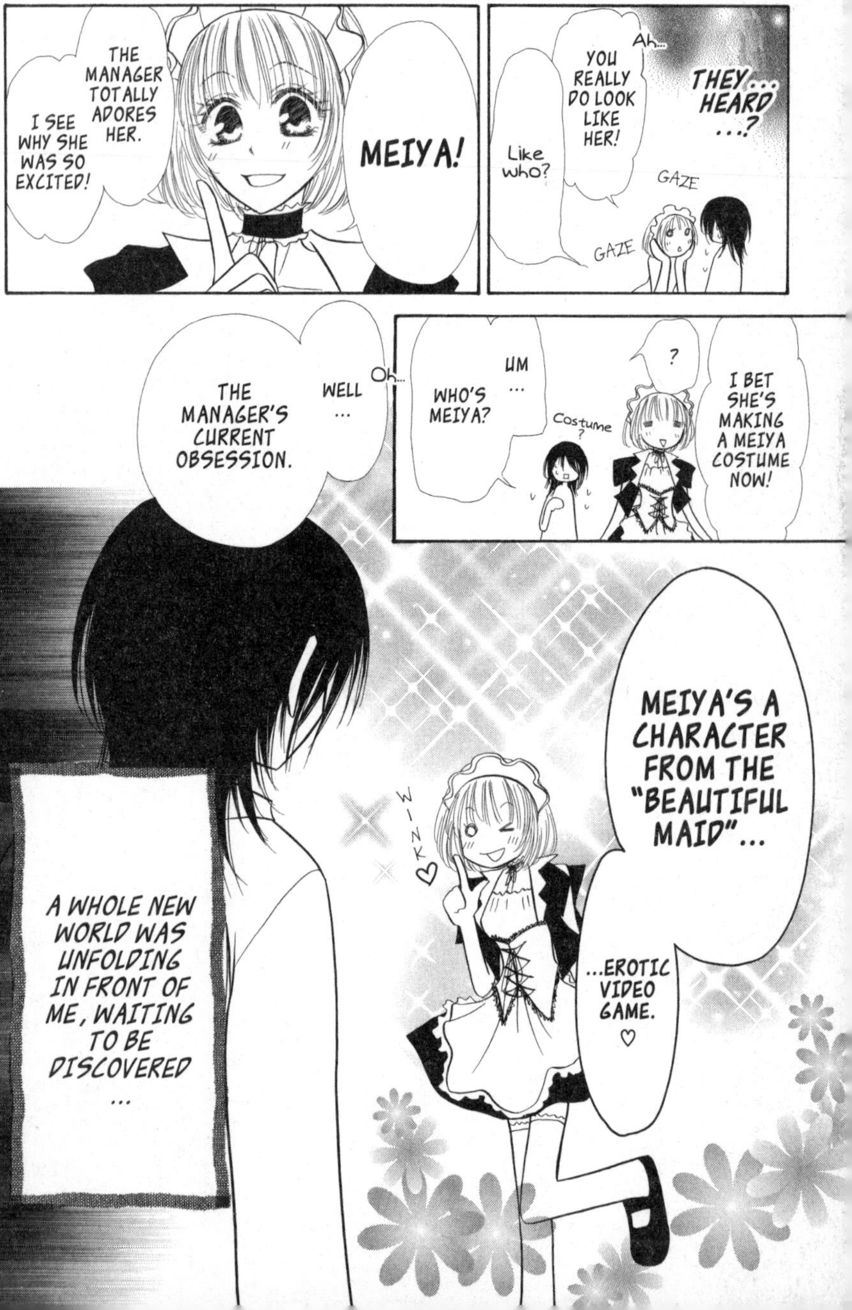
THEY... HEARD...?
Ah...
YOU REALLY DO LOOK LIKE HER!
Like who?
GAZE
GAZE
MEIYA!
THE MANAGER TOTALLY ADORES HER.
I SEE WHY SHE WAS SO EXCITED!
I BET SHE'S MAKING A MEIYA COSTUME NOW!
?
UM ...
WHO'S MEIYA?
Costume?
Oh...
WELL ...
THE MANAGER'S CURRENT OBSESSION.
MEIYA'S A CHARACTER FROM THE "BEAUTIFUL MAID"...
WINK ♡
...EROTIC VIDEO GAME. ♡
A WHOLE NEW WORLD WAS UNFOLDING IN FRONT OF ME, WAITING TO BE DISCOVERED ...

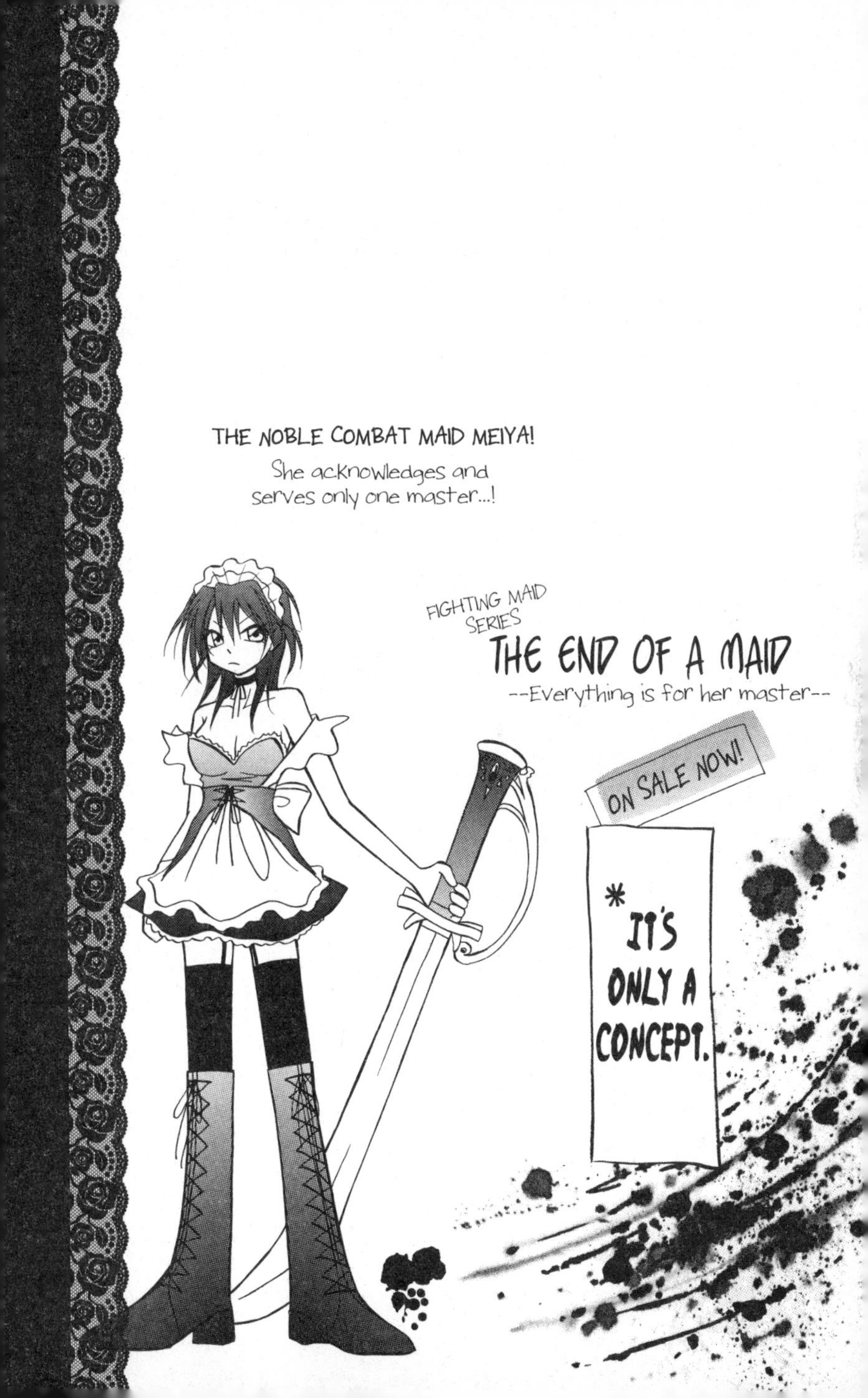
THE NOBLE COMBAT MAID MEIYA!
She acknowledges and serves only one master...!
FIGHTING MAID SERIES
THE END OF A MAID
--Everything is for her master--
ON SALE NOW!
*IT'S ONLY A CONCEPT.

Thank you for reading right to the end! Who would've expected my first-ever manga to have such an outrageous title?

I'm going to let my hair down and have fun with this, so I hope you'll all come along for the ride.

I'd love to hear from you! If you write to me, I'll cry from sheer joy. It might take me a while, but I'll write back for sure!

∘ **Address** ∘

Hiro Fujiwara
c/o Maid-sama! Editor
Viz Media
P.O. Box 77010
San Francisco, CA 94107

▶ **Special Thanks**

Research Assistance

Maid Café Chocolatte
Café and Reflexology Garden Fairy

• The Staff
• Mother and K

CLOSING TIME... / THE END

Shojo Beat

Maid-sama!

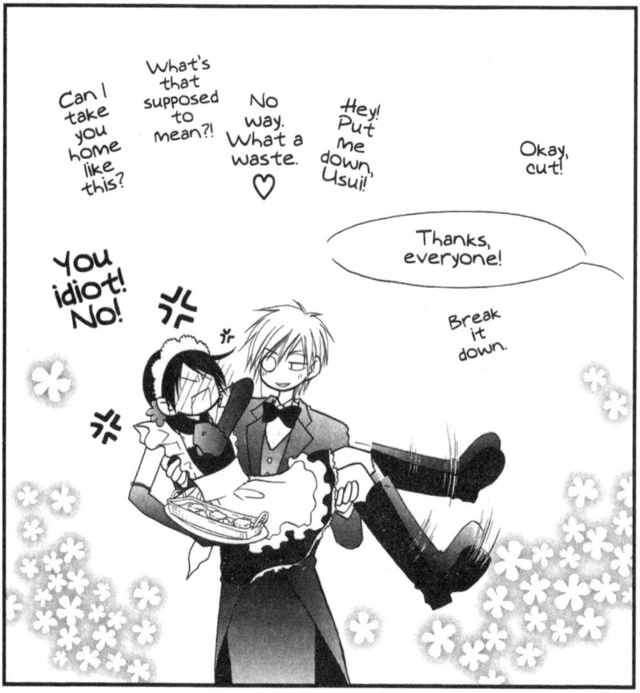
Okay, cut!
Thanks, everyone!
Break it down.
Hey! Put me down, Usui!
No way. What a waste. ♡
What's that supposed to mean?!
Can I take you home like this?
You idiot! No!

Vol.2

Story & Art by

Hiro Fujiwara

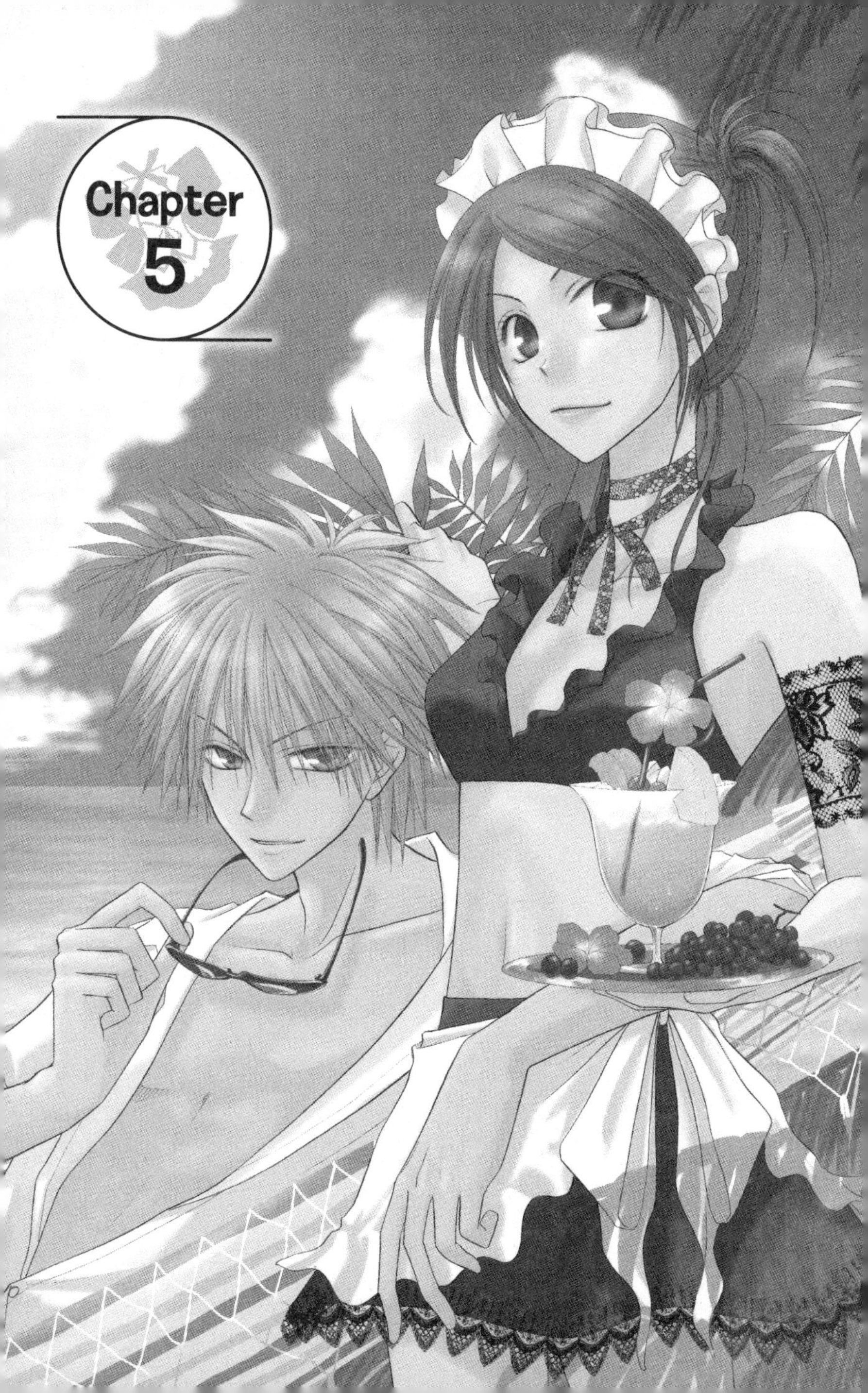
Chapter
5

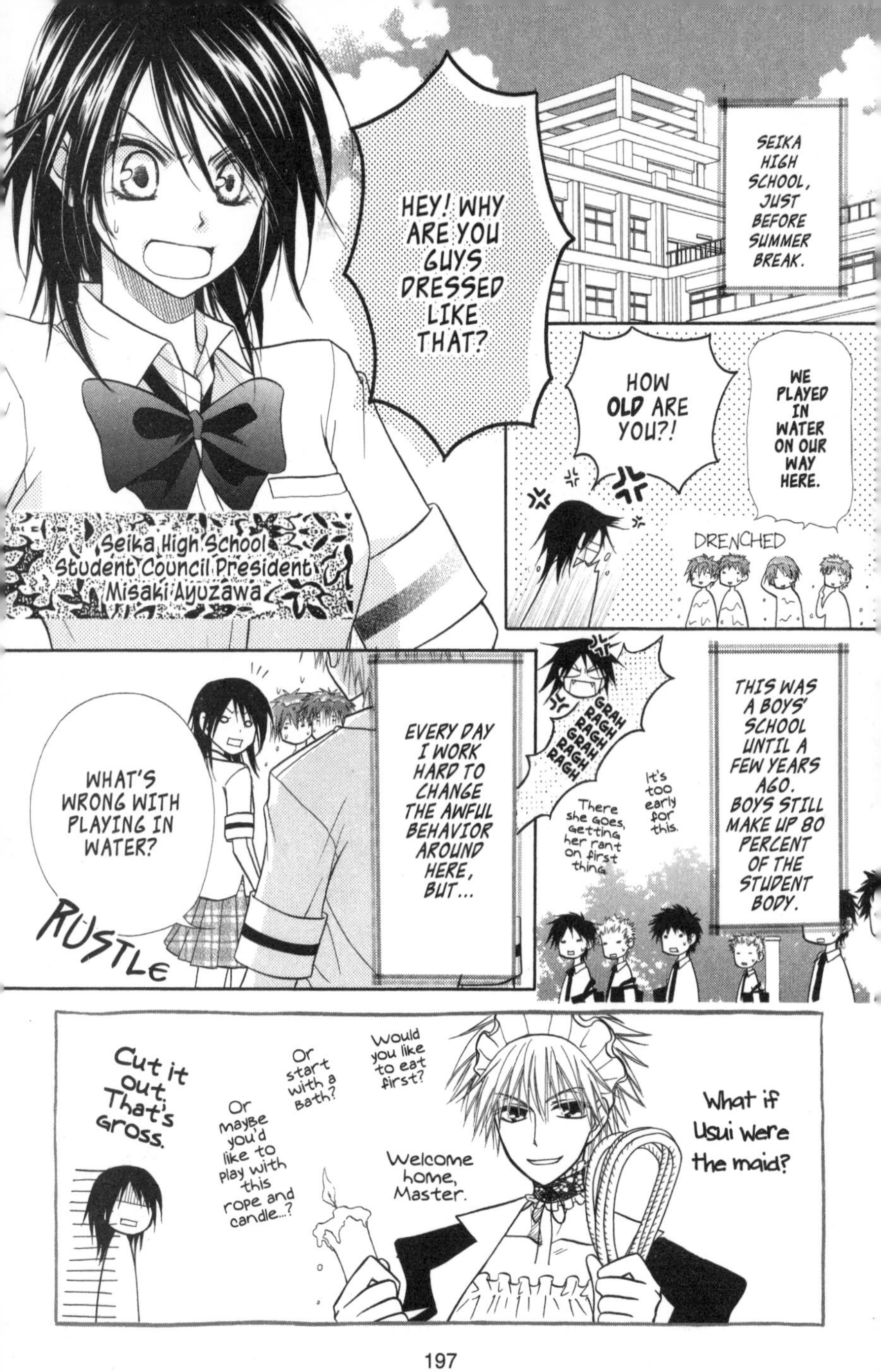
SEIKA HIGH SCHOOL, JUST BEFORE SUMMER BREAK.
WE PLAYED IN WATER ON OUR WAY HERE.
HOW OLD ARE YOU?!
DRENCHED
HEY! WHY ARE YOU GUYS DRESSED LIKE THAT?
Seika High School Student Council President Misaki Ayuzawa
THIS WAS A BOYS' SCHOOL UNTIL A FEW YEARS AGO. BOYS STILL MAKE UP 80 PERCENT OF THE STUDENT BODY.
GRAH RAGH RAGH GRAH RAGH RAGH
It's too early for this.
There she goes, getting her rant on first thing.
EVERY DAY I WORK HARD TO CHANGE THE AWFUL BEHAVIOR AROUND HERE, BUT...
WHAT'S WRONG WITH PLAYING IN WATER?
RUSTLE
What if Usui were the maid?
Would you like to eat first?
Welcome home, Master.
Or start with a Bath?
Or maybe you'd like to play with this rope and candle...?
Cut it out. That's gross.

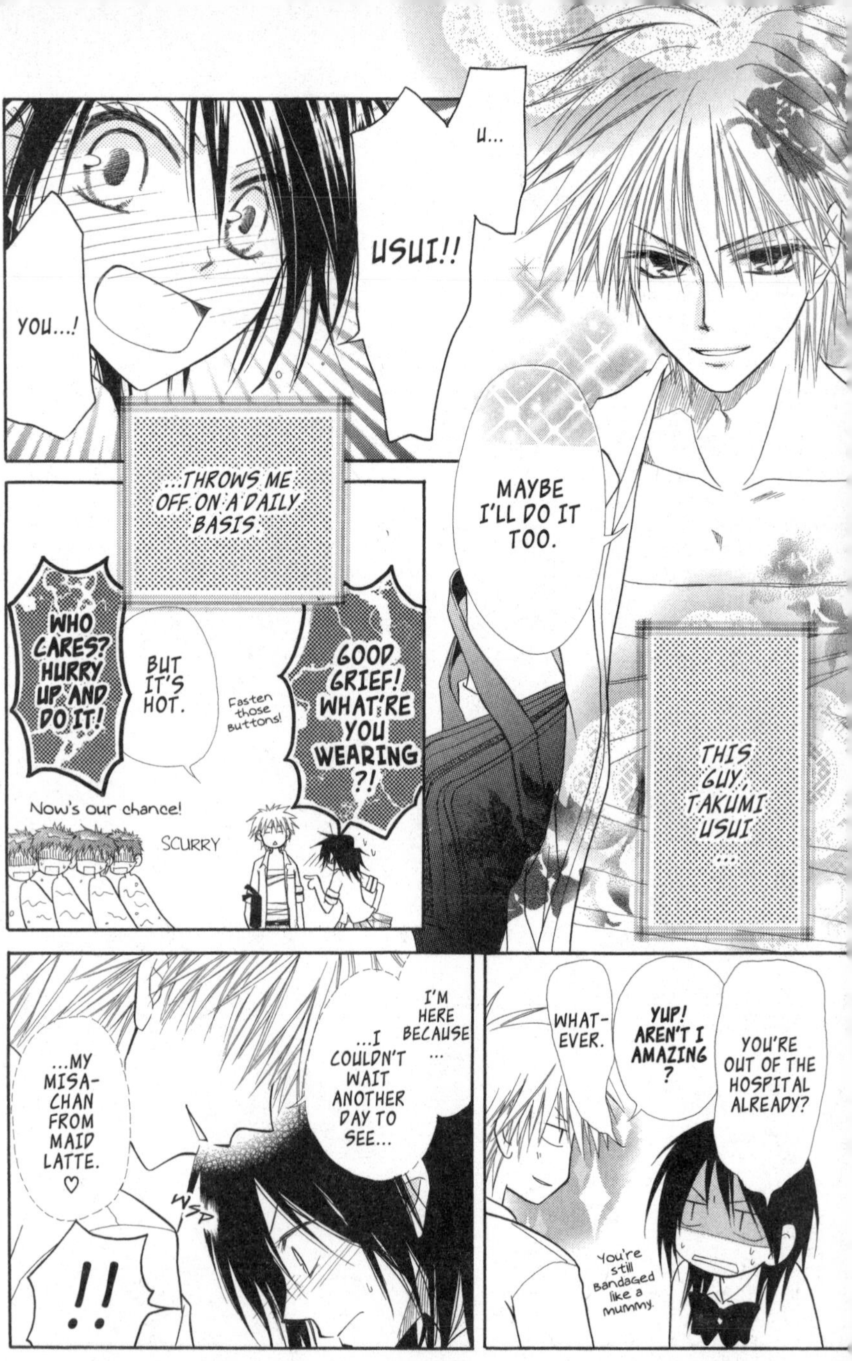

YOU...!
U...
USUI!!
THIS GUY, TAKUMI USUI...
...THROWS ME OFF ON A DAILY BASIS.
MAYBE I'LL DO IT TOO.
GOOD GRIEF! WHAT'RE YOU WEARING?!
Fasten those buttons!
BUT IT'S HOT.
WHO CARES? HURRY UP AND DO IT!
Now's our chance!
SCURRY
YOU'RE OUT OF THE HOSPITAL ALREADY?
YUP! AREN'T I AMAZING?
WHAT-EVER.
You're still bandaged like a mummy.
I'M HERE BECAUSE...
...I COULDN'T WAIT ANOTHER DAY TO SEE...
...MY MISA-CHAN FROM MAID LATTE. ♡
WSP
!!

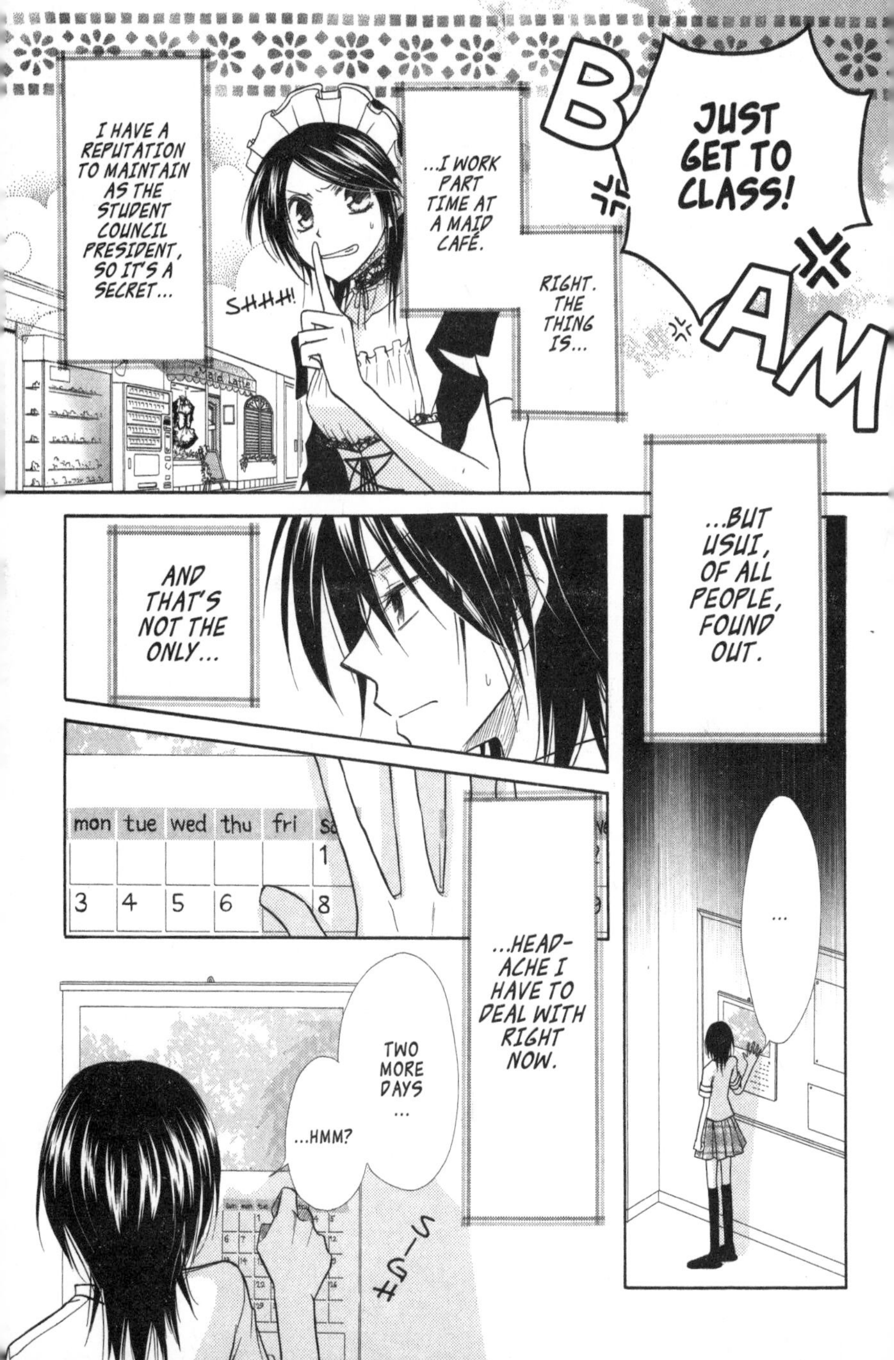
BAM
JUST GET TO CLASS!
RIGHT. THE THING IS...
...I WORK PART TIME AT A MAID CAFÉ.
SHHH!
I HAVE A REPUTATION TO MAINTAIN AS THE STUDENT COUNCIL PRESIDENT, SO IT'S A SECRET...
Maid Latte
...BUT USUI, OF ALL PEOPLE, FOUND OUT.
...
AND THAT'S NOT THE ONLY...
...HEAD-ACHE I HAVE TO DEAL WITH RIGHT NOW.
mon tue wed thu fri
1
3 4 5 6 8
TWO MORE DAYS ...
...HMM?
SIGH

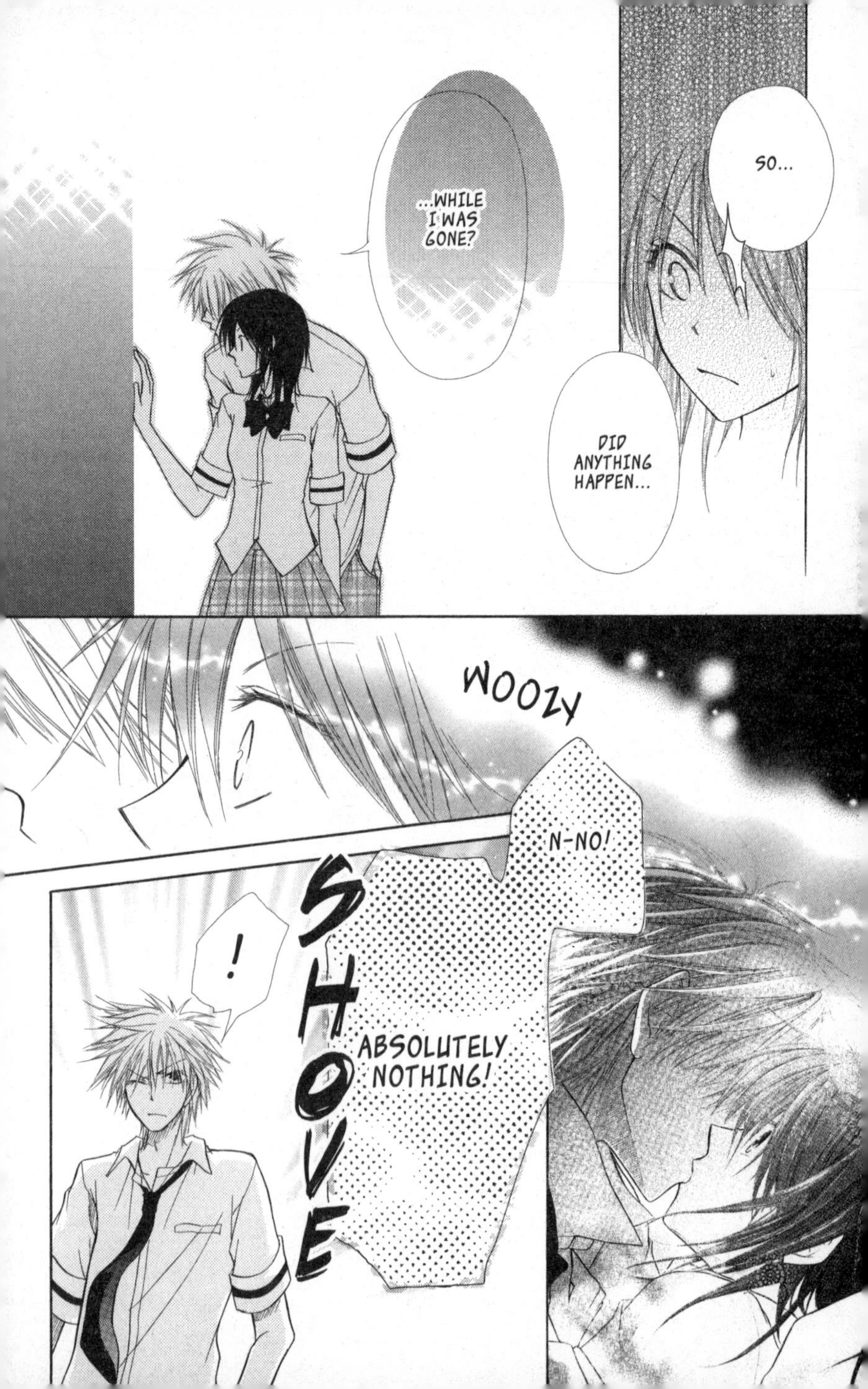
SO...
DID ANYTHING HAPPEN...
...WHILE I WAS GONE?
WOOZY
N-NO!
ABSOLUTELY NOTHING!
SHOVE
!

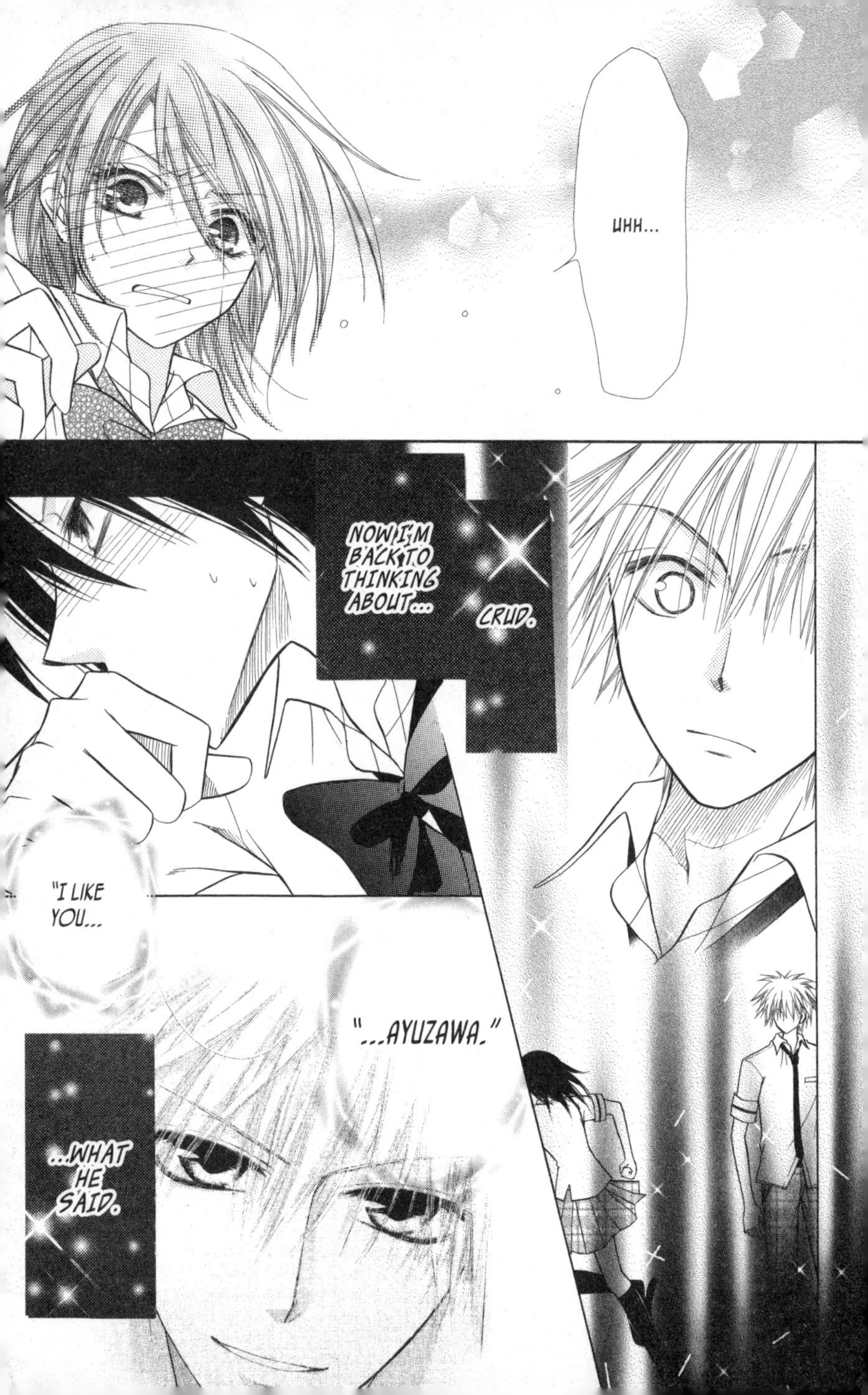
UHH...
NOW I'M BACK TO THINKING ABOUT...
CRUD.
"I LIKE YOU...
"...AYUZAWA."
...WHAT HE SAID.

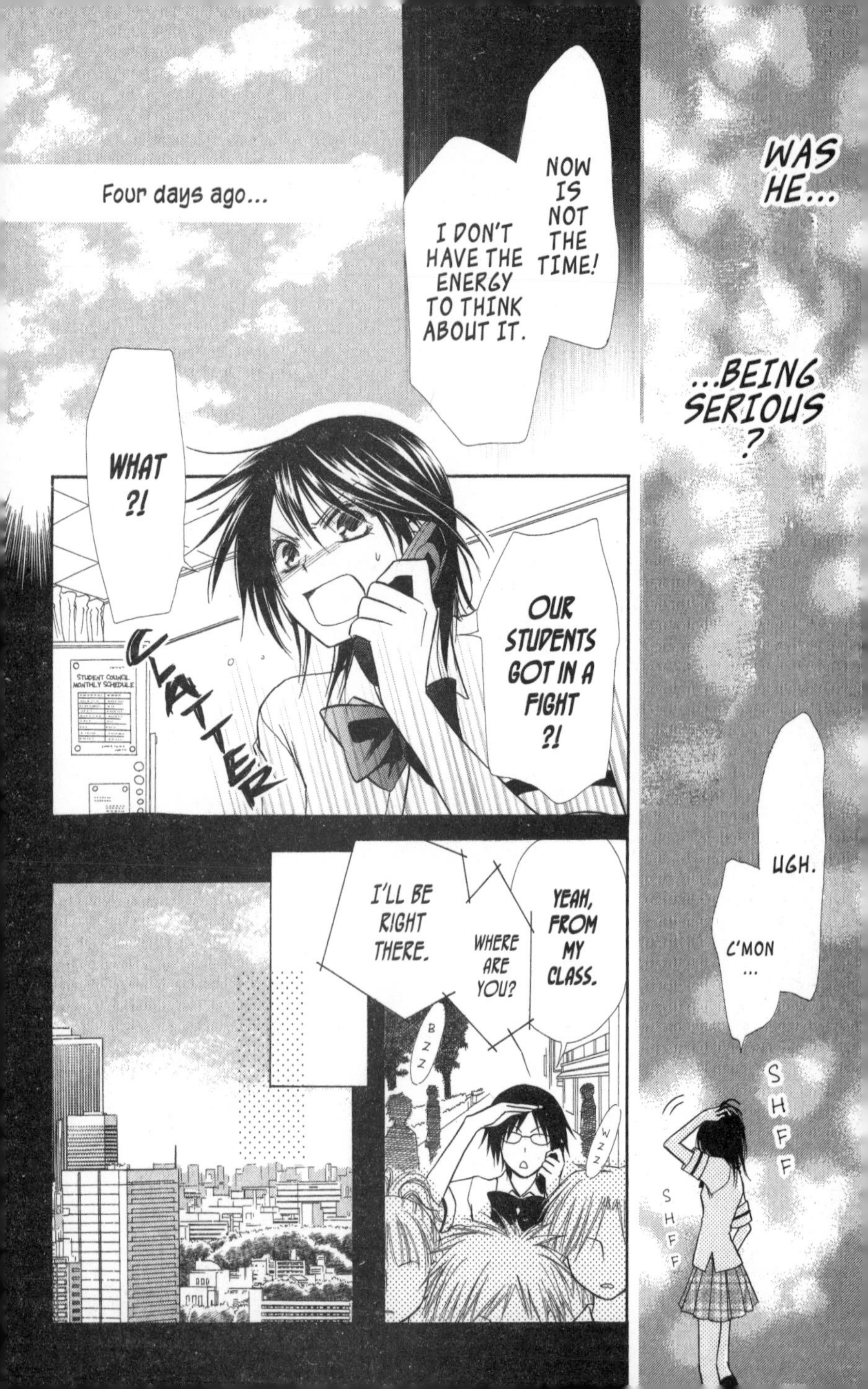
WAS HE...
...BEING SERIOUS?
UGH.
C'MON...
SHFF
SHFF
NOW IS NOT THE TIME!
I DON'T HAVE THE ENERGY TO THINK ABOUT IT.
Four days ago...
WHAT ?!
OUR STUDENTS GOT IN A FIGHT ?!
CLATTER
STUDENT COUNCIL MONTHLY SCHEDULE
YEAH, FROM MY CLASS.
WHERE ARE YOU?
I'LL BE RIGHT THERE.
BZZ
WZZ

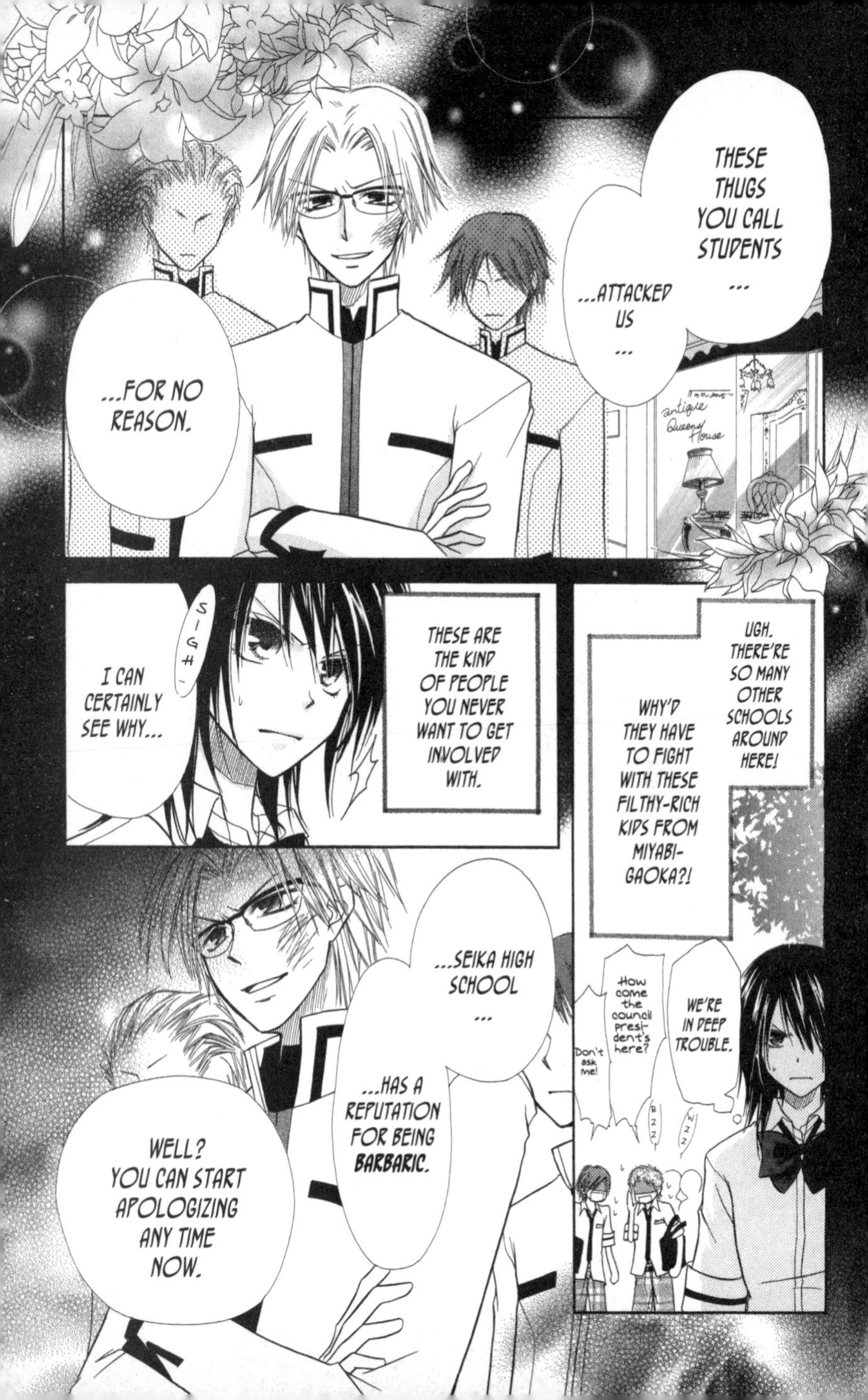
THESE THUGS YOU CALL STUDENTS ...
...ATTACKED US ...
...FOR NO REASON.
antique Queens House
UGH. THERE'RE SO MANY OTHER SCHOOLS AROUND HERE!
WHY'D THEY HAVE TO FIGHT WITH THESE FILTHY-RICH KIDS FROM MIYABI-GAOKA?!
WE'RE IN DEEP TROUBLE.
How come the council president's here?
Don't ask me!
BZZ
WZZ
THESE ARE THE KIND OF PEOPLE YOU NEVER WANT TO GET INVOLVED WITH.
SIGH...
I CAN CERTAINLY SEE WHY...
...SEIKA HIGH SCHOOL ...
...HAS A REPUTATION FOR BEING **BARBARIC.**
WELL? YOU CAN START APOLOGIZING ANY TIME NOW.

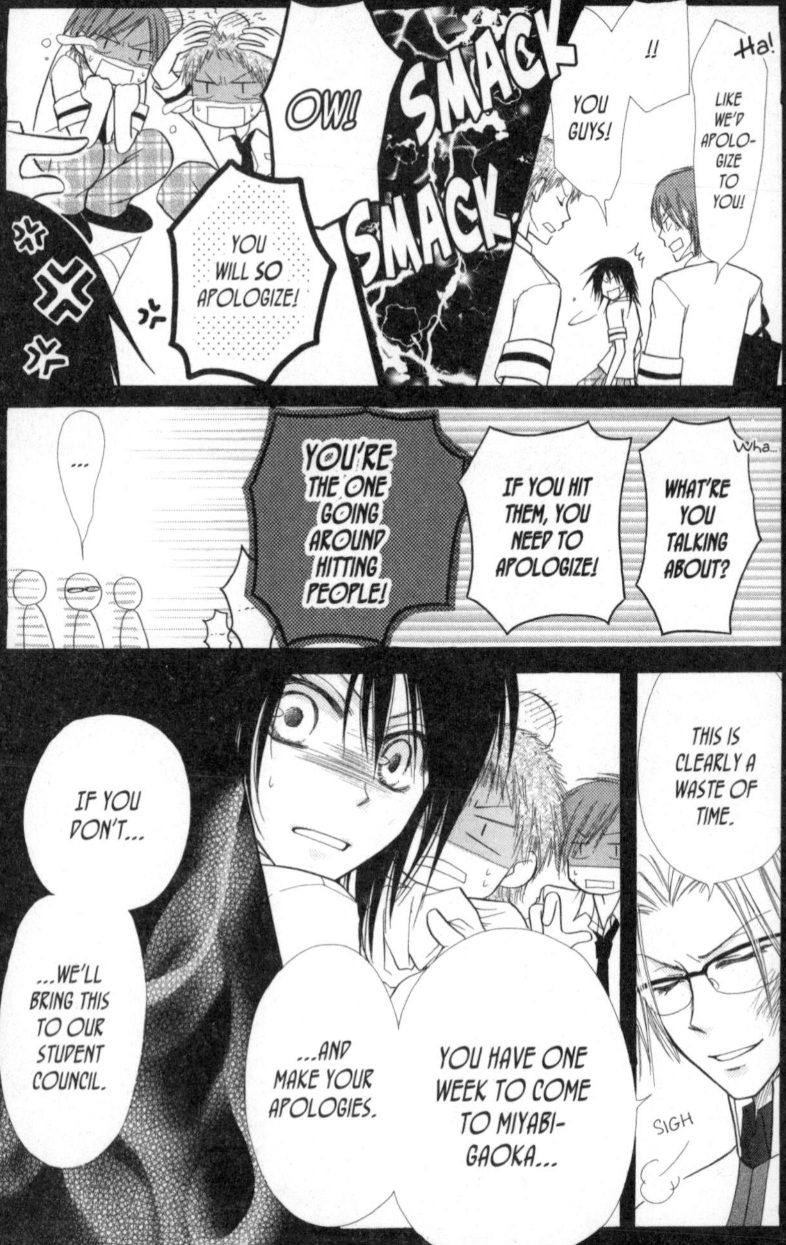
Ha!
LIKE WE'D APOLO-GIZE TO YOU!
!!
YOU GUYS!
SMACK
SMACK
OW!
YOU WILL SO APOLOGIZE!
Wha...
WHAT'RE YOU TALKING ABOUT?
IF YOU HIT THEM, YOU NEED TO APOLOGIZE!
YOU'RE THE ONE GOING AROUND HITTING PEOPLE!
...
THIS IS CLEARLY A WASTE OF TIME.
SIGH
YOU HAVE ONE WEEK TO COME TO MIYABI-GAOKA...
...AND MAKE YOUR APOLOGIES.
IF YOU DON'T...
...WE'LL BRING THIS TO OUR STUDENT COUNCIL.

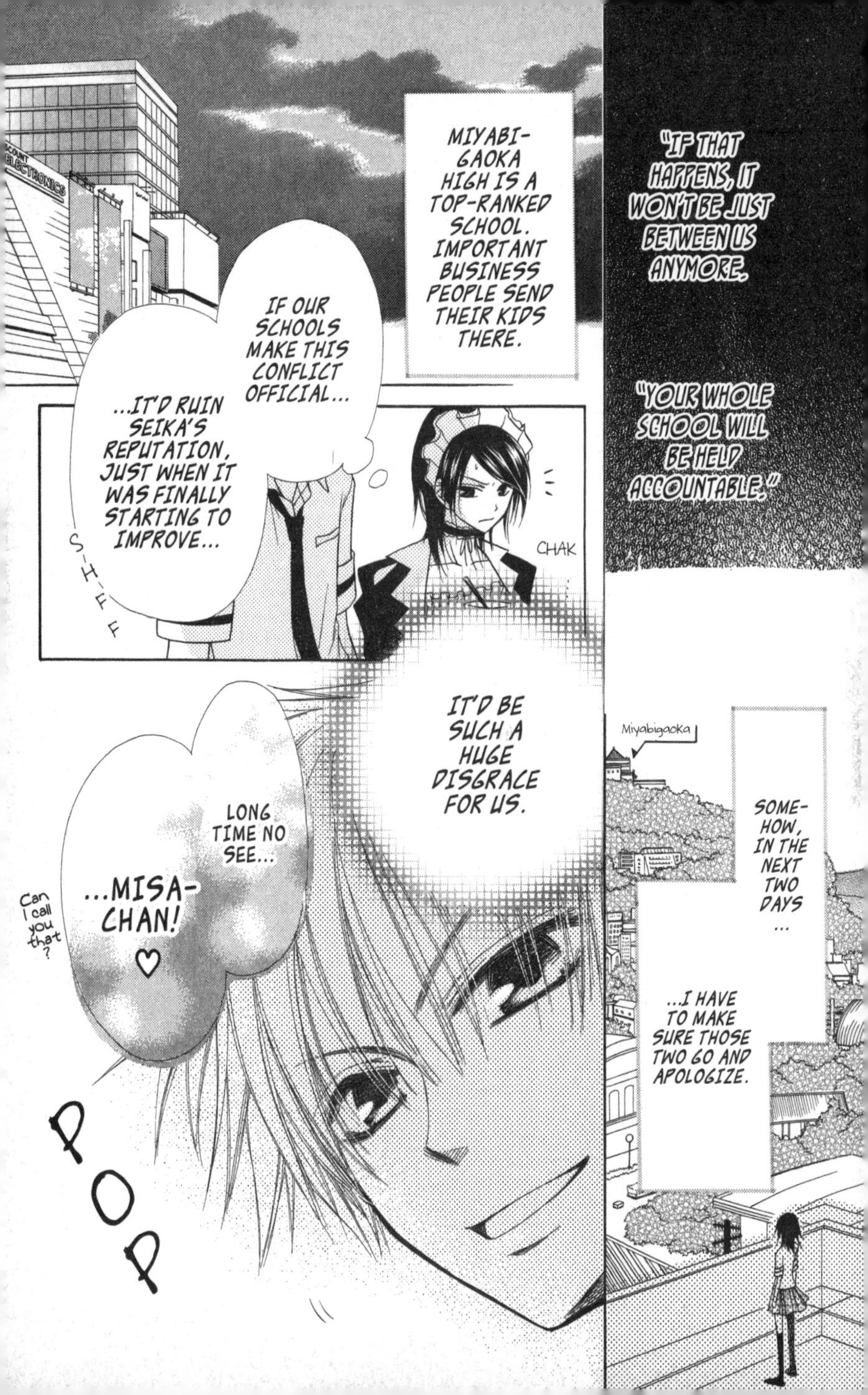
"IF THAT HAPPENS, IT WON'T BE JUST BETWEEN US ANYMORE.
"YOUR WHOLE SCHOOL WILL BE HELD ACCOUNTABLE."
MIYABI-GAOKA HIGH IS A TOP-RANKED SCHOOL. IMPORTANT BUSINESS PEOPLE SEND THEIR KIDS THERE.
IF OUR SCHOOLS MAKE THIS CONFLICT OFFICIAL...
...IT'D RUIN SEIKA'S REPUTATION, JUST WHEN IT WAS FINALLY STARTING TO IMPROVE...
CHAK
S-H-F-F
IT'D BE SUCH A HUGE DISGRACE FOR US.
Miyabigaoka
SOME-HOW, IN THE NEXT TWO DAYS...
...I HAVE TO MAKE SURE THOSE TWO GO AND APOLOGIZE.
LONG TIME NO SEE...
...MISA-CHAN! ♡
Can I call you that?
POP

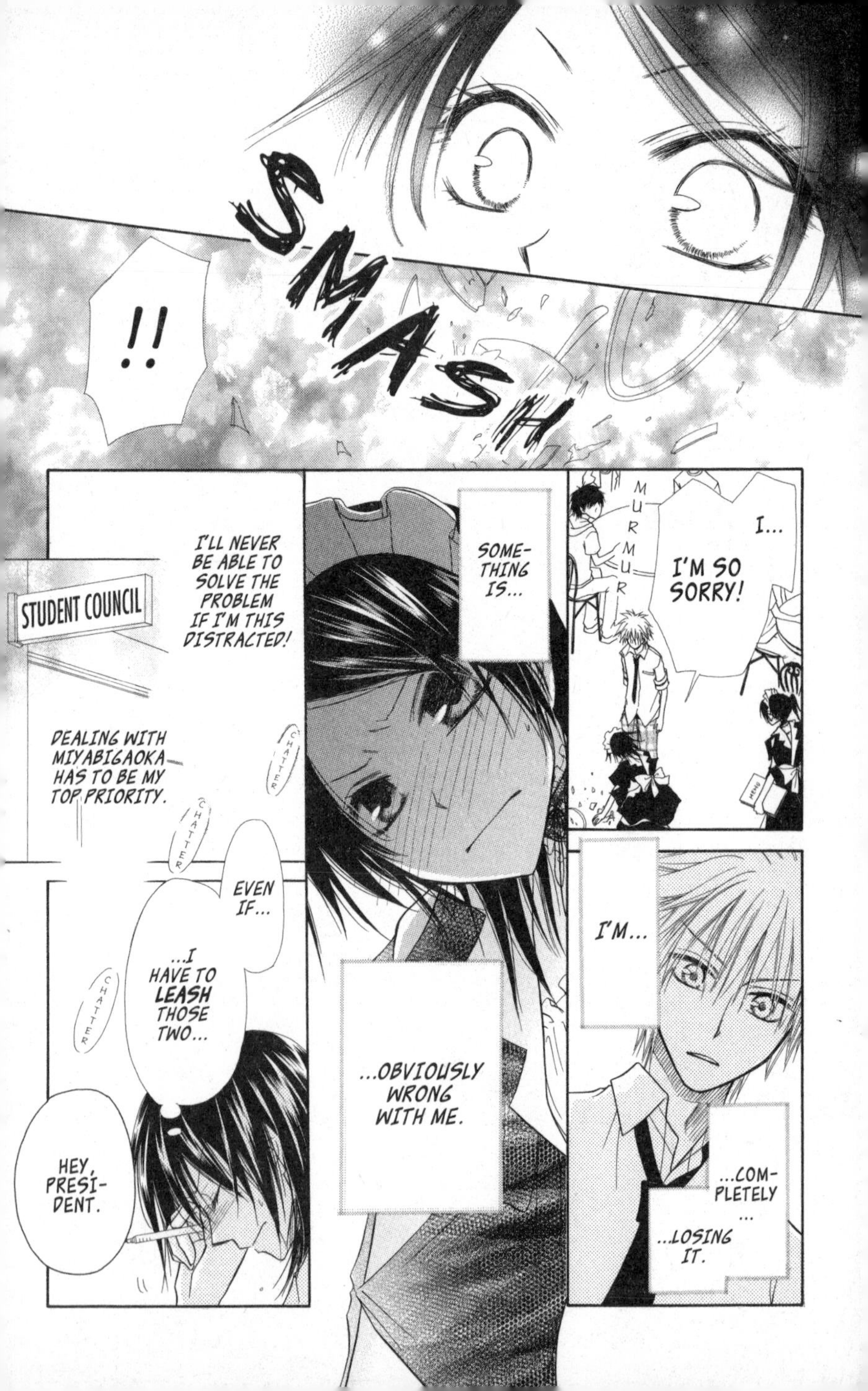
SMASH
!!
I...
I'M SO SORRY!
MURMUR
MURMUR
I'M...
...COMPLETELY...
...LOSING IT.
SOME-THING IS...
...OBVIOUSLY WRONG WITH ME.
STUDENT COUNCIL
I'LL NEVER BE ABLE TO SOLVE THE PROBLEM IF I'M THIS DISTRACTED!
DEALING WITH MIYABIGAOKA HAS TO BE MY TOP PRIORITY.
CHATTER
CHATTER
EVEN IF...
...I HAVE TO LEASH THOSE TWO...
CHATTER
HEY, PRESI-DENT.

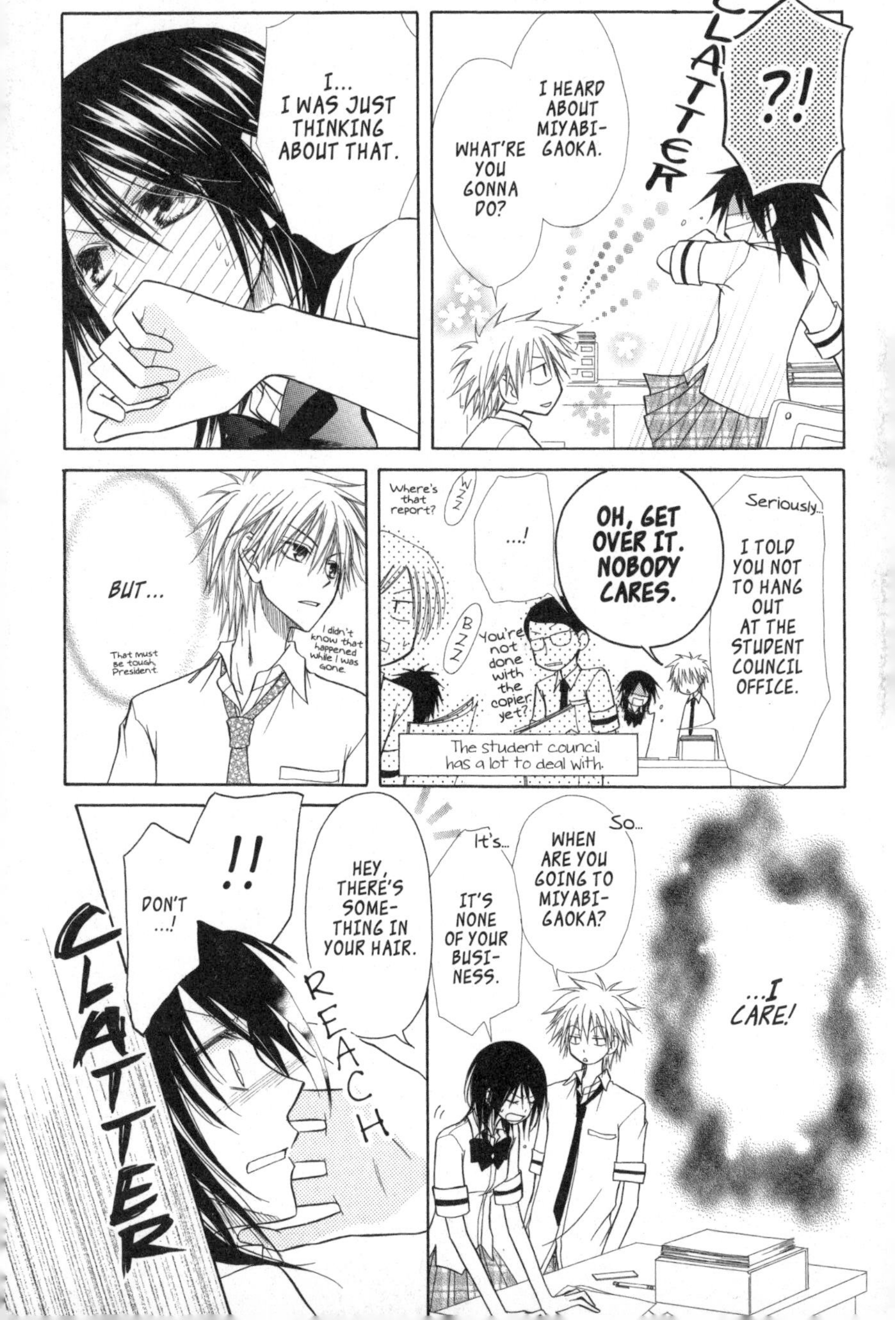
CLATTER
?!
I HEARD ABOUT MIYABI-GAOKA.
WHAT'RE YOU GONNA DO?
I... I WAS JUST THINKING ABOUT THAT.
Seriously...
I TOLD YOU NOT TO HANG OUT AT THE STUDENT COUNCIL OFFICE.
OH, GET OVER IT. NOBODY CARES.
...!
WZZ
Where's that report?
BZZ
You're not done with the copier yet?
The student council has a lot to deal with.
BUT...
I didn't know that happened while I was gone.
That must be tough, President.
...I CARE!
So...
WHEN ARE YOU GOING TO MIYABI-GAOKA?
It's...
IT'S NONE OF YOUR BUSI-NESS.
HEY, THERE'S SOME-THING IN YOUR HAIR.
REACH
!!
DON'T ...!
CLATTER

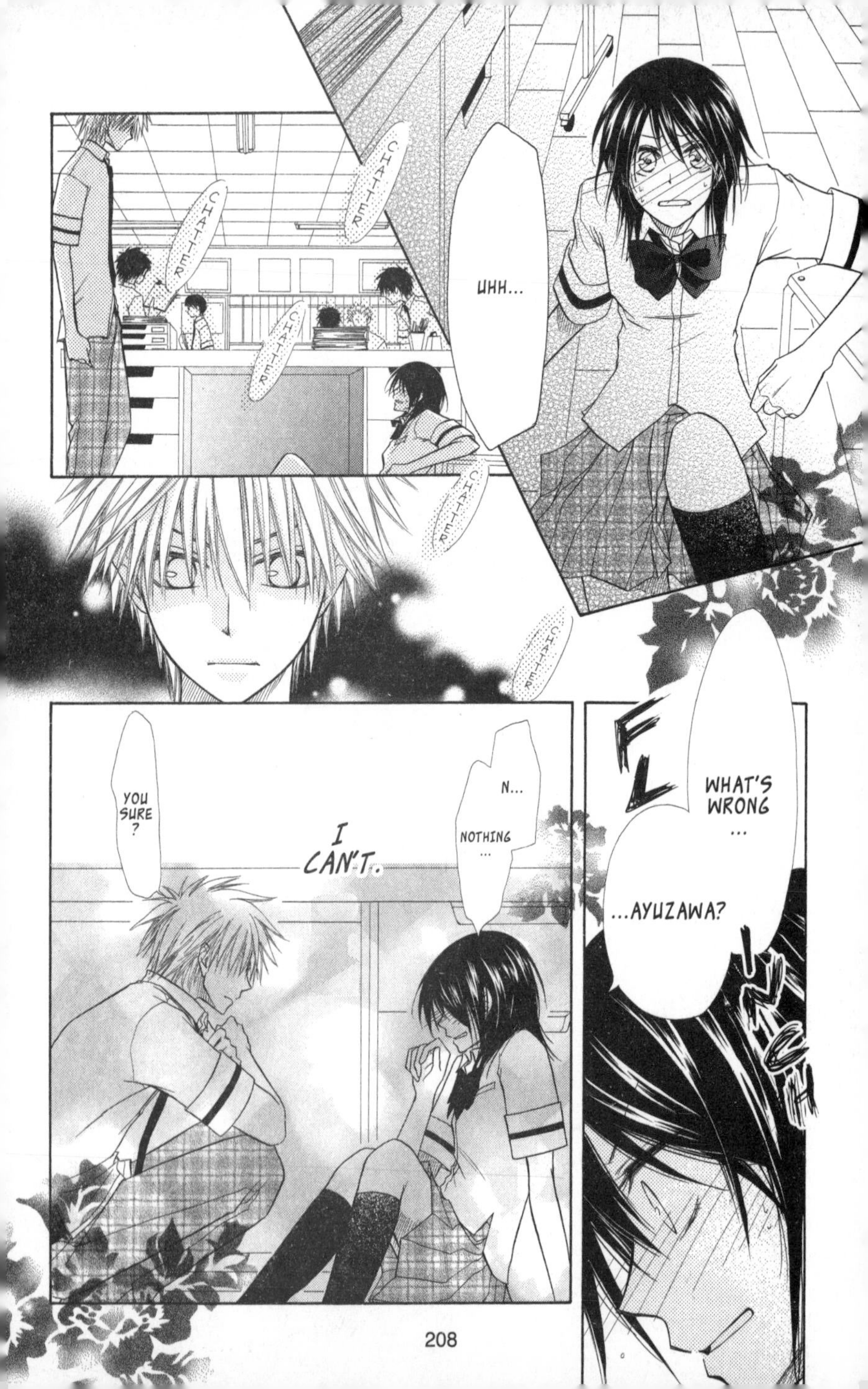
UHH...
CHATTER
CHATTER
CHATTER
CHATTER
CHATTER
WHAT'S WRONG ...
...AYUZAWA?
N...
NOTHING ...
I CAN'T.
YOU SURE?

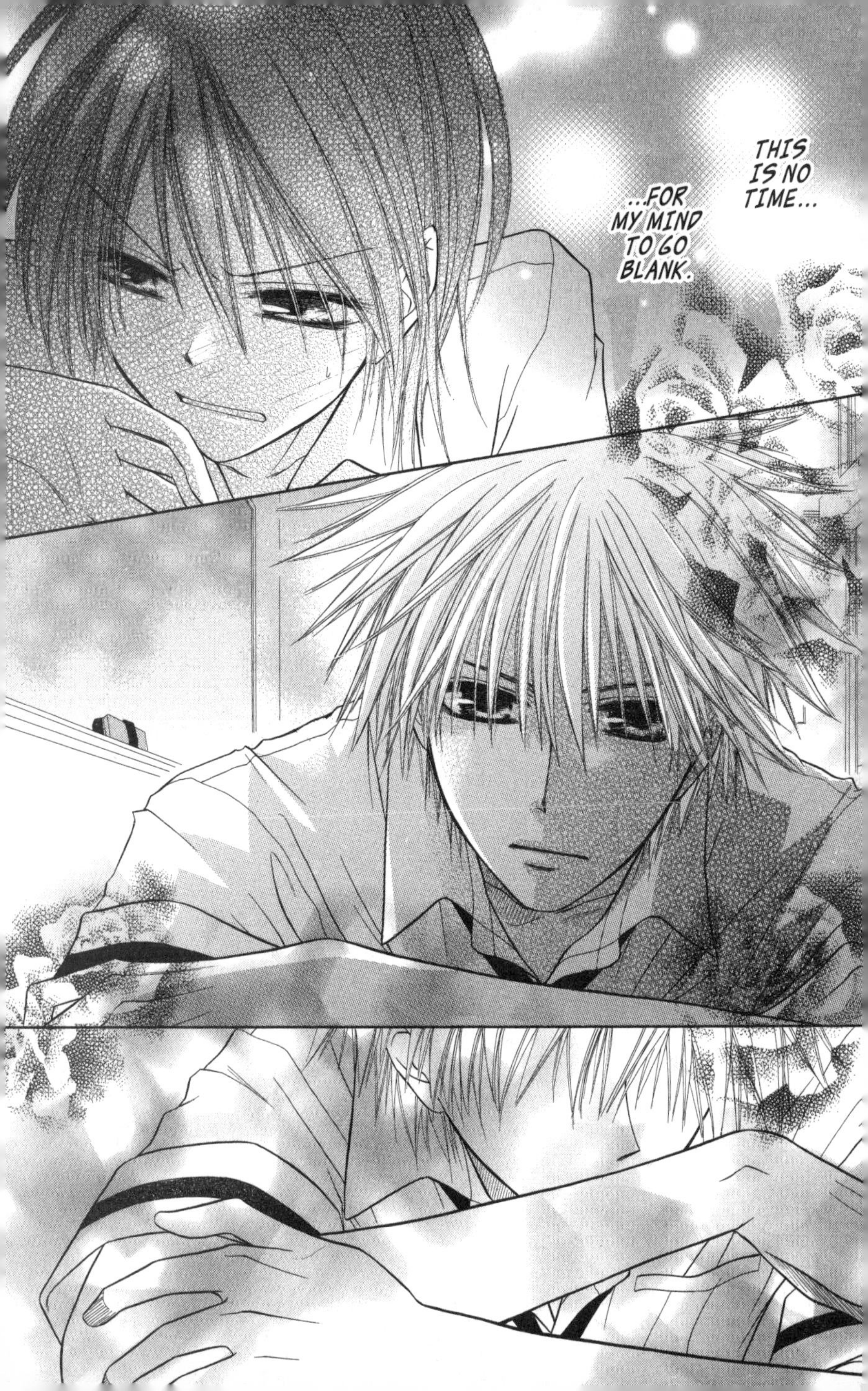
THIS IS NO TIME...
...FOR MY MIND TO GO BLANK.

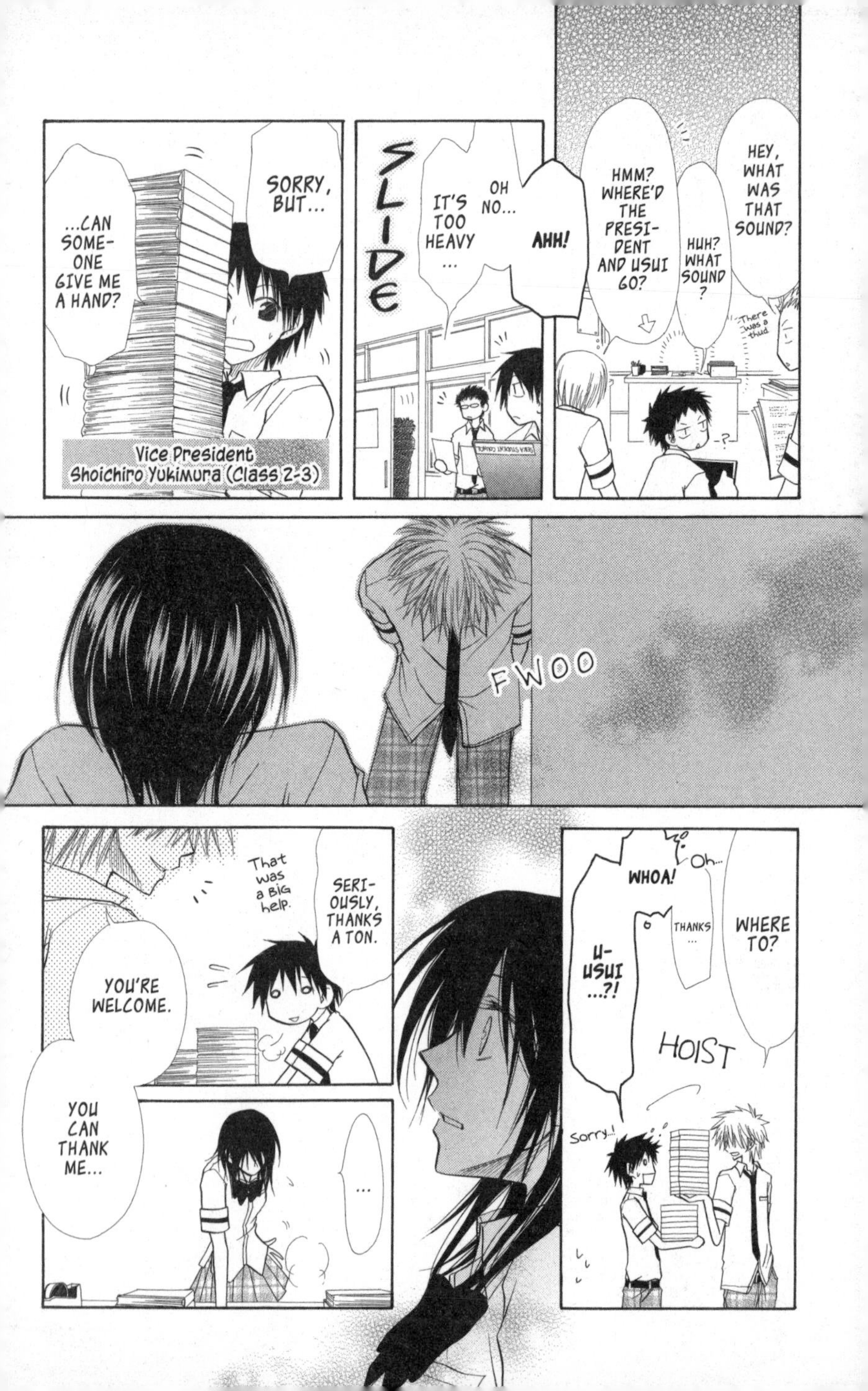
HEY, WHAT WAS THAT SOUND?
HUH? WHAT SOUND?
There was a thud
HMM? WHERE'D THE PRESIDENT AND USUI GO?
AHH!
OH NO...
IT'S TOO HEAVY...
SLIDE
SORRY, BUT...
...CAN SOMEONE GIVE ME A HAND?
Vice President Shoichiro Yukimura (Class 2-3)
FWOO
WHERE TO?
Oh...
THANKS...
WHOA!
U-USUI...?!
HOIST
Sorry...!
SERIOUSLY, THANKS A TON.
That was a big help.
YOU'RE WELCOME.
YOU CAN THANK ME...
...

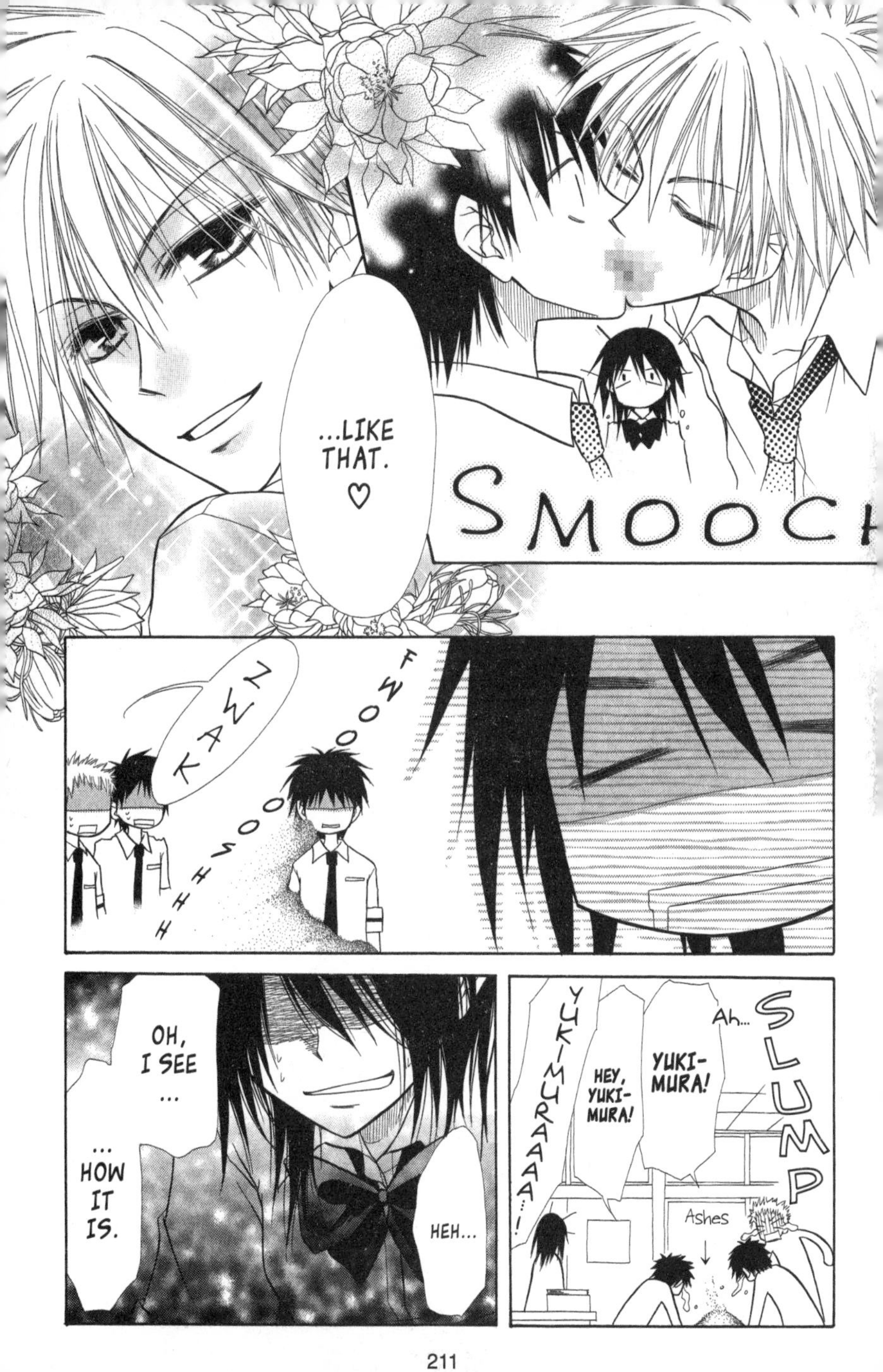
...LIKE THAT. ♡
SMOOCH
FWOOOOSHHHH
KAZAN
Ah...
SLUMP
YUKIMURA!
HEY, YUKIMURA!
YUKIMURAAAA...!
Ashes
OH, I SEE ...
... HOW IT IS.
HEH...

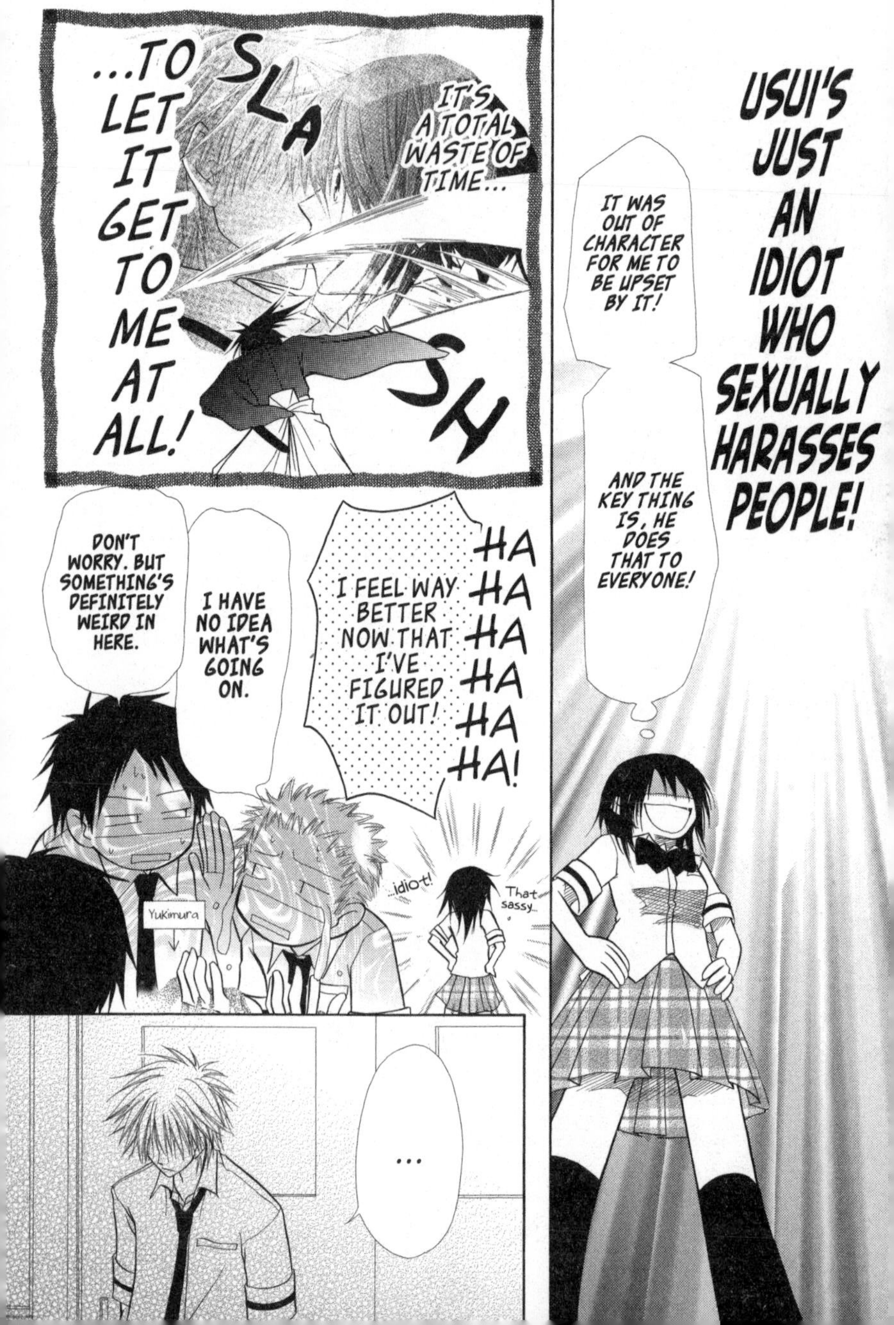
USUI'S JUST AN IDIOT WHO SEXUALLY HARASSES PEOPLE!
IT WAS OUT OF CHARACTER FOR ME TO BE UPSET BY IT!
AND THE KEY THING IS, HE DOES THAT TO EVERYONE!
IT'S A TOTAL WASTE OF TIME...
SLA
SH
...TO LET IT GET TO ME AT ALL!
HA HA HA HA HA HA!
I FEEL WAY BETTER NOW THAT I'VE FIGURED IT OUT!
I HAVE NO IDEA WHAT'S GOING ON.
DON'T WORRY. BUT SOMETHING'S DEFINITELY WEIRD IN HERE.
That sassy...
...idiot!
Yukimura
...

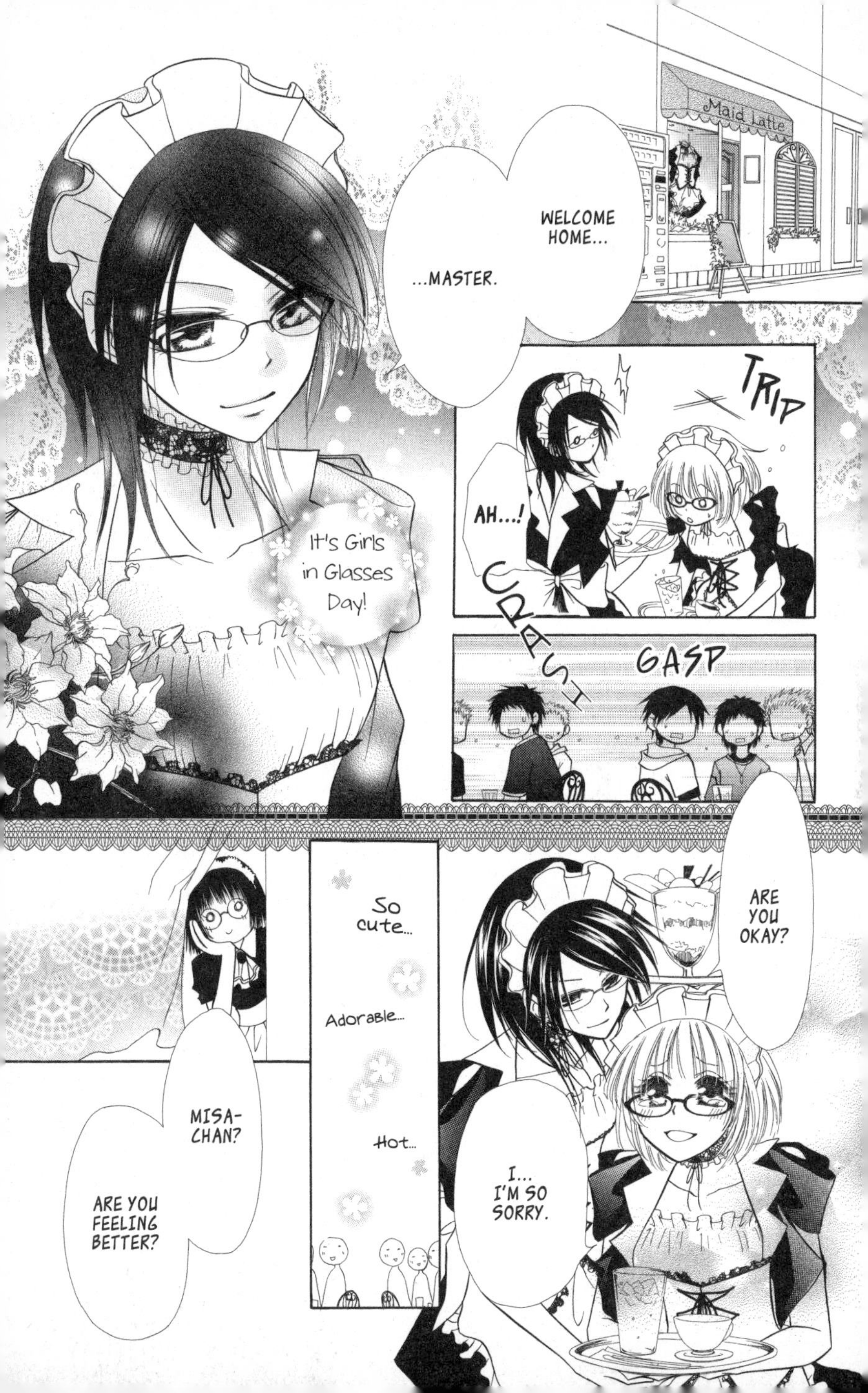

Maid Latte
WELCOME HOME...
...MASTER.
TRIP
AH...!
CRASH
GASP
It's Girls in Glasses Day!
ARE YOU OKAY?
I... I'M SO SORRY.
So cute...
Adorable...
Hot...
MISA-CHAN?
ARE YOU FEELING BETTER?

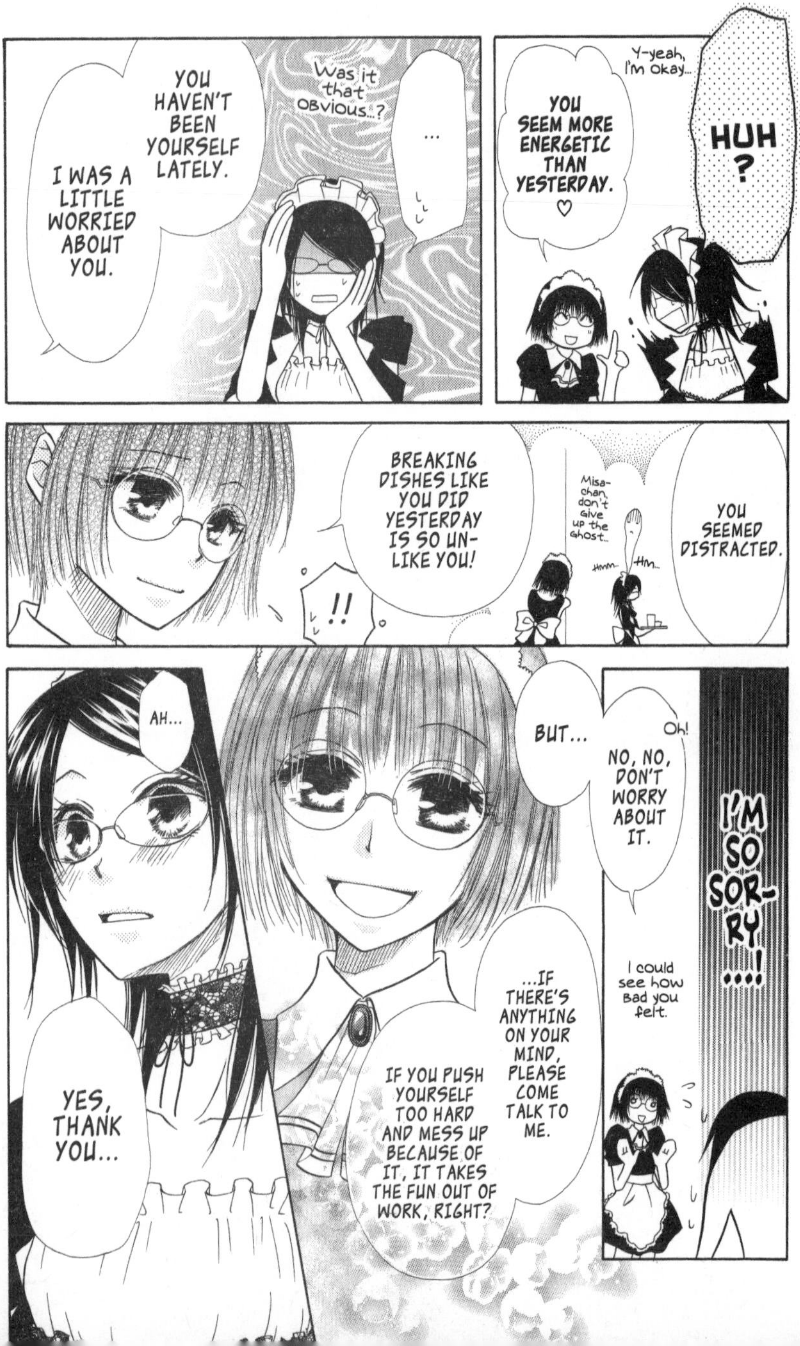
HUH?
Y-yeah, I'm okay...
YOU SEEM MORE ENERGETIC THAN YESTERDAY. ♡
...
Was it that obvious...?
YOU HAVEN'T BEEN YOURSELF LATELY.
I WAS A LITTLE WORRIED ABOUT YOU.
YOU SEEMED DISTRACTED.
Misa-chan, don't give up the ghost...
Hm...
Hmm...
BREAKING DISHES LIKE YOU DID YESTERDAY IS SO UN-LIKE YOU!
!!
I'M SO SOR-RY...!
Oh!
NO, NO, DON'T WORRY ABOUT IT.
I could see how bad you felt.
BUT...
AH...
...IF THERE'S ANYTHING ON YOUR MIND, PLEASE COME TALK TO ME.
IF YOU PUSH YOURSELF TOO HARD AND MESS UP BECAUSE OF IT, IT TAKES THE FUN OUT OF WORK, RIGHT?
YES, THANK YOU...

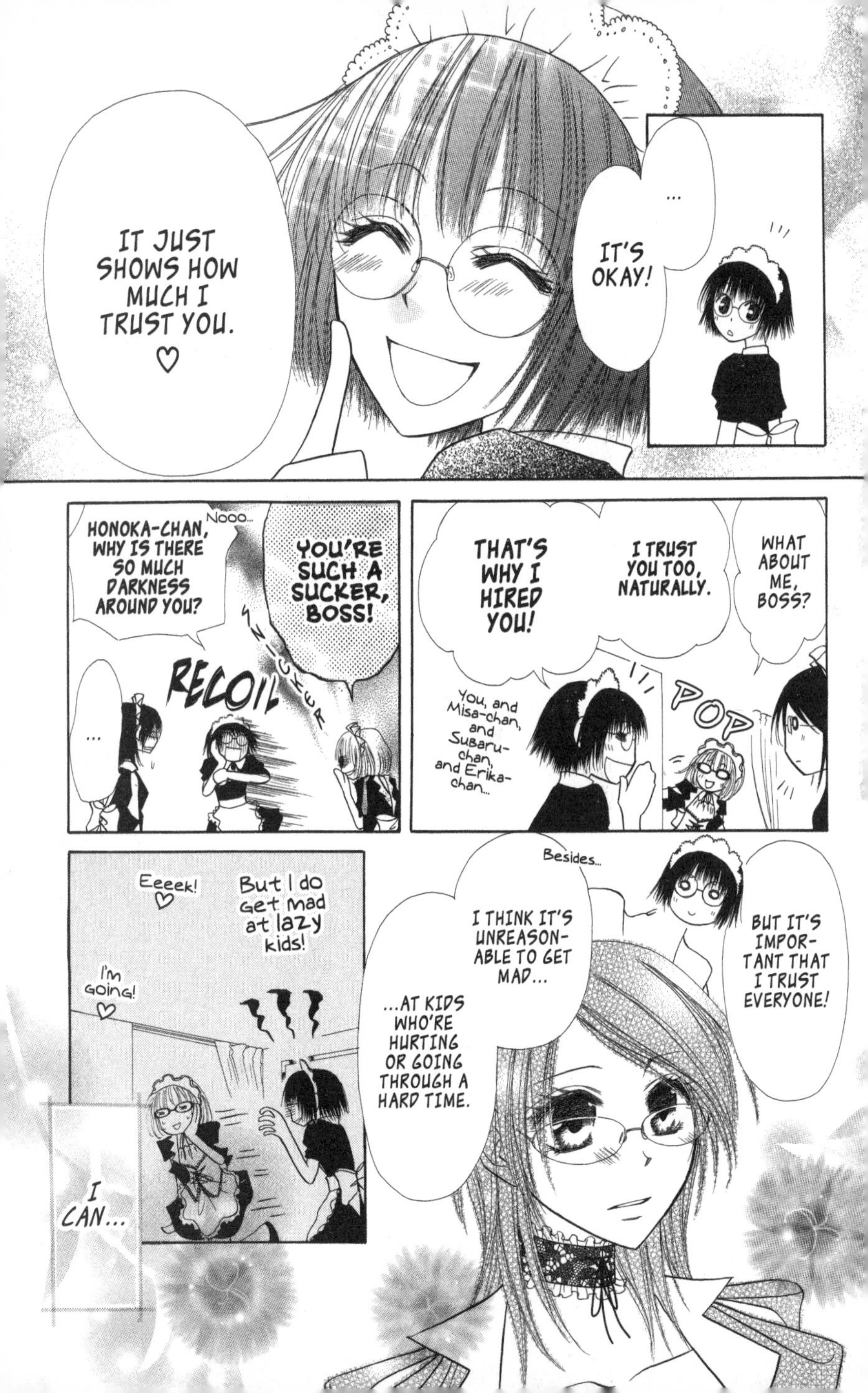
...
IT'S OKAY!
IT JUST SHOWS HOW MUCH I TRUST YOU. ♡
WHAT ABOUT ME, BOSS?
I TRUST YOU TOO, NATURALLY.
THAT'S WHY I HIRED YOU!
POP
You, and Misa-chan, and Subaru-chan, and Erika-chan...
YOU'RE SUCH A SUCKER, BOSS!
Nooo...
HONOKA-CHAN, WHY IS THERE SO MUCH DARKNESS AROUND YOU?
SNICKER
RECOIL
...
Besides...
BUT IT'S IMPOR-TANT THAT I TRUST EVERYONE!
I THINK IT'S UNREASON-ABLE TO GET MAD...
...AT KIDS WHO'RE HURTING OR GOING THROUGH A HARD TIME.
But I do get mad at lazy kids!
Eeeek! ♡
I'm going! ♡
I CAN...

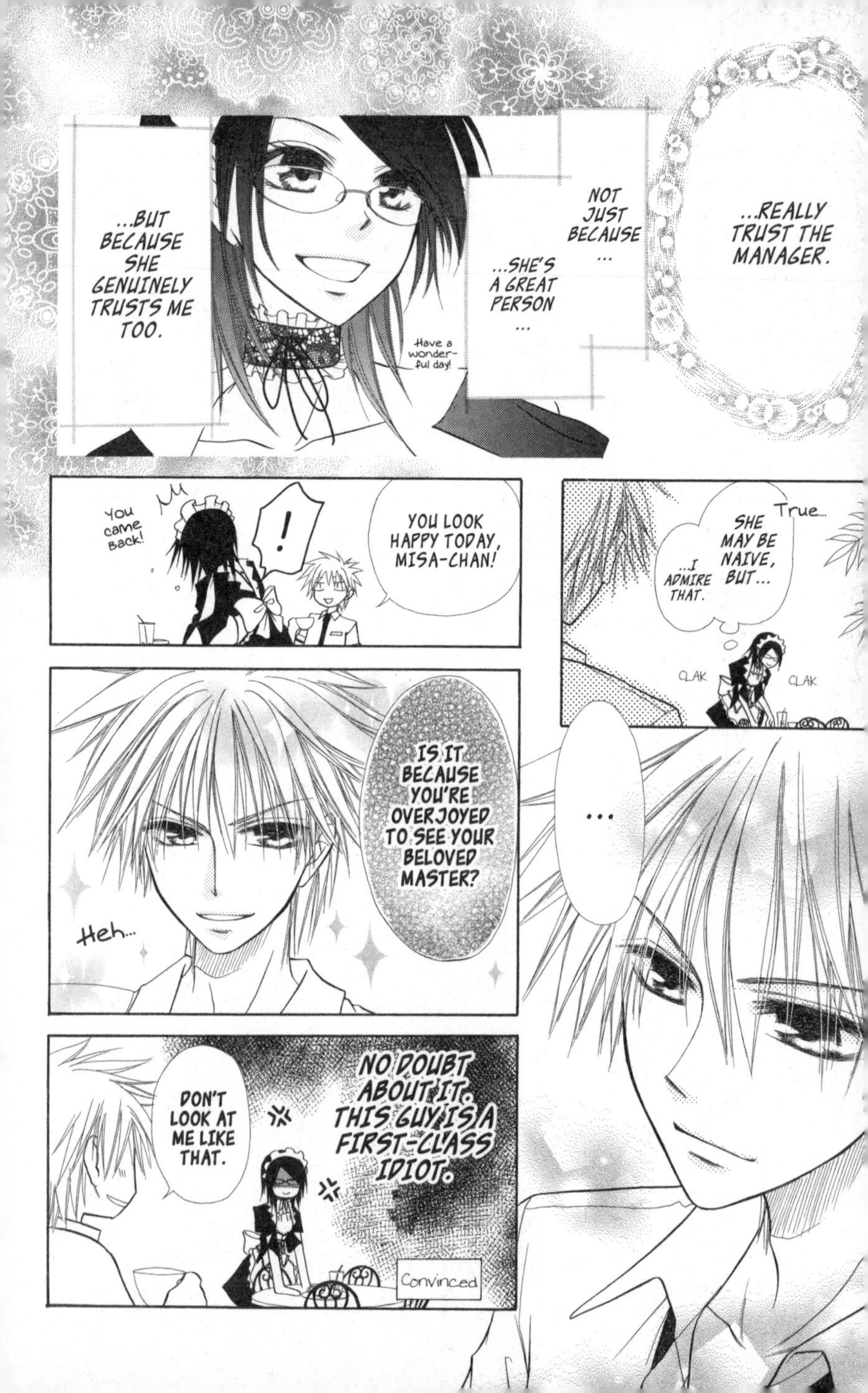
...REALLY TRUST THE MANAGER.
NOT JUST BECAUSE...
...SHE'S A GREAT PERSON...
Have a wonderful day!
...BUT BECAUSE SHE GENUINELY TRUSTS ME TOO.
True...
SHE MAY BE NAIVE, BUT...
...I ADMIRE THAT.
CLAK
CLAK
YOU LOOK HAPPY TODAY, MISA-CHAN!
!
You came back!
...
IS IT BECAUSE YOU'RE OVERJOYED TO SEE YOUR BELOVED MASTER?
Heh...
NO DOUBT ABOUT IT. THIS GUY IS A FIRST-CLASS IDIOT.
DON'T LOOK AT ME LIKE THAT.
Convinced

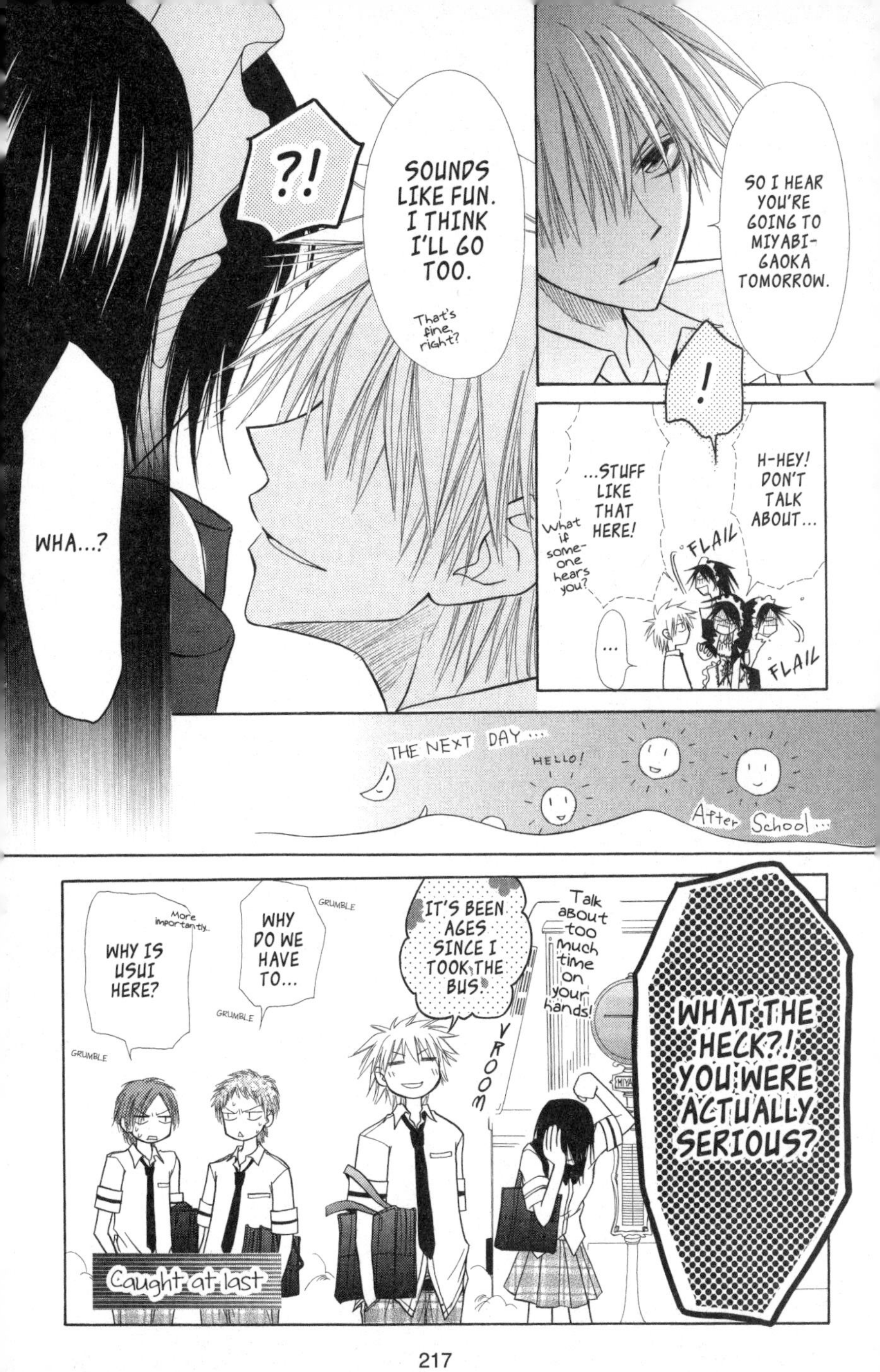

SO I HEAR YOU'RE GOING TO MIYABI-GAOKA TOMORROW.
SOUNDS LIKE FUN. I THINK I'LL GO TOO.
That's fine, right?
?!
WHA...?
!
H-HEY! DON'T TALK ABOUT...
...STUFF LIKE THAT HERE!
What if someone hears you?
FLAIL
FLAIL
...
THE NEXT DAY...
HELLO!
After School...
WHAT THE HECK?! YOU WERE ACTUALLY SERIOUS?
Talk about too much time on your hands!
IT'S BEEN AGES SINCE I TOOK THE BUS.
VROOOM
GRUMBLE
WHY DO WE HAVE TO...
GRUMBLE
More importantly..
WHY IS USUI HERE?
GRUMBLE
Caught at last

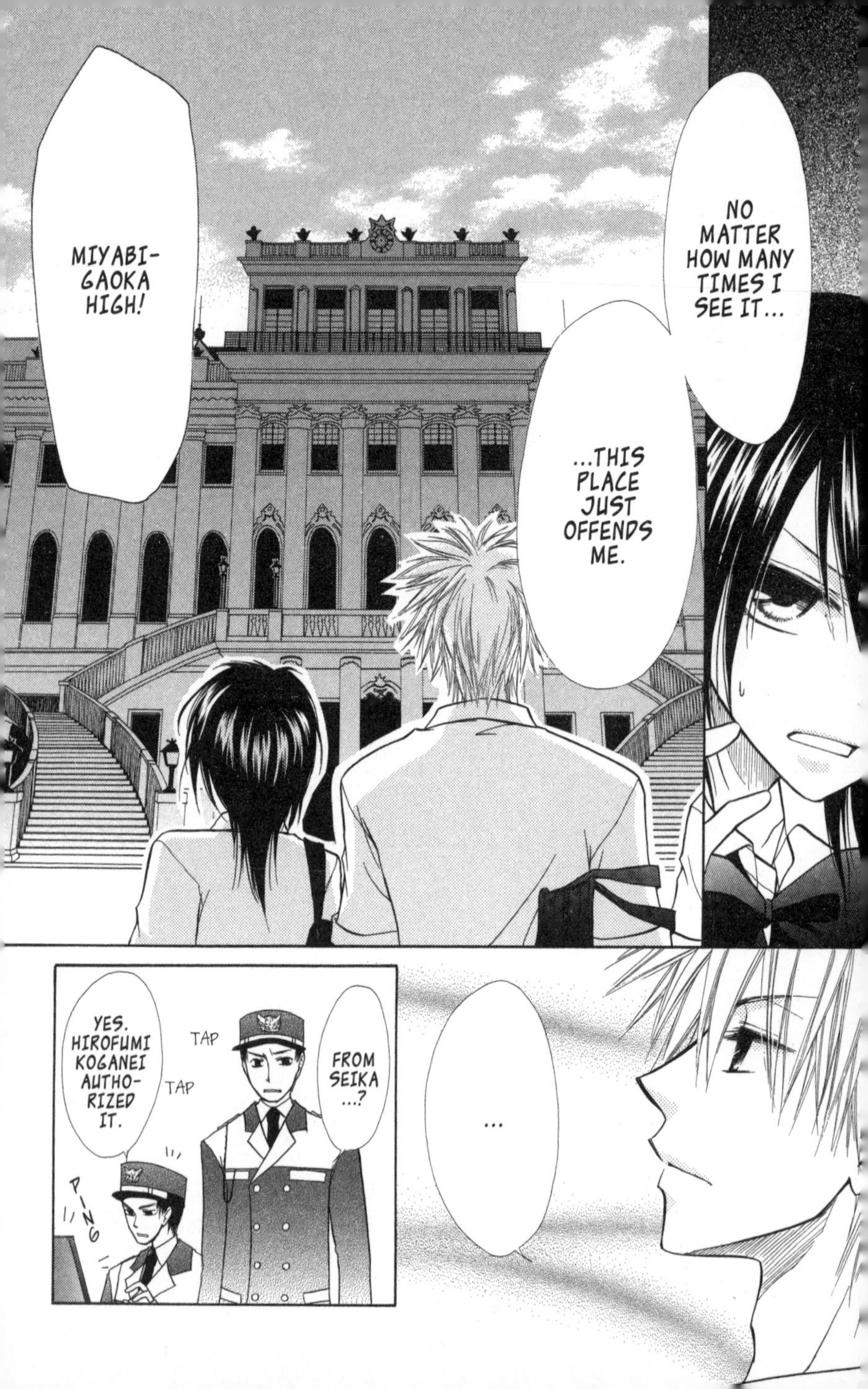
NO MATTER HOW MANY TIMES I SEE IT...
...THIS PLACE JUST OFFENDS ME.
MIYABI-GAOKA HIGH!
...
FROM SEIKA ...?
TAP
TAP
YES. HIROFUMI KOGANEI AUTHO-RIZED IT.
PING

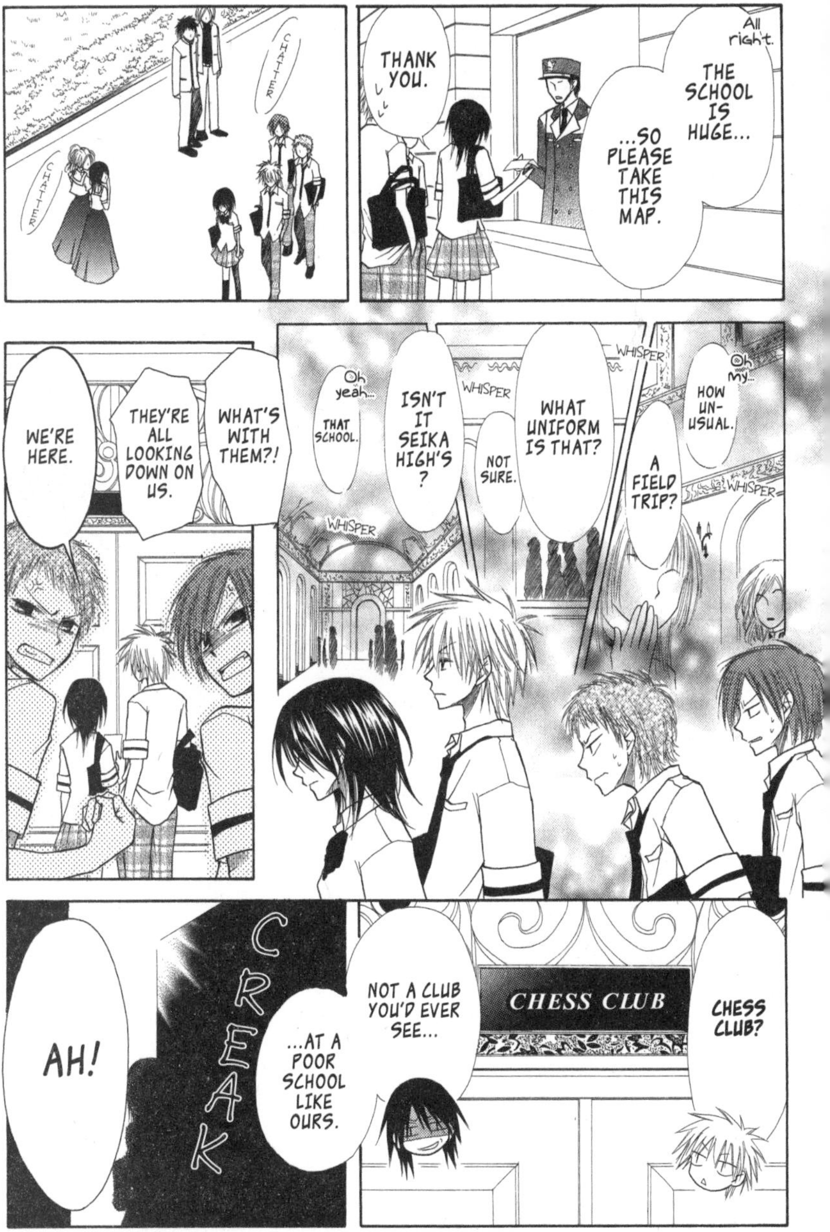
All right.
THE SCHOOL IS HUGE...
...SO PLEASE TAKE THIS MAP.
THANK YOU.
CHATTER
CHATTER
Oh my...
HOW UN-USUAL.
WHISPER
A FIELD TRIP?
WHISPER
WHAT UNIFORM IS THAT?
NOT SURE.
WHISPER
ISN'T IT SEIKA HIGH'S?
Oh yeah...
THAT SCHOOL.
WHISPER
WHAT'S WITH THEM?!
THEY'RE ALL LOOKING DOWN ON US.
WE'RE HERE.
CHESS CLUB?
CHESS CLUB
NOT A CLUB YOU'D EVER SEE...
...AT A POOR SCHOOL LIKE OURS.
CREAK
AH!

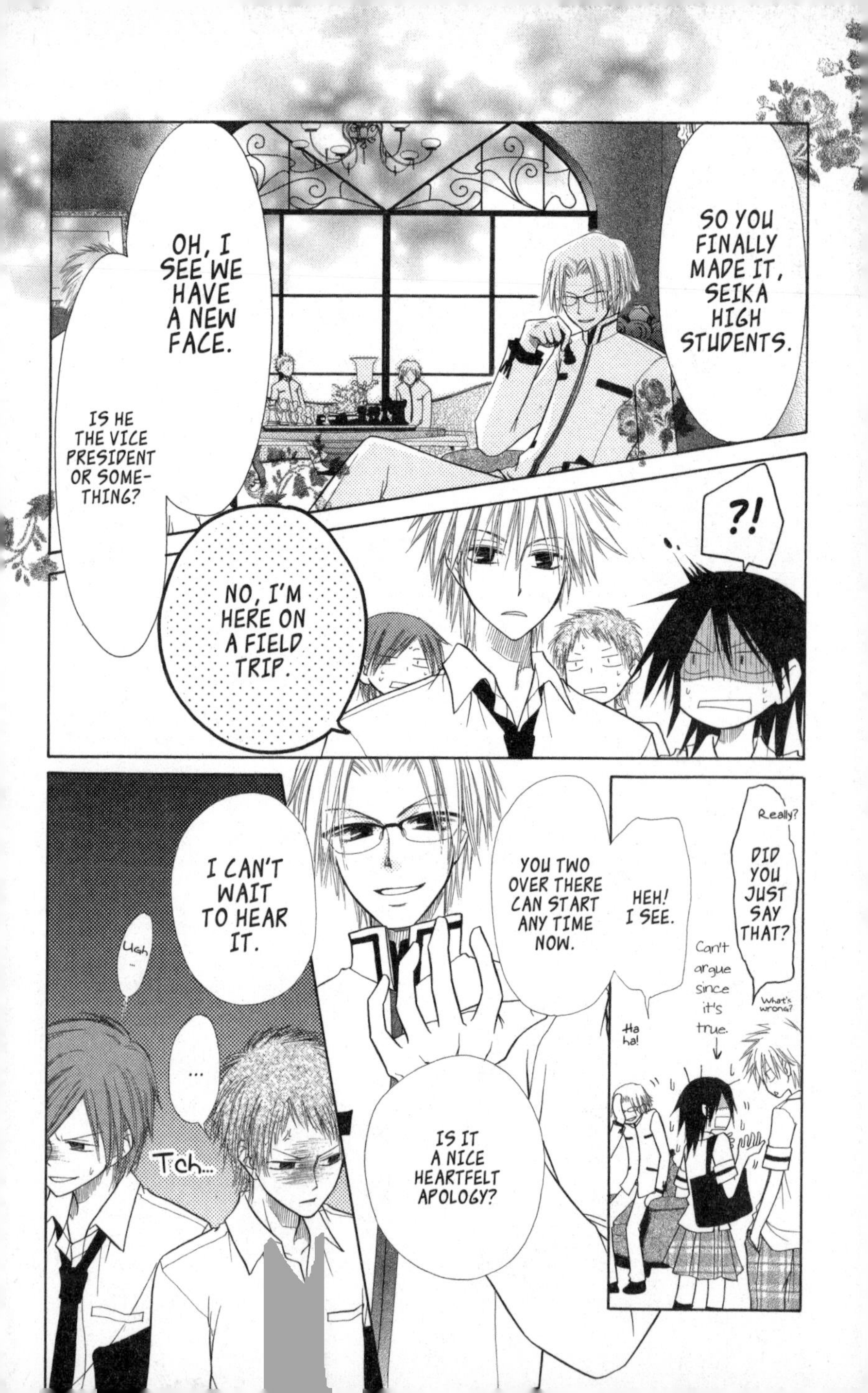
SO YOU FINALLY MADE IT, SEIKA HIGH STUDENTS.
OH, I SEE WE HAVE A NEW FACE.
IS HE THE VICE PRESIDENT OR SOME-THING?
?!
NO, I'M HERE ON A FIELD TRIP.
Really?
DID YOU JUST SAY THAT?
What's wrong?
Can't argue since it's true.
Ha ha!
HEH! I SEE.
YOU TWO OVER THERE CAN START ANY TIME NOW.
I CAN'T WAIT TO HEAR IT.
IS IT A NICE HEARTFELT APOLOGY?
Ugh...
...
Tch...

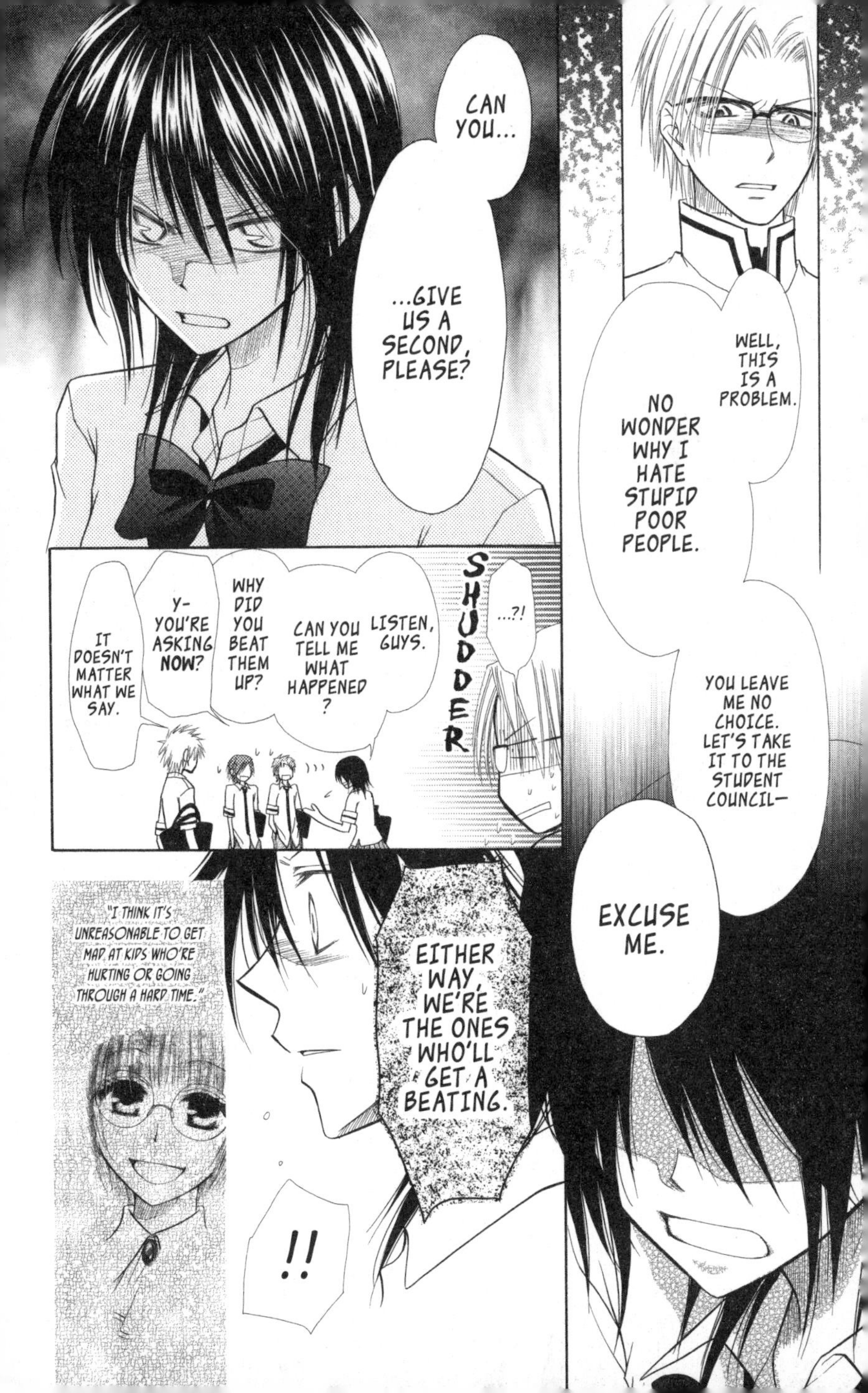
WELL, THIS IS A PROBLEM.
NO WONDER WHY I HATE STUPID POOR PEOPLE.
YOU LEAVE ME NO CHOICE. LET'S TAKE IT TO THE STUDENT COUNCIL—
EXCUSE ME.
CAN YOU...
...GIVE US A SECOND, PLEASE?
...?!
SHUDDER
LISTEN, GUYS.
CAN YOU TELL ME WHAT HAPPENED?
WHY DID YOU BEAT THEM UP?
Y-YOU'RE ASKING NOW?
IT DOESN'T MATTER WHAT WE SAY.
EITHER WAY, WE'RE THE ONES WHO'LL GET A BEATING.
!!
"I THINK IT'S UNREASONABLE TO GET MAD AT KIDS WHO'RE HURTING OR GOING THROUGH A HARD TIME."

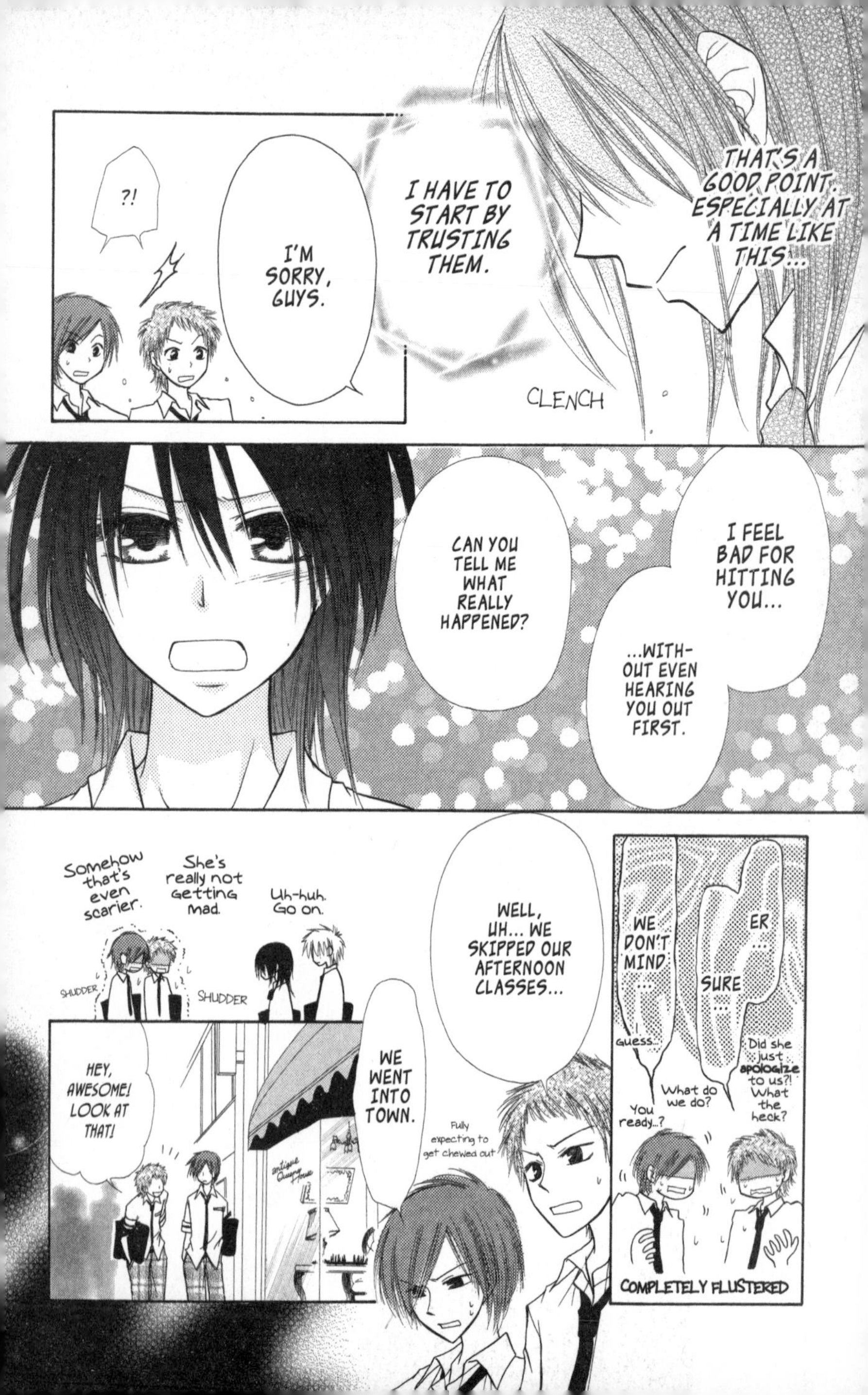
THAT'S A GOOD POINT. ESPECIALLY AT A TIME LIKE THIS...
I HAVE TO START BY TRUSTING THEM.
CLENCH
I'M SORRY, GUYS.
?!
I FEEL BAD FOR HITTING YOU...
...WITHOUT EVEN HEARING YOU OUT FIRST.
CAN YOU TELL ME WHAT REALLY HAPPENED?
ER... SURE...
WE DON'T MIND... I guess...
Did she just apologize to us?! What the heck?
What do we do?
You ready...?
COMPLETELY FLUSTERED
WELL, UH... WE SKIPPED OUR AFTERNOON CLASSES...
Fully expecting to get chewed out
Uh-huh. Go on.
She's really not getting mad.
Somehow that's even scarier.
SHUDDER
SHUDDER
WE WENT INTO TOWN.
HEY, AWESOME! LOOK AT THAT!

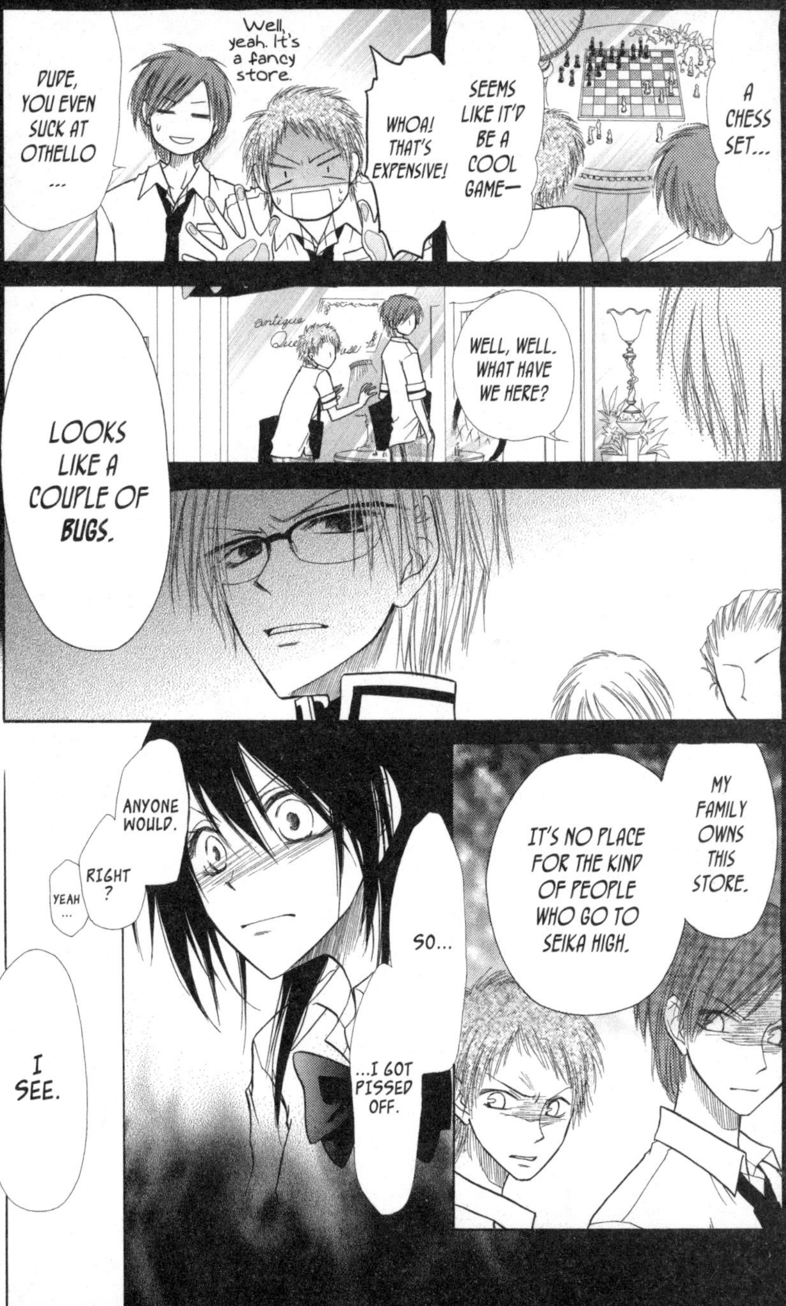
A CHESS SET...
SEEMS LIKE IT'D BE A COOL GAME—
WHOA! THAT'S EXPENSIVE!
Well, yeah. It's a fancy store.
DUDE, YOU EVEN SUCK AT OTHELLO ...
WELL, WELL. WHAT HAVE WE HERE?
LOOKS LIKE A COUPLE OF BUGS.
MY FAMILY OWNS THIS STORE.
IT'S NO PLACE FOR THE KIND OF PEOPLE WHO GO TO SEIKA HIGH.
SO...
...I GOT PISSED OFF.
ANYONE WOULD.
RIGHT?
YEAH...
I SEE.

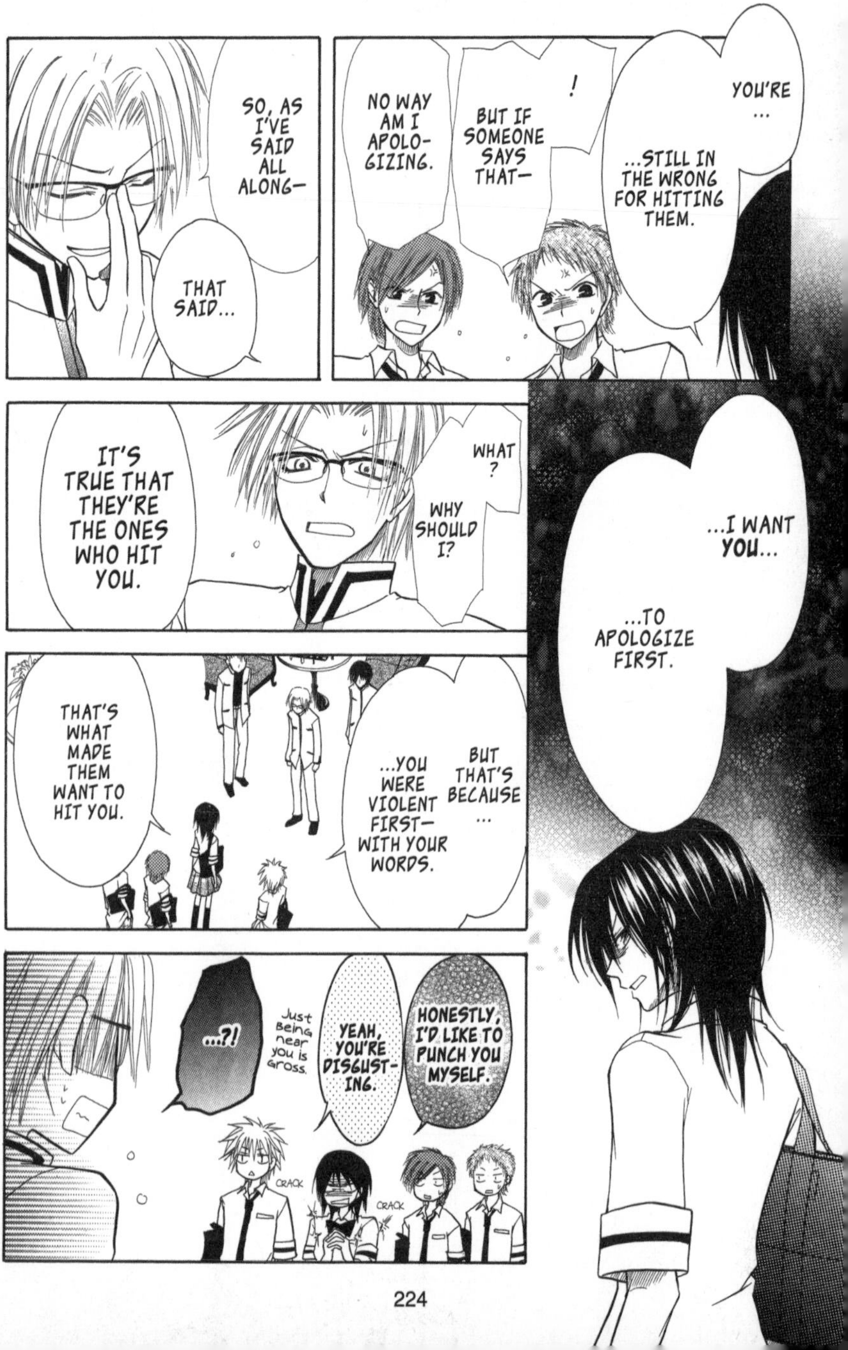
YOU'RE ...
...STILL IN THE WRONG FOR HITTING THEM.
!
BUT IF SOMEONE SAYS THAT—
NO WAY AM I APOLOGIZING.
SO, AS I'VE SAID ALL ALONG—
THAT SAID...
...I WANT YOU...
...TO APOLOGIZE FIRST.
WHAT?
WHY SHOULD I?
IT'S TRUE THAT THEY'RE THE ONES WHO HIT YOU.
BUT THAT'S BECAUSE...
...YOU WERE VIOLENT FIRST— WITH YOUR WORDS.
THAT'S WHAT MADE THEM WANT TO HIT YOU.
HONESTLY, I'D LIKE TO PUNCH YOU MYSELF.
YEAH, YOU'RE DISGUSTING.
Just being near you is gross.
...?!
CRACK
CRACK

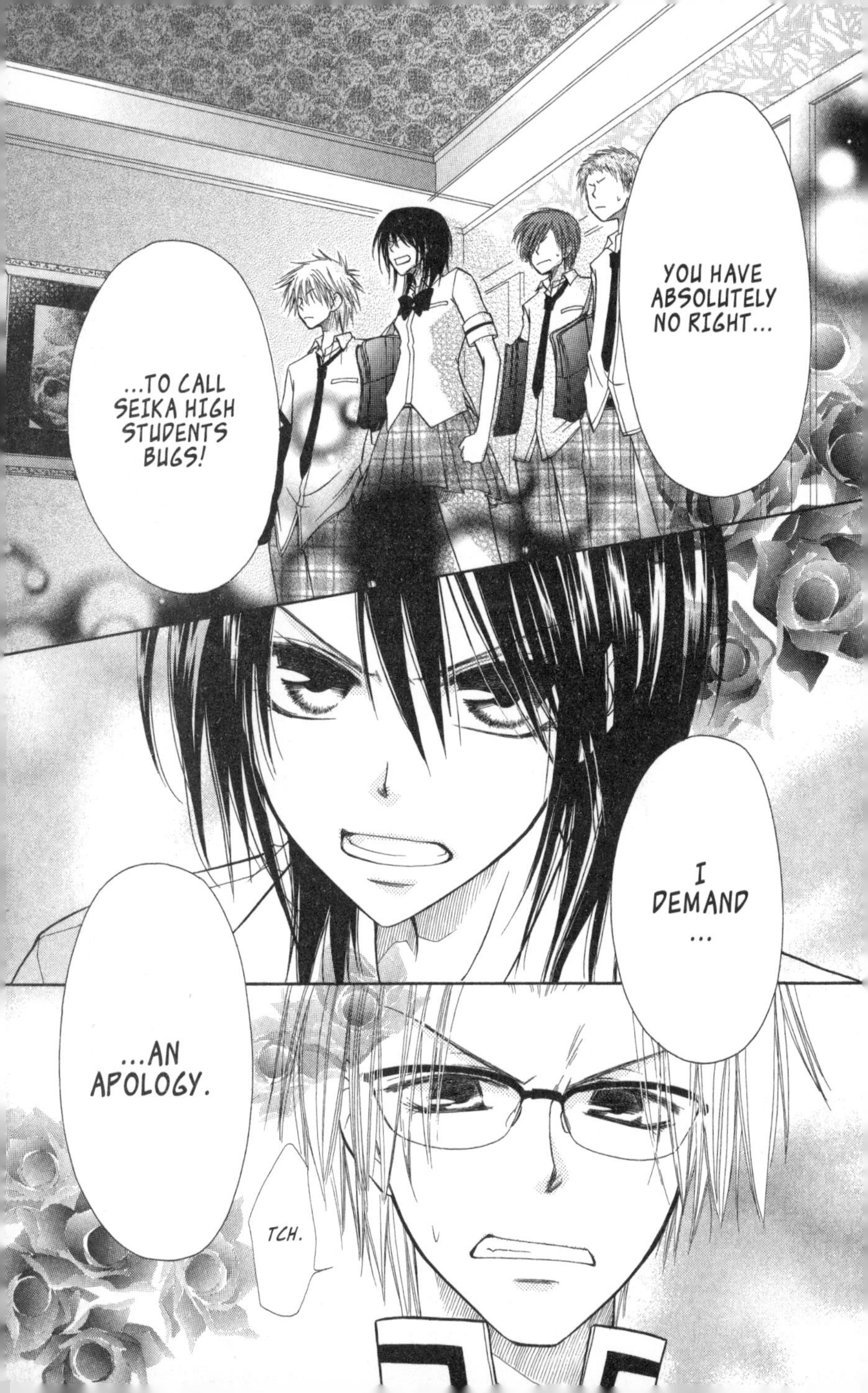
YOU HAVE ABSOLUTELY NO RIGHT...
...TO CALL SEIKA HIGH STUDENTS BUGS!
I DEMAND ...
...AN APOLOGY.
TCH.

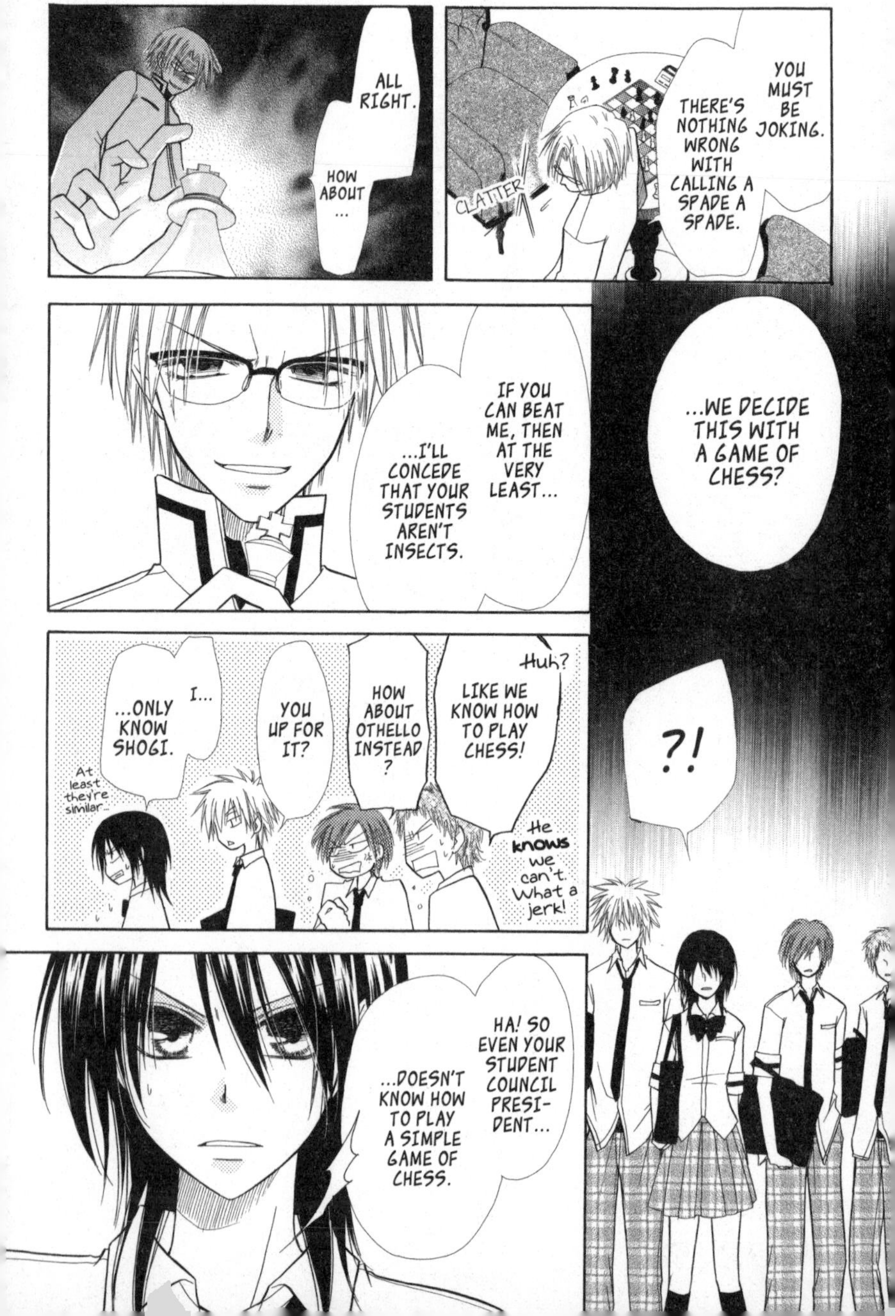
YOU MUST BE JOKING.
THERE'S NOTHING WRONG WITH CALLING A SPADE A SPADE.
CLATTER
ALL RIGHT.
HOW ABOUT...
...WE DECIDE THIS WITH A GAME OF CHESS?
?!
IF YOU CAN BEAT ME, THEN AT THE VERY LEAST...
...I'LL CONCEDE THAT YOUR STUDENTS AREN'T INSECTS.
Huh?
LIKE WE KNOW HOW TO PLAY CHESS!
He knows we can't. What a jerk!
HOW ABOUT OTHELLO INSTEAD?
YOU UP FOR IT?
I...
...ONLY KNOW SHOGI.
At least they're similar...
HA! SO EVEN YOUR STUDENT COUNCIL PRESIDENT...
...DOESN'T KNOW HOW TO PLAY A SIMPLE GAME OF CHESS.

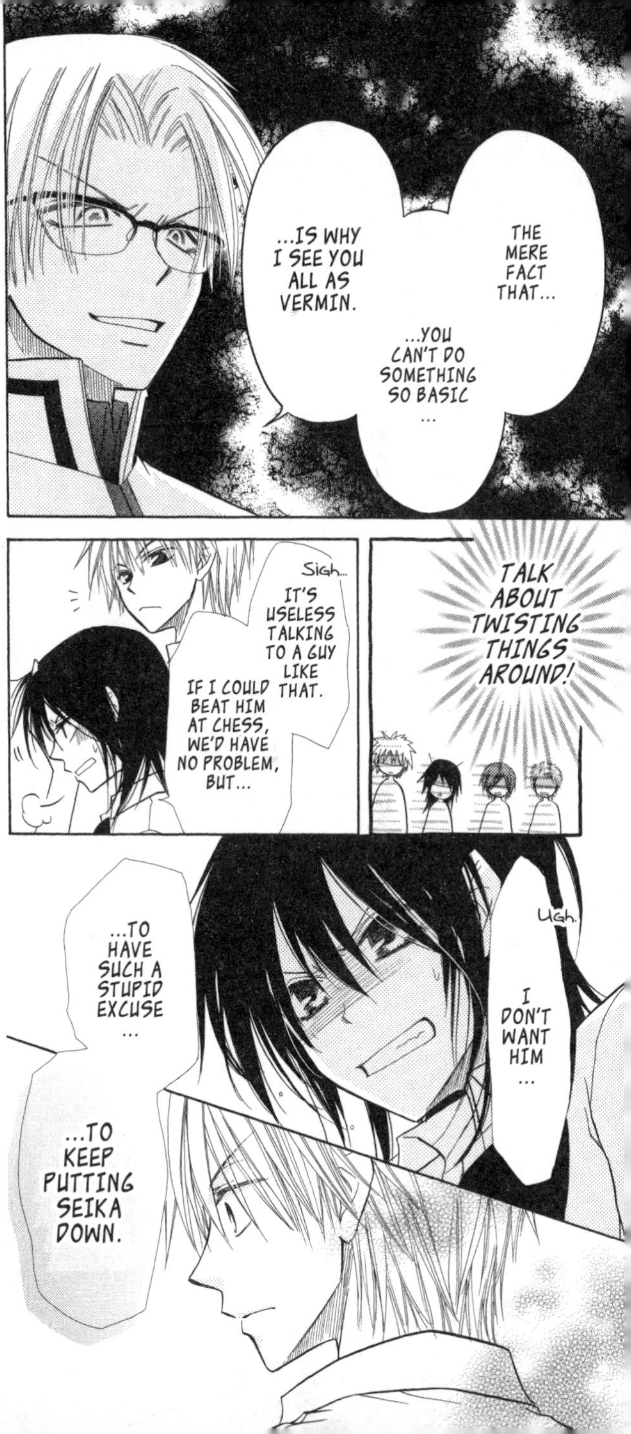
THE MERE FACT THAT...
...YOU CAN'T DO SOMETHING SO BASIC ...
...IS WHY I SEE YOU ALL AS VERMIN.
TALK ABOUT TWISTING THINGS AROUND!
Sigh...
IT'S USELESS TALKING TO A GUY LIKE THAT.
IF I COULD BEAT HIM AT CHESS, WE'D HAVE NO PROBLEM, BUT...
Ugh.
I DON'T WANT HIM ...
...TO HAVE SUCH A STUPID EXCUSE ...
...TO KEEP PUTTING SEIKA DOWN.

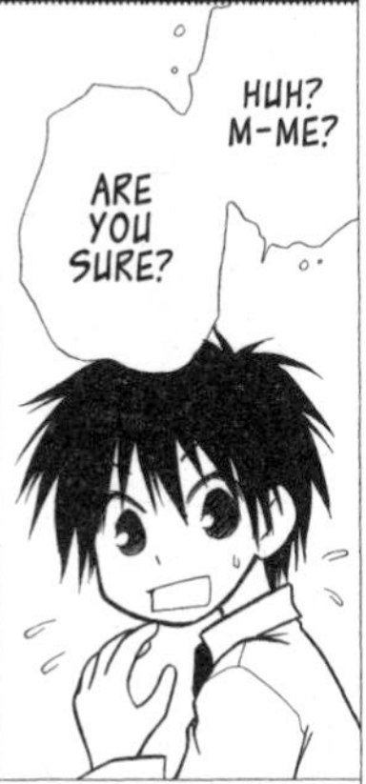
HUH? M-ME?
ARE YOU SURE?

NAME

Shoichiro Yukimura

AGE (CLASS)

16 (2-3)

BLOOD TYPE

A

HEIGHT

164 cm

WEIGHT

48 Kg

SPECIAL SKILL

Mental arithmetic

FAVORITE THING

CLERICAL WORK

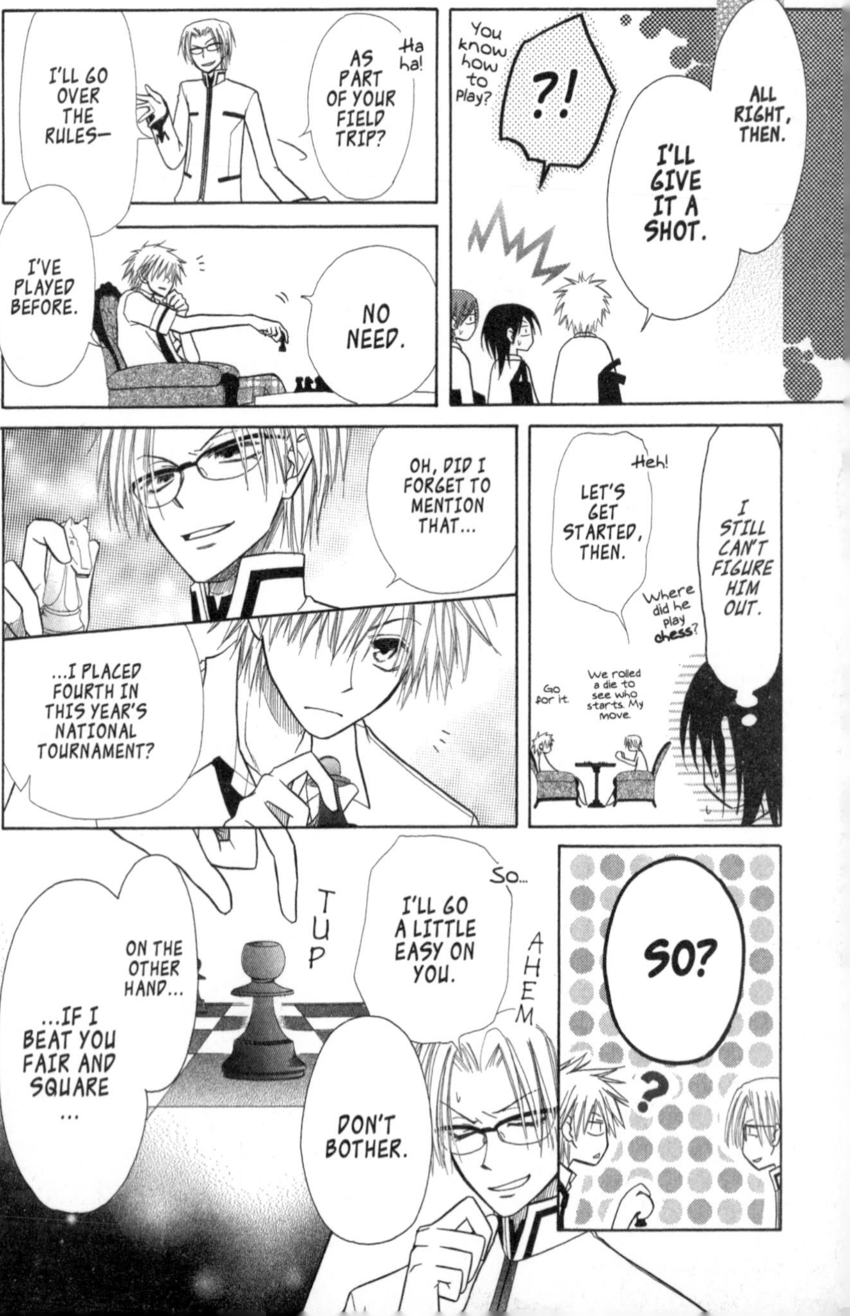
ALL RIGHT, THEN.
I'LL GIVE IT A SHOT.
?!
You know how to play?
Ha ha!
AS PART OF YOUR FIELD TRIP?
I'LL GO OVER THE RULES—
NO NEED.
I'VE PLAYED BEFORE.
I STILL CAN'T FIGURE HIM OUT.
Heh!
LET'S GET STARTED, THEN.
Where did he play chess?
We rolled a die to see who starts. My move.
Go for it.
OH, DID I FORGET TO MENTION THAT...
...I PLACED FOURTH IN THIS YEAR'S NATIONAL TOURNAMENT?
SO?
So...
I'LL GO A LITTLE EASY ON YOU.
AHEM
DON'T BOTHER.
TUP
ON THE OTHER HAND...
...IF I BEAT YOU FAIR AND SQUARE ...

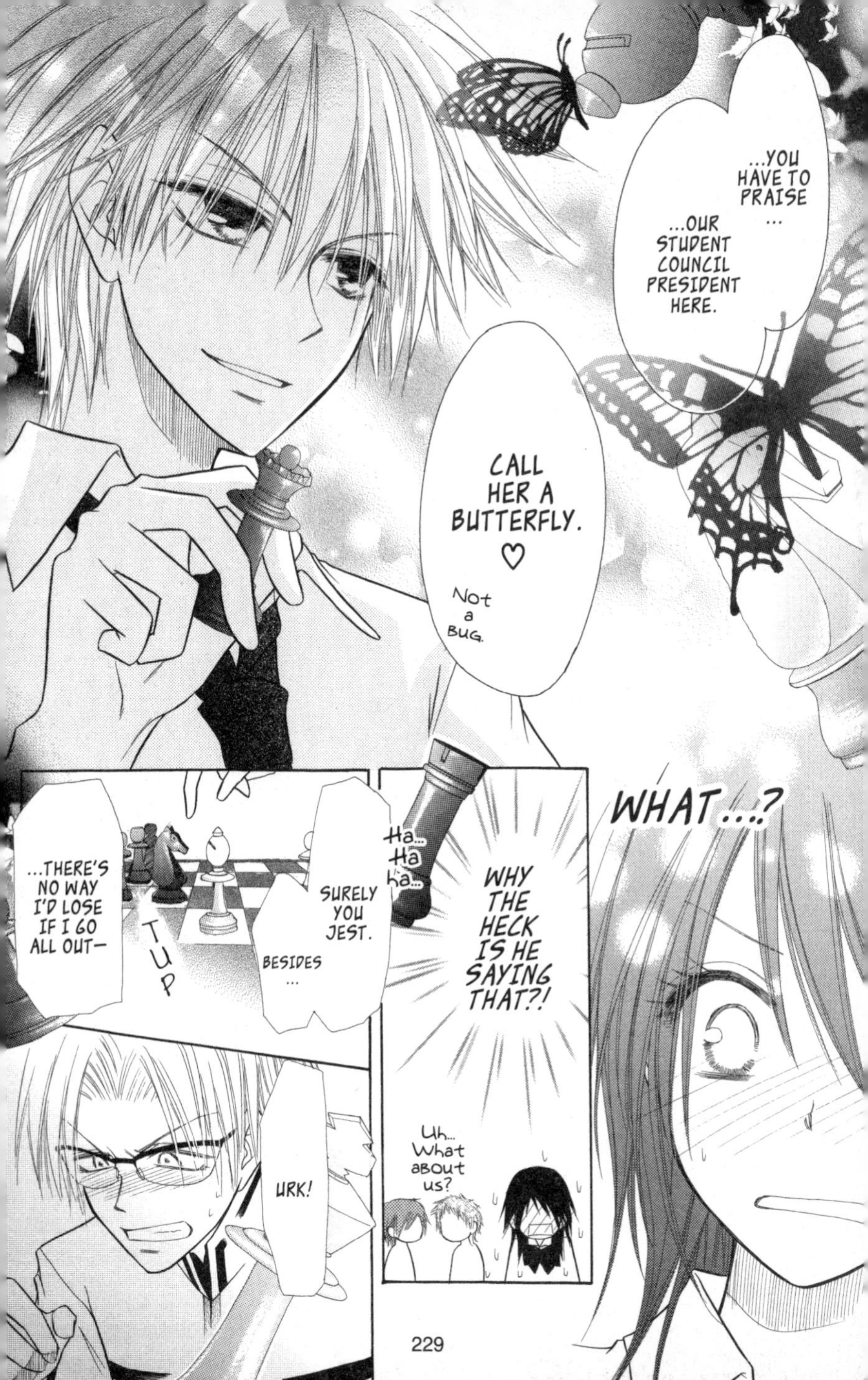

...YOU HAVE TO PRAISE...
...OUR STUDENT COUNCIL PRESIDENT HERE.
CALL HER A BUTTERFLY. ♡
Not a bug.
WHAT...?
WHY THE HECK IS HE SAYING THAT?!
Ha... Ha ha...
Uh... What about us?
SURELY YOU JEST.
BESIDES...
...THERE'S NO WAY I'D LOSE IF I GO ALL OUT—
TUP
URK!

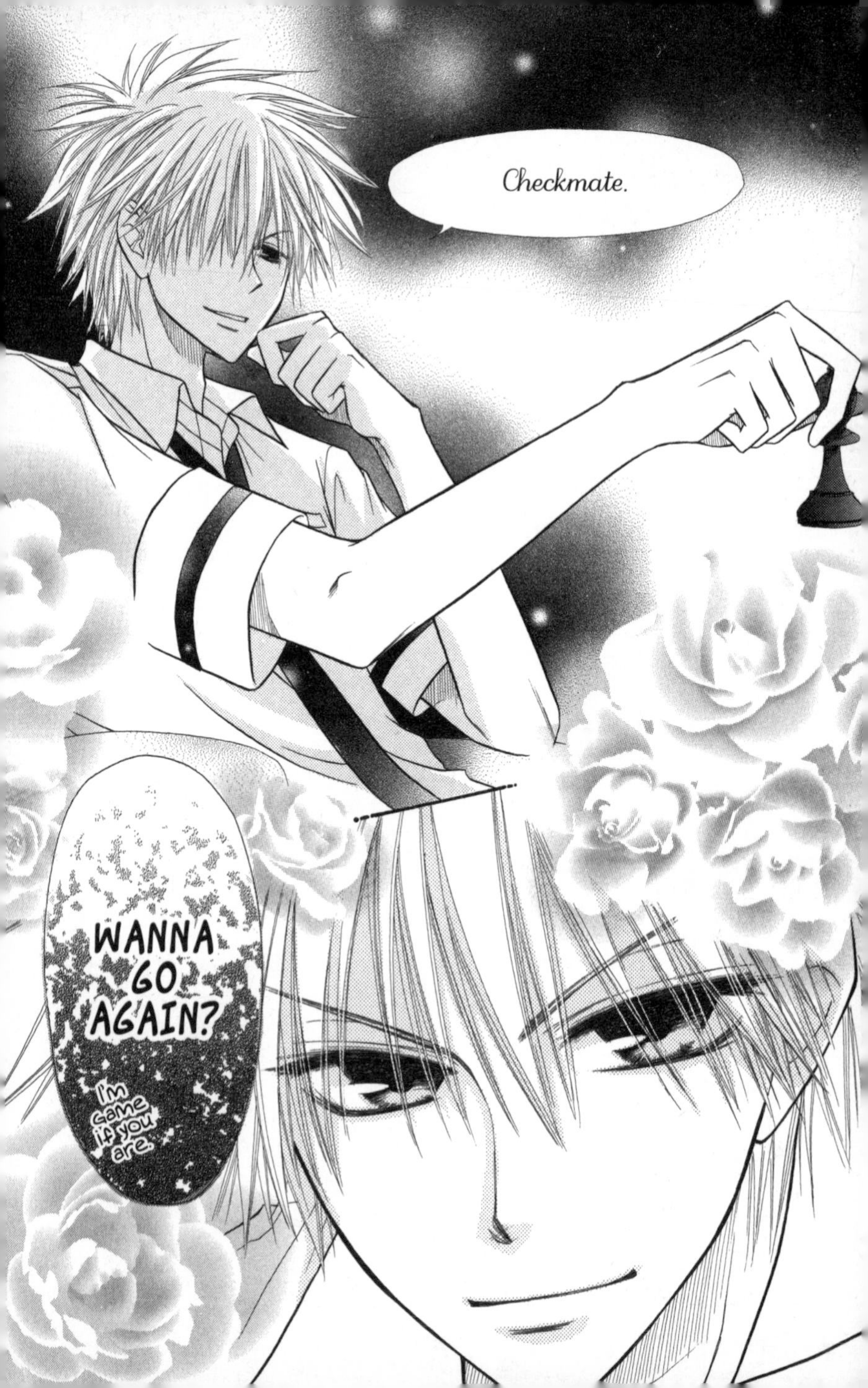
Checkmate.
WANNA GO AGAIN?
I'm game if you are.

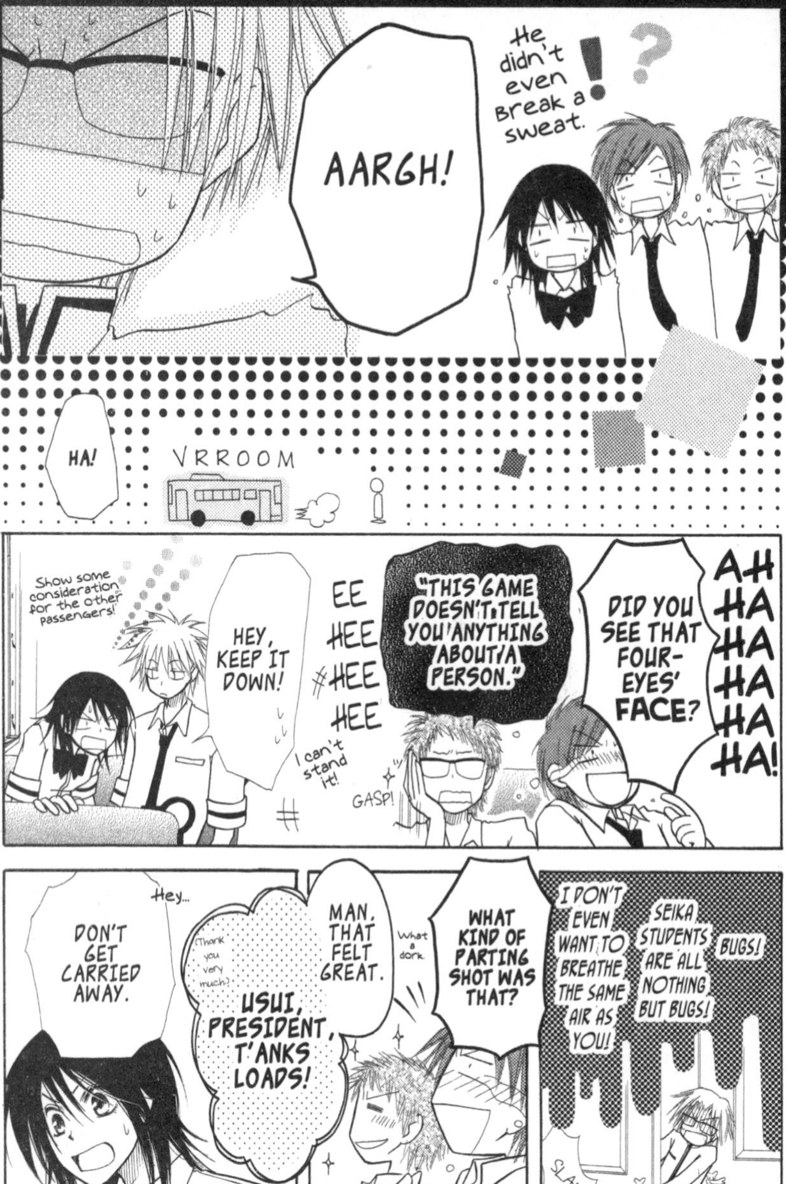
He didn't even break a sweat.
AARGH!
VRROOM
HA!
AHAHAHAHAHAHA!
DID YOU SEE THAT FOUR-EYES' FACE?
"THIS GAME DOESN'T TELL YOU ANYTHING ABOUT A PERSON."
GASP!
EE HEE HEE HEE
I can't stand it!
HEY, KEEP IT DOWN!
Show some consideration for the other passengers!
BUGS!
SEIKA STUDENTS ARE ALL NOTHING BUT BUGS!
I DON'T EVEN WANT TO BREATHE THE SAME AIR AS YOU!
SLAM
WHAT KIND OF PARTING SHOT WAS THAT?
What a dork.
MAN, THAT FELT GREAT.
USUI, PRESIDENT, T'ANKS LOADS!
(Thank you very much.)
Hey...
DON'T GET CARRIED AWAY.

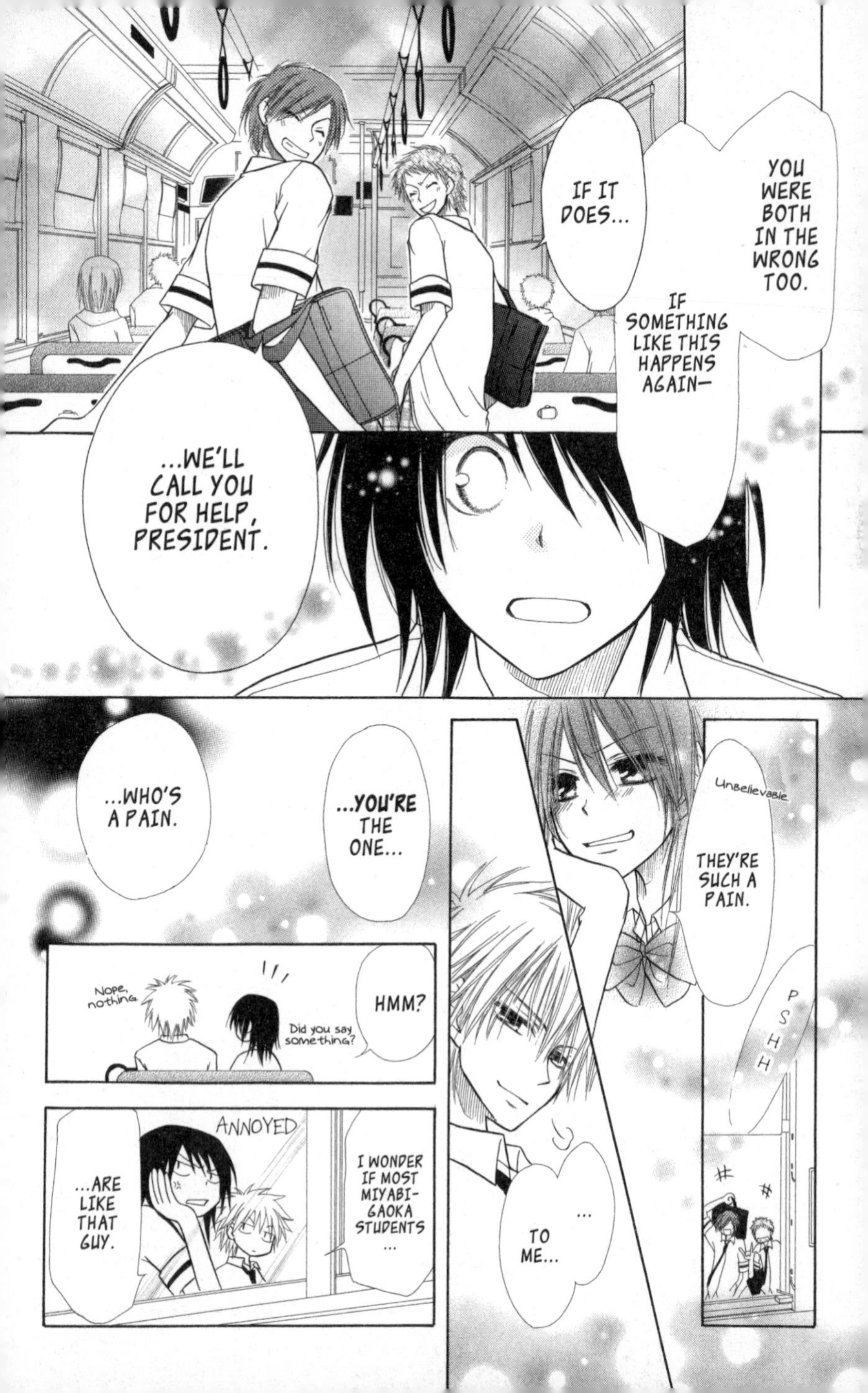
YOU WERE BOTH IN THE WRONG TOO.
IF SOMETHING LIKE THIS HAPPENS AGAIN—
IF IT DOES...
...WE'LL CALL YOU FOR HELP, PRESIDENT.
Unbelievable
THEY'RE SUCH A PAIN.
PSHH
...
TO ME...
...YOU'RE THE ONE...
...WHO'S A PAIN.
HMM?
Did you say something?
Nope, nothing.
I WONDER IF MOST MIYABI-GAOKA STUDENTS...
ANNOYED
...ARE LIKE THAT GUY.

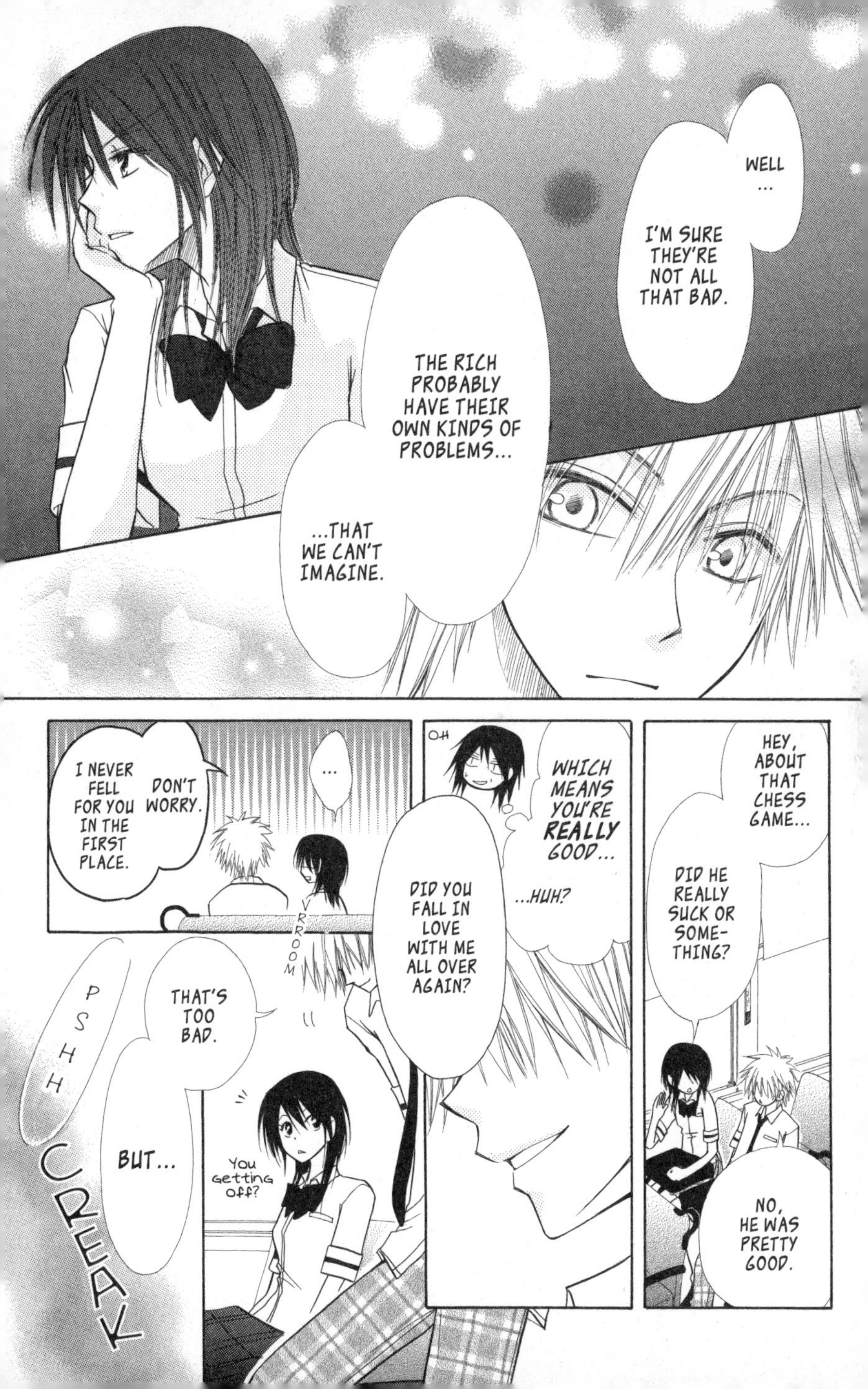
WELL ...
I'M SURE THEY'RE NOT ALL THAT BAD.
THE RICH PROBABLY HAVE THEIR OWN KINDS OF PROBLEMS...
...THAT WE CAN'T IMAGINE.
HEY, ABOUT THAT CHESS GAME...
DID HE REALLY SUCK OR SOME-THING?
NO, HE WAS PRETTY GOOD.
OH
WHICH MEANS YOU'RE REALLY GOOD...
...HUH?
DID YOU FALL IN LOVE WITH ME ALL OVER AGAIN?
...
DON'T WORRY.
I NEVER FELL FOR YOU IN THE FIRST PLACE.
VRROOM
THAT'S TOO BAD.
BUT...
You getting off?
PSHH
CREAK

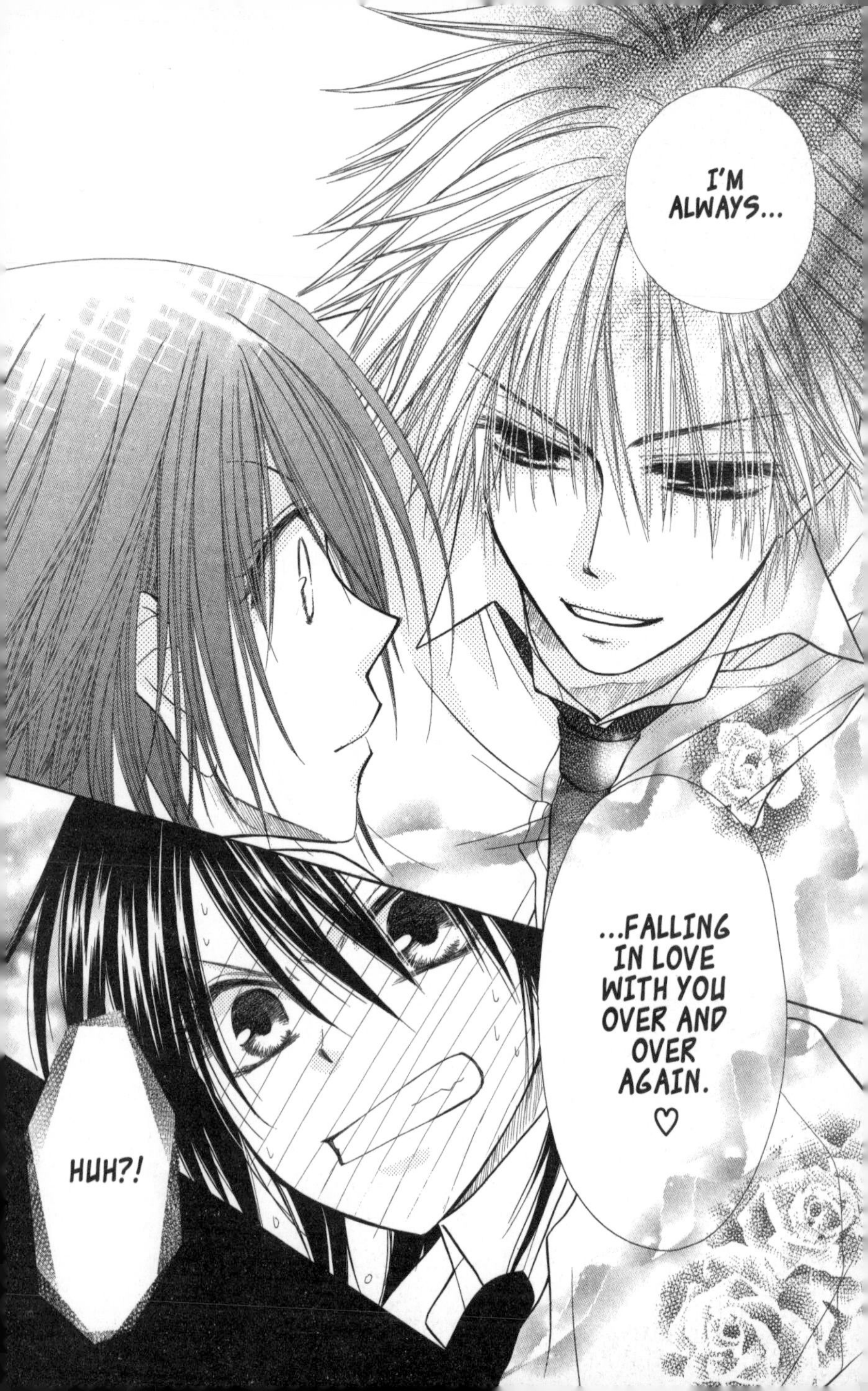
I'M ALWAYS...
...FALLING IN LOVE WITH YOU OVER AND OVER AGAIN. ♡
HUH?!

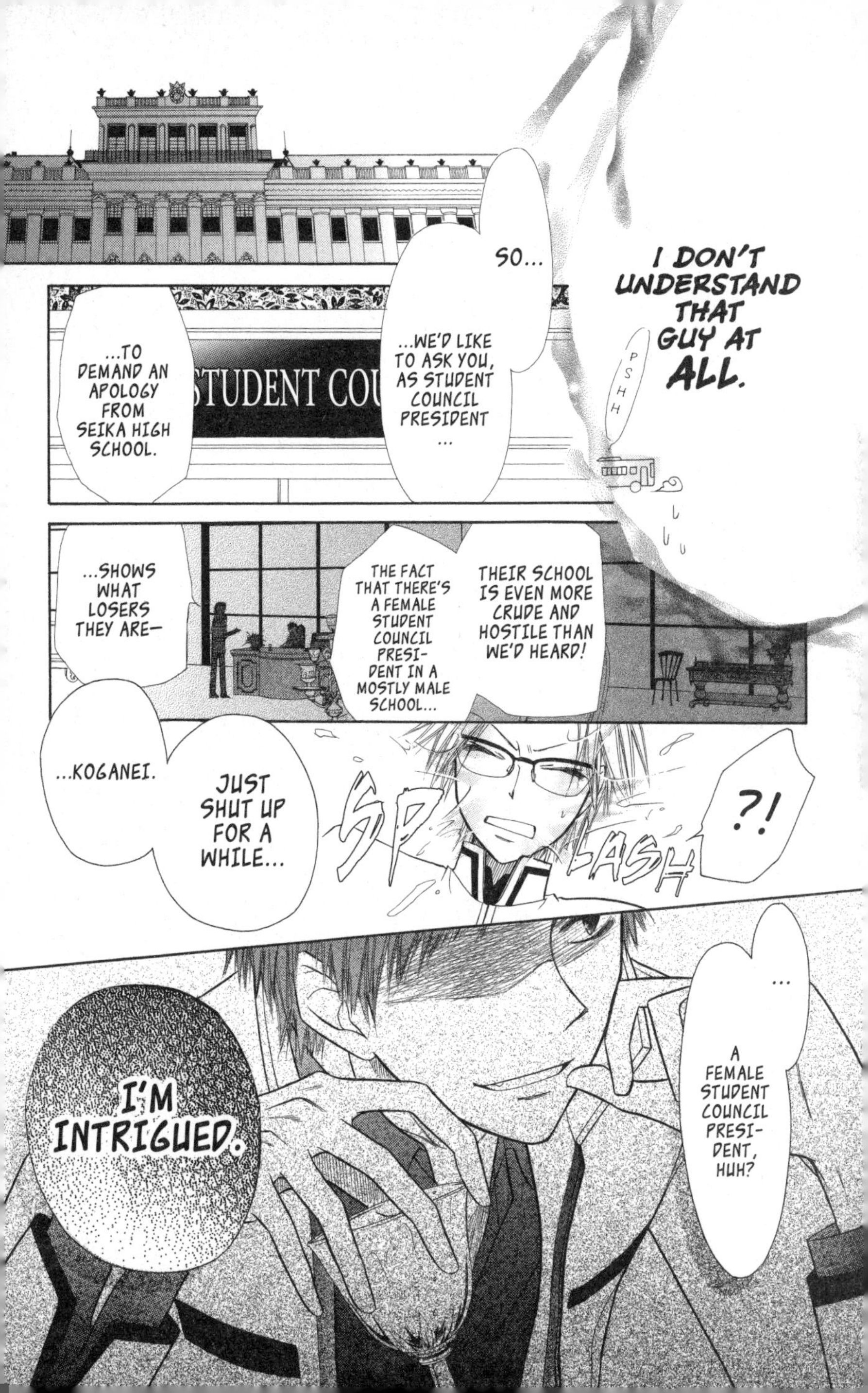
I DON'T UNDERSTAND THAT GUY AT ALL.
PSHH
SO...
...WE'D LIKE TO ASK YOU, AS STUDENT COUNCIL PRESIDENT...
STUDENT COU
...TO DEMAND AN APOLOGY FROM SEIKA HIGH SCHOOL.
THEIR SCHOOL IS EVEN MORE CRUDE AND HOSTILE THAN WE'D HEARD!
THE FACT THAT THERE'S A FEMALE STUDENT COUNCIL PRESI-DENT IN A MOSTLY MALE SCHOOL...
...SHOWS WHAT LOSERS THEY ARE—
?!
SPLASH
JUST SHUT UP FOR A WHILE...
...KOGANEI.
...
A FEMALE STUDENT COUNCIL PRESI-DENT, HUH?
I'M INTRIGUED.

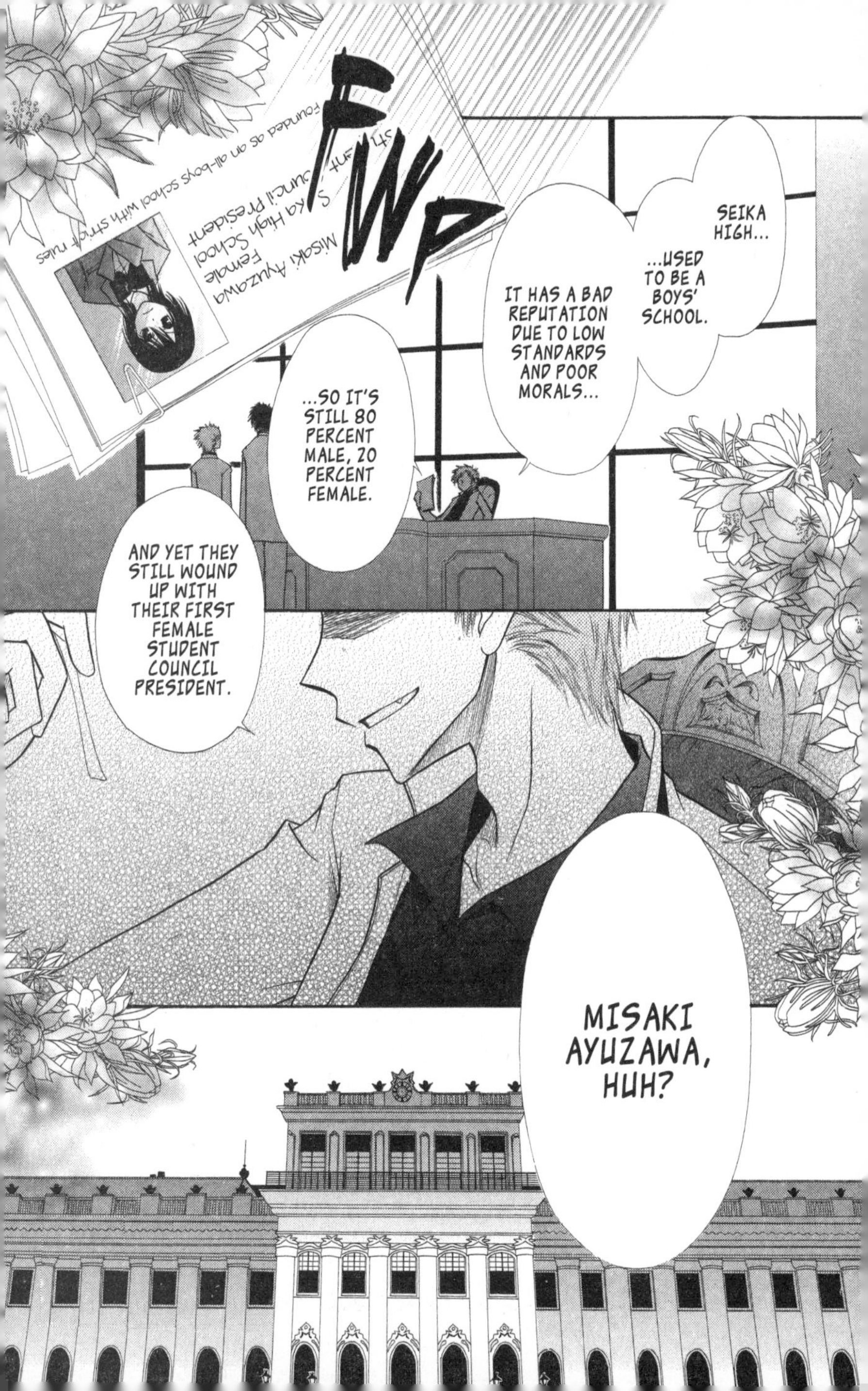
SEIKA HIGH...
...USED TO BE A BOYS' SCHOOL.
IT HAS A BAD REPUTATION DUE TO LOW STANDARDS AND POOR MORALS...
FWP
Misaki Ayuzawa
Female
ka High School
Founded as an all-boys school with strict rules
...SO IT'S STILL 80 PERCENT MALE, 20 PERCENT FEMALE.
AND YET THEY STILL WOUND UP WITH THEIR FIRST FEMALE STUDENT COUNCIL PRESIDENT.
MISAKI AYUZAWA, HUH?

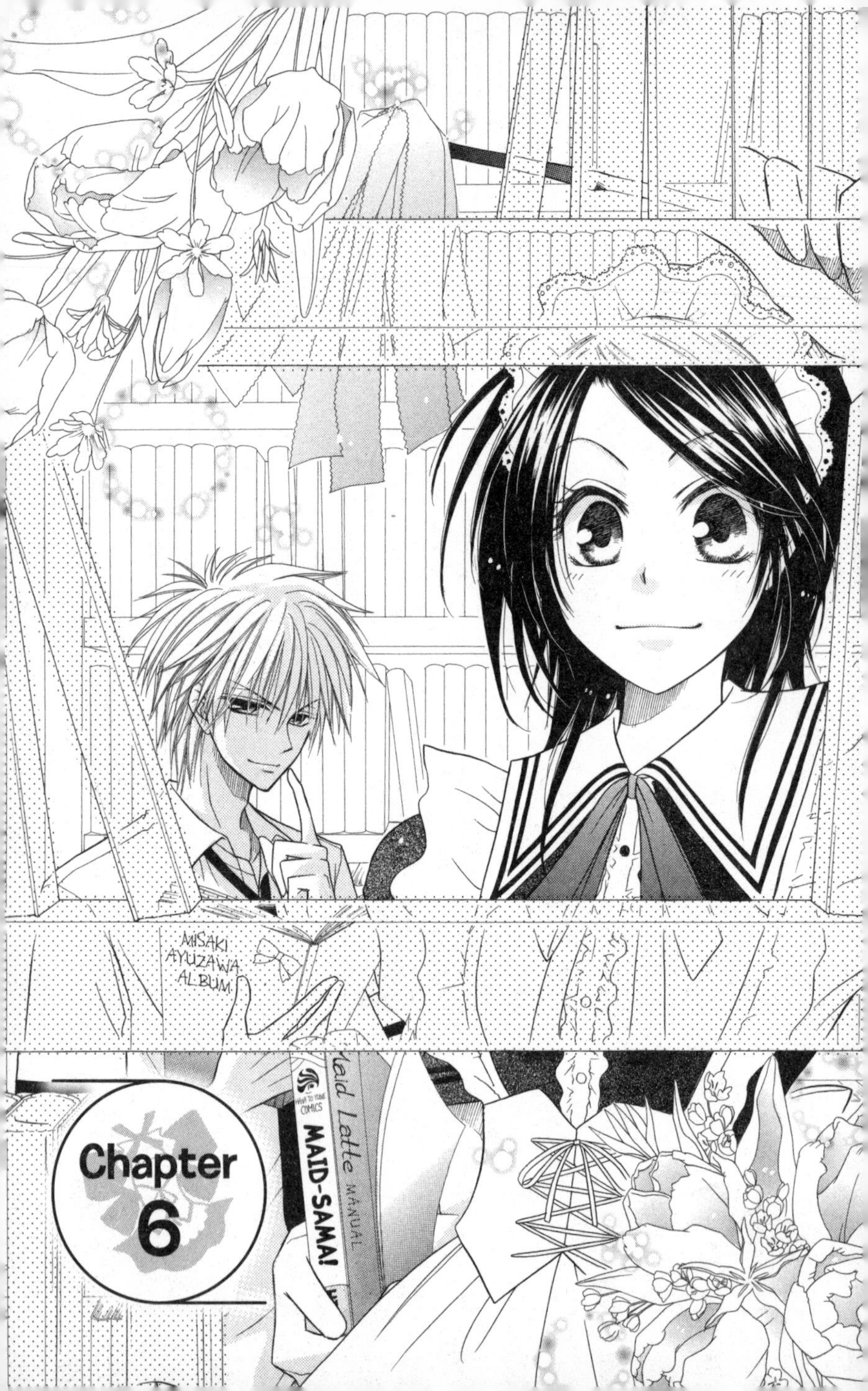
MISAKI AYUZAWA ALBUM
Maid Latte MANUAL
HANA TO YUME COMICS
MAID-SAMA!
Chapter 6

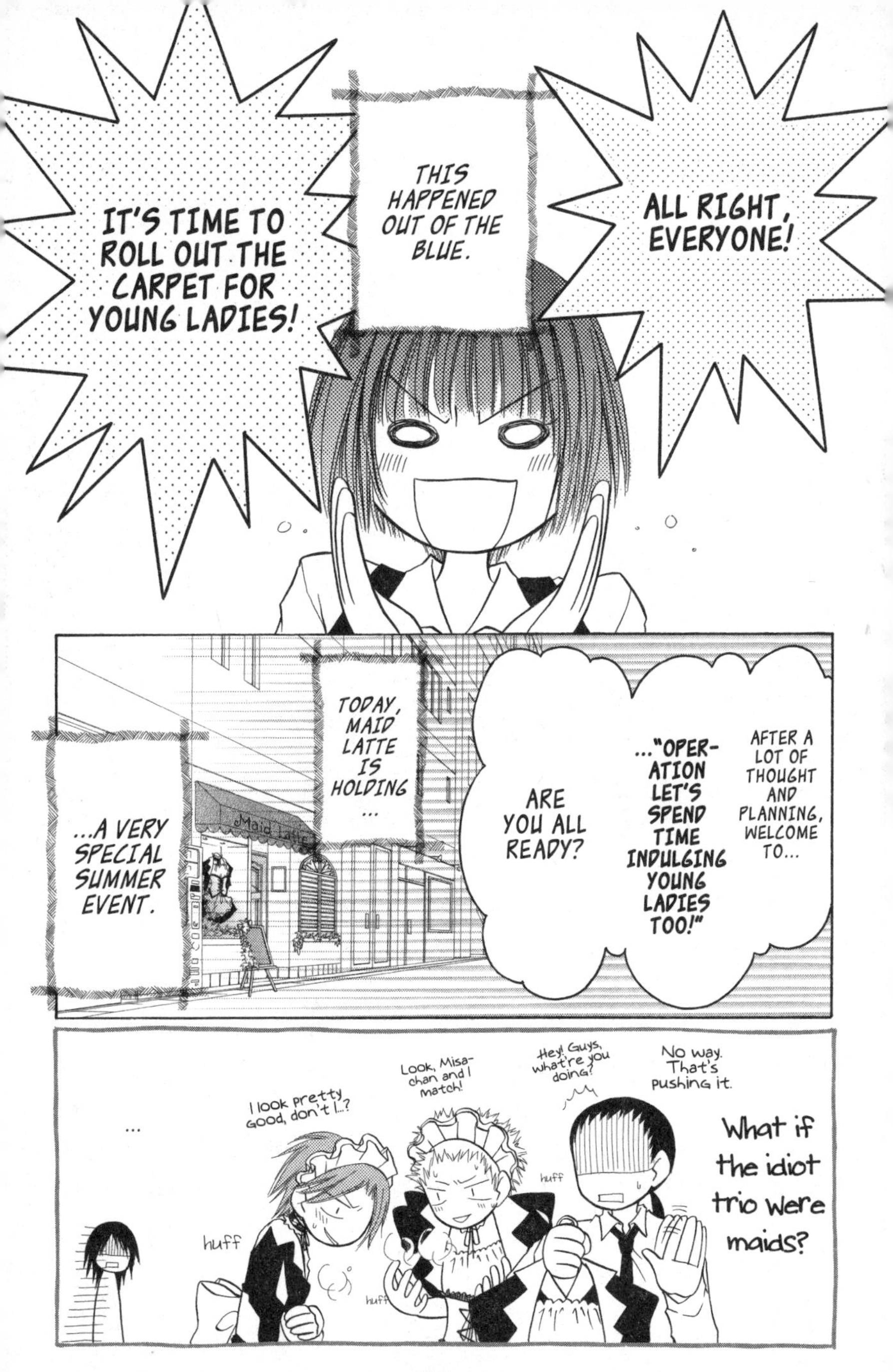
ALL RIGHT, EVERYONE!
THIS HAPPENED OUT OF THE BLUE.
IT'S TIME TO ROLL OUT THE CARPET FOR YOUNG LADIES!
AFTER A LOT OF THOUGHT AND PLANNING, WELCOME TO...
..."OPERATION LET'S SPEND TIME INDULGING YOUNG LADIES TOO!"
ARE YOU ALL READY?
TODAY, MAID LATTE IS HOLDING...
Maid latte
...A VERY SPECIAL SUMMER EVENT.
What if the idiot trio were maids?
No way. That's pushing it.
Hey! Guys, what're you doing?
huff
Look, Misa-chan and I match!
huff
I look pretty good, don't I...?
huff
...

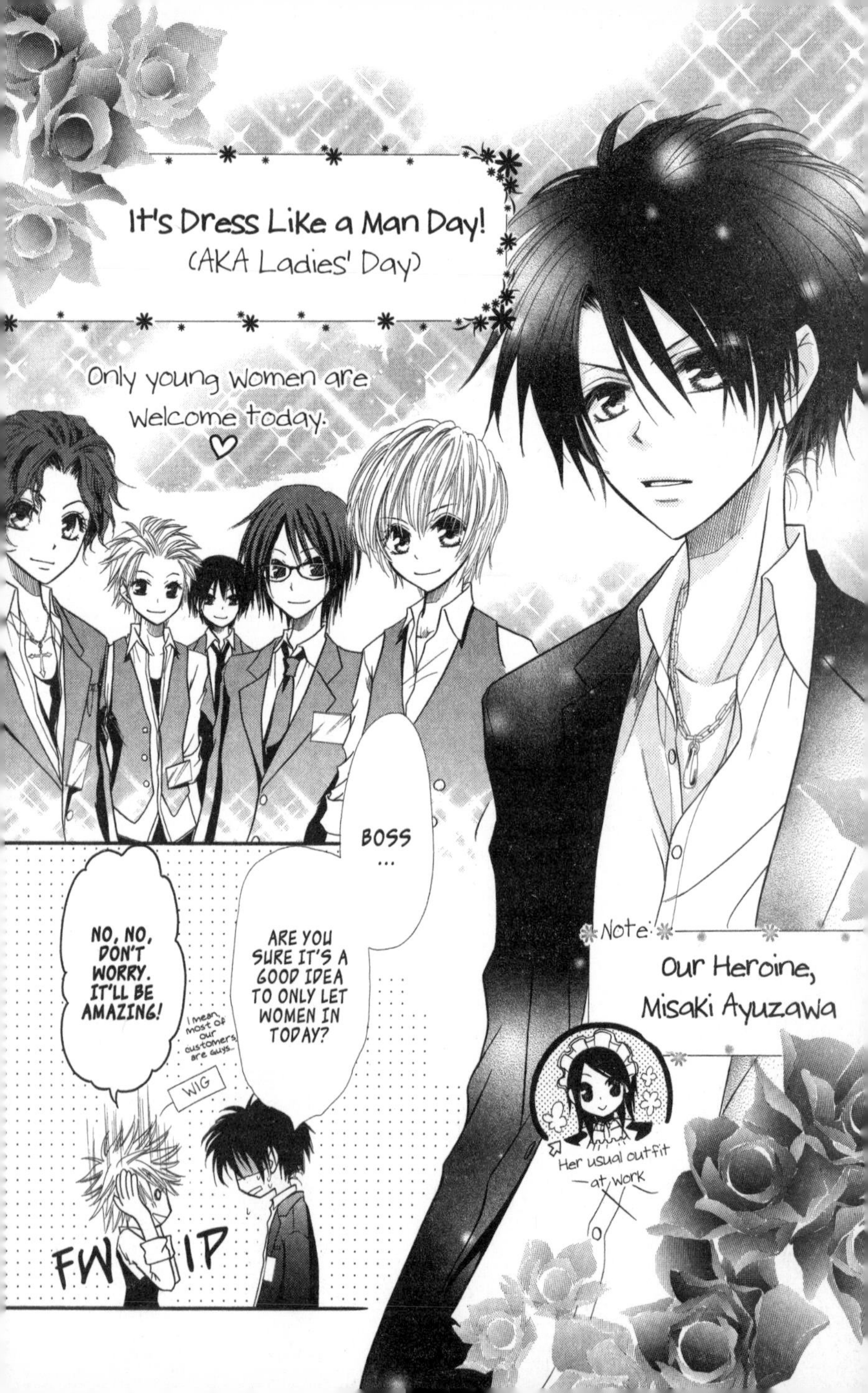

It's Dress Like a Man Day!
(AKA Ladies' Day)
Only young women are welcome today. ♡
Note:
Our Heroine, Misaki Ayuzawa
Her usual outfit at work
BOSS ...
ARE YOU SURE IT'S A GOOD IDEA TO ONLY LET WOMEN IN TODAY?
I mean, most of our customers are guys...
NO, NO, DON'T WORRY. IT'LL BE AMAZING!
WIG
FWIP

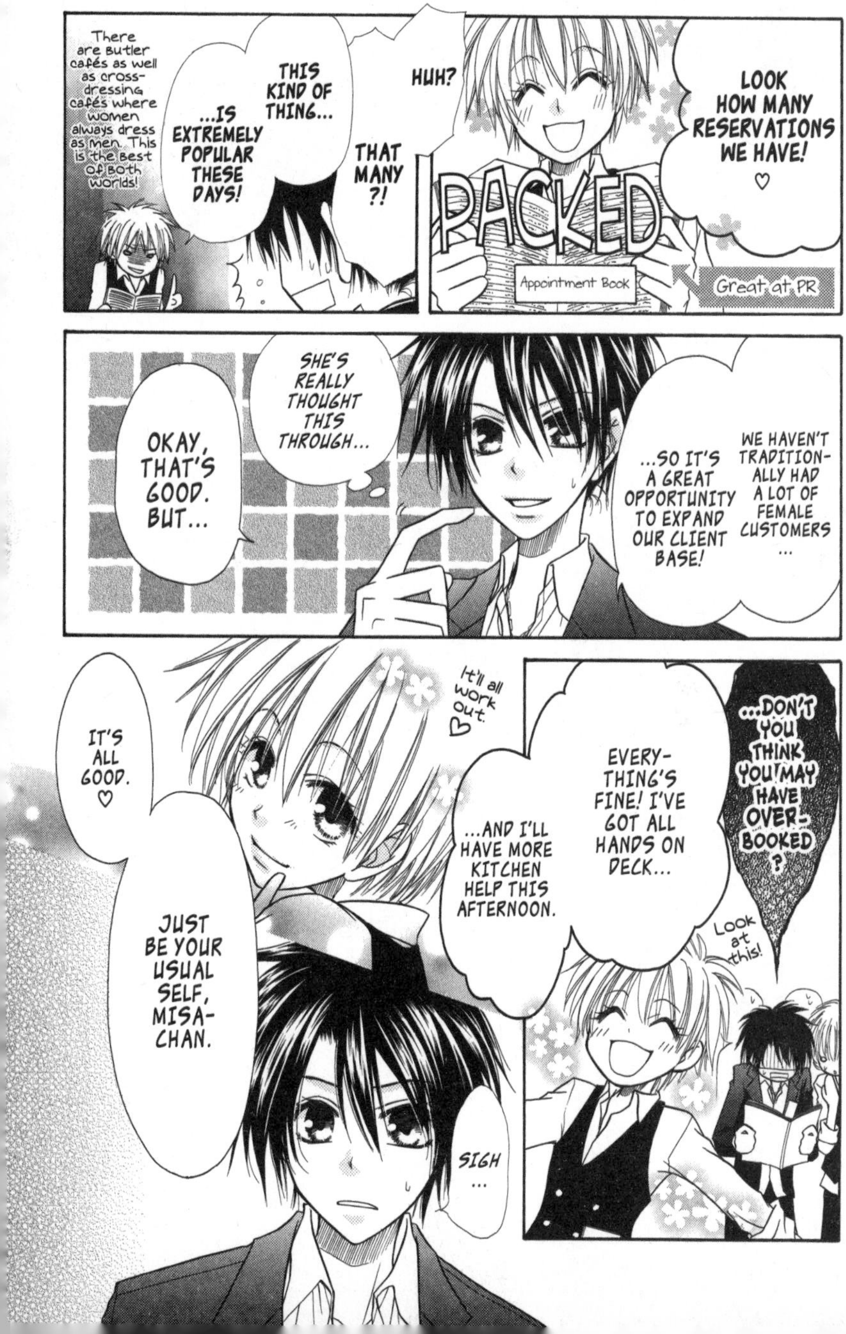
LOOK HOW MANY RESERVATIONS WE HAVE! ♡
PACKED
Appointment Book
Great at PR
HUH?
THAT MANY?!
THIS KIND OF THING...
...IS EXTREMELY POPULAR THESE DAYS!
There are butler cafés as well as cross-dressing cafés where women always dress as men. This is the best of both worlds!
WE HAVEN'T TRADITIONALLY HAD A LOT OF FEMALE CUSTOMERS...
...SO IT'S A GREAT OPPORTUNITY TO EXPAND OUR CLIENT BASE!
SHE'S REALLY THOUGHT THIS THROUGH...
OKAY, THAT'S GOOD. BUT...
...DON'T YOU THINK YOU MAY HAVE OVERBOOKED?
Look at this!
EVERYTHING'S FINE! I'VE GOT ALL HANDS ON DECK...
...AND I'LL HAVE MORE KITCHEN HELP THIS AFTERNOON.
It'll all work out. ♡
IT'S ALL GOOD. ♡
JUST BE YOUR USUAL SELF, MISA-CHAN.
SIGH...

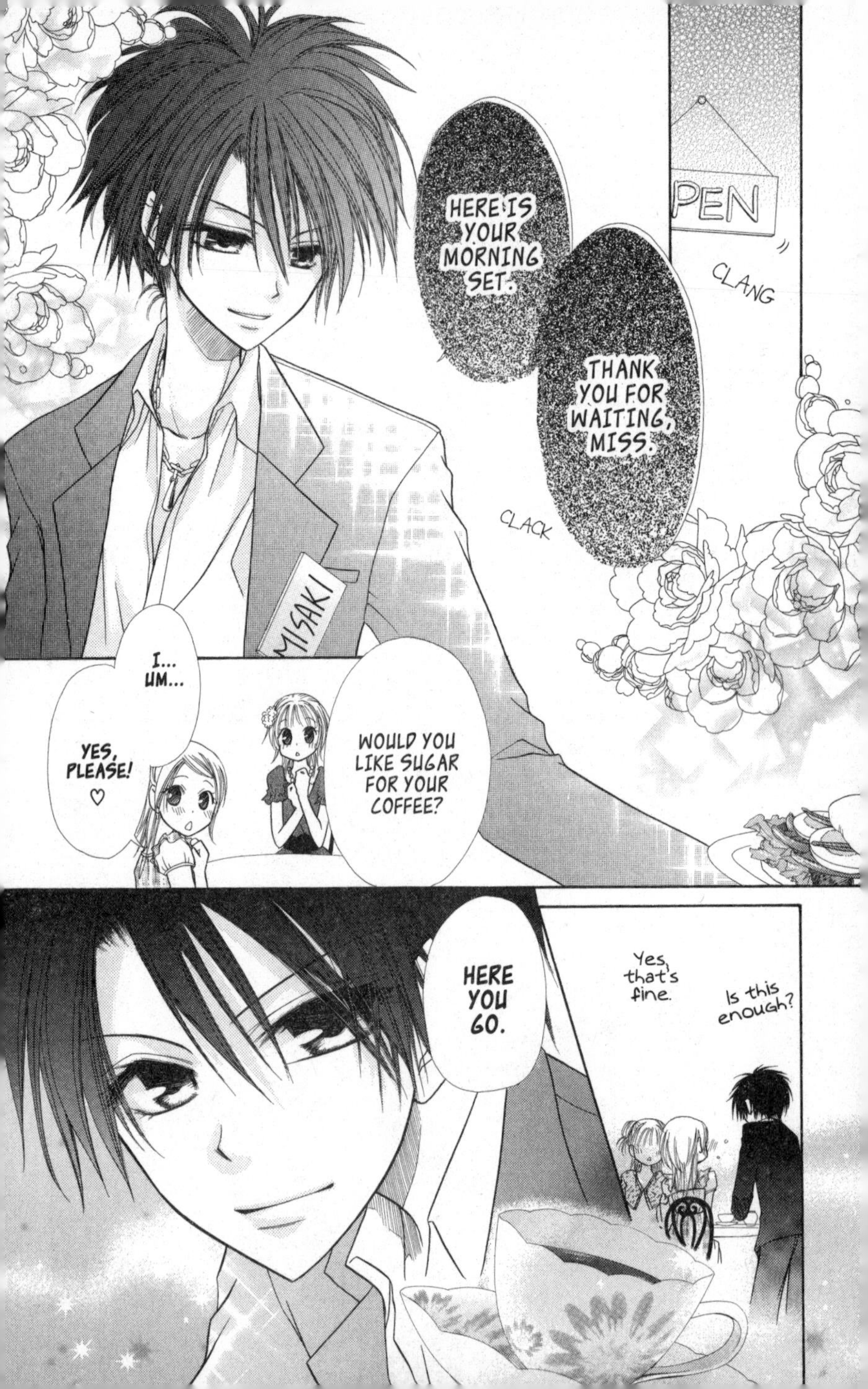
PEN
CLANG
THANK YOU FOR WAITING, MISS.
HERE IS YOUR MORNING SET.
CLACK
MISAKI
WOULD YOU LIKE SUGAR FOR YOUR COFFEE?
I... UM...
YES, PLEASE! ♡
Is this enough?
Yes, that's fine.
HERE YOU GO.

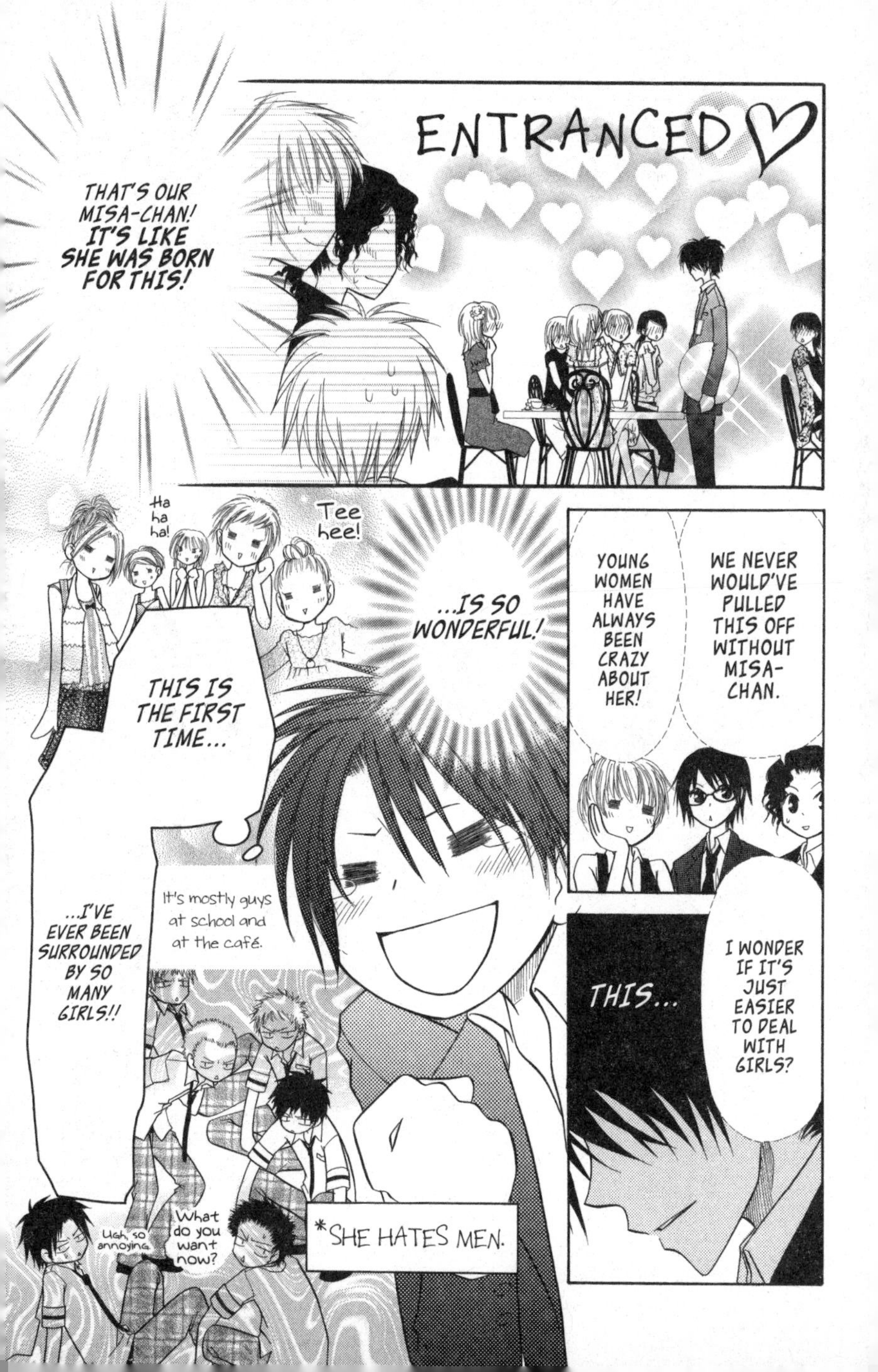
ENTRANCED ♡
THAT'S OUR MISA-CHAN! IT'S LIKE SHE WAS BORN FOR THIS!
WE NEVER WOULD'VE PULLED THIS OFF WITHOUT MISA-CHAN.
YOUNG WOMEN HAVE ALWAYS BEEN CRAZY ABOUT HER!
I WONDER IF IT'S JUST EASIER TO DEAL WITH GIRLS?
THIS...
...IS SO WONDERFUL!
Tee hee!
Ha ha ha!
THIS IS THE FIRST TIME...
...I'VE EVER BEEN SURROUNDED BY SO MANY GIRLS!!
It's mostly guys at school and at the café.
*SHE HATES MEN.
What do you want now?
Ugh, so annoying.

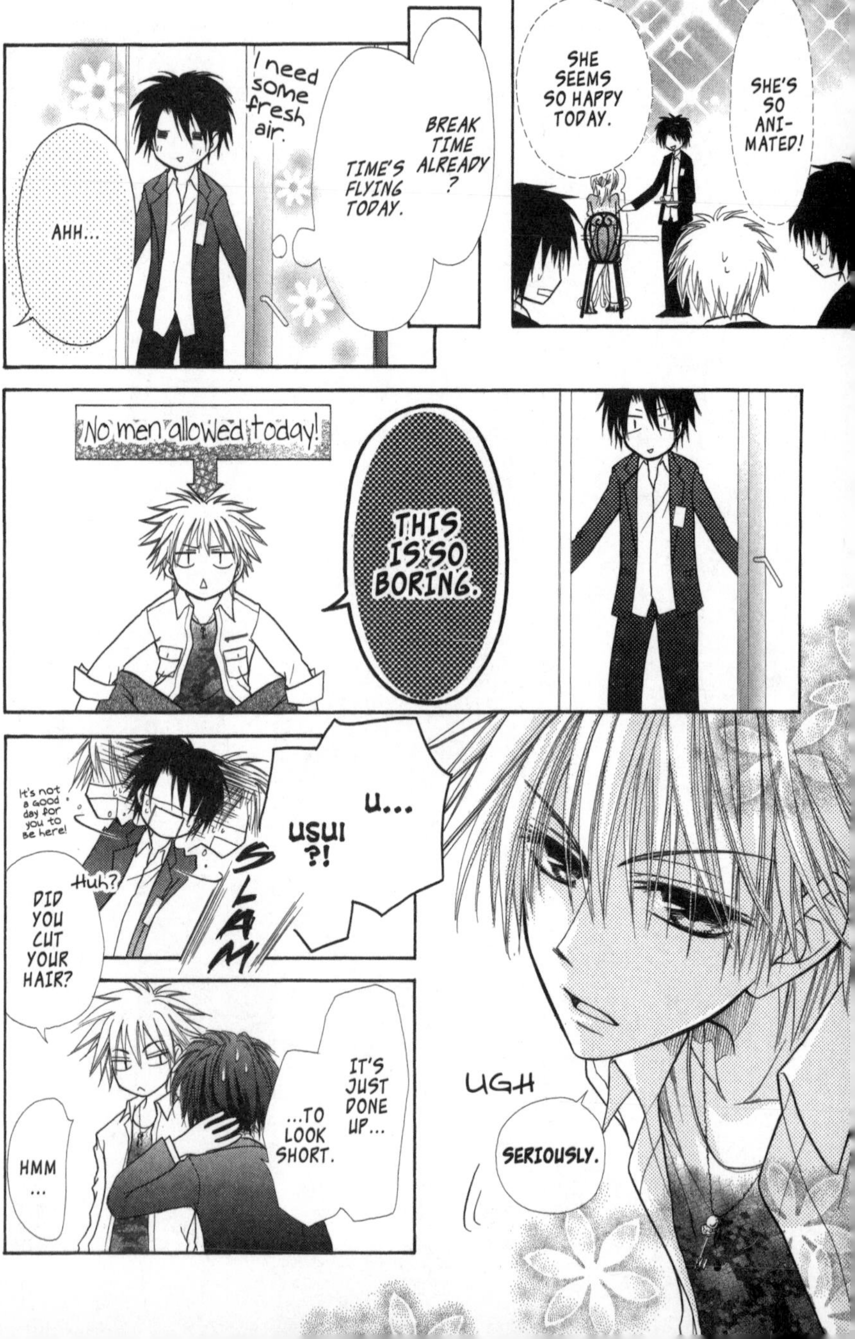
SHE'S SO ANI-MATED!
SHE SEEMS SO HAPPY TODAY.
BREAK TIME ALREADY?
TIME'S FLYING TODAY.
I need some fresh air.
AHH...
THIS IS SO BORING.
No men allowed today!
UGH
SERIOUSLY.
U...
USUI?!
SLAM
It's not a good day for you to be here!
Huh?
DID YOU CUT YOUR HAIR?
IT'S JUST DONE UP...
...TO LOOK SHORT.
HMM...

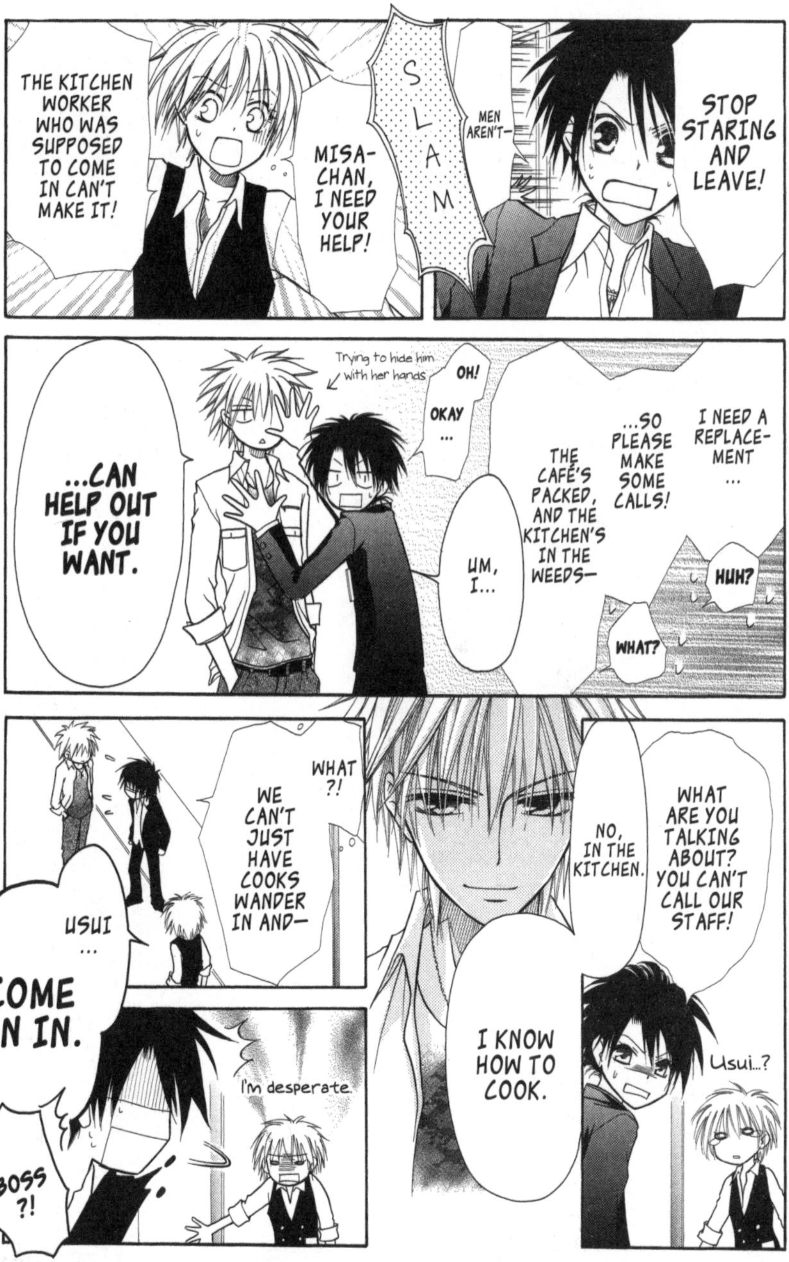

STOP STARING AND LEAVE!
MEN AREN'T—
SLAM
MISA-CHAN, I NEED YOUR HELP!
THE KITCHEN WORKER WHO WAS SUPPOSED TO COME IN CAN'T MAKE IT!
I NEED A REPLACEMENT...
HUH?
...SO PLEASE MAKE SOME CALLS!
THE CAFÉ'S PACKED, AND THE KITCHEN'S IN THE WEEDS—
WHAT?
UM, I...
OH!
OKAY...
Trying to hide him with her hands
...CAN HELP OUT IF YOU WANT.
WHAT ARE YOU TALKING ABOUT? YOU CAN'T CALL OUR STAFF!
NO, IN THE KITCHEN.
I KNOW HOW TO COOK.
Usui...?
WHAT?!
WE CAN'T JUST HAVE COOKS WANDER IN AND—
USUI...
COME ON IN.
I'm desperate.
BOSS?!

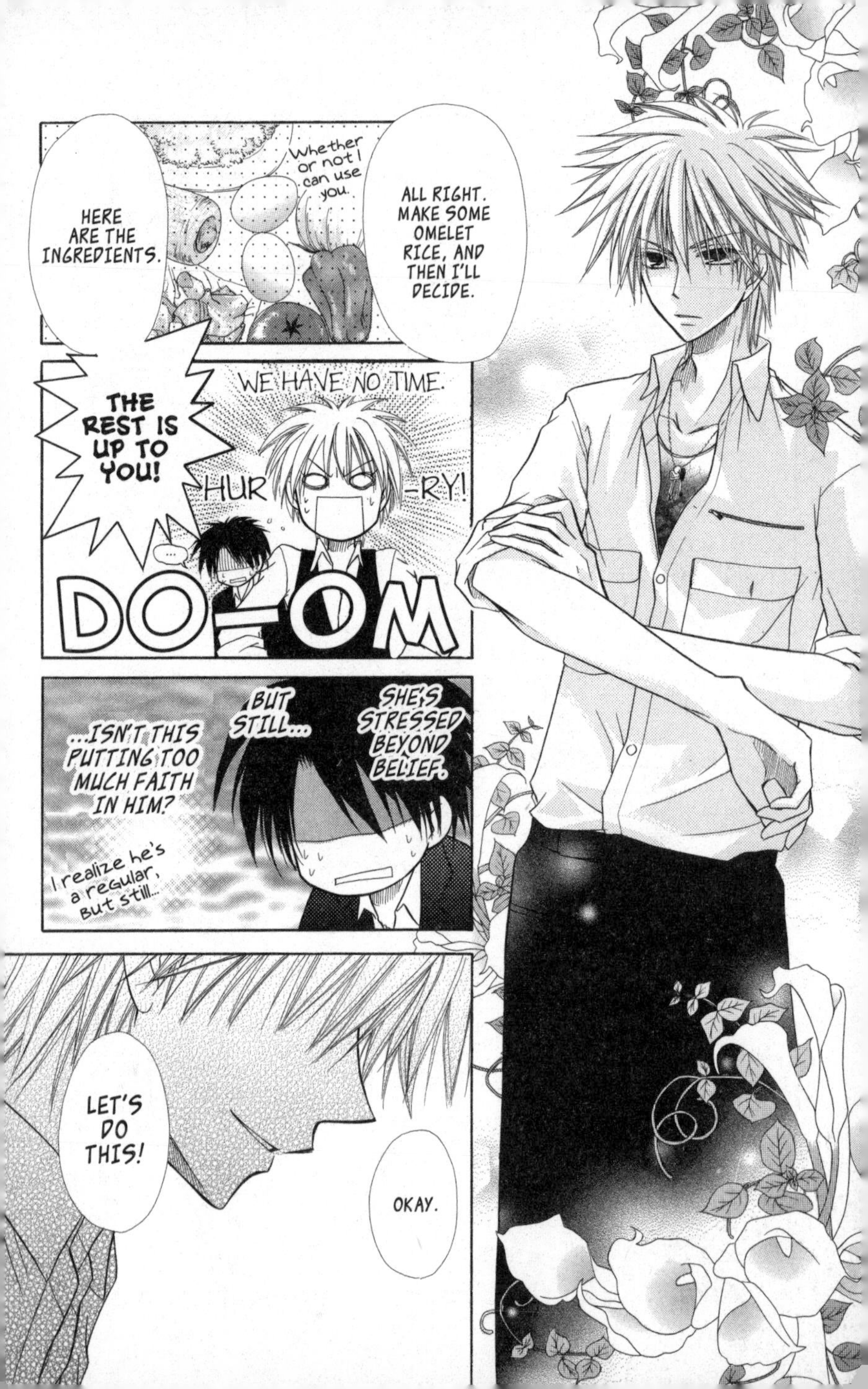
ALL RIGHT. MAKE SOME OMELET RICE, AND THEN I'LL DECIDE.
Whether or not I can use you.
HERE ARE THE INGREDIENTS.
WE HAVE NO TIME.
THE REST IS UP TO YOU!
HUR-RY!
...
DO-OM
SHE'S STRESSED BEYOND BELIEF.
BUT STILL...
...ISN'T THIS PUTTING TOO MUCH FAITH IN HIM?
I realize he's a regular, but still...
OKAY.
LET'S DO THIS!

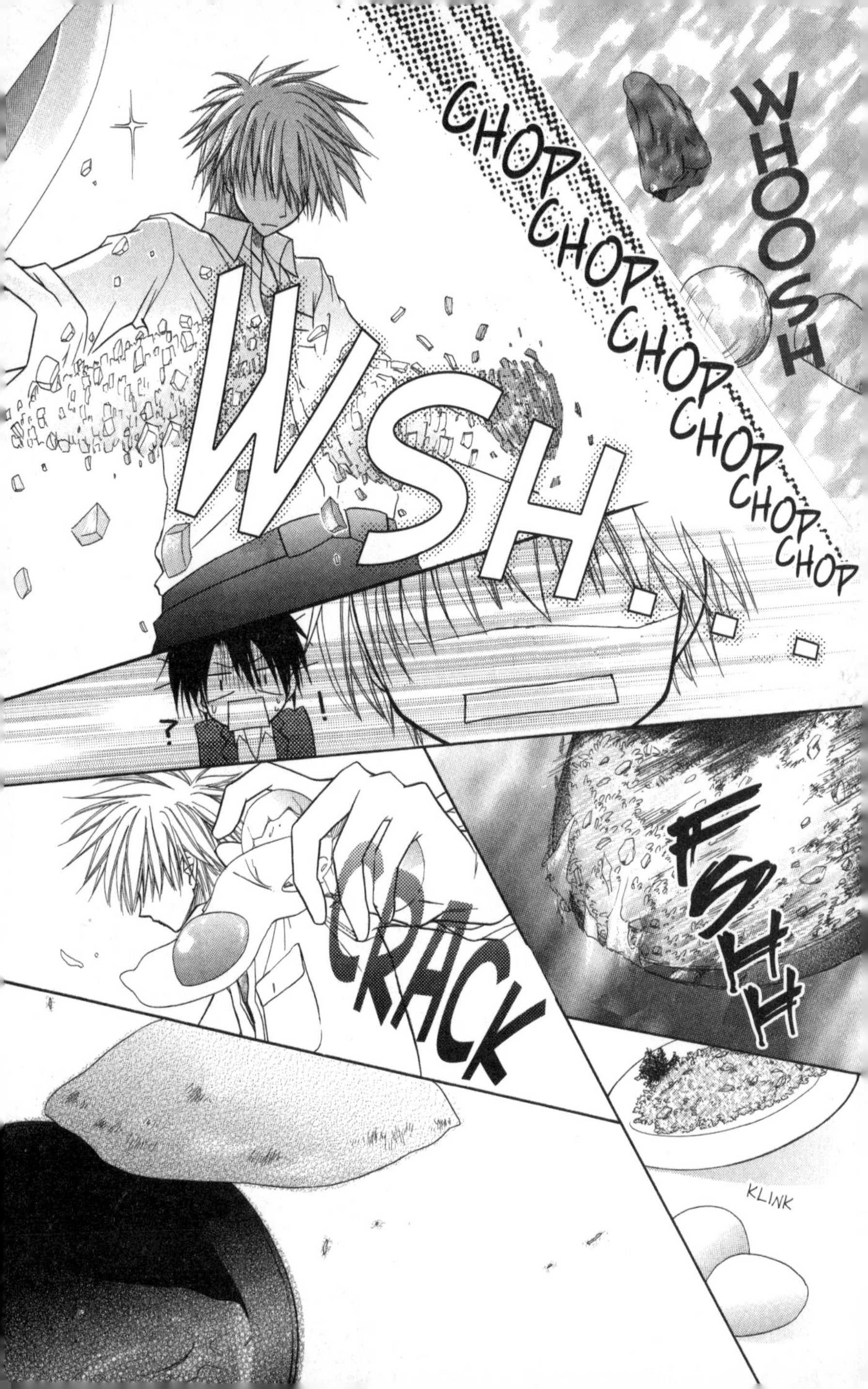
WHOOSH
CHOP CHOP CHOP CHOP CHOP CHOP CHOP
WSH
FSHH
CRACK
KLINK

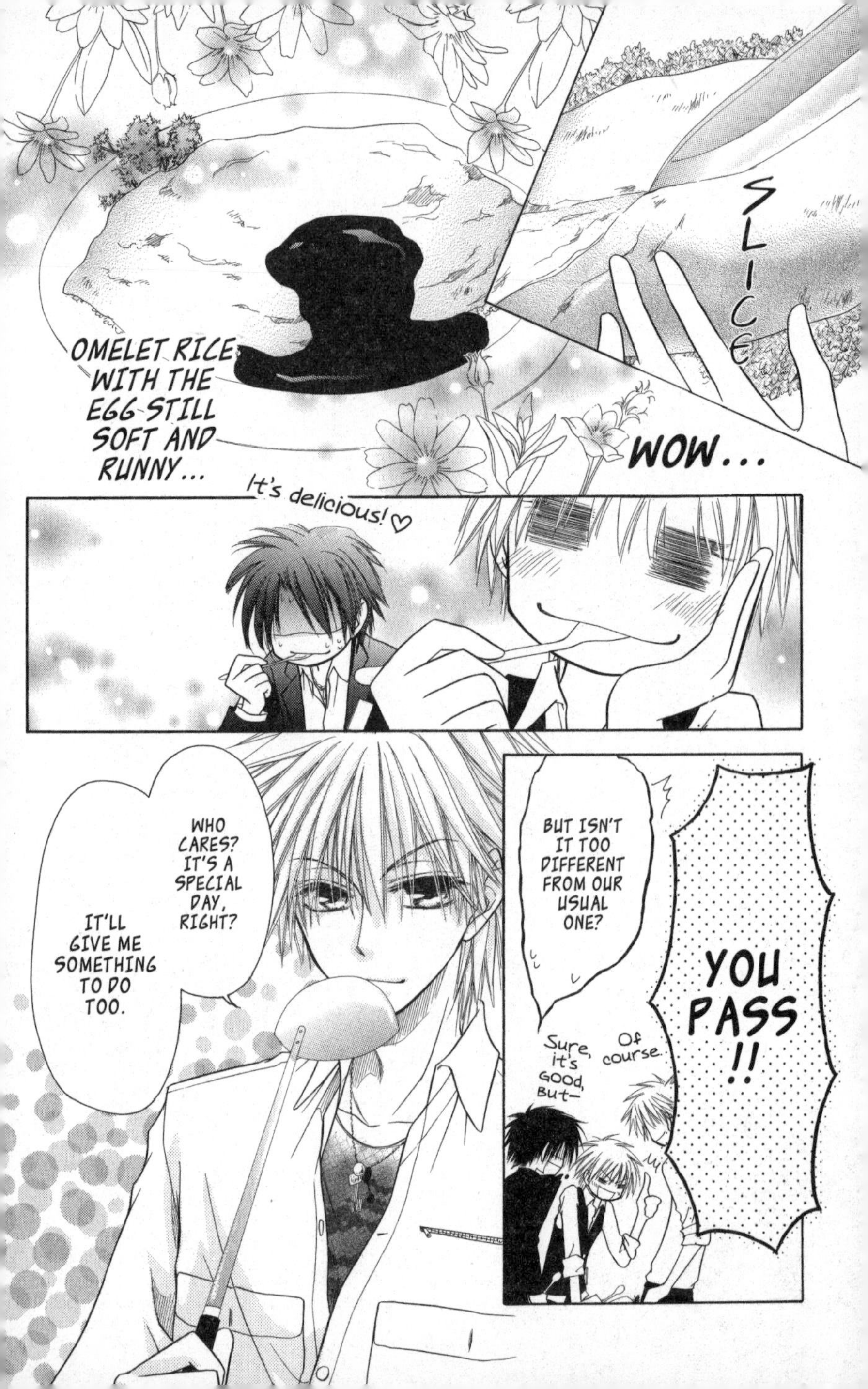
SLICE
OMELET RICE WITH THE EGG STILL SOFT AND RUNNY...
WOW...
It's delicious! ♡
YOU PASS!!
Of course.
Sure, it's good, but—
BUT ISN'T IT TOO DIFFERENT FROM OUR USUAL ONE?
WHO CARES? IT'S A SPECIAL DAY, RIGHT?
IT'LL GIVE ME SOMETHING TO DO TOO.

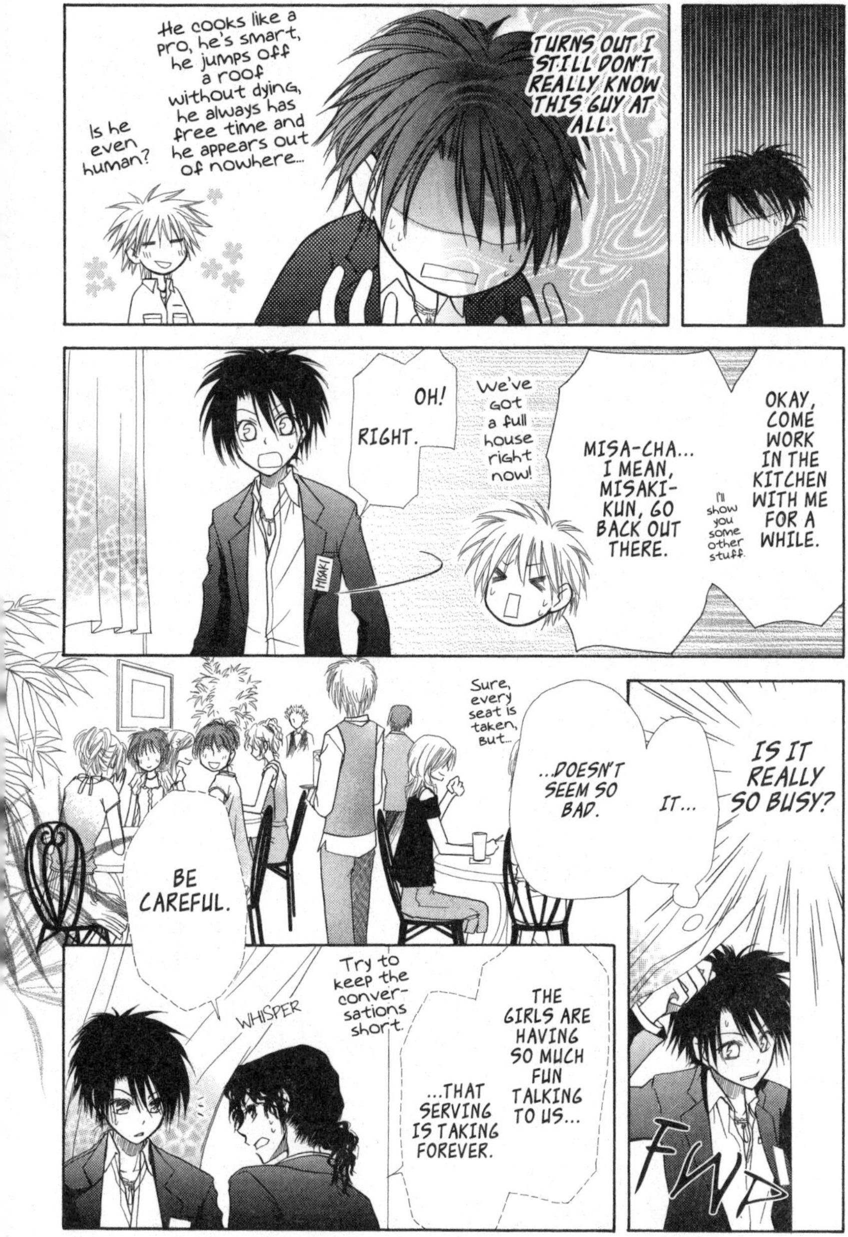
TURNS OUT I STILL DON'T REALLY KNOW THIS GUY AT ALL.
He cooks like a pro, he's smart, he jumps off a roof without dying, he always has free time and he appears out of nowhere...
Is he even human?
OKAY, COME WORK IN THE KITCHEN WITH ME FOR A WHILE.
I'll show you some other stuff.
MISA-CHA... I MEAN, MISAKI-KUN, GO BACK OUT THERE.
We've got a full house right now!
OH!
RIGHT.
MISAKI
IS IT REALLY SO BUSY?
IT...
...DOESN'T SEEM SO BAD.
Sure, every seat is taken, but...
FWP
BE CAREFUL.
THE GIRLS ARE HAVING SO MUCH FUN TALKING TO US...
...THAT SERVING IS TAKING FOREVER.
Try to keep the conversations short.
WHISPER

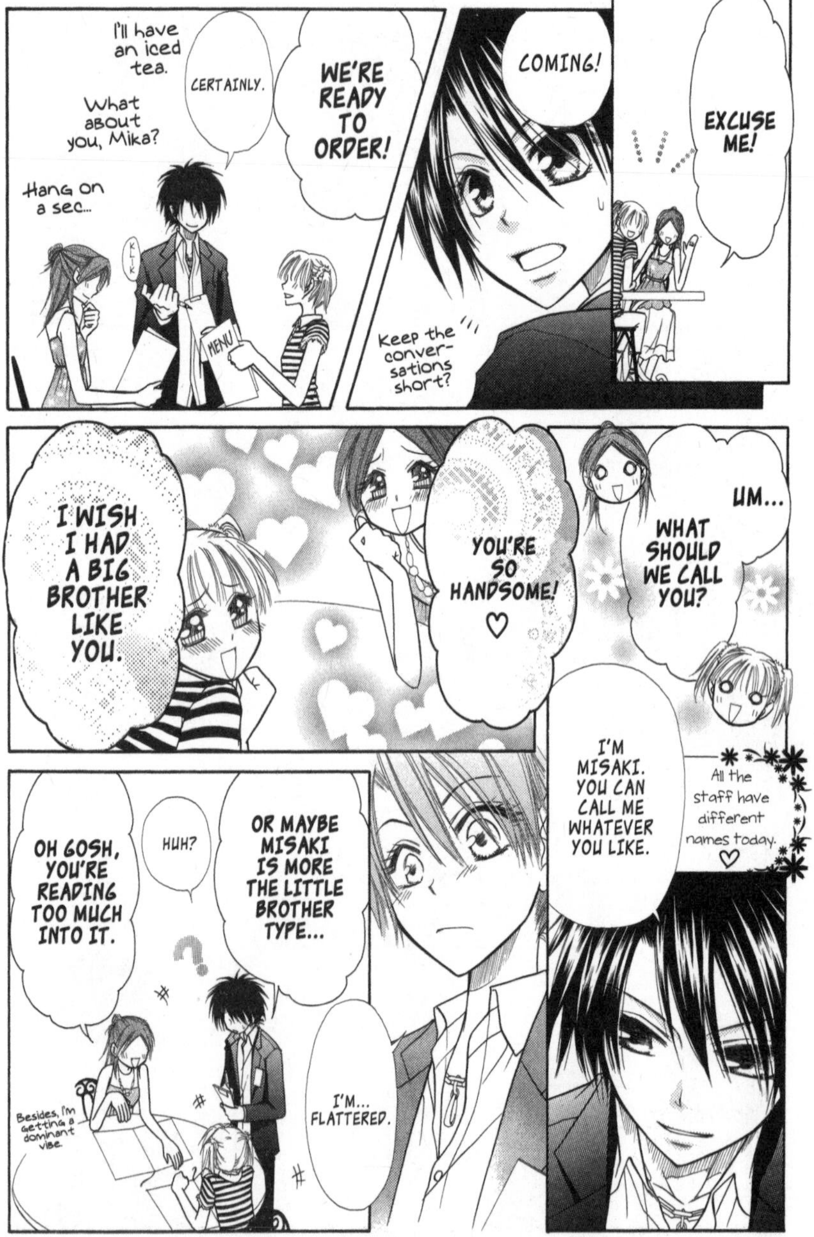
EXCUSE ME!
COMING!
Keep the conver-sations short?
WE'RE READY TO ORDER!
CERTAINLY.
I'll have an iced tea.
What about you, Mika?
Hang on a sec...
KLIK
MENU
UM...
WHAT SHOULD WE CALL YOU?
YOU'RE SO HANDSOME! ♡
I WISH I HAD A BIG BROTHER LIKE YOU.
I'M MISAKI. YOU CAN CALL ME WHATEVER YOU LIKE.
All the staff have different names today. ♡
OR MAYBE MISAKI IS MORE THE LITTLE BROTHER TYPE...
HUH?
OH GOSH, YOU'RE READING TOO MUCH INTO IT.
I'M... FLATTERED.
Besides, I'm getting a dominant vibe.

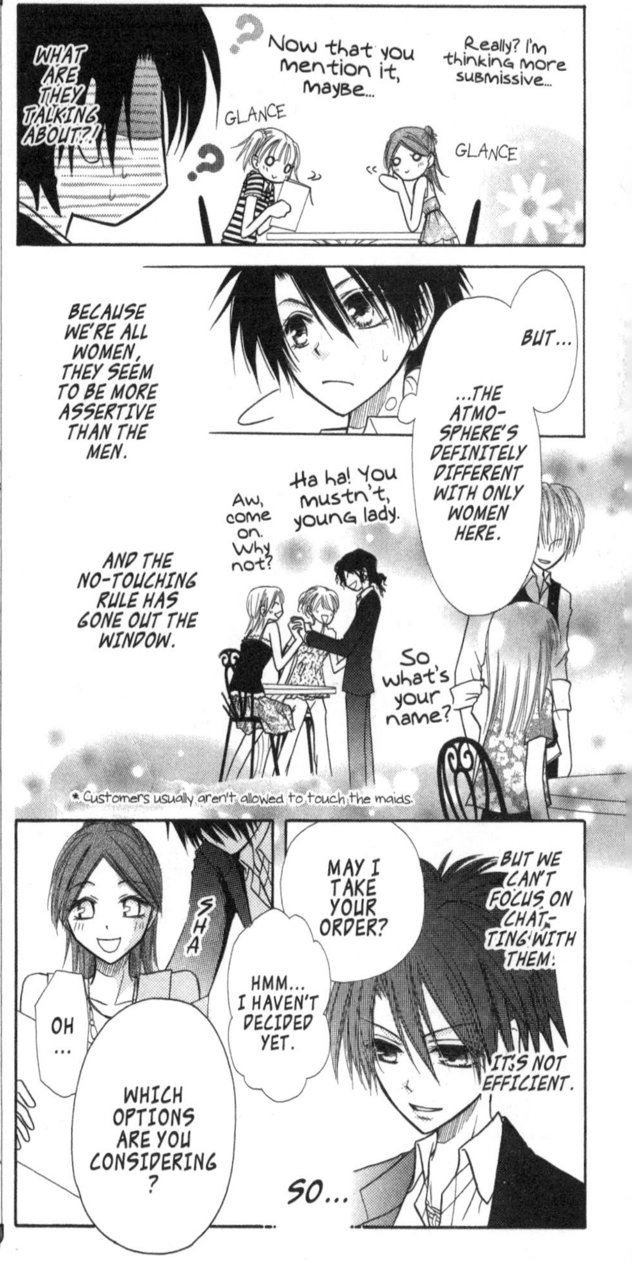
Really? I'm thinking more submissive...
GLANCE
Now that you mention it, maybe...
GLANCE
WHAT ARE THEY TALKING ABOUT?!
BUT...
...THE ATMOSPHERE'S DEFINITELY DIFFERENT WITH ONLY WOMEN HERE.
BECAUSE WE'RE ALL WOMEN, THEY SEEM TO BE MORE ASSERTIVE THAN THE MEN.
So what's your name?
Ha ha! You mustn't, young lady.
Aw, come on. Why not?
AND THE NO-TOUCHING RULE HAS GONE OUT THE WINDOW.
* Customers usually aren't allowed to touch the maids.
MAY I TAKE YOUR ORDER?
BUT WE CAN'T FOCUS ON CHATTING WITH THEM.
IT'S NOT EFFICIENT.
HMM... I HAVEN'T DECIDED YET.
SO...
SHA
OH...
WHICH OPTIONS ARE YOU CONSIDERING?

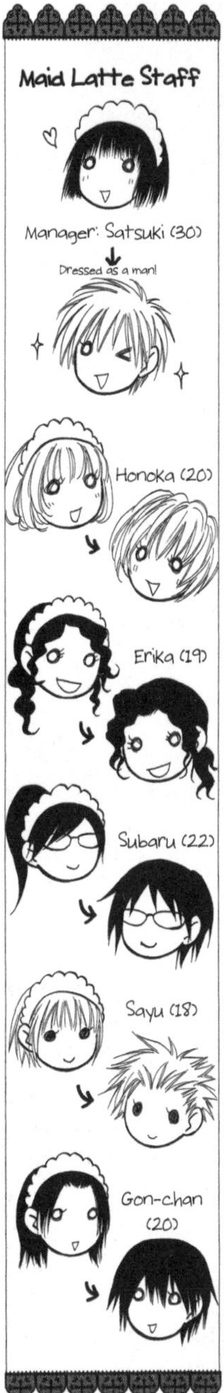
Maid Latte Staff
Manager: Satsuki (30)
Dressed as a man!
Honoka (20)
Erika (19)
Subaru (22)
Sayu (18)
Gon-chan (20)

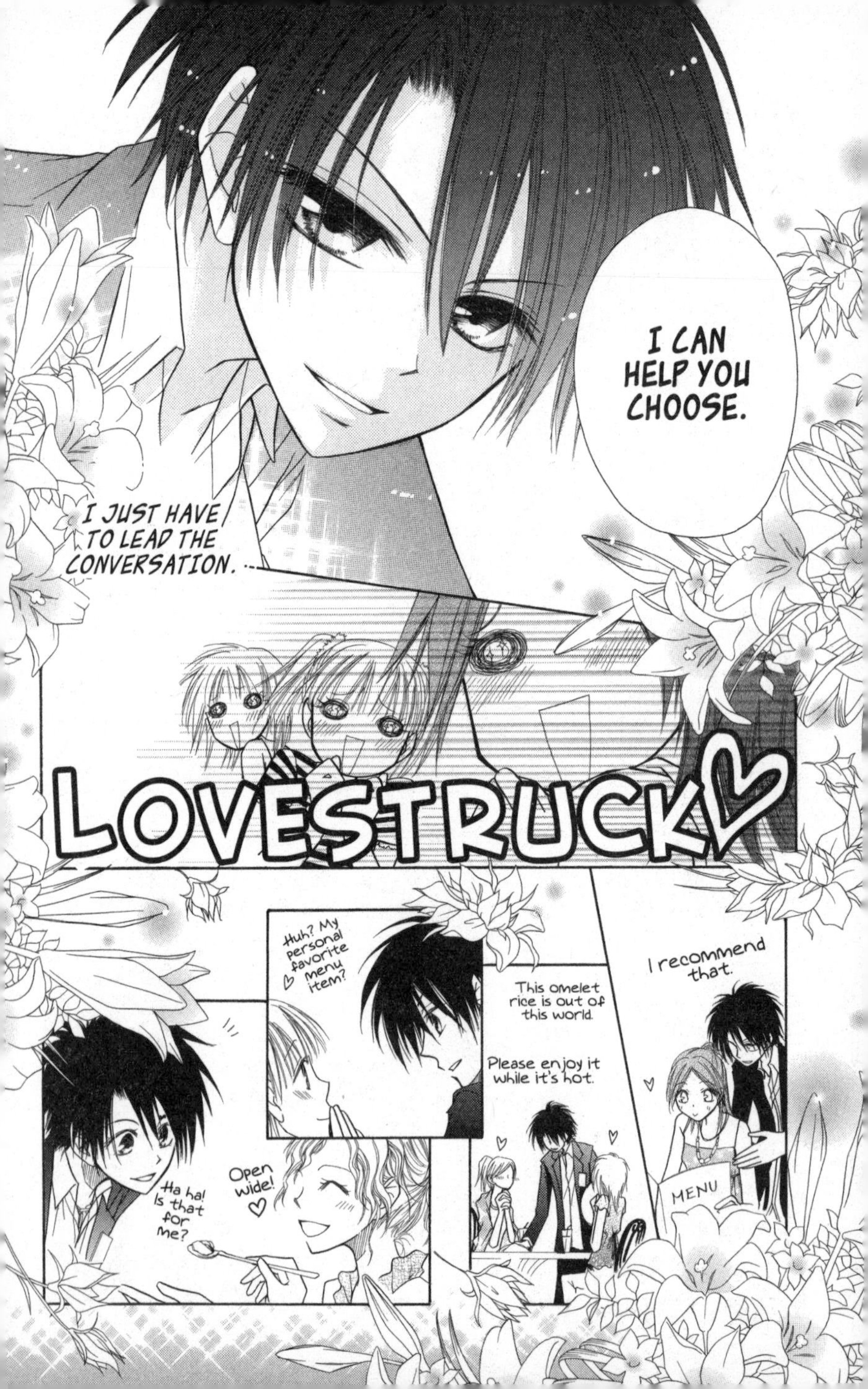
I CAN HELP YOU CHOOSE.
I JUST HAVE TO LEAD THE CONVERSATION...
LOVESTRUCK♥
I recommend that.
MENU
This omelet rice is out of this world.
Please enjoy it while it's hot.
Huh? My personal favorite menu item?
Open wide! ♥
Ha ha! Is that for me?

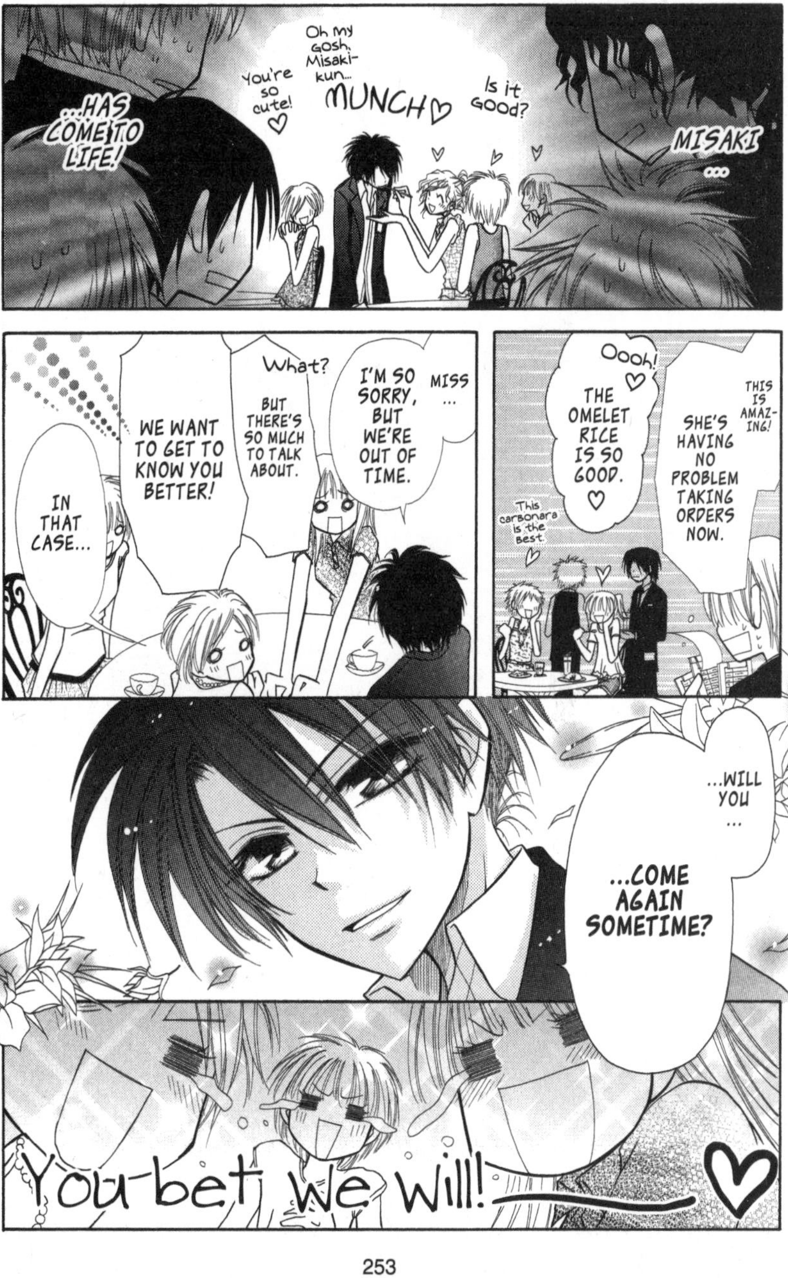
MISAKI...
Is it good?
MUNCH♥
Oh my gosh, Misaki-kun...
You're so cute! ♥
...HAS COME TO LIFE!
THIS IS AMAZING!
SHE'S HAVING NO PROBLEM TAKING ORDERS NOW.
Oooh! ♥
THE OMELET RICE IS SO GOOD. ♥
This carbonara is the best. ♥
MISS...
I'M SO SORRY, BUT WE'RE OUT OF TIME.
What?
BUT THERE'S SO MUCH TO TALK ABOUT.
WE WANT TO GET TO KNOW YOU BETTER!
IN THAT CASE...
...WILL YOU...
...COME AGAIN SOMETIME?
You bet we will! ♥

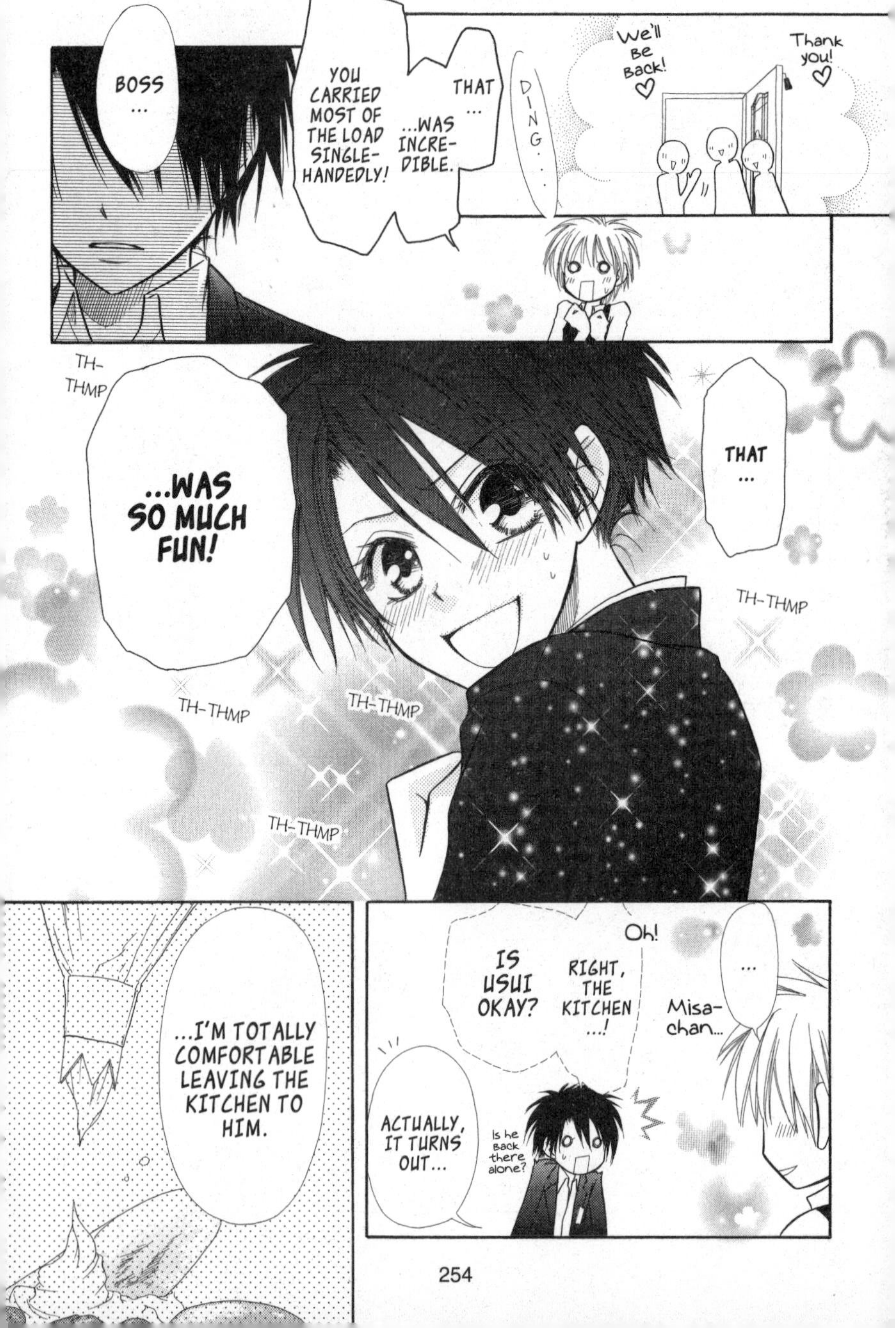

Thank you! ♡
We'll be back! ♡
DING...
THAT ...
...WAS INCREDIBLE.
YOU CARRIED MOST OF THE LOAD SINGLE-HANDEDLY!
BOSS ...
TH-THMP
THAT ...
...WAS SO MUCH FUN!
TH-THMP
TH-THMP
TH-THMP
TH-THMP
... Misa-chan...
Oh!
RIGHT, THE KITCHEN ...!
IS USUI OKAY?
Is he back there alone?
ACTUALLY, IT TURNS OUT...
...I'M TOTALLY COMFORTABLE LEAVING THE KITCHEN TO HIM.

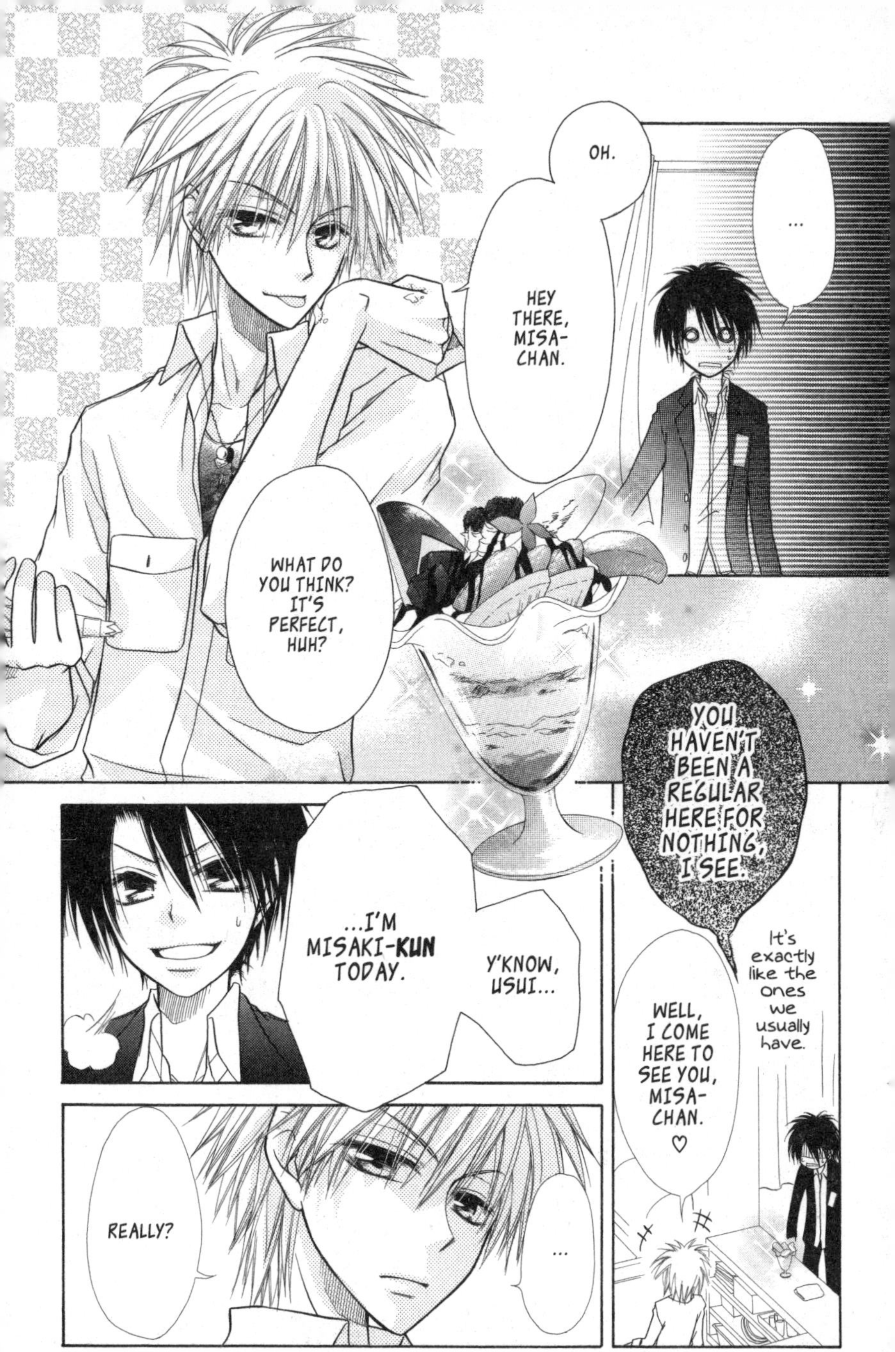
...
OH.
HEY THERE, MISA-CHAN.
WHAT DO YOU THINK? IT'S PERFECT, HUH?
YOU HAVEN'T BEEN A REGULAR HERE FOR NOTHING, I SEE.
It's exactly like the ones we usually have.
WELL, I COME HERE TO SEE YOU, MISA-CHAN. ♡
Y'KNOW, USUI...
...I'M MISAKI-**KUN** TODAY.
...
REALLY?

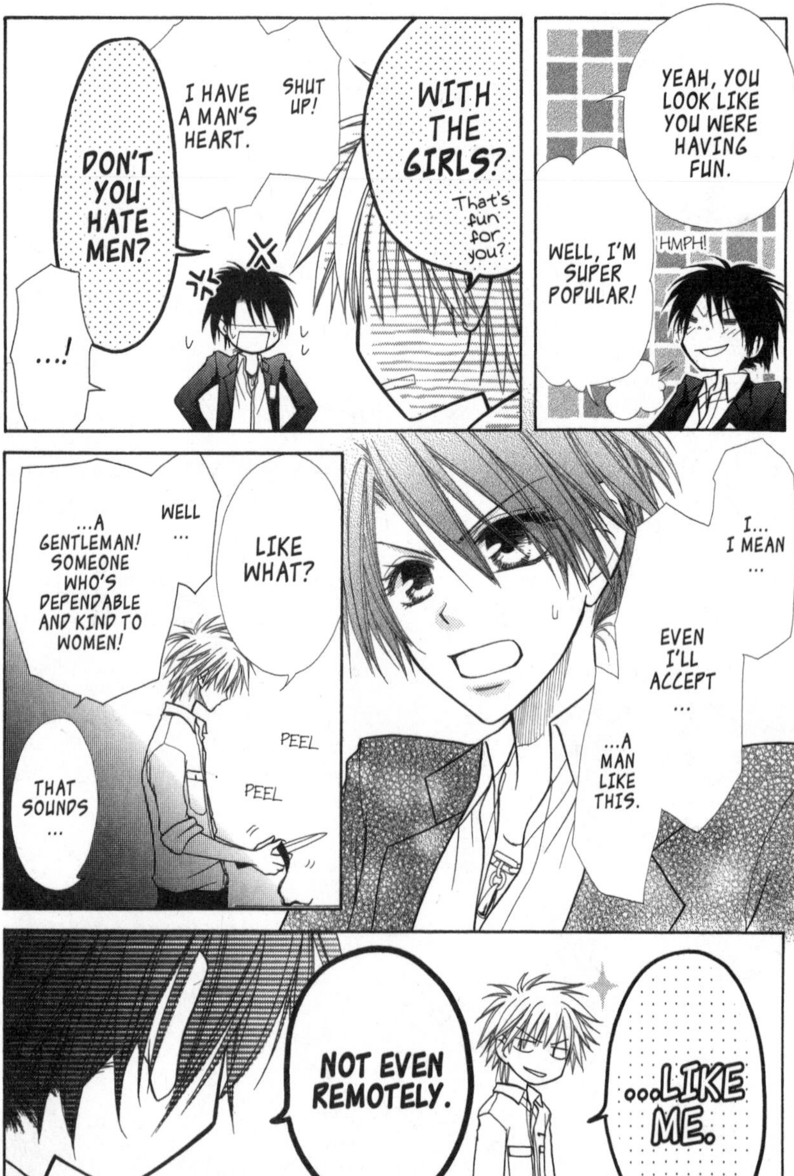
YEAH, YOU LOOK LIKE YOU WERE HAVING FUN.
HMPH!
WELL, I'M SUPER POPULAR!
WITH THE GIRLS?
That's fun for you?
SHUT UP!
I HAVE A MAN'S HEART.
DON'T YOU HATE MEN?
...!
I... I MEAN ...
EVEN I'LL ACCEPT ...
...A MAN LIKE THIS.
LIKE WHAT?
WELL ...
...A GENTLEMAN! SOMEONE WHO'S DEPENDABLE AND KIND TO WOMEN!
PEEL
PEEL
THAT SOUNDS ...
...LIKE ME.
NOT EVEN REMOTELY.

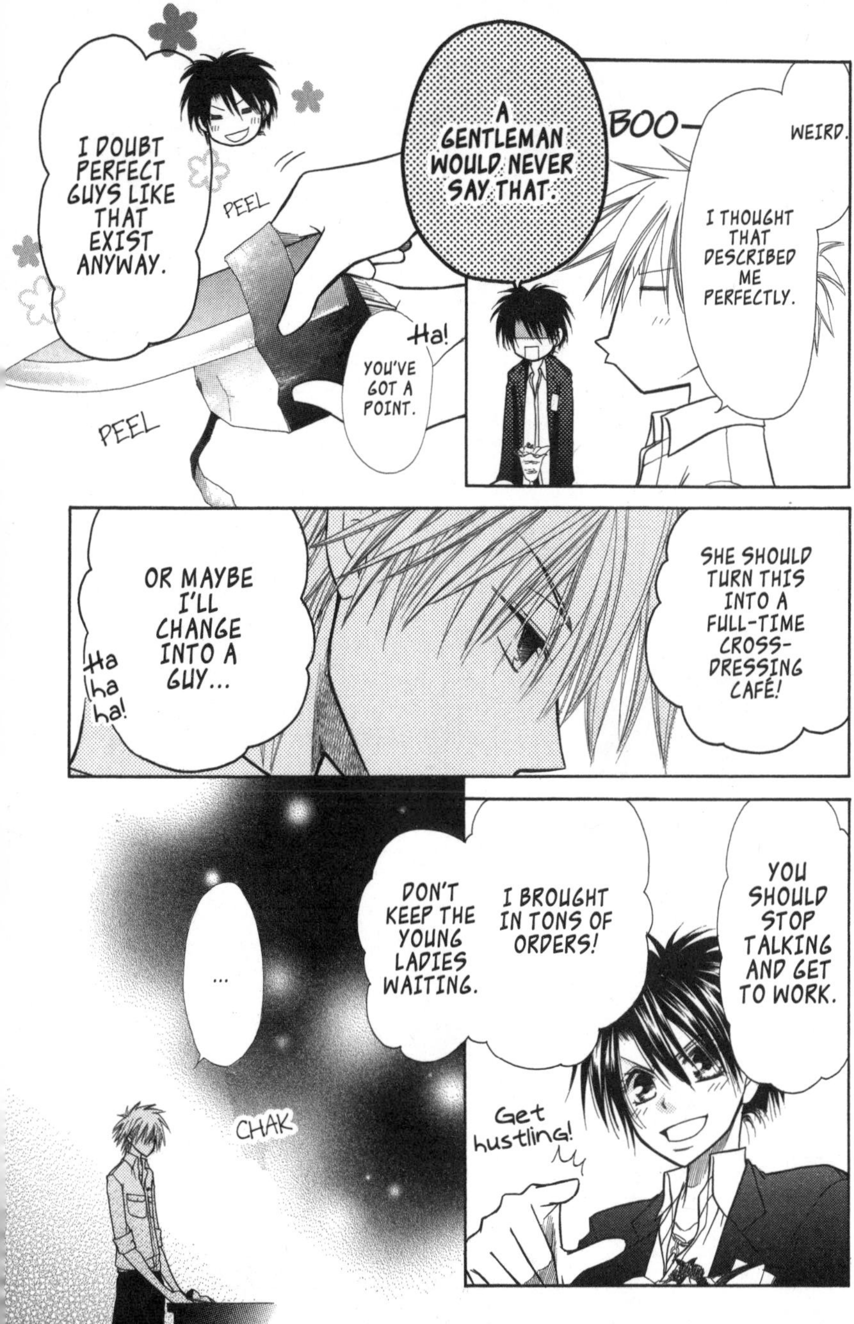
WEIRD.
I THOUGHT THAT DESCRIBED ME PERFECTLY.
BOO—
A GENTLEMAN WOULD NEVER SAY THAT.
I DOUBT PERFECT GUYS LIKE THAT EXIST ANYWAY.
PEEL
Ha!
YOU'VE GOT A POINT.
PEEL
SHE SHOULD TURN THIS INTO A FULL-TIME CROSS-DRESSING CAFÉ!
OR MAYBE I'LL CHANGE INTO A GUY...
Ha ha ha!
YOU SHOULD STOP TALKING AND GET TO WORK.
I BROUGHT IN TONS OF ORDERS!
DON'T KEEP THE YOUNG LADIES WAITING.
Get hustling!
...
CHAK

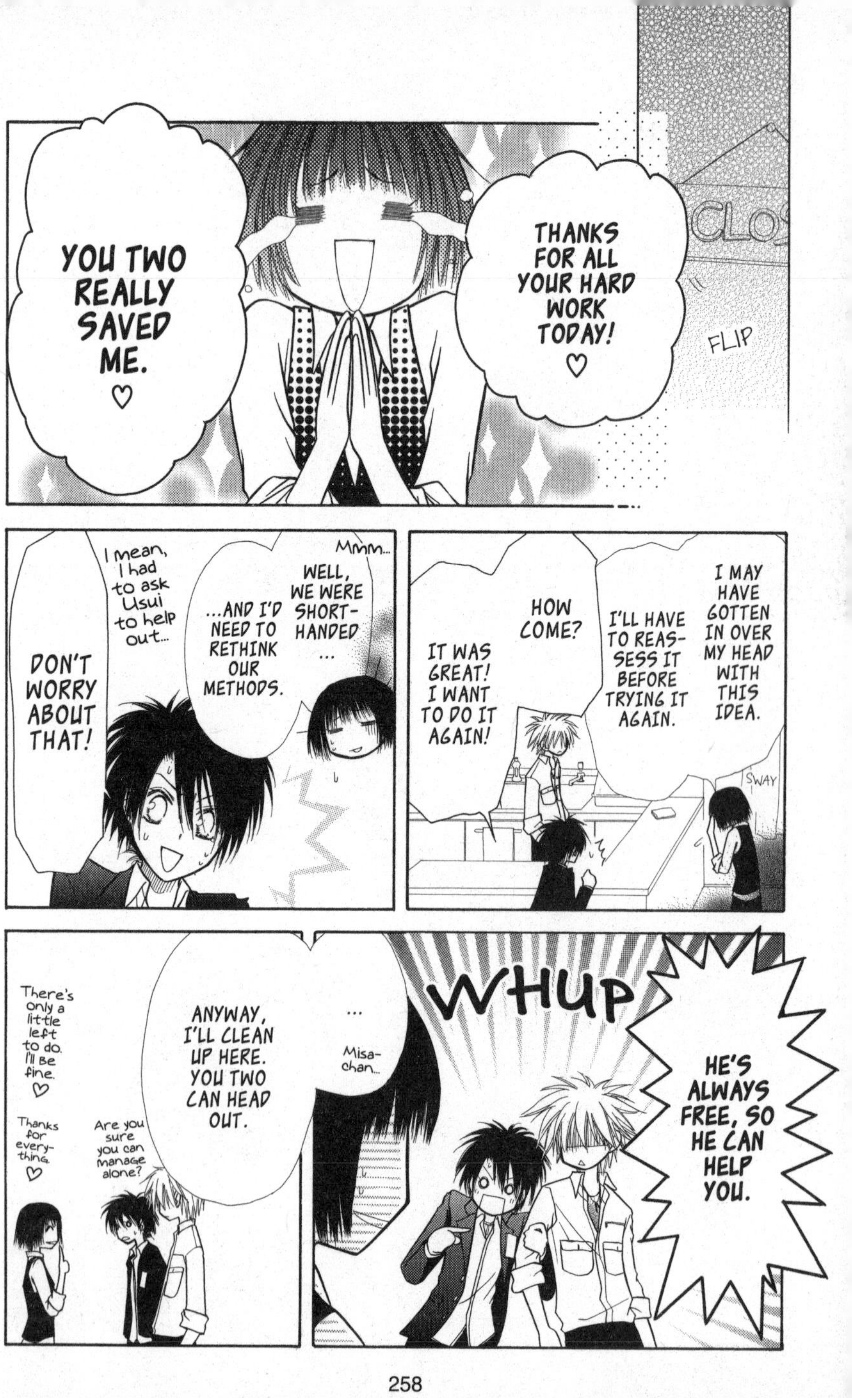
THANKS FOR ALL YOUR HARD WORK TODAY! ♡
FLIP
YOU TWO REALLY SAVED ME. ♡
I MAY HAVE GOTTEN IN OVER MY HEAD WITH THIS IDEA.
SWAY
I'LL HAVE TO REASSESS IT BEFORE TRYING IT AGAIN.
HOW COME?
IT WAS GREAT! I WANT TO DO IT AGAIN!
Mmm...
WELL, WE WERE SHORT-HANDED ...
...AND I'D NEED TO RETHINK OUR METHODS.
I mean, I had to ask Usui to help out...
DON'T WORRY ABOUT THAT!
HE'S ALWAYS FREE, SO HE CAN HELP YOU.
WHUP
...
Misa-chan...
ANYWAY, I'LL CLEAN UP HERE. YOU TWO CAN HEAD OUT.
Are you sure you can manage alone?
There's only a little left to do. I'll be fine. ♡
Thanks for everything. ♡

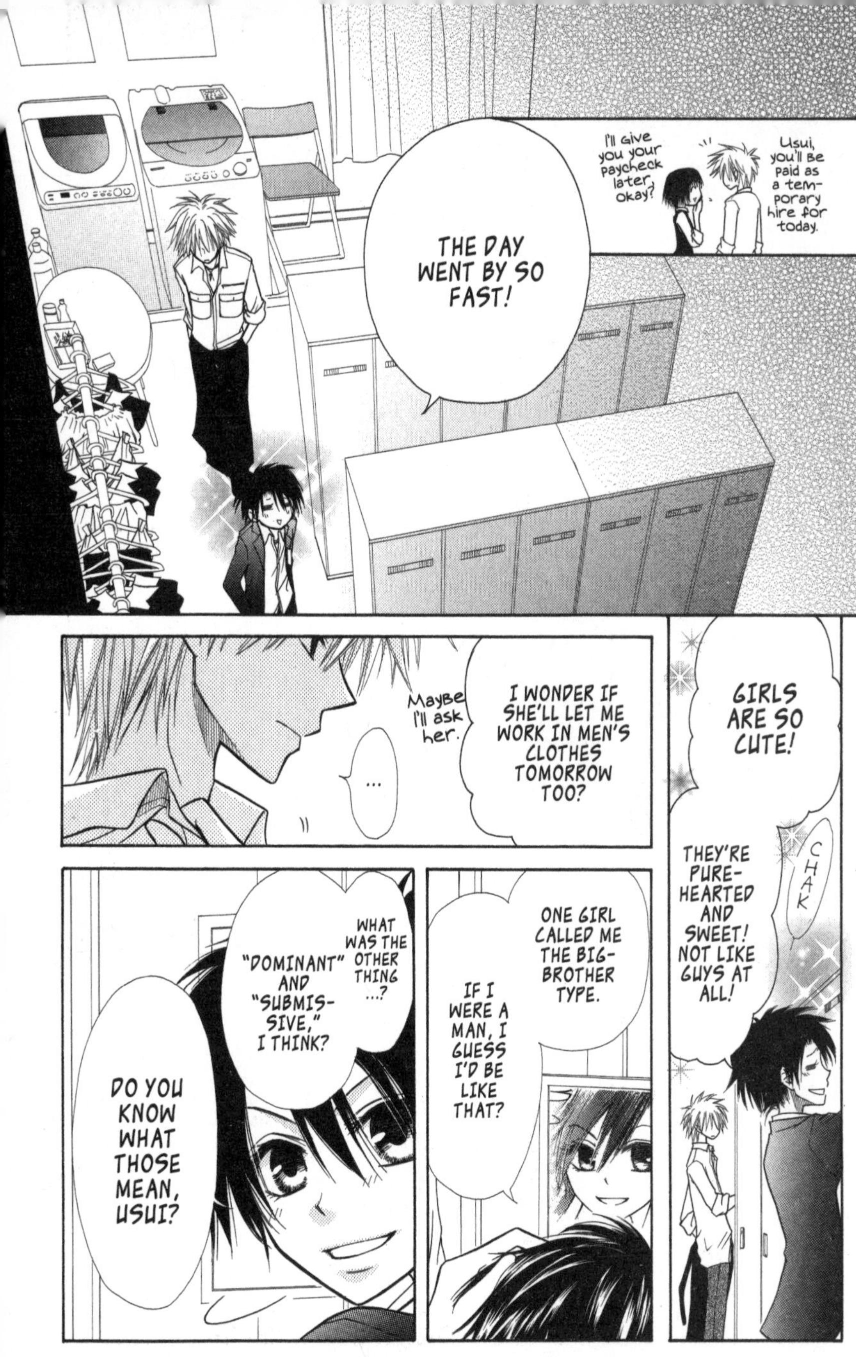
THE DAY WENT BY SO FAST!
Usui, you'll be paid as a temporary hire for today.
I'll give you your paycheck later, okay?
GIRLS ARE SO CUTE!
CHAK
THEY'RE PURE-HEARTED AND SWEET! NOT LIKE GUYS AT ALL!
I WONDER IF SHE'LL LET ME WORK IN MEN'S CLOTHES TOMORROW TOO?
Maybe I'll ask her.
...
ONE GIRL CALLED ME THE BIG-BROTHER TYPE.
IF I WERE A MAN, I GUESS I'D BE LIKE THAT?
WHAT WAS THE OTHER THING ...?
"DOMINANT" AND "SUBMISSIVE," I THINK?
DO YOU KNOW WHAT THOSE MEAN, USUI?

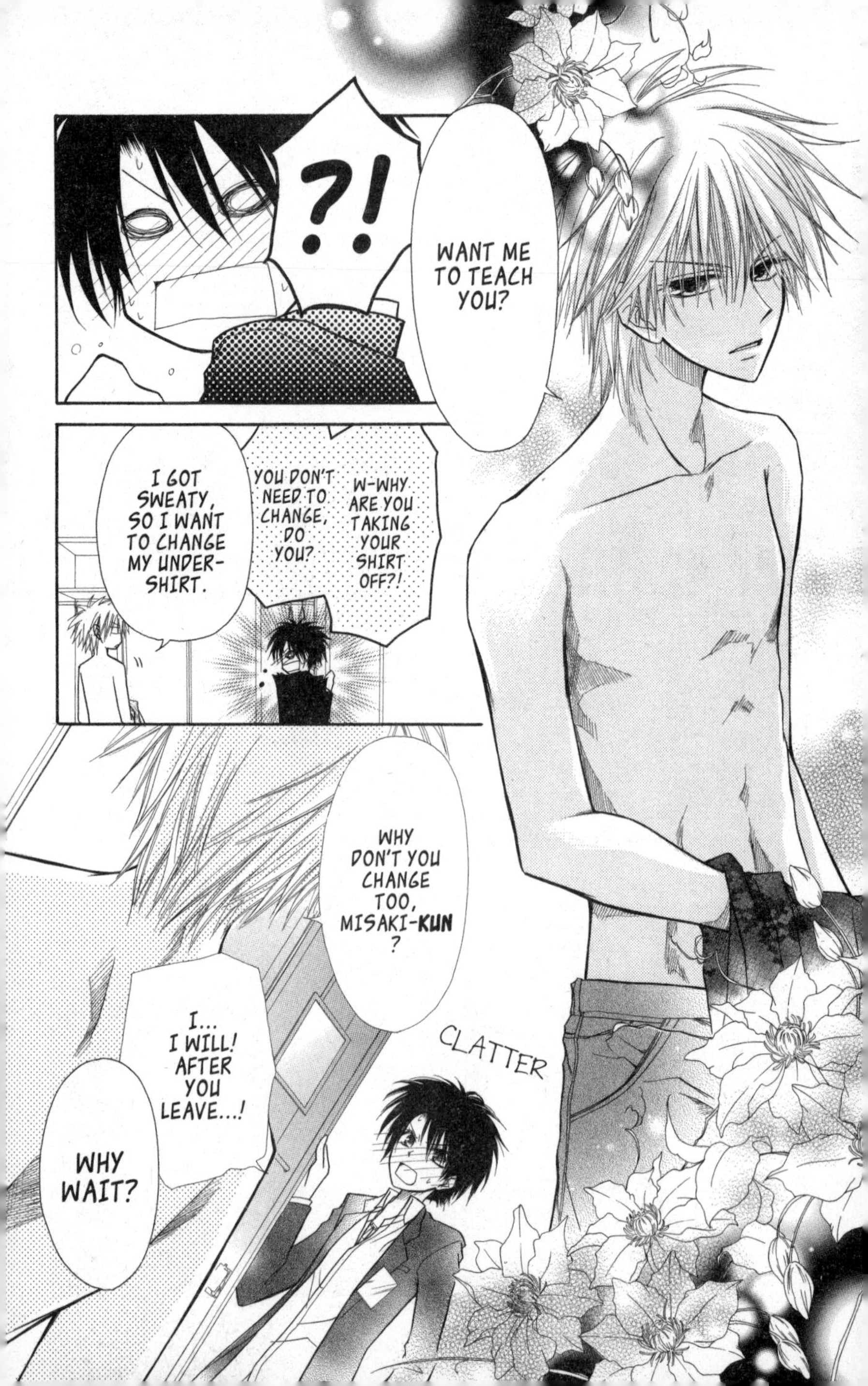
WANT ME TO TEACH YOU?
?!
W-WHY ARE YOU TAKING YOUR SHIRT OFF?!
YOU DON'T NEED TO CHANGE, DO YOU?
I GOT SWEATY, SO I WANT TO CHANGE MY UNDER-SHIRT.
WHY DON'T YOU CHANGE TOO, MISAKI-KUN?
CLATTER
I... I WILL! AFTER YOU LEAVE...!
WHY WAIT?

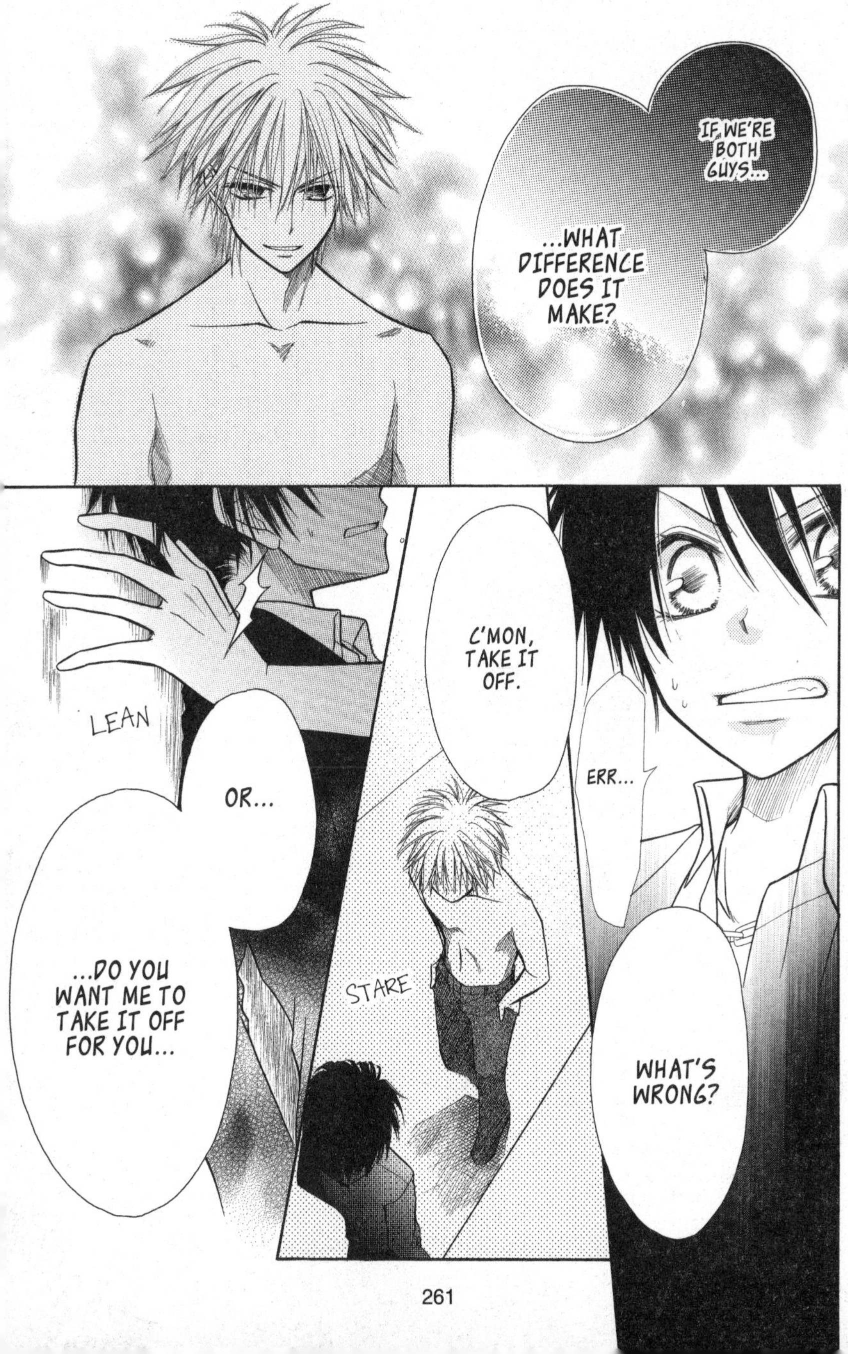
IF WE'RE BOTH GUYS...
...WHAT DIFFERENCE DOES IT MAKE?
ERR...
WHAT'S WRONG?
C'MON, TAKE IT OFF.
STARE
LEAN
OR...
...DO YOU WANT ME TO TAKE IT OFF FOR YOU...

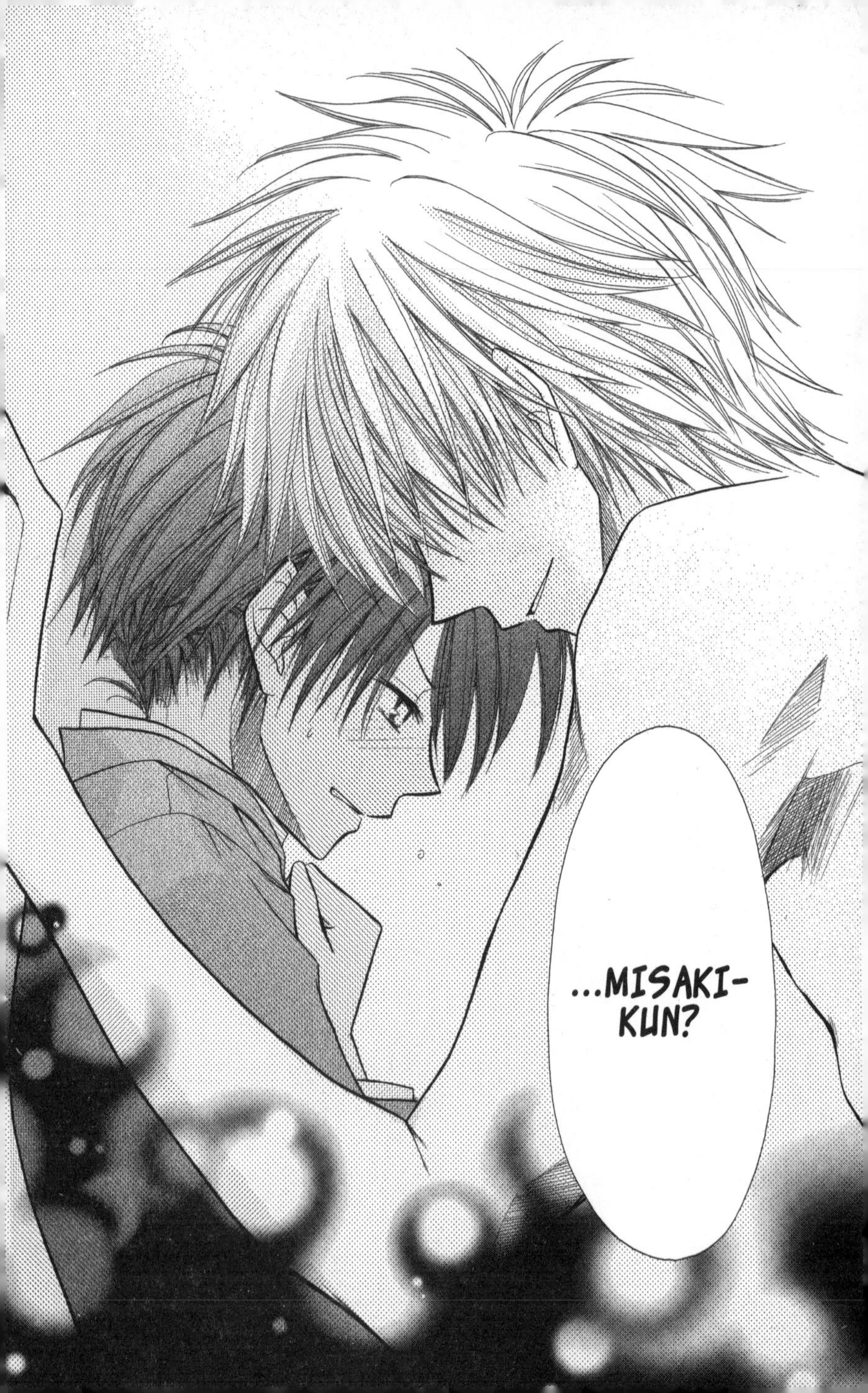
...MISAKI-KUN?

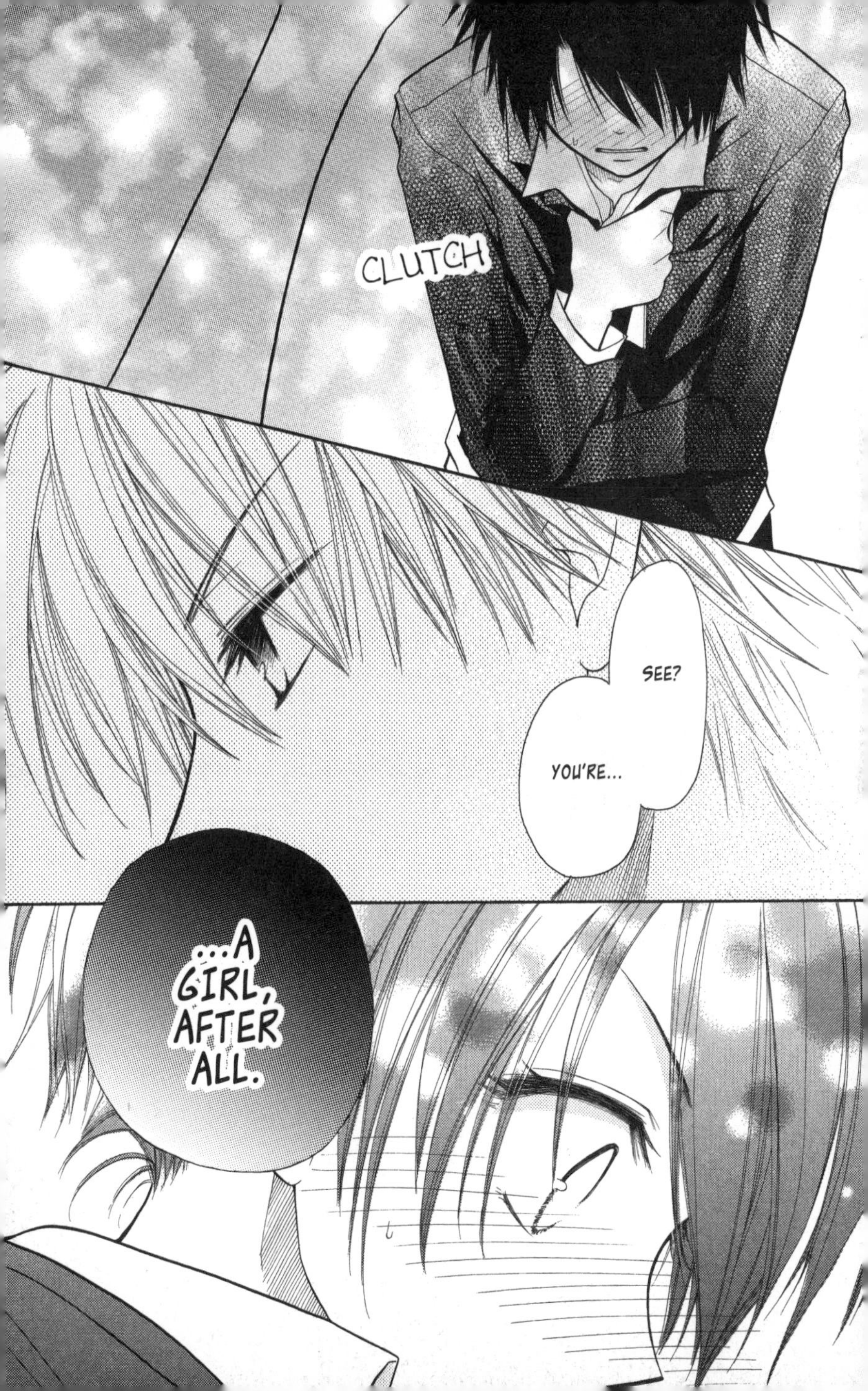
CLUTCH
SEE?
YOU'RE...
...A GIRL, AFTER ALL.

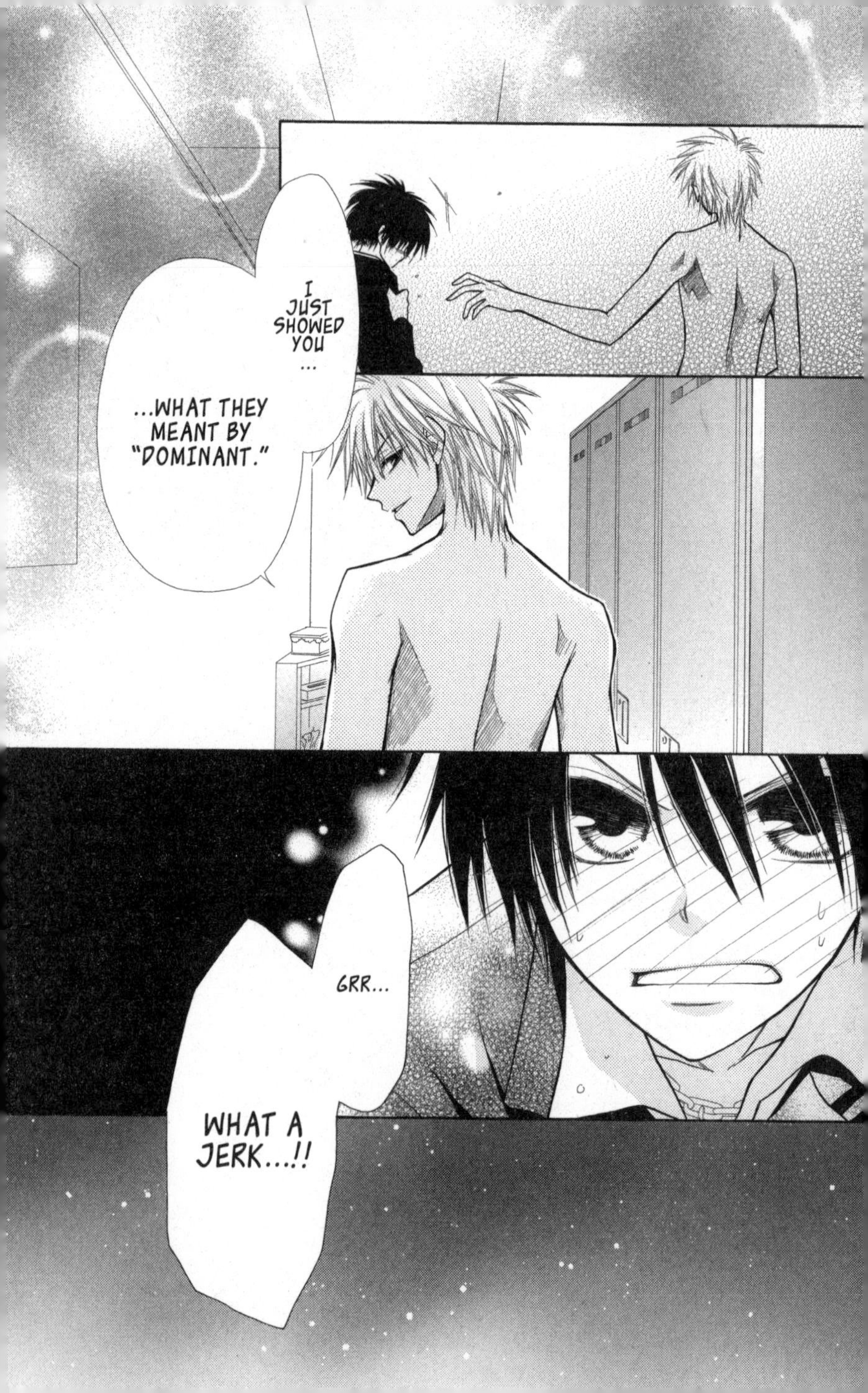
I JUST SHOWED YOU ...
...WHAT THEY MEANT BY "DOMINANT."
GRR...
WHAT A JERK...!!

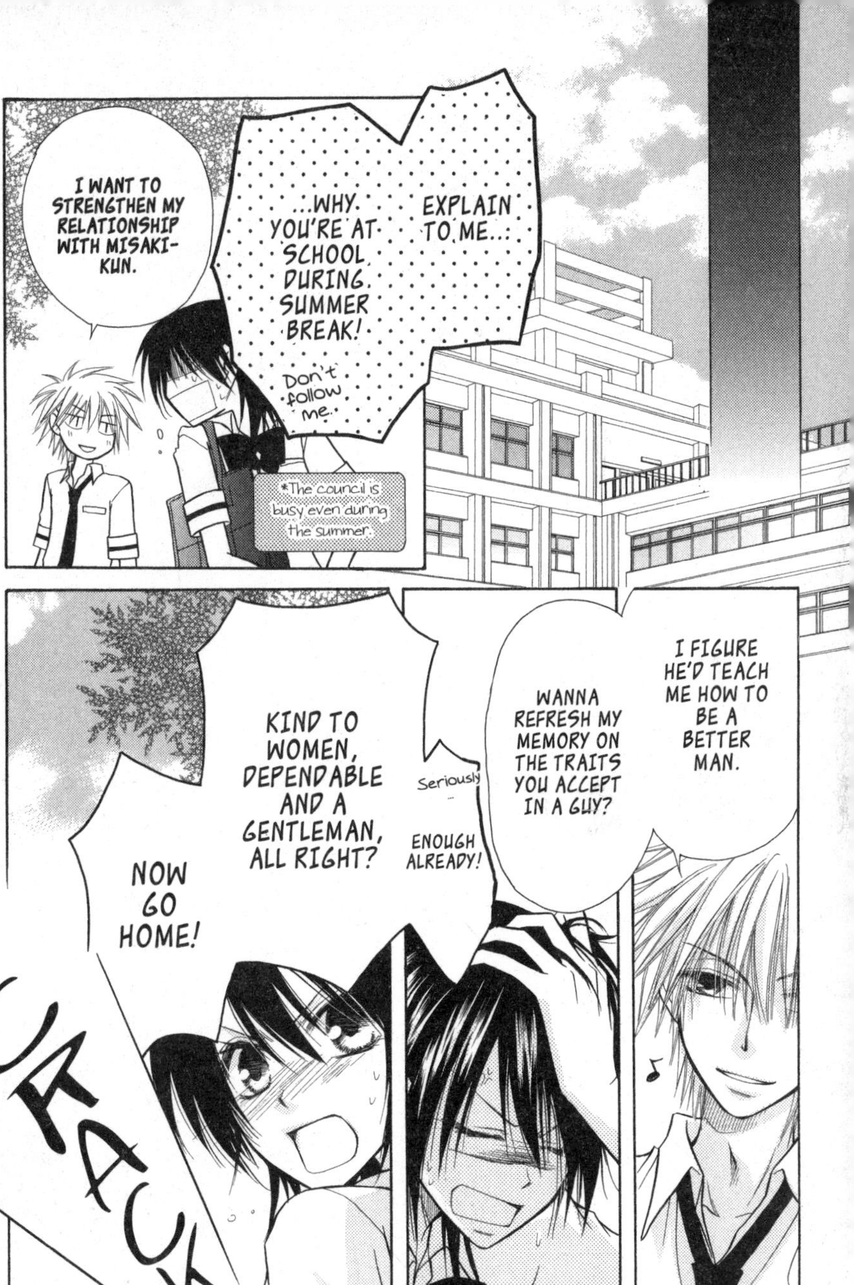
EXPLAIN TO ME...
...WHY YOU'RE AT SCHOOL DURING SUMMER BREAK!
Don't follow me.
I WANT TO STRENGTHEN MY RELATIONSHIP WITH MISAKI-KUN.
*The council is busy even during the summer.
I FIGURE HE'D TEACH ME HOW TO BE A BETTER MAN.
WANNA REFRESH MY MEMORY ON THE TRAITS YOU ACCEPT IN A GUY?
Seriously...
ENOUGH ALREADY!
KIND TO WOMEN, DEPENDABLE AND A GENTLEMAN, ALL RIGHT?
NOW GO HOME!
WHACK

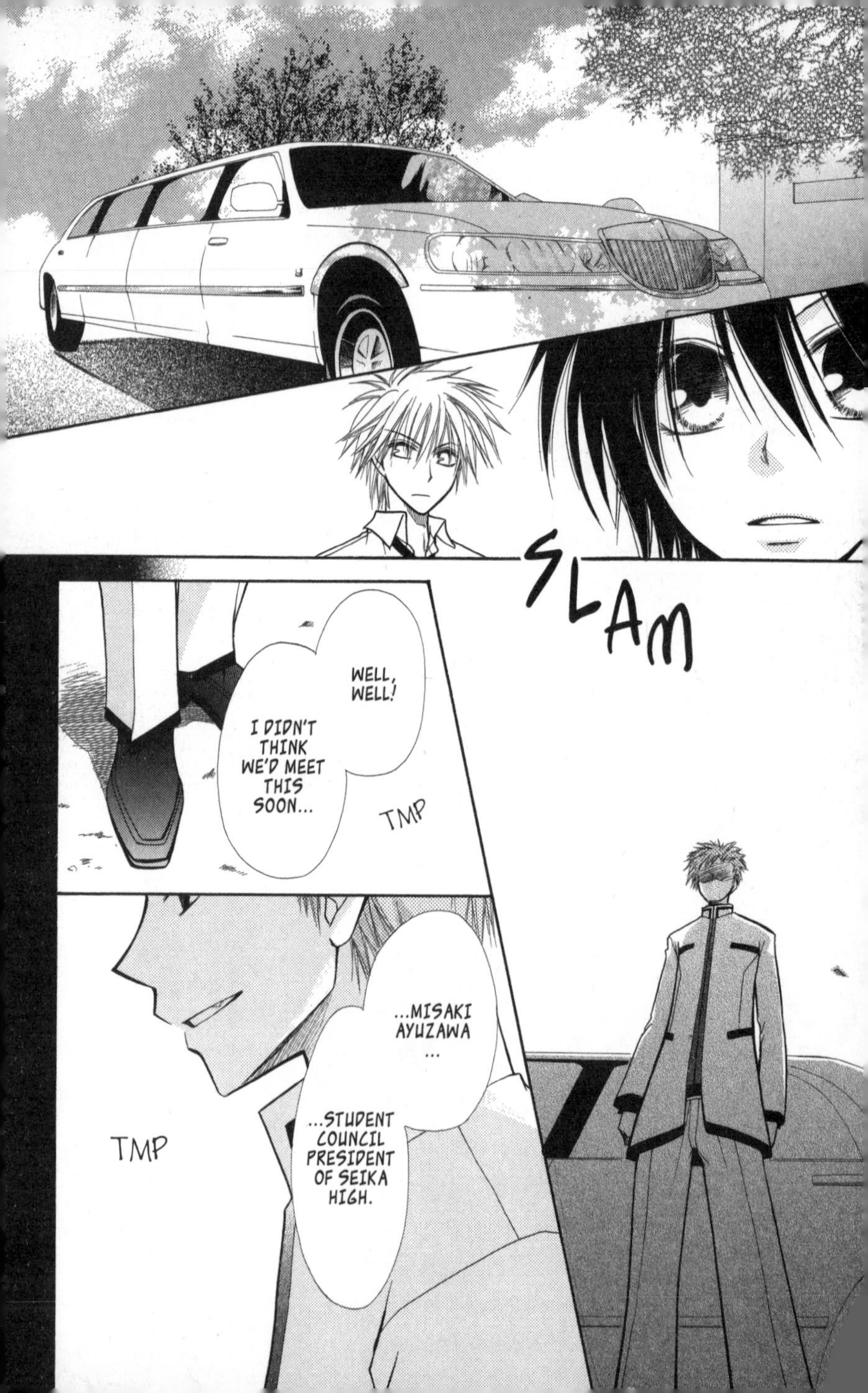
SLAM
WELL, WELL!
I DIDN'T THINK WE'D MEET THIS SOON...
TMP
...MISAKI AYUZAWA ...
...STUDENT COUNCIL PRESIDENT OF SEIKA HIGH.
TMP

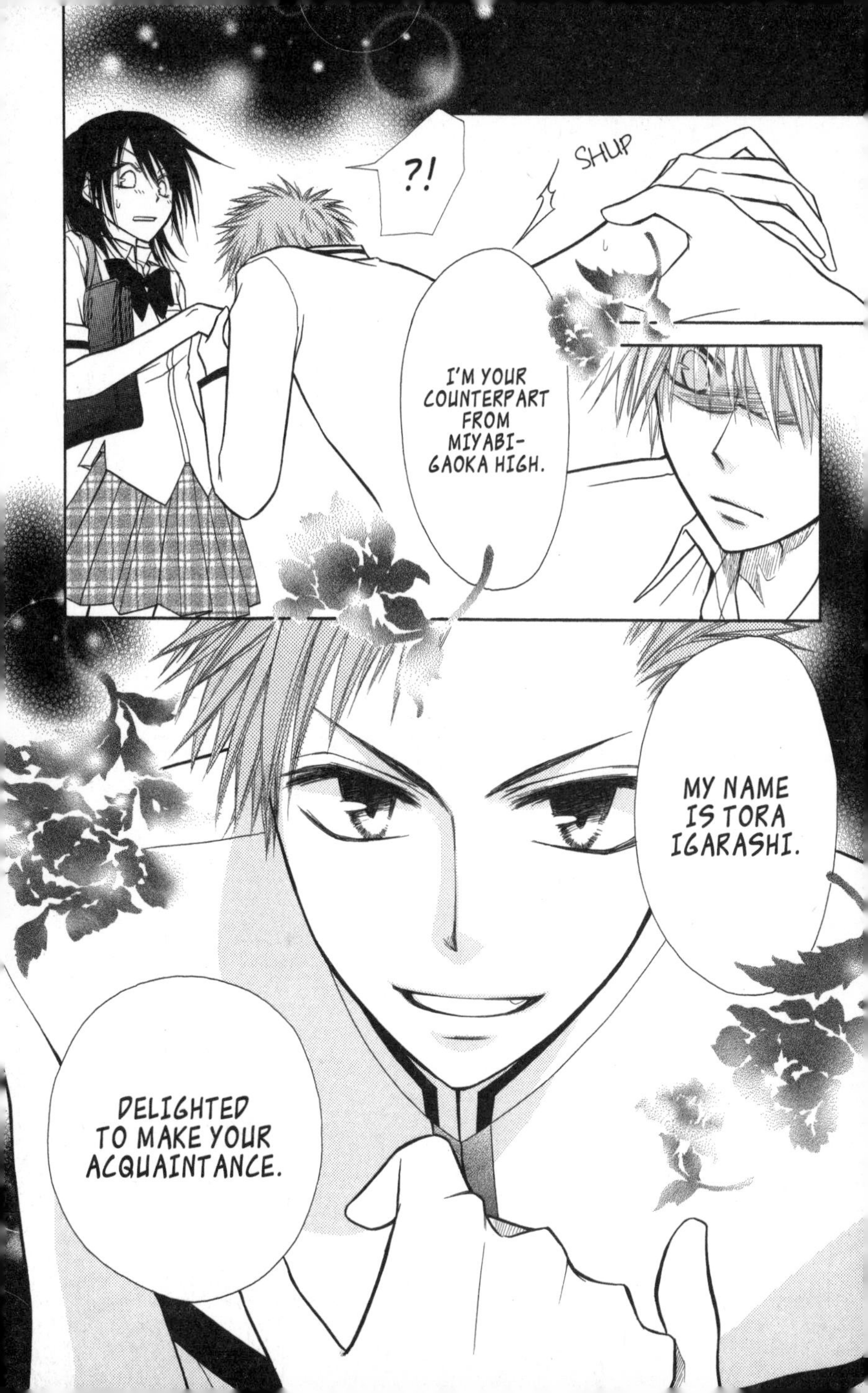
SHUP
?!
I'M YOUR COUNTERPART FROM MIYABI-GAOKA HIGH.
MY NAME IS TORA IGARASHI.
DELIGHTED TO MAKE YOUR ACQUAINTANCE.

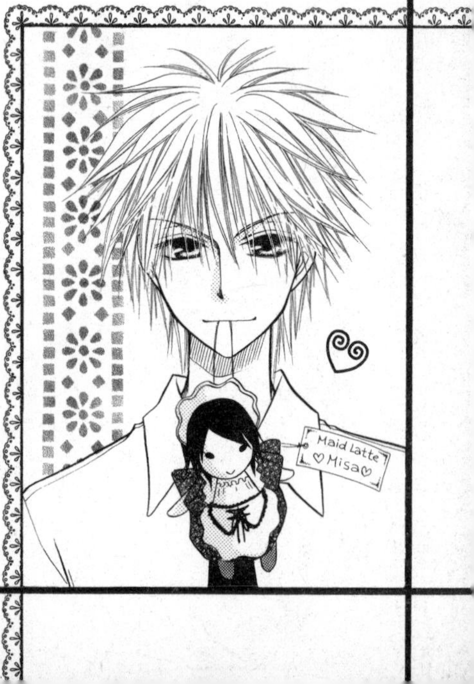
Maid Latte
♡Misa♡

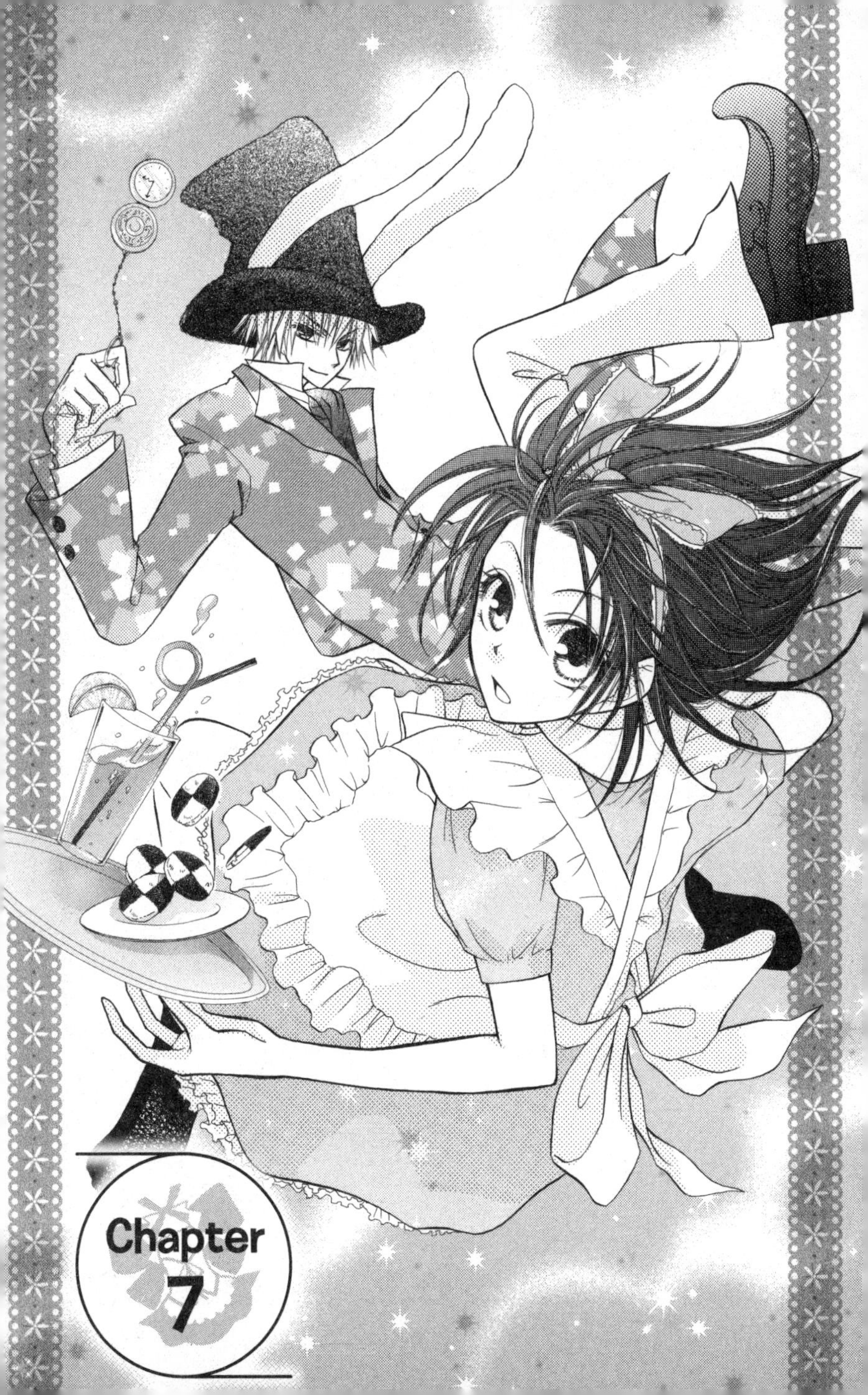
Chapter
7

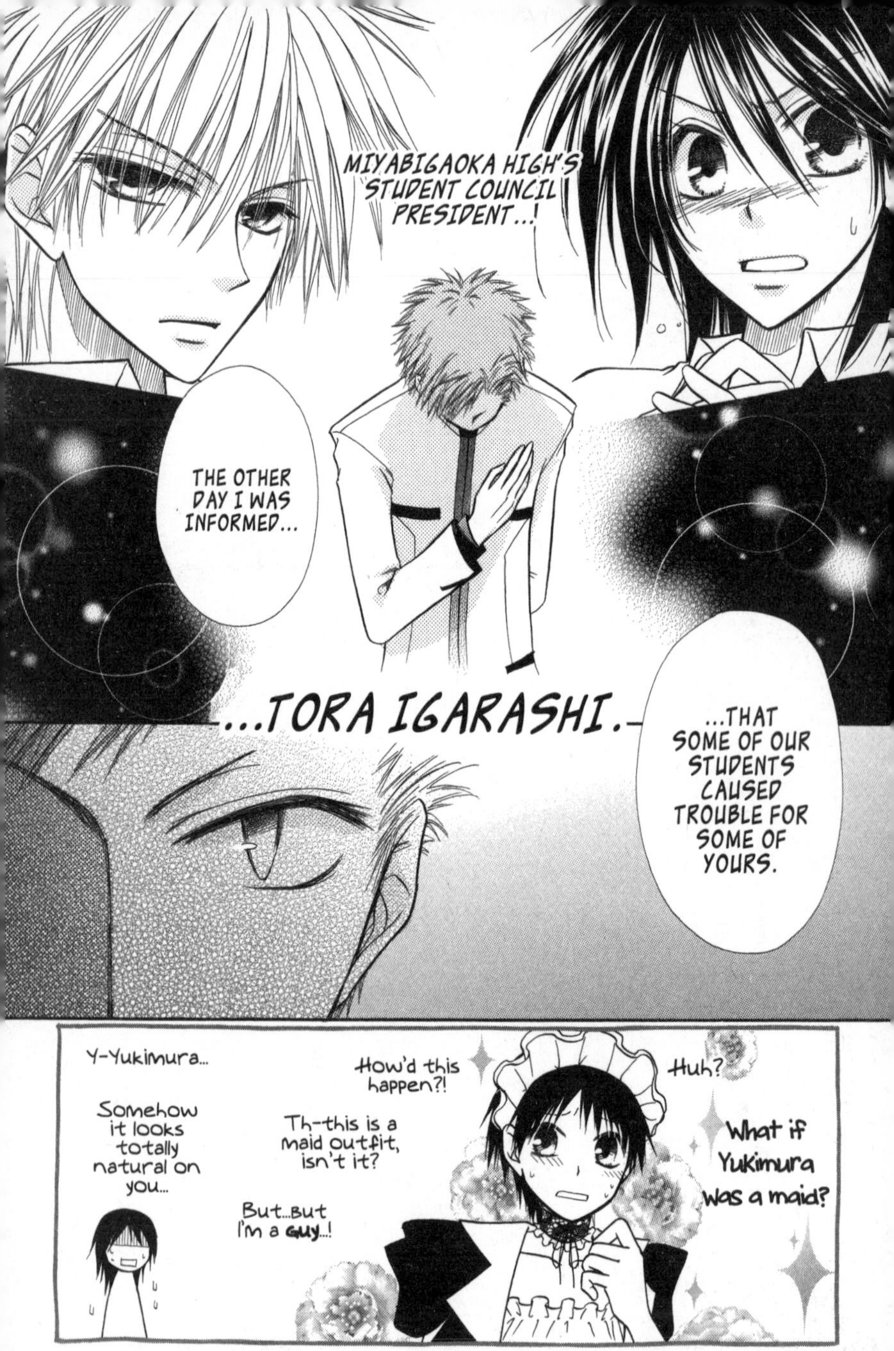
MIYABIGAOKA HIGH'S STUDENT COUNCIL PRESIDENT...!
...TORA IGARASHI.
THE OTHER DAY I WAS INFORMED...
...THAT SOME OF OUR STUDENTS CAUSED TROUBLE FOR SOME OF YOURS.
What if Yukimura was a maid?
Huh?
How'd this happen?!
Th-this is a maid outfit, isn't it?
But...but I'm a guy...!
Y-Yukimura...
Somehow it looks totally natural on you...

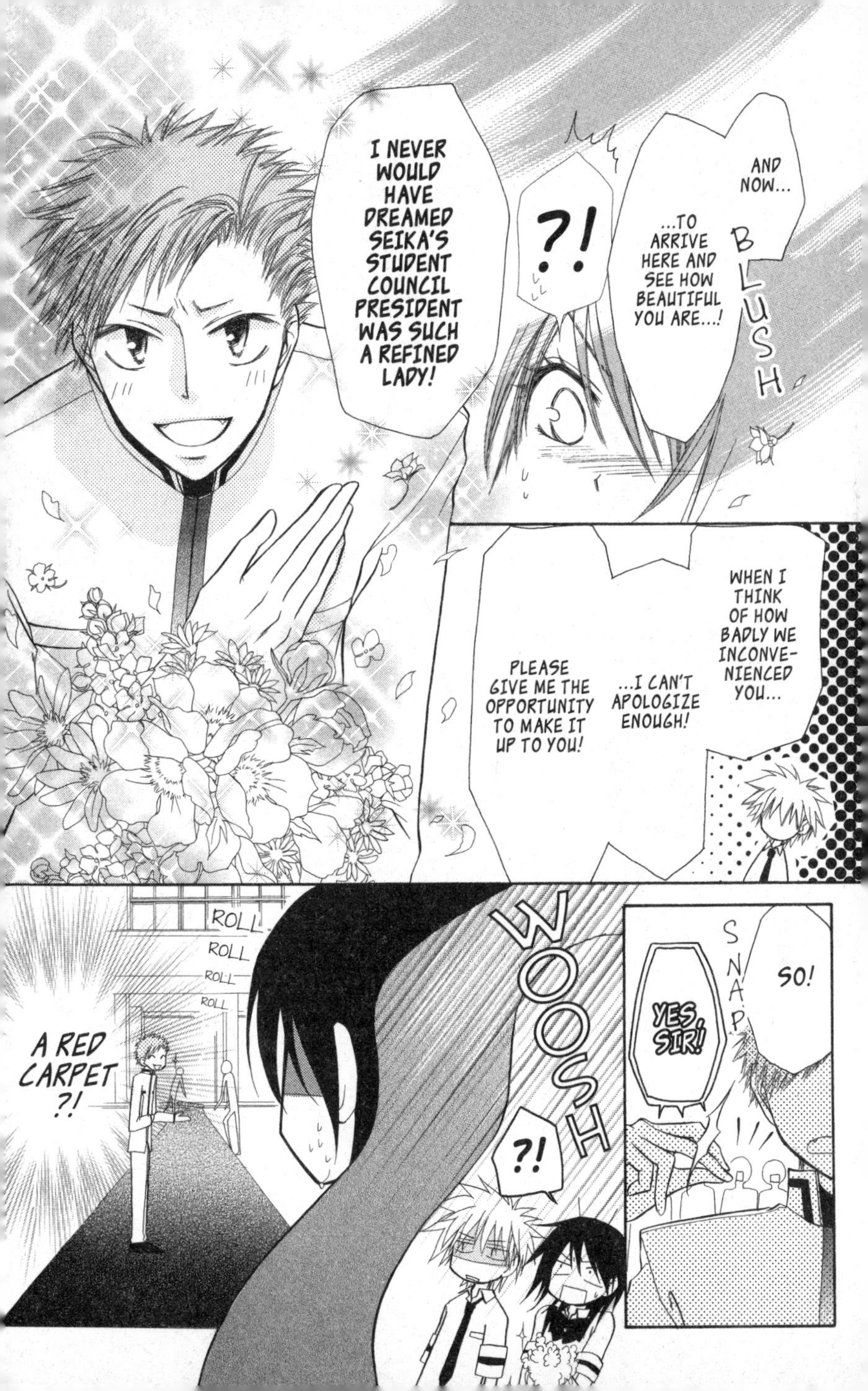
I NEVER WOULD HAVE DREAMED SEIKA'S STUDENT COUNCIL PRESIDENT WAS SUCH A REFINED LADY!
AND NOW...
...TO ARRIVE HERE AND SEE HOW BEAUTIFUL YOU ARE...!
BLUSH
?!
WHEN I THINK OF HOW BADLY WE INCONVENIENCED YOU...
...I CAN'T APOLOGIZE ENOUGH!
PLEASE GIVE ME THE OPPORTUNITY TO MAKE IT UP TO YOU!
SO!
SNAP
YES, SIR!
WOOSH
?!
ROLL
ROLL
ROLL
ROLL
A RED CARPET ?!

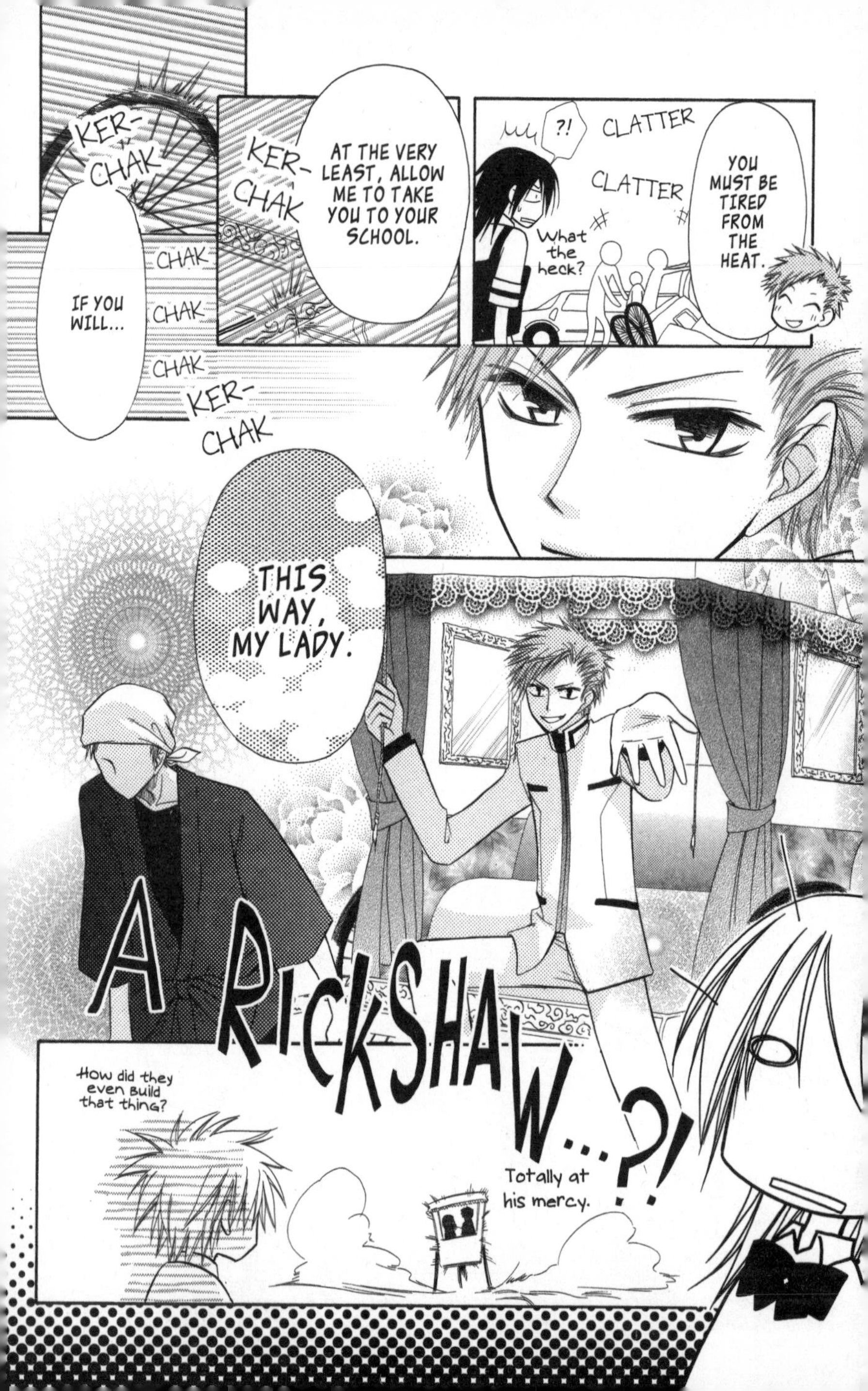
?!
CLATTER
CLATTER
YOU MUST BE TIRED FROM THE HEAT.
What the heck?
KER-CHAK
AT THE VERY LEAST, ALLOW ME TO TAKE YOU TO YOUR SCHOOL.
KER-CHAK
IF YOU WILL...
CHAK
CHAK
CHAK
KER-CHAK
THIS WAY, MY LADY.
A RICKSHAW...?!
Totally at his mercy.
How did they even build that thing?

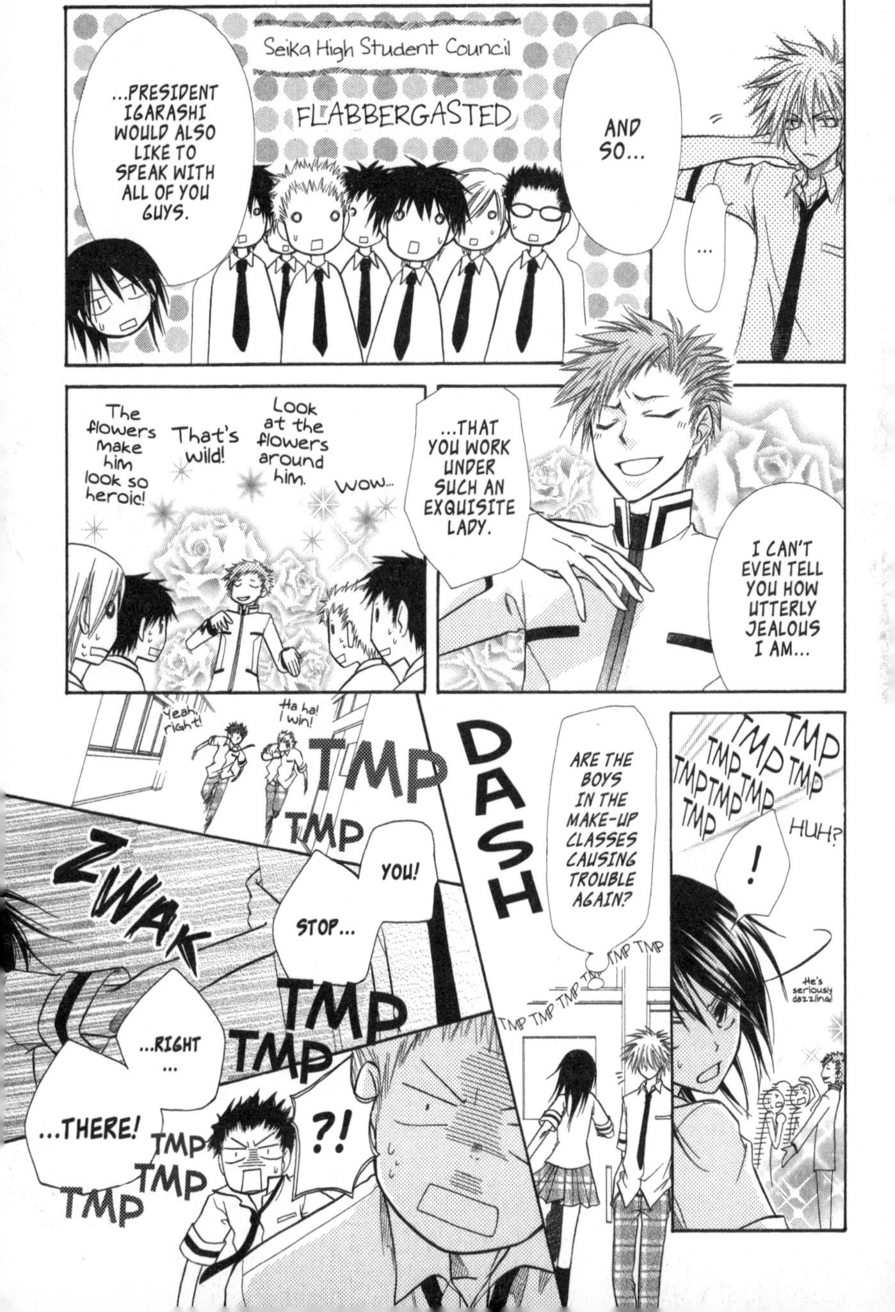

...
AND SO...
Seika High Student Council
FLABBERGASTED
...PRESIDENT IGARASHI WOULD ALSO LIKE TO SPEAK WITH ALL OF YOU GUYS.
I CAN'T EVEN TELL YOU HOW UTTERLY JEALOUS I AM...
...THAT YOU WORK UNDER SUCH AN EXQUISITE LADY.
WOW...
Look at the flowers around him.
That's wild!
The flowers make him look so heroic!
TMP TMP TMP TMP TMP TMP TMP TMP TMP
HUH?
!
He's seriously dazzling!
ARE THE BOYS IN THE MAKE-UP CLASSES CAUSING TROUBLE AGAIN?
TMP TMP TMP TMP TMP TMP TMP
DASH
Ha ha! I win!
Yeah, right!
TMP
TMP
YOU!
STOP...
ZWAK
TMP
TMP
...RIGHT ...
...THERE!
?!
TMP
TMP
TMP

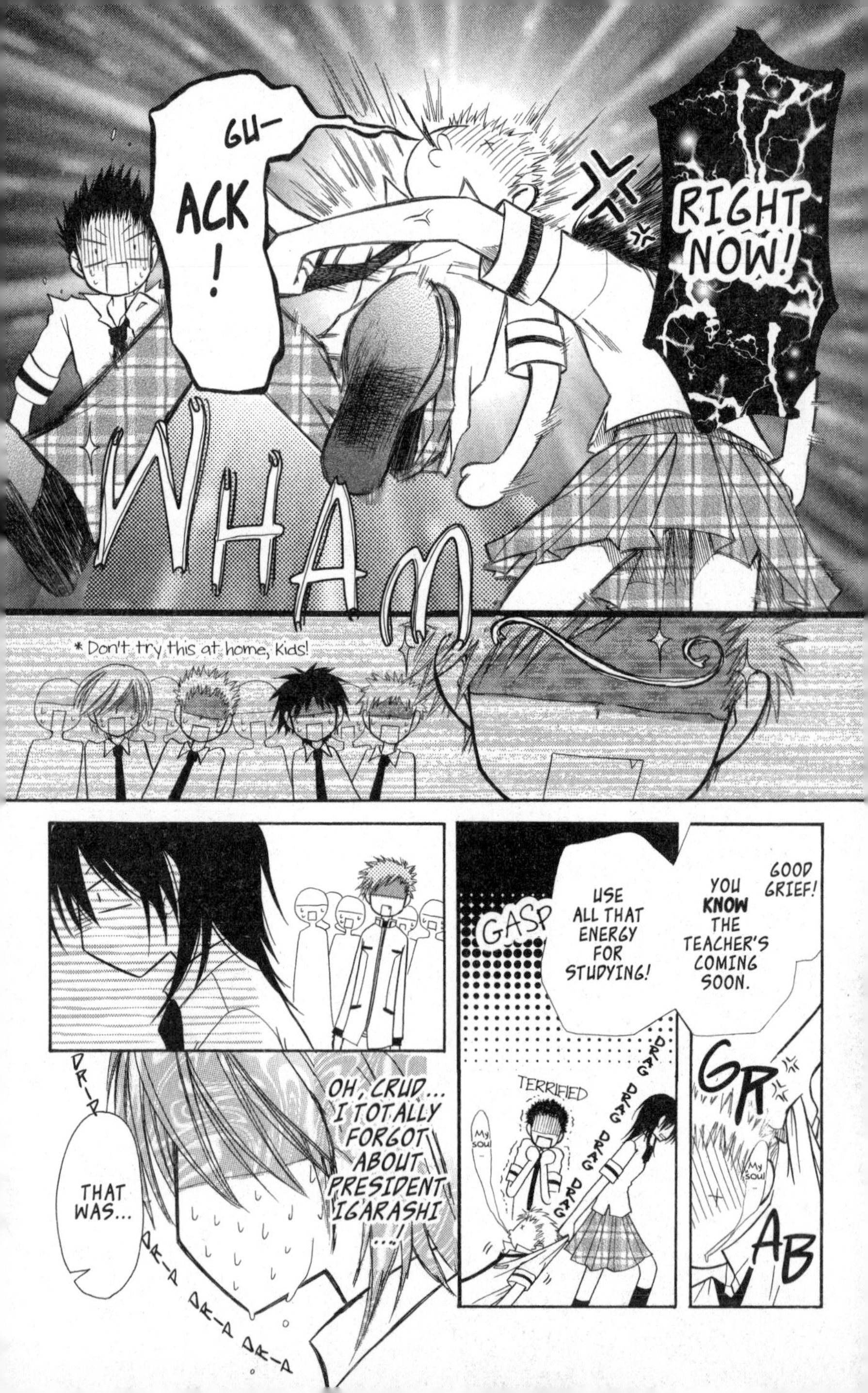
RIGHT NOW!
GU-ACK!
WHAM
* Don't try this at home, Kids!
GOOD GRIEF!
YOU KNOW THE TEACHER'S COMING SOON.
USE ALL THAT ENERGY FOR STUDYING!
GASP
GR
AB
My soul...
DRAG DRAG DRAG DRAG DRAG
TERRIFIED
My soul...
OH, CRUD... I TOTALLY FORGOT ABOUT PRESIDENT IGARASHI...
DRIP
THAT WAS...
DR-A DR-A DR-A DR-A

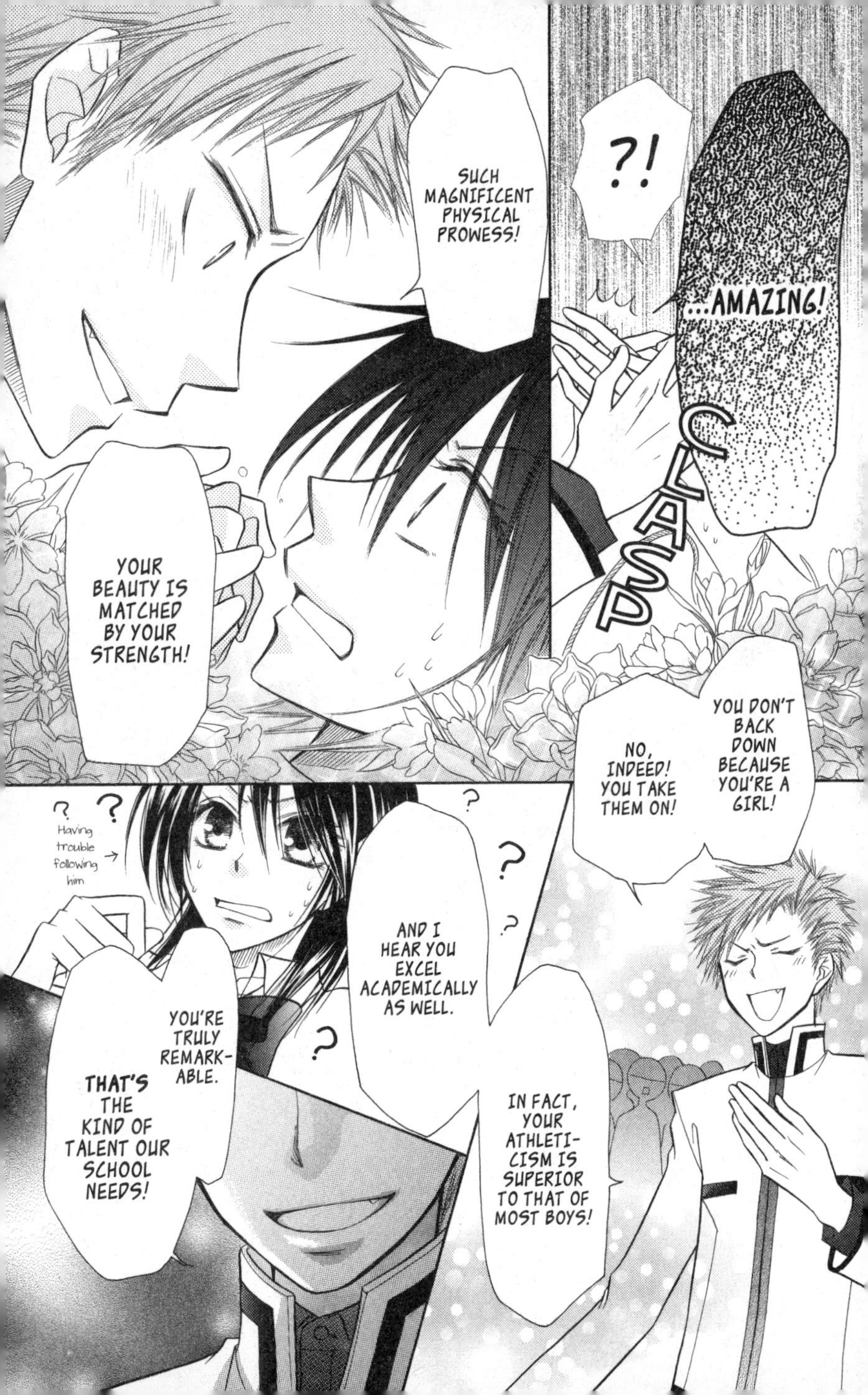
?!
...AMAZING!
CLASP
SUCH MAGNIFICENT PHYSICAL PROWESS!
YOUR BEAUTY IS MATCHED BY YOUR STRENGTH!
YOU DON'T BACK DOWN BECAUSE YOU'RE A GIRL!
NO, INDEED! YOU TAKE THEM ON!
IN FACT, YOUR ATHLETICISM IS SUPERIOR TO THAT OF MOST BOYS!
AND I HEAR YOU EXCEL ACADEMICALLY AS WELL.
YOU'RE TRULY REMARKABLE.
THAT'S THE KIND OF TALENT OUR SCHOOL NEEDS!
? ?
Having trouble following him
?
?
?
?

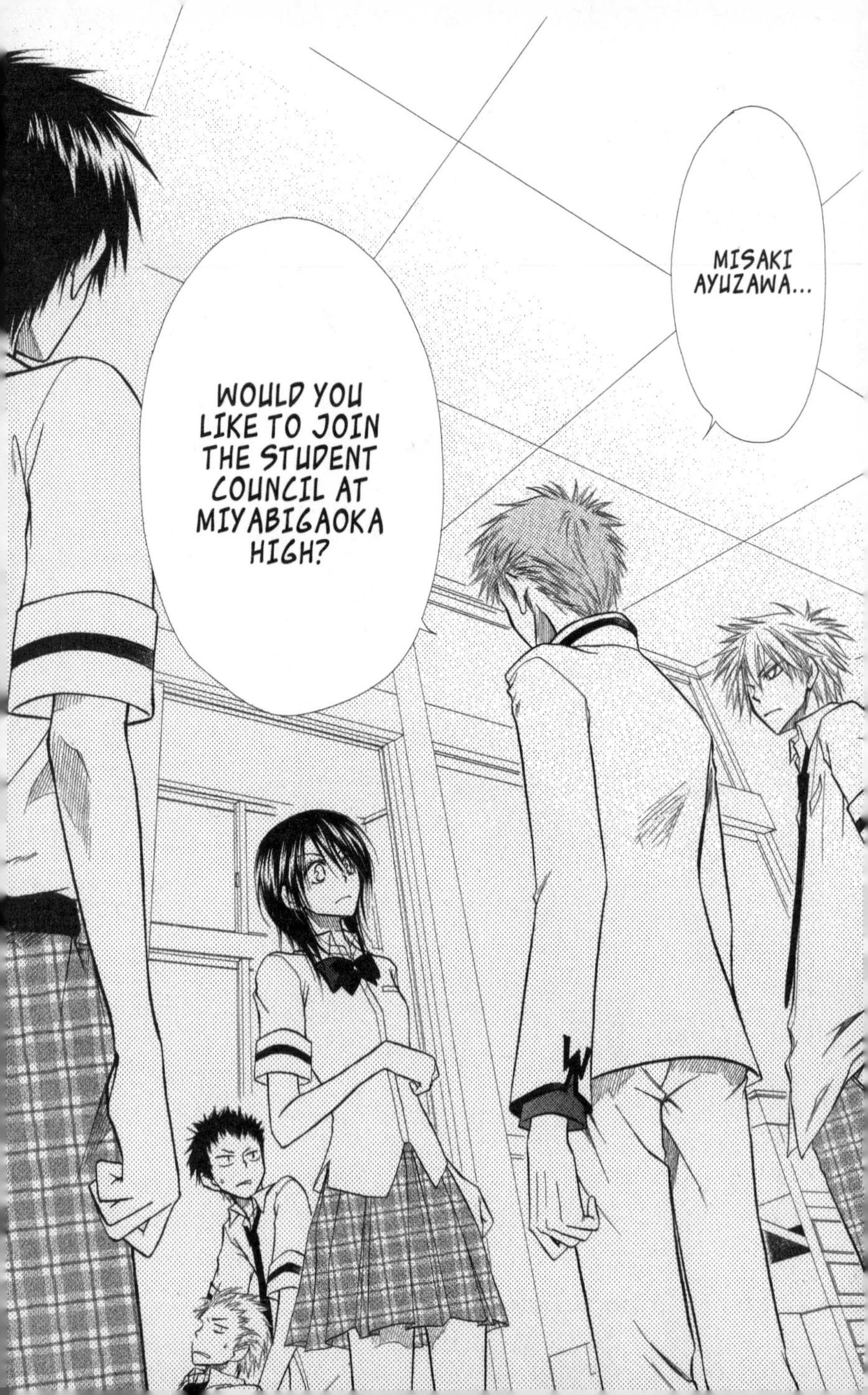
MISAKI AYUZAWA...
WOULD YOU LIKE TO JOIN THE STUDENT COUNCIL AT MIYABIGAOKA HIGH?

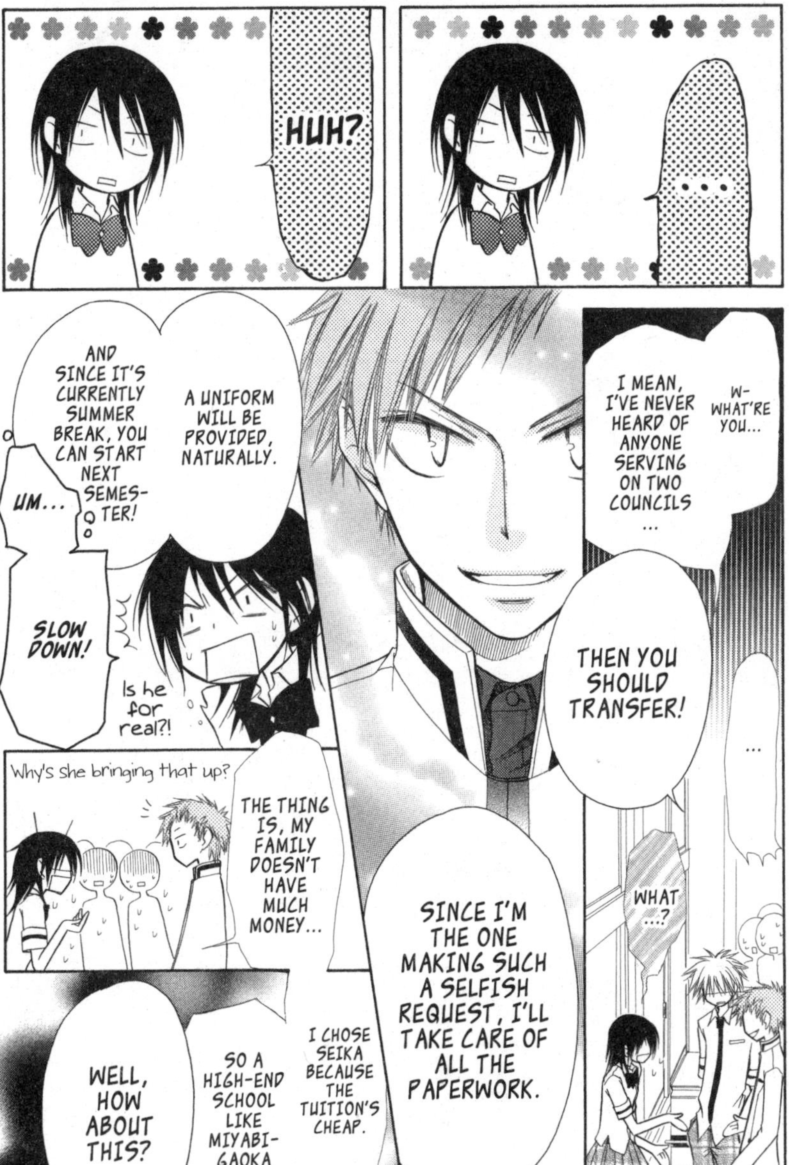
...
HUH?
W-WHAT'RE YOU...
I MEAN, I'VE NEVER HEARD OF ANYONE SERVING ON TWO COUNCILS ...
...
WHAT ...?
THEN YOU SHOULD TRANSFER!
SINCE I'M THE ONE MAKING SUCH A SELFISH REQUEST, I'LL TAKE CARE OF ALL THE PAPERWORK.
A UNIFORM WILL BE PROVIDED, NATURALLY.
AND SINCE IT'S CURRENTLY SUMMER BREAK, YOU CAN START NEXT SEMES-TER!
UM...
SLOW DOWN!
Is he for real?!
THE THING IS, MY FAMILY DOESN'T HAVE MUCH MONEY...
Why's she bringing that up?
I CHOSE SEIKA BECAUSE THE TUITION'S CHEAP.
SO A HIGH-END SCHOOL LIKE MIYABI-GAOKA ISN'T—
WELL, HOW ABOUT THIS?

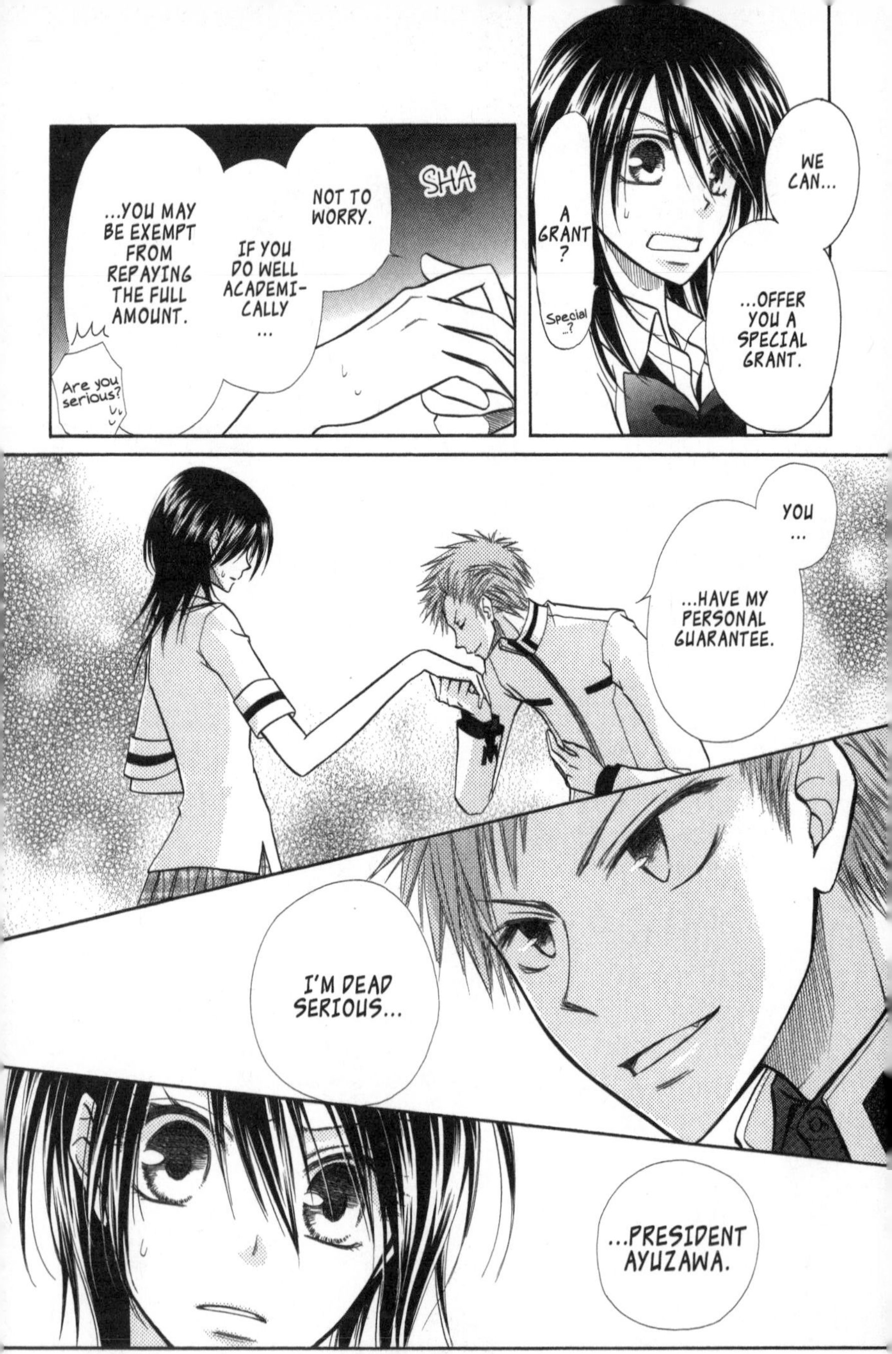
WE CAN...
...OFFER YOU A SPECIAL GRANT.
A GRANT?
Special...?
SHA
NOT TO WORRY.
IF YOU DO WELL ACADEMICALLY...
...YOU MAY BE EXEMPT FROM REPAYING THE FULL AMOUNT.
Are you serious?
YOU...
...HAVE MY PERSONAL GUARANTEE.
I'M DEAD SERIOUS...
...PRESIDENT AYUZAWA.

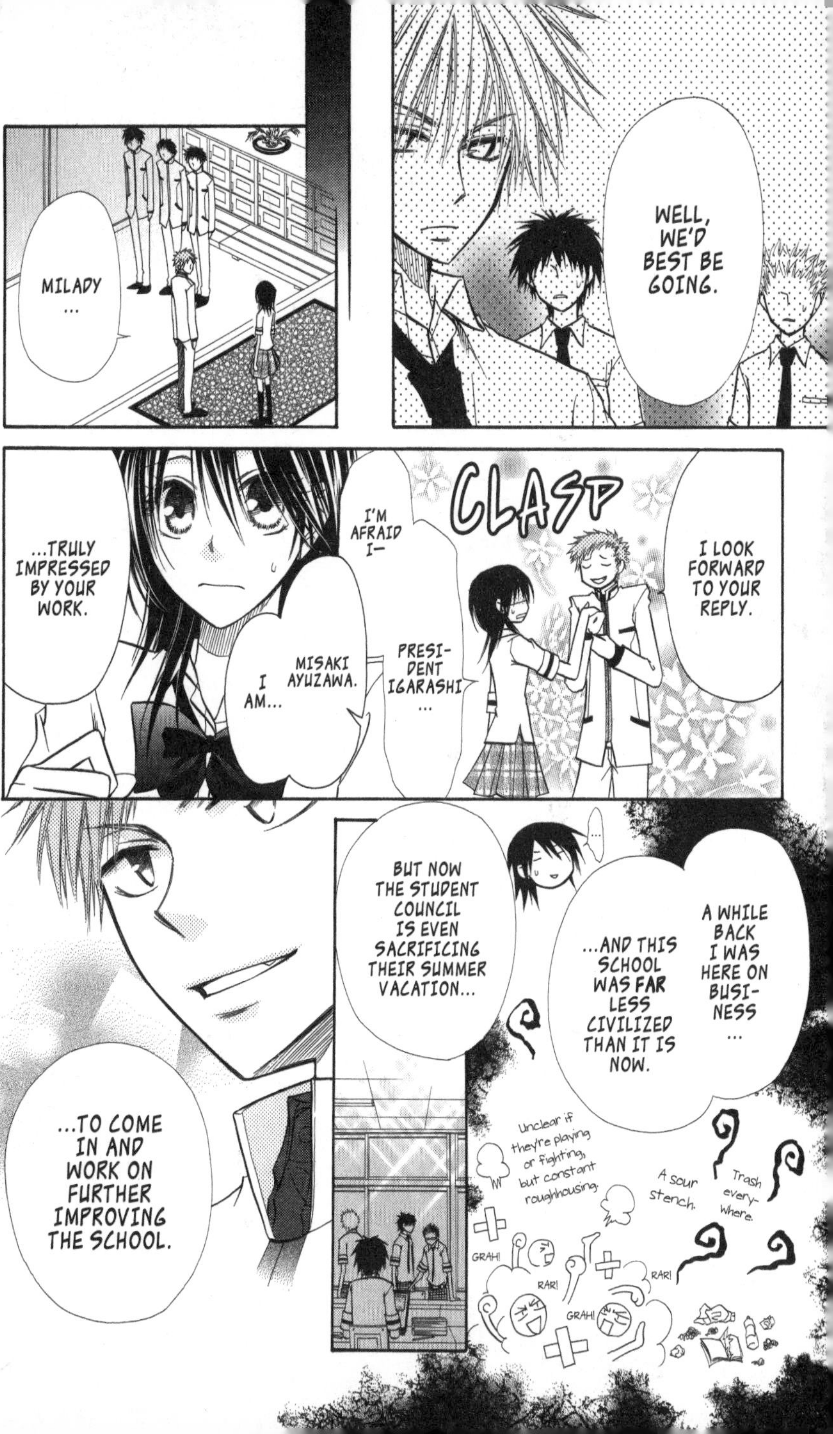
WELL, WE'D BEST BE GOING.
MILADY ...
I LOOK FORWARD TO YOUR REPLY.
CLASP
PRESIDENT IGARASHI ...
I'M AFRAID I—
MISAKI AYUZAWA.
I AM...
...TRULY IMPRESSED BY YOUR WORK.
A WHILE BACK I WAS HERE ON BUSINESS ...
...AND THIS SCHOOL WAS FAR LESS CIVILIZED THAN IT IS NOW.
...
Trash everywhere.
A sour stench.
Unclear if they're playing or fighting, but constant roughhousing.
RAR!
GRAH!
RAR!
GRAH!
GRAH!
BUT NOW THE STUDENT COUNCIL IS EVEN SACRIFICING THEIR SUMMER VACATION...
...TO COME IN AND WORK ON FURTHER IMPROVING THE SCHOOL.

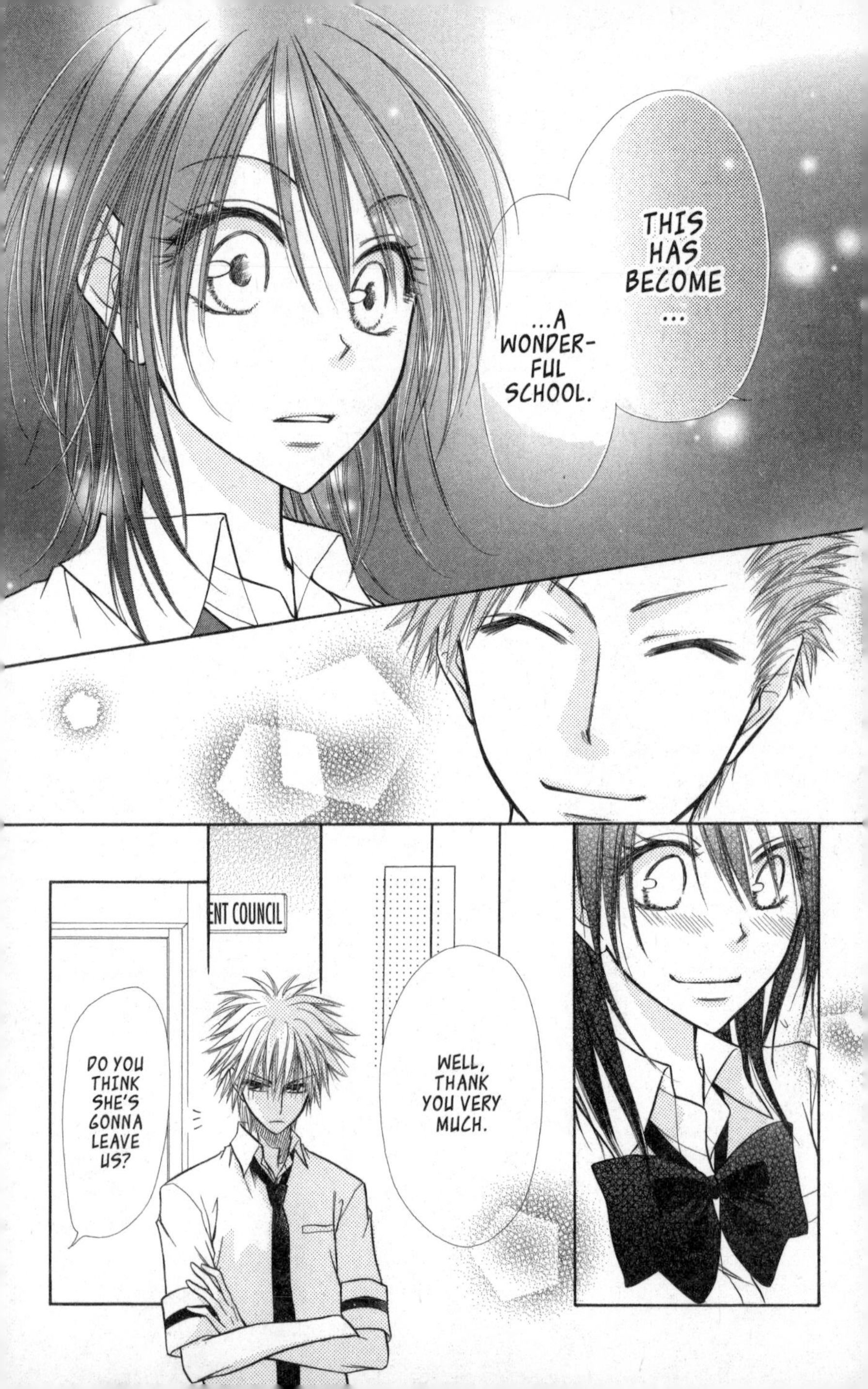
THIS HAS BECOME ...
...A WONDERFUL SCHOOL.
ENT COUNCIL
WELL, THANK YOU VERY MUCH.
DO YOU THINK SHE'S GONNA LEAVE US?

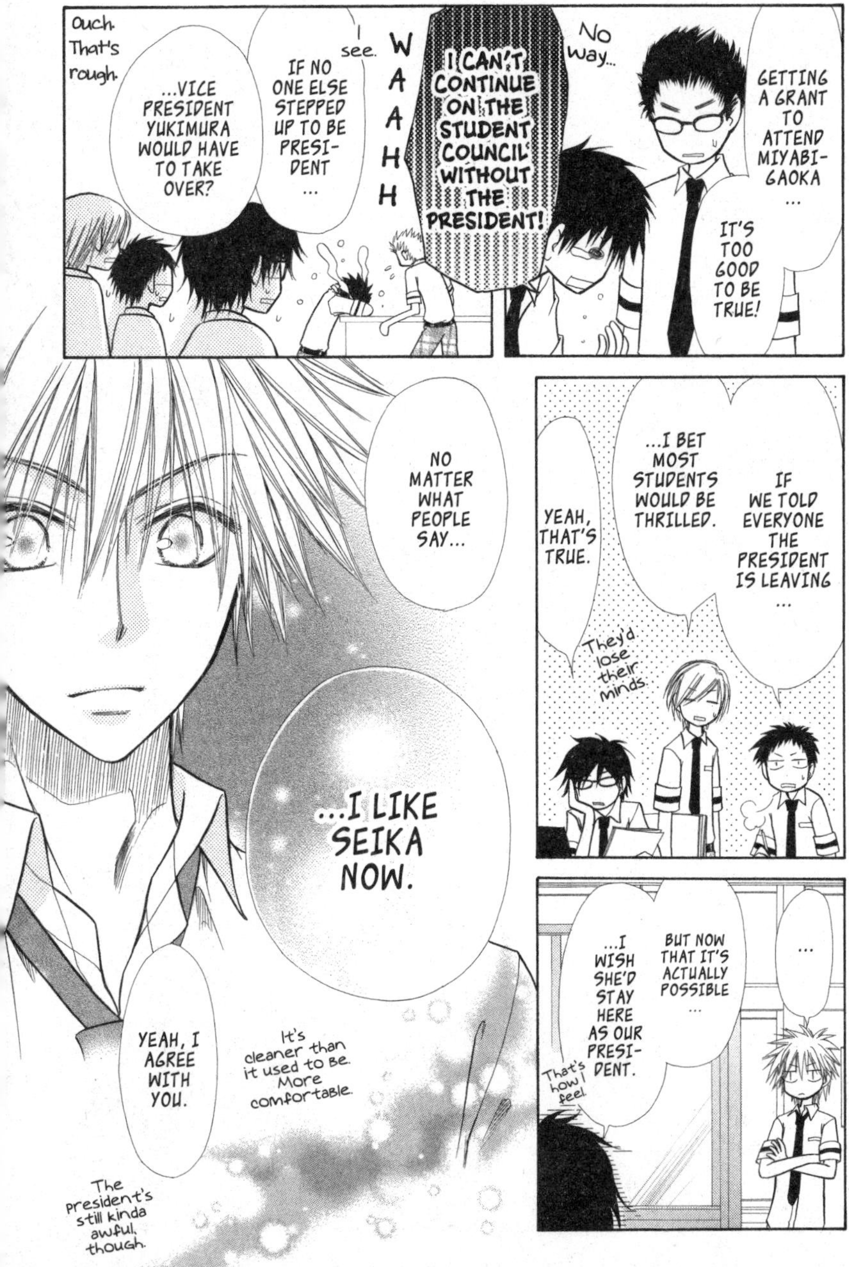
GETTING A GRANT TO ATTEND MIYABI-GAOKA...
IT'S TOO GOOD TO BE TRUE!
No way...
I CAN'T CONTINUE ON THE STUDENT COUNCIL WITHOUT THE PRESIDENT!
WAAHH
I see.
IF NO ONE ELSE STEPPED UP TO BE PRESIDENT...
...VICE PRESIDENT YUKIMURA WOULD HAVE TO TAKE OVER?
Ouch. That's rough.
IF WE TOLD EVERYONE THE PRESIDENT IS LEAVING...
...I BET MOST STUDENTS WOULD BE THRILLED.
YEAH, THAT'S TRUE.
They'd lose their minds.
...
BUT NOW THAT IT'S ACTUALLY POSSIBLE...
...I WISH SHE'D STAY HERE AS OUR PRESIDENT.
That's how I feel.
NO MATTER WHAT PEOPLE SAY...
...I LIKE SEIKA NOW.
It's cleaner than it used to be. More comfortable.
YEAH, I AGREE WITH YOU.
The president's still kinda awful, though.

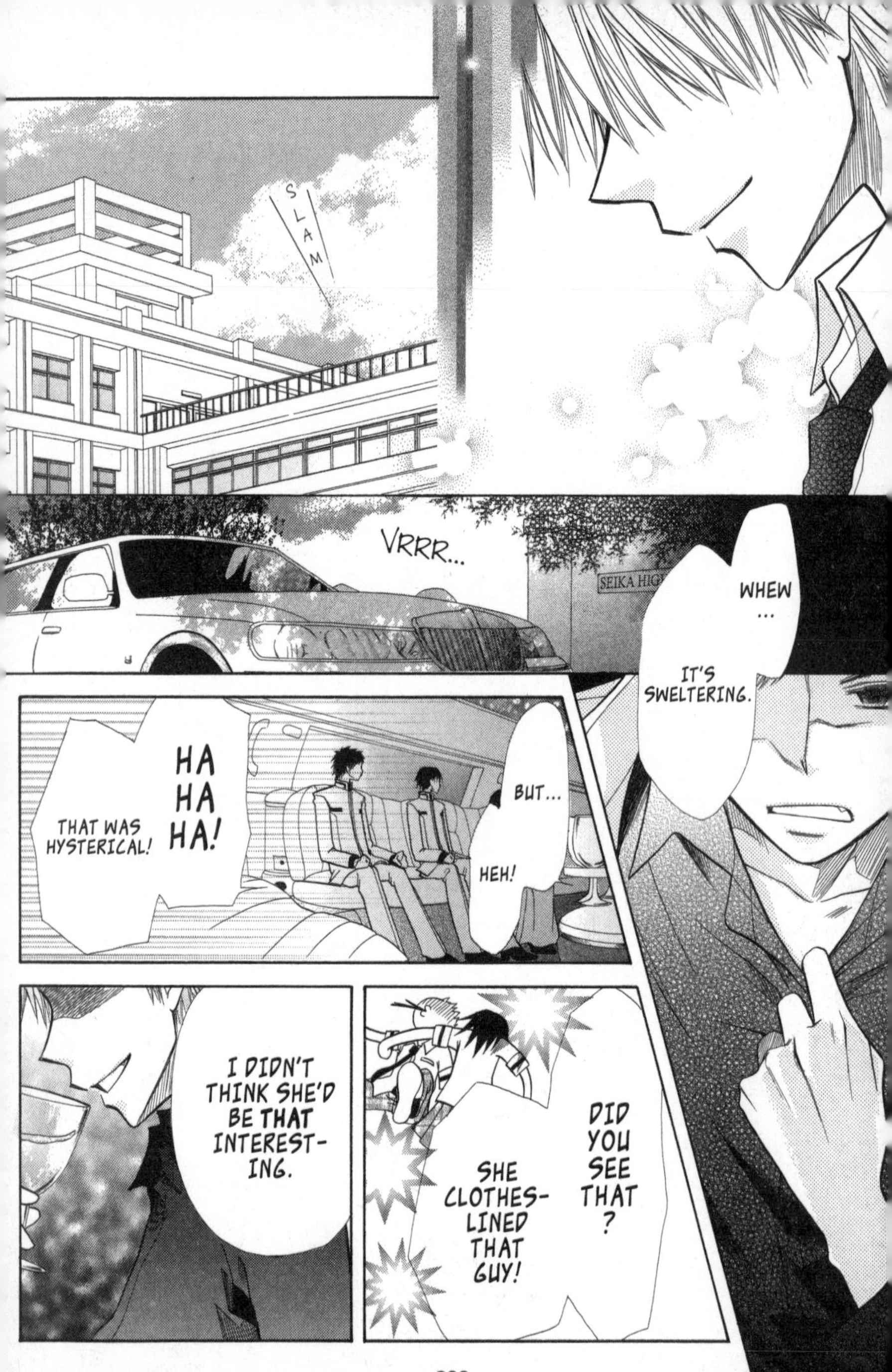
SLAM
VRRR...
WHEW...
IT'S SWELTERING.
BUT...
HEH!
HA HA HA!
THAT WAS HYSTERICAL!
DID YOU SEE THAT?
SHE CLOTHES-LINED THAT GUY!
I DIDN'T THINK SHE'D BE THAT INTEREST-ING.

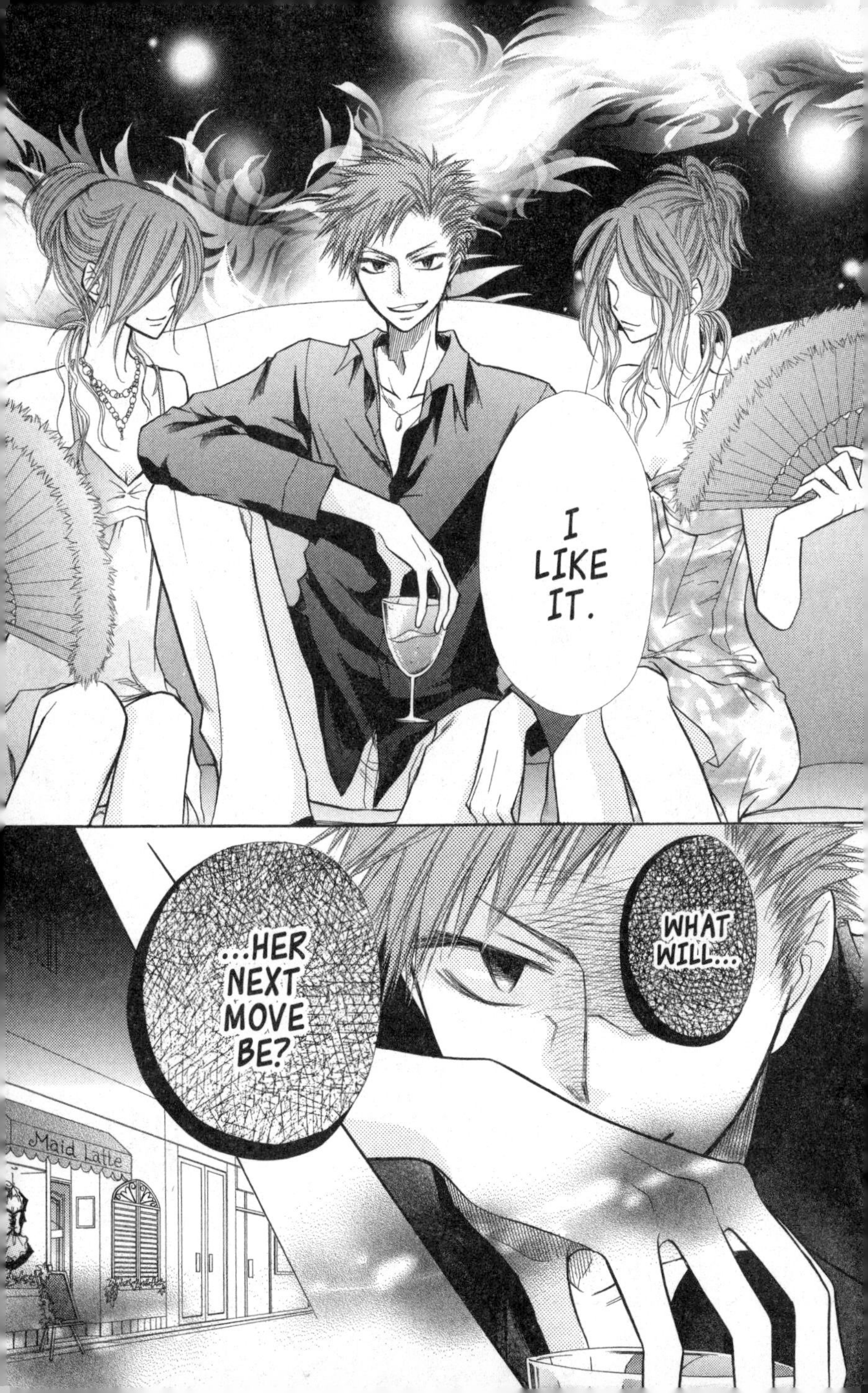
I LIKE IT.
WHAT WILL...
...HER NEXT MOVE BE?
Maid Latte

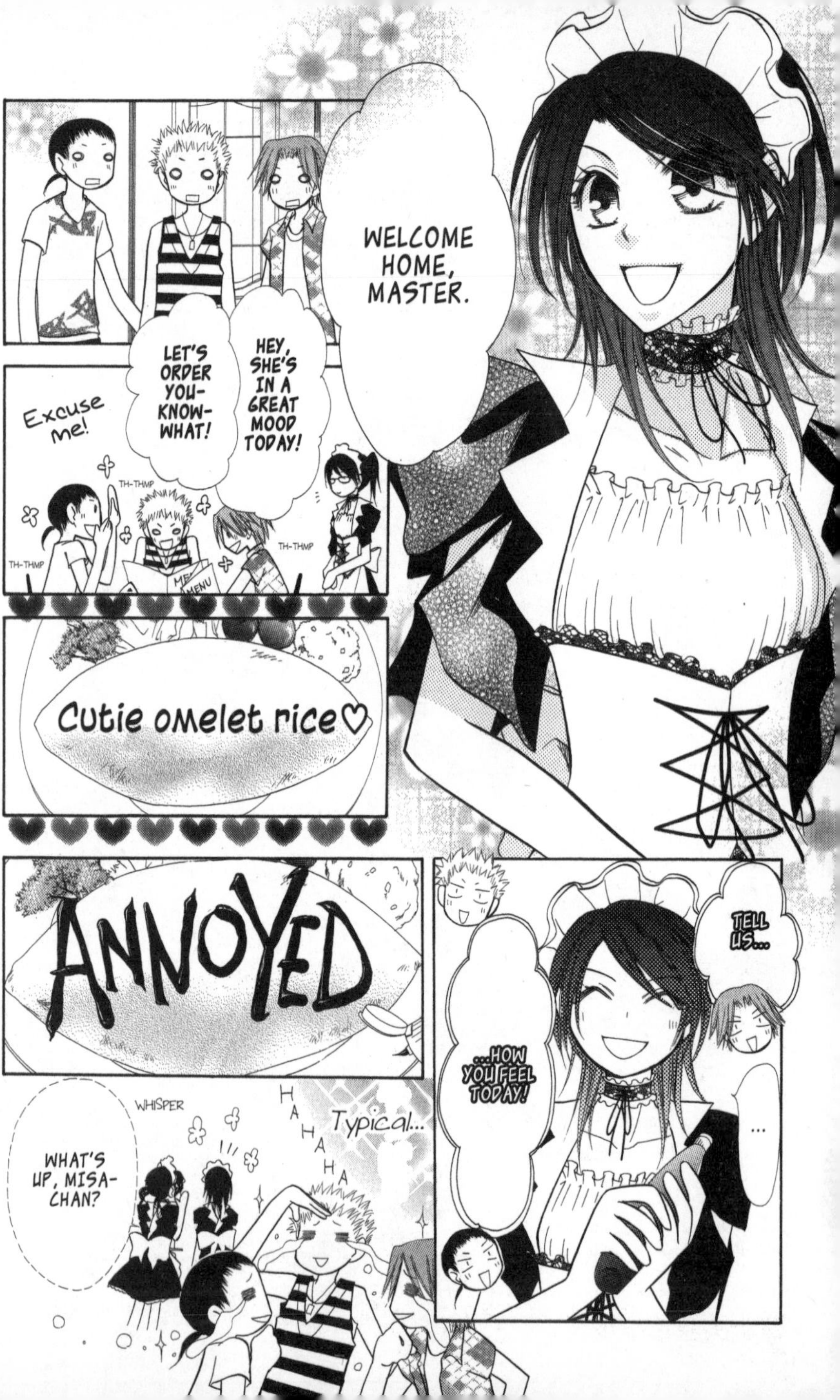
WELCOME HOME, MASTER.
HEY, SHE'S IN A GREAT MOOD TODAY!
LET'S ORDER YOU-KNOW-WHAT!
Excuse me!
TH-THMP
TH-THMP
TH-THMP
MENU
MENU
Cutie omelet rice♡
TELL US...
...HOW YOU FEEL TODAY!
...
ANNOYED
Typical...
HAHAHA
WHISPER
WHAT'S UP, MISA-CHAN?

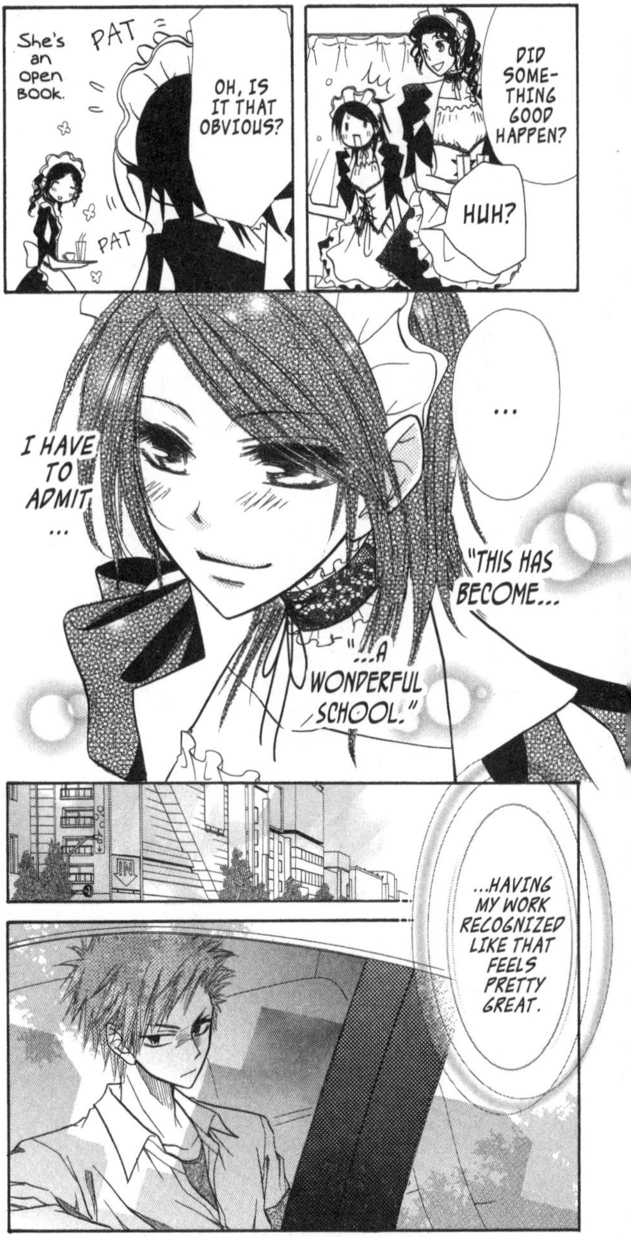
DID SOME-THING GOOD HAPPEN?
HUH?
OH, IS IT THAT OBVIOUS?
PAT
PAT
She's an open book.
...
I HAVE TO ADMIT...
"THIS HAS BECOME...
"...A WONDERFUL SCHOOL."
...HAVING MY WORK RECOGNIZED LIKE THAT FEELS PRETTY GREAT.

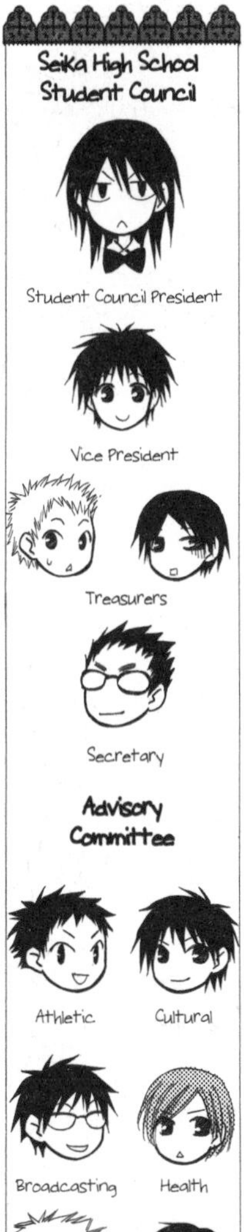
Seika High School Student Council
Student Council President
Vice President
Treasurers
Secretary
Advisory Committee
Athletic
Cultural
Broadcasting
Health
Grounds Improvement
Library
Discipline

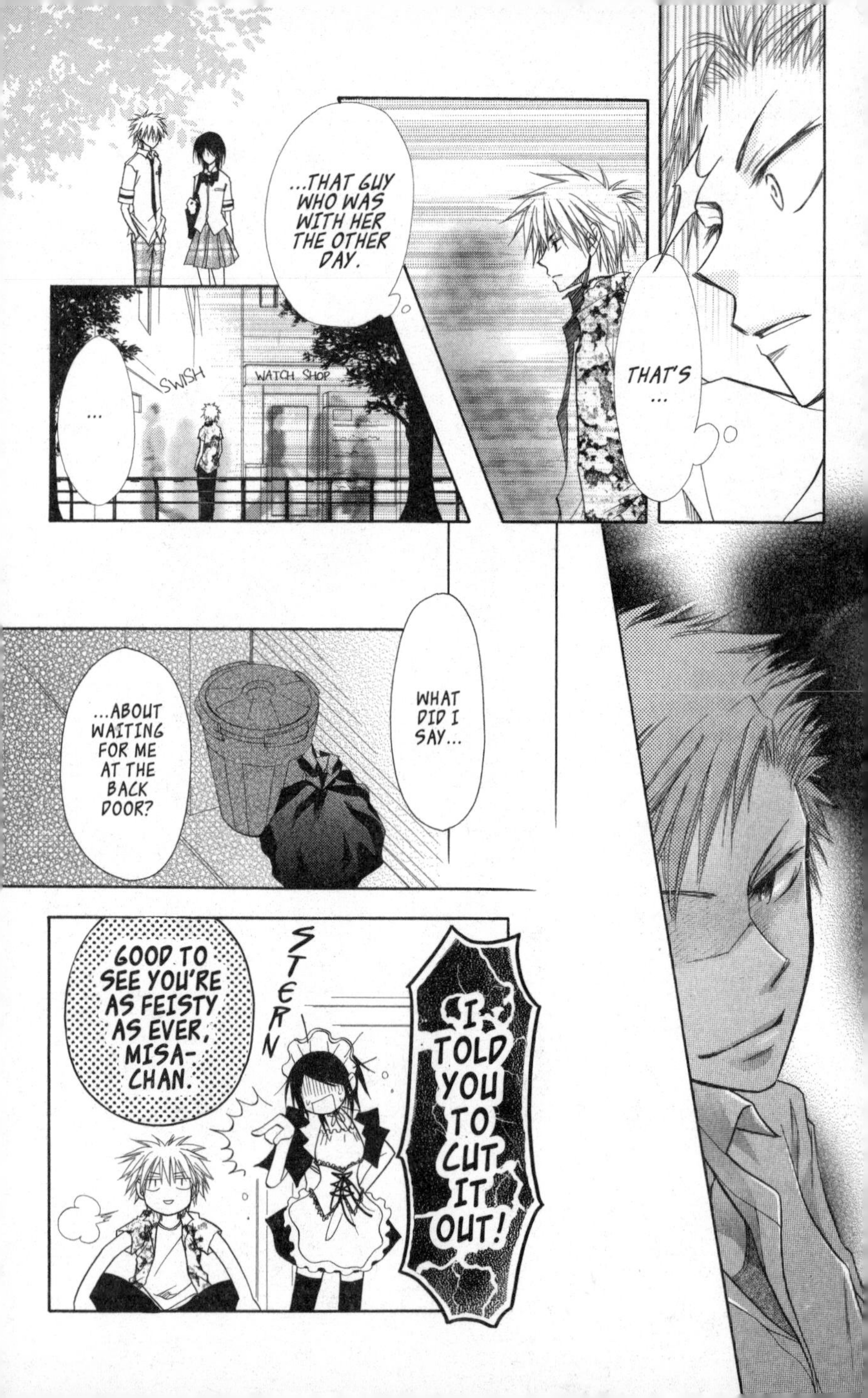
THAT'S ...
...THAT GUY WHO WAS WITH HER THE OTHER DAY.
SWISH
WATCH SHOP
...
WHAT DID I SAY...
...ABOUT WAITING FOR ME AT THE BACK DOOR?
I TOLD YOU TO CUT IT OUT!
STERN
...GOOD TO SEE YOU'RE AS FEISTY AS EVER, MISA-CHAN.

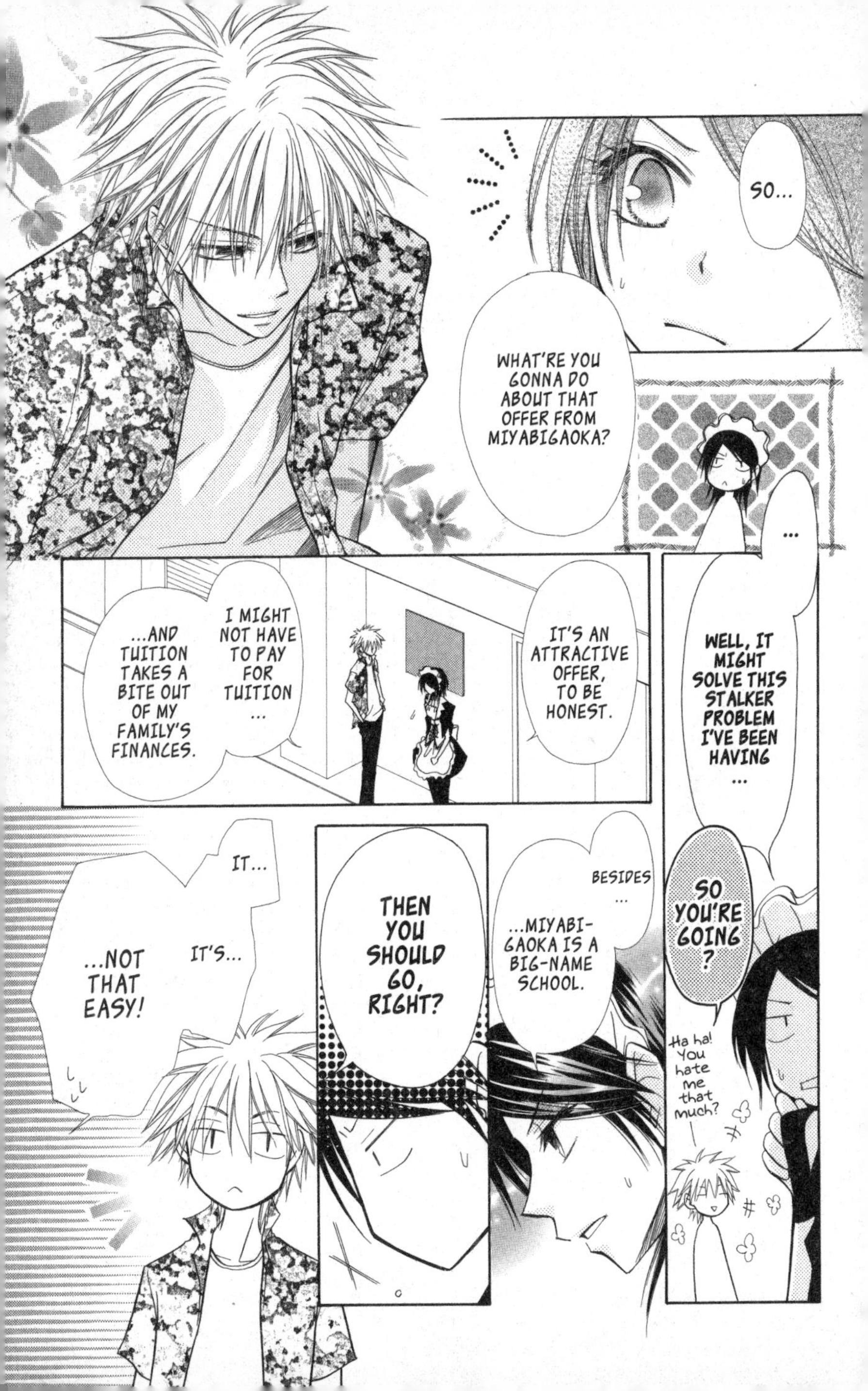
SO...
WHAT'RE YOU GONNA DO ABOUT THAT OFFER FROM MIYABIGAOKA?
...
WELL, IT MIGHT SOLVE THIS STALKER PROBLEM I'VE BEEN HAVING...
SO YOU'RE GOING?
Ha ha! You hate me that much?
IT'S AN ATTRACTIVE OFFER, TO BE HONEST.
I MIGHT NOT HAVE TO PAY FOR TUITION...
...AND TUITION TAKES A BITE OUT OF MY FAMILY'S FINANCES.
BESIDES...
...MIYABIGAOKA IS A BIG-NAME SCHOOL.
THEN YOU SHOULD GO, RIGHT?
IT...
IT'S...
...NOT THAT EASY!

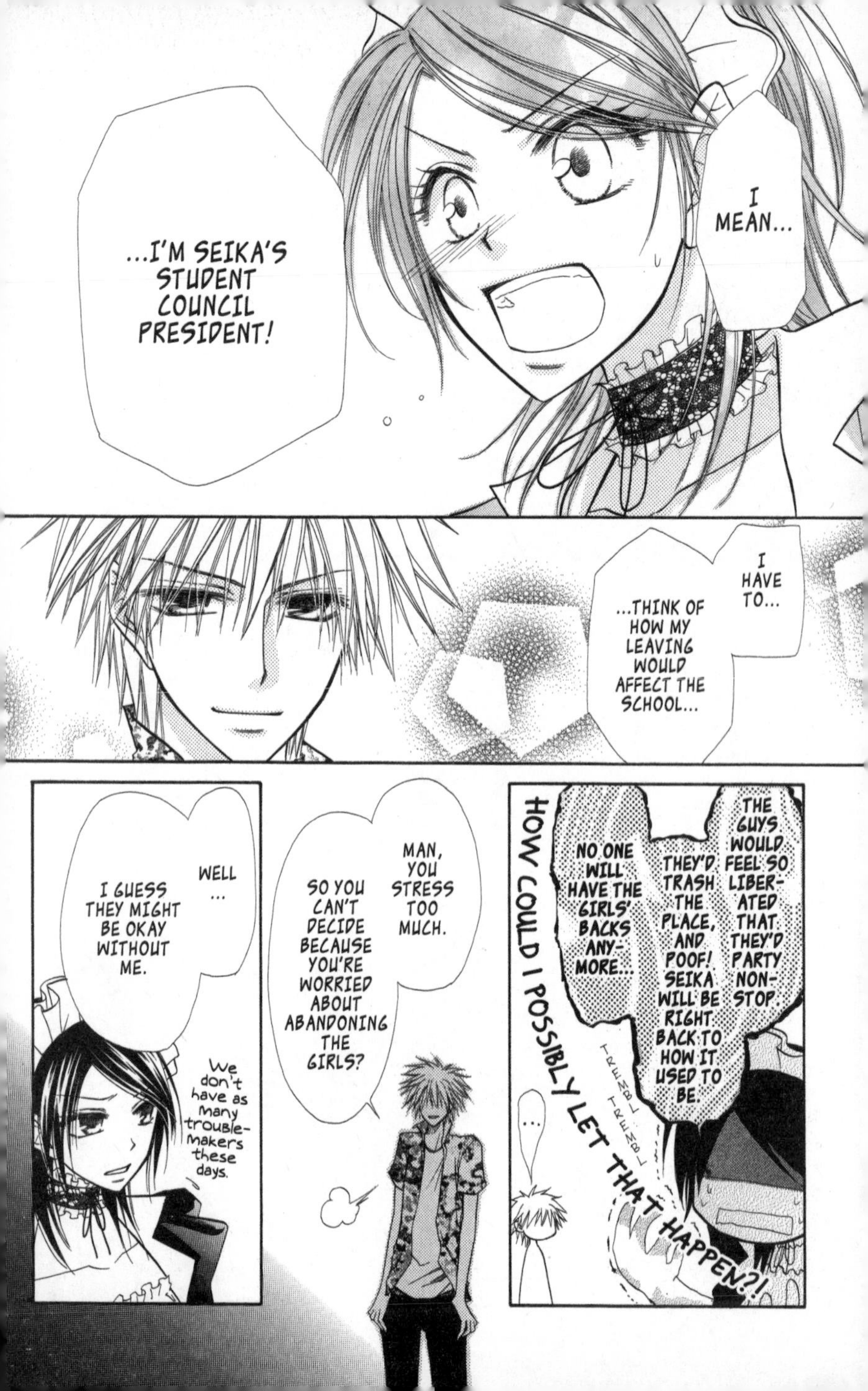
I MEAN...
...I'M SEIKA'S STUDENT COUNCIL PRESIDENT!
I HAVE TO...
...THINK OF HOW MY LEAVING WOULD AFFECT THE SCHOOL...
THE GUYS WOULD FEEL SO LIBER-ATED THAT THEY'D PARTY NON-STOP
THEY'D TRASH THE PLACE, AND POOF! SEIKA WILL BE RIGHT BACK TO HOW IT USED TO BE.
NO ONE WILL HAVE THE GIRLS' BACKS ANY-MORE...
HOW COULD I POSSIBLY LET THAT HAPPEN?!
TREMBL TREMBL
...
MAN, YOU STRESS TOO MUCH.
SO YOU CAN'T DECIDE BECAUSE YOU'RE WORRIED ABOUT ABANDONING THE GIRLS?
WELL...
I GUESS THEY MIGHT BE OKAY WITHOUT ME.
We don't have as many trouble-makers these days.

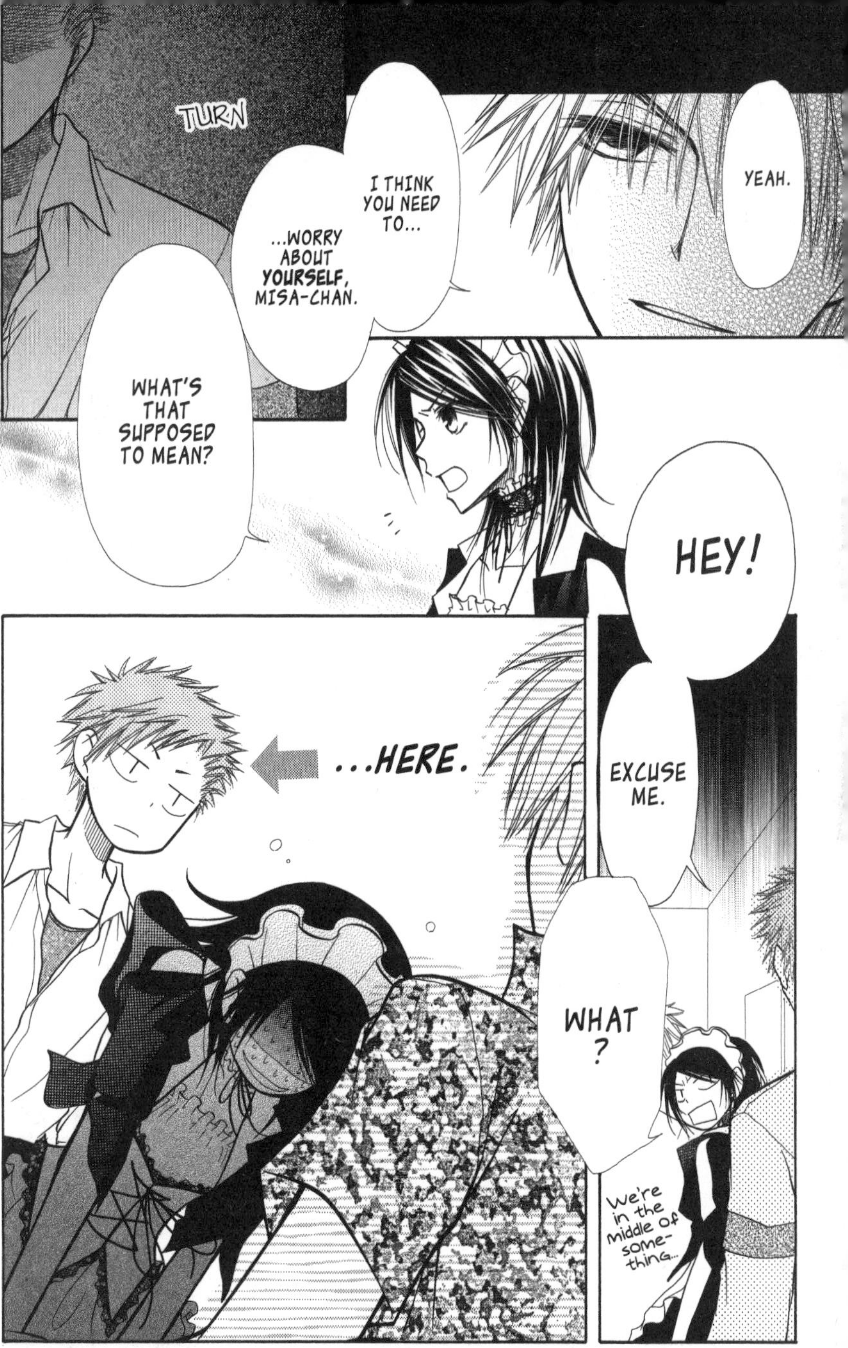
YEAH.
TURN
I THINK YOU NEED TO...
...WORRY ABOUT **YOURSELF**, MISA-CHAN.
WHAT'S THAT SUPPOSED TO MEAN?
HEY!
EXCUSE ME.
WHAT?
We're in the middle of something...
...HERE.

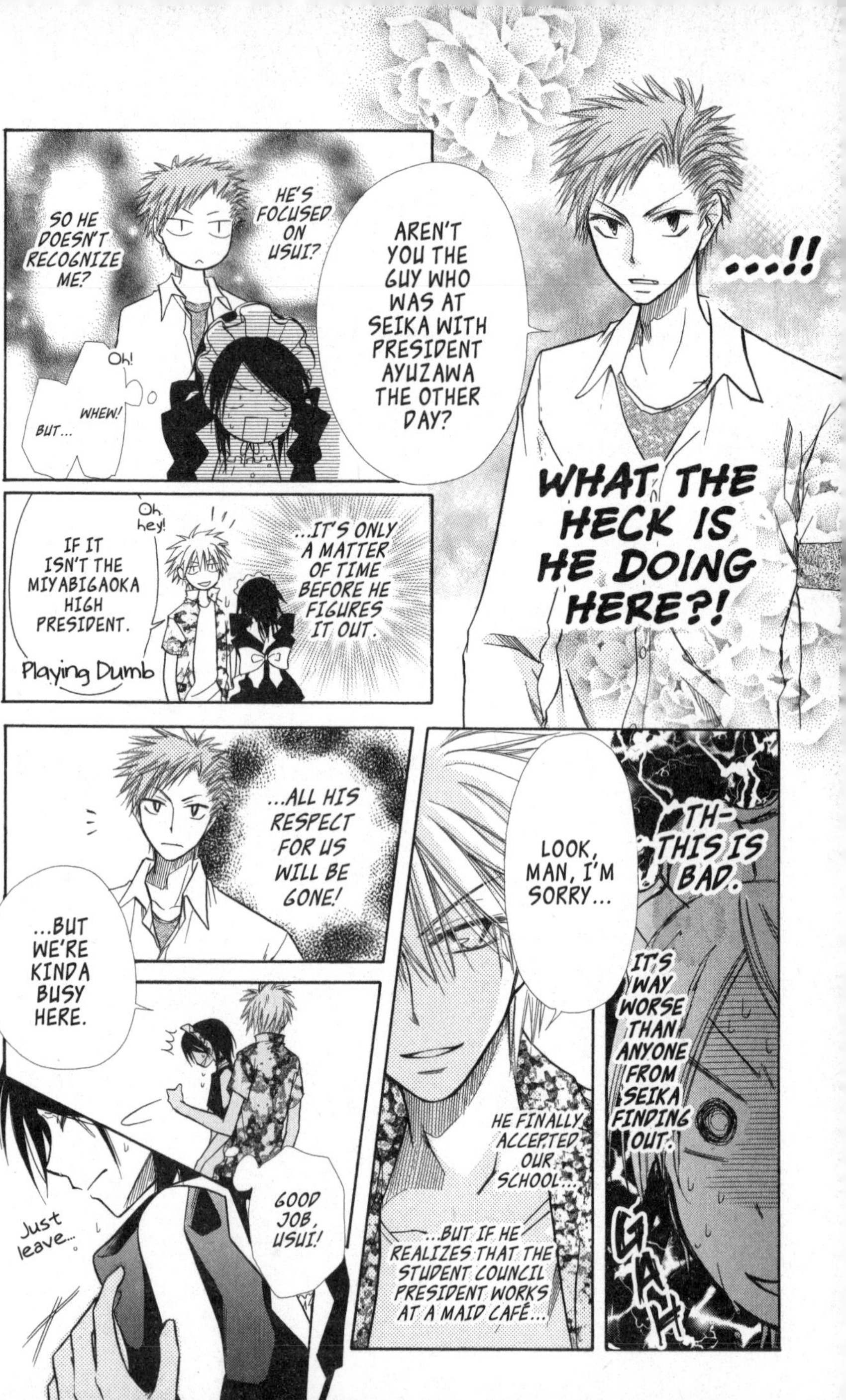

...!!
WHAT THE HECK IS HE DOING HERE?!
AREN'T YOU THE GUY WHO WAS AT SEIKA WITH PRESIDENT AYUZAWA THE OTHER DAY?
HE'S FOCUSED ON USUI?
SO HE DOESN'T RECOGNIZE ME?
Oh!
WHEW!
BUT...
...IT'S ONLY A MATTER OF TIME BEFORE HE FIGURES IT OUT.
Oh, hey!
IF IT ISN'T THE MIYABIGAOKA HIGH PRESIDENT.
Playing Dumb
TH- THIS IS BAD.
IT'S WAY WORSE THAN ANYONE FROM SEIKA FINDING OUT.
GAH
LOOK, MAN, I'M SORRY...
HE FINALLY ACCEPTED OUR SCHOOL...
...BUT IF HE REALIZES THAT THE STUDENT COUNCIL PRESIDENT WORKS AT A MAID CAFÉ...
...ALL HIS RESPECT FOR US WILL BE GONE!
...BUT WE'RE KINDA BUSY HERE.
GOOD JOB, USUI!
Just leave...

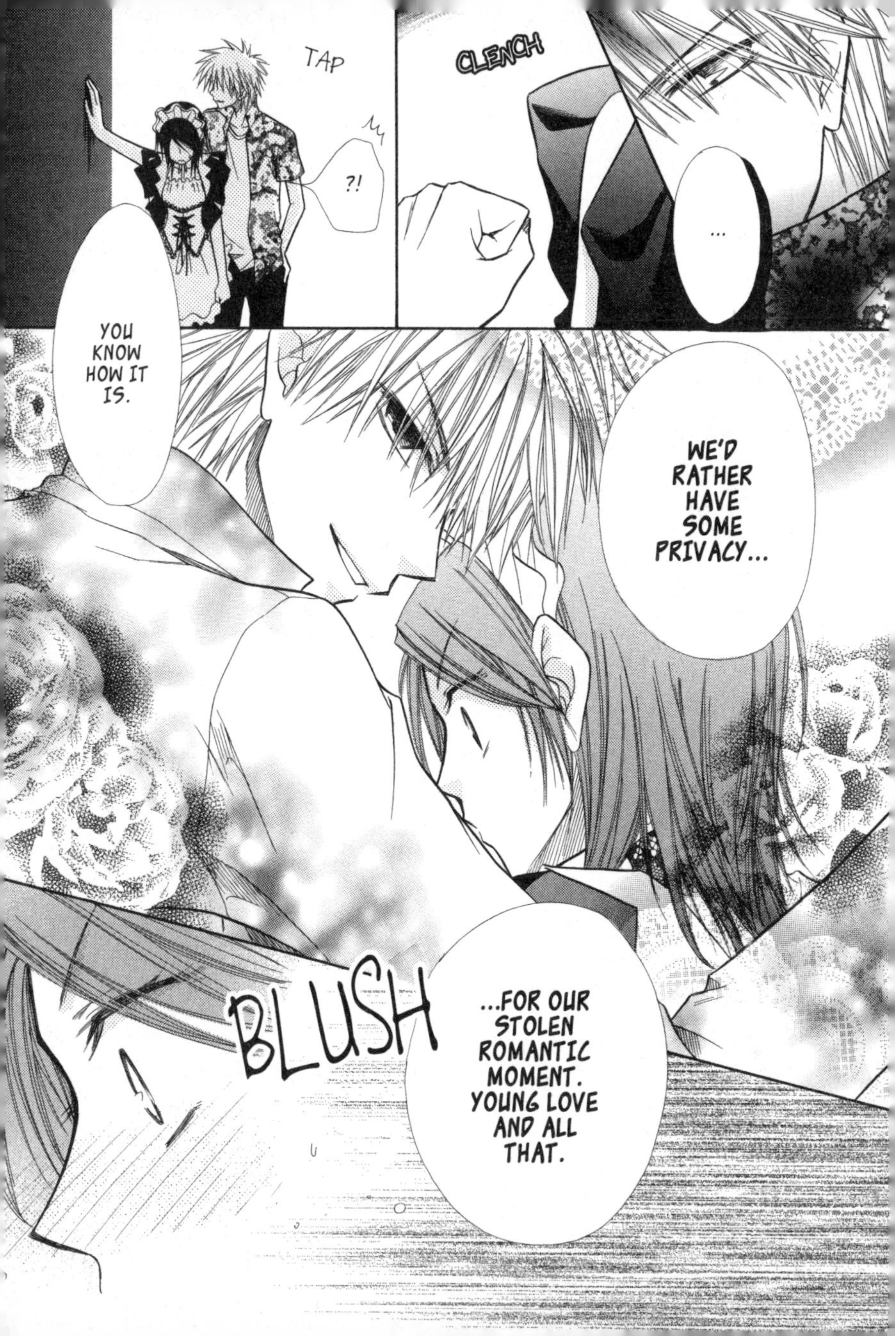
CLENCH
...
TAP
?!
YOU KNOW HOW IT IS.
WE'D RATHER HAVE SOME PRIVACY...
BLUSH
...FOR OUR STOLEN ROMANTIC MOMENT. YOUNG LOVE AND ALL THAT.

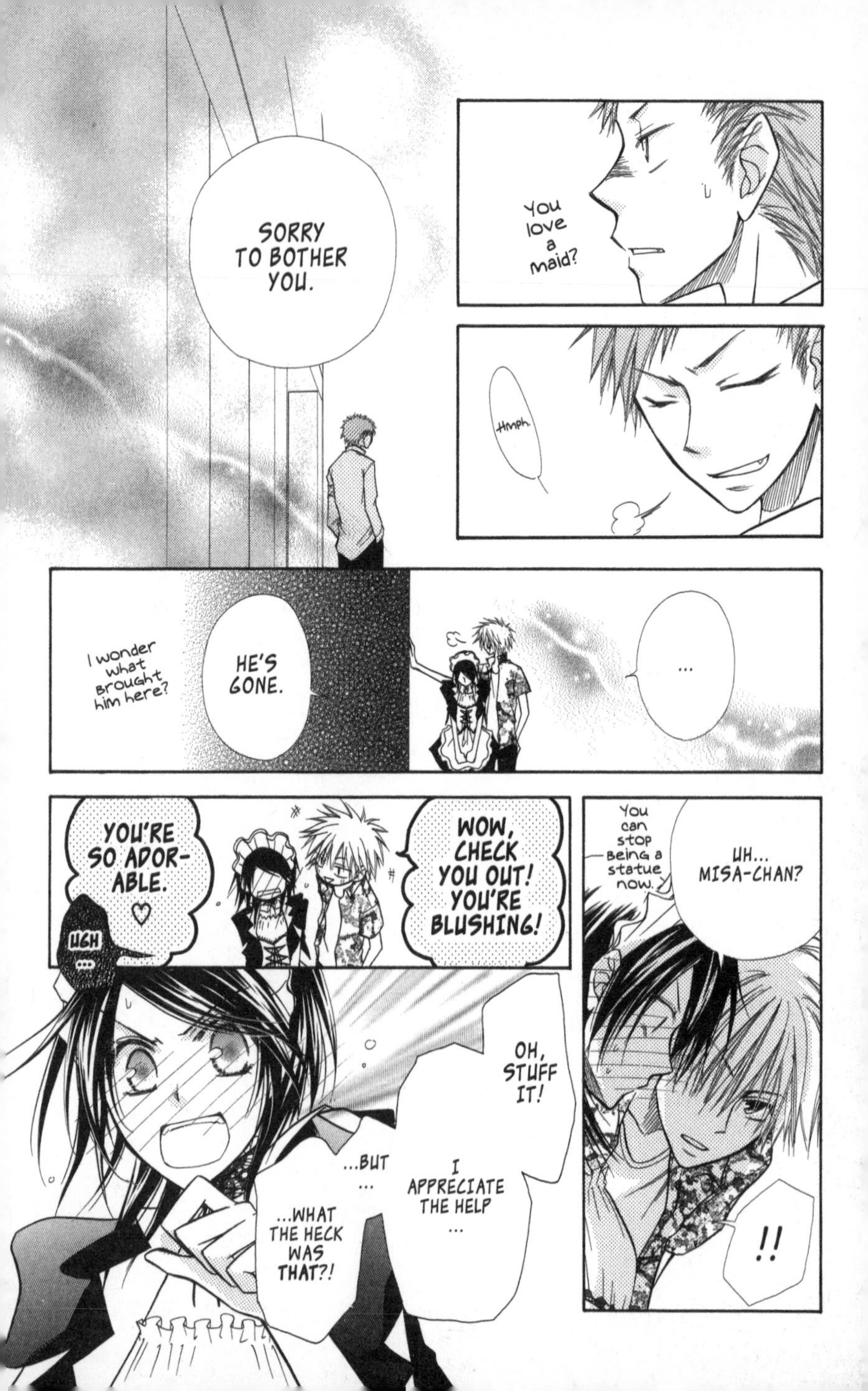
You love a maid?
Hmph.
SORRY TO BOTHER YOU.
...
HE'S GONE.
I wonder what brought him here?
UH... MISA-CHAN?
You can stop being a statue now.
!!
WOW, CHECK YOU OUT! YOU'RE BLUSHING!
YOU'RE SO ADORABLE.
UGH ...
OH, STUFF IT!
I APPRECIATE THE HELP ...
...BUT ...
...WHAT THE HECK WAS THAT?!

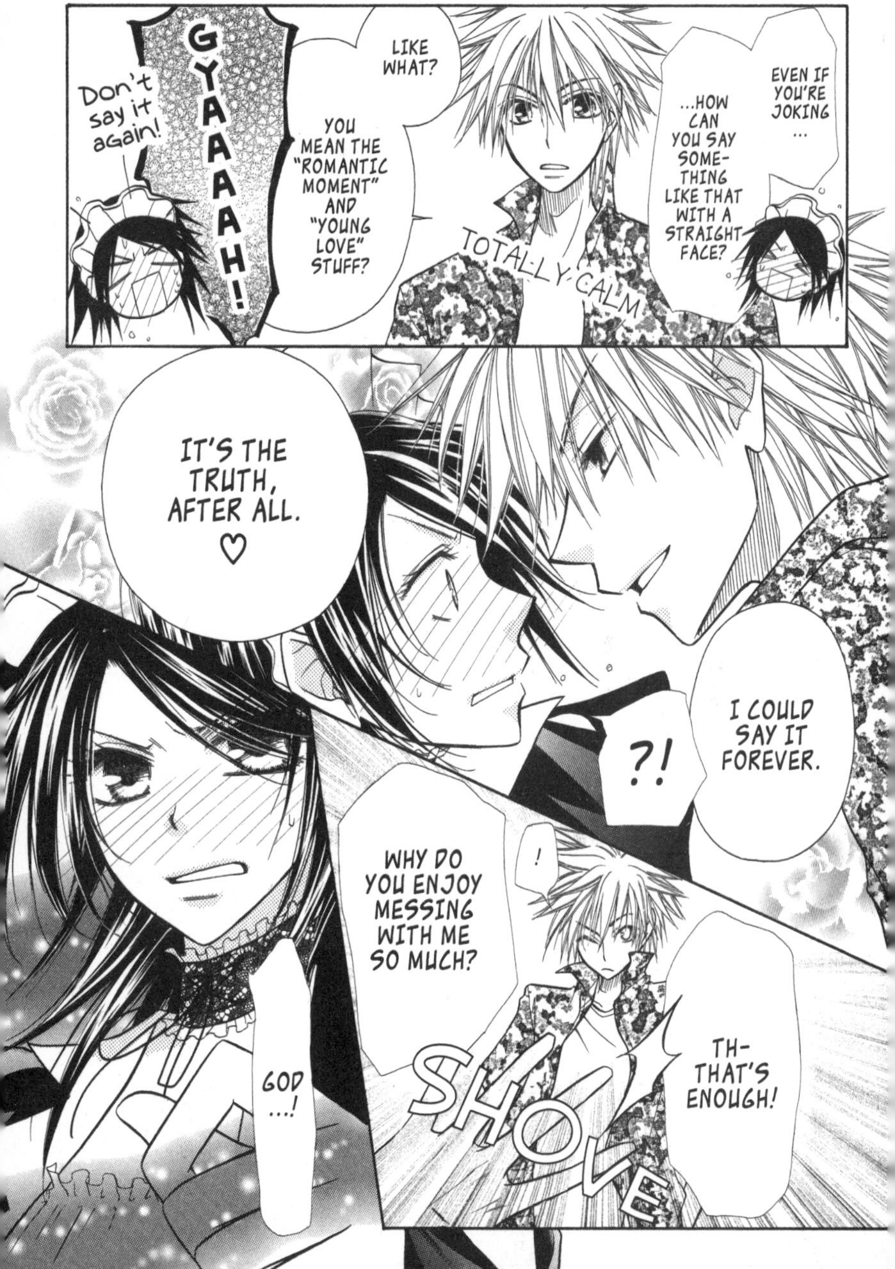
EVEN IF YOU'RE JOKING ...
...HOW CAN YOU SAY SOME-THING LIKE THAT WITH A STRAIGHT FACE?
TOTAL-LY-CALM
LIKE WHAT?
YOU MEAN THE "ROMANTIC MOMENT" AND "YOUNG LOVE" STUFF?
GYAAAAH!
Don't say it again!
IT'S THE TRUTH, AFTER ALL. ♡
I COULD SAY IT FOREVER.
?!
!
TH-THAT'S ENOUGH!
SHOVE
WHY DO YOU ENJOY MESSING WITH ME SO MUCH?
GOD ...!

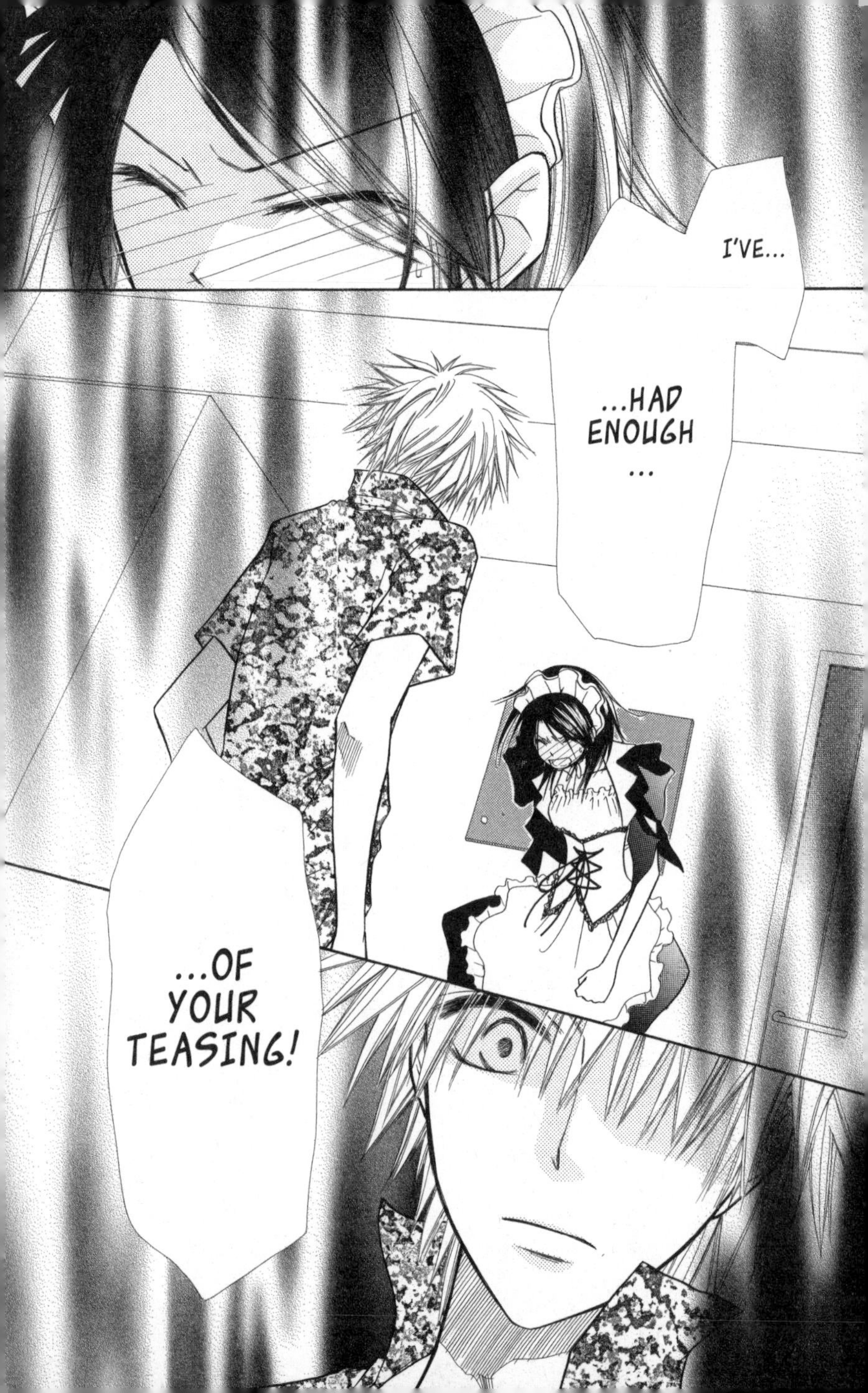
I'VE...
...HAD ENOUGH ...
...OF YOUR TEASING!

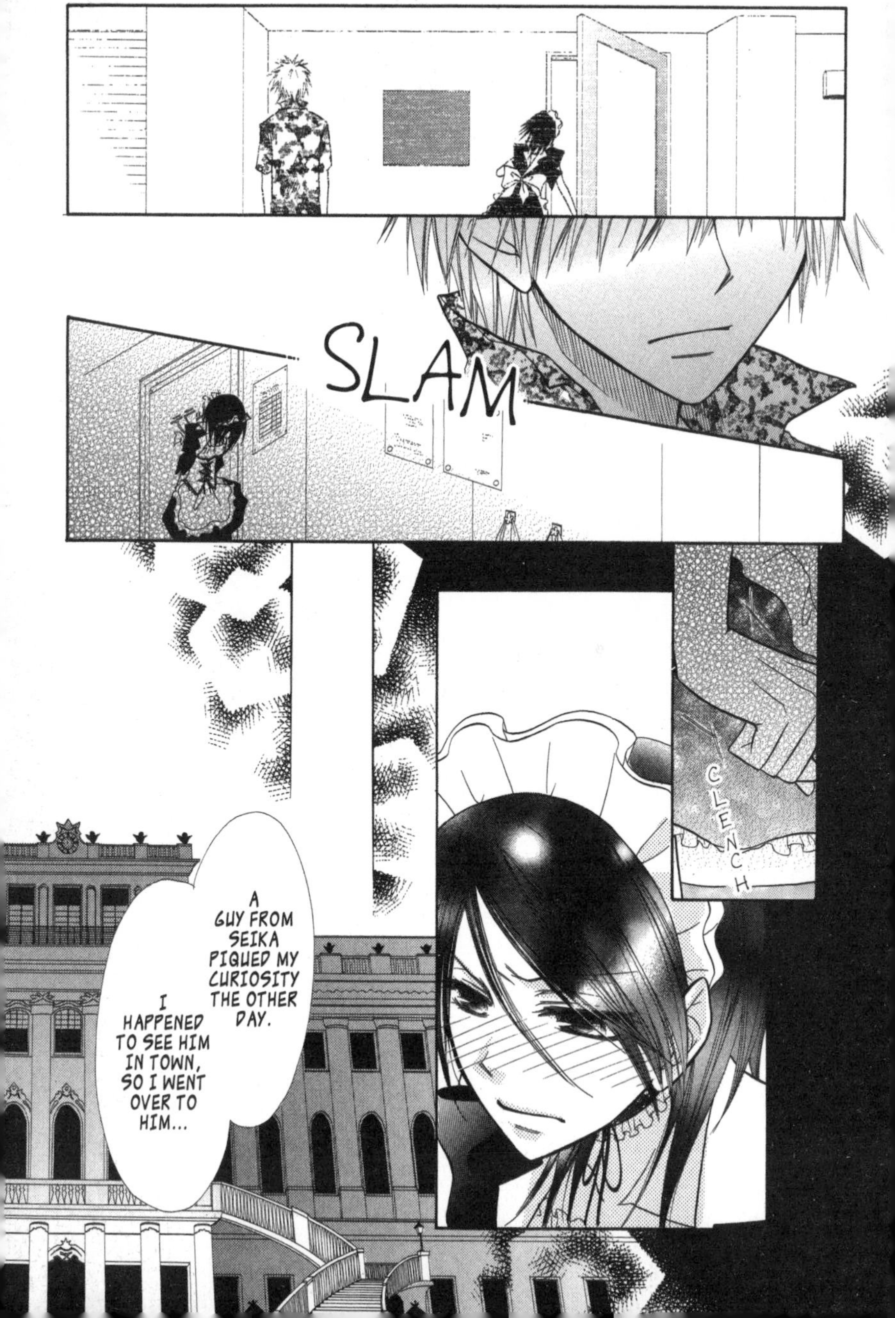
SLAM
CLENCH
A GUY FROM SEIKA PIQUED MY CURIOSITY THE OTHER DAY.
I HAPPENED TO SEE HIM IN TOWN, SO I WENT OVER TO HIM...

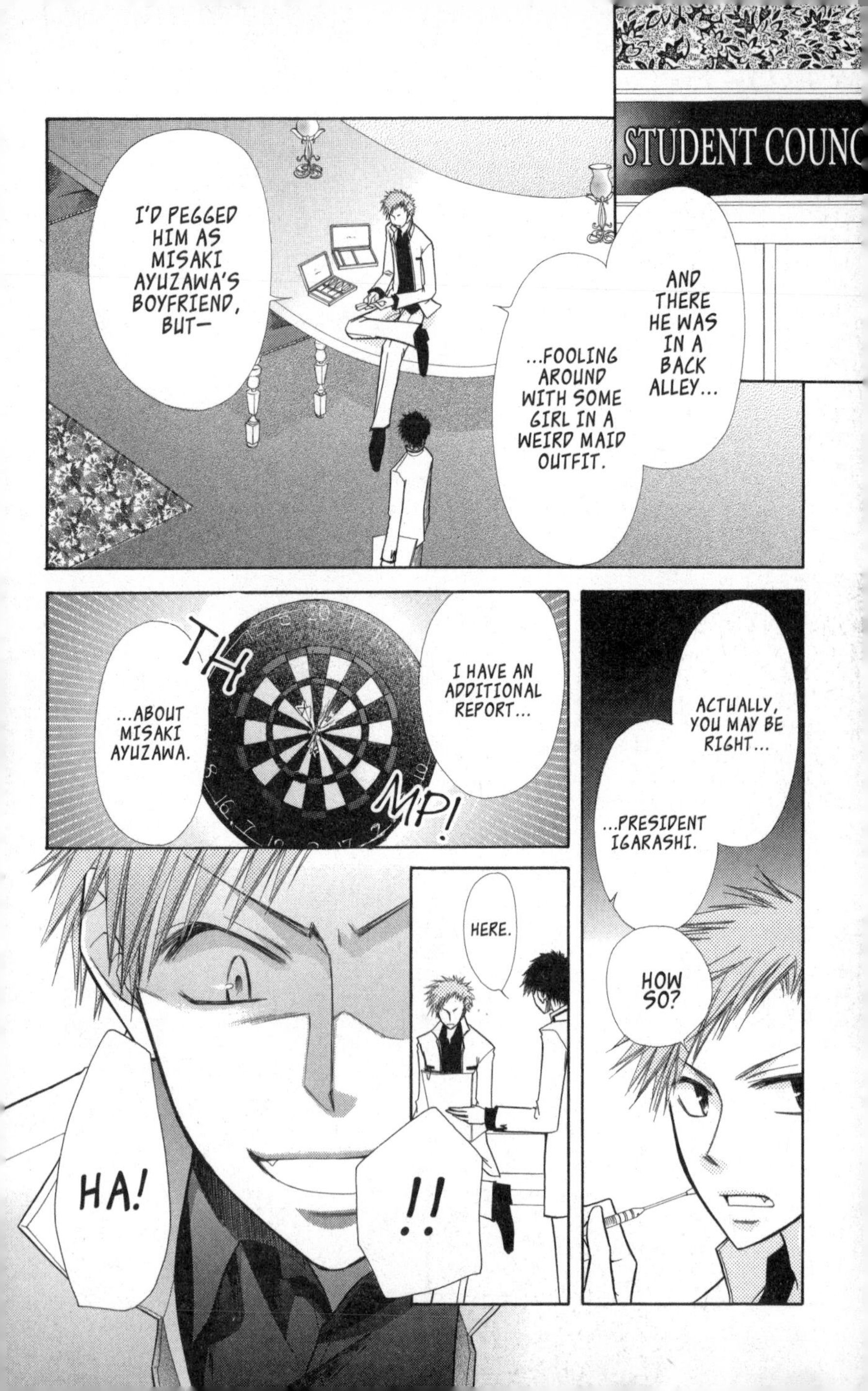
STUDENT COUNC
AND THERE HE WAS IN A BACK ALLEY...
...FOOLING AROUND WITH SOME GIRL IN A WEIRD MAID OUTFIT.
I'D PEGGED HIM AS MISAKI AYUZAWA'S BOYFRIEND, BUT—
ACTUALLY, YOU MAY BE RIGHT...
...PRESIDENT IGARASHI.
HOW SO?
I HAVE AN ADDITIONAL REPORT...
THMP!
...ABOUT MISAKI AYUZAWA.
HERE.
!!
HA!

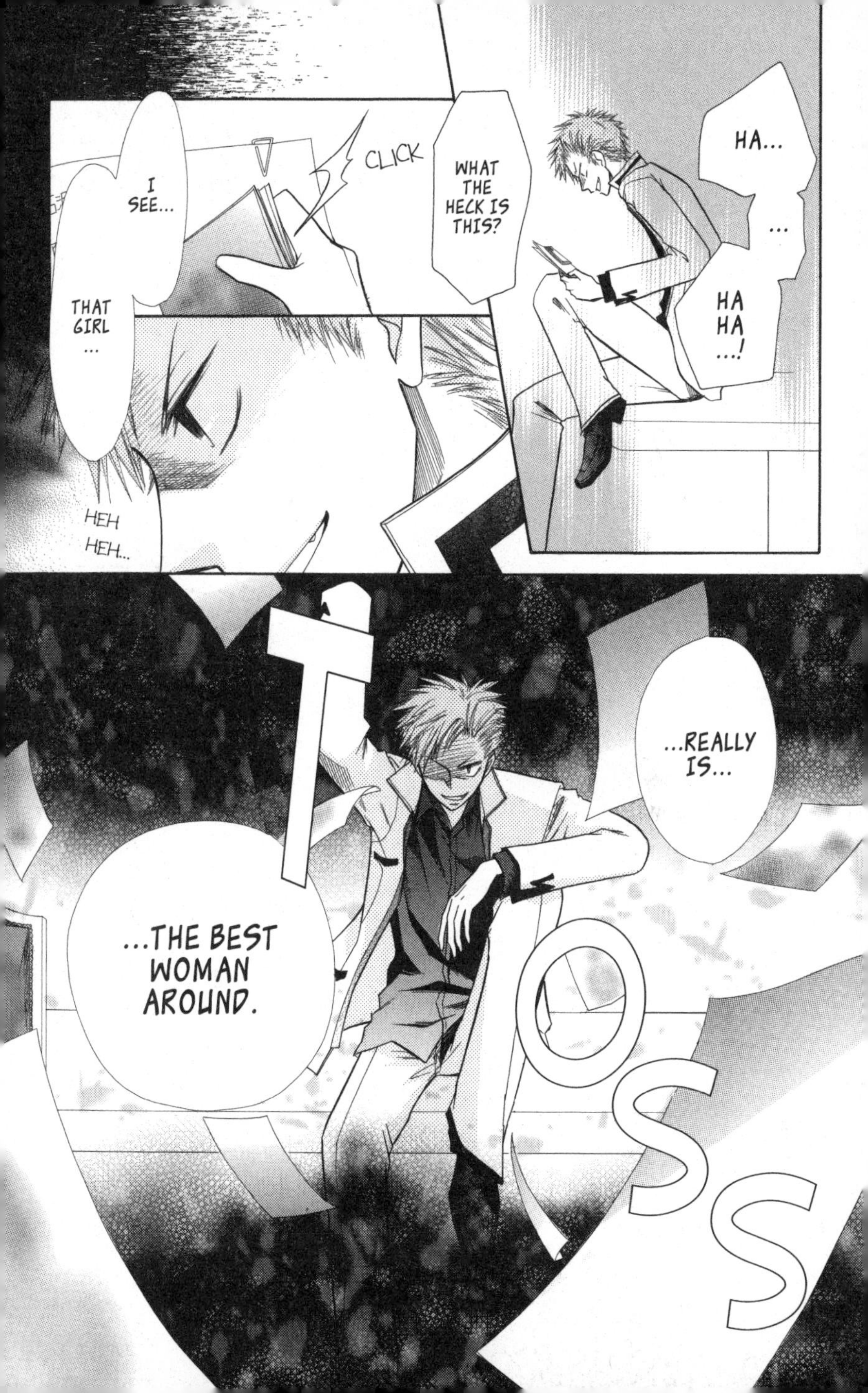
HA...
...
HA HA...!
WHAT THE HECK IS THIS?
CLICK
I SEE...
THAT GIRL...
HEH HEH...
...REALLY IS...
...THE BEST WOMAN AROUND.
TOSS

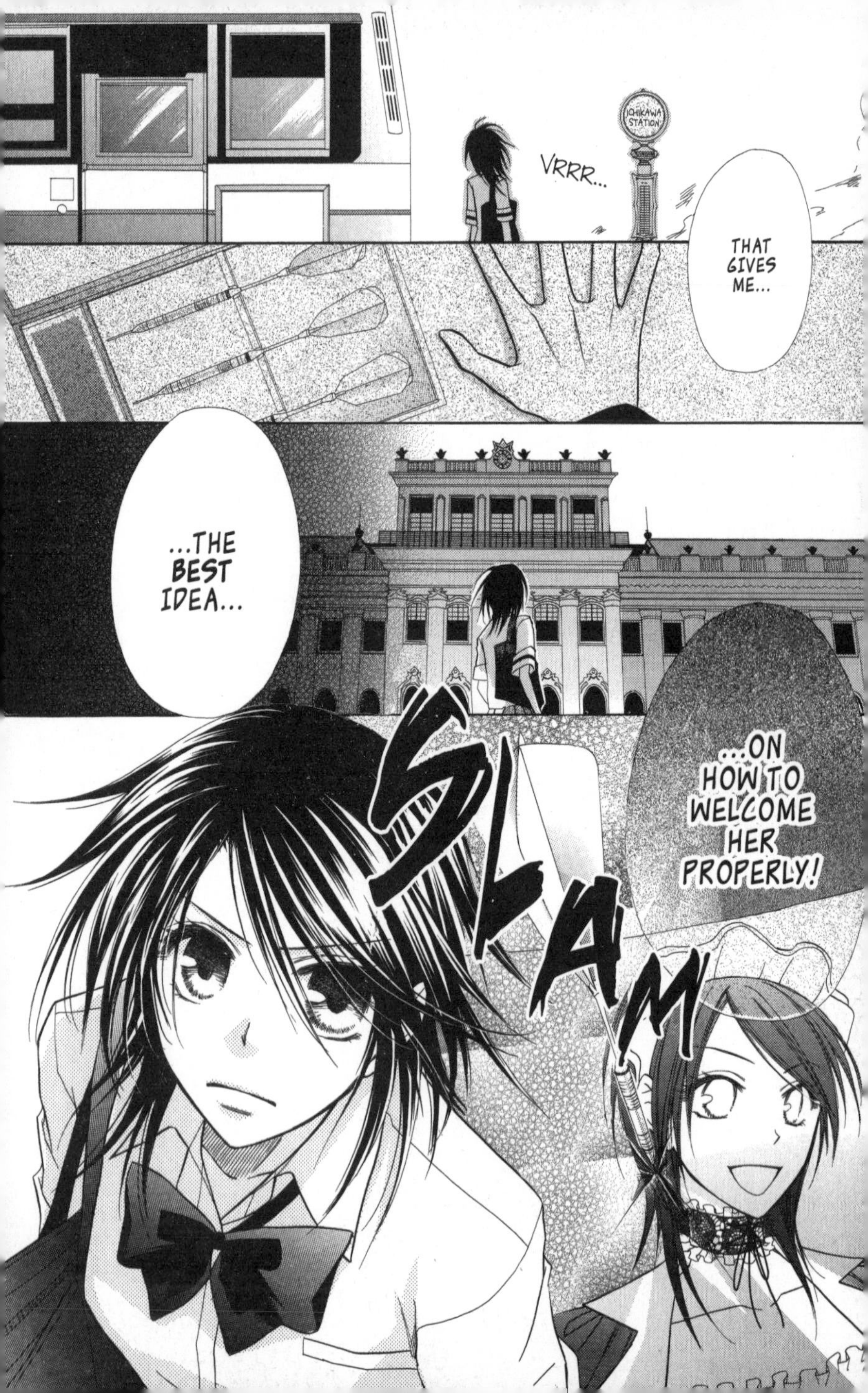
ICHIKAWA STATION
VRRR...
THAT GIVES ME...
...THE BEST IDEA...
...ON HOW TO WELCOME HER PROPERLY!
SLAM

Chapter 8

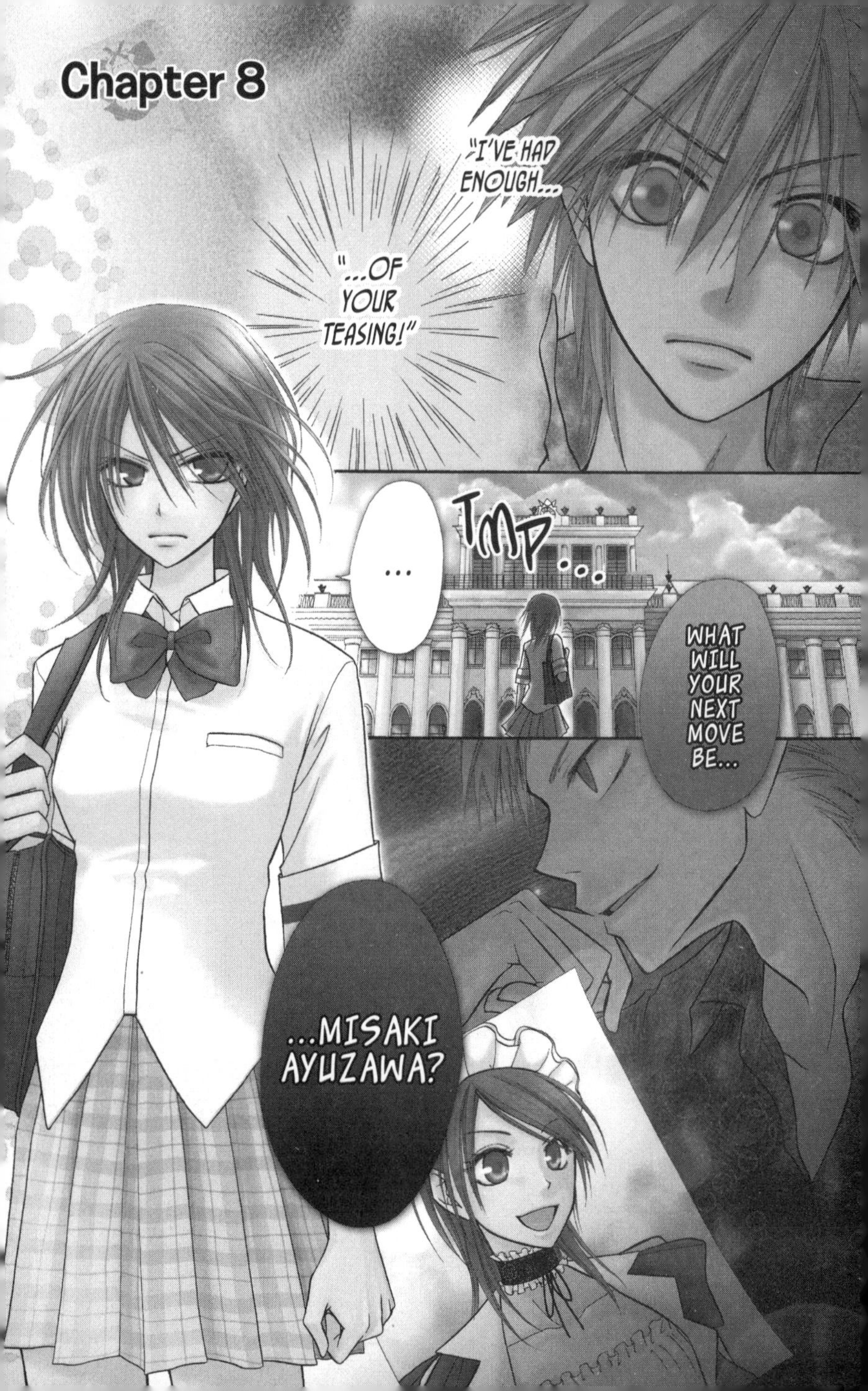
"I'VE HAD ENOUGH...
"...OF YOUR TEASING!"
...
TMP...
WHAT WILL YOUR NEXT MOVE BE...
...MISAKI AYUZAWA?

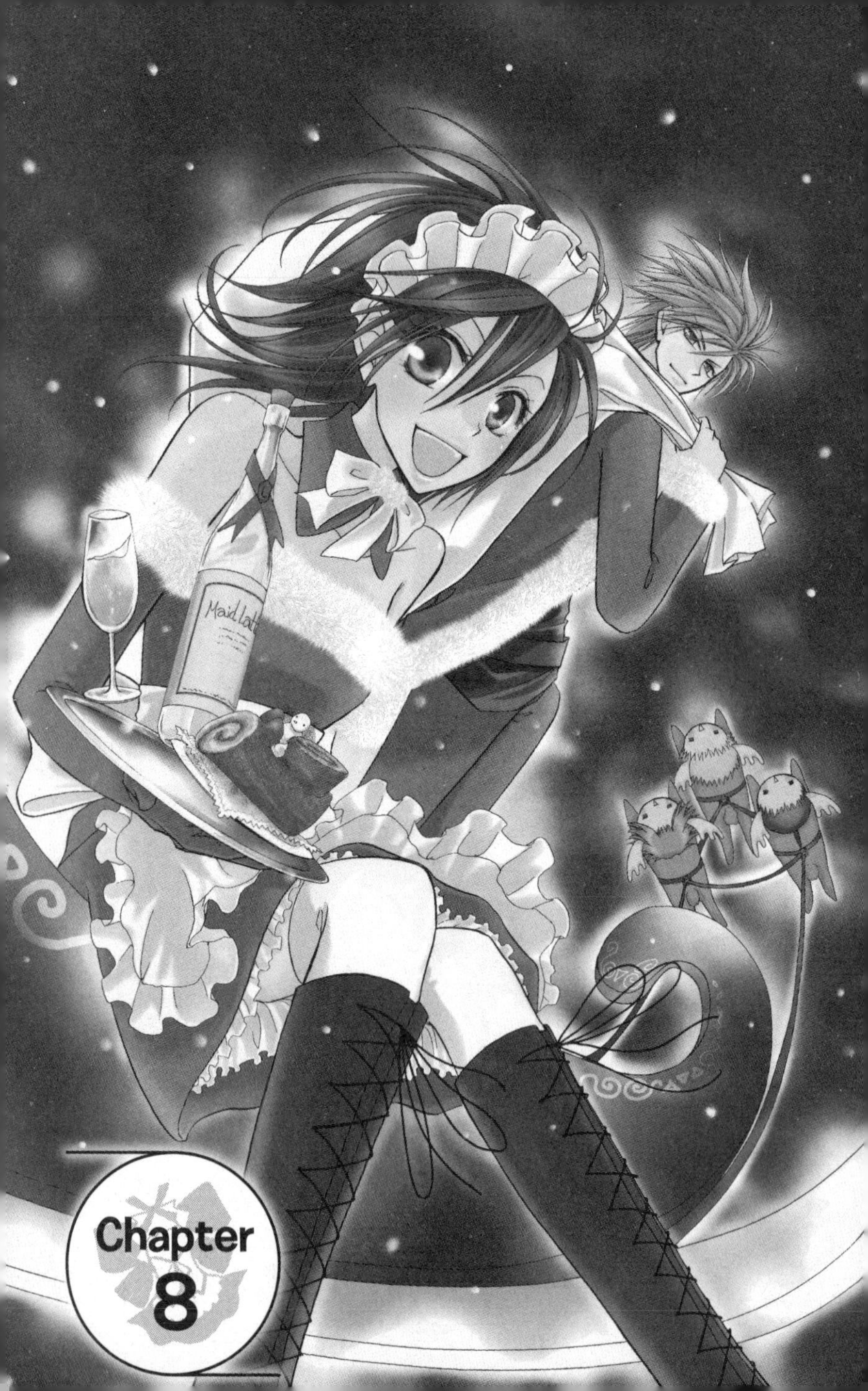
Maid latte
Chapter
8

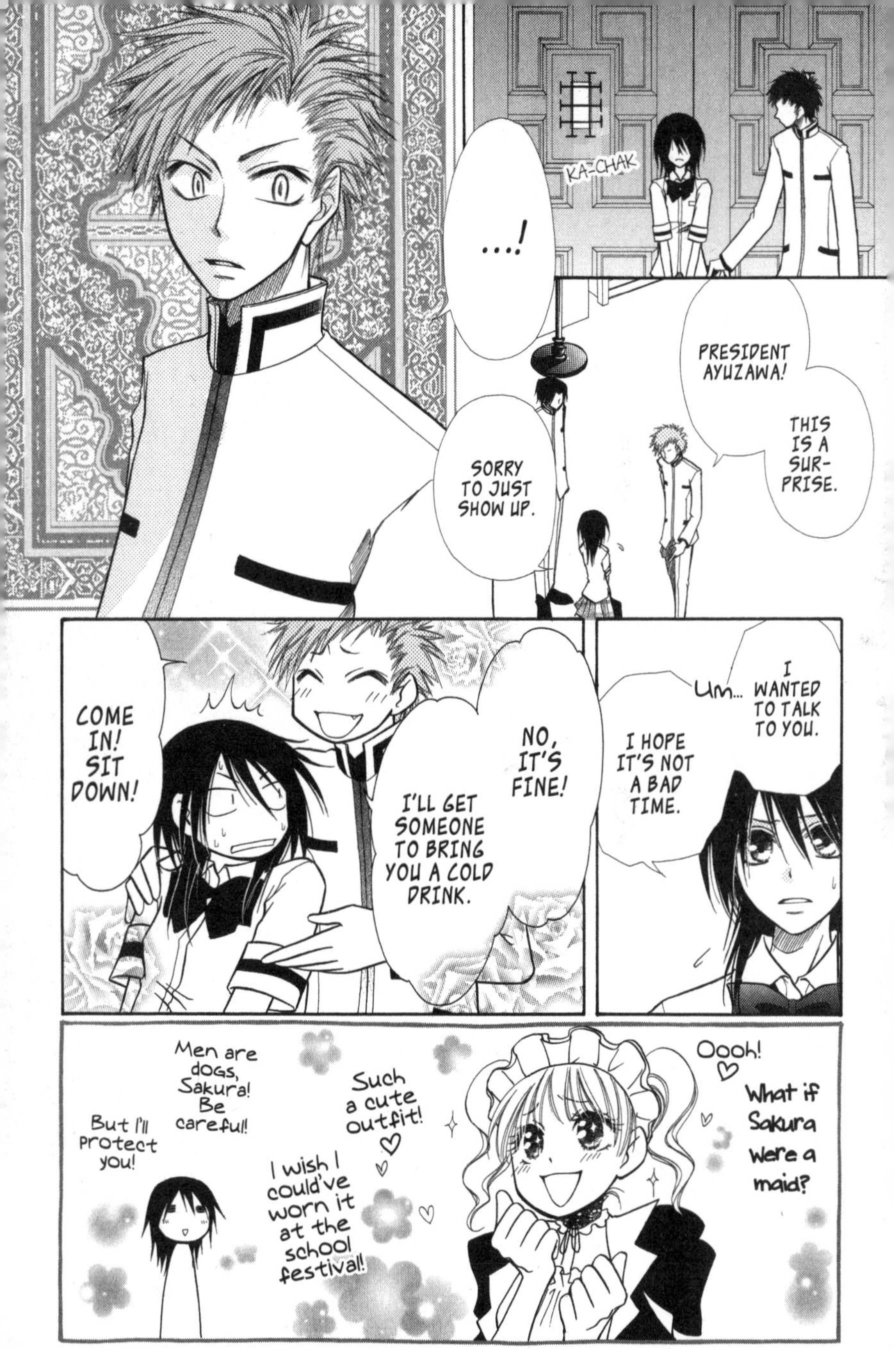
KA-CHAK
PRESIDENT AYUZAWA!
THIS IS A SURPRISE.
SORRY TO JUST SHOW UP.
...!
I WANTED TO TALK TO YOU.
Um...
I HOPE IT'S NOT A BAD TIME.
NO, IT'S FINE!
I'LL GET SOMEONE TO BRING YOU A COLD DRINK.
COME IN! SIT DOWN!
Oooh! ♡
What if Sakura were a maid?
Such a cute outfit! ♡
I wish I could've worn it at the school festival!
Men are dogs, Sakura! Be careful!
But I'll protect you!

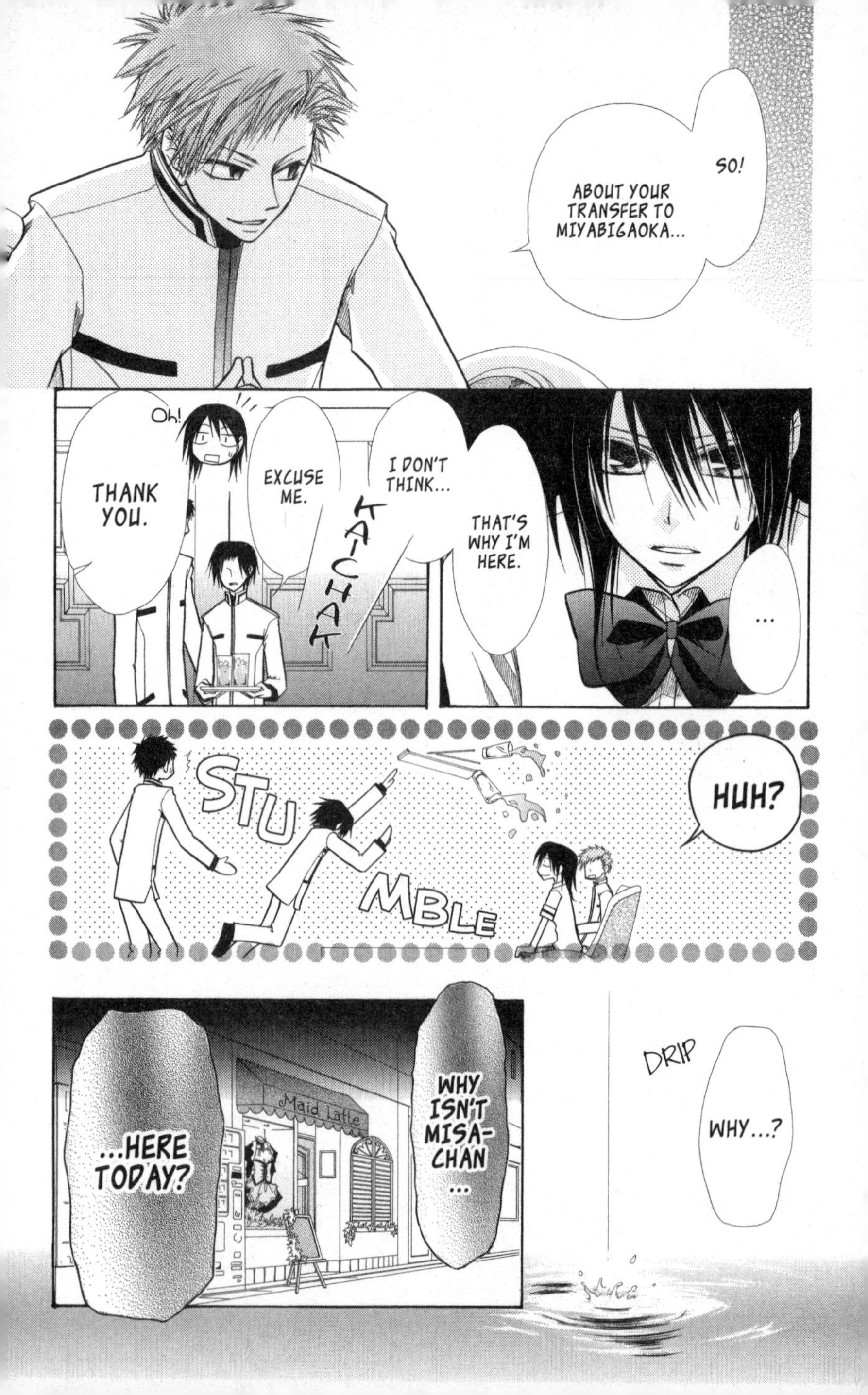
SO! ABOUT YOUR TRANSFER TO MIYABIGAOKA...
...
I DON'T THINK...
THAT'S WHY I'M HERE.
KAICHAK
EXCUSE ME.
Oh!
THANK YOU.
HUH?
STU
MBLE
DRIP
WHY...?
WHY ISN'T MISA-CHAN ...
...HERE TODAY?
Maid Latte

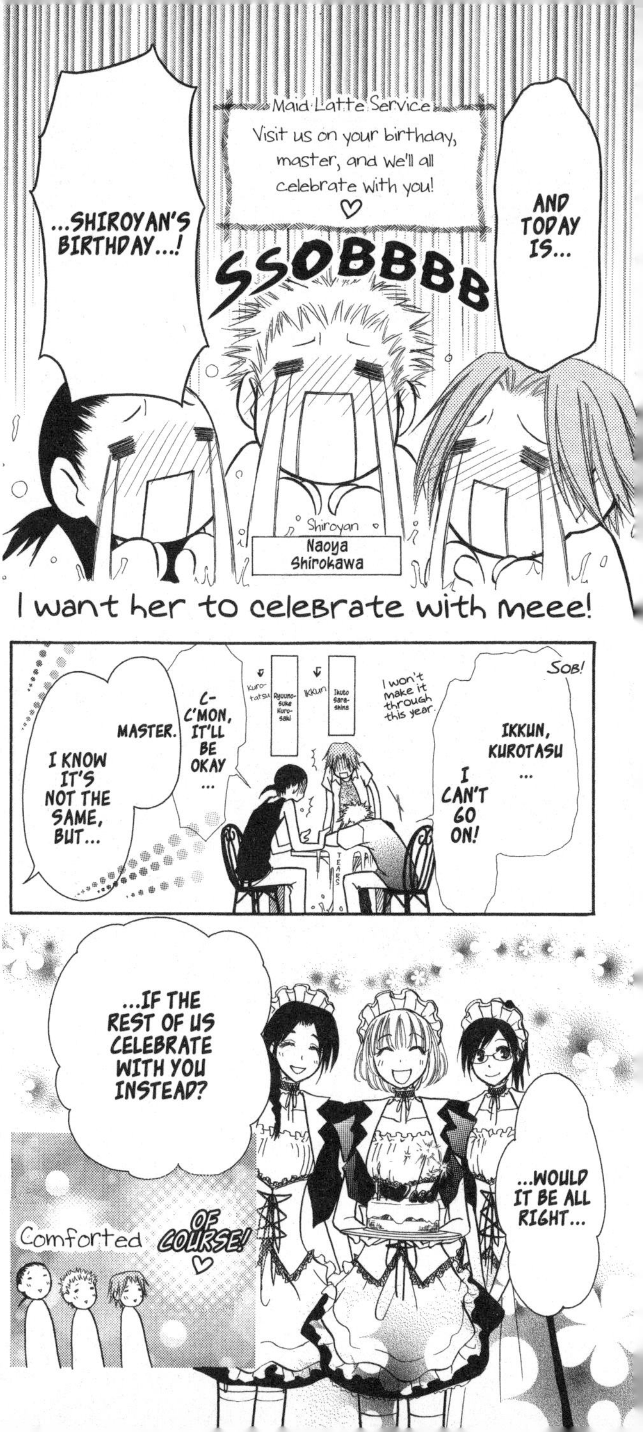
AND TODAY IS...
Maid Latte Service
Visit us on your birthday, master, and we'll all celebrate with you!
...SHIROYAN'S BIRTHDAY...!
SSOBBBB
Shiroyan
Naoya Shirokawa
I want her to celebrate with meee!
SOB!
IKKUN, KUROTASU ...
I CAN'T GO ON!
I won't make it through this year.
Ikuto Sarashina
Ikkun
Ryuunosuke Kurosaki
Kurotatsu
C-C'MON, IT'LL BE OKAY ...
TEARS
MASTER.
I KNOW IT'S NOT THE SAME, BUT...
...IF THE REST OF US CELEBRATE WITH YOU INSTEAD?
...WOULD IT BE ALL RIGHT...
OF COURSE!
Comforted

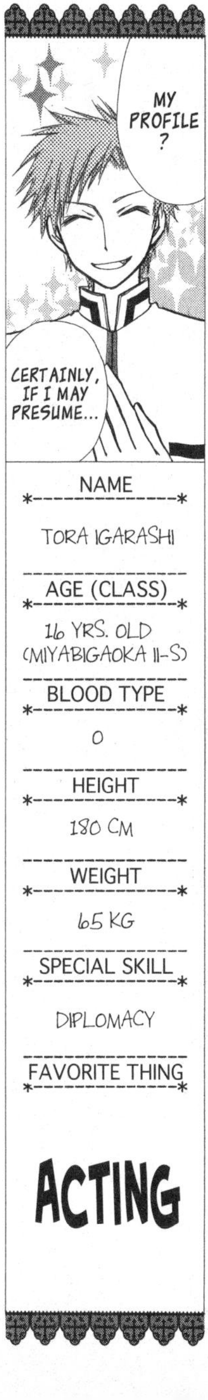
MY PROFILE?
CERTAINLY, IF I MAY PRESUME...

NAME

TORA IGARASHI

AGE (CLASS)

16 YRS. OLD (MIYABIGAOKA II-S)

BLOOD TYPE

O

HEIGHT

180 CM

WEIGHT

65 KG

SPECIAL SKILL

DIPLOMACY

FAVORITE THING

ACTING

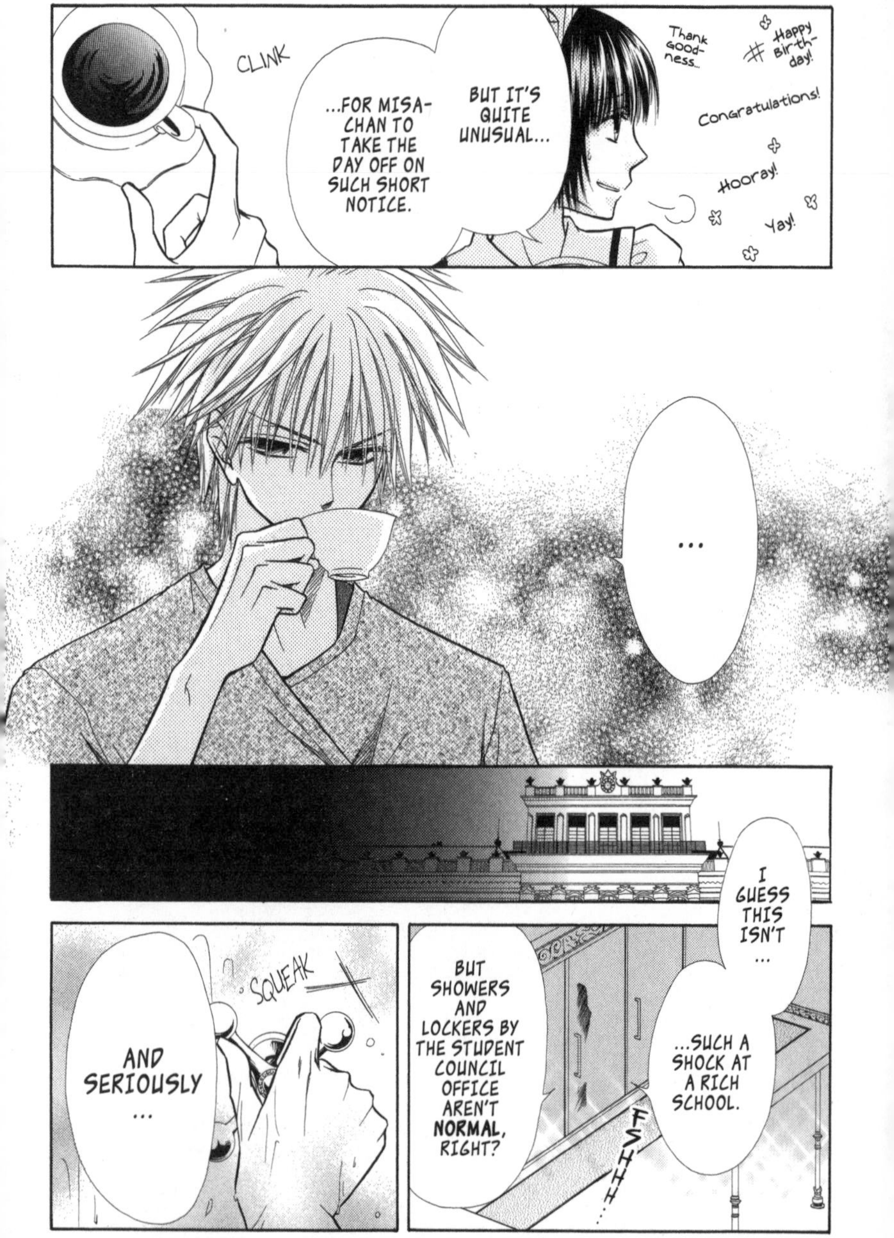
Happy Birth-day!
Thank Good-ness...
Congratulations!
Hooray!
Yay!
BUT IT'S QUITE UNUSUAL...
...FOR MISA-CHAN TO TAKE THE DAY OFF ON SUCH SHORT NOTICE.
CLINK
...
I GUESS THIS ISN'T ...
...SUCH A SHOCK AT A RICH SCHOOL.
FSHHHH...
BUT SHOWERS AND LOCKERS BY THE STUDENT COUNCIL OFFICE AREN'T **NORMAL**, RIGHT?
SQUEAK
AND SERIOUSLY ...

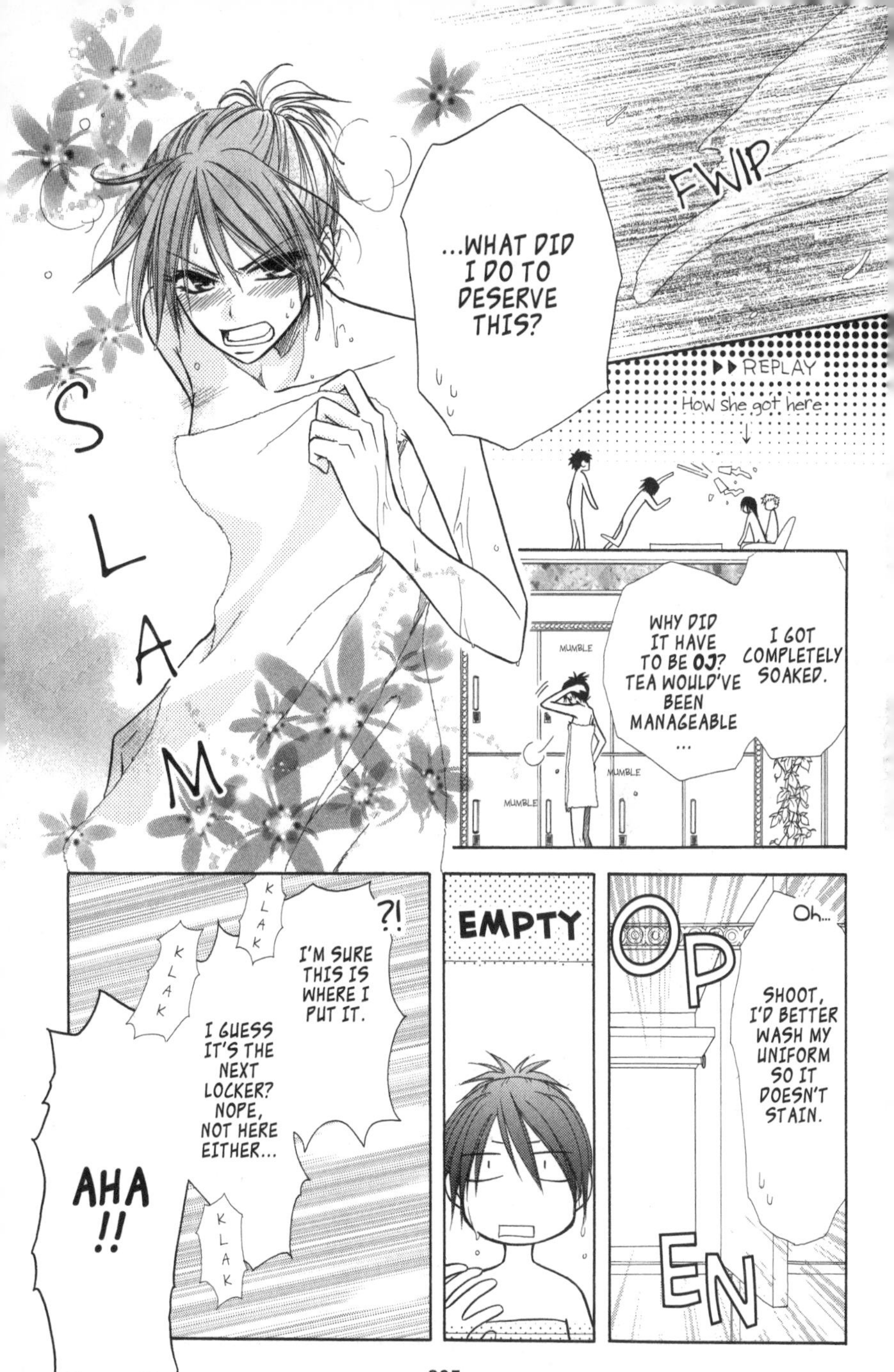
FWIP
▶▶ REPLAY
How she got here
MUMBLE
MUMBLE
MUMBLE
I GOT COMPLETELY SOAKED.
WHY DID IT HAVE TO BE OJ? TEA WOULD'VE BEEN MANAGEABLE ...
...WHAT DID I DO TO DESERVE THIS?
SLAM
Oh...
SHOOT, I'D BETTER WASH MY UNIFORM SO IT DOESN'T STAIN.
OPEN
EMPTY
?!
I'M SURE THIS IS WHERE I PUT IT.
KLAK
KLAK
I GUESS IT'S THE NEXT LOCKER? NOPE, NOT HERE EITHER...
KLAK
AHA !!

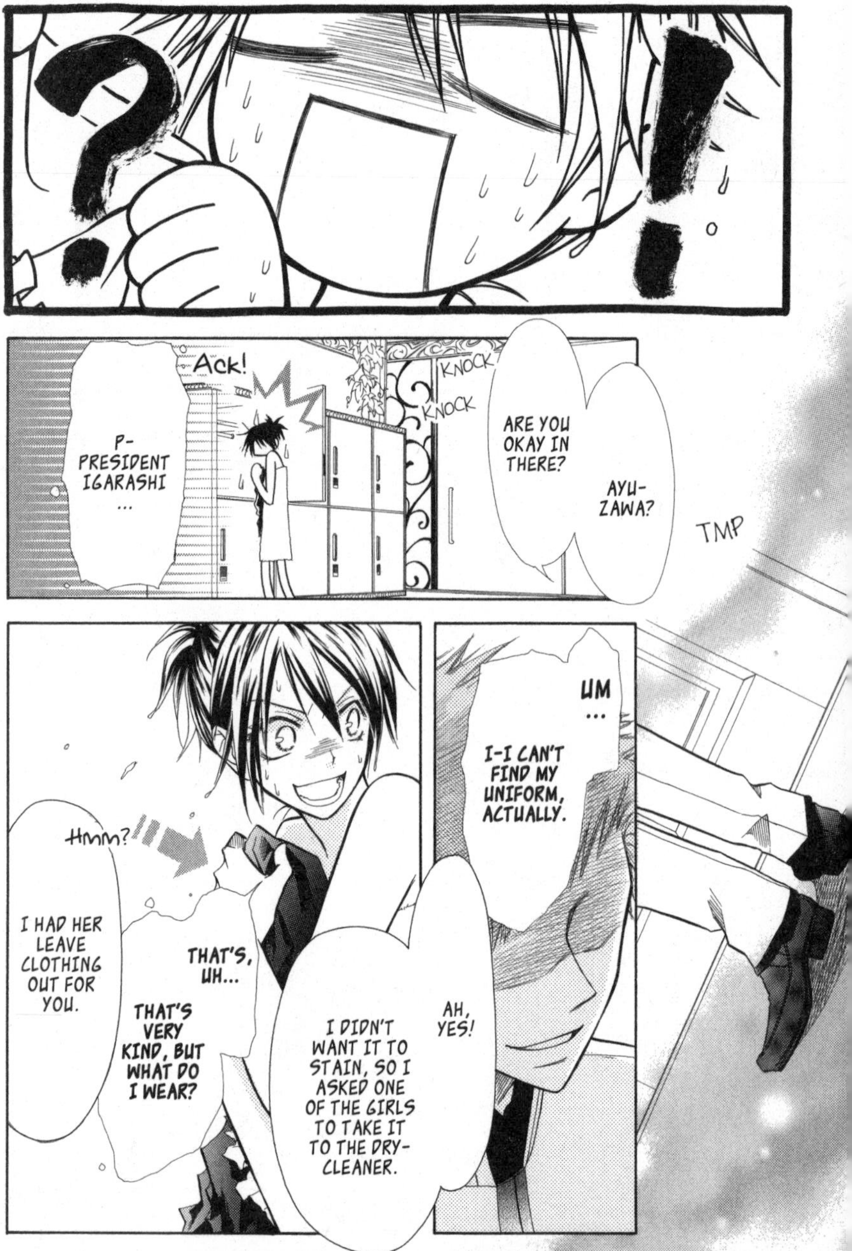
KNOCK
KNOCK
ARE YOU OKAY IN THERE?
AYU-ZAWA?
ACK!
P-PRESIDENT IGARASHI ...
TMP
UM ...
I-I CAN'T FIND MY UNIFORM, ACTUALLY.
AH, YES!
I DIDN'T WANT IT TO STAIN, SO I ASKED ONE OF THE GIRLS TO TAKE IT TO THE DRY-CLEANER.
THAT'S, UH...
THAT'S VERY KIND, BUT WHAT DO I WEAR?
HMM?
I HAD HER LEAVE CLOTHING OUT FOR YOU.

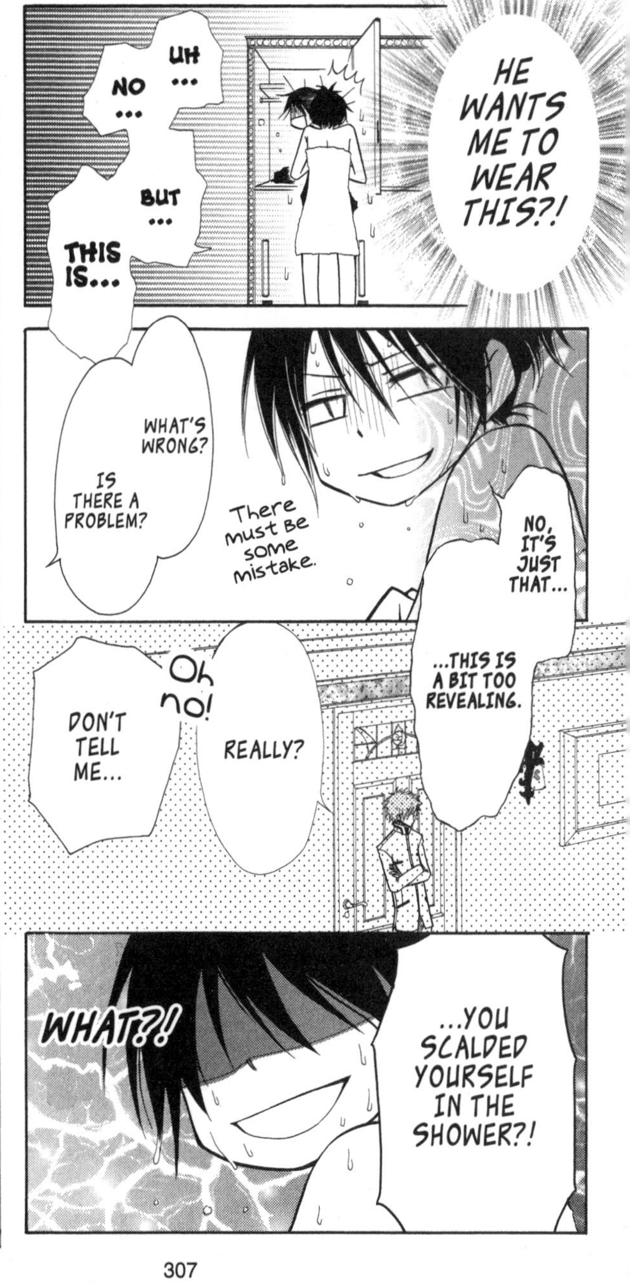
HE WANTS ME TO WEAR THIS?!
UH...
NO...
BUT...
THIS IS...
WHAT'S WRONG?
IS THERE A PROBLEM?
There must be some mistake.
NO, IT'S JUST THAT...
...THIS IS A BIT TOO REVEALING.
REALLY?
Oh no!
DON'T TELL ME...
...YOU SCALDED YOURSELF IN THE SHOWER?!
WHAT?!

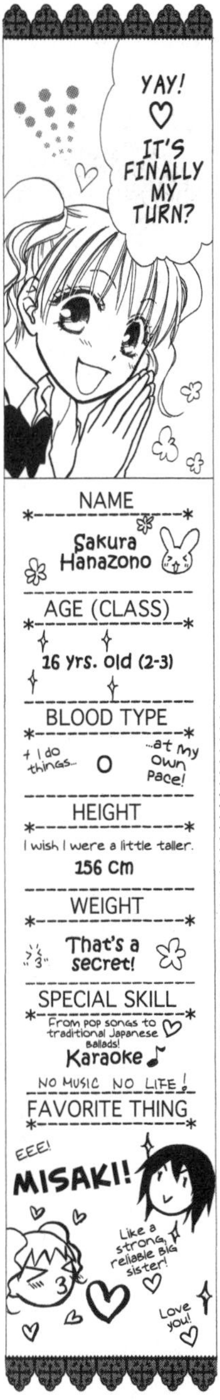
YAY! ♡ IT'S FINALLY MY TURN?
NAME
Sakura Hanazono
AGE (CLASS)
16 yrs. old (2-3)
BLOOD TYPE
I do things... O ...at my own pace!
HEIGHT
I wish I were a little taller.
156 cm
WEIGHT
That's a secret!
SPECIAL SKILL
From pop songs to traditional Japanese ballads!
Karaoke
NO MUSIC NO LIFE!
FAVORITE THING
EEE!
MISAKI!
Like a strong, reliable big sister!
Love you!

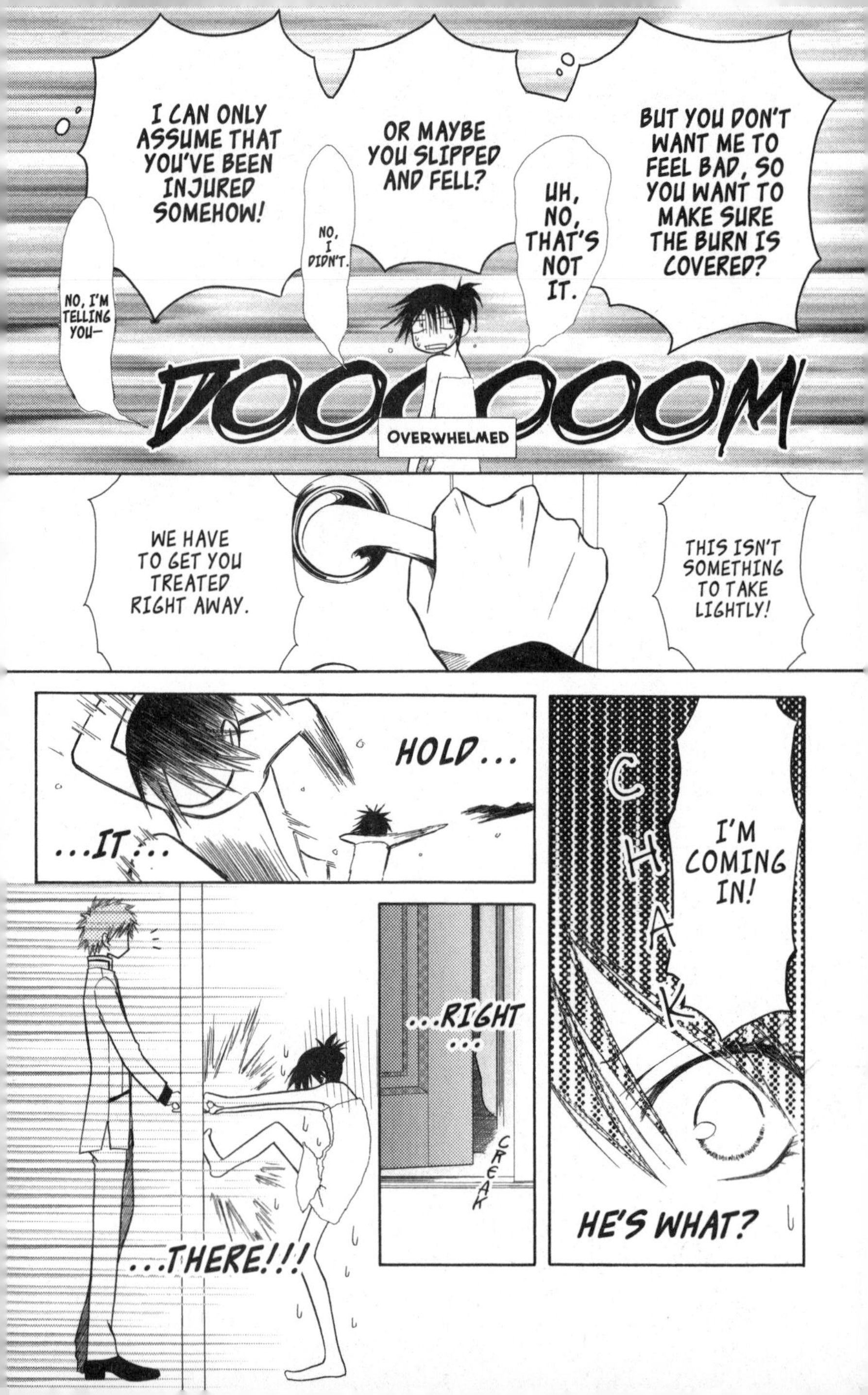
BUT YOU DON'T WANT ME TO FEEL BAD, SO YOU WANT TO MAKE SURE THE BURN IS COVERED?
UH, NO, THAT'S NOT IT.
OR MAYBE YOU SLIPPED AND FELL?
NO, I DIDN'T.
I CAN ONLY ASSUME THAT YOU'VE BEEN INJURED SOMEHOW!
NO, I'M TELLING YOU—
DOOOOOOOM
OVERWHELMED
THIS ISN'T SOMETHING TO TAKE LIGHTLY!
WE HAVE TO GET YOU TREATED RIGHT AWAY.
CHAK
I'M COMING IN!
HE'S WHAT?
HOLD...
...IT...
...RIGHT...
CREAK
...THERE!!!

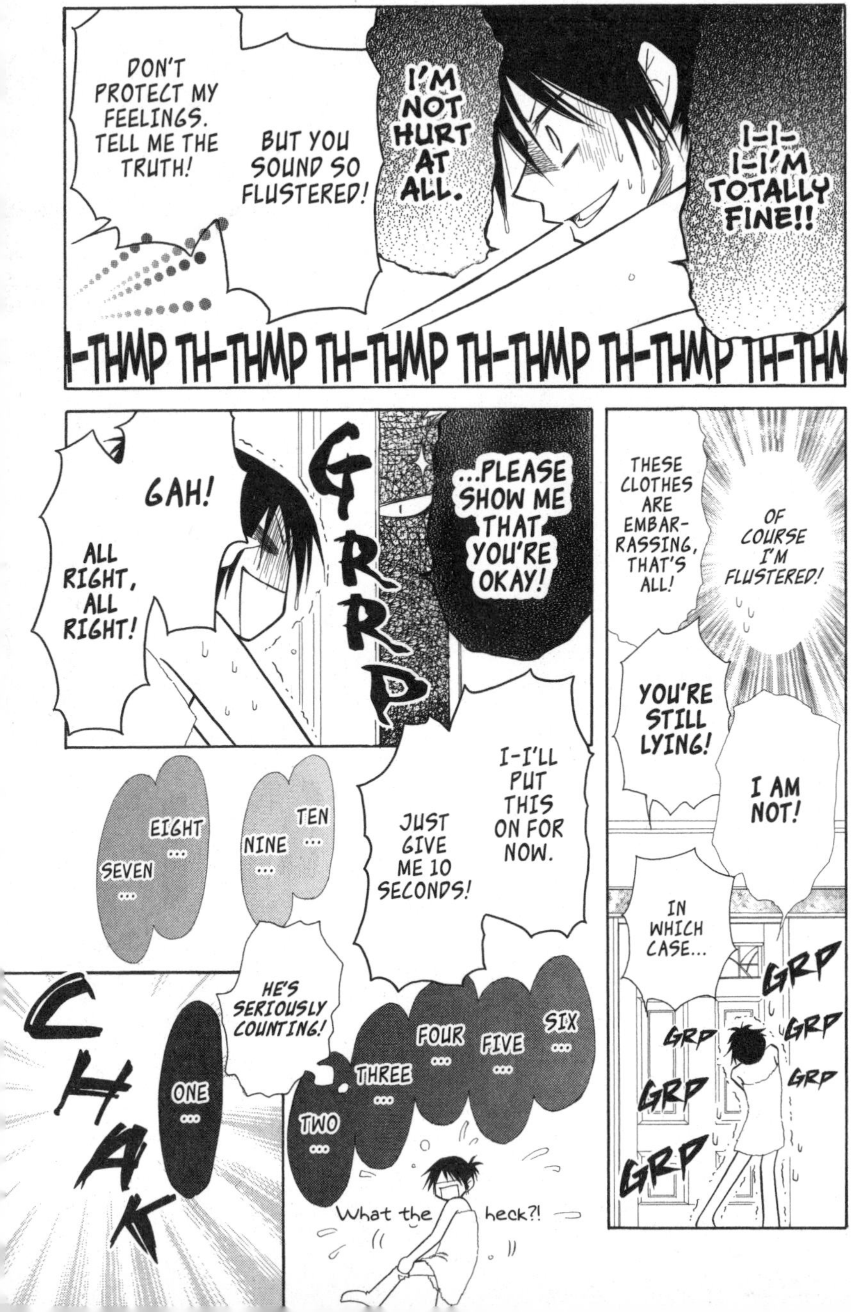
I-I-I-I'M TOTALLY FINE!!
I'M NOT HURT AT ALL.
BUT YOU SOUND SO FLUSTERED!
DON'T PROTECT MY FEELINGS. TELL ME THE TRUTH!
TH-THMP TH-THMP TH-THMP TH-THMP TH-THMP TH-THM
OF COURSE I'M FLUSTERED!
THESE CLOTHES ARE EMBARRASSING, THAT'S ALL!
YOU'RE STILL LYING!
I AM NOT!
IN WHICH CASE...
GRP
GRP
GRP
GRP
GRP
GRP
...PLEASE SHOW ME THAT YOU'RE OKAY!
GRRP
GAH!
ALL RIGHT, ALL RIGHT!
I-I'LL PUT THIS ON FOR NOW.
JUST GIVE ME 10 SECONDS!
TEN ...
NINE ...
EIGHT ...
SEVEN ...
SIX ...
FIVE ...
FOUR ...
THREE ...
HE'S SERIOUSLY COUNTING!
TWO ...
What the heck?!
ONE ...
CHAK

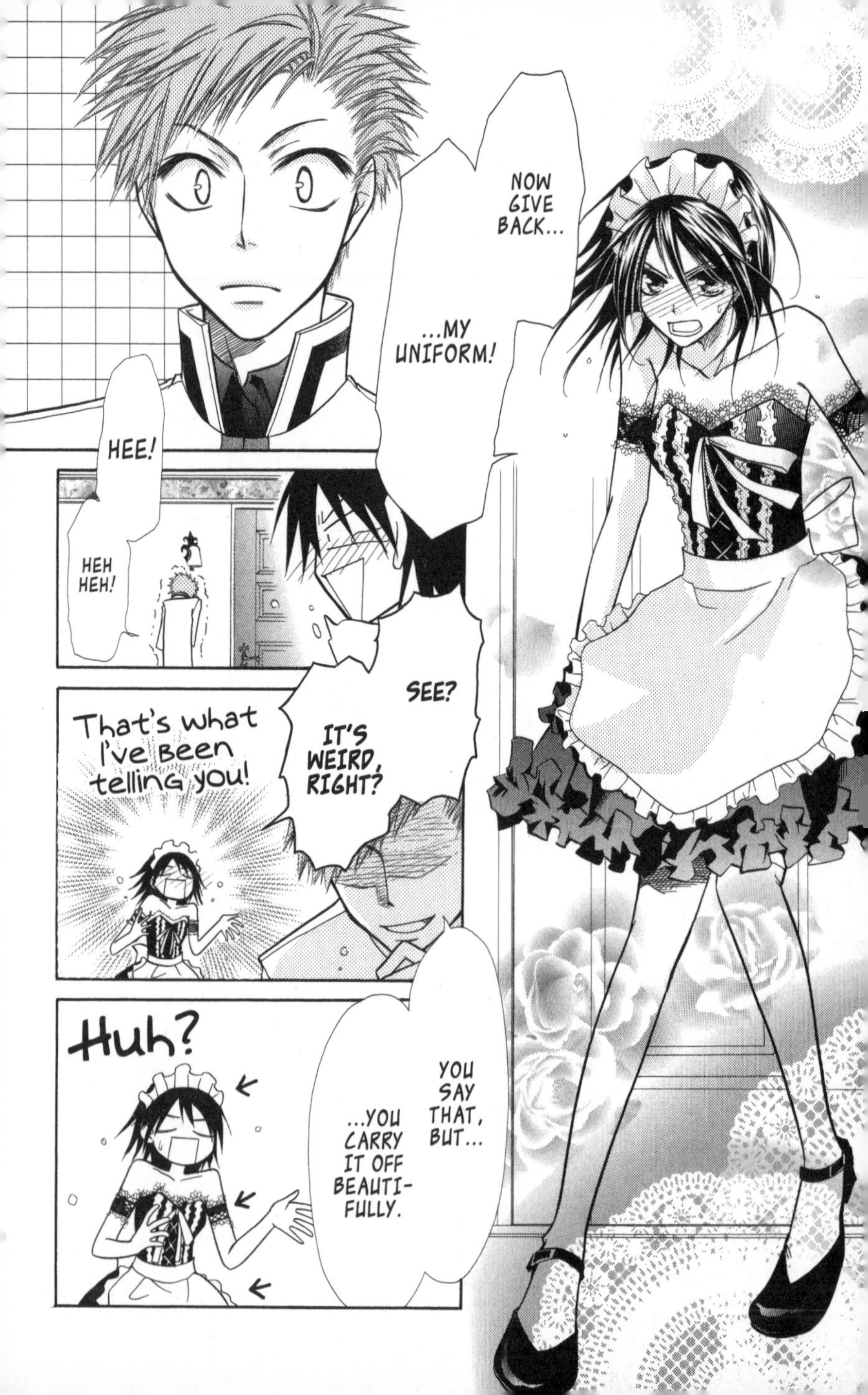
NOW GIVE BACK...
...MY UNIFORM!
HEE!
HEH HEH!
SEE?
IT'S WEIRD, RIGHT?
That's what I've been telling you!
YOU SAY THAT, BUT...
...YOU CARRY IT OFF BEAUTI-FULLY.
Huh?

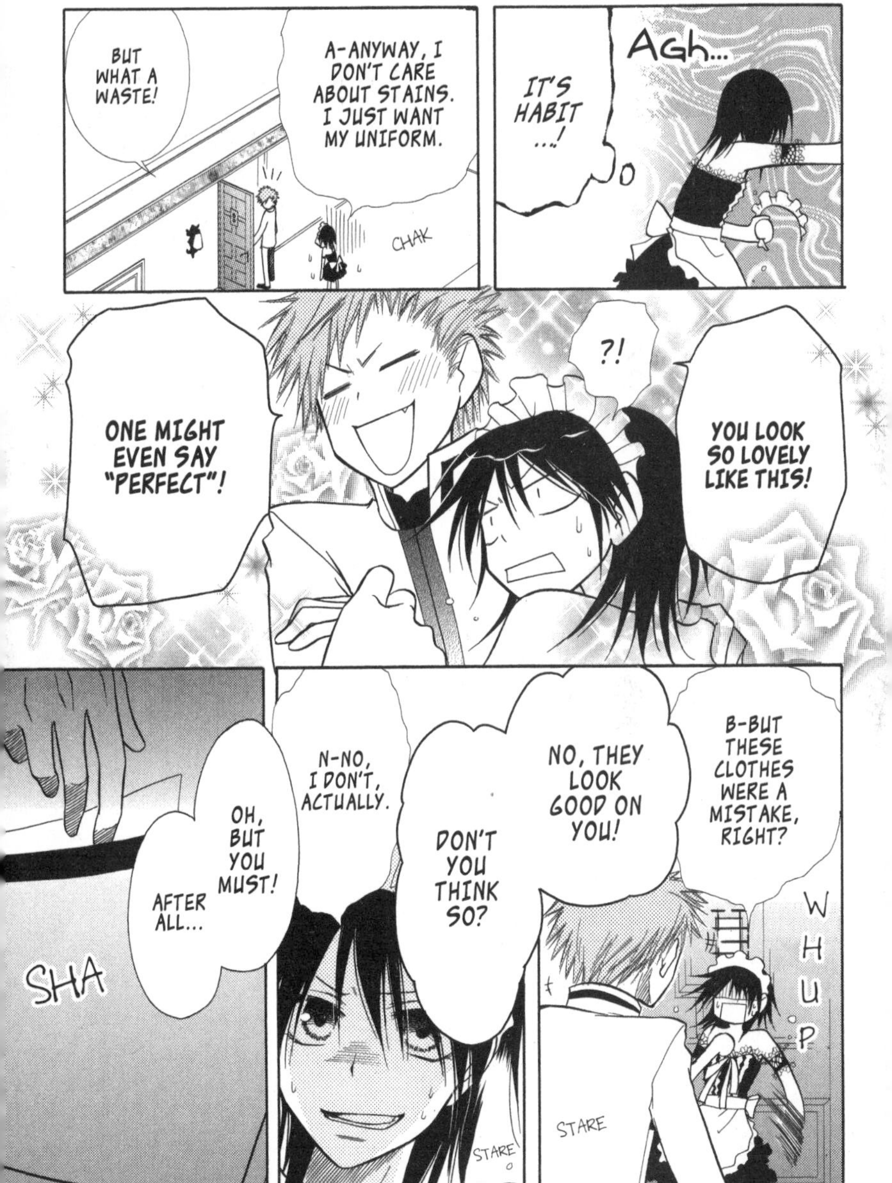
Agh...
IT'S HABIT ...!
A-ANYWAY, I DON'T CARE ABOUT STAINS. I JUST WANT MY UNIFORM.
BUT WHAT A WASTE!
CHAK
YOU LOOK SO LOVELY LIKE THIS!
?!
ONE MIGHT EVEN SAY "PERFECT"!
B-BUT THESE CLOTHES WERE A MISTAKE, RIGHT?
WHUP
STARE
NO, THEY LOOK GOOD ON YOU!
DON'T YOU THINK SO?
N-NO, I DON'T, ACTUALLY.
STARE
OH, BUT YOU MUST!
AFTER ALL...
SHA

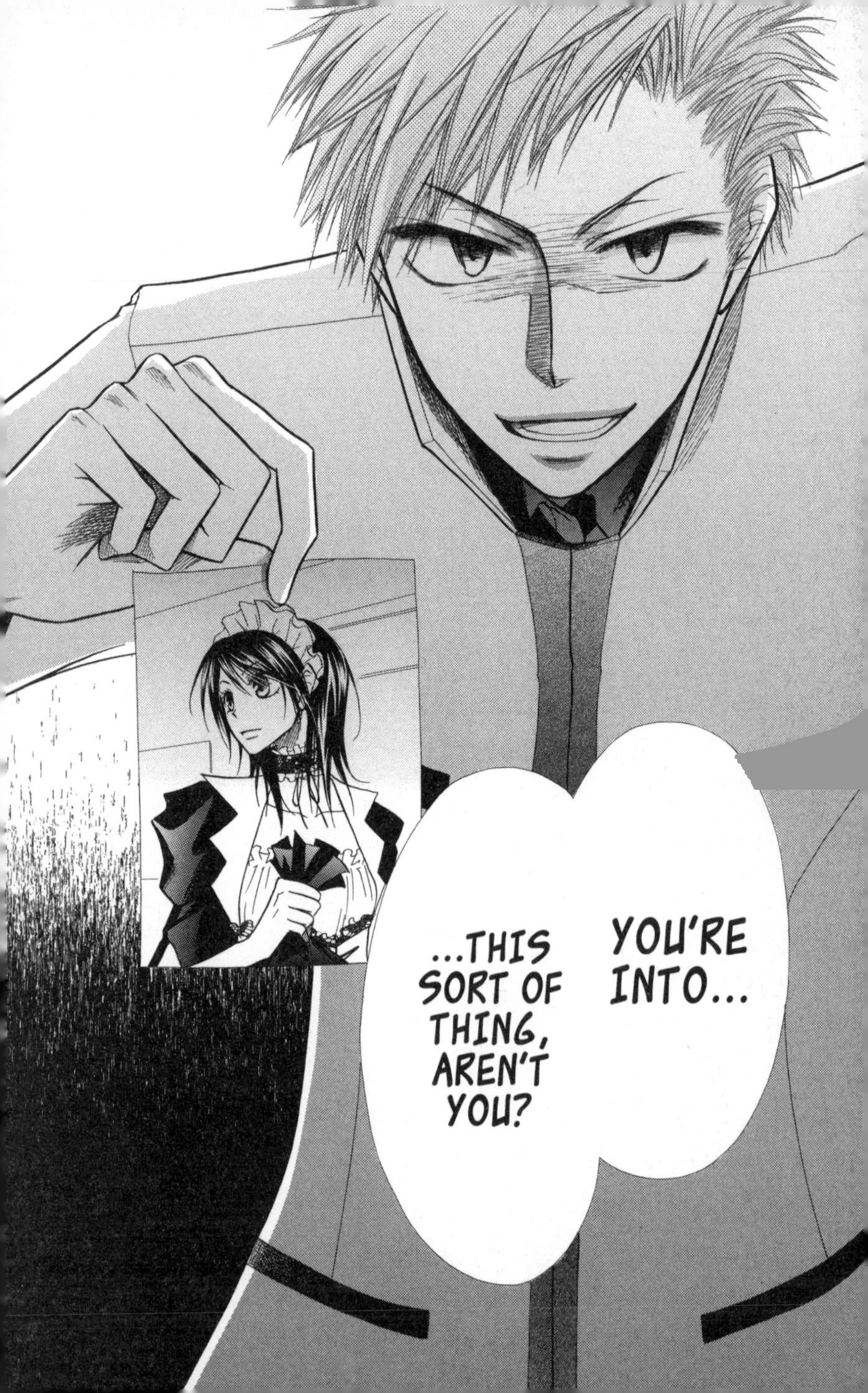
YOU'RE INTO...
...THIS SORT OF THING, AREN'T YOU?

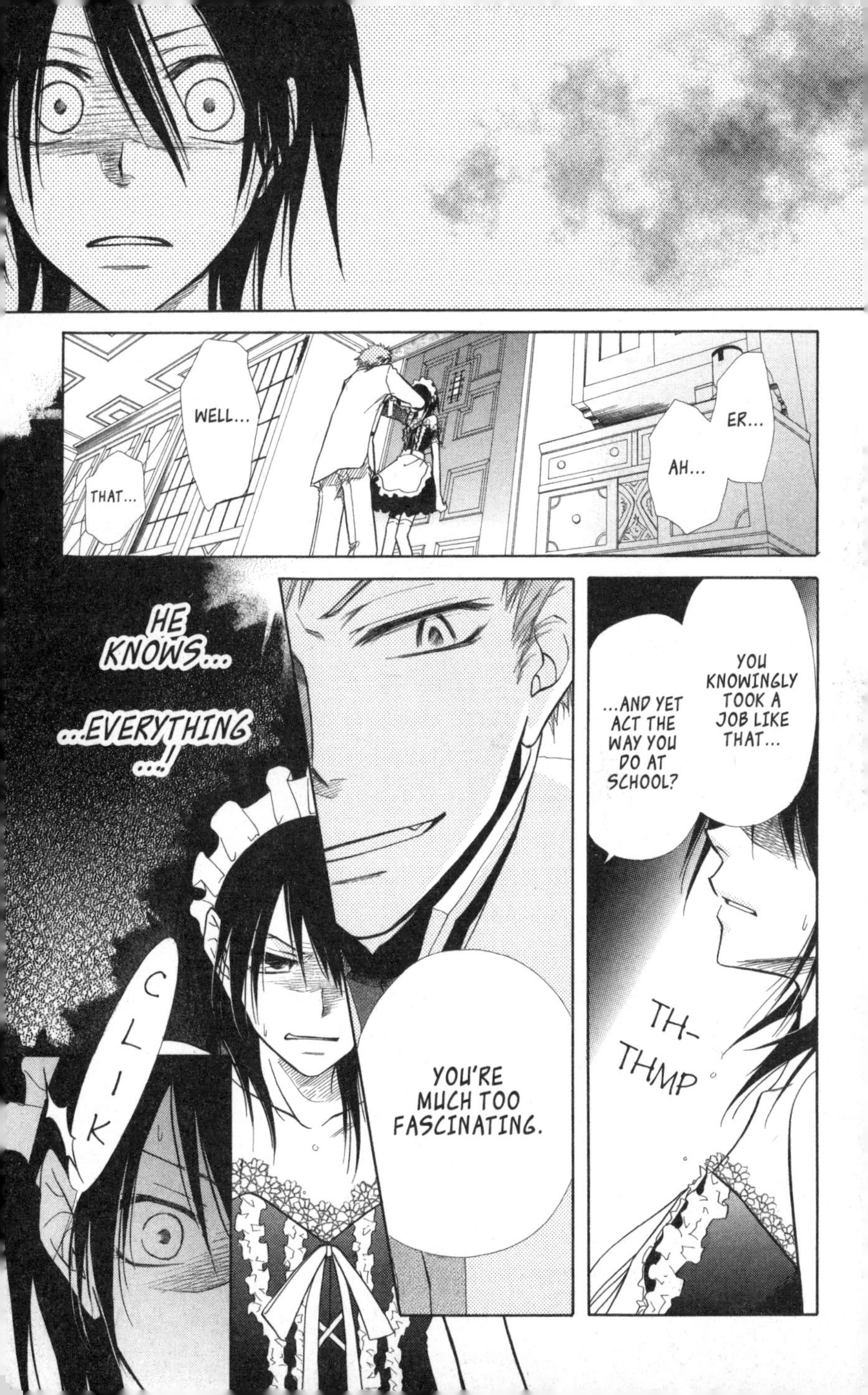
ER...
AH...
WELL...
THAT...
YOU KNOWINGLY TOOK A JOB LIKE THAT...
...AND YET ACT THE WAY YOU DO AT SCHOOL?
TH-THMP
YOU'RE MUCH TOO FASCINATING.
HE KNOWS...
...EVERYTHING...!
CLIK

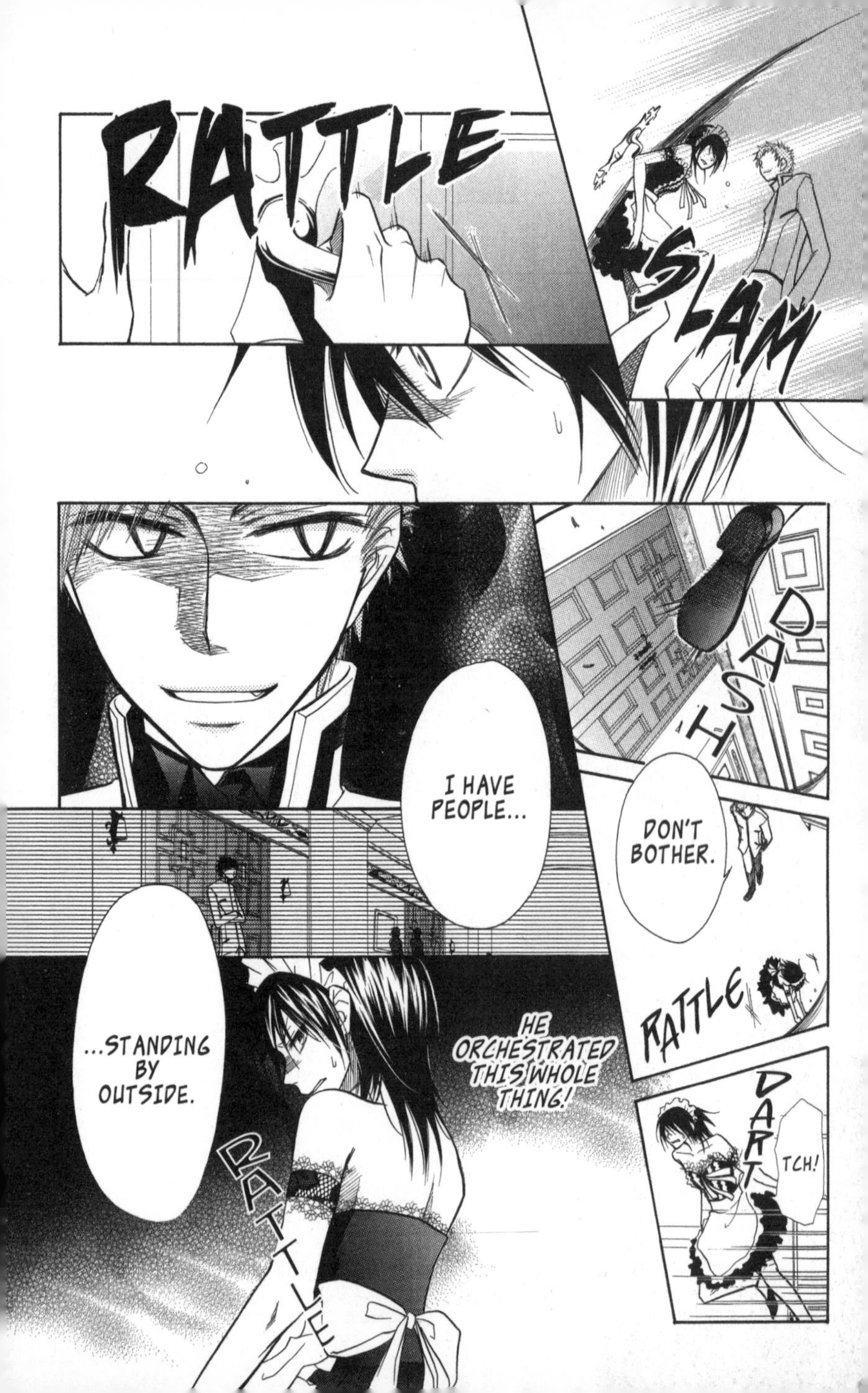
SLAM
RATTLE
DASH
DON'T BOTHER.
RATTLE
DART
TCH!
I HAVE PEOPLE...
...STANDING BY OUTSIDE.
HE ORCHESTRATED THIS WHOLE THING!
RATTLE

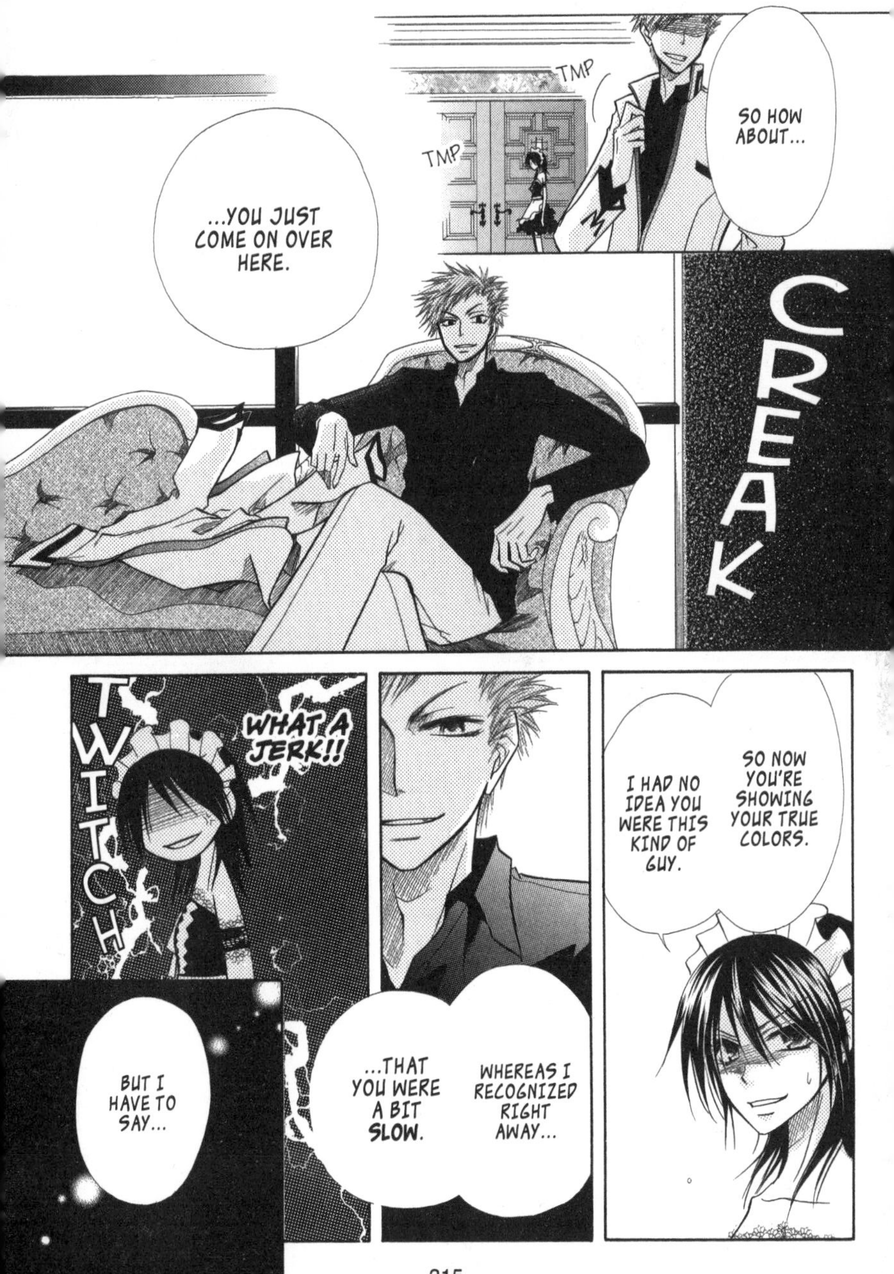
SO HOW ABOUT...
TMP
TMP
...YOU JUST COME ON OVER HERE.
CREAK
SO NOW YOU'RE SHOWING YOUR TRUE COLORS.
I HAD NO IDEA YOU WERE THIS KIND OF GUY.
WHEREAS I RECOGNIZED RIGHT AWAY...
...THAT YOU WERE A BIT **SLOW**.
TWITCH
WHAT A JERK!!
BUT I HAVE TO SAY...

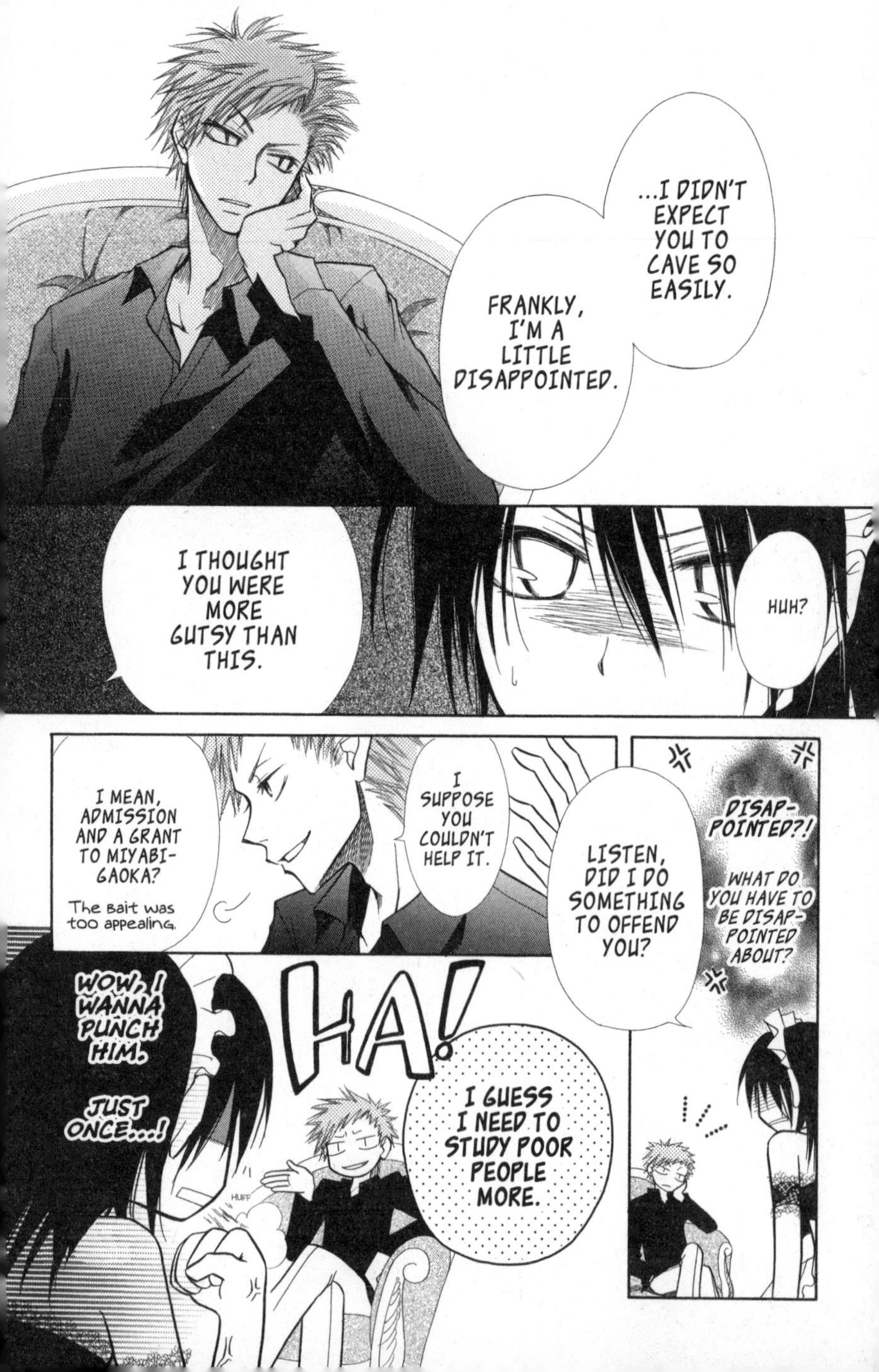
...I DIDN'T EXPECT YOU TO CAVE SO EASILY.
FRANKLY, I'M A LITTLE DISAPPOINTED.
HUH?
I THOUGHT YOU WERE MORE GUTSY THAN THIS.
DISAP-POINTED?!
WHAT DO YOU HAVE TO BE DISAP-POINTED ABOUT?
LISTEN, DID I DO SOMETHING TO OFFEND YOU?
I SUPPOSE YOU COULDN'T HELP IT.
I MEAN, ADMISSION AND A GRANT TO MIYABI-GAOKA?
The bait was too appealing.
HA!
I GUESS I NEED TO STUDY POOR PEOPLE MORE.
HUFF
WOW, I WANNA PUNCH HIM.
JUST ONCE...!

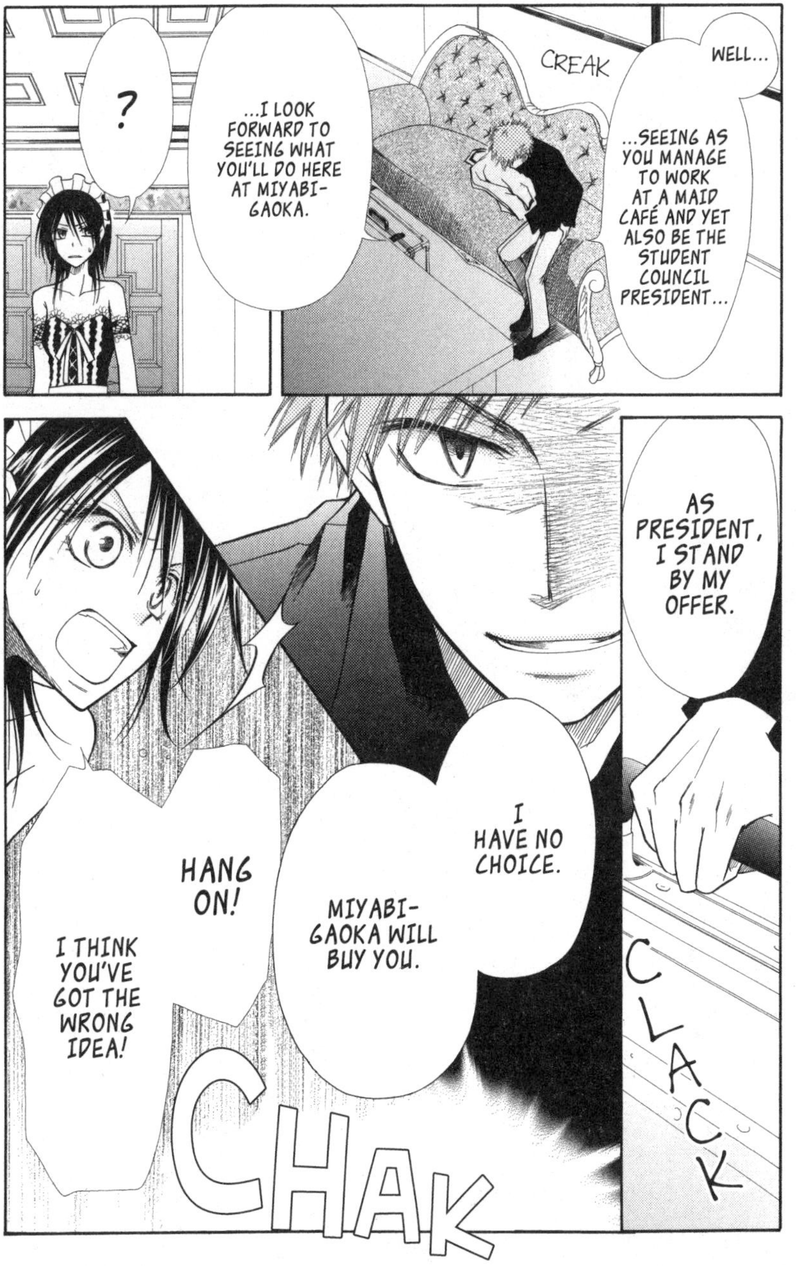
WELL...
...SEEING AS YOU MANAGE TO WORK AT A MAID CAFÉ AND YET ALSO BE THE STUDENT COUNCIL PRESIDENT...
CREAK
...I LOOK FORWARD TO SEEING WHAT YOU'LL DO HERE AT MIYABI-GAOKA.
?
AS PRESIDENT, I STAND BY MY OFFER.
CLACK
I HAVE NO CHOICE.
MIYABI-GAOKA WILL BUY YOU.
HANG ON!
I THINK YOU'VE GOT THE WRONG IDEA!
CHAK

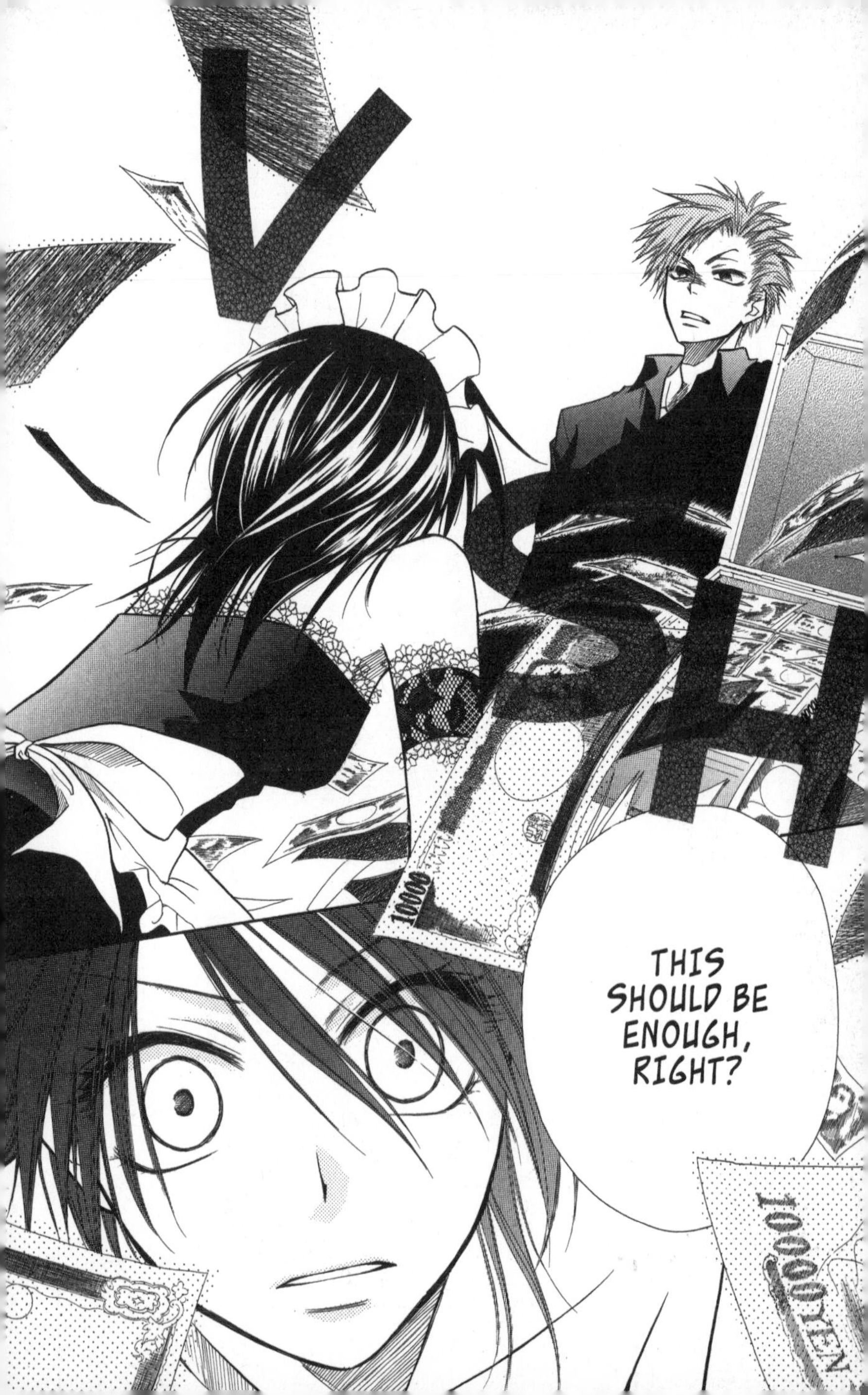
THIS SHOULD BE ENOUGH, RIGHT?
10000YEN

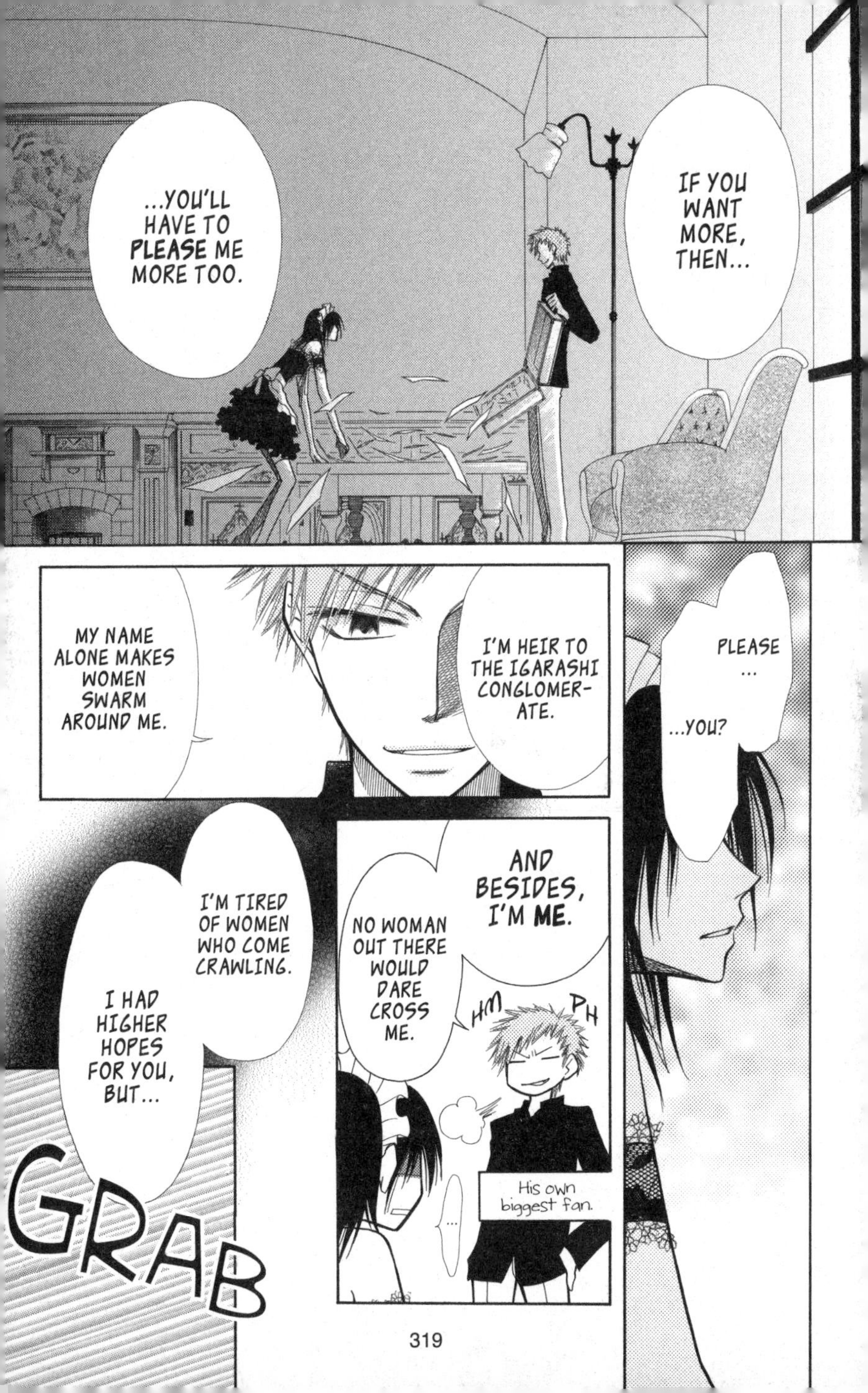
IF YOU WANT MORE, THEN...
...YOU'LL HAVE TO **PLEASE** ME MORE TOO.
PLEASE ...
...YOU?
I'M HEIR TO THE IGARASHI CONGLOMER-ATE.
MY NAME ALONE MAKES WOMEN SWARM AROUND ME.
AND BESIDES, I'M **ME**.
NO WOMAN OUT THERE WOULD DARE CROSS ME.
HMPH
His own biggest fan.
...
I'M TIRED OF WOMEN WHO COME CRAWLING.
I HAD HIGHER HOPES FOR YOU, BUT...
GRAB

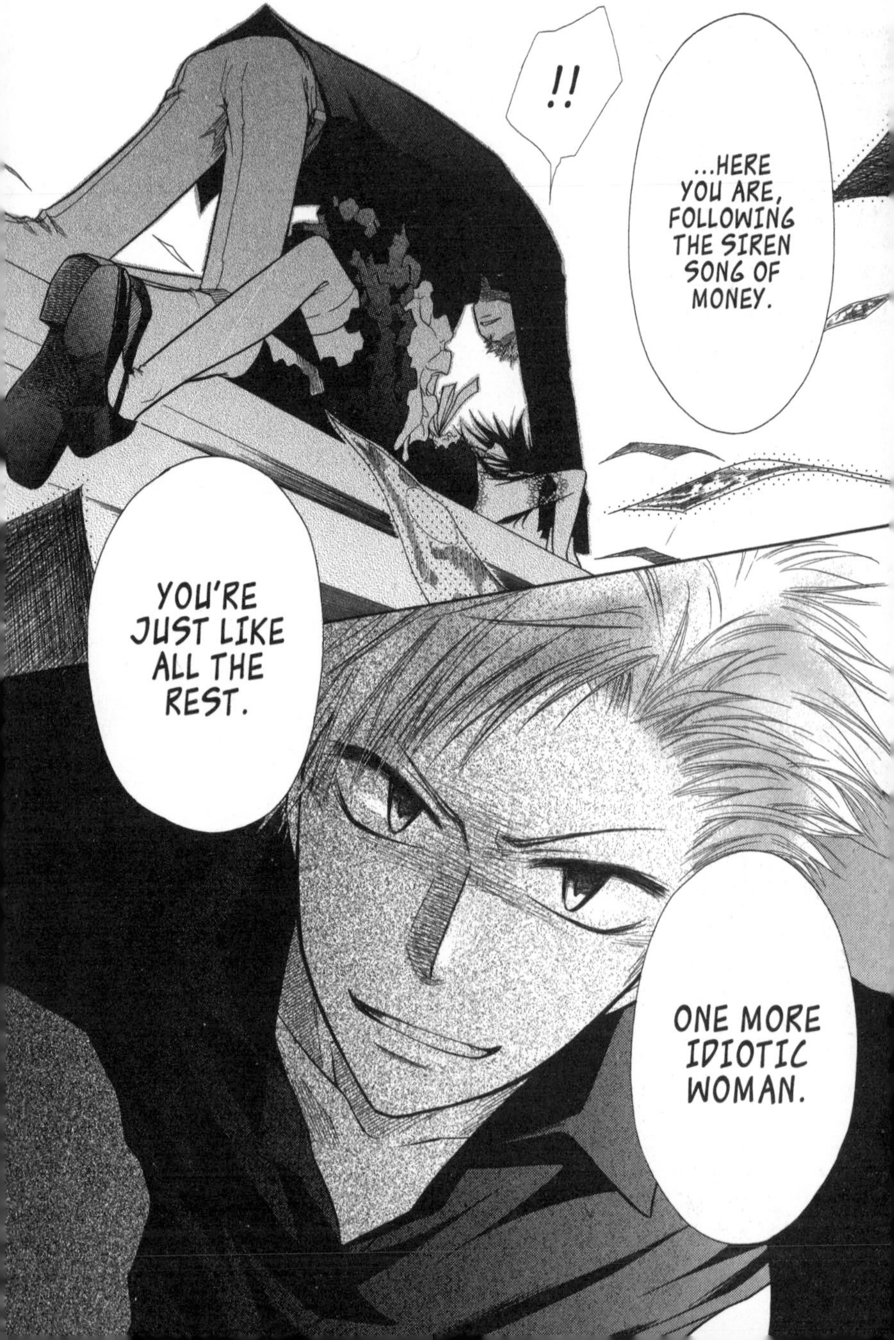
...HERE YOU ARE, FOLLOWING THE SIREN SONG OF MONEY.
!!
YOU'RE JUST LIKE ALL THE REST.
ONE MORE IDIOTIC WOMAN.

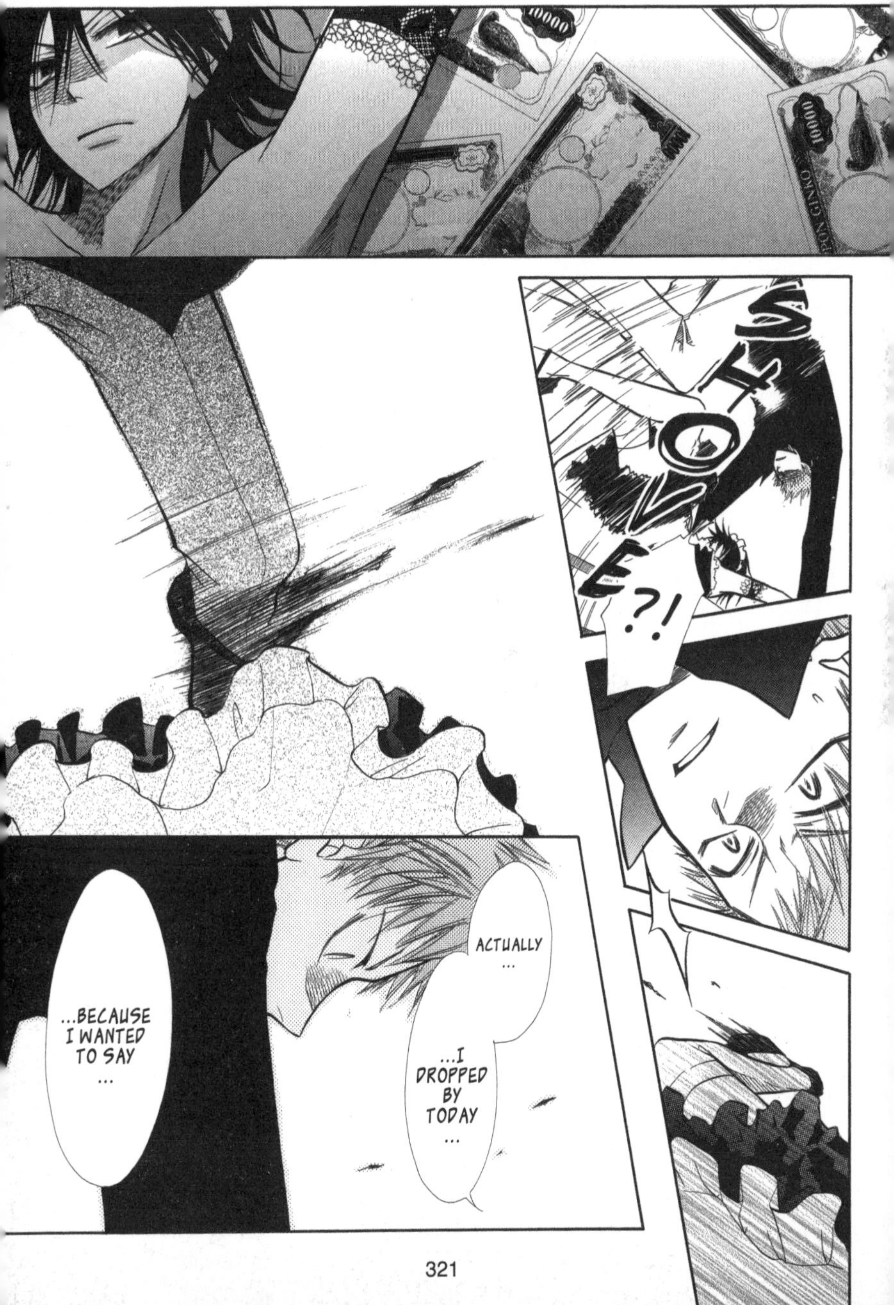
SHOVE ?!
ACTUALLY ...
...I DROPPED BY TODAY ...
...BECAUSE I WANTED TO SAY ...

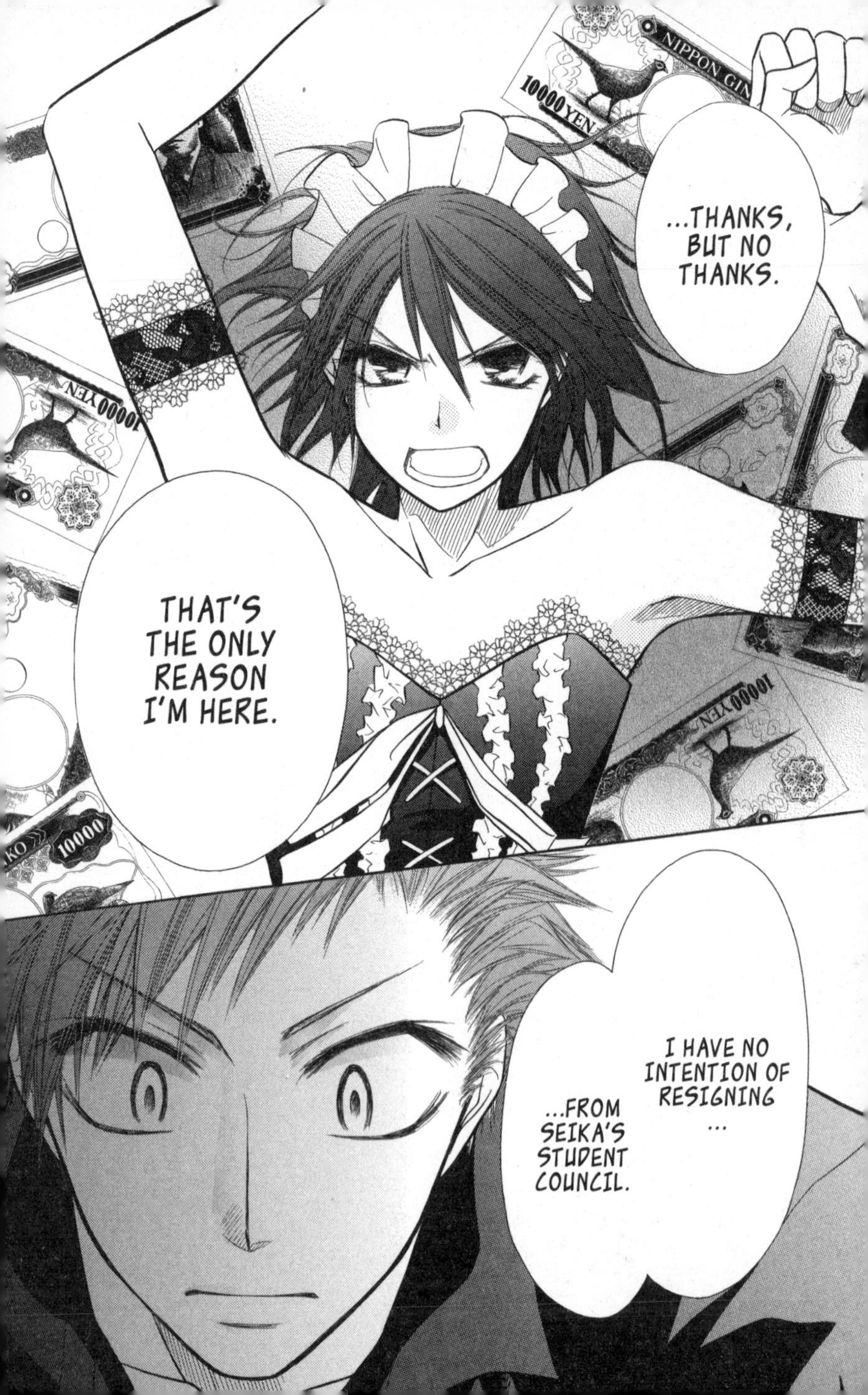
...THANKS, BUT NO THANKS.
THAT'S THE ONLY REASON I'M HERE.
I HAVE NO INTENTION OF RESIGNING ...
...FROM SEIKA'S STUDENT COUNCIL.
NIPPON GIN
10000 YEN
10000 YEN
10000 YEN
10000

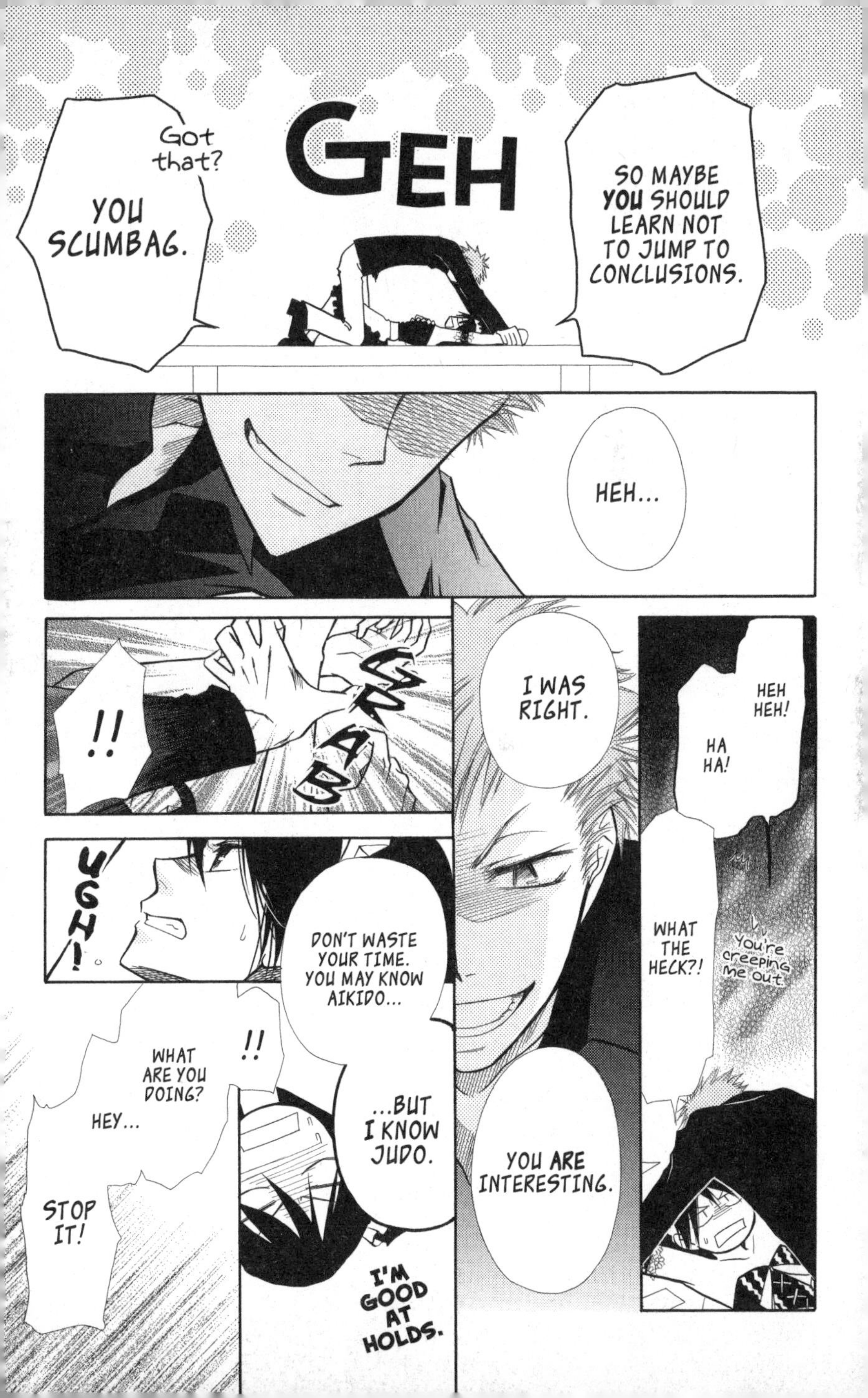
SO MAYBE YOU SHOULD LEARN NOT TO JUMP TO CONCLUSIONS.
GEH
Got that?
YOU SCUMBAG.
HEH...
HEH HEH!
HA HA!
WHAT THE HECK?!
You're creeping me out.
I WAS RIGHT.
YOU ARE INTERESTING.
GRAB
!!
UGH!
DON'T WASTE YOUR TIME. YOU MAY KNOW AIKIDO...
...BUT I KNOW JUDO.
I'M GOOD AT HOLDS.
!!
WHAT ARE YOU DOING?
HEY...
STOP IT!

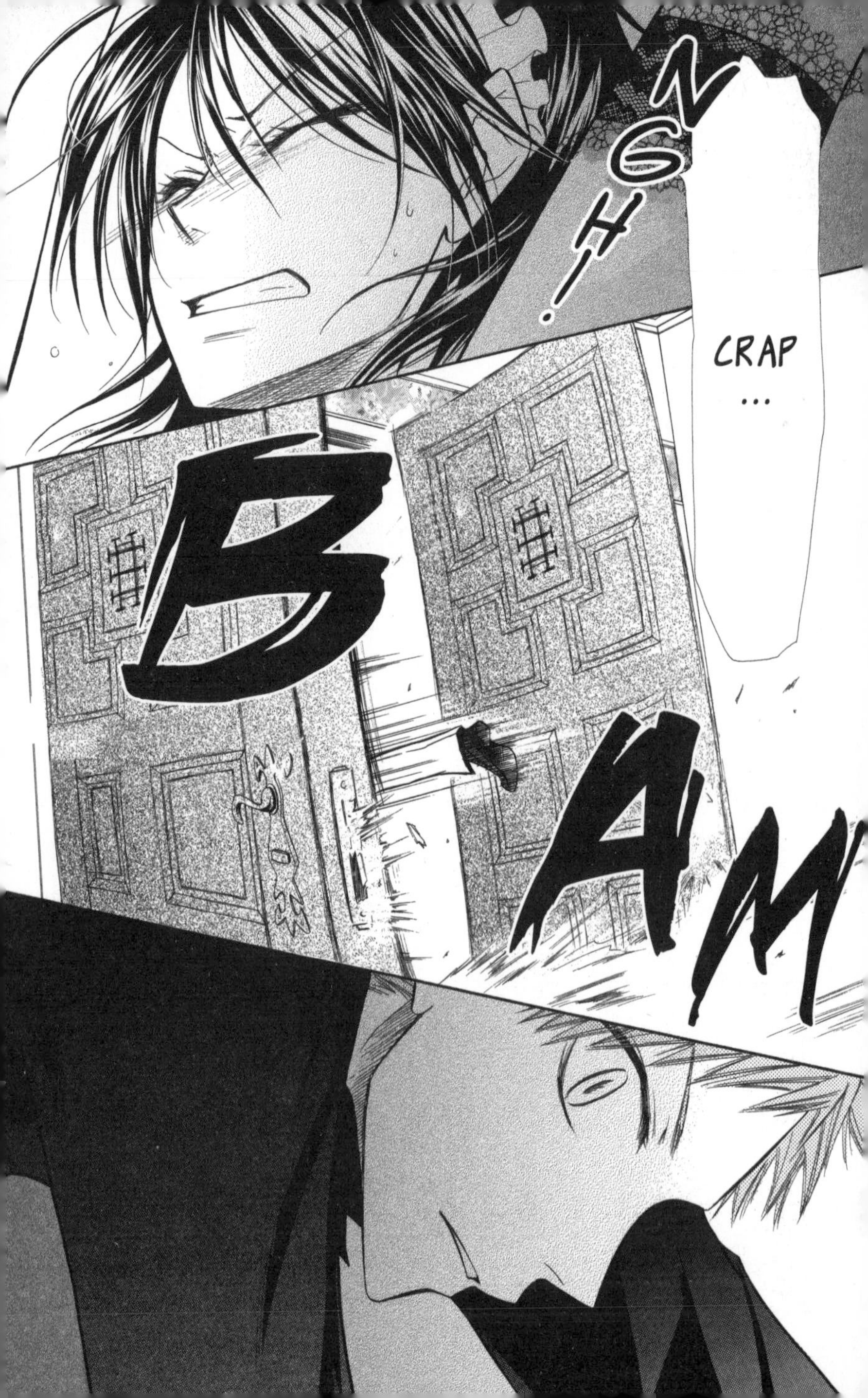
NNGH!
CRAP ...
BAM

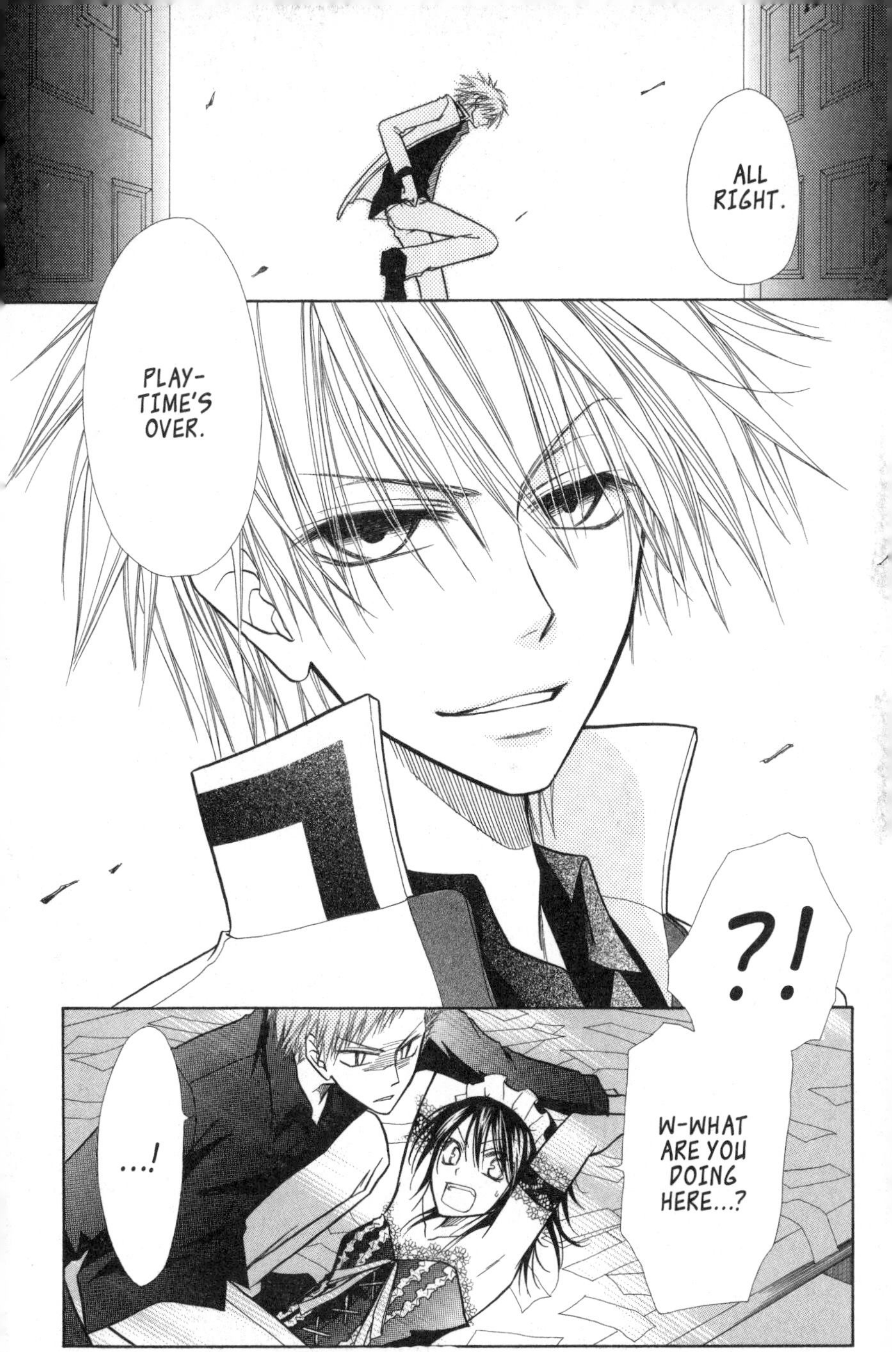
ALL RIGHT.
PLAY-TIME'S OVER.
?!
W-WHAT ARE YOU DOING HERE...?
...!

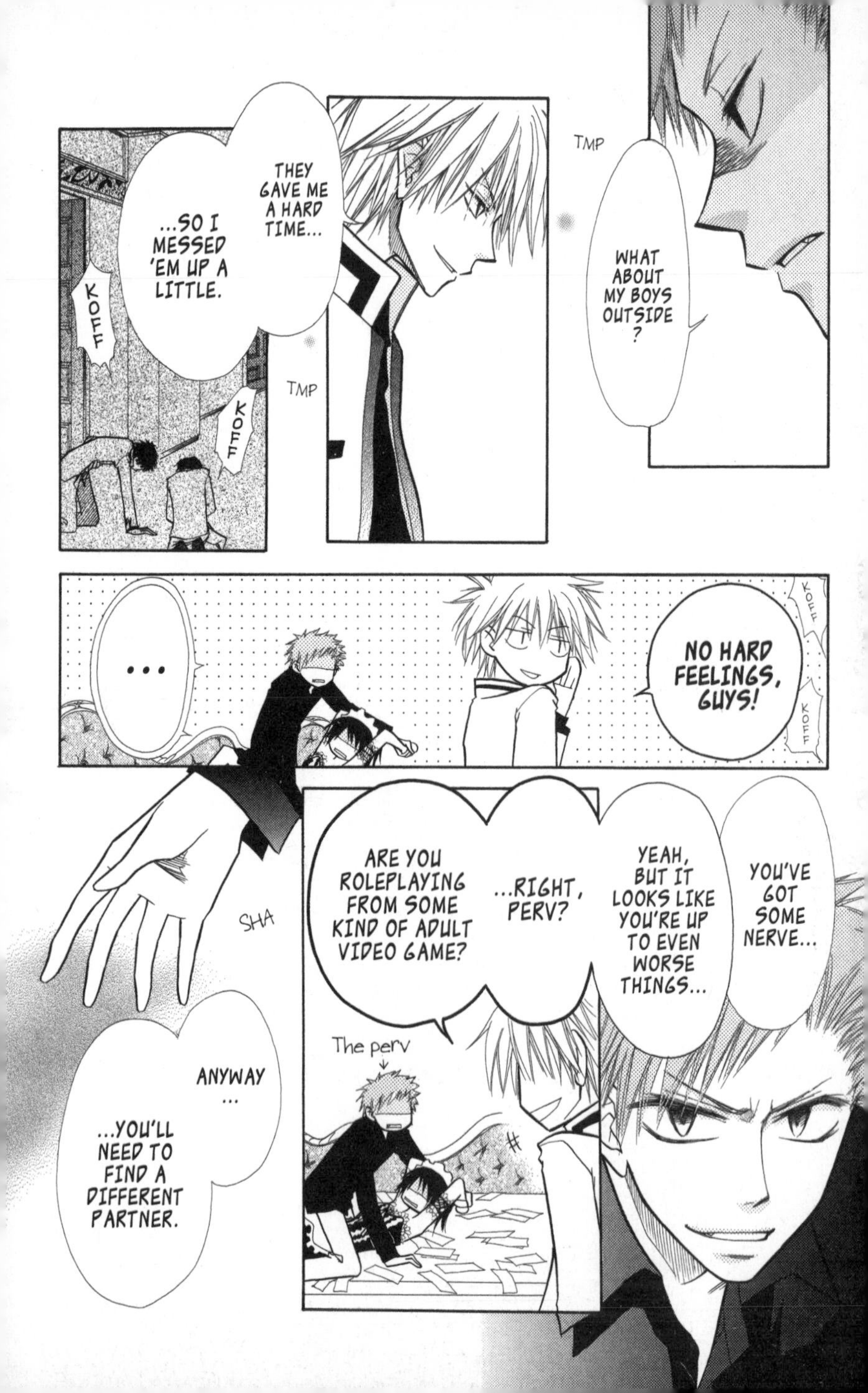
TMP
WHAT ABOUT MY BOYS OUTSIDE?
THEY GAVE ME A HARD TIME...
TMP
...SO I MESSED 'EM UP A LITTLE.
KOFF
KOFF
KOFF
KOFF
NO HARD FEELINGS, GUYS!
...
YOU'VE GOT SOME NERVE...
YEAH, BUT IT LOOKS LIKE YOU'RE UP TO EVEN WORSE THINGS...
...RIGHT, PERV?
ARE YOU ROLEPLAYING FROM SOME KIND OF ADULT VIDEO GAME?
The perv
SHA
ANYWAY...
...YOU'LL NEED TO FIND A DIFFERENT PARTNER.

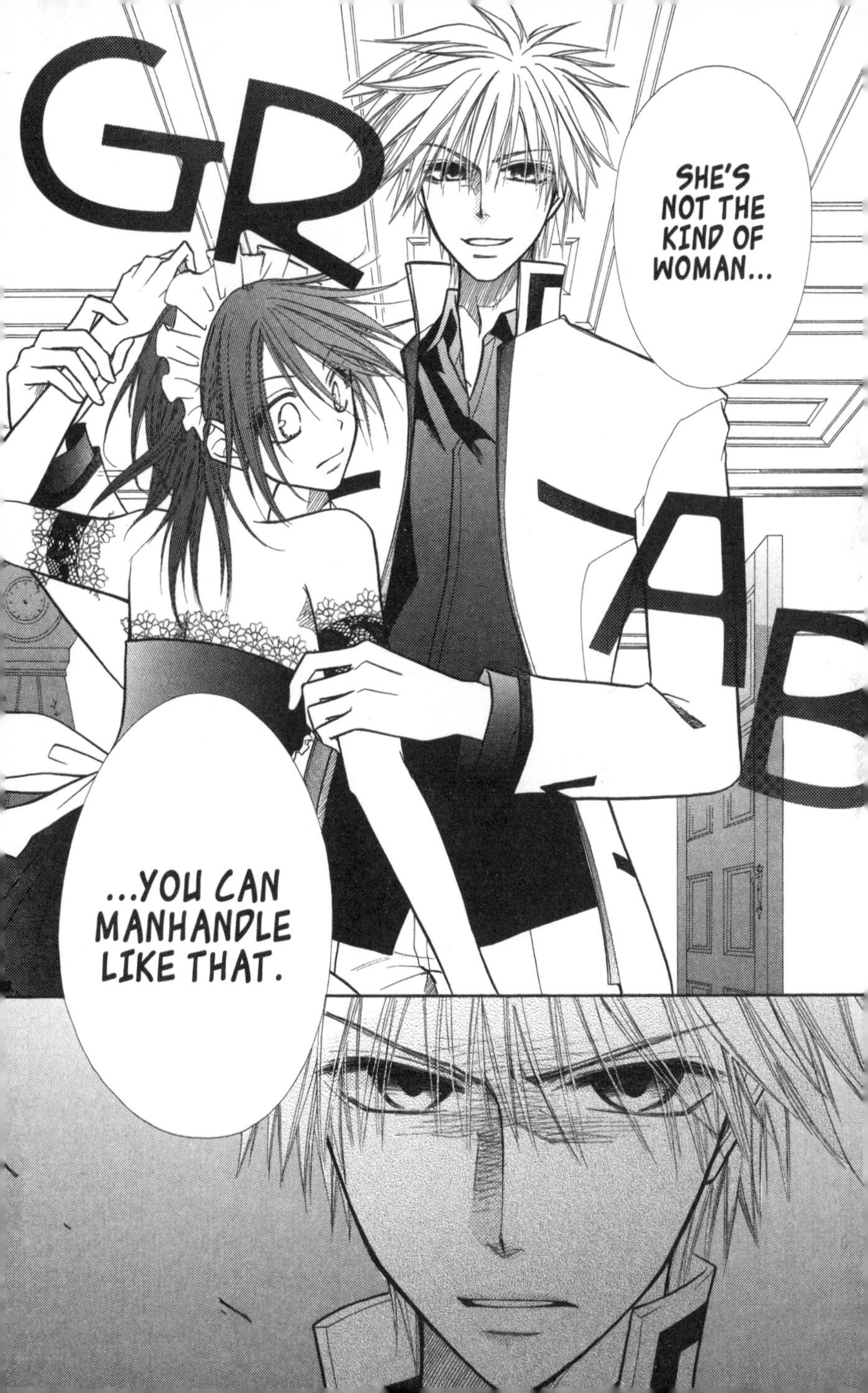
SHE'S NOT THE KIND OF WOMAN...
GRAB
...YOU CAN MANHANDLE LIKE THAT.

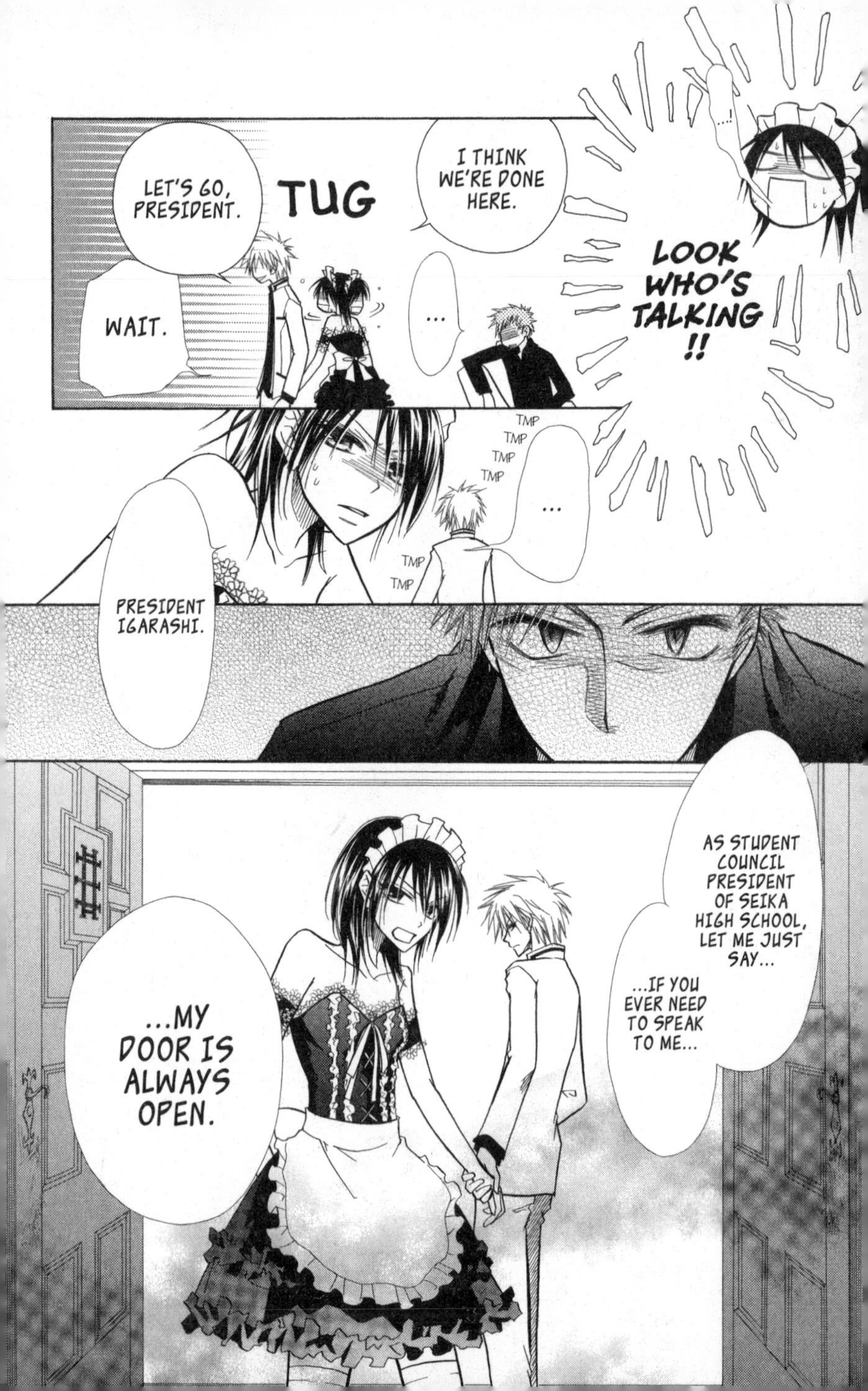
LOOK WHO'S TALKING!!
I THINK WE'RE DONE HERE.
TUG
LET'S GO, PRESIDENT.
...
WAIT.
TMP TMP TMP TMP
...
TMP TMP
PRESIDENT IGARASHI.
AS STUDENT COUNCIL PRESIDENT OF SEIKA HIGH SCHOOL, LET ME JUST SAY...
...IF YOU EVER NEED TO SPEAK TO ME...
...MY DOOR IS ALWAYS OPEN.

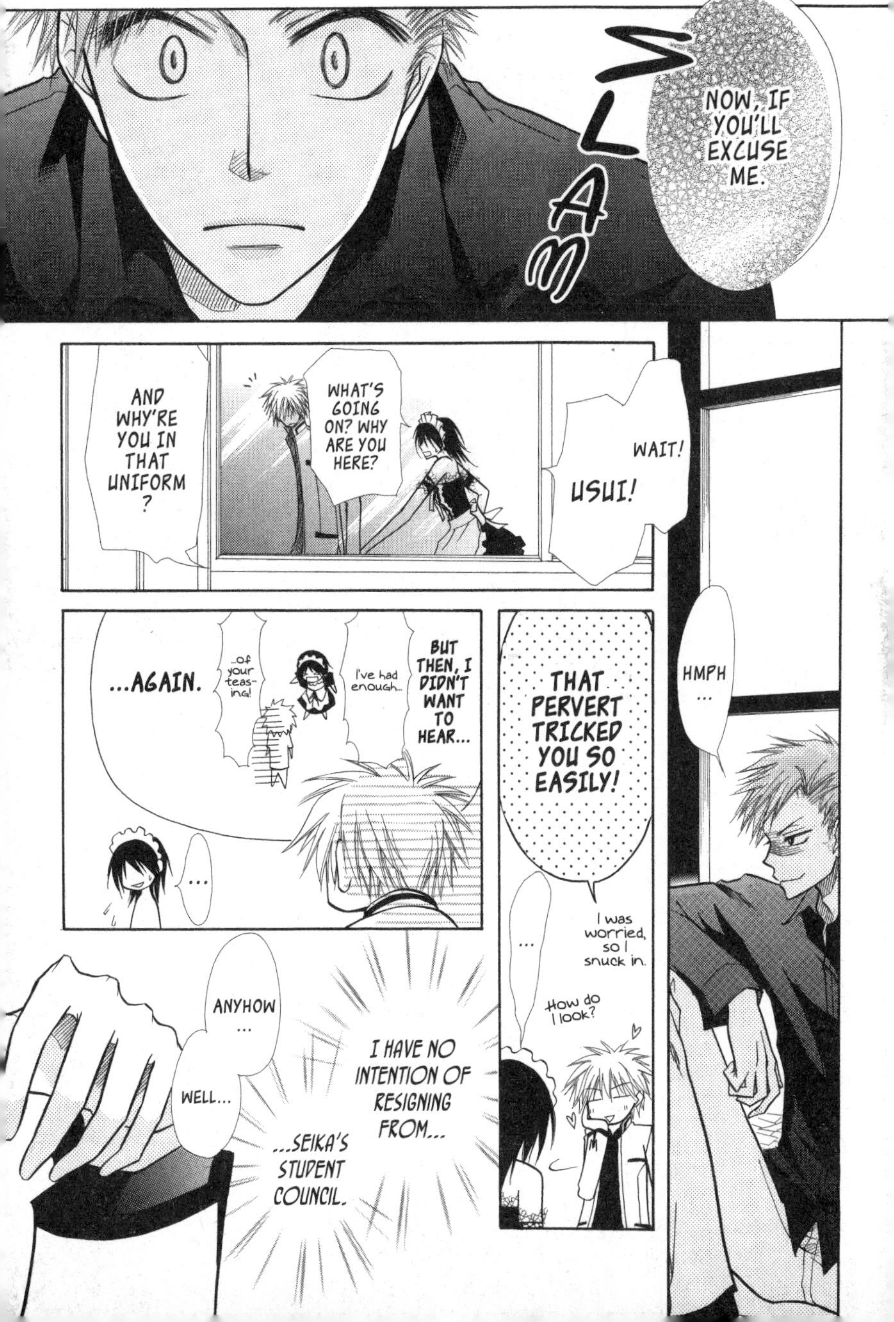
NOW, IF YOU'LL EXCUSE ME.
SLAM
WAIT!
USUI!
WHAT'S GOING ON? WHY ARE YOU HERE?
AND WHY'RE YOU IN THAT UNIFORM?
HMPH...
THAT PERVERT TRICKED YOU SO EASILY!
BUT THEN, I DIDN'T WANT TO HEAR...
I've had enough...
...of your teasing!
...AGAIN.
...
I was worried, so I snuck in.
...
How do I look?
ANYHOW...
WELL...
I HAVE NO INTENTION OF RESIGNING FROM...
...SEIKA'S STUDENT COUNCIL.

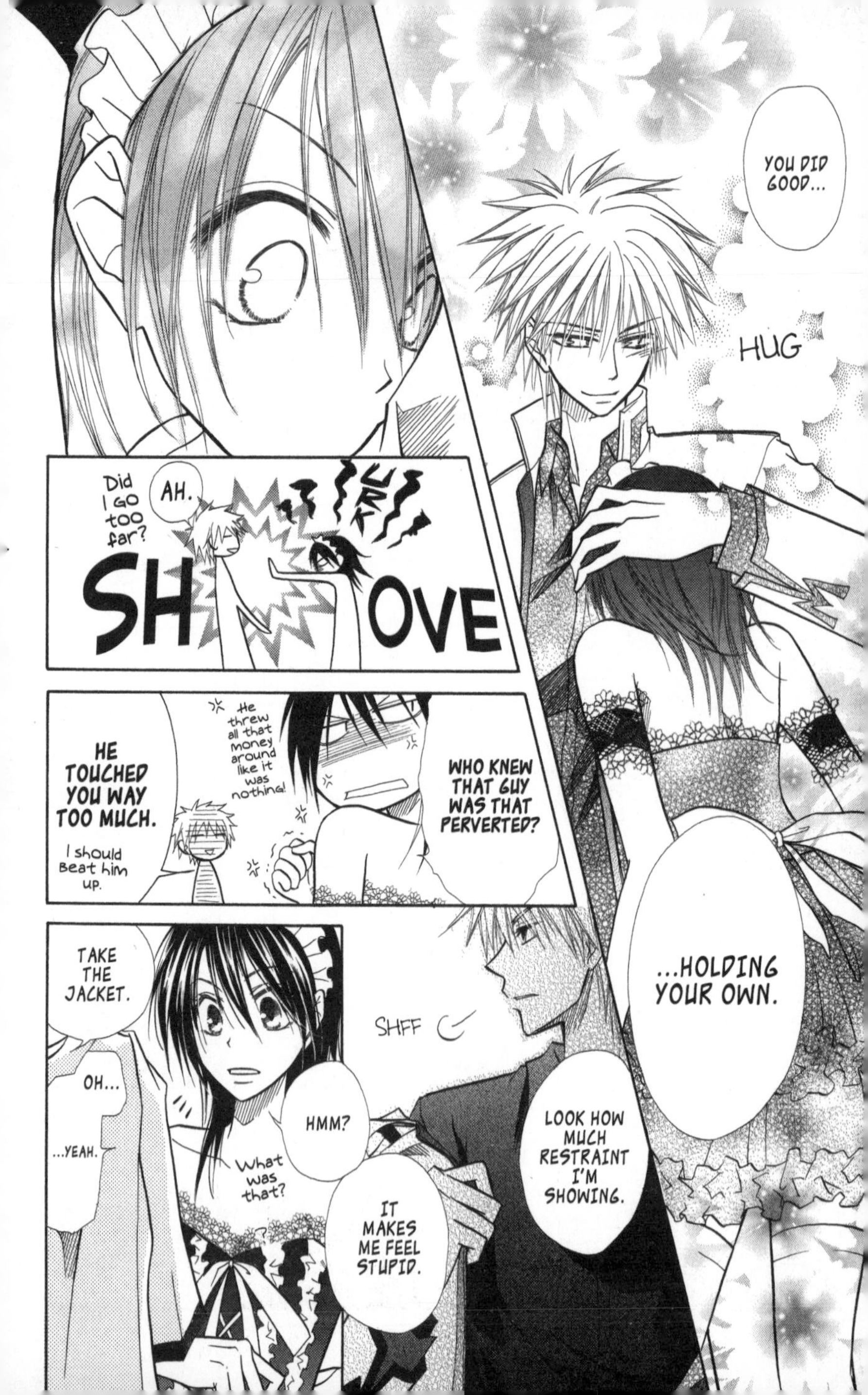

YOU DID GOOD...
HUG
...HOLDING YOUR OWN.
URK
AH.
Did I go too far?
SHOVE
WHO KNEW THAT GUY WAS THAT PERVERTED?
He threw all that money around like it was nothing!
HE TOUCHED YOU WAY TOO MUCH.
I should beat him up.
LOOK HOW MUCH RESTRAINT I'M SHOWING.
IT MAKES ME FEEL STUPID.
HMM?
What was that?
SHFF
TAKE THE JACKET.
OH...
...YEAH.

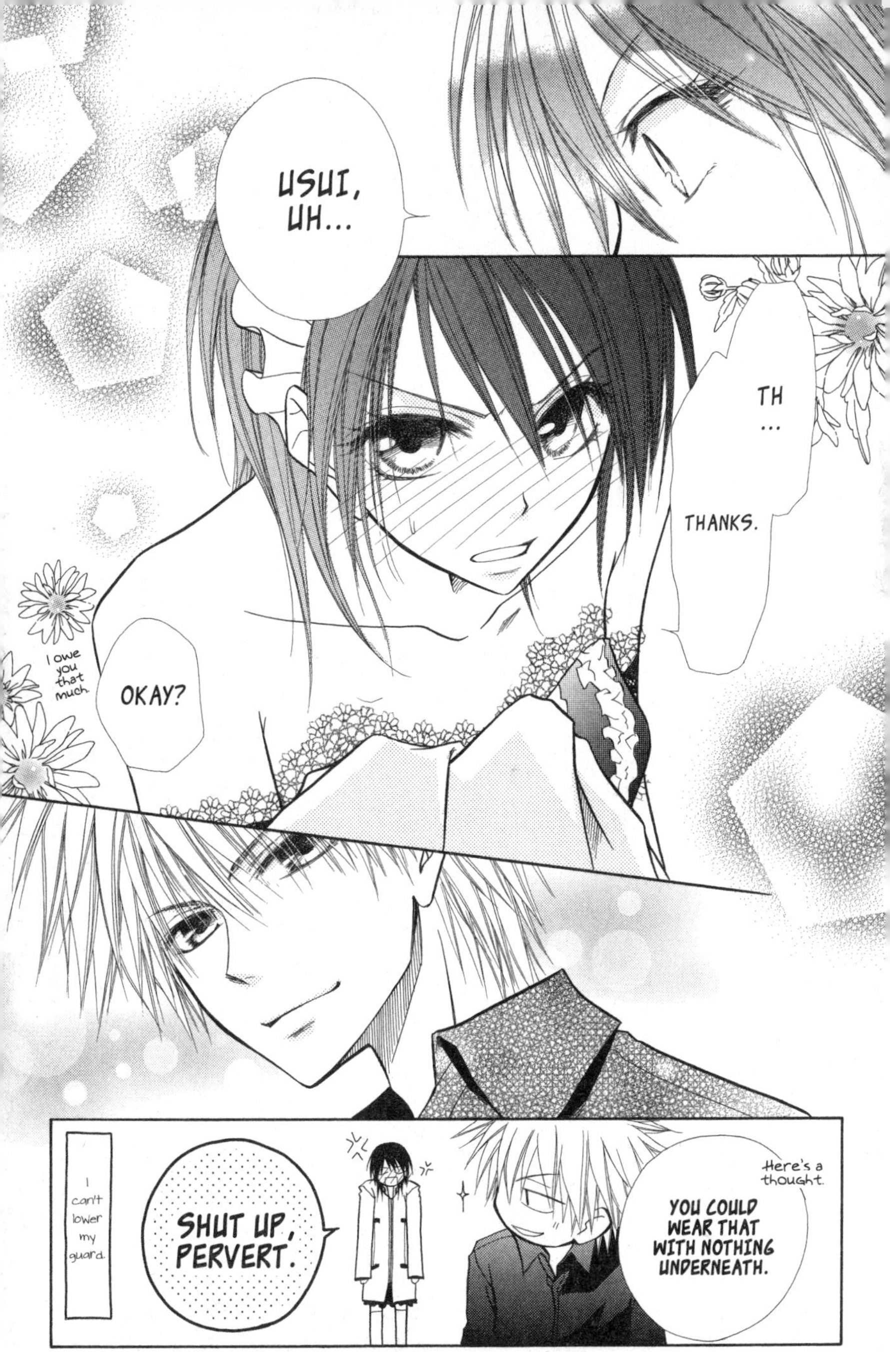
USUI, UH...
TH ...
THANKS.
I owe you that much.
OKAY?
Here's a thought.
YOU COULD WEAR THAT WITH NOTHING UNDERNEATH.
SHUT UP, PERVERT.
I can't lower my guard.

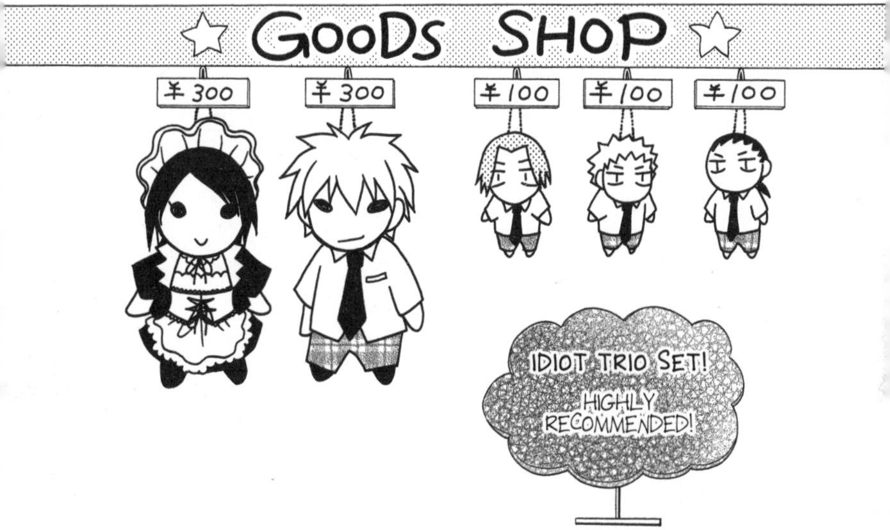
GOODS SHOP
¥300
¥300
¥100
¥100
¥100
IDIOT TRIO SET!
HIGHLY RECOMMENDED!

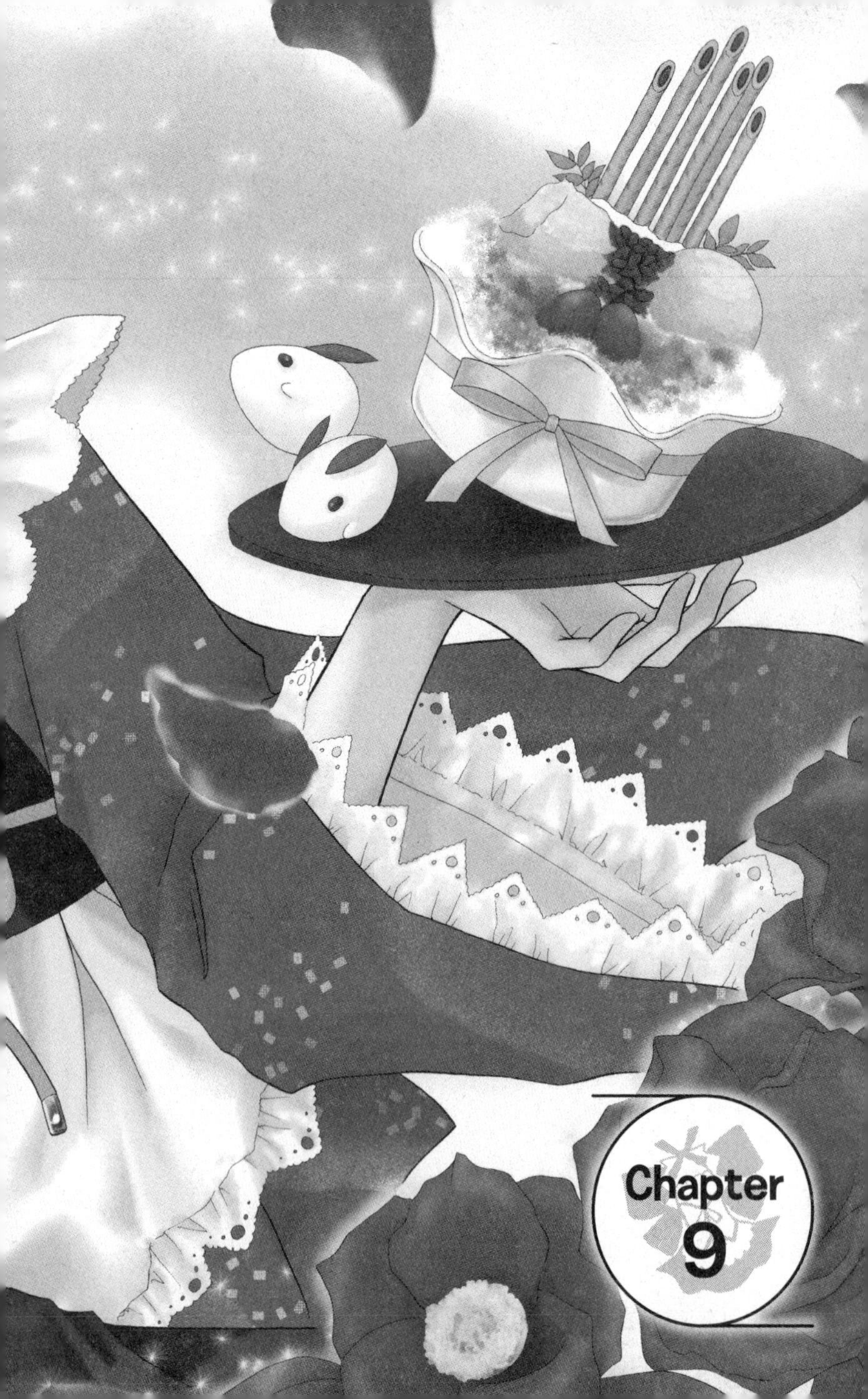
Chapter
9

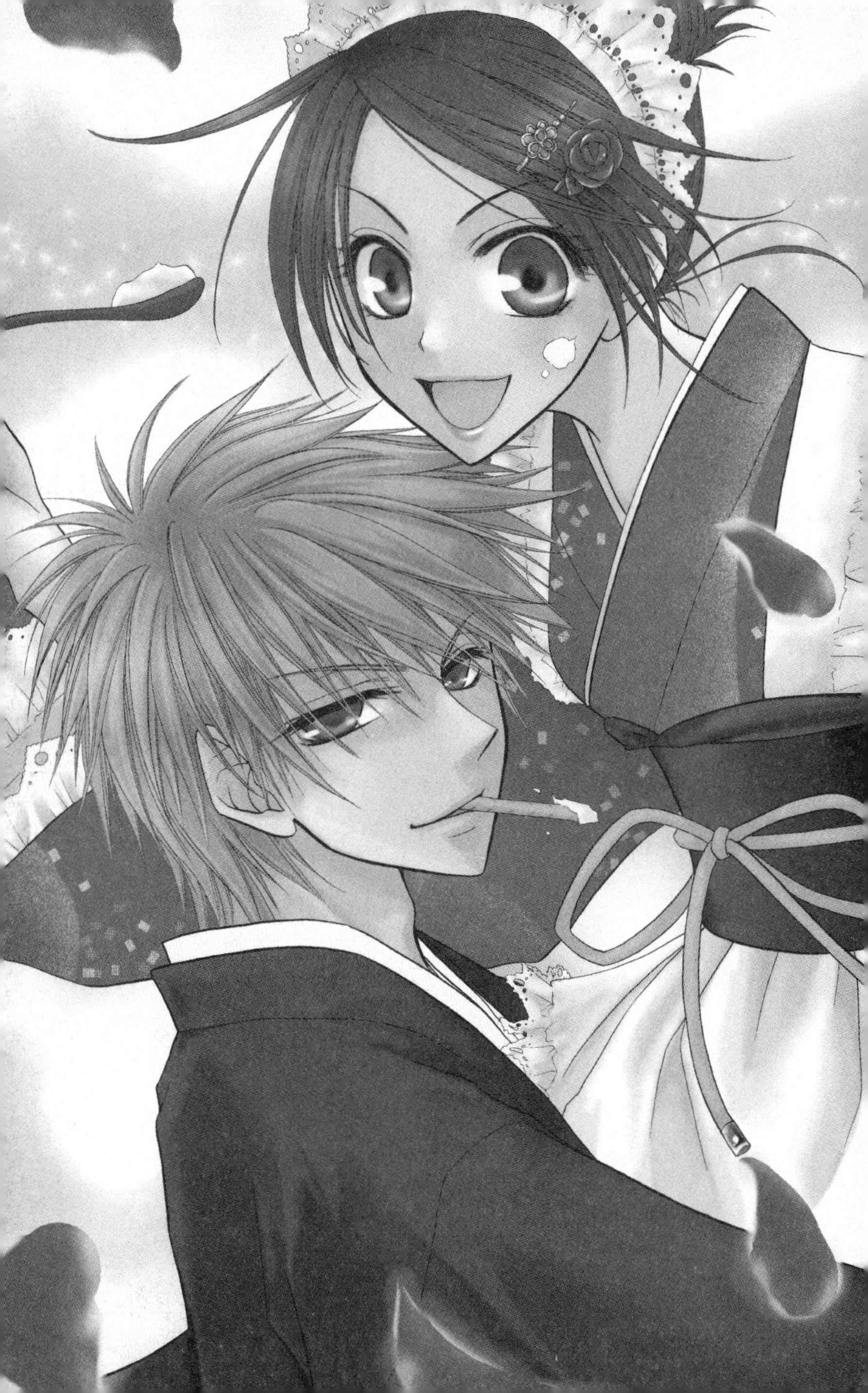

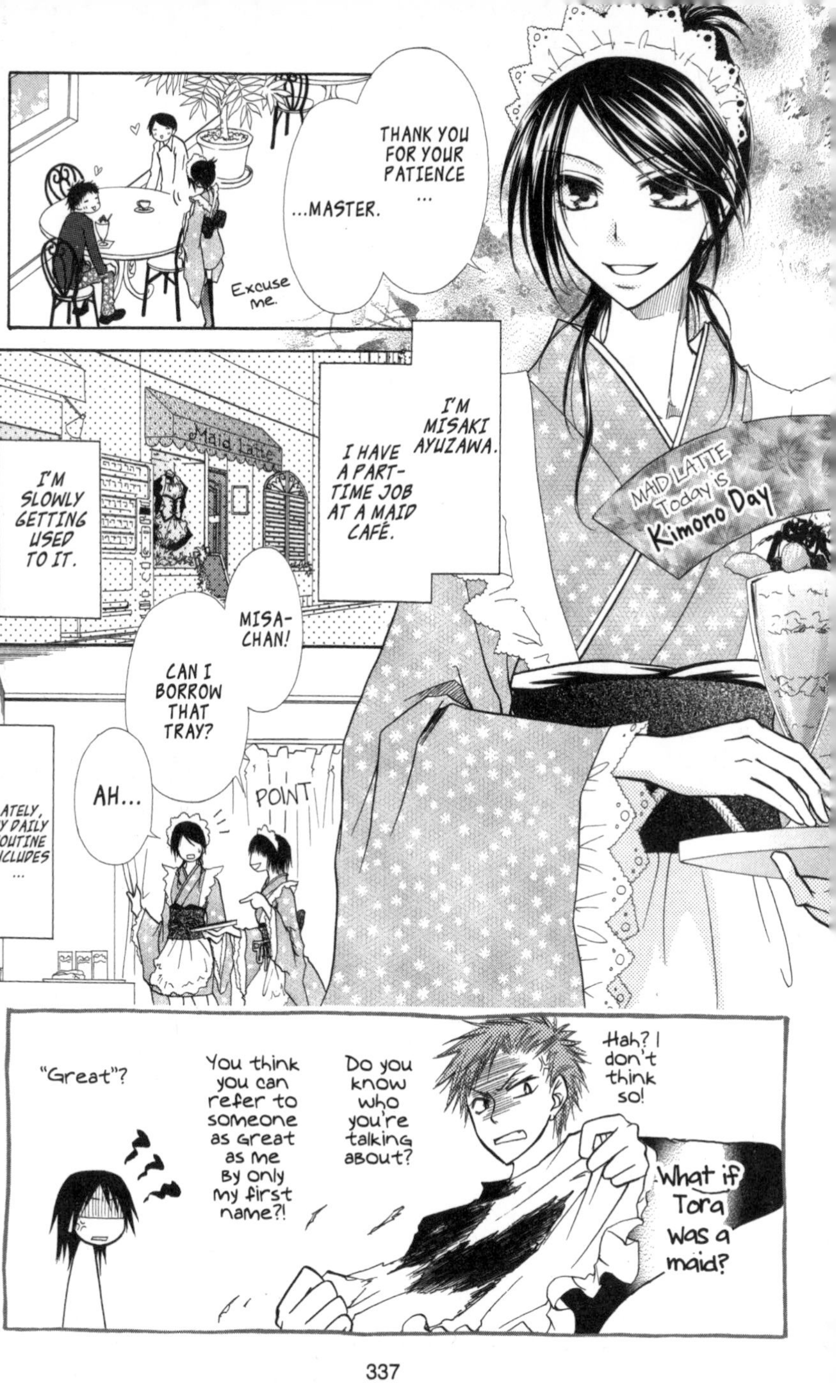
THANK YOU FOR YOUR PATIENCE ...
...MASTER.
Excuse me.
I'M MISAKI AYUZAWA.
I HAVE A PART-TIME JOB AT A MAID CAFÉ.
MAID LATTE Today is Kimono Day
Maid Latte
I'M SLOWLY GETTING USED TO IT.
MISA-CHAN!
CAN I BORROW THAT TRAY?
POINT
AH...
LATELY, MY DAILY ROUTINE INCLUDES ...
Hah? I don't think so!
What if Tora was a maid?
Do you know who you're talking about?
You think you can refer to someone as great as me by only my first name?!
"Great"?

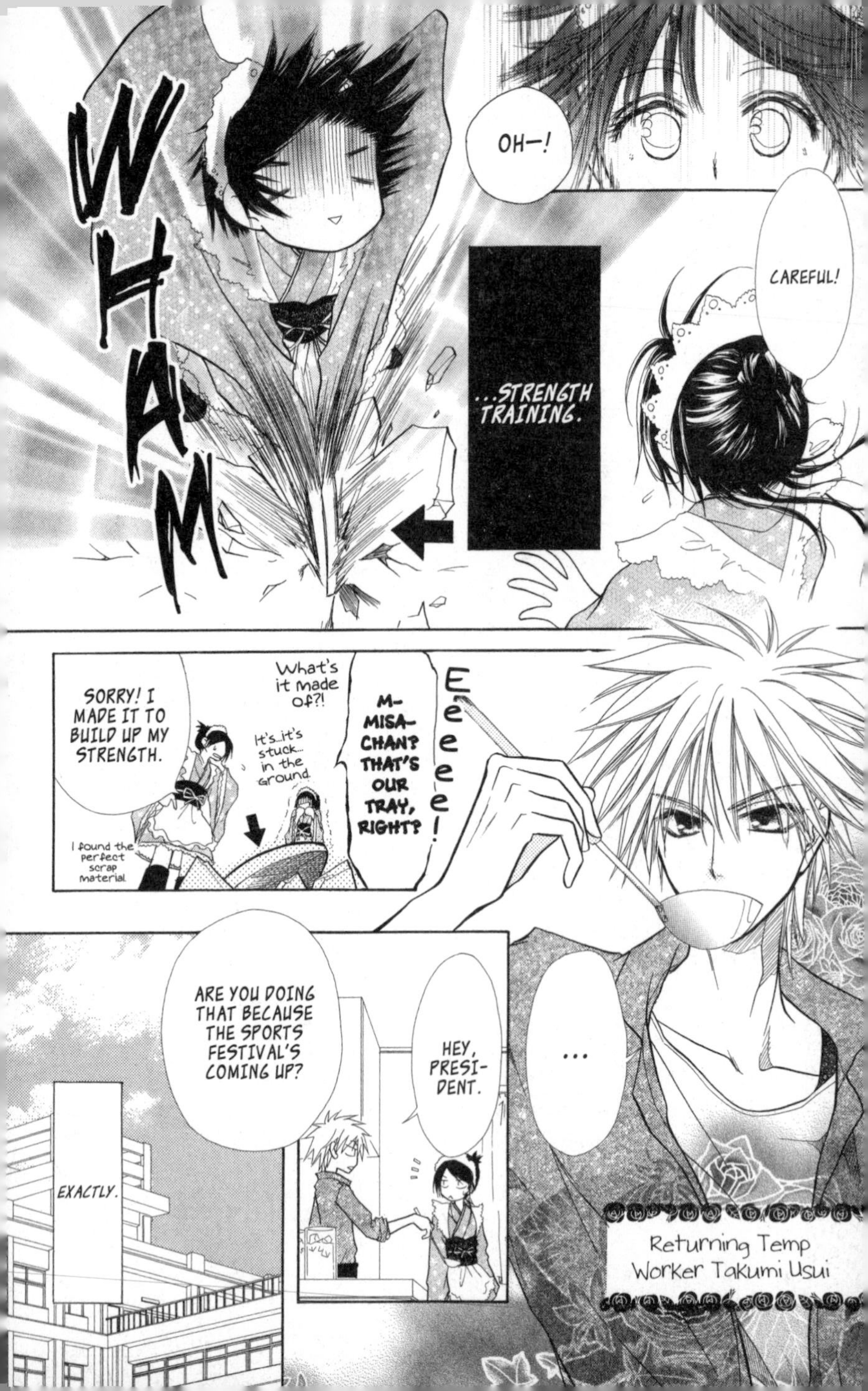
OH—!
CAREFUL!
...STRENGTH TRAINING.
WHAM
...
Returning Temp Worker Takumi Usui
Eeeeee!
M-MISA-CHAN? THAT'S OUR TRAY, RIGHT?
What's it made of?!
It's...it's stuck... in the ground.
SORRY! I MADE IT TO BUILD UP MY STRENGTH.
I found the perfect scrap material.
HEY, PRESIDENT.
ARE YOU DOING THAT BECAUSE THE SPORTS FESTIVAL'S COMING UP?
EXACTLY.

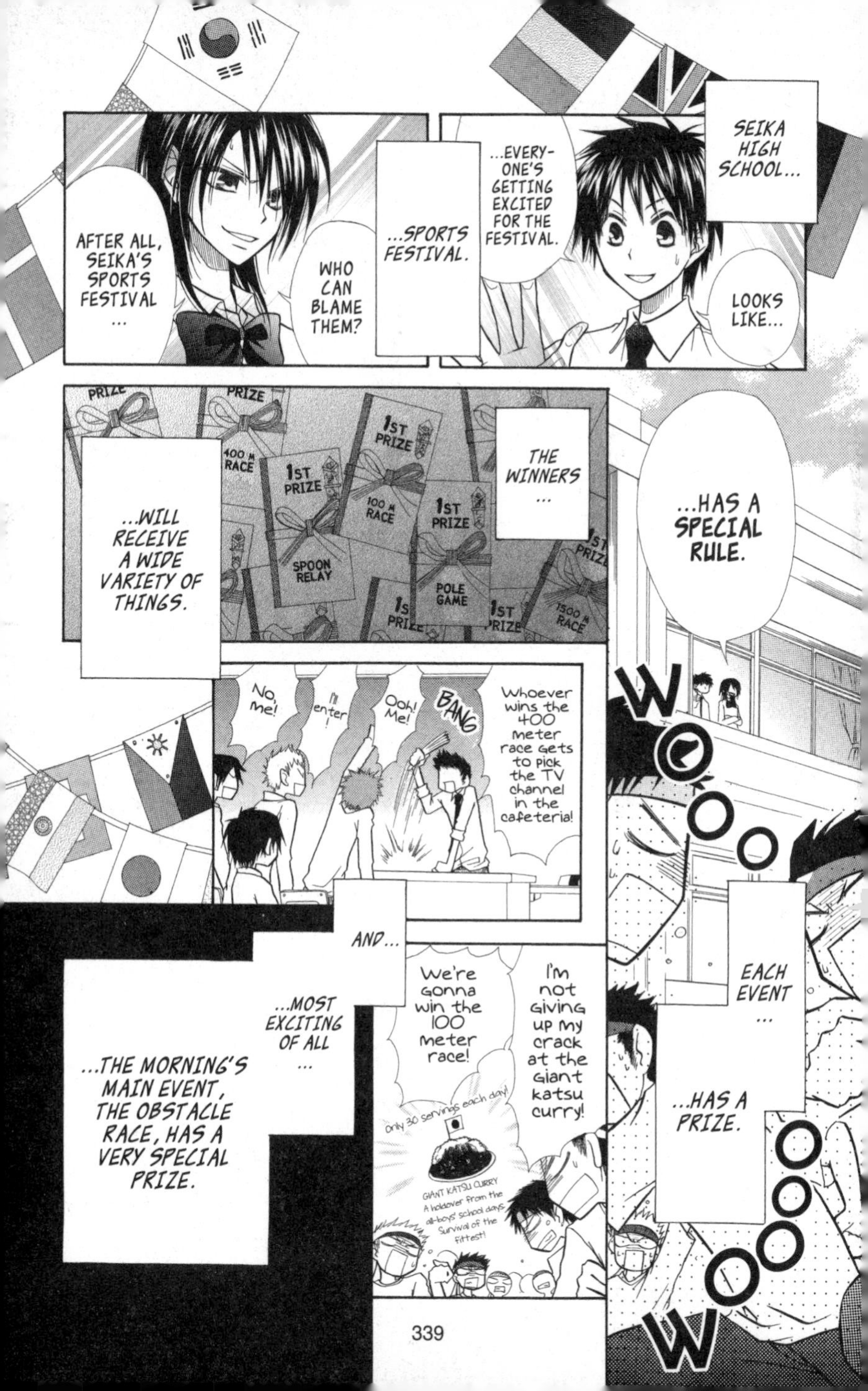
SEIKA HIGH SCHOOL...
LOOKS LIKE...
...EVERY-ONE'S GETTING EXCITED FOR THE FESTIVAL.
...SPORTS FESTIVAL.
WHO CAN BLAME THEM?
AFTER ALL, SEIKA'S SPORTS FESTIVAL ...
...HAS A SPECIAL RULE.
WOOOOOOOOW
EACH EVENT ...
...HAS A PRIZE.
THE WINNERS ...
...WILL RECEIVE A WIDE VARIETY OF THINGS.
PRIZE
PRIZE
400 M RACE
1ST PRIZE
100 M RACE
1ST PRIZE
SPOON RELAY
1ST PRIZE
POLE GAME
1ST PRIZE
1ST PRIZE
1ST PRIZE
1500 M RACE
Whoever wins the 400 meter race gets to pick the TV channel in the cafeteria!
BANG
Ooh! Me!
I'll enter!
No, me!
I'm not giving up my crack at the Giant katsu curry!
We're gonna win the 100 meter race!
Only 30 servings each day!
GIANT KATSU CURRY
A holdover from the all-boys' school days. Survival of the fittest!
AND...
...MOST EXCITING OF ALL ...
...THE MORNING'S MAIN EVENT, THE OBSTACLE RACE, HAS A VERY SPECIAL PRIZE.

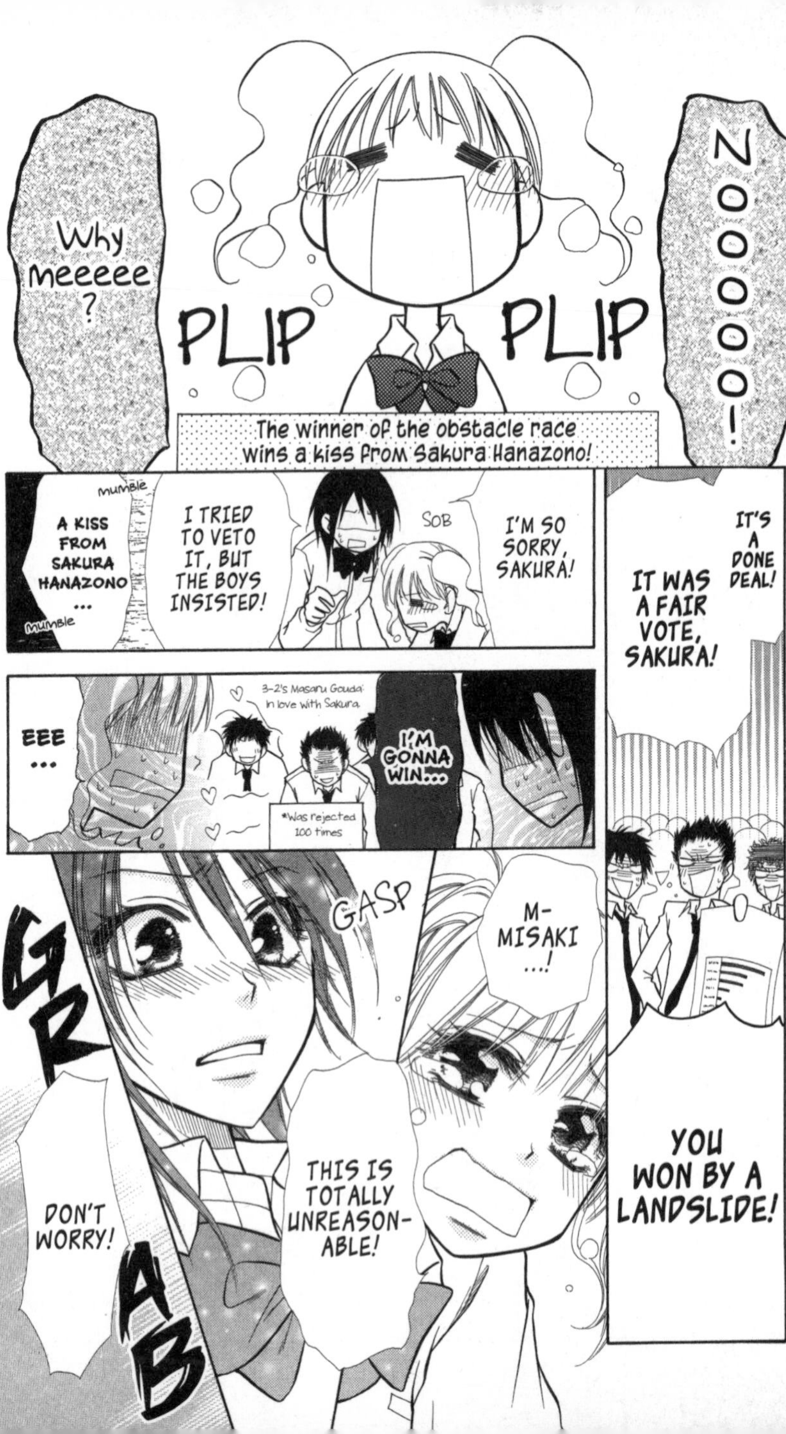
NOOOOO!
PLIP PLIP
Why meeeee?
The winner of the obstacle race wins a kiss from Sakura Hanazono!
IT'S A DONE DEAL!
IT WAS A FAIR VOTE, SAKURA!
YOU WON BY A LANDSLIDE!
I'M SO SORRY, SAKURA!
SOB
I TRIED TO VETO IT, BUT THE BOYS INSISTED!
mumble
A KISS FROM SAKURA HANAZONO ...
mumble
I'M GONNA WIN...
3-2's Masaru Gouda: In love with Sakura.
*Was rejected 100 times
EEE ...
M-MISAKI ...!
GASP
THIS IS TOTALLY UNREASON-ABLE!
GRAB
DON'T WORRY!

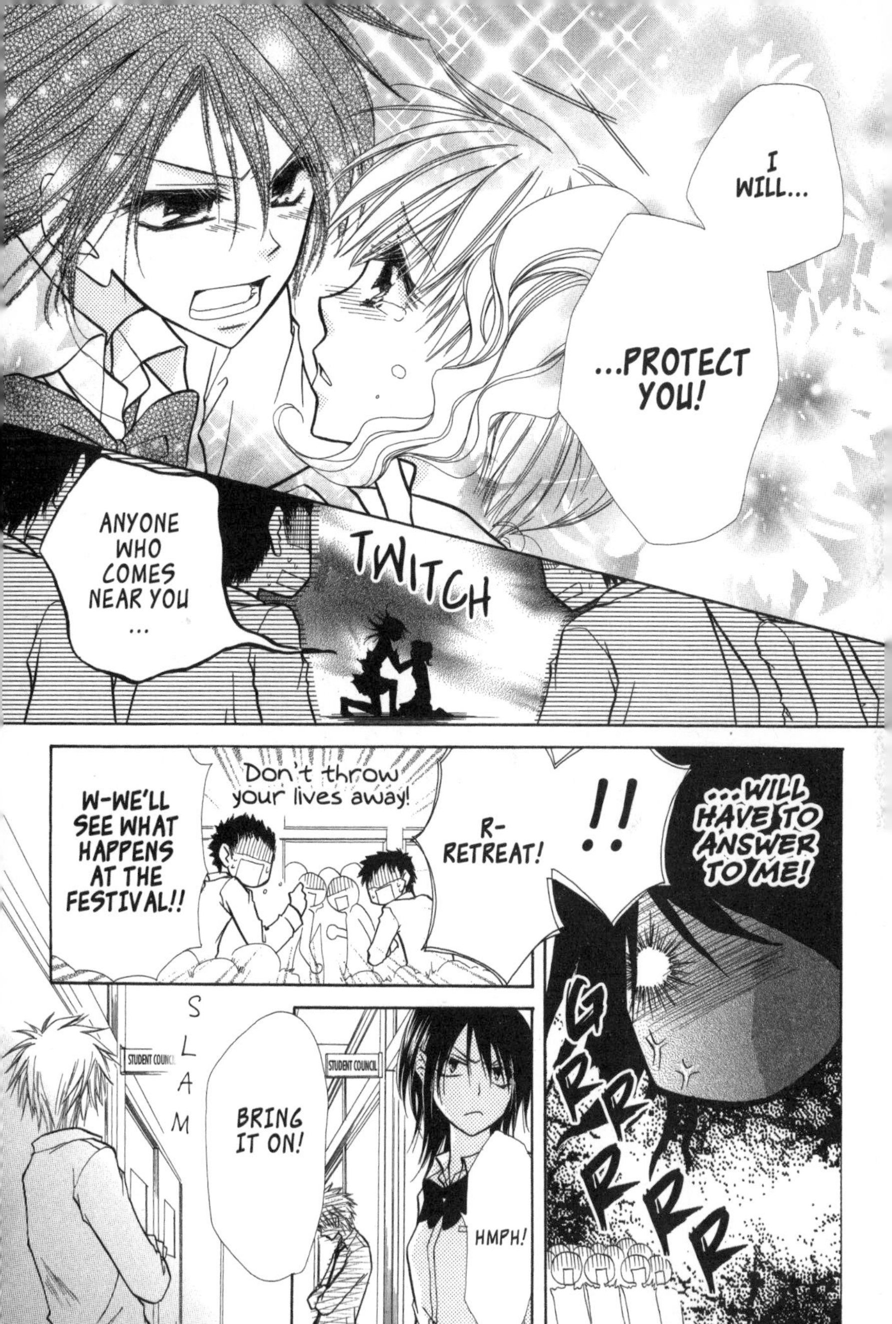
I WILL...
...PROTECT YOU!
ANYONE WHO COMES NEAR YOU ...
TWITCH
...WILL HAVE TO ANSWER TO ME!
GRRRRRR
!!
R-RETREAT!
Don't throw your lives away!
W-WE'LL SEE WHAT HAPPENS AT THE FESTIVAL!!
SLAM
BRING IT ON!
STUDENT COUNCIL
HMPH!

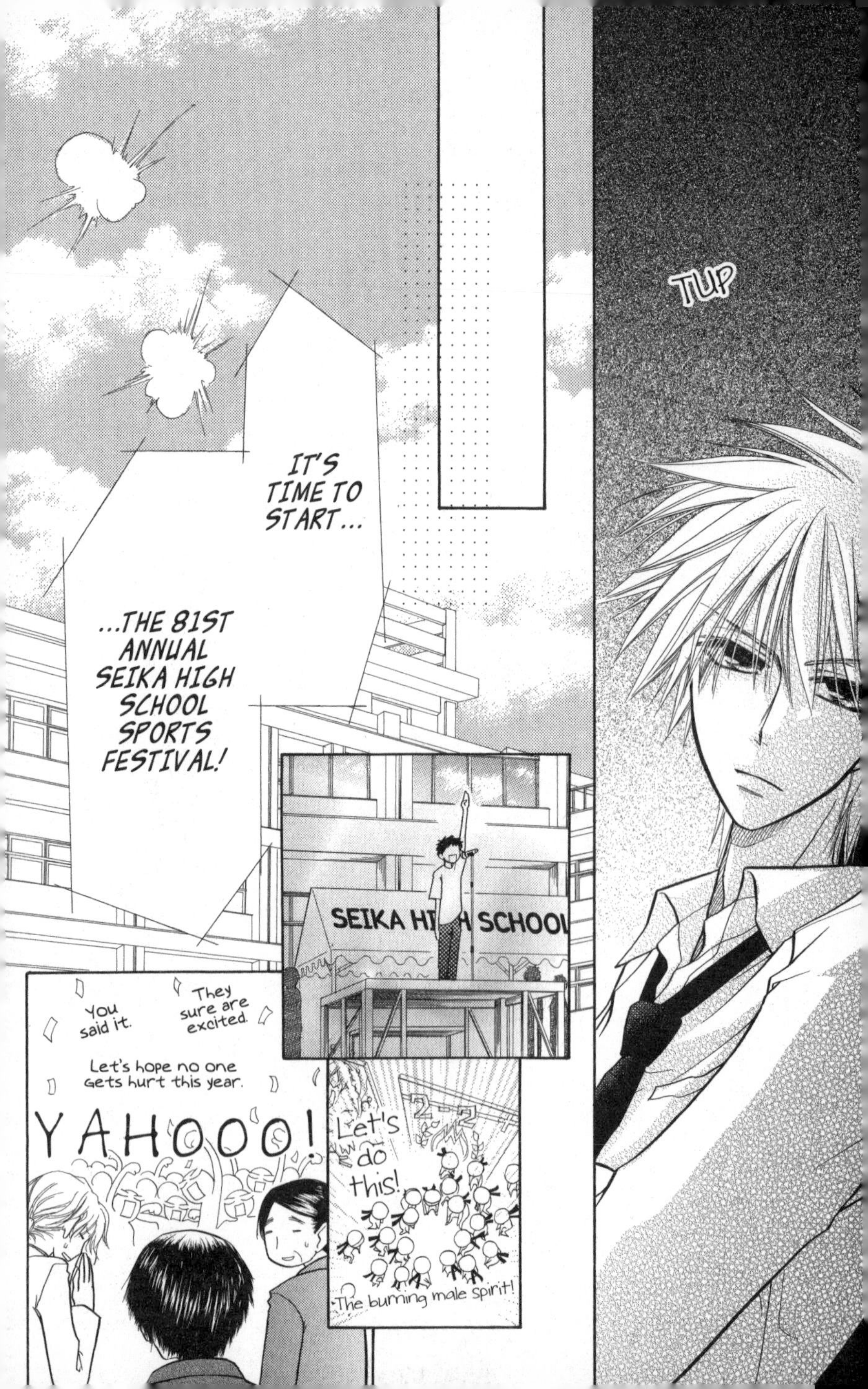
TUP
IT'S TIME TO START...
...THE 81ST ANNUAL SEIKA HIGH SCHOOL SPORTS FESTIVAL!
SEIKA HIGH SCHOOL
Let's do this!
The burning male spirit!
They sure are excited.
You said it.
Let's hope no one gets hurt this year.
YAHOOO!

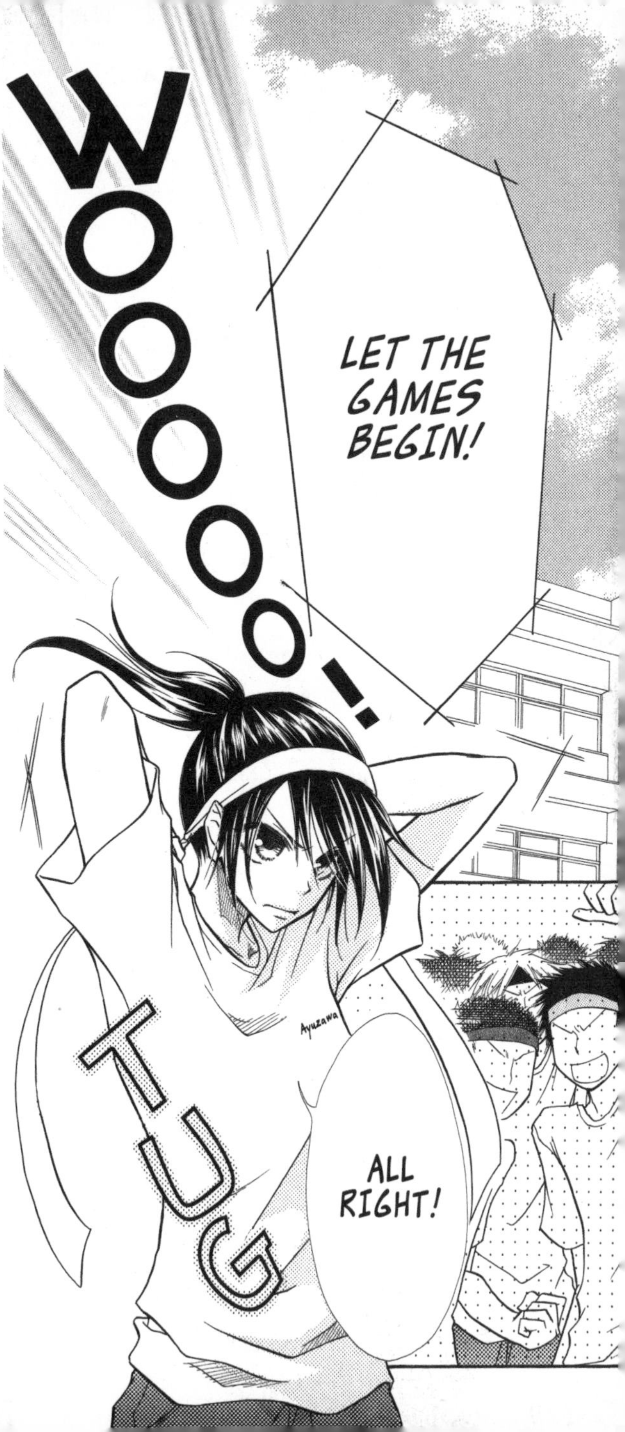
WOOOOO!!
LET THE GAMES BEGIN!
TUG
Ayuzawa
ALL RIGHT!

Words of ☆ Appreciation

Hi, it's Fujiwara!

In September 2006, my first manga, Maid-sama! volume 1, was released.

I've always told my friends and family that I create manga, so my sweet friends made a point of calling from the bookstore to say, "I bought it!" (Often accompanied by a photo!)

As for me, I'd go to the bookstore to see that my manga was, in fact, on the shelves.

A weird aura makes it hard to look straight at it.

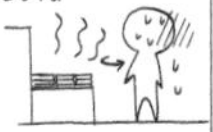

Heroes... You're all heroes, seriously.

My best friend, M, went above and beyond by going to two stores and buying ten books!

Thanks to all you heroes!

I mean it...!! ✧✧

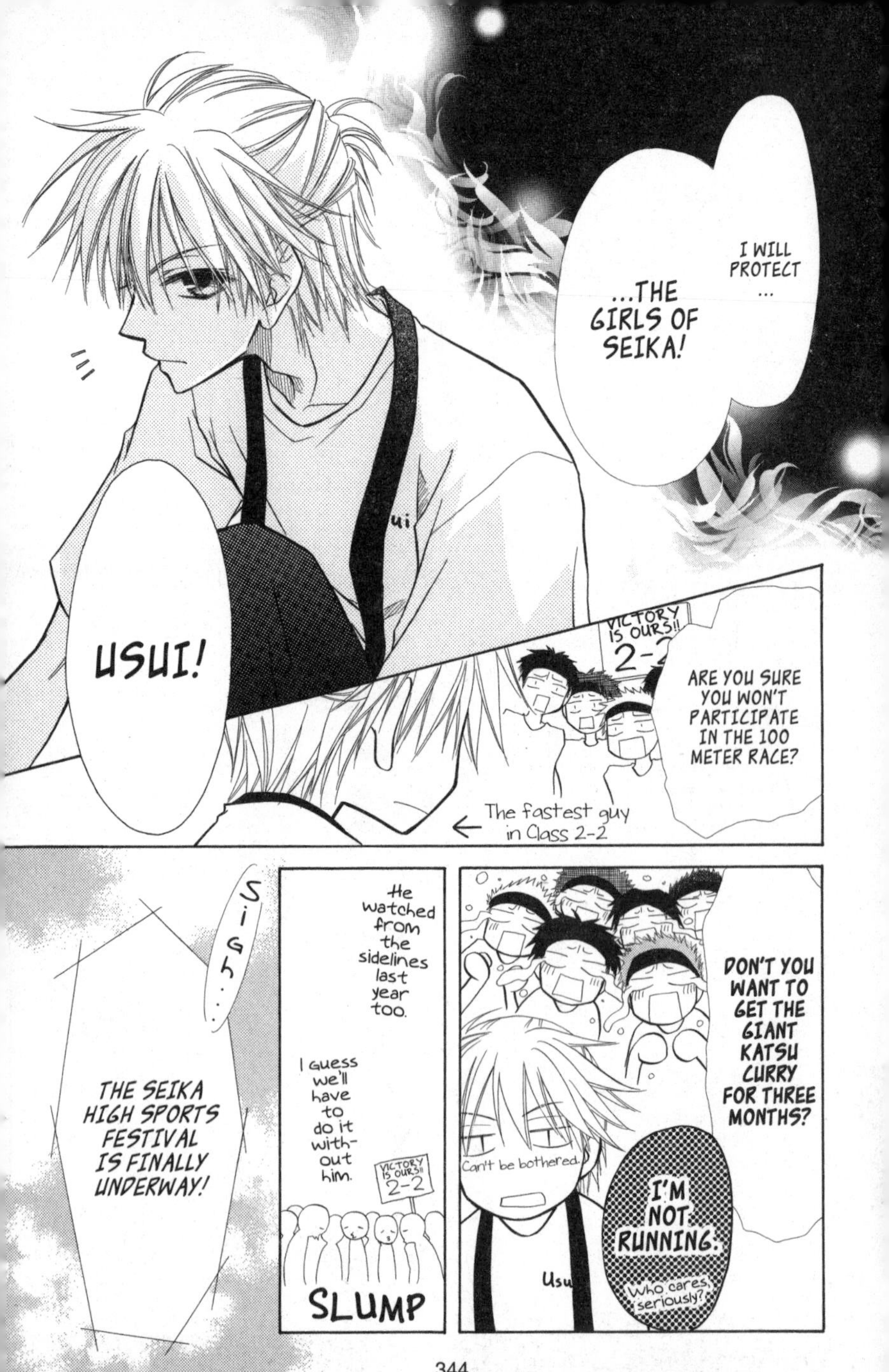
I WILL PROTECT ...
...THE GIRLS OF SEIKA!
ui
USUI!
VICTORY IS OURS!! 2-2
ARE YOU SURE YOU WON'T PARTICIPATE IN THE 100 METER RACE?
← The fastest guy in Class 2-2
DON'T YOU WANT TO GET THE GIANT KATSU CURRY FOR THREE MONTHS?
Can't be bothered.
I'M NOT RUNNING.
Who cares, seriously?
Usu
He watched from the sidelines last year too.
I guess we'll have to do it without him.
VICTORY IS OURS!! 2-2
SLUMP
Sigh...
THE SEIKA HIGH SPORTS FESTIVAL IS FINALLY UNDERWAY!

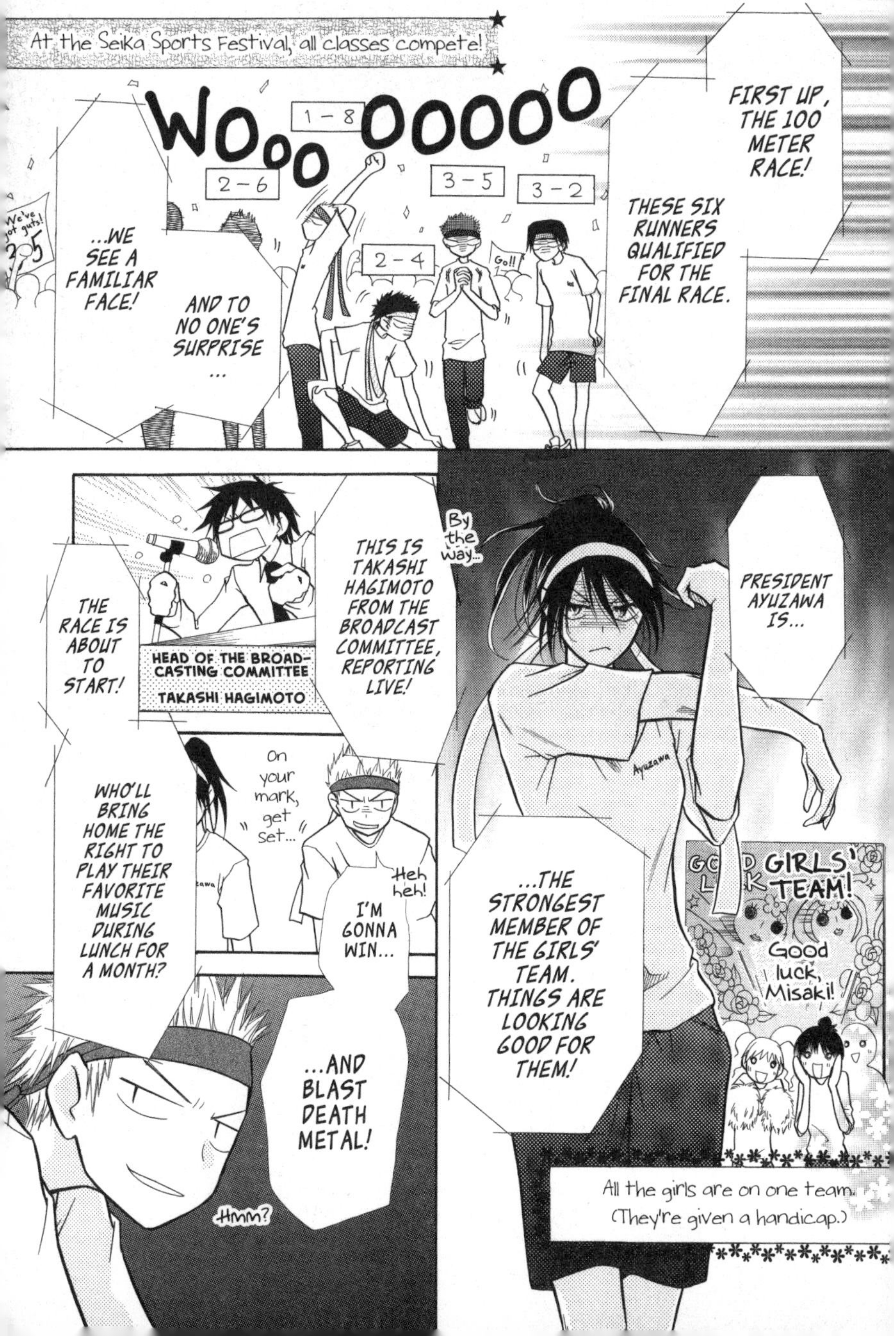

At the Seika Sports Festival, all classes compete!
FIRST UP, THE 100 METER RACE!
THESE SIX RUNNERS QUALIFIED FOR THE FINAL RACE.
WOOOOOOOO
1-8
3-2
3-5
2-6
2-4
Go!!
We've got guts! 2-5
AND TO NO ONE'S SURPRISE ...
...WE SEE A FAMILIAR FACE!
By the way...
PRESIDENT AYUZAWA IS...
...THE STRONGEST MEMBER OF THE GIRLS' TEAM. THINGS ARE LOOKING GOOD FOR THEM!
GOOD LUCK GIRLS' TEAM!
Good luck, Misaki!
Ayuzawa
All the girls are on one team. (They're given a handicap.)
THIS IS TAKASHI HAGIMOTO FROM THE BROADCAST COMMITTEE, REPORTING LIVE!
THE RACE IS ABOUT TO START!
HEAD OF THE BROAD-CASTING COMMITTEE
TAKASHI HAGIMOTO
On your mark, get set...
Heh heh!
I'M GONNA WIN...
WHO'LL BRING HOME THE RIGHT TO PLAY THEIR FAVORITE MUSIC DURING LUNCH FOR A MONTH?
...AND BLAST DEATH METAL!
Hmm?

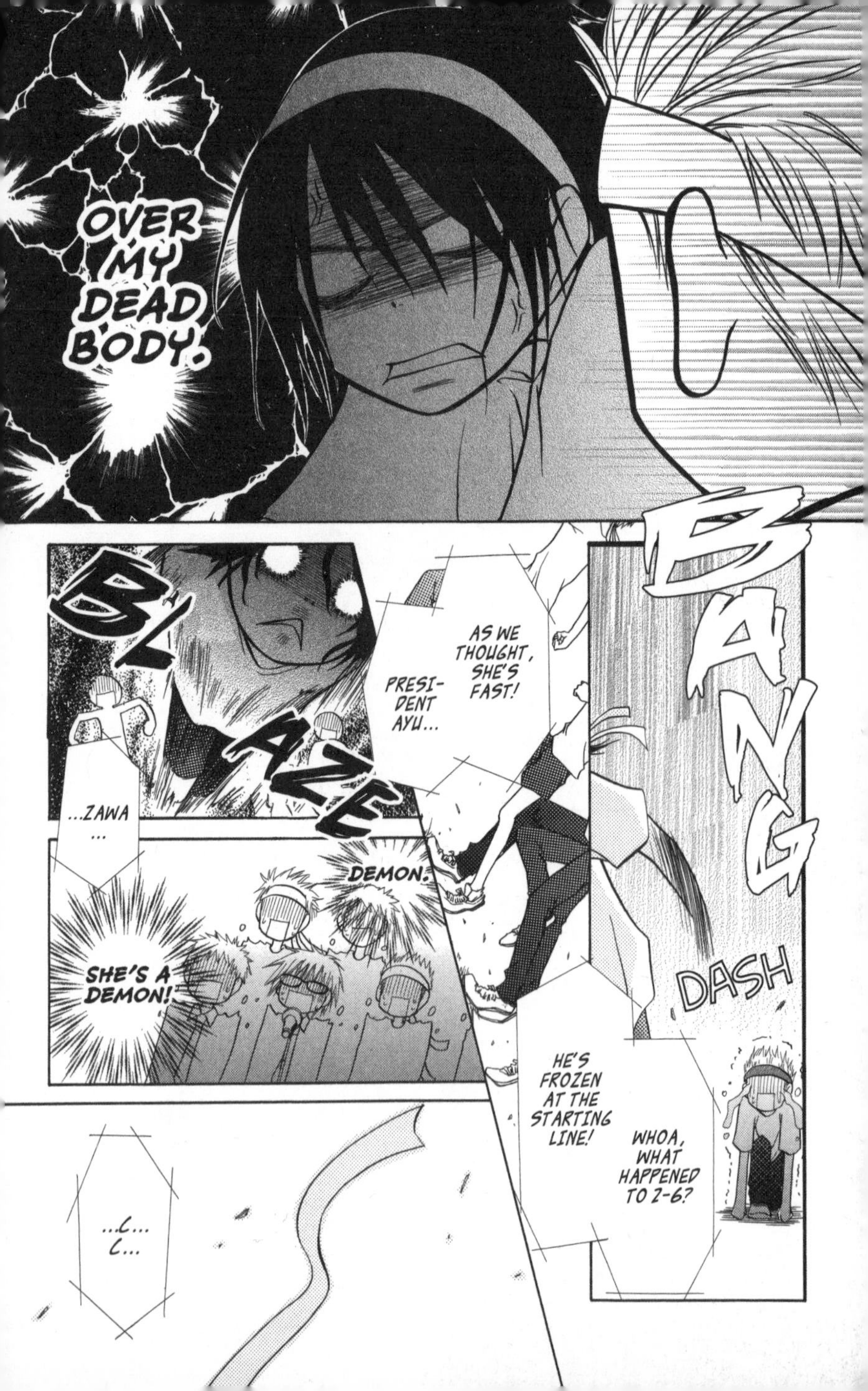
OVER MY DEAD BODY.
BANG
DASH
WHOA, WHAT HAPPENED TO 2-6?
HE'S FROZEN AT THE STARTING LINE!
AS WE THOUGHT, SHE'S FAST!
PRESI-DENT AYU...
BLAZE
...ZAWA ...
DEMON.
SHE'S A DEMON!
...C... C...

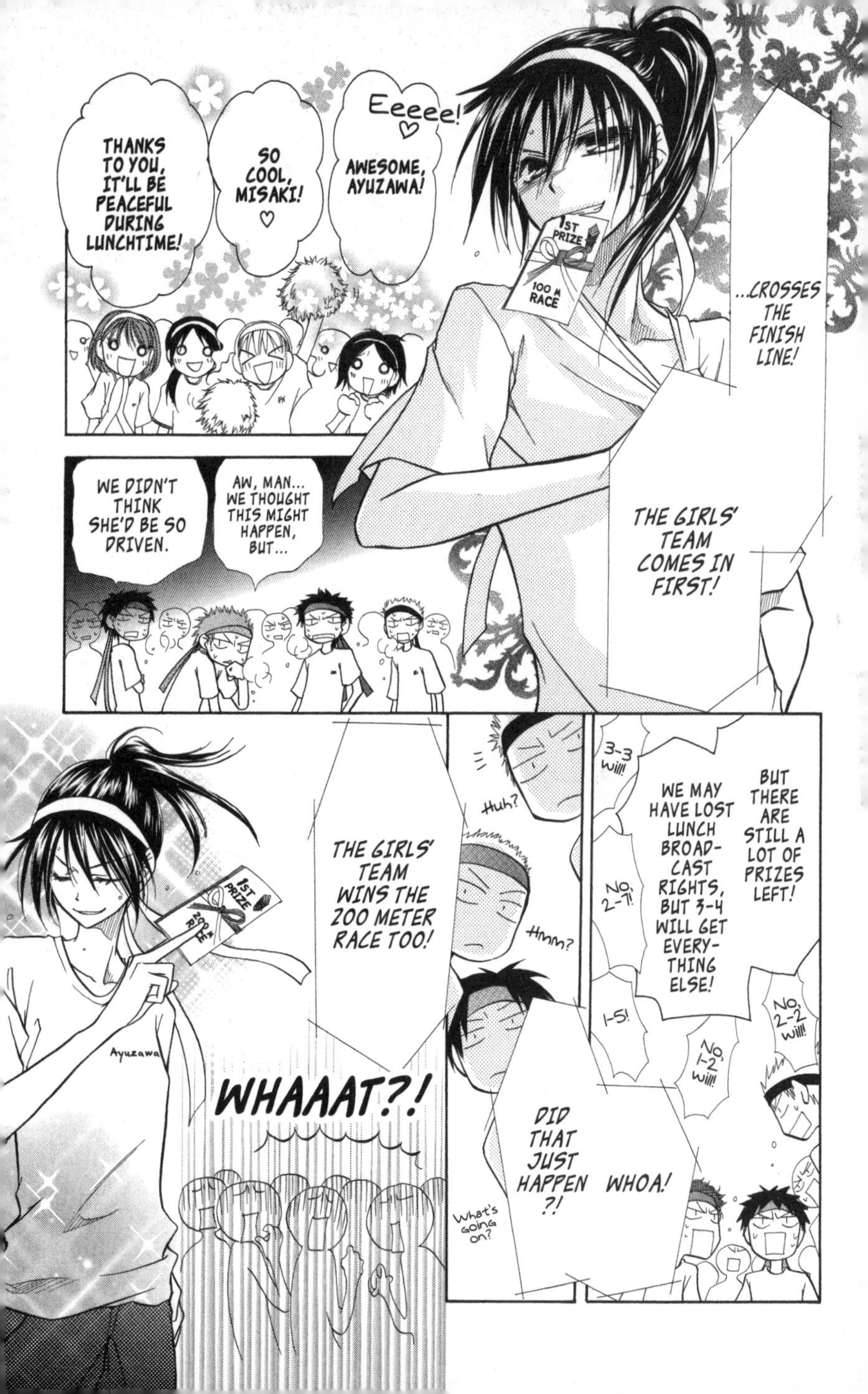

...CROSSES THE FINISH LINE!
THE GIRLS' TEAM COMES IN FIRST!
1ST PRIZE 100 M RACE
Eeeee! ♡
AWESOME, AYUZAWA!
SO COOL, MISAKI! ♡
THANKS TO YOU, IT'LL BE PEACEFUL DURING LUNCHTIME!
AW, MAN... WE THOUGHT THIS MIGHT HAPPEN, BUT...
WE DIDN'T THINK SHE'D BE SO DRIVEN.
3-3 will!
BUT THERE ARE STILL A LOT OF PRIZES LEFT!
WE MAY HAVE LOST LUNCH BROAD-CAST RIGHTS, BUT 3-4 WILL GET EVERY-THING ELSE!
No, 2-7!
1-5!
No, 2-2 will!
No, 1-2 will!
Huh?
Hmm?
WHOA!
DID THAT JUST HAPPEN ?!
What's going on?
THE GIRLS' TEAM WINS THE 200 METER RACE TOO!
1ST PRIZE
Ayuzawa
WHAAAT?!

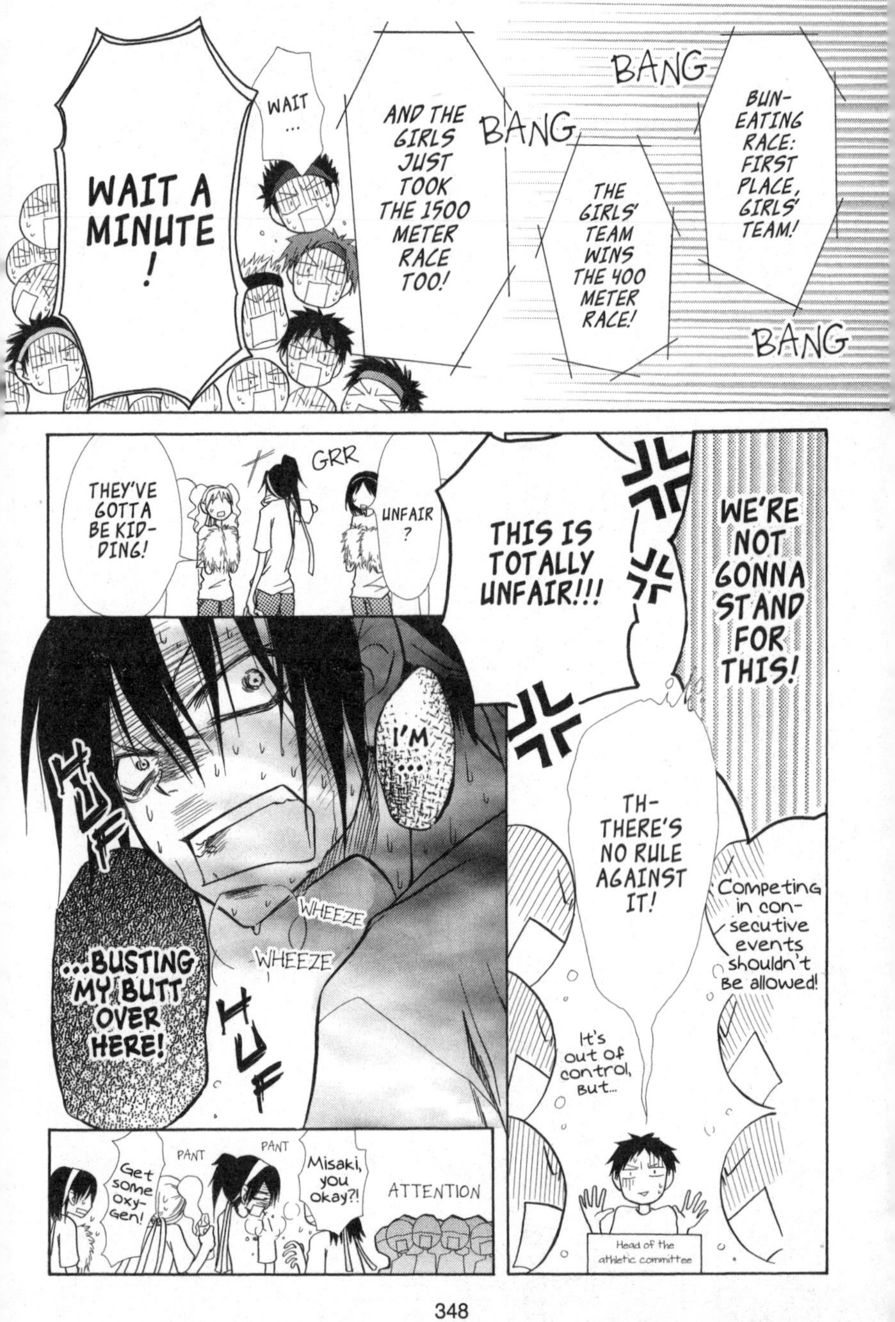
BUN-EATING RACE: FIRST PLACE, GIRLS' TEAM!
BANG
BANG
BANG
THE GIRLS' TEAM WINS THE 400 METER RACE!
AND THE GIRLS JUST TOOK THE 1500 METER RACE TOO!
WAIT ...
WAIT A MINUTE!
WE'RE NOT GONNA STAND FOR THIS!
THIS IS TOTALLY UNFAIR!!!
Competing in consecutive events shouldn't be allowed!
TH-THERE'S NO RULE AGAINST IT!
It's out of control, but...
Head of the athletic committee
UNFAIR?
GRR
THEY'VE GOTTA BE KIDDING!
I'M ...
...BUSTING MY BUTT OVER HERE!
HUF
WHEEZE
WHEEZE
HUF
ATTENTION
Misaki, you okay?!
PANT
PANT
Get some oxy-gen!

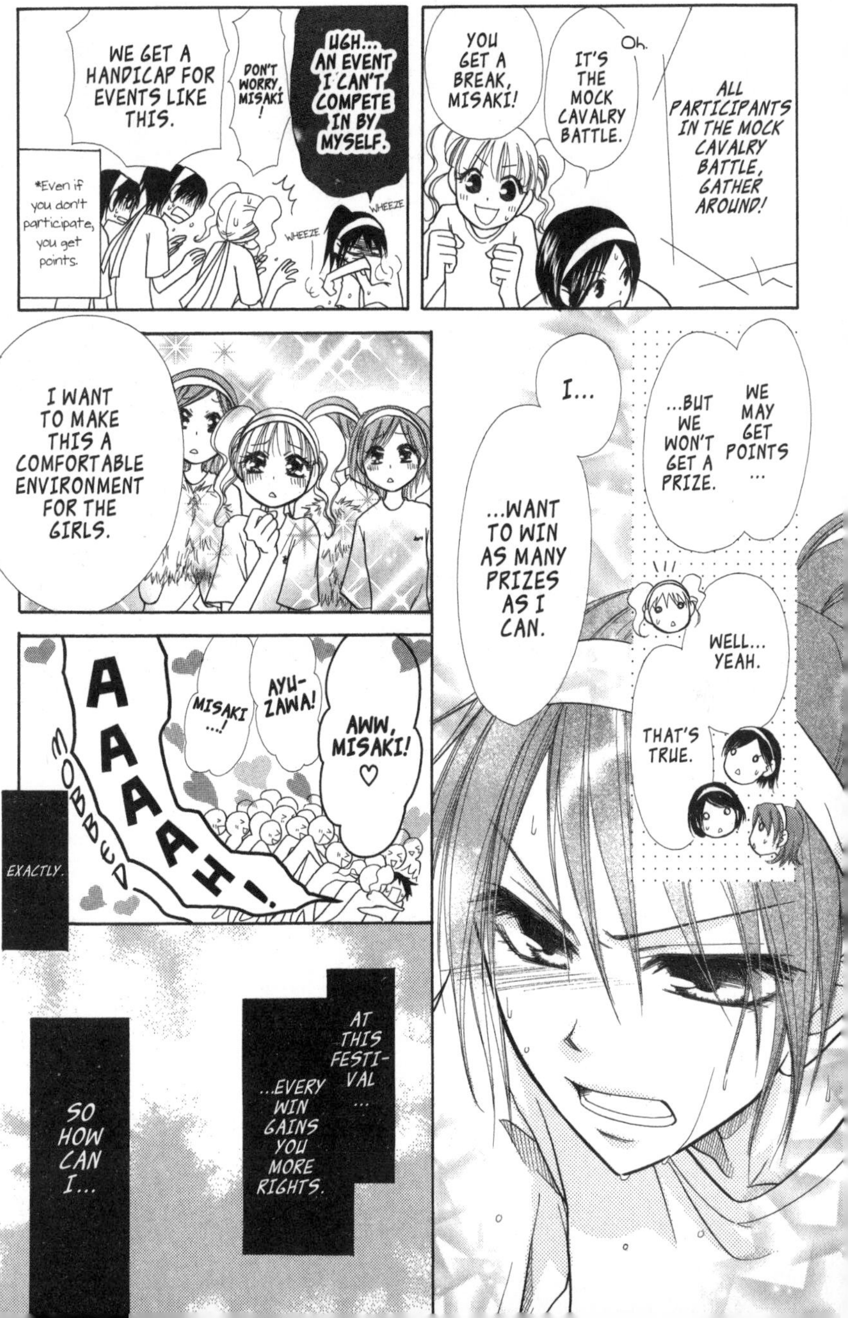
ALL PARTICIPANTS IN THE MOCK CAVALRY BATTLE, GATHER AROUND!
Oh.
IT'S THE MOCK CAVALRY BATTLE.
YOU GET A BREAK, MISAKI!
UGH... AN EVENT I CAN'T COMPETE IN BY MYSELF.
WHEEZE
WHEEZE
DON'T WORRY, MISAKI!
WE GET A HANDICAP FOR EVENTS LIKE THIS.
*Even if you don't participate, you get points.
WE MAY GET POINTS...
...BUT WE WON'T GET A PRIZE.
WELL... YEAH.
THAT'S TRUE.
I...
...WANT TO WIN AS MANY PRIZES AS I CAN.
I WANT TO MAKE THIS A COMFORTABLE ENVIRONMENT FOR THE GIRLS.
AWW, MISAKI! ♡
AYU-ZAWA!
MISAKI...!
AAAAAH!
MOBBED
EXACTLY.
AT THIS FESTIVAL...
...EVERY WIN GAINS YOU MORE RIGHTS.
SO HOW CAN I...

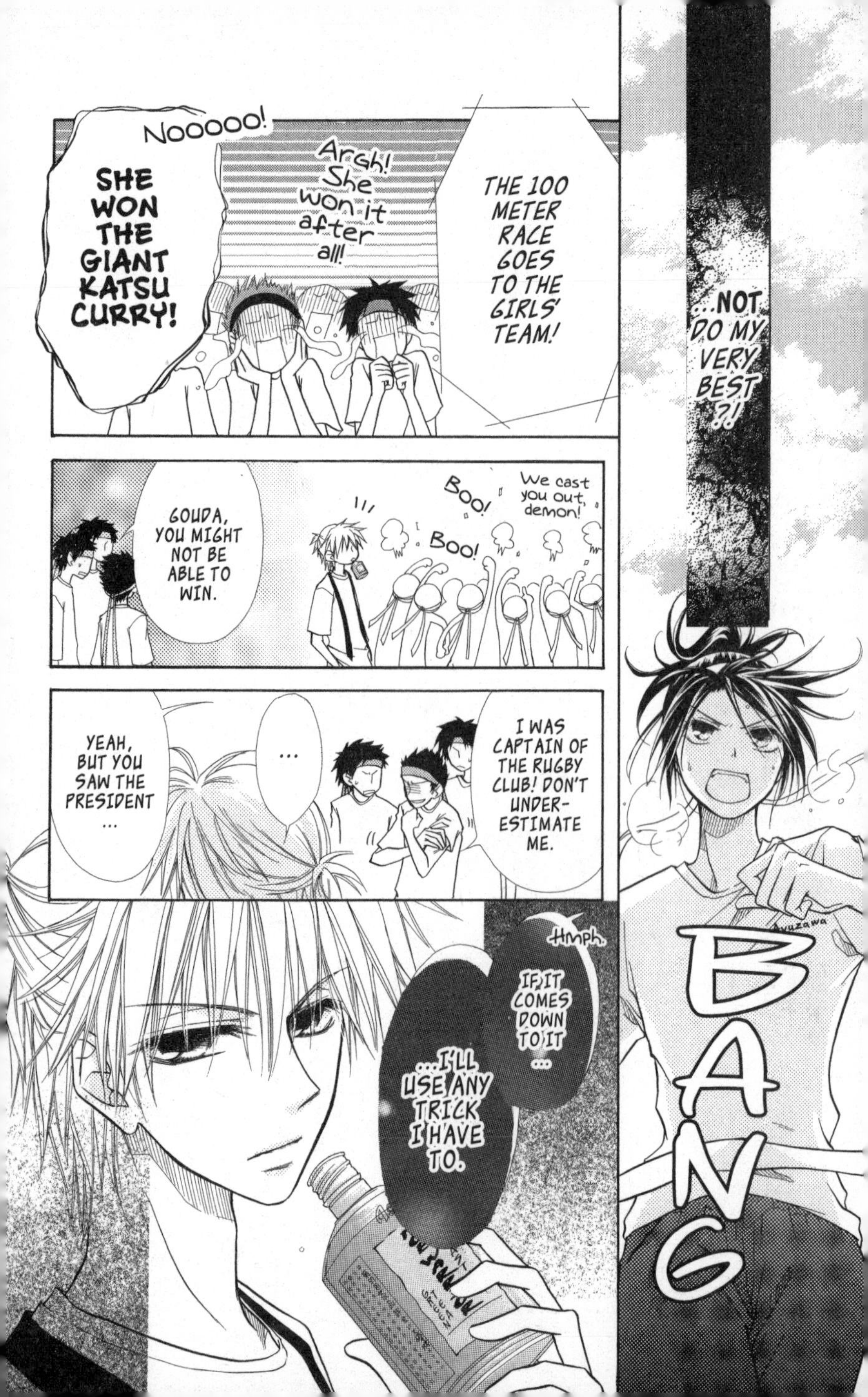
...NOT DO MY VERY BEST ?!
Ayuzawa
BANG
THE 100 METER RACE GOES TO THE GIRLS' TEAM!
Argh! She won it after all!
Nooooo!
SHE WON THE GIANT KATSU CURRY!
We cast you out, demon!
Boo!
Boo!
GOUDA, YOU MIGHT NOT BE ABLE TO WIN.
I WAS CAPTAIN OF THE RUGBY CLUB! DON'T UNDER-ESTIMATE ME.
...
YEAH, BUT YOU SAW THE PRESIDENT ...
Hmph.
IF IT COMES DOWN TO IT ...
...I'LL USE ANY TRICK I HAVE TO.

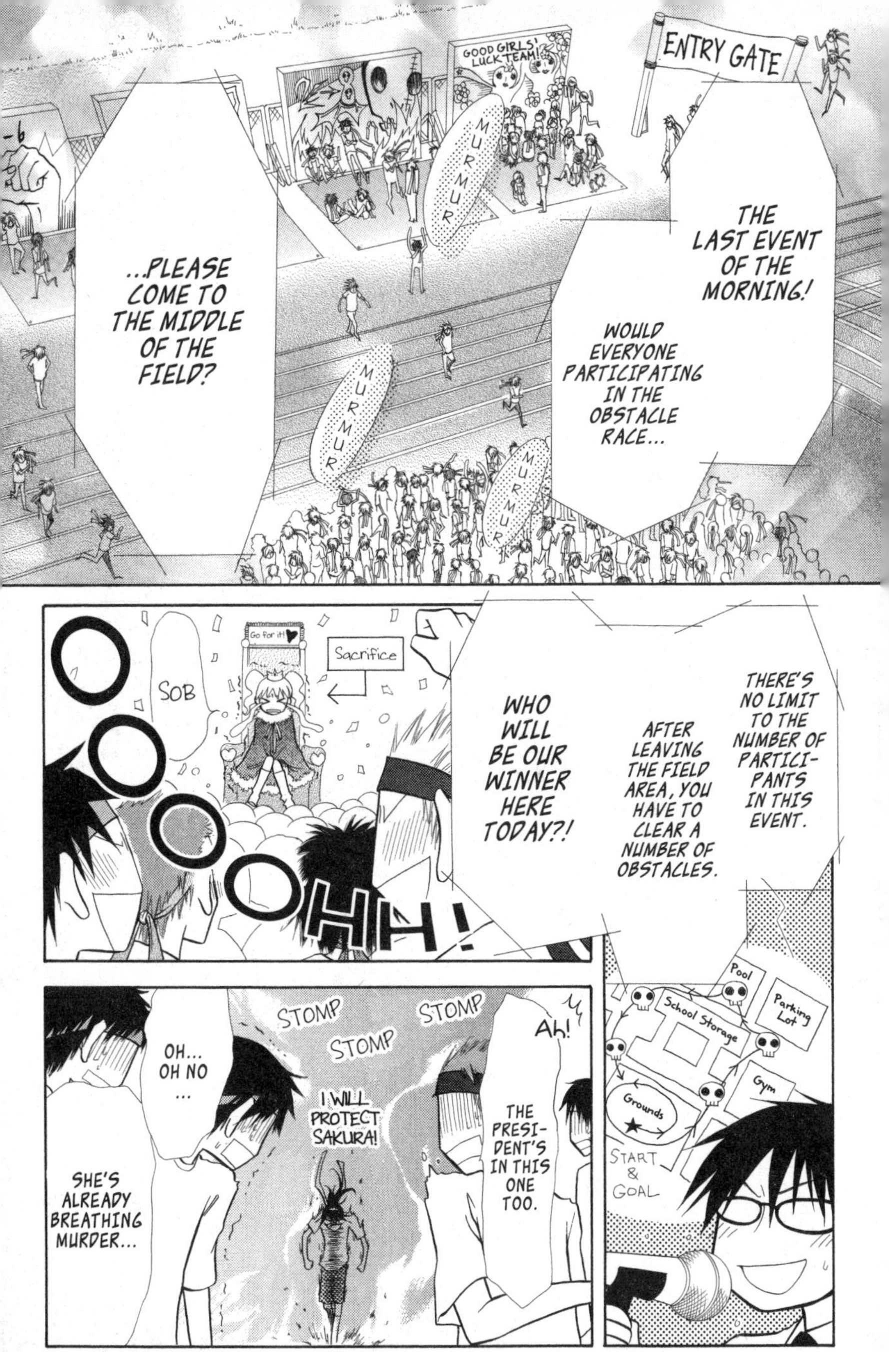
ENTRY GATE
GOOD GIRLS' LUCK TEAM!
THE LAST EVENT OF THE MORNING!
WOULD EVERYONE PARTICIPATING IN THE OBSTACLE RACE...
MURMUR
MURMUR
MURMUR
...PLEASE COME TO THE MIDDLE OF THE FIELD?
THERE'S NO LIMIT TO THE NUMBER OF PARTICI-PANTS IN THIS EVENT.
AFTER LEAVING THE FIELD AREA, YOU HAVE TO CLEAR A NUMBER OF OBSTACLES.
WHO WILL BE OUR WINNER HERE TODAY?!
Pool
Parking Lot
School Storage
Gym
Grounds
START & GOAL
Sacrifice
Go for it!
SOB
OOOOOHH!
Ah!
THE PRESI-DENT'S IN THIS ONE TOO.
STOMP
STOMP
STOMP
I WILL PROTECT SAKURA!
OH... OH NO ...
SHE'S ALREADY BREATHING MURDER...

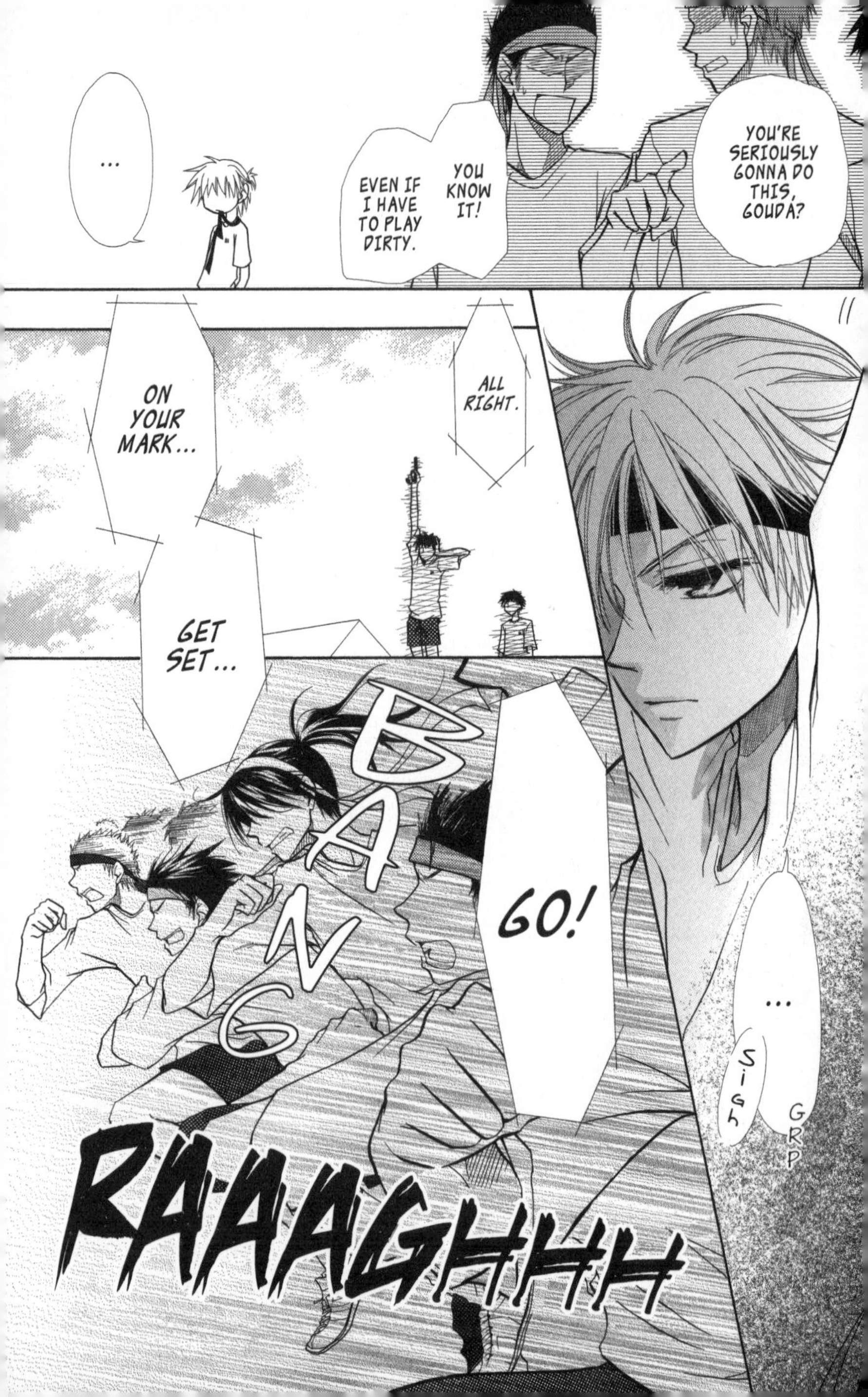
YOU'RE SERIOUSLY GONNA DO THIS, GOUDA?
YOU KNOW IT!
EVEN IF I HAVE TO PLAY DIRTY.
...
...
Sigh
GRP
ALL RIGHT.
ON YOUR MARK...
GET SET...
BANG
GO!
RAAAGHHHH

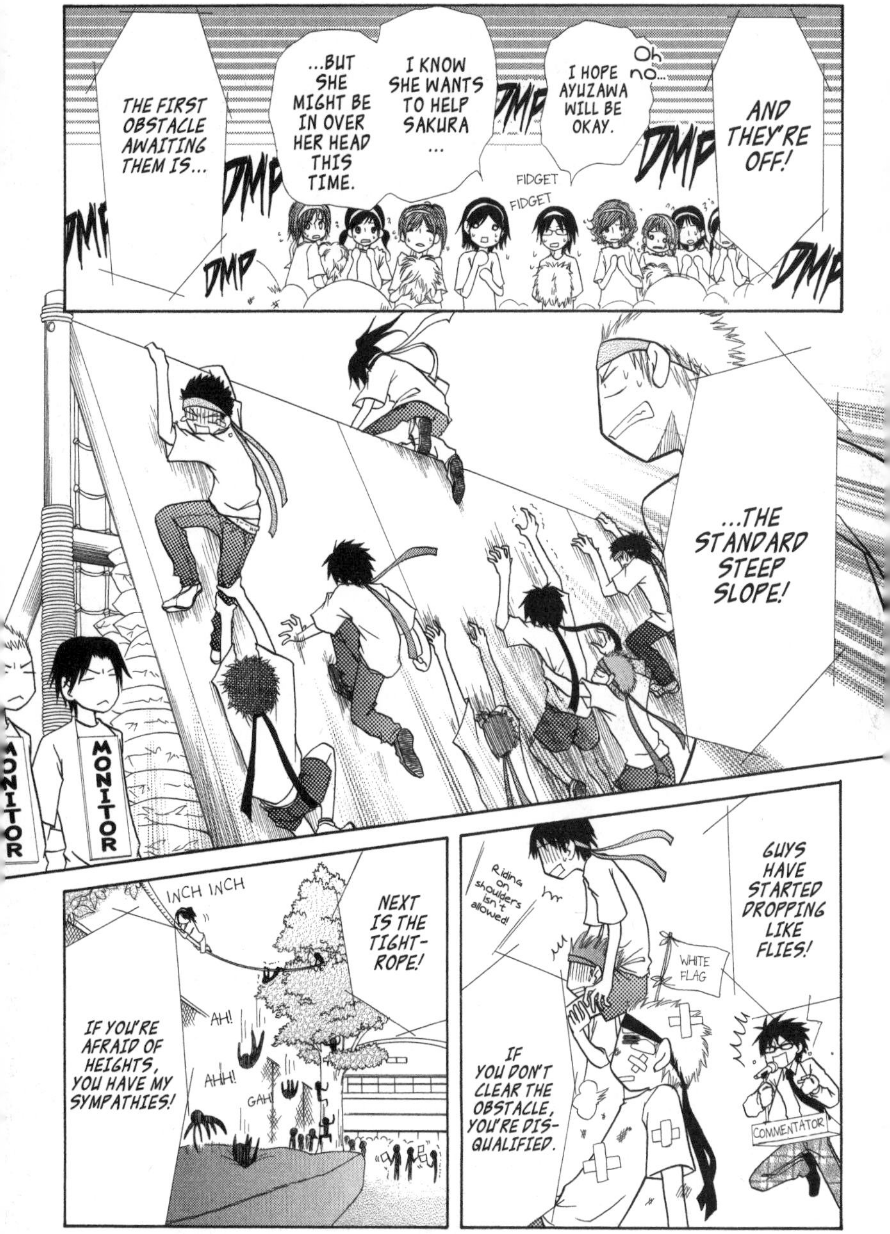
AND THEY'RE OFF!
DMP
Oh no...
I HOPE AYUZAWA WILL BE OKAY.
FIDGET
FIDGET
I KNOW SHE WANTS TO HELP SAKURA...
...BUT SHE MIGHT BE IN OVER HER HEAD THIS TIME.
DMP
THE FIRST OBSTACLE AWAITING THEM IS...
DMP
DMP
DMP
...THE STANDARD STEEP SLOPE!
MONITOR
MONITOR
GUYS HAVE STARTED DROPPING LIKE FLIES!
WHITE FLAG
Riding on shoulders isn't allowed!
COMMENTATOR
IF YOU DON'T CLEAR THE OBSTACLE, YOU'RE DISQUALIFIED.
NEXT IS THE TIGHTROPE!
INCH INCH
AH!
AHH!
GAH
IF YOU'RE AFRAID OF HEIGHTS, YOU HAVE MY SYMPATHIES!

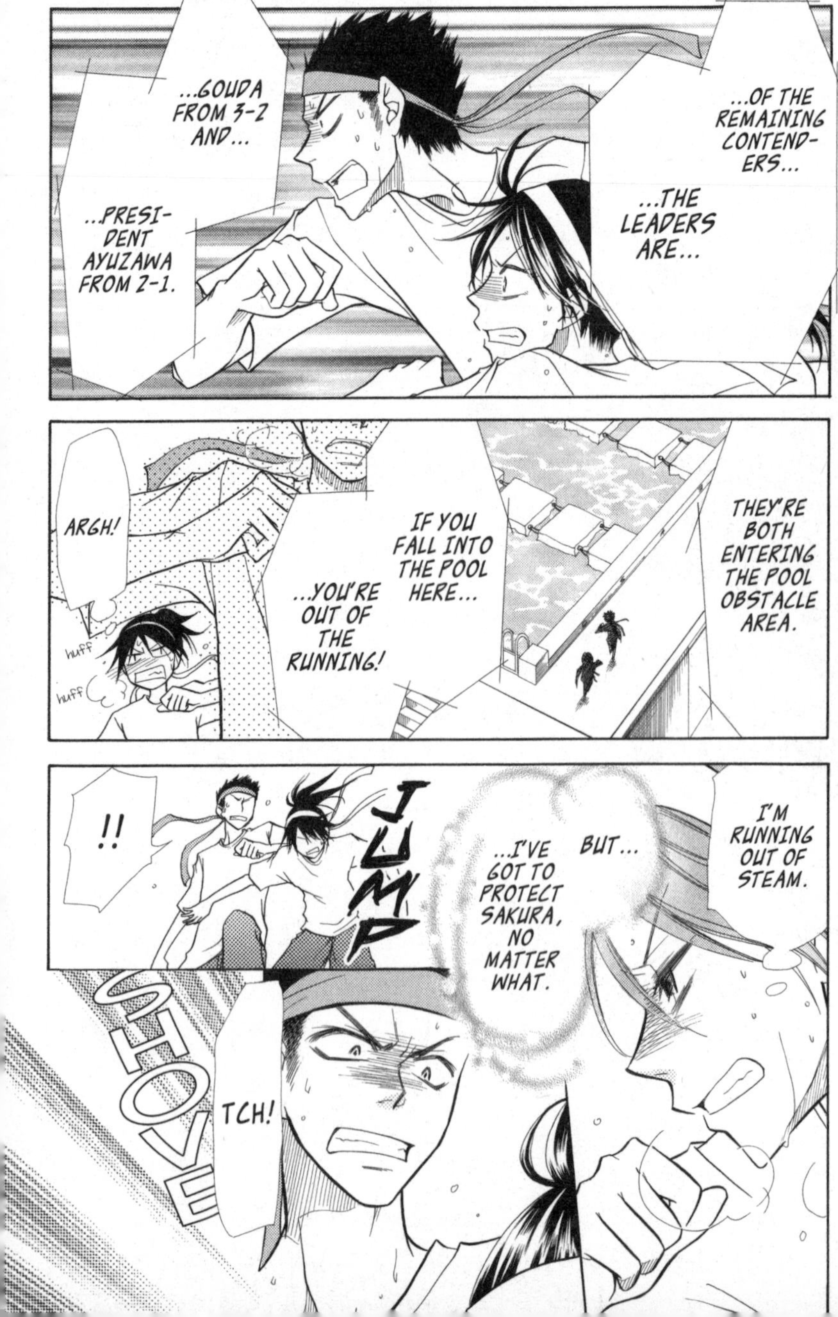
...OF THE REMAINING CONTENDERS...
...THE LEADERS ARE...
...GOUDA FROM 3-2 AND...
...PRESIDENT AYUZAWA FROM 2-1.
THEY'RE BOTH ENTERING THE POOL OBSTACLE AREA.
IF YOU FALL INTO THE POOL HERE...
...YOU'RE OUT OF THE RUNNING!
ARGH!
huff
huff
I'M RUNNING OUT OF STEAM.
BUT...
...I'VE GOT TO PROTECT SAKURA, NO MATTER WHAT.
!!
JUMP
SHOVE
TCH!

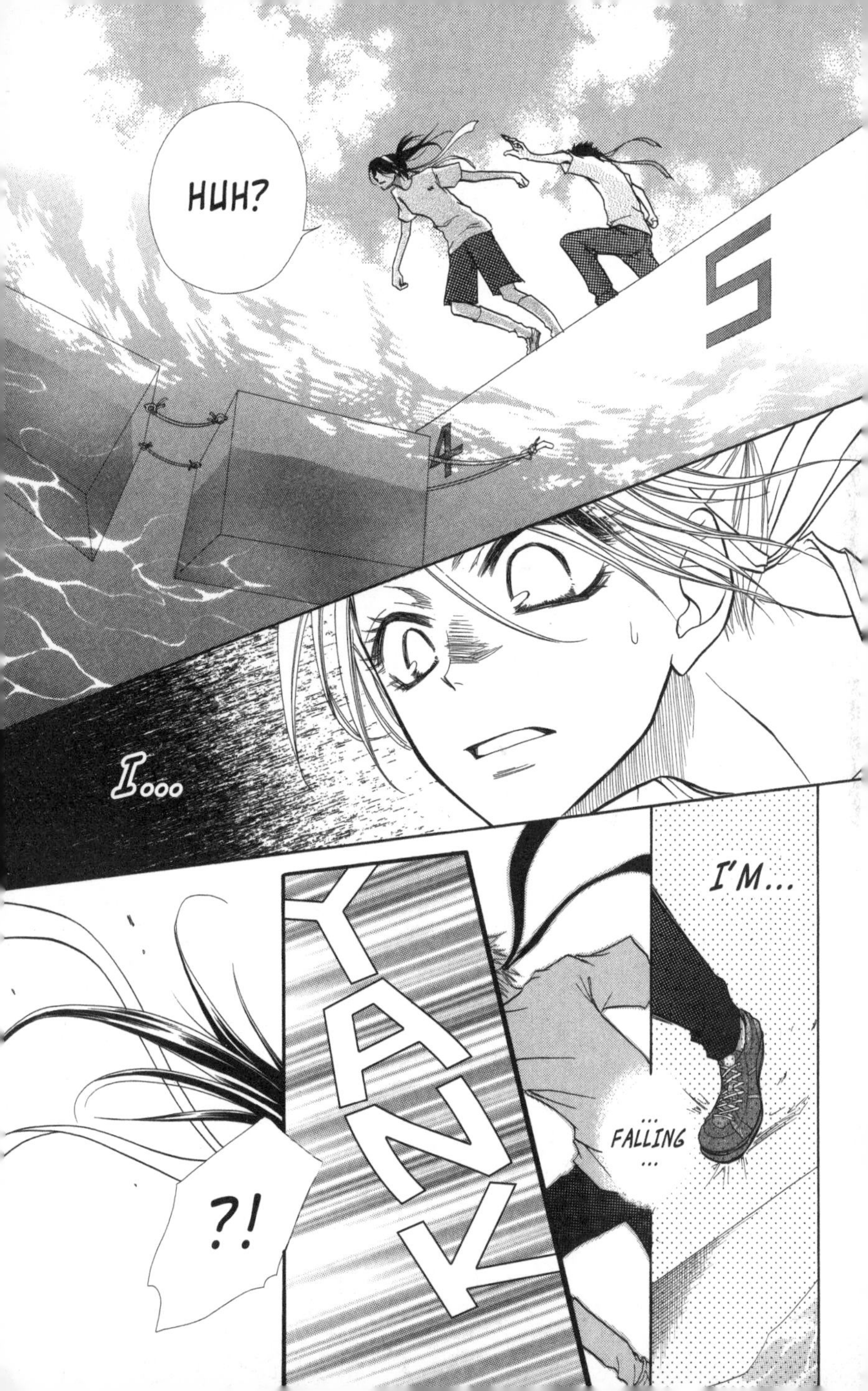
HUH?
I...
I'M...
...FALLING...
YANK
?!

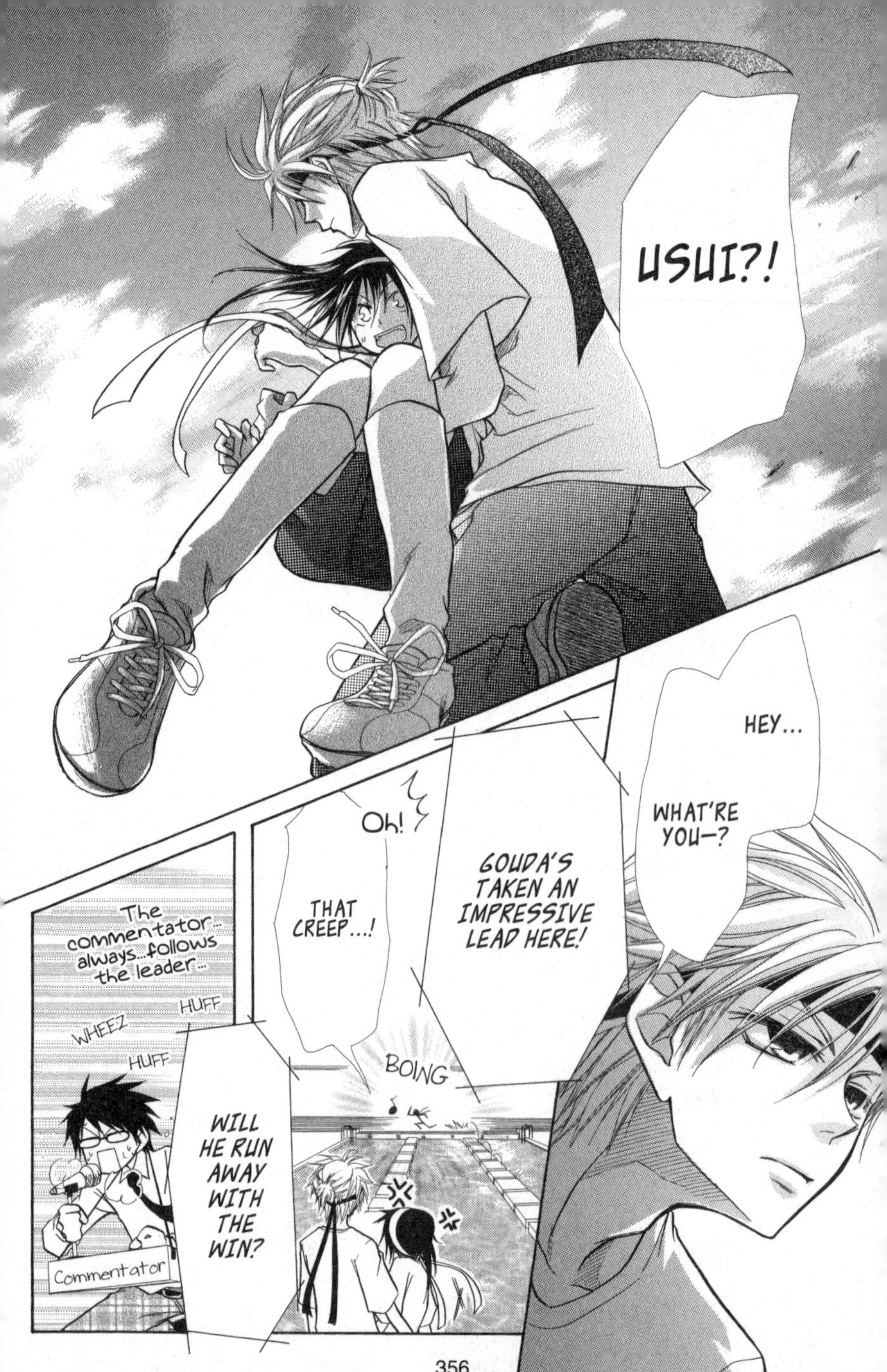
USUI?!
HEY...
WHAT'RE YOU—?
GOUDA'S TAKEN AN IMPRESSIVE LEAD HERE!
Oh!
THAT CREEP...!
BOING
WILL HE RUN AWAY WITH THE WIN?
The commentator... always...follows the leader...
HUFF
WHEEZ
HUFF
Commentator

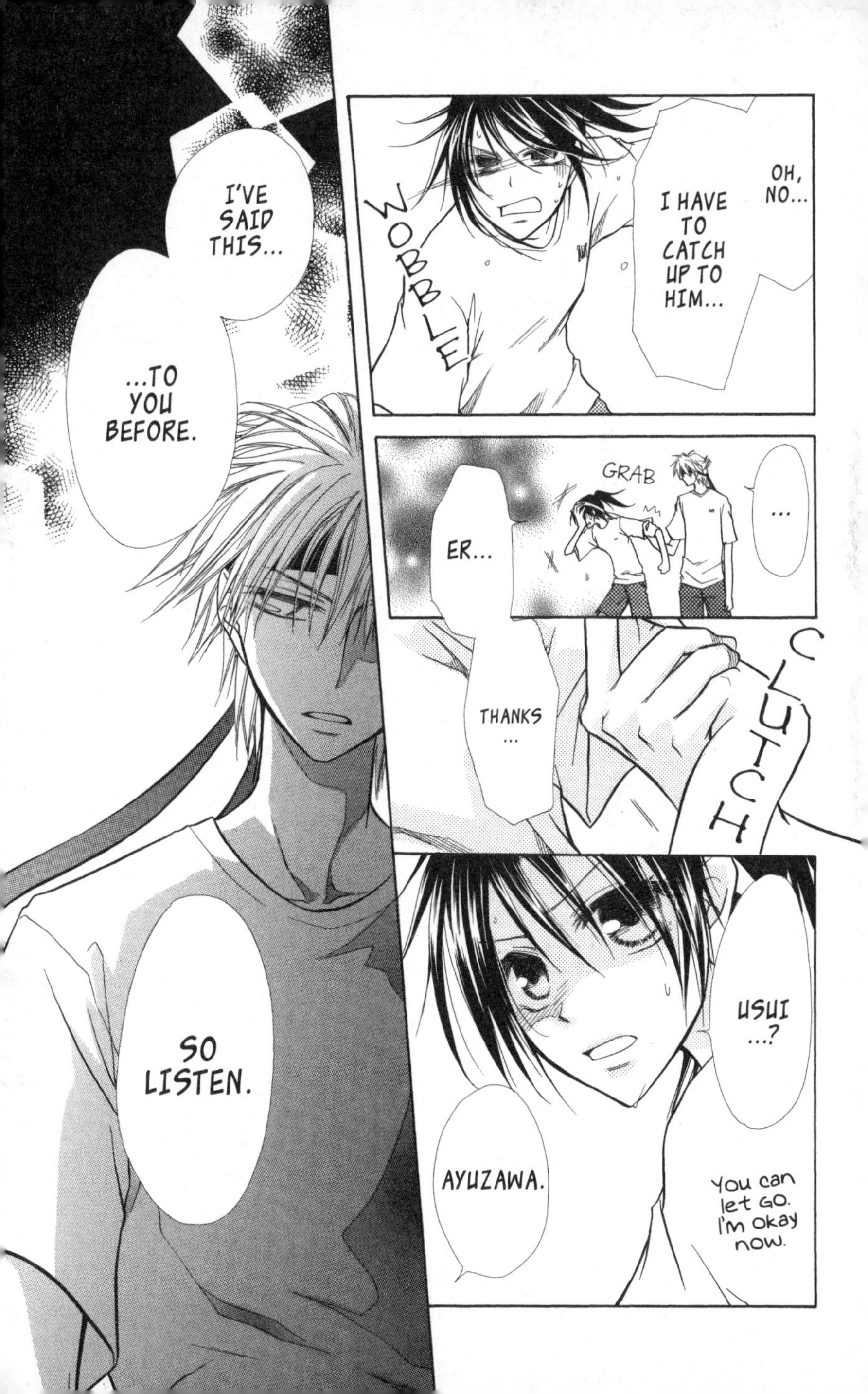
OH, NO...
I HAVE TO CATCH UP TO HIM...
WOBBLE
...
GRAB
ER...
CLUTCH
THANKS ...
USUI ...?
You can let GO. I'm okay now.
AYUZAWA.
I'VE SAID THIS...
...TO YOU BEFORE.
SO LISTEN.

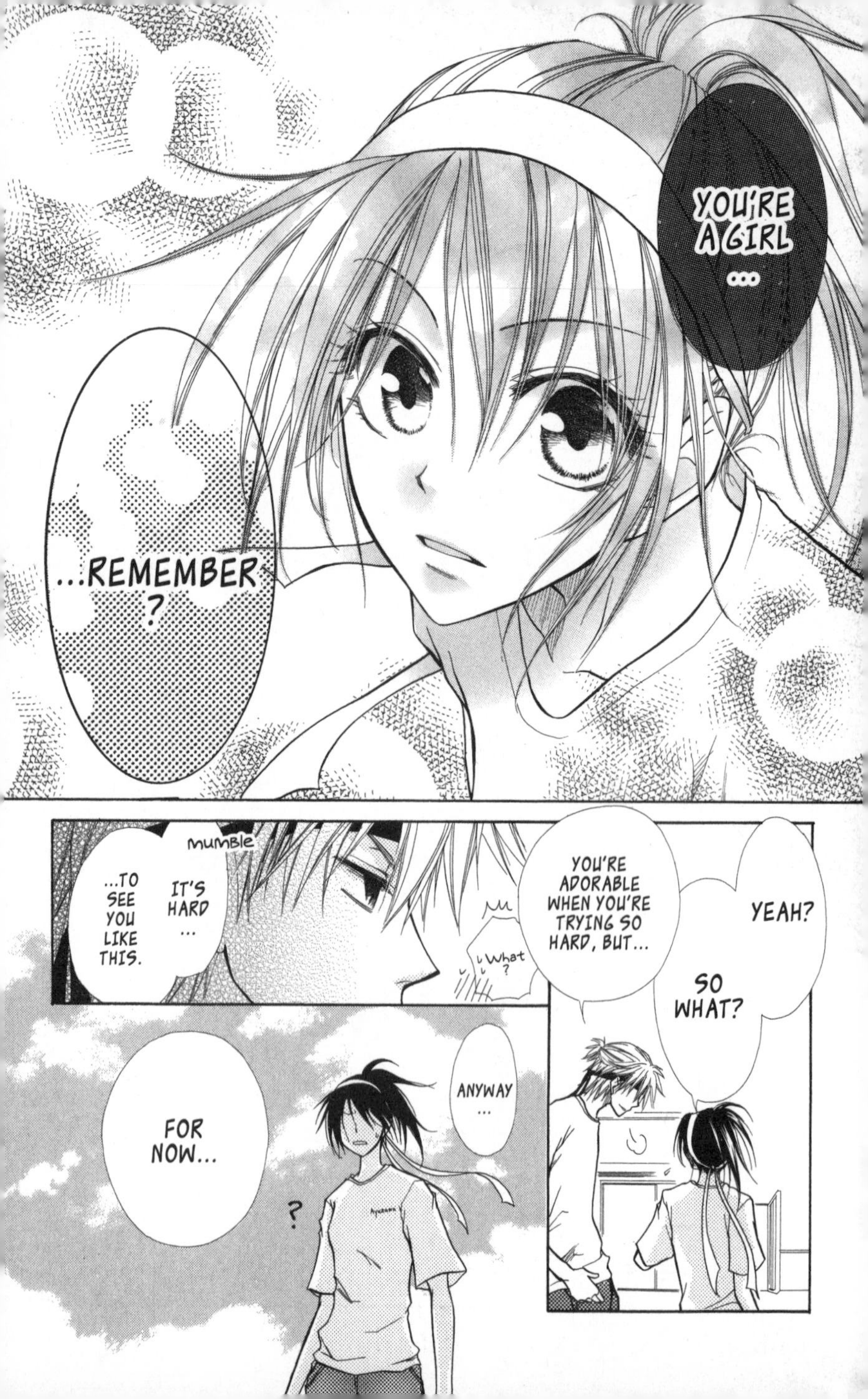
YOU'RE A GIRL ...
...REMEMBER ?
YEAH?
YOU'RE ADORABLE WHEN YOU'RE TRYING SO HARD, BUT...
SO WHAT?
What ?
Mumble
IT'S HARD ...
...TO SEE YOU LIKE THIS.
ANYWAY ...
FOR NOW...
?

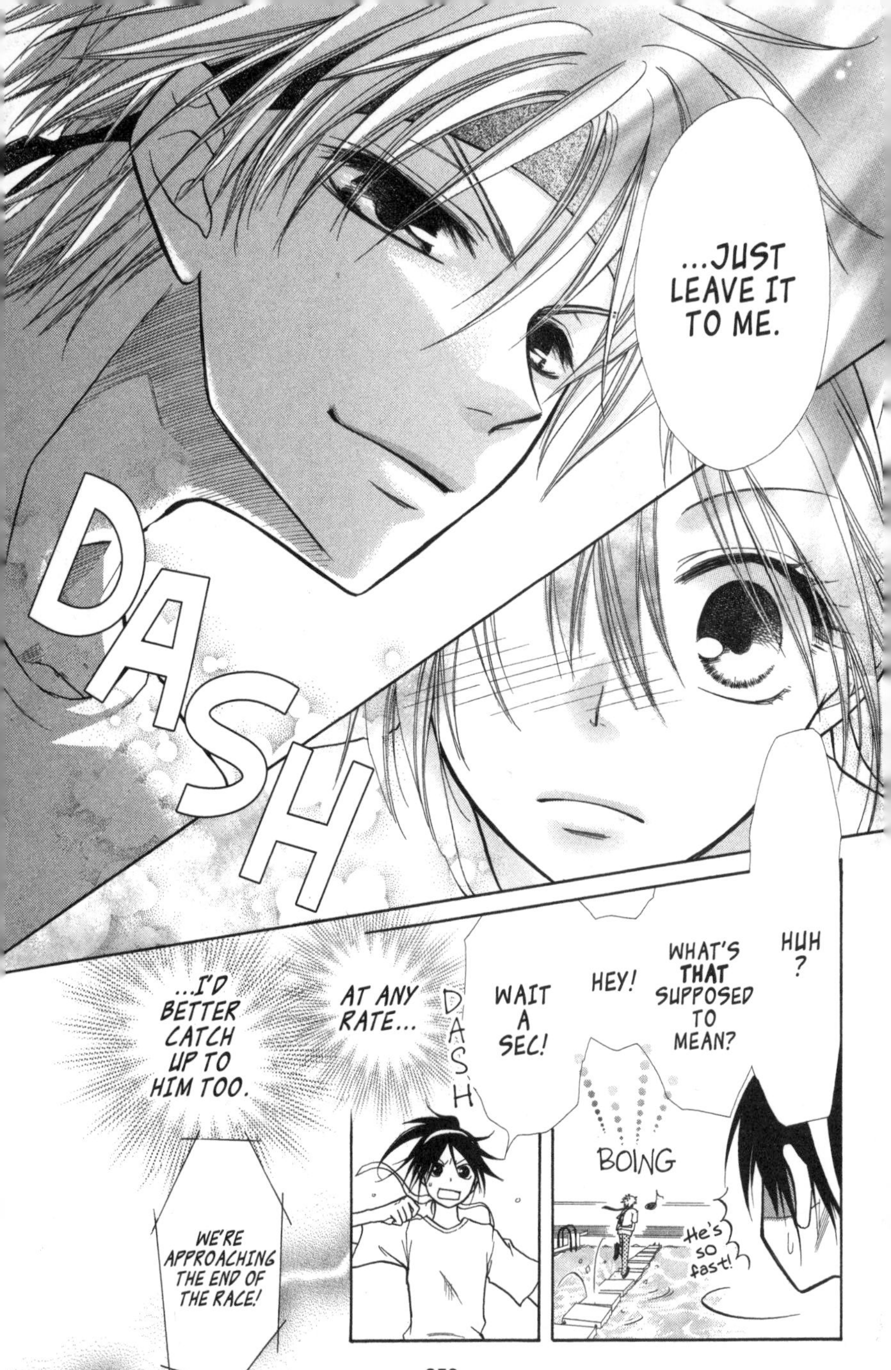
...JUST LEAVE IT TO ME.
DASH
HUH?
WHAT'S THAT SUPPOSED TO MEAN?
BOING
He's so fast!
HEY!
WAIT A SEC!
DASH
AT ANY RATE...
...I'D BETTER CATCH UP TO HIM TOO.
WE'RE APPROACHING THE END OF THE RACE!

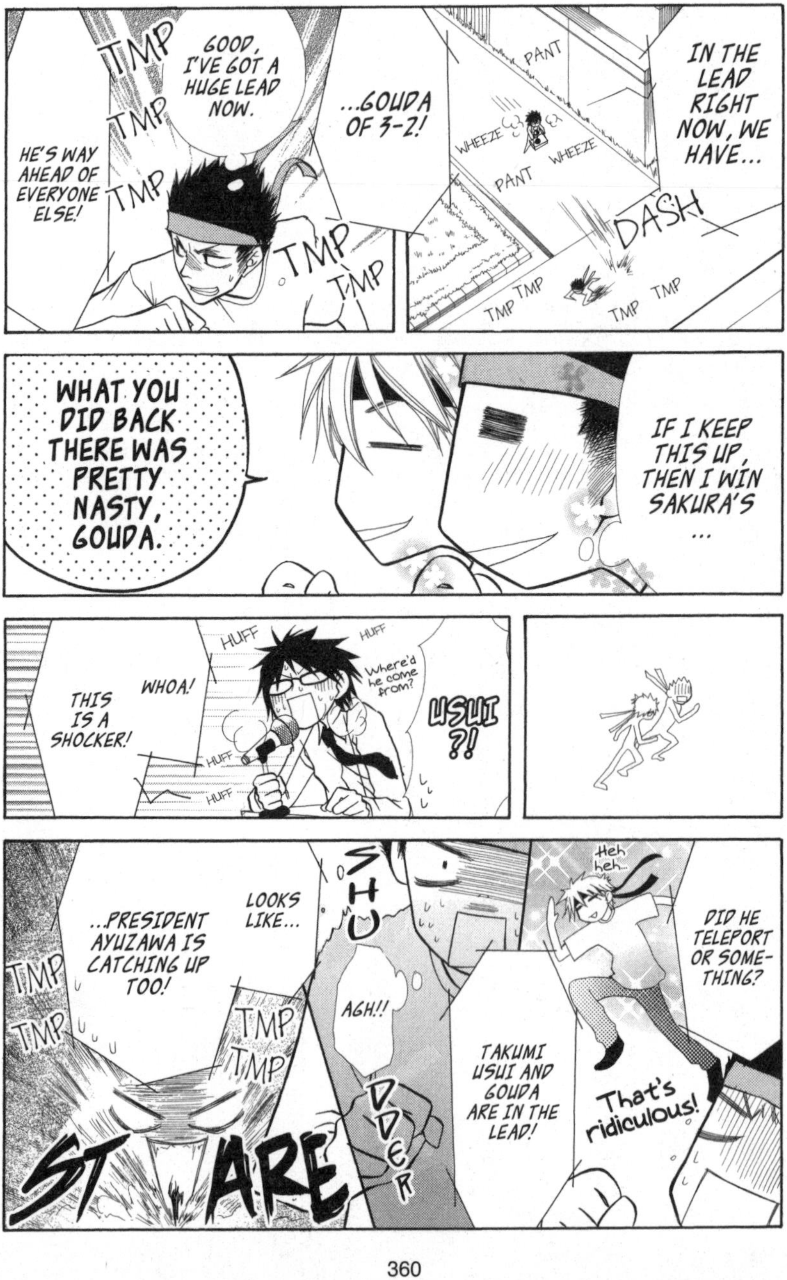
IN THE LEAD RIGHT NOW, WE HAVE...
PANT
WHEEZE
PANT
WHEEZE
DASH
TMP TMP
TMP TMP
...GOUDA OF 3-2!
GOOD, I'VE GOT A HUGE LEAD NOW.
TMP
TMP
TMP
HE'S WAY AHEAD OF EVERYONE ELSE!
TMP
TMP
IF I KEEP THIS UP, THEN I WIN SAKURA'S ...
WHAT YOU DID BACK THERE WAS PRETTY NASTY, GOUDA.
USUI ?!
Where'd he come from?
HUFF
HUFF
WHOA!
HUFF
HUFF
THIS IS A SHOCKER!
DID HE TELEPORT OR SOME-THING?
Heh heh...
That's ridiculous!
TAKUMI USUI AND GOUDA ARE IN THE LEAD!
SHUDDER
AGH!!
LOOKS LIKE...
...PRESIDENT AYUZAWA IS CATCHING UP TOO!
TMP
TMP
TMP
TMP
STARE

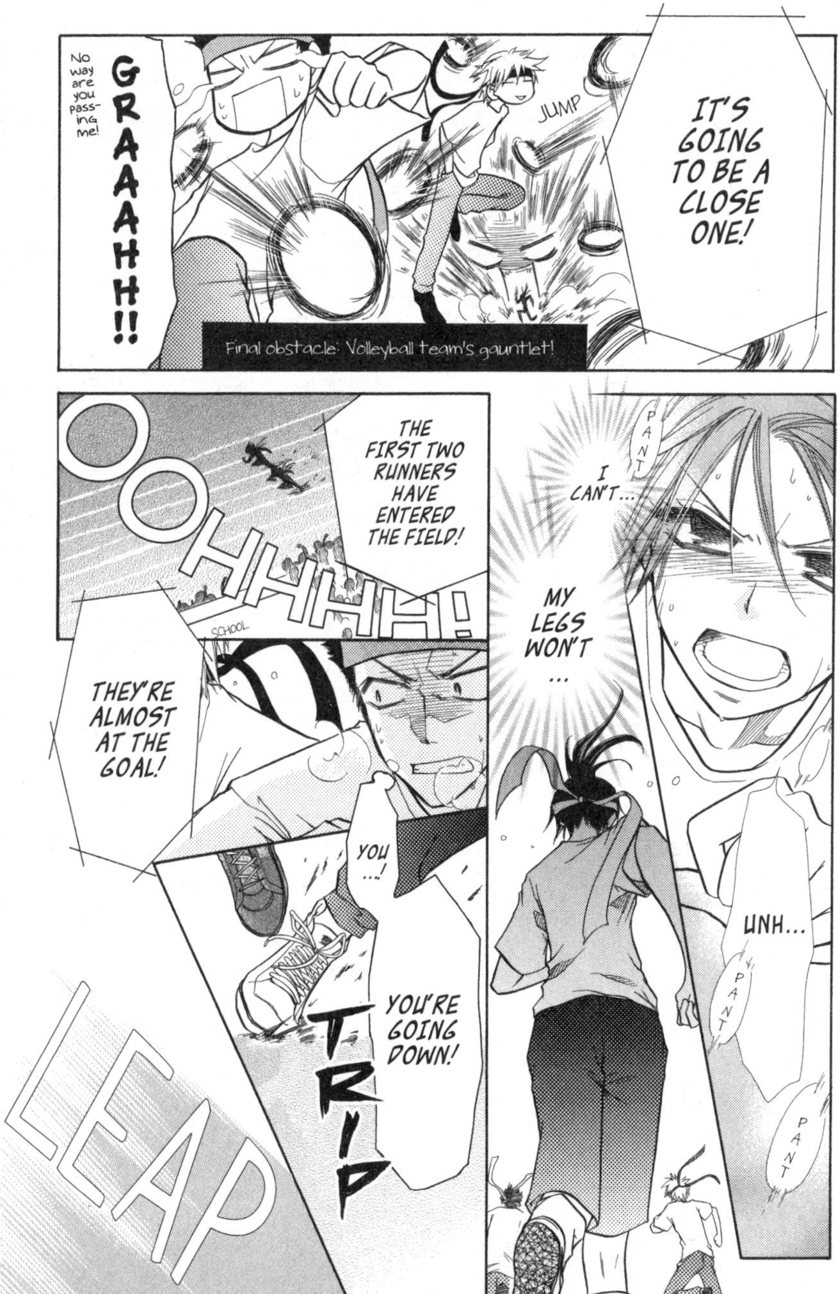
IT'S GOING TO BE A CLOSE ONE!
JUMP
No way are you pass-ing me!
GRAAAAHH!!
Final obstacle: Volleyball team's gauntlet!
PANT
I CAN'T...
MY LEGS WON'T...
UNH...
PANT
PANT
THE FIRST TWO RUNNERS HAVE ENTERED THE FIELD!
OOHHHHHH!
SCHOOL
THEY'RE ALMOST AT THE GOAL!
YOU...!
YOU'RE GOING DOWN!
TRIP
LEAP

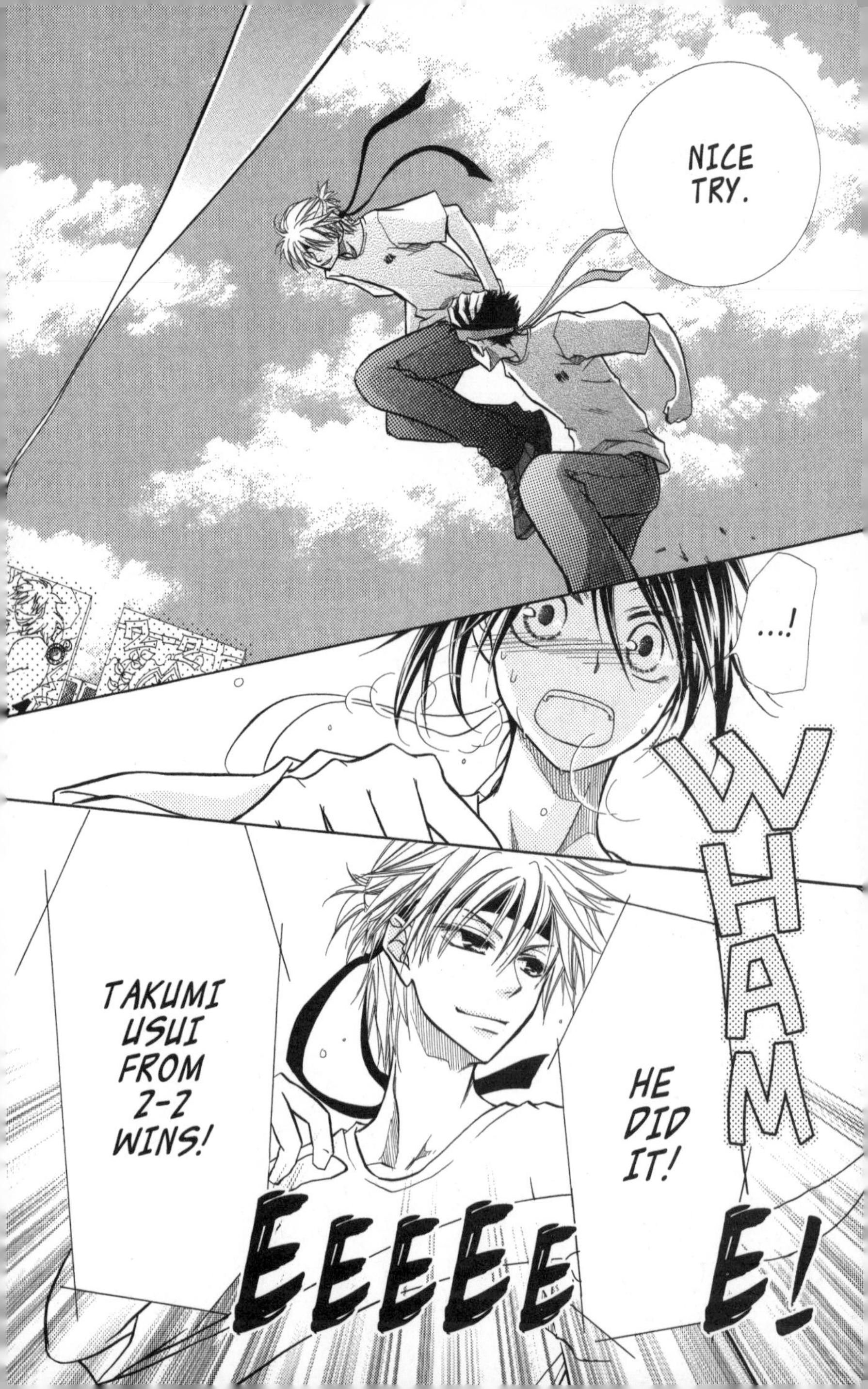
NICE TRY.
...!
WHAM
HE DID IT!
TAKUMI USUI FROM 2-2 WINS!
EEEEE E!

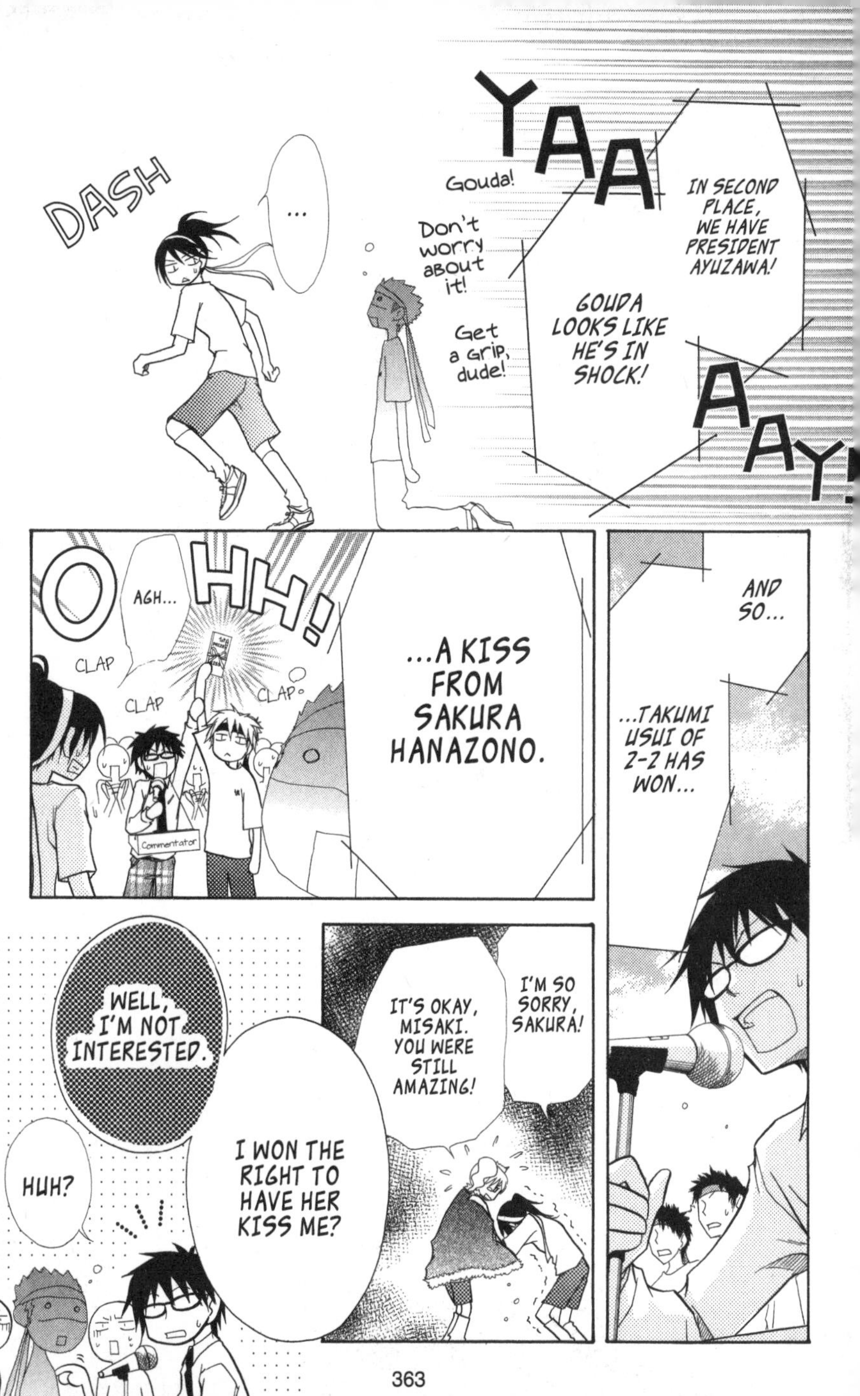
YAAAAAY!
IN SECOND PLACE, WE HAVE PRESIDENT AYUZAWA!
GOUDA LOOKS LIKE HE'S IN SHOCK!
Gouda!
Don't worry about it!
Get a grip, dude!
...
DASH
AND SO...
...TAKUMI USUI OF 2-2 HAS WON...
...A KISS FROM SAKURA HANAZONO.
OHH!
AGH...
CLAP
CLAP
CLAP
Commentator
I'M SO SORRY, SAKURA!
IT'S OKAY, MISAKI. YOU WERE STILL AMAZING!
WELL, I'M NOT INTERESTED.
I WON THE RIGHT TO HAVE HER KISS ME?
HUH?

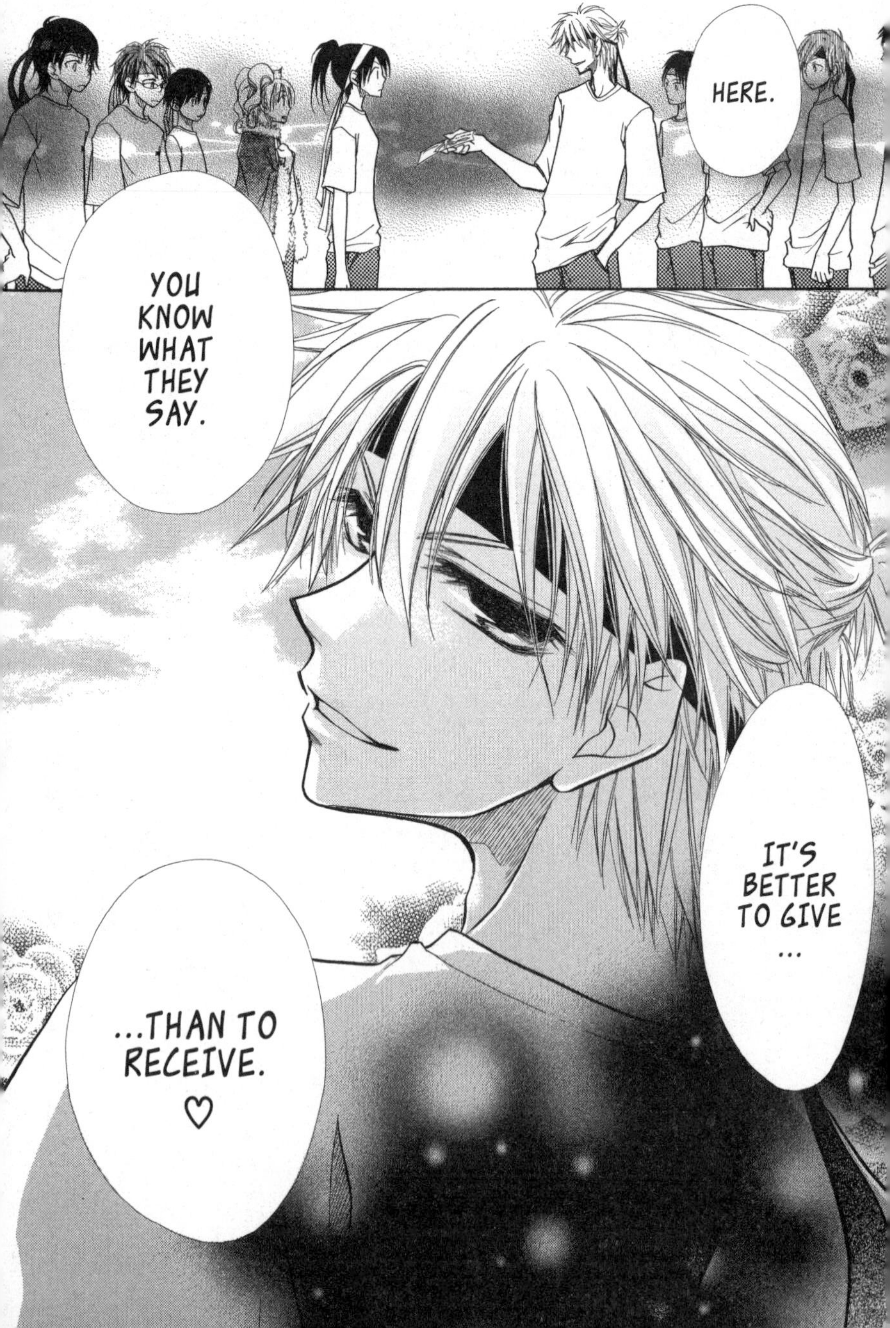
HERE.
YOU KNOW WHAT THEY SAY.
IT'S BETTER TO GIVE...
...THAN TO RECEIVE. ♡

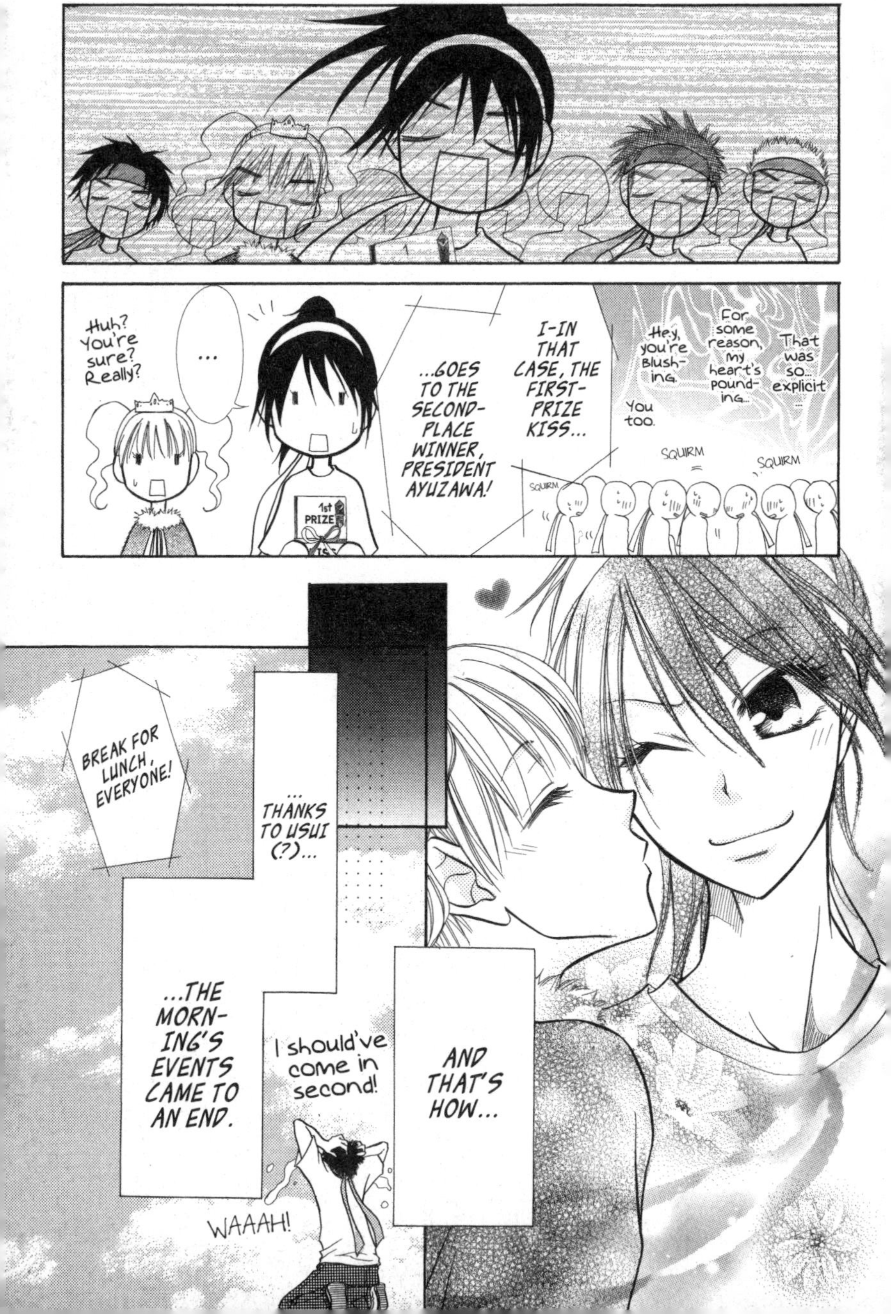
That was so... explicit...
For some reason, my heart's pounding...
Hey, you're blushing.
You too.
SQUIRM
SQUIRM
SQUIRM
I-IN THAT CASE, THE FIRST-PRIZE KISS...
...GOES TO THE SECOND-PLACE WINNER, PRESIDENT AYUZAWA!
1st PRIZE
...
Huh? You're sure? Really?
AND THAT'S HOW...
...THANKS TO USUI (?)...
...THE MORNING'S EVENTS CAME TO AN END.
BREAK FOR LUNCH, EVERYONE!
I should've come in second!
WAAAH!

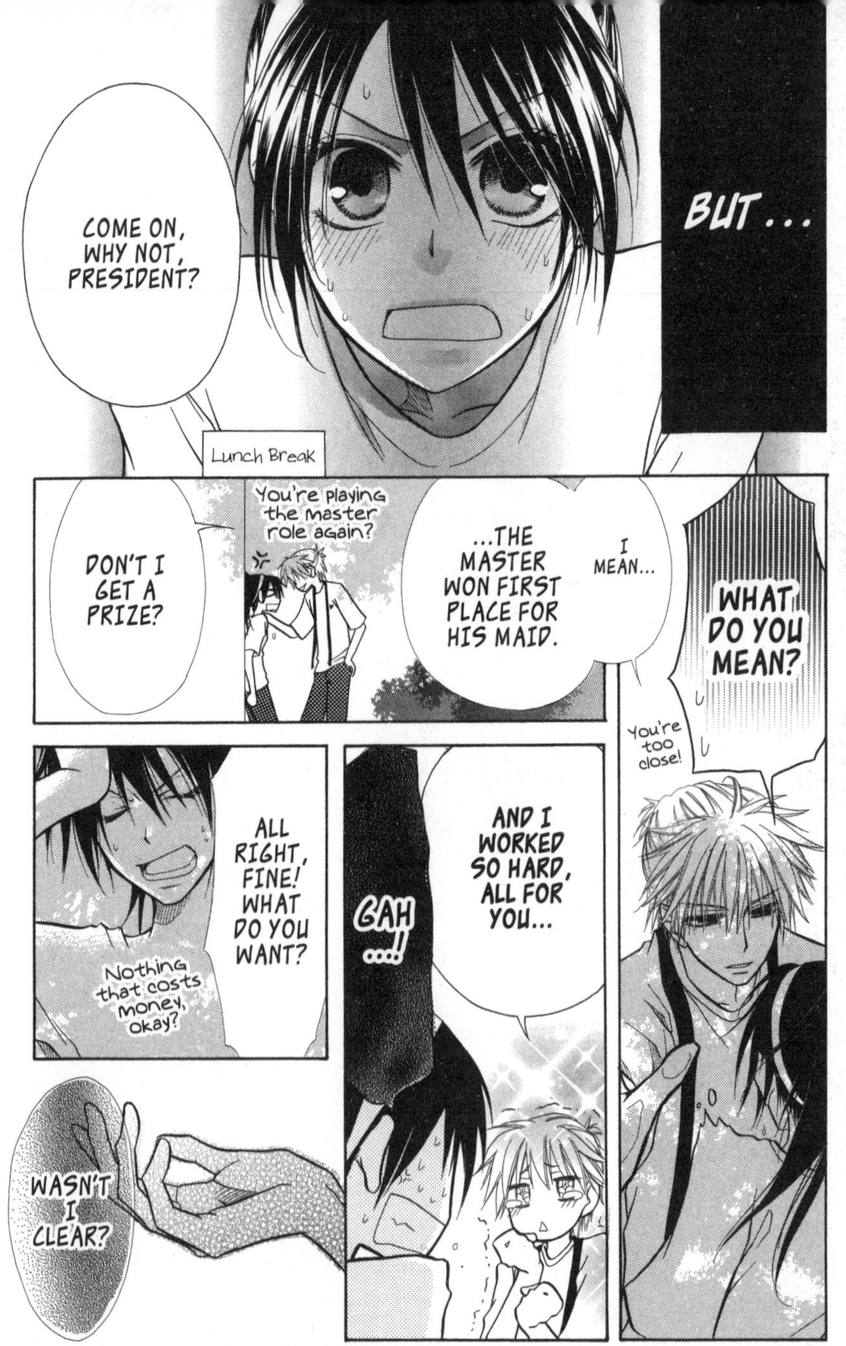
BUT...
COME ON, WHY NOT, PRESIDENT?
Lunch Break
WHAT DO YOU MEAN?
You're too close!
I MEAN...
...THE MASTER WON FIRST PLACE FOR HIS MAID.
You're playing the master role again?
DON'T I GET A PRIZE?
AND I WORKED SO HARD, ALL FOR YOU...
GAH...!!
ALL RIGHT, FINE! WHAT DO YOU WANT?
Nothing that costs money, okay?
WASN'T I CLEAR?

I'D...

...RATHER GIVE...

...THAN RECEIVE.

81ST SPORTS FESTI

●AFTERNOON EVENTS●
10. PARADE OF CLUBS AND RELAY RACE
11. TUG-OF-WAR
12. COSTUME RACE
13. CENTIPEDE RACE
14. THREE-LEGGED RACE
SPORT
BOYS

THE SPORTS FESTIVAL ISN'T OVER.

I DON'T THINK WE'RE OUT OF THE WOODS YET!

GET OUT OF MY FACE!

ON TO THE AFTERNOON EVENTS!

SHOVE

But it's an order from your master!

Commentator

MAID-SAMA! ② / THE END

closing time...

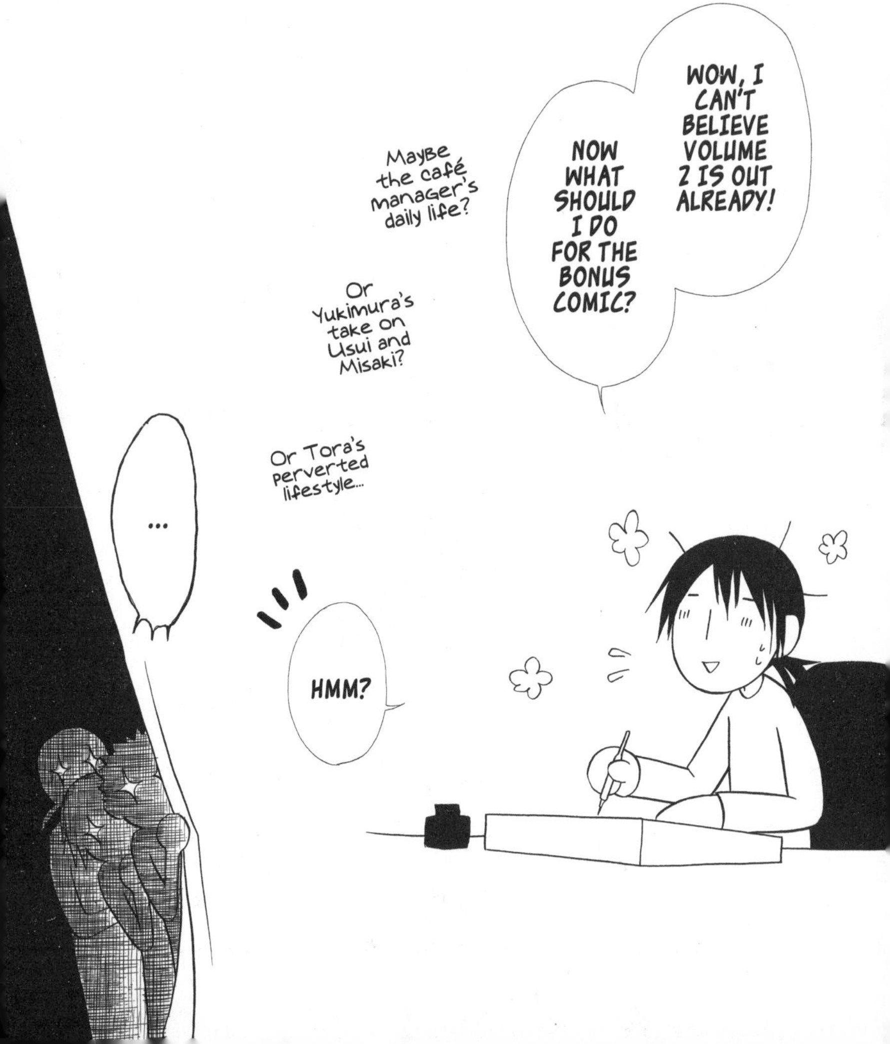
WOW, I CAN'T BELIEVE VOLUME 2 IS OUT ALREADY!
NOW WHAT SHOULD I DO FOR THE BONUS COMIC?
Maybe the café manager's daily life?
Or Yukimura's take on Usui and Misaki?
Or Tora's perverted lifestyle...
...
HMM?

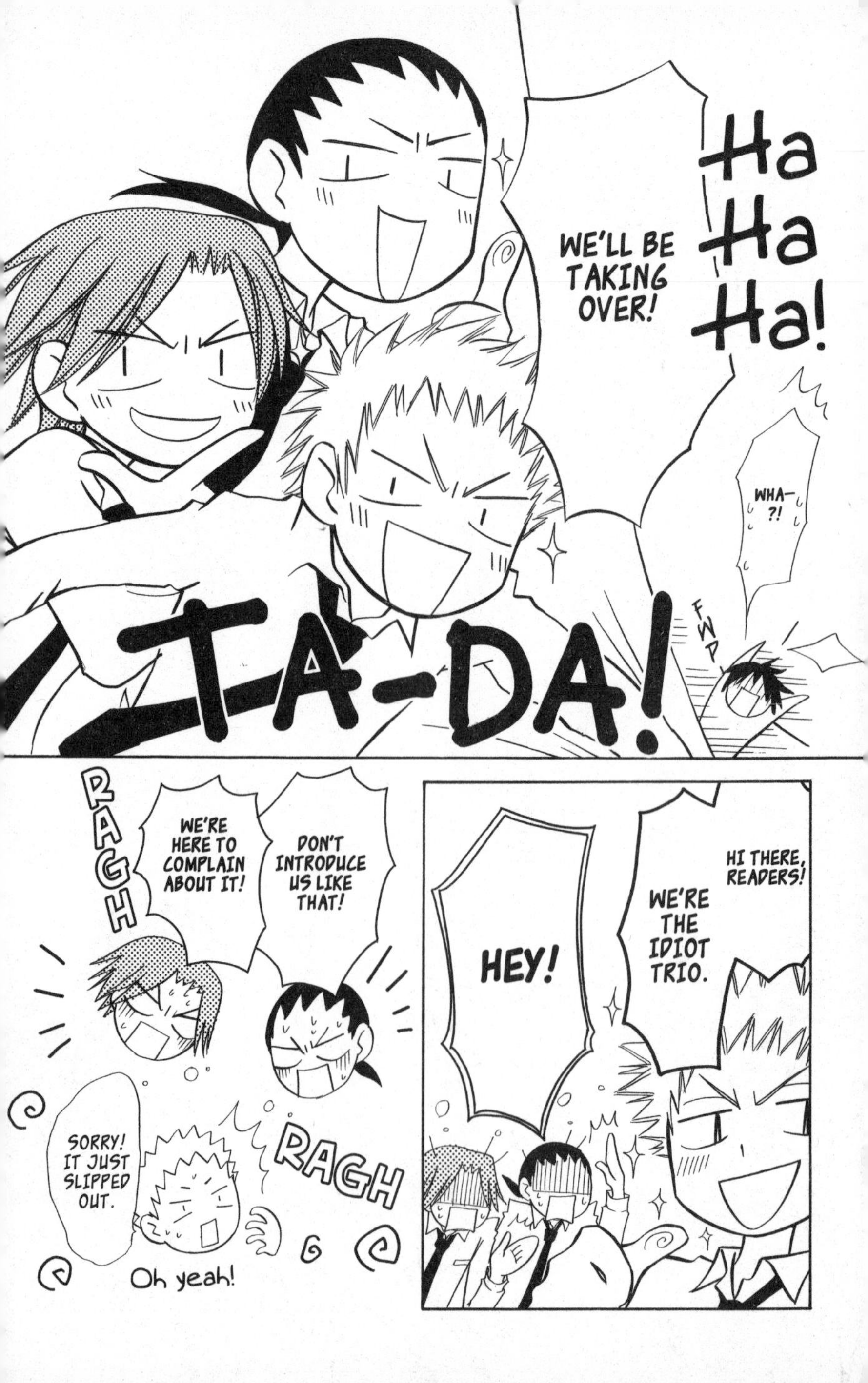
Ha Ha Ha!
WE'LL BE TAKING OVER!
WHA—?!
FWP
TA-DA!
HI THERE, READERS!
WE'RE THE IDIOT TRIO.
HEY!
DON'T INTRODUCE US LIKE THAT!
WE'RE HERE TO COMPLAIN ABOUT IT!
RAGH
RAGH
SORRY! IT JUST SLIPPED OUT.
Oh yeah!

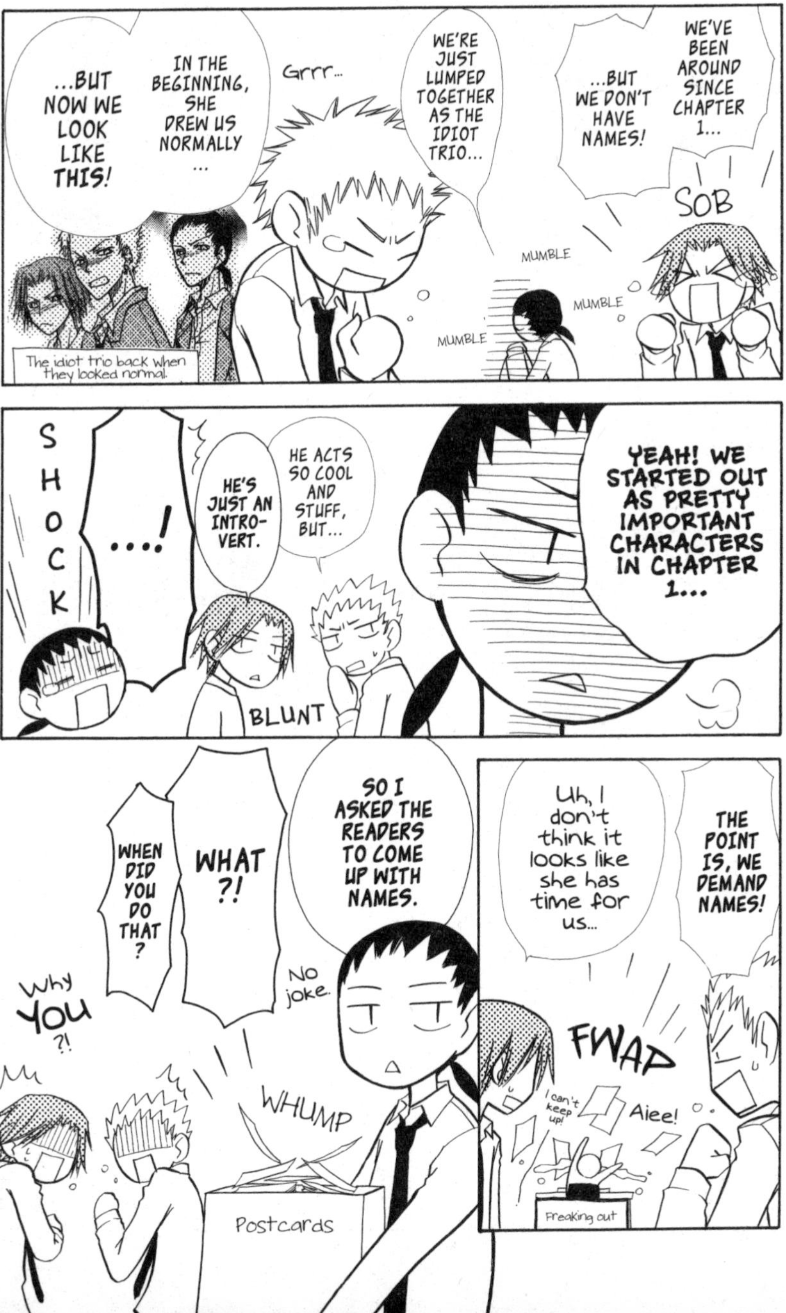
WE'VE BEEN AROUND SINCE CHAPTER 1...
...BUT WE DON'T HAVE NAMES!
SOB
MUMBLE
MUMBLE
MUMBLE
WE'RE JUST LUMPED TOGETHER AS THE IDIOT TRIO...
Grrr...
IN THE BEGINNING, SHE DREW US NORMALLY...
...BUT NOW WE LOOK LIKE THIS!
The idiot trio back when they looked normal.
YEAH! WE STARTED OUT AS PRETTY IMPORTANT CHARACTERS IN CHAPTER 1...
HE ACTS SO COOL AND STUFF, BUT...
HE'S JUST AN INTRO-VERT.
BLUNT
...!
SHOCK
THE POINT IS, WE DEMAND NAMES!
Uh, I don't think it looks like she has time for us...
FWAP
Aiee!
I can't keep up!
Freaking out
SO I ASKED THE READERS TO COME UP WITH NAMES.
No joke.
WHAT?!
WHEN DID YOU DO THAT?
WHUMP
Postcards
Why YOU?!

A meeting to pick names for the Idiot Trio!

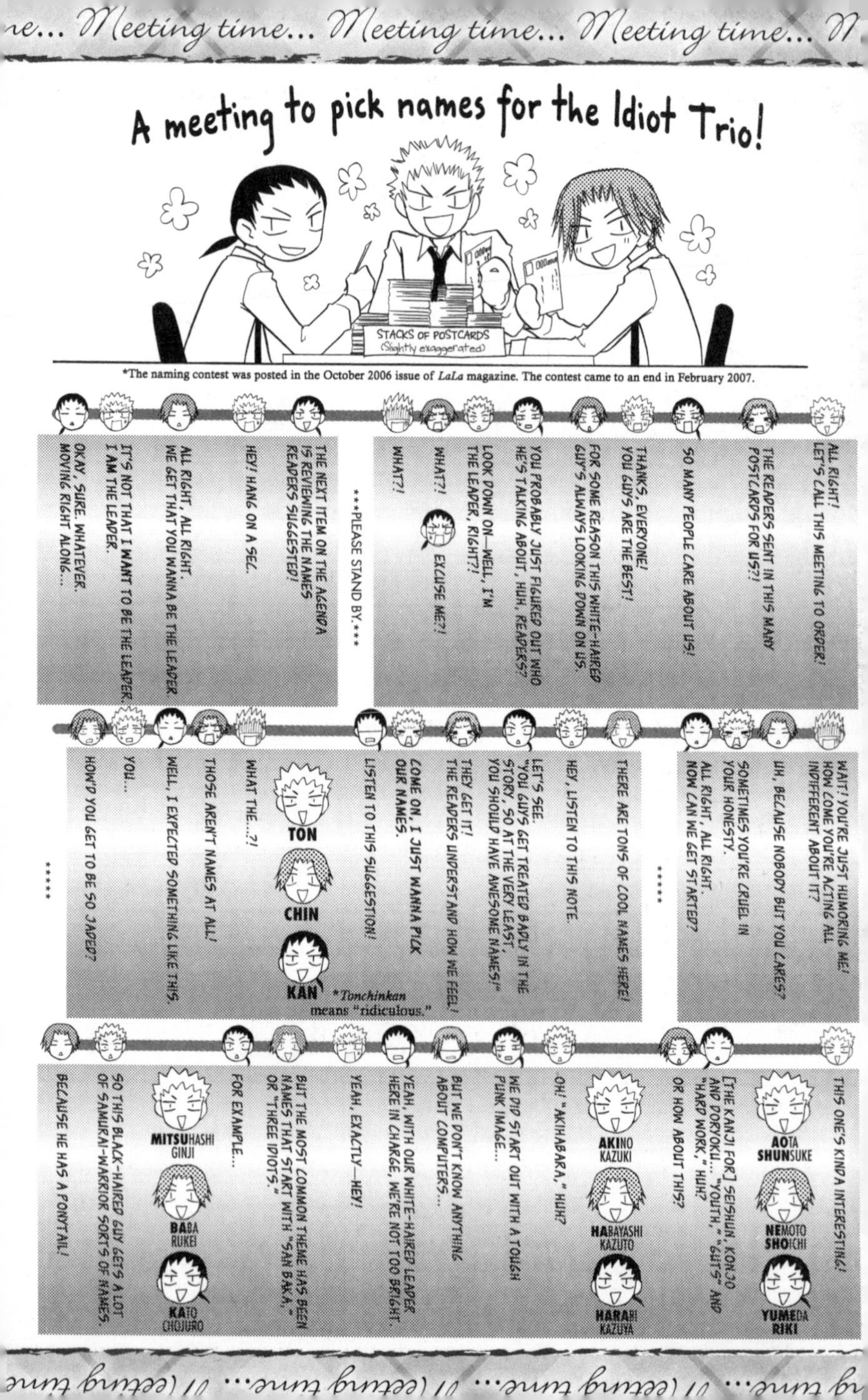
STACKS OF POSTCARDS
(Slightly exaggerated)

*The naming contest was posted in the October 2006 issue of *LaLa* magazine. The contest came to an end in February 2007.

ALL RIGHT! LET'S CALL THIS MEETING TO ORDER!

THE READERS SENT IN THIS MANY POSTCARDS FOR US?!

SO MANY PEOPLE CARE ABOUT US!

THANKS, EVERYONE! YOU GUYS ARE THE BEST!

FOR SOME REASON THIS WHITE-HAIRED GUY'S ALWAYS LOOKING DOWN ON US.

YOU PROBABLY JUST FIGURED OUT WHO HE'S TALKING ABOUT, HUH, READERS?

LOOK DOWN ON—WELL, I'M THE LEADER, RIGHT?!

WHAT?! EXCUSE ME?!

WHAT?!

PLEASE STAND BY.

THE NEXT ITEM ON THE AGENDA IS REVIEWING THE NAMES READERS SUGGESTED!

HEY! HANG ON A SEC.

ALL RIGHT, ALL RIGHT. WE GET THAT YOU WANNA BE THE LEADER.

IT'S NOT THAT I WANT TO BE THE LEADER. I AM THE LEADER.

OKAY, SURE. WHATEVER. MOVING RIGHT ALONG...

WAIT! YOU'RE JUST HUMORING ME! HOW COME YOU'RE ACTING ALL INDIFFERENT ABOUT IT?

UH, BECAUSE NOBODY BUT YOU CARES?

SOMETIMES YOU'RE CRUEL IN YOUR HONESTY.

ALL RIGHT, ALL RIGHT. NOW CAN WE GET STARTED?

*****

THERE ARE TONS OF COOL NAMES HERE!

HEY, LISTEN TO THIS NOTE.

LET'S SEE. "YOU GUYS GET TREATED BADLY IN THE STORY, SO AT THE VERY LEAST, YOU SHOULD HAVE AWESOME NAMES!"

THEY GET IT! THE READERS UNDERSTAND HOW WE FEEL!

COME ON, I JUST WANNA PICK OUR NAMES.

LISTEN TO THIS SUGGESTION!

TON
CHIN
KAN

*Tonchinkan means "ridiculous."

WHAT THE...?!

THOSE AREN'T NAMES AT ALL!

WELL, I EXPECTED SOMETHING LIKE THIS.

YOU...

HOW'D YOU GET TO BE SO JADED?

*****

THIS ONE'S KINDA INTERESTING!

AOTA SHUNSUKE
NEMOTO SHOICHI
YUMEDA RIKI

[THE KANJI FOR] SEISHUN, KONJO AND DORYOKU... "YOUTH," "GUTS" AND "HARD WORK," HUH?

OR HOW ABOUT THIS?

AKINO KAZUKI
HABAYASHI KAZUTO
HARAHI KAZUYA

OH! "AKIHABARA," HUH?

WE DID START OUT WITH A TOUGH PUNK IMAGE...

BUT WE DON'T KNOW ANYTHING ABOUT COMPUTERS...

YEAH, WITH OUR WHITE-HAIRED LEADER HERE IN CHARGE, WE'RE NOT TOO BRIGHT.

YEAH, EXACTLY—HEY!

BUT THE MOST COMMON THEME HAS BEEN NAMES THAT START WITH "SAN BAKA," OR "THREE IDIOTS."

FOR EXAMPLE...

MITSUHASHI GINJI
BABA RUKEI
KATO CHOJURO

SO THIS BLACK-HAIRED GUY GETS A LOT OF SAMURAI-WARRIOR SORTS OF NAMES.

BECAUSE HE HAS A PONYTAIL!

I BET THIS IS HOW EVERYONE IMAGINES ME...

WHAAAAAAT?!

YOU DON'T GET TO MAKE YOURSELF LOOK BETTER THAN US!

YEAH, NO ONE'S ALLOWED TO STAND OUT LIKE THAT.

BUT THERE ARE FANS WHO SEND IN DRAWINGS OF ME BY MYSELF...

SHUT UP, YOU TRAITOR!

GO BACK TO THE WARRIOR ERAS AND GET CUT DOWN!

THEN YOU GUYS ARE THE EVIL MAGISTRATE AND THE EVIL MERCHANT...

STOP ASSIGNING US ROLES!

*****

COME ON, WE'VE GOTTA DECIDE SOON.

WE'RE RUNNING OUT OF PAGES.

WE TOOK OVER THE BONUS CHAPTER FOR THIS, SO WE'D BETTER FIND GREAT NAMES.

HURRY UP! READ ALL THE POSTCARDS ASAP!

OH, HOW ABOUT THIS ONE?

NO, THIS ONE!

THIS ONE'S NOT BAD EITHER.

HOW ABOUT WE SHUT OUR EYES AND PICK AT RANDOM?

HUH?

THAT'D MEAN WE DID ALL THIS WORK FOR NOTHING.

BUT THE THING IS, THEY ALL SOUND SO COOL THAT WE CAN'T POSSIBLY DECIDE. OKAY? YOU READY?

ARE YOU SERIOUS?

THAT'S SO RECKLESS.

OKAY, HERE IT IS!

PATTSUN
THOROUGHBRED
MA-GE

... ...

UM...

OF ALL THESE CHOICES...

...YOU PICKED THOSE?

I'M... PATTSUN?

I'M A... HORSE?

MINE JUST SOUNDS WEAK AND PATHETIC.

THAT WORKS.

THAT'S PERFECT FOR YOU!

...

NO...!

THIS SUCKS!

I DEMAND A DO-OVER!

WHY'RE YOU GUYS BEING SO LOUD?

WELL...

M...

MISA-CHAN...

I TOLD YOU TO NEVER CALL ME THAT OUTSIDE THE CAFE.

WHY'RE YOU HERE?

THE AUTHOR SAID YOU GUYS WERE CHOOSING YOUR NAMES, SO I CAME TO CHECK IT OUT.

YOU...YOU CAME ALL THE WAY OVER HERE FOR US, MISA-CHAN?

I JUST SAID NOT TO CALL ME THAT. SO DID YOU PICK?

WELL... WE HAVE TEMPORARY NAMES.

GREAT! WHAT ARE THEY?

I'M, UH...PATTSUN.

THOROUGHBRED.

MA-GE...

HUH?

WELL, IT'S PATTS...

ARE YOU MESSING WITH ME?

YIKES!

I KNEW I COULDN'T LEAVE IT UP TO YOU GUYS. GIVE ME THAT.

SHE TOOK ALL THE POSTCARDS!

OKAY, LISTEN. I'LL GO HAVE A SERIOUS TALK WITH THE AUTHOR ABOUT THIS. YOU THREE SIT TIGHT, OKAY?

HUH?

M...MISA-CHAN...

THERE SHE GOES.

I...GUESS WE'LL WAIT...?

O-OKAY.

SO WHAT WAS THE POINT OF THIS MEETING?

Meeting adjourned.

Meeting time... Meeting time... Meeting time... Meeting time...

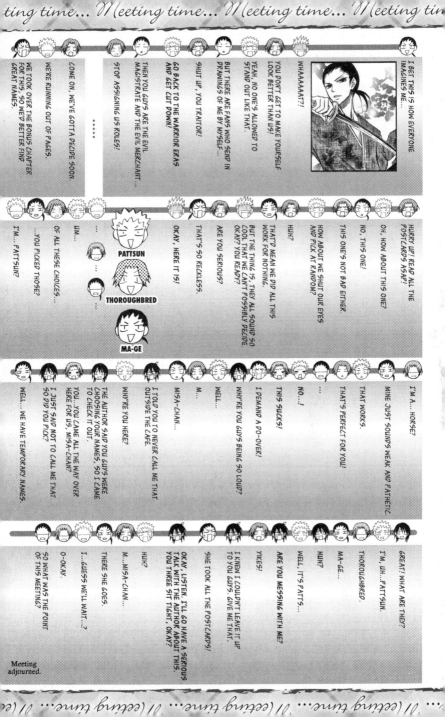

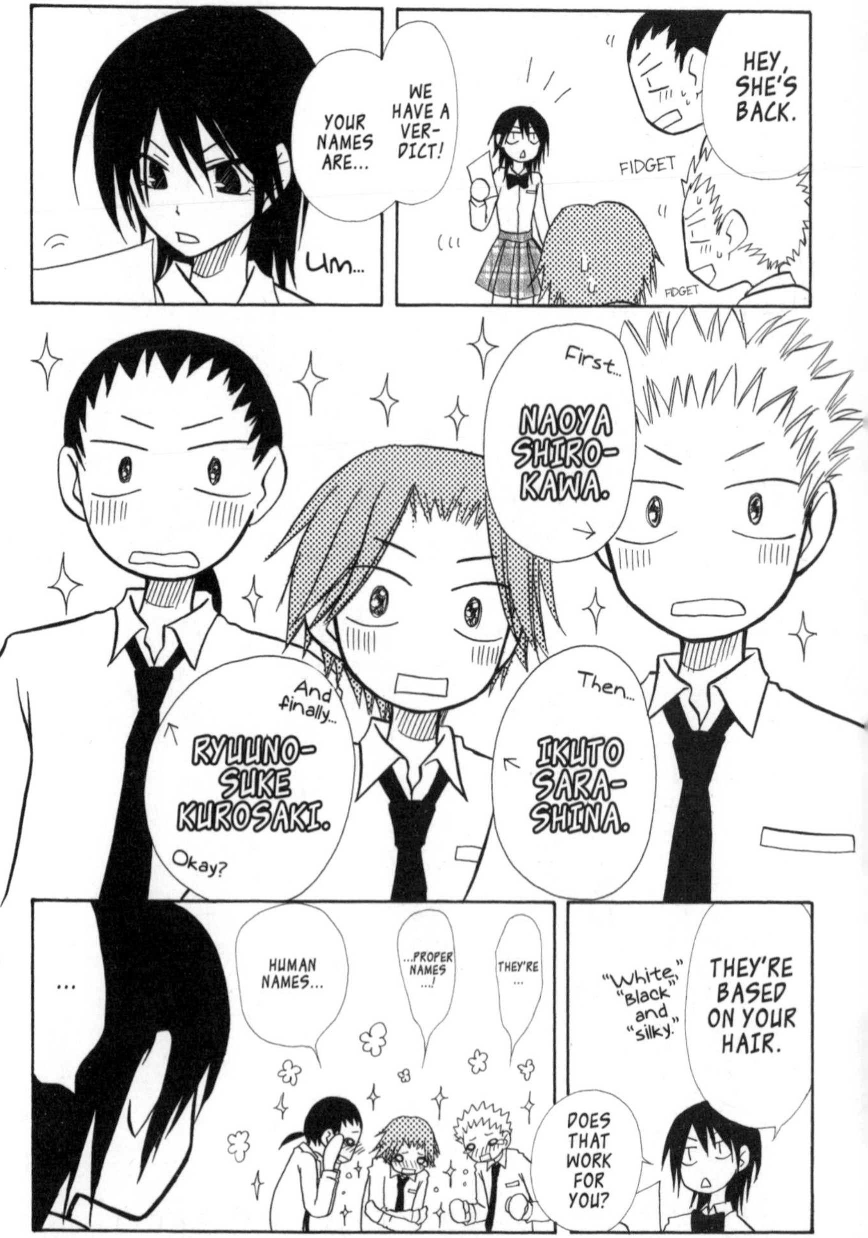
HEY, SHE'S BACK.
FIDGET
FIDGET
WE HAVE A VER-DICT!
YOUR NAMES ARE...
Um...
First...
NAOYA SHIRO-KAWA.
Then...
IKUTO SARA-SHINA.
And finally...
RYUUNO-SUKE KUROSAKI.
Okay?
THEY'RE BASED ON YOUR HAIR.
"White," "black" and "silky."
DOES THAT WORK FOR YOU?
THEY'RE...
...PROPER NAMES...!
HUMAN NAMES...
...

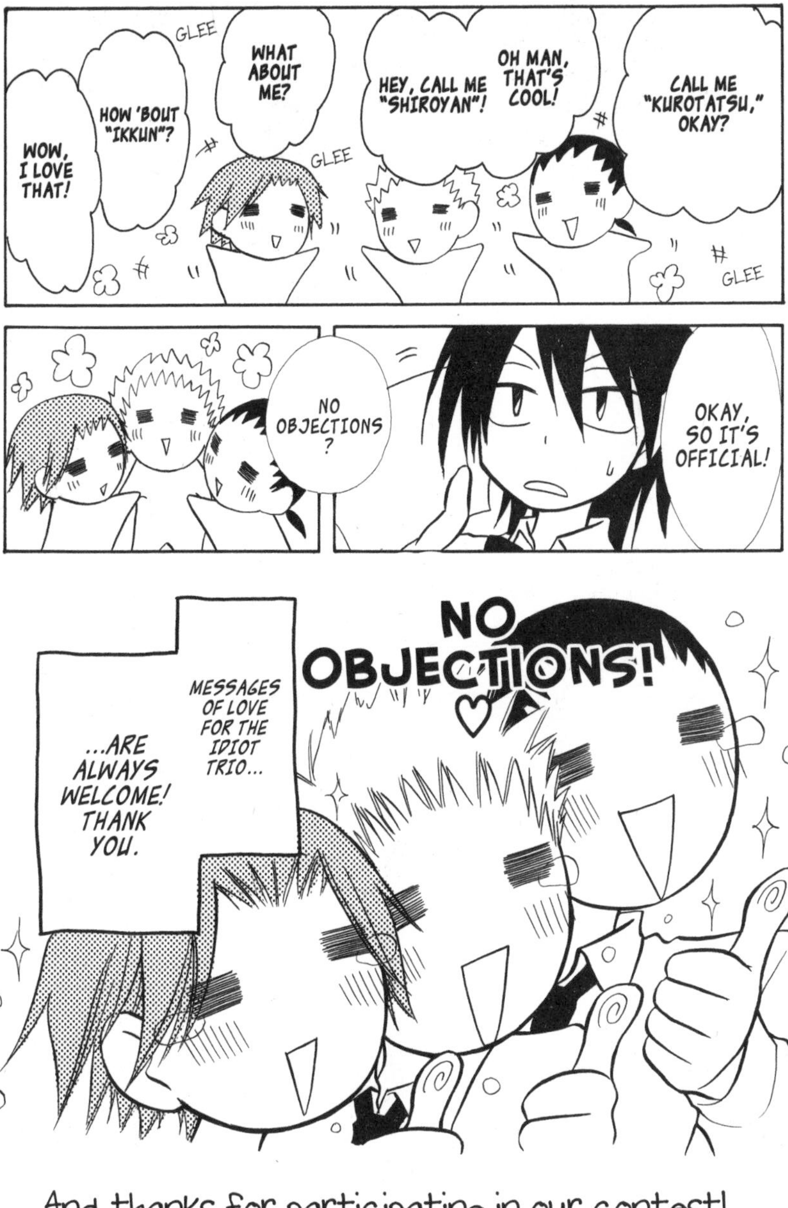
CALL ME "KUROTATSU," OKAY?
GLEE
OH MAN, THAT'S COOL!
HEY, CALL ME "SHIROYAN"!
GLEE
WHAT ABOUT ME?
GLEE
HOW 'BOUT "IKKUN"?
WOW, I LOVE THAT!
OKAY, SO IT'S OFFICIAL!
NO OBJECTIONS?
NO OBJECTIONS!
MESSAGES OF LOVE FOR THE IDIOT TRIO...
...ARE ALWAYS WELCOME! THANK YOU.

And thanks for participating in our contest!

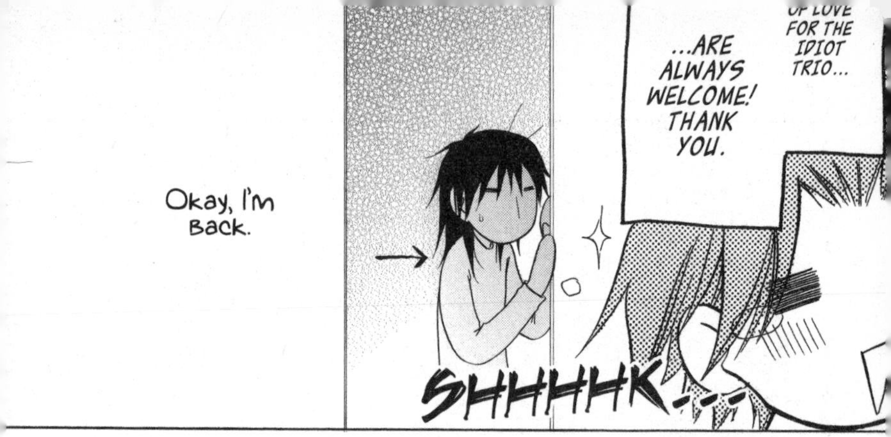
FOR THE IDIOT TRIO...
...ARE ALWAYS WELCOME! THANK YOU.
SHHHHK...
Okay, I'm Back.

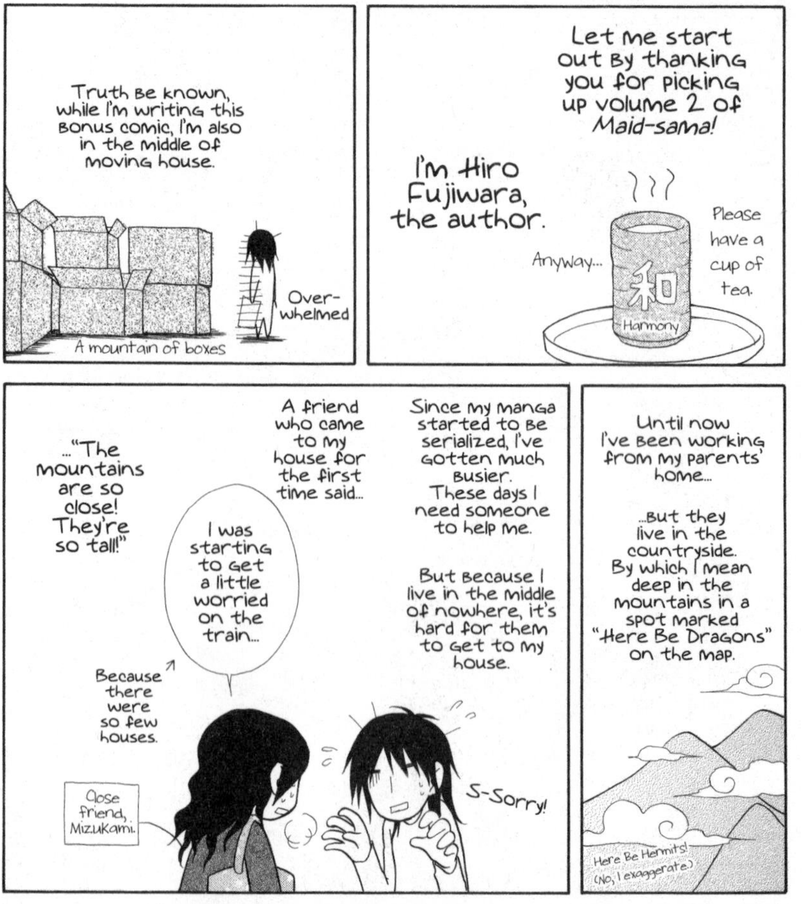
Let me start out By thanking you for picking up volume 2 of Maid-sama!
I'm Hiro Fujiwara, the author.
Anyway...
Please have a cup of tea.
和
Harmony
Truth Be known, while I'm writing this Bonus comic, I'm also in the middle of moving house.
Over-whelmed
A mountain of boxes
Until now I've Been working from my parents' home...
...But they live in the countryside. By which I mean deep in the mountains in a spot marked "Here Be Dragons" on the map.
Here Be Hermits! (No, I exaggerate.)
Since my manga started to Be serialized, I've gotten much Busier. These days I need someone to help me.
But Because I live in the middle of nowhere, it's hard for them to get to my house.
A friend who came to my house for the first time said...
..."The mountains are so close! They're so tall!"
I was starting to get a little worried on the train...
Because there were so few houses.
S-Sorry!
Close friend, Mizukami.

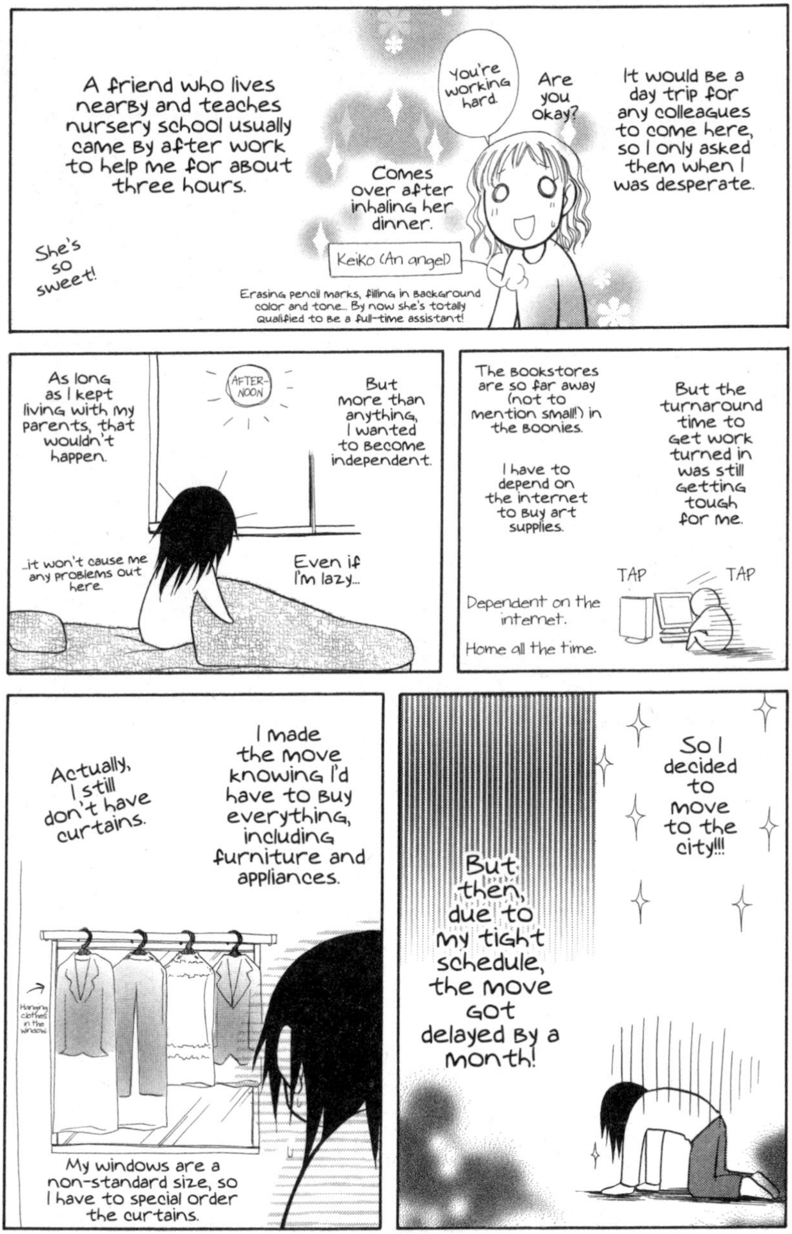
It would be a day trip for any colleagues to come here, so I only asked them when I was desperate.
Are you okay?
You're working hard.
Comes over after inhaling her dinner.
A friend who lives nearby and teaches nursery school usually came by after work to help me for about three hours.
She's so sweet!
Keiko (An angel)
Erasing pencil marks, filling in background color and tone... By now she's totally qualified to be a full-time assistant!
But the turnaround time to get work turned in was still getting tough for me.
The bookstores are so far away (not to mention small!) in the boonies.
I have to depend on the internet to buy art supplies.
TAP
TAP
Dependent on the internet.
Home all the time.
But more than anything, I wanted to become independent.
AFTER-NOON
As long as I kept living with my parents, that wouldn't happen.
Even if I'm lazy...
...it won't cause me any problems out here.
So I decided to move to the city!!!
But then, due to my tight schedule, the move got delayed by a month!
I made the move knowing I'd have to buy everything, including furniture and appliances.
Actually, I still don't have curtains.
Hanging clothes in the window
My windows are a non-standard size, so I have to special order the curtains.

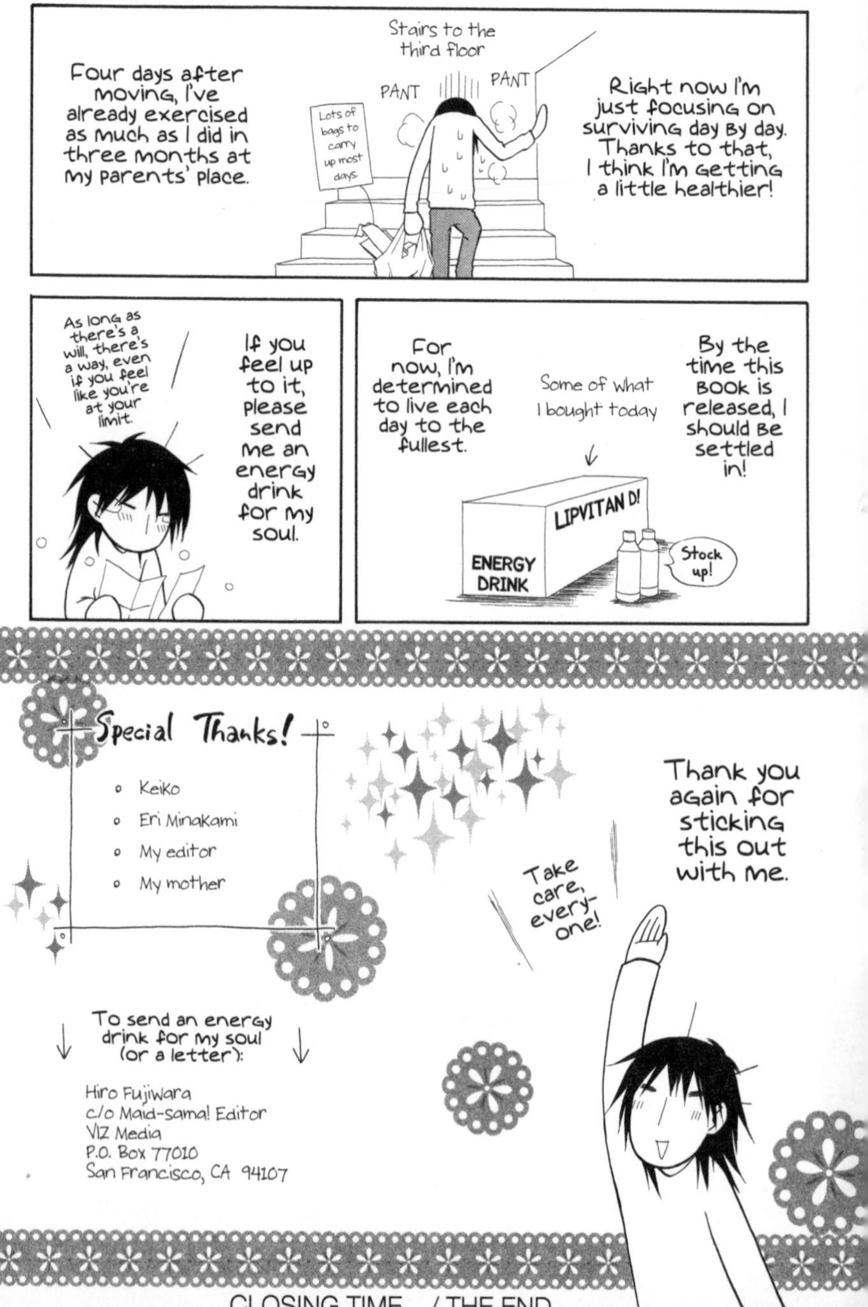

Right now I'm just focusing on surviving day by day. Thanks to that, I think I'm getting a little healthier!
Stairs to the third floor
PANT
PANT
Lots of bags to carry up most days.
Four days after moving, I've already exercised as much as I did in three months at my parents' place.
By the time this book is released, I should be settled in!
Some of what I bought today
LIPVITAN D!
ENERGY DRINK
Stock up!
For now, I'm determined to live each day to the fullest.
If you feel up to it, please send me an energy drink for my soul.
As long as there's a will, there's a way, even if you feel like you're at your limit.
Thank you again for sticking this out with me.
Take care, every-one!
Special Thanks!
Keiko
Eri Minakami
My editor
My mother
To send an energy drink for my soul (or a letter):
Hiro Fujiwara
c/o Maid-sama! Editor
VIZ Media
P.O. Box 77010
San Francisco, CA 94107

CLOSING TIME... / THE END

Hiro Fujiwara is from Hyogo Prefecture in Japan
and was born on December 23. *Maid-sama!*
(originally published as *Kaicho wa Maid Sama!*
in Hakusensha's *LaLa* magazine) is her first
long-running manga series and is available in
North America from VIZ Media.

MAID-SAMA!
2-in-1 Edition
Volume 1
A compilation of graphic novel volumes 1–2

STORY AND ART BY
HIRO FUJIWARA

English Adaptation/Ysabet Reinhardt MacFarlane
Translation/JN Productions
Touch-Up Art & Lettering/Joanna Estep
Design/Yukiko Whitley
Editor/Amy Yu

Kaicho wa Maid Sama! by Hiro Fujiwara
© Hiro Fujiwara 2006, 2007
All rights reserved.
First published in Japan in 2006, 2007 by HAKUSENSHA, Inc., Tokyo.
English language translation rights arranged with HAKUSENSHA, Inc., Tokyo.

Printed in the U.S.A.

Published by VIZ Media, LLC
P.O. Box 77010
San Francisco, CA 94107

10 9 8 7
First printing, August 2015
Seventh printing, October 2021

www.viz.com   www.shojobeat.com

IDOL dreams

STORY & ART BY
ARINA TANEMURA

At age 31, office worker Chikage Deguchi feels she missed her chances at love and success. When word gets out that she's a virgin, Chikage is humiliated and wishes she could turn back time to when she was still young and popular. She takes an experimental drug that changes her appearance back to when she was 15. Now Chikage is determined to pursue everything she missed out on all those years ago—including becoming a star!

www.viz.com

Ouran High School

Host Club BOX SET

Story and Art by
Bisco Hatori

Escape to the world of the young, rich and sexy

All 18 volumes
in a collector's box
with an Ouran High
School stationery
notepad!

In this screwball romantic
comedy, Haruhi, a poor girl at
a rich kids' school, is forced to
repay an $80,000 debt by working
for the school's swankiest, all-
male club—as a boy! There she
discovers just how wealthy the six
members are and how different
the rich are from everybody else...

www.viz.com

Surprise!

You may be reading the wrong way!

It's true: In keeping with the original Japanese comic format, this book reads from right to left—so action, sound effects and word balloons are completely reversed. This preserves the orientation of the original artwork—plus, it's fun! Check out the diagram shown here to get the hang of things, and then turn to the other side of the book to get started!